Catalogue of Vocal Solos and Duets Arranged in Biblical Order

Second Edition

James H. Laster
Diana Reed Strommen

The Scarecrow Press, Inc.
Lanham, Maryland, and Oxford
2003

SCARECROW PRESS, INC.

Published in the United States of America
by Scarecrow Press, Inc.
A Member of the Rowman & Littlefield Publishing Group
4501 Forbes Boulevard, Suite 200, Lanham, MD 20706
www.scarecrowpress.com

PO Box 317
Oxford
OX2 9RU, UK

British Library Cataloguing-in-Publication Information Available

Library of Congress Cataloging-in-Publication Data

Laster, James, 1934
Catalogue of vocal solos and duets arranged in Biblical order / James H. Laster, Diana Reed Strommen.—2nd ed.
p. cm.
Includes indexes.
ISBN 0-8108-4838-4 (alk. paper)
1. Sacred songs–Bibliography. 2. Sacred vocal duets–Bibliography. I. Strommen, Diana Reed, 1955– II. Title.
ML128.S3L38 2003
016.7832'295–dc21 2003052645

First edition: Catalogue of Vocal Solos and Duets Arranged in Biblical Order
James H. Laster, Scarecrow Press, Metuchen, N.J., 1984 ISBN 0-8108-1748-9

™ The paper used in this publication meets the minimum requirements of American National Standard for Information Sciences—Permanence of Paper for Printed Library Materials, ANSI/NISO Z39.48-1992.
Manufactured in the United States of America.

Contents

Preface v

Acknowledgments vii

List of Abbreviations ix

The Old Testament

Genesis 1
Exodus 2
Leviticus 3
Numbers 3
Deuteronomy 4
Joshua 5
Ruth 5
I Samuel 7
II Samuel 7
I Kings 7
II Kings 8
I Chronicles 8
II Chronicles 9
Nehemiah 9
Esther 9
Job 9
Psalms 11
Proverbs 78
Ecclesiastes 80
Song of Songs 80
Isaiah 83
Jeremiah 95
Lamentations 96
Ezekiel 97
Daniel 97
Hosea 97
Joel 98
Amos 98
Micah 98
Habakkuk 99
Zephaniah 99
Haggai 99
Zechariah 99
Malachi 99

The Apocrypha

Tobit 100
Ecclesiasticus 100
I Macabees 100

The New Testament

Matthew 101
Mark 111
Luke 112
John 121
Acts 128
Romans 129
I Corinthians 130
II Corinthians 134
Galatians 134
Ephesians 135
Philippians 136
Colossians 137
I Thessalonians 138
I Timothy 138
II Timothy 138
Hebrews 138
James 139
I Peter 139
II Peter 140
I John 140
Jude 141
Revelation 141

Composer Index 147

Title Index 183

Collections 219

About the Compilers 225

PREFACE

When the *Catalogue of Vocal Solos and Duets Arranged in Biblical Order* was published in 1984, there was no immediate plan for a second edition. Sometime in the early 1990s, Diana Reed Strommen requested permission to use the *Catalogue* as a basis for her master's thesis that would include titles published since 1984 as well as to correct errors found in the original book. Permission was granted with the offer that when the thesis was completed to convert it into the second edition of the *Catalogue.* Although the thesis, *Revised Catalogue of Vocal Solos and Duets arranged in Biblical Order,* was completed in 1995 at the University of Wisconsin—Stevens Point, circumstances prevented meeting the publisher's original deadline.

It has been gratifying to note that there is still interest in this volume, as there have been many inquiries about the availability of the 1984 *Catalogue,* out of print for a number of years. It is with pleasure, as well as relief, that the second edition has finally come to fruition.

The format used in the earlier *Catalogue* is continued in this volume: e.g., the texts of the solos/duets are arranged in Biblical Order, followed by the name of the composer, the title, the vocal range, the accompaniment, and the publisher information. Texts for each entry are assumed to be in English unless otherwise indicated. There is a title index as well as a composer index and in each of these the scripture source is given, which serve as an entry point into the main body.

There are two types of entries found in the *Catalogue*: a Main Entry and a SEE Reference. An annotated Main Entry is as follows:

(1) Deuteronomy 29:30. (2) (Job 23:3; Joel 2:13). (3) Mendelssohn, Felix.
(4) *If With All Your Hearts* (from *Elijah*). (5) Kbd: (6) T: (7) f♯1–a♭3.
(8) G. Schirmer (1949), found in *52 Sacred Songs; Anthology of Sacred Song–Tenor*

(1) Biblical Reference—Book, Chapter, Verse(s).
(2) Additional Scripture used in the solo; or the name of the author of paraphrased text, or a translator of a text will appear here.
(3) Composer's Name, including arranger and editor, if appropriate.
(4) Title of composition followed by translated title along with the major work in which it appears, if appropriate; and language of text if not in English.
(5) Accompaniment. Organ and piano are the most common accompanying instruments, but if other instruments are used, they will appear here.
(6) Voice type. Specific voice type will be indicated as well as general terms such as High or Medium.
(7) Vocal range. Highest and lowest notes are given according to the vocal chart found on the next page.
(8) The name of the publisher, the most recent date of publication, and the publisher's number appear at the end of each citation. If the title is published in a collection, this information is also included at this point. Items where no date is given are listed as (n.d.) or left blank. Items for which there is no publisher's number are listed as (n.#.) or left blank. If the title was found in a publisher's catalog, but not actually examined by one of the two authors, it is indicated as not viewed (n.v.).

An Annotated SEE Reference is as follows:

(1) Job 23:3. (2) SEE: Deuteronomy 29:30. (3) Mendelssohn, Felix. (4) *If With All Your Hearts.*

(1) Biblical Reference—Book, Chapter, Verse(s).
(2) The SEE Reference refers to the Main Scripture Heading where the complete citation is located.
(3) Composer and (4) Title for the Main Heading are repeated in the SEE Reference.

The following chart for vocal ranges is used:

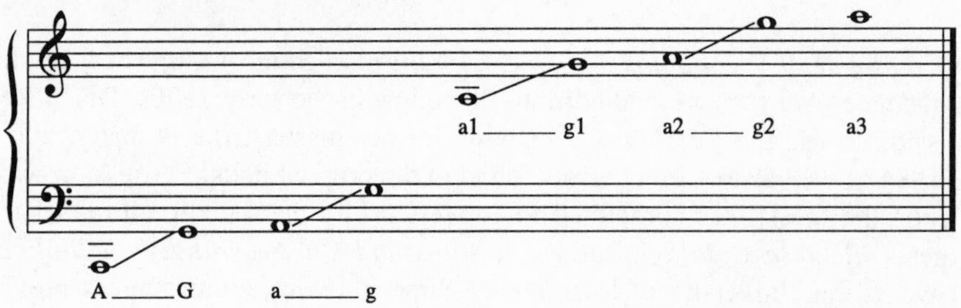

As in the first edition of *A Catalogue of Vocal Solos and Duets Arranged in Biblical Order,* the entry point for each citation is the Biblical passage as it appears in the music. When there were obvious errors, every attempt was made to correct them. There are variations in the way publishers list scripture sources that account for irregularities in listings. Many titles give the text as "the Psalms," "from the Bible," or "from Scripture." When this occurs, every effort has been made to locate the specific passages. When the text could be found, the title is included in the *Catalogue.* By the same token, there are solos and duets that use Biblical texts that were such a pastiche that no definitive reference could be determined. In these instances, the title was omitted.

All titles from the first edition of the *Catalogue* are included in the second edition. Every attempt has been made to correct errors that were found in the first edition as well as to supply the missing data.

There are some titles from choral literature for unison or for two-part voices that are often appropriate for use as vocal solos or duets. There are examples of this type of literature included in this edition, especially if they are octavo publications of solos from major choral works. However, if any of these titles were already listed in *A Catalogue of Choral Music Arranged in Biblical Order,* 2nd edition, or in *A Catalogue of Choral Music Arranged in Biblical Order—Supplement,* they were omitted.

Material for the second edition was obtained through the generosity of many publishers. Expression of gratitude is extended to: AMSI, Abingdon Press, Alfred Publishing, American Composers Editions, Augsburg Fortress, Bärenreiter, Beckenhorst, Boosey & Hawkes, Boston Music, Brodt Music, Canadian Music Centre, Carl Fischer, Chantry, Choristers Guild, Concordia, Darcy, Gregorian Institute of America, Harmony House Music, Hope, Hal Leonard, Kevin Mayhew, Kjos, Leyerle Publications, Lillenas Publishing, Lorenz, Manna Music, Maranatha Music, Mark Foster, MorningStar, NATS Publications, North American Liturgy Resources, Oregon Catholic Publishing, Oxford University Press, Paraclete Press, Theodore Presser, Randall Egan, Seesaw, Selah, Southern Music, Tempo Music, Transcontinental Music, Western International Music, Walton, Willis, and Word.

Publisher's names are written out in the citation. For the following publishers, abbreviations are used: GIA—Gregorian Institute of America; OCP—Oregon Catholic Press; NALR—North American Liturgy Resources; and WIM—Western International Music.

The Collections section, found at the back of the volume, is a list of collections that contain titles by more than one composer. Collections of songs by a single composer are omitted. Bibliographical information for collections by a single composer is found in the citation.

Finally, it should be remembered that works such as this are always out of date the minute they are frozen into print. Due to the vast amount of solo literature, there are numerous titles that have been overlooked. Please share what you have found so that it can be included in the next revision.

ACKNOWLEDGMENTS

JAMES H. LASTER: would like to express his appreciation to Diana Reed Strommen for initially taking on the task of revising and updating the *Catalogue of Vocal Solos and Duets Arranged in Biblical Order* as the topic of her master's thesis. Her thesis forms the core of additional material found in the second edition, although altered for publication purposes. My responsibility in this volume has been primarily that of editor of the manuscript, as well as overseeing the document through publication. When appropriate, I have contributed additional titles that have been brought to my attention.

I concur with Ms. Strommen's list of expressions of gratitude to those who have contributed to this project. In addition, I must add my sincere thanks to the staff of Scarecrow Press who have supported this endeavor, and to graphic artist, Susan Lee, for her work in preparing the manuscript into camera-ready format.

DIANA REED STROMMEN: expresses considerable recognition and heartfelt thanks to James Laster for his dedication to the music ministry, for his vision set forth in the first edition of *Catalogue of Vocal Solos and Duets Arranged in Biblical Order*, and for his enthusiastic support of this current endeavor. Without his permission and encouragement, my participation in this project would not have been possible.

I extend appreciation to the many publishers and their supporting staff who donated time and materials toward the successful completion of the thesis. Further thanks are extended to those who supplied supporting information: to Gerald H. Iversen, who provided his research on vocal repertoire resources, to Joan Welles for her *Soloists' Guide to Selecting Sacred Solos,* and to James Sampson and the Whitefish Bay Christian Science Church for opening their solo library to this project; to the staff and facilities of Ward-Brodt Music Mall, Madison, Wisconsin, and JW Pepper of Indianapolis for opening their stock shelves to us.

My gratitude is offered to those who provided hours of technical and academic support: to my graduate advisor, Dr. William Lavonis, whose gift of time and example in dedicated music education will remain indelible; to my husband Doug and brother-in-law Randy who enabled the database project from its onset; and finally, in memory of my mother, Beverly, and to my family and friends, who made many sacrifices while this work was being completed.

LIST OF ABBREVIATIONS

The following list contains abbreviations used throughout the *Catalogue.*

VOICING

Bar	baritone voice
Bbar	bass baritone
Cant	cantor
Desc	descant
H	high voice
L	low voice
Med	medium voice
Mez	mezzo-soprano
MH	medium high voice
ML	medium low voice
SAB	three part choral voicing
SATB	four part choral voicing
Sop	soprano voice
U	unison voices
U/2 Pt	unison or two part voices

GENERAL

acc.	accompanied
bk	book
har.	harmonized
Ms	manuscript
red.	reduction
n.d.	no date
n.v.	not viewed
n.#.	no number
unacc.	unaccompanied
vol.	volume

INSTRUMENTS

bng	bongos
bsn	bassoon
cas	cassette
cl	clarinet
cont	continuo
cym	cymbal
db	double or string bass
drm	drum
fl	flute
gtr	guitar
hb	handbells
hn	french horn
inst	instruments
kbd	keyboard
opt	optional
obd	oboe d'amore
orch	orchestra
org	organ
perc	percussion
pno	piano
qnt	quintet
qt	quartet
rec	recorder
st	string
tbn	trombone
trpt(s)	trumpet(s)
vc	violoncello
vla(s)	viola(s)
vln(s)	violin(s)
stg qt	string quartet

The Old Testament

GENESIS

1:00 (Genesis 2:1-3)
Haugen, Marty. *Creation.* U/2-part. Kbd, gtr, opt duet: a1-e2. GIA (1989), found in *Tales of Wonder*

1:1-3 Haydn, F. Joseph. *In the Beginning* (from *The Creation*). Kbd: H:c1-g2; M:a1-e2. Carl Fischer (1939), found in *Sacred Hour of Song*

1:1-3 (adapted; Deuteronomy 7:21)
Mullins, Rich. *Awesome God.* Kbd or Trax: ML:e1-c♯2; L:d1-b2. Edward Grant, Inc. (1988), found in *40 Contemporary Hits; Fifty Contemporary Favorites for Low Voice* (ML); *Songs for Praise and Worship* (L); *WOW Worship Songbook* (ML)

1:1-3 (adapted; Deuteronomy 7:21)
Mullins, Rich (arr. Bryce Inman). *Awesome God.* Pno, gtr: c1-c2. BMG (1988) HL00309882, found in *50 EZ Inspirational Favorites*

1:1-3 (adapted; Deuteronomy 7:21)
Mullins, Rich (choral arr. Steven V. Taylor). *Awesome God.* 2-part-Kbd or Trax: e1-d2/c-c♯1. Word (1988, 1990), found in *25 Songs for Two-Part Choir,* vol. II; solos arrangements available

1:3 (Mary Baker Eddy, based on Genesis 9:13; Psalm 91:5)
MacDermid, James G. *Love (Brood O'er Us).* Kbd: Low. Henry Hunt (1932) 4157-6 (n.v.)

1:3 (Mary Baker Eddy, based on Genesis 9:13; Psalm 91:5)
Roberts, John Varley. *Love (Brood O'er Us).* Kbd: Med. Coburn Press (n.v.)

1:3 (Mary Baker Eddy, based on Genesis 9:13; Psalm 91:5)
Root, Frederic W. *Love (Brood O'er Us).* Kbd: Alto. Summy (1927) (n.v.)

1:9 Haydn, F. Joseph. *And God Said, Let the Waters Under the Heavens* (from *The Creation*). Kbd: Bass:G-f1. G. Schirmer (1977), found in *Schirmer's Singer's Library: Bass Arias from Oratorios; Oratorio Repertoire,* vol. IV

1:11 Haydn, F. Joseph. *And God Said, Let the Earth Bring Forth Grass* (from *The Creation*). Kbd: Sop:e1-e♭2(b♭3). G. Schirmer (1977), found in *Schirmer's Singer's Library: Soprano Arias from Oratorios*

1:20 Haydn, F. Joseph. *And God Said, Let the Waters Bring Forth Abundantly* (from *The Creation*). Kbd: Sop:f1-f2(a3). G. Schirmer (1977), found in *Schirmer's Singer's Library: Sop Arias from Oratorios*

1:24 Haydn, F. Joseph. *And God Said, Let the Earth Bring Forth Living Creatures* (from *The Creation*). Kbd: Bass:F♯-f♯1. G. Schirmer (1977), found in *Schirmer's Singer's Library: Bass Arias from Oratorios; Oratorio Reperoitre,* vol. IV

1:26, 27 (I John 3:1, 3)
MacDermid, James G. *Behold What Manner of Love.* Kbd: H:e1-g2; L:c1-e2. Forster (1913, 1942)

1:27 (Psalm 8:3-6)
Humphreys, Don. *Man.* Kbd: H:d1-g2; L:b1-e2. R. D. Row (1953), found in *Don Humphrey's Song Book* (H/L); *Songs for Christian Science Service,* bk 1

1:28 Haydn, F. Joseph. *And God Created Man* (Recitative for *In Native Worth* from *The Creation*). Kbd: Tenor:g-f2. Presser (1923), found in *Oratorio Repertoire,* vol. III

2:1-3 SEE: Genesis 1:00. Haugen, Marty. *Creation*

4:9 (other)
Barrett-Ayres, Reginald. *Am I My Brother's Keeper?* Kbd, gtr: d1-d♭2. Galaxy (1969), found in *Scripture Solos for All Seasons*

7:4 (based on)
Spiritual (arr. Harry T. Burleigh). *Oh, Didn't It Rain.* Pno: H:f1-f2(b♭3); L:(g)d1-d2(g2). Belwin Mills (1919), found in *The Spirituals of Harry T. Burleigh* (H/L)

9:13 SEE: Genesis 1:3. MacDermid, James G. *Love*

9:13 SEE: Genesis 1:3. Roberts, John Varley. *Love*

9:13 SEE: Genesis 1:3. Root, Frederic W. *Love*

12:1-2 (Genesis 13:14-17; Genesis 15:1-6)
Schutte, Daniel L. *Yahweh, the Faithful One.* U/2-part. Gtr, w/cong: a1-b2. NALR (1974) 10485CC, also found in *Neither Silver Nor Gold*

13:14-17 SEE: Genesis 12:1-2. Schutte, Daniel L. *Yahweh, the Faithful One*

15:1-6 SEE: Genesis 12:1-2. Schutte, Daniel L. *Yahweh, the Faithful One*

22:2-19 (based on)
Britten, Benjamin. *Canticle II–Abraham and Isaac,* op. 51. Duet-Pno: A:b1-e2/T:f♯1-a2. Boosey & Hawkes (1953)

28:16-17 Colvin, Herbert (arr. Richard Huggins) *Surely the Lord Is in This Place* 2-part-Kbd, gtr; Trax or orch: b♭1-f2/b♭-d1(f1). Word (1977, 1978, 1995) Orch: 301 0384 254, also found in *The Best of Times*

28:16-17 (other)
Lister, Mosie. *The Lord Is in This Place.* Kbd: L:b♭1-c2. Lillenas (1985) MB-545, found in *Low Voice Classics*

28:16-17 (Psalm 134:00)
Powell, Robert J. *Surely the Lord Is in This Place* (from *Surely The Lord Is in This Place*). Kbd: M:c1-g2. Augsburg (1995) 11-10607

48:16 (Luke 1:46-49, 76-77; Luke 10:23-24; John 17:11, 15; based on)
Schutte, Daniel L. *Blessed Are You.* U/2-part-Gtr: b1-d2. NALR (1974), found in *Neither Silver Nor Gold*

EXODUS

8:1 (based on)
Spiritual (arr. Edward Boatner). *Go Down Moses.* Kbd: f1-f2. Belwin Mills (1973), found in *The Story of the Spirituals*

8:1 (based on)
Spiritual (comp. Joan Frey Boytim). *Go Down Moses.* Kbd. or CD: Bar/Bass. Hal Leonard (2000), found in *Easy Songs for the Beginning Baritone/Bass*

8:1 (based on)
Spiritual (arr. Harry T. Burleigh). *Go Down Moses.* Kbd: M. Hal Leonard (2001), found in *The Sacred Collection* (H/L)

8:1 (based on)
Spiritual (arr. Michael Johnson). *Go Down Moses.* Kbd: b1-b2. Portside Music (1996), found in *All-American Gospel*

8:1 (based on)
Spiritual (arr. Florence Price). *Go Down Moses* (from *Four Songs*). Kbd: M. Southern Music

8:1 (paraphrased)
Spiritual (ed. Jay Althouse). *Little David, Play On Your Harp.* Kbd or CD: MH; ML. Alfred (1997) MH: 11696 or w/CD 16915; ML: 11698 or w/CD 11916, found in *Spirituals for Solo Singers* (MH/ML)

8:1 (paraphrased)
Spiritual (arr. Harry T. Burleigh). *Little David, Play on Your Harp.* Pno: H:e♭1-f2(a♭3); L:c1-d2(f2). Belwin Mills (1921), found in *The Spirituals of Harry T. Burleigh; The Sacred Collection* (H/L)

13:2, 12-13 (based on)
SEE: Luke 2:22-35. Card, Michael. *Now That I've Held Him in My Arms (Simeon's Song)*

13:14 (I Corinthians 10:11; other)
Hayford, Jack (arr. Paul Johnson). *Tell Ye This Story.* Kbd, gtr: a1-d♭2. Lillenas (1980), found in *Scripture Solos for All Seasons*

14:22 (I Samuel 17:49; based on)
Spiritual (arr. Harry T. Burleigh). *He's Jus' De Same Today.* Pno: H:f1-f2; L:d1-d2. Belwin Mills (1919), found in *The Spirituals of Harry T. Burleigh* (H/L)

15:00 (taken from)
Cumming, Richard. *The Song of Moses* (from *We Happy Few,* no. 10). Pno: Bass:G-e1. Boosey & Hawkes (1969)

15:1 (based on)
Talbot, John Michael. *Let Us Sing to the Lord.* Gtr: c1-c2. Birdwing (1985), found in *Praise, Praise the Lord, O My Soul and Worship*

15:1-2 Viadana, Ludovico (ed. Rudolf Ewerhart). *Cantemus Domino* (from *Drei geistliche Konzerte*) (Latin). Cont: Bass:G-b♭1. Edmund Bieler Verlag (1958) 5

15:2 Handel, G. F. *The Lord Is My Strength* (from *Israel in Egypt*). Duet-Kbd: Equal Voices: e1-a3/d1-g2. John Church (1902), found in *Sacred Duets,* vol. I (H/H); *Sacred Duets,* vol. II (H/L)

15:3 (Psalm 46:10; Psalm 74:20; Psalm 12:5; Psalm 76:6)
Anonymous (ed. Marilyn Gombosi). *The Lord Is a Mighty Warrior*. Kbd: Bass:A-d1. Boosey & Hawkes (1975), found in *Psalm of Joy*

15:4 (based on)
Handel, G. F. (ed. Bernard Taylor). *Thou Didst Blow* (from *Israel in Egypt*). Kbd: Sop:e♭1-b♭3. G. Schirmer (1968), found in *Solos from the Great Oratorios for Soprano*

15:9 (based on)
Handel, G. F. *The Enemy Said* (from *Israel in Egypt*). Kbd: Tenor:d-a. Hal Leonard (1994), found in *Oratorio Anthology: Tenor*

15:17 Handel, G. F. *Thou Shalt Bring Them in* (from *Israel in Egypt*). Kbd: Alto:b1- c♯3. G. Schirmer (1977), found in *Anthology of Sacred Song–Alto; Schirmer's Singer's Library: Alto Arias from Oratorios*

15:26b (Psalm 46:10; Jeremiah 31:3; other)
Chapman, Steve Curtis (arr. Bryce Inman). *Be Still and Know*. Kbd, gtr: d1-d2. Sparrow (1999) HL00309882, found in *50 EZ Inspirational Favorites*

15:26b (Psalm 46:10; Jeremiah 31:3; other)
Chapman, Steve Curtis and Tom Fettke (arr. Tom Fettke). *Be Still and Know*. Kbd, gtr: d1-e♭2. Lillenas (1999), found in *24 Songs for Solo Ministry*

15:26b (Psalm 46:10; Jeremiah 31:3; other)
Chapman, Steve Curtis and Tom Fettke (arr. Lee Herrington). *Be Still and Know*. Kbd, gtr, (opt orch): d1-d2. Word (1992), found in *Songs for Praise and Worship*

23:20, 22, 25 (other)
Head, Michael. *Behold, I Send an Angel*. Kbd: Med. Boosey & Hawkes (1964)

32:10 (Psalm 69:24; based on)
Mendelssohn, Felix. *Consume Them All, Lord Sabaoth* (*O Lord They Prophesy Against Thee*) (from *St. Paul*). Kbd: H:d1-g2; L:b1-e2; Bass:b-d1. G. Schirmer, found in *Anthology of Sacred Song–Bass; Schirmer's Singer's Library: Bass Arias from Oratorios; Sacred Hour of Song* (H/M)

32:11, 13-14
Foley, John B. *Why, O Lord*. Gtr: c1-d2. NARL (1974), found in *Neither Silver Nor Gold*

LEVITICUS

8:35 (C. Wesley)
Mason, Lowell (arr. Rhonda Sandberg). *A Charge to Keep Have I*. 2-part -Kbd: H:c1-c2/L:e♭-d1. Plymouth (1992) RS-107

NUMBERS

6:22-27 Walker, Christopher. *May God Bless and Keep You*. Kbd, vc, cl, inst in c, gtr: c1-c2. OCP (1989), found in *Out of Darkness; United as One,* vol. 2

6:24 Card, Michael. *Barocha*. Kbd, gtr: Bass:A-b1. Birdwing (1989), found in *Greatest Songs of Michael Card*

6:24 Lutkin, Peter C. *The Lord Bless You and Keep You*. Kbd: c1-e2. Creative Concepts (1997) 07-1107, found in *Joy, Joy, Joy*

6:24 Lutkin, Peter C. (arr. William Stickles). *The Lord Bless You and Keep You*. Pno: c1-e2. Boston Music (1963), found in *Wedding Music for Piano*

6:24 Smith, Gregg. *The Lord Bless Thee and Keep Thee*. Kbd: Sop:d1-a♭3. G. Schirmer (1964) 11160

6:24-26 (other)
Cohen, Gerald. *Y'varech'cha (May Adonai Bless You)*. (Hebrew transliterated). Pno: Med:f1-f2. Oxford (2001), found in *Come Before God with Joyous Song*

6:24-26 SEE: Romans 8:38, d39. Floyd, Carlisle. *For I Am Persuaded*

24:5 (Psalm 5:8; Psalm 26:8; Psalm 69:14)
Gottlieb, Jack. *Ma Tovu (How Lovely Are Your Tents)* (Hebrew/English). Transcontinental (1979) 983025 (n.v.)

24:5 (Psalm 95:6; from the Liturgy)
Pasternak, Velvel. *Ma Tõvu (How Goodly Are Your Tents)* (Hebrew transliterated). Gtr: M:a1-b2. Bloch (1971), found in *Songs of the Chassidim II*

24:5 (Psalm 5:8; Psalm 26:8; Psalm 69:14)
Steinberg, Ben. *Mah Tovu (How Goodly Are Thy Tents)* (Hebrew). Transcontinental (1988), found in *A Ben Steinberg Solo Collection*

24:5 (Psalm 5:8; Psalm 26:8; Psalm 69:14)
Weiner, Lazar. *Mah Tovu* (from *Anim Z'Miros*) (Hebrew). Transcontinental (1964) (n.v.)

DEUTERONOMY

4:29 SEE: Jeremiah 29:11-14. Courtney, Craig. *If You Search With All Your Heart*

4:29 (Job 23:3; Joel 2:13)
Mendelssohn, Felix. *If With All Your Hearts* (from *Elijah*) (English/German). Kbd: Tenor: f♯1-a♭3; MH:d1-f2; L:c♯1-e♭2. Found in *52 Sacred Songs; Anthology of Sacred Song–Tenor; The Church Soloist* (MH); *Everything for the Church Soloist; Everybody's Favorite Sacred Songs* (H); *Favorite Sacred Classics for Solo Singers* (MH/ML); *The Lord Is My Light* (L); *Oratorio Anthology:* Tenor (Eng/Ger); *Oratorio Repertoire,* vol. III; *Seventeen Sacred Songs For Church and General Use* (H, L); *Sing Solo Tenor* (H); *Solo Singer; Soloist Practical Library,* bk 2; *Solos from the Word*

4:29 (Job 23:3; Joel 2:13)
Mendelssohn, Felix. (arr. Lynn Hodges). *If With All Your Hearts* (from *Elijah*). U-Kbd: c♯1-e2. Intrada (1993), found in *Mendelssohn's ELIJAH for Young Voices*

4:29 (Job 23:3; Joel 2:13)
Mendelssohn, Felix. (arr. Harrison Oxley). *If With All Your Hearts* (from *Elijah*). U-Org: e♯1-g2. Kevin Mayhew (1992) found in *Favorite Anthems,* bk 2

4:29 (Jeremiah 29:13; Job 23:3)
Mendelssohn, Felix. (arr. Leonard Van Camp). *If Your Heart and Soul Both Truly Seek Me (So ihr mich von ganzem Herzen suchet)* (from *Elijah*) (English/German). Kbd: Tenor: d♯-f1. Laudamus Press (1993), found in *Songs for Youthful Tenors of All Ages*

4:29 Reinthaler, C. *The Lord Will Not Be Ever Wroth* (from *Jephtha and His Daughter*). Kbd: c1-e2. Stainer (1929), found in *Anthology of Sacred Song–Alto*

4:29 (Job 23:3)
Roberts, J. E. *If With All Your Hearts.* Kbd: H:e1-g2; L:b1-d2. Presser (1936)

4:39 Weiner, Lazar. *Adoration* (from *Anim Z'Miros*) (Hebrew). Transcontinental (1964) (n.v.)

6:1-5 SEE: Matthew 6:33. Pendleton, Emmet. *The Kingdom of God*

6:4-5 (Mark 12:31)
Haas, David. *Hear, O Israel.* Kbd, vc, bsn: d1-c2. GIA (1989), found in *Creating God*

6:4-5 (Psalm 8:3-9)
Tindall, Adrienne M. *Hear, O Israel.* Kbd: d1-e2. Adrienne Tindall (1987), found in *Sacred Solos by Adrienne Tindall,* vol. I

6:5 Hatton, Ray D. *Love the Lord.* 2-part-Kbd: H: c1-e♭2/L:b♭1-c2. GlorySound (1987) EA-5072

6:5-9 Gottlieb, Jack. *Veahavta (And You Shall Love)* (Hebrew/English). Transcontinental (1991) 983031

7:21 (adapted)
SEE: Genesis 1:1-3. Mullins, Rich. *Awesome God*

7:21 (adapted)
SEE: Genesis 1:1-3. Mullins, Rich (arr. Bryce Inman). *Awesome God*

7:21 (adapted)
SEE: Genesis 1:1-3. Mullins, Rich (arr. Steven V. Taylor). *Awesome God*

8:3b SEE: Matthew 6:33. Lafferty, Karen. *Seek Ye First*

16:14 Pasternak, Velvel. *V'Somachto B; Chagecho,* no. 1 *(And Thou Shalt Rejoice in Thy Feast)* (Hebrew transliterated). Gtr: M:d1-d2. Bloch (1971), found in *Songs of the Chassidim II*

16:14 Pasternak, Velvel. *V'Somachto B; Chagecho,* no. 2 *(And Thou Shalt Rejoice In Thy Feast)* (Hebrew transliterated). Gtr: M:c♯1-d2. Bloch (1971), found in *Songs of the Chassidim II*

16:14 Taub, Rabbi S. E. (arr. Velvel Pasternak). *V'Somachto B; Chagecho,* no. 3 *(And Thou Shalt Rejoice in Thy Feast)* (Hebrew transliterated). Gtr: M:c1-e♭2. Bloch (1971), found in *Songs of the Chassidim II*

28:67 SEE: Psalm 27:4. Talma, Louise. *Cantata: All the Days of My Life*

31:6 SEE: Psalm 31:19, 24. Beaumont, Vivian. *Be of Good Courage*

32:1-3 MacDermid, James G. *My Speech Shall Distill As the Dew.* Kbd: H:c1-d♯2; L:a1-f2. Forster (1943)

32:1-4, 9-12
Selby, Peter H. *Give Ear Oh Ye Heaven.* Kbd: b-e2. Willis Music (1973)

32:11 (Hebrews 8:10)
Mendelssohn, Felix. *God Hath Led His People On.* Kbd: c1-f2. Coburn Press (1971), found in *Lift Up Your Voice* (M)

JOSHUA

1:5-7 Butt, James. *Courage*. Kbd: e1-e2. Sphemusations (1965)

1:8-9 Ultan, Lloyd. *I Will Give You Shepherds*. Kbd: d1-g2. American Composers Alliance (1985)

1:9 (based on)
Chapman, Morris. *Be Bold, Be Strong*. U-kbd: g1-d2. Word (1984), found in *Face to Face*

1:9 Chiasson, Basil (arr. Carl Seal). *Be Strong and Take Courage*. Kbd, gtr: c1-f2. Lillenas (1999), found in *Solos from the Word*

6:00 (based on)
Spiritual (arr. Bond). *Joshua Fit Da Battle of Jericho*. Pno: Bar. Presser (n.d.) 151099495

6:00 (based on)
Spiritual (arr. Harry T. Burleigh). *Joshua Fit Da Battle of Jericho*. Pno: d♯1-e2. Belwin Mills (1935) found in *The Spirituals of Harry T. Burleigh*

6:00 (based on)
Spiritual (arr. Mark Hayes). *Joshua Fit Da Battle of Jericho*. Pno: g♯-c♯2. Alfred (1998) MH:17954; ML:17959, found in *The Mark Hayes Vocal Solo Collection: 10 Spirituals* (MH/ML)

24:15 (other)
Sheppard, Tim. *Me and My House*. Kbd: c1-e♭2. Tim Sheppard Music (1981), found in *42 Songs for All Occasions; 50 Great Songs of Commitment; The Lord Is My Light*

RUTH

1:8 (other)
Gaul, Alfred Robert. *Now Go Your Ways (O Gracious Lord)* (from *Ruth*). Kbd: Alto:e♭1-d2. G. Schirmer (1977), found in *Schirmer's Singer's Library: Alto Arias from Oratorios*

1:16 (Rory Cooney)
Daigle, Gary. *Covenant Hymn*. U-Kbd, gtr, vc, inst in c: c1-c2. GIA (1993) G-3977

1:16 (and other)
Dewey, Richard A. *Whither Thou Goest*. Org: e♭1-e♭2. Intrada (1977), found in *Whom God Hath Joined Together*

1:16 (and other)
Hallquist, Gary. *Song of Ruth*. Kbd: d1-b2. Sonlife Music (1976), found in *Everything for the Wedding Soloist*

1:16 Liljestrand, Paul. *Whither Thou Goest*. Kbd: c1-e2. Hope (1980), found in *Everything for the Church Soloist; Everything for the Wedding Soloist*

1:16 Roff, Joseph. *Entreat Me Not to Leave You*. Duet, pno: M:d1-d2/L:b1-b2. FitzSimons (1989) F0115

1:16 Schütz, Heinrich. *Wedding Song*. Kbd: d1-d2. Augsburg (2001), found in *To God Will I Sing*

1:16-17 Avery, Lawrence. *Entreat Me Not to Leave Thee (Al Tifigi vi Le-Ozveich)* (English/Hebrew). Kbd: e♭1-e♭2. Transcontinental (1979)

1:16, 17 Avery, Richard and Donald Marsh. *I Will Follow*. Kbd: c1-e2. Hope (1980), found in *Everything for the Wedding Soloist*

1:16-17 Birch, Robert Fairfax. *Entreat Me Not to Leave Thee*. Kbd: H:e1-f♯2. Presser (n.v.)

1:16-17 Black, Jennie Prince. *The Pledge*. Pno: H:d1-g2; L:b1-e2. G. Schirmer (1943)

1:16-17 Cassler, G. Winston. *Whither Thou Goest*. Org: M:c1-f2; L:a1-d2. Augsburg (1955) 11-0700

1:16-17 Cook, Gerald. *Ruth (to Naomi)*. Kbd: f1-f2. American Music Centre (n.d.)

1:16-17 Damrosch, Leopold (ed. Bernard Taylor). *Entreat Me Not to Leave Thee* (from *Ruth and Naomi*). Kbd: Sop: d♭1-b♭3. G. Schirmer (1968), found in *Solos from the Great Oratorios for Soprano*

1:16-17 Eben, Petr. *Lied der Ruth (Song of Ruth)* (German/English). Org: c1-f2. Universal (1970, 1980) 17161

1:16-17 (KJV)
Engel, James. *Whither Thou Goest*. Org, fl: M:e1-e2. Augsburg (1979) 11-9478, also found in *Three Solos for Medium Voice*

1:16-17 Gieseke, Richard W. *Wedding Song*. Org: M:c1-f2. Concordia (1983) 97-5786

1:16-17 Goldman, Maurice. *Song of Ruth (Entreat Me Not to Leave Thee)*. Pno: H:d1-g2; M:b1-e2. Transcontinental (1950) 990476

1:16-17 Gore, Richard T. *Entreat Me Not to Leave Thee*. Kbd: H:d♯1-g2; L:b1-e♭2. Concordia (1959) 97-9345; 97-9346

1:16-17 Gounod, Charles. *Entreat Me Not to Leave Thee*. Pno: H:e1-g♯2; M:d1-f♯2; L:c1-e2. Found in *The Church Soloist* (L); *Everybody's Favorite Sacred Songs* (M); *Everything for the Wedding Soloist; Famous Sacred Songs; The Sacred Collection* (H/L); *Singer's Wedding Anthology* (H/L); *Together* (M); *Wedding Classics* (H/L); *A Wedding Garland*

1:16-17 Gounod, Charles. *Entreat Me Not to Leave Thee*. Pno: L:c1-e2. Hal Leonard (1992), found in *The Bride's Guide to Wedding Music*

1:16-17 Groton, Frederic. *Entreat Me Not,* op. 10. Kbd: g-f♭2. Huntzinger (1931), found in *Choice Sacred Songs for Home or Church Services* (H/L)

1:16-17 (Song of Songs 2:10-12; Song of Songs 7:6-7)
Haas, David. *Whereever You Go*. Duet-Pno or harp, gtr, inst in c: c1-d2/b1-f♯1. GIA (1993), found in *When Love Is Found*

1:16-17 (other)
Hallquist, Gary (arr. Paul Johnson). *Song of Ruth*. Kbd, gtr: d1-b2. Sonlife Music (1976), found in *Everything for the Wedding Soloist*

1:16-17 Hildach, Eugen. *Where'er Thou Goest*. Kbd: H:d1-g2; M:c1-f2; L: b♭1-e 2. Heinrichshofen (Peters)

1:16-17 (Song of Songs 6:12)
Hurd, Bob (arr. Craig S. Kingsbury). *Where You Go*. Org, gtr: d1-d2. OCP (1988) 9111, found in *United as One,* vol. 2

1:16-17 (Song of Songs 6:12)
Hurd, Bob (arr. Craig S. Kingsbury). *Where You Go*. U/2-part-Org, gtr: d1-d2 (b1-c2). OCP (1988) OCP 9111, also found in *Everlasting Your Love*

1:16-17 (Song of Songs 6:12)
Hurd, Bob (arr. Craig S. Kingsbury). *Where You Go*. Duet-Org, gtr: M:d1-d2/ML:b1-c2. OCP (1988), found in *United as One,* vol. 2

1:16-17 Norbet, Gregory and Mary David Callahan. *Wherever You Go*. Kbd or gtr: b♭1-c1. Weston Priory (1972), found in *United as One,* vol. 1

1:16-17 Peeters, Flor. *Wedding Song,* op. 103B. Org: H:f1-a3; M:d1-f 2; L:c1-e2. C. F. Peters (1962)

1:16-17 Pendleton, Emmet. *Song of Ruth,* op. 12, no. 2 (from *The Light of the Lord*). Pno: c1-f2. Bruce Humphries (1945)

1:16-17 Poulsen, James. *Entreat Me Not to Leave You*. Kbd: M: d♯1-e2. Randall M. Egan (1991) 32-21-611

1:16-17 Samama, Leo. *Whither Thou Goest,* mvt. 3 (from *Wedding Cantata*). Org: Tenor:g1-e♭2. WIM (1974) 118

1:16-17 Schütz, Heinrich. *A Wedding Song (Zur Trauung)*. Kbd: L:d1-d2. G. Schirmer (1978), found in *The Church Year in Song*

1:16-17 (English adaptation by Ruth Michaelis)
Schütz, Heinrich. *Wedding Song (Zur Trauung)* (English/German). Kbd: MH:f1-f2; ML:d1-d2. Augsburg (1951) MH: 90-5115; ML: 90-5116

1:16-17 Schütz, Heinrich. *Wedding Song (Zur Trauung)* (English/German). Kbd: H:f1-f2; L:d1-d2. Chantry (1951) MH: EK12-905115; ML: EK12-905116

1:16-17 (taken from)
Singer, Guy. *Whither Thou Goest*. Pno: M: b♭1-e♭2; L:g-c1. Hal Leonard (1987), found in *50 Great Wedding Favorites; From This Day Forward* (M); *New Love & Wedding Songbook* (M); *Singer's Wedding Anthology* (H/L); *We Will Serve the Lord* (M); *Wedding & Love* (M); *Wedding Collection: 52 Solos* (M/L); *Wedding Music*, vol. 2; *Wedding Songbook* (M)

1:16-17 (taken from)
Singer, Guy. *Whither Thou Goest*. Pno: M:b♭1-e♭2 (g2). Hal Leonard (1986) HL00305570

1:16-17 (taken from)
Singer, Guy. *Whither Thou Goest.* Duet Pno: M:b♭1-e♭2/L:b♭1-c2. Hal Leonard (1987), found in *Singer's Wedding Anthology-Duet*

1:16-17 Stern, Robert. *Al Tifg'i Vi* (from *Two Hebrew Songs*) (Hebrew). Kbd: H. Transcontinental (1992)

1:16-17 Watts, Wintter. *Intreat Me Not to Leave Thee*. Pno: L:a1-e♭2. G. Schirmer (1923)

1:16-17 Weiner, Lazar. *Ruth*. Kbd: e1-b♭3. Transcontinental (1972)

1:16-17 White, Louie. *Entreat Me Not to Leave Thee*. Org: H:e1-f2; L:c1-d♭2. Concordia (1980), found in *Seven Wedding Songs*

1:16-17 Young, Gordon. *Entreat Me Not to Leave Thee*. Kbd: f1-f2. Galaxy (1961)

I SAMUEL

1:00 Plantavsky, Peter. *Hannu und Eli.* Org: Sop:c♯1-a3. Doblinger (1982) 08-868

2:1-2 Schütz, Heinrich. *Exultavit cor meum,* SWV258 (Latin/German). Cont, 2 vlns: Sop:c1-f2. Bärenreiter (1956) BA29

2:1-10 (verses by Emily R. Brink)
Lovelace, Austin C. *My Soul Is Filled with Joy (Song of Hannah).* Kbd: c1-e♭2. Darcy Press (1993), found in *Sacred Solos by Austin C. Lovelace*

15:22 Gates, Crawford. *To Obey Is Better Than Sacrifice* (from *Three Songs for the Young Heart,* op. 49). Kbd: M:d1-e2. Jackman Music (1992) S-0180, found in *Scripture Settings for Solo Voice*

17:47 (Revelation 7:12; based on)
Owens, Jimmy and Jamie Collins. *The Battle Belongs to the Lord.* Kbd: b1-d2. Fairhill Music (1984, 1990), found in *Face to Face*

17:49 SEE: Exodus 14:22. Spiritual (arr. Harry T. Burleigh). *He's Jus' De Same Today*

25:32 Steinberg, Ben. *Vayomer David L'Avigayil (And David Said to Abigail)* (Hebrew). Transcontinental (1988), found in *A Ben Steinberg Solo Collection* (n.v.)

II SAMUEL

1:19-27 Adler, Samuel. *Laments.* Chamber orch: Bar. Ms (1968), copy found in Sibley Library, Eastman

1:19-27 Rorem, Ned. *Mourning Scene.* Stg qt: c1-g2. C. F. Peters (1963) 6374

2:2-3, 7, 18
SEE: Psalm 18:00. Cornelius, Peter. *I Love Thee, Lord, My Strength,* op. 2, no. 2

18:33 DeLong, Richard. *Absalom* (from *Five Sacred Songs*). Kbd: M:f1-d♯2. E. C. Schirmer (1993) 4759

18:33 Diamond, David. *David Mourns for Absalom.* Pno: Tenor:d1-a3. Mercury (1947)

18:33 Schütz, Heinrich. *Fili mi, Absalom,* SWV 269 (from *Symphoniae Sacrae* I) (Latin). Cont, 4 tbns: Bass:a-d1. Bärenreiter (1949) BA40

19:27 Fromm, Herbert. *Lamentation of David* (from *Five Songs of Worship*). Kbd: a1-e2. Transcontinental (1946) TV 474

22:2-3 SEE: Psalm 18:2. Nelhybel, Vaclav. *The Lord Is My Rock*

22:3 (Psalm 18:2; Psalm 23:2-3; Psalm 28:7; Psalm 34:1)
Bach, J. S. *Ever Will I Praise.* Duet-Kbd: b♭1-a/c-d1. Heritage (Lorenz) (1991), found in *Selected Duets for Contest:* set 1

22:4 (Psalm 18:3, 46; adapted)
O'Shields, Michael. *I Will Call Upon the Lord (The Lord Liveth).* Kbd, gtr, (opt orch): d1-d2. Sound III, Inc. (1981), found in *Songs for Praise and Worship*

22:4 (Psalm 18:3, 46; adapted)
O'Shields, Michael (arr. Gary Rhodes). *I Will Call Upon the Lord (The Lord Liveth).* 2-part-Kbd or Trax: c1-d2/c-d1. Sound III (1981, 1991), found in *The Two Part Collection*

23:1-5 Freudenthal, Josef. *Last Words of David.* Kbd: H:g1-g2; M. Transcontinental (1964) TV 565

I KINGS

3:5, 7, 9, 10-14
Miller, Merle. *Solomon's Prayer.* Kbd: H:d1-f2; L:b1-d2. R. D. Row (1947)

3:9 Rubenstein, Anton (arr. Carl Fredrickson). *Give Me an Understanding Heart.* Kbd: M. R. D. Row (1959), found in *Sacred Song Masterpieces,* bk 1

18:36-37 Mendelssohn, Felix. *Lord God of Abraham (Herr Gott Abrahams)* (from *Elijah*) (English/German). Kbd: Bass: b♭-e♭1. G. Schirmer; H. W. Gray; Novello, found in *Anthology of Sacred Song–Bass; Oratorio Anthology: Baritone/Bass; Oratorio Repertoire,* vol. IV; *Schirmer's Singer's Library: Bass Arias from Oratorios; Second Book of Baritone/Bass Solos; The Second Book of Tenor Solos*

18:36-37 Mendelssohn, Felix (arr. Lynn Hodges). *Lord God of Abraham (Draw Near, All Ye People)* (from *Elijah*). Kbd: b1-d2. Integra (1993), found in *Mendelssohn's ELIJAH for Young Voices*

18:43-44 (based on)
Mendelssohn, Felix (arr. Lynn Hodges). *Go Up, Child (There Is Nothing)* (from *Elijah*). Duet-Kbd: c♯1-c♯2/e1-a2. Integra (1993), found in *Mendelssohn's ELIJAH for Young Voices*

19:4, 10 Mendelssohn, Felix. *It Is Enough (Es ist genug!)* (from *Elijah*) (English/German). Kbd: Bass:a-e1. G. Schirmer; H. W. Gray; Novello, found in *52 Sacred Songs; Anthology of Sacred Song–Bass; Everybody's Favorite Sacred Songs; Oratorio Anthology: Baritone/Bass; Oratorio Repertoire,* vol. IV; *Schirmer's Singer's Library: Bass Arias from Oratorios*

19:4, 10 Mendelssohn, Felix (arr. Lynn Hodges). *It Is Enough* (from *Elijah*). Kbd: c1-d2. Integra (1993), found in *Mendelssohn's ELIJAH for Young Voices*

II KINGS

2:9-13 (other; based on)
Hawkins, Floyd (trans. Lyndell Leatherman). *Let Thy Mantle Fall on Me*. Kbd: c1-f2. Lillenas (1990), found in *Solos from the Word*

2:11 (based on)
Spiritual. *Swing Low, Sweet Chariot*. Kbd or CD: L:c1-c2. Hal Leonard (1997) found in *Classical Contest Solos–Baritone/Bass*

2:11 (based on)
Spiritual (arr. Edward Boatner). *Swing Low, Sweet Chariot*. Pno, gtr: d1-e2. Belwin Mills (1973), found in *The Story of the Spirituals*

2:11 (based on)
Spiritual (arr. Harry T. Burleigh). *Swing Low, Sweet Chariot*. Kbd: H:e♭1-e♭2; L:c1-c2. Belwin Mills (1917), found in *Thirty Spirituals; The Sacred Collection* (H/L)

2:11 (based on)
Spiritual (arr. Hall Johnson). *Swing Low, Sweet Chariot*. Kbd: e1-e2(a3). G. Schirmer (1949), found in *The Spirituals of Harry T. Burleigh* (H/L)

2:11 (based on)
Spiritual (ed. Jean Anne Shafferman). *Chariot's Comin' (Swing Low, Sweet Chariot)*. Duet-Kbd or CD: M/M. Alfred (1997), found in *Spirituals for Two*

2:11 (based on)
Spiritual (arr. Hall Johnson). *Swing Low, Sweet Chariot*. Kbd: e1-e2(a3). G. Schirmer (1949), found in *The Spirituals of Harry T. Burleigh* (H/L)

I CHRONICLES

4:10 Beck, Joe and Tom Lane. *The Prayer of Jabez*. Kbd, gtr: d1-f♯2. Hal Leonard (2001), found in *The Prayer of Jabez*

4:10 Cooper, Jim and Regie Hamm. *Beyond the Borders*. Kbd, gtr: Tenor:e♭-f♯2. Hal Leonard (2001), found in *The Prayer of Jabez*

4:10 Hartley, John and Gary Sadler. *This Is My Prayer*. Kbd, gtr: a-b2. Hal Leonard (2001), found in *The Prayer of Jabez*

16:8-9 (and other based on)
Carswell, Eddie and Oliver Wells. *Come Let's Worship Him*. Kbd, gtr or Trax: c1-g2. Word (1987), found in *Sandi Patti: Anthology*

16:23-25, 27, 31
Dengler, Lee. *Sing Unto the Lord*. Kbd: M:b1-g2. Augsburg (1995) 11-10608, found in *Songs of David*

16:29 (Psalm 29:2, Psalm 96:9)
Handel, G. F. *O Worship the Lord*. 2-part mixed-Kbd: H:a1-d2/L:c-e1. Beckenhorst (1984) BP1235

16:29 SEE: Job 22:21. Head, Michael. *Acquaint Now Thyself With Him*

16:29 (Psalm 104:1; Psalm 145:13; adapted)
Schubert, Franz (arr. Carl Fredrickson). *The Grand Alleluia*. Kbd: b♭1-f2. R. D. Row (1964), found in *Sacred Song Masterpieces*, bk 2

16:29 (and other based on)
Tunney, Dick and Melodie Tunney. *Come Before Him*. Kbd or Trax: c1-b♭3. Pamela Kay Music/Dick and Mel Music (1988), found in *Sandi Patti: Anthology*

16:29 SEE: Psalm 113:3. VanDyke, May. *In the Beauty of Holiness*. Kbd: H:e1-g2; L:b1-d2 Boosey & Hawkes (1937)

29:10-11, 13-14
Greenfield, Alfred M. *Blessed Be Thou Lord God of Israel*. Org: c♯1-f2. H. W. Gray (1932)

29:11 Weiner, Lazar. *L'Cho Adonoy* (from *Anim Z'Miros*) (Hebrew). Transcontinental (1964) (n.v.)

29:11-13 MacDermid, James G. *Thine, O Lord Is the Greatness*. Kbd: H:f$^{\sharp}$1-a3; L:d1-f2. Forster (1944)

29:15 SEE: Psalm 27:4. Talma, Louise. *Cantata: All the Days of My Life*

II CHRONICLES

6:14, 19-21
Pisk, Paul A. *Solomon's Prayer*. Kbd: c1-f$^{\sharp}$2. American Composers Alliance

7:14 (other)
Brooks, Tom and Robin Brooks (arr. Tom Fettke). *Heal Our Land* (incorporates song, *America the Beautiful*). Kbd, gtr: a1-e$^{\flat}$2(f2). Integrity (1988), found in *The Solo Book*

7:14 Owens, Jimmy. *If My People Will Pray*. Kbd: c1-g2. Found in *The Church Soloist; Everything for the Church Soloist; Gospel & Inspirational Showstoppers; How Majestic Is Your Name; Scripture Solos for All Seasons; Solos from the Word*

20:15b, 17 (Isaiah 41:10, 13; II Timothy 1:7)
Koch, Frederick. *Be Not Afraid*. Kbd: H:e$^{\flat}$1-a$^{\flat}$3. Boosey & Hawkes (1963)

NEHEMIAH

8:10 (based on)
Vale, Alliene G. *The Joy of the Lord*. Kbd, gtr, (opt orch): a1-d2. Word (1982), found in *Songs for Praise and Worship*

ESTHER

4:14 (based on; other)
Craig, Shawn and Don Koch. *A Time Such as This*. Kbd, gtr: a1-f2(a$^{\flat}$3). Lillenas (1999), found in *Solos from the Word*

8:16 Horowitz, Rabbi M. (arr. Velvel Pasternak). *La-y'hudim*, no. 2 *(The Jews Had Lightness)* (Hebrew transliterated). Gtr: M:b1-e2. Bloch (1971), found in *Songs of the Chassidim II*

8:16 Portugal, Rabbi E. (arr. Velvel Pasternak). *La-y'hudim*, no. 1 *(The Jews Had Lightness)* (Hebrew transliterated). Gtr: M:b1-e2. Bloch (1971), found in *Songs of the Chassidim II*

9:1 Benet, Ch. (arr. Velvel Pasternak). *V'nahafõch*, no. 2 *(It Was Turned to the Contrary)* (Hebrew transliterated). Gtr: H:f1-f2. Bloch (1971), found in *Songs of the Chassidim II*

9:1 Pasternak, Velvel. *V'nahafõch*, no. 2 *(It Was Turned to the Contrary)* (Hebrew transliterated). Gtr: M:a1-d2. Bloch (1971), found in *Songs of the Chassidim II*

JOB

1:21a (Psalm 113:2; other)
Rogers, Dawn and Tricia Walker. *Baruch Hashem Adonai*. Kbd, gtr: b1-c2. Word (1984), found in *Our God Reigns*

7:6 SEE: Psalm 27:4. Talma, Louise. *Cantata: All the Days of My Life*

8:5 SEE: Job 22:21. Way, Arthur. *Acquaint Now Thyself With Him*

9:10 Portugal, Rabbi E. (arr. Velvel Pasternak). *Ho-õse g'dõlõs (Who Does Great Things)* (Hebrew transliterated). Gtr: M:b1-e2. Bloch (1971), found in *Songs of the Chassidim II*

11:7, 13-15, 17
MacDermid, James G. *Cans't Thou By Searching Find Our God?* Kbd: Med. Forster (1956)

11:13, 15, 17, 19
SEE: Job 22:21. Way, Arthur. *Acquaint Now Thyself With Him*

11:13-19 Parker, Clifton. *If Thou Prepare Thine Heart*. Kbd: c1-e$^{\flat}$2. Carl Fischer (1934)

11:16 (Matthew 6:25-34; John 14:18)
Hurd, Bob (acc. Laura Wasson). *God's Eye Is on the Sparrow*. Pno, gtr, inst in c: b1-c$^{\sharp}$2. OCP (1990), found in *Behold the Cross*

11:17 SEE: Psalm 27:4. Talma, Louise. *Cantata: All the Days of My Life*

14:1-2 Pinkham, Daniel. *Man That Is Born of a Woman* (from *Man That Is Born of a Woman*). Gtr: g1-e2. E. C. Schirmer (1971)

14:1, 2, 7-12
Floyd, Carlisle. *Man That Is Born of a Woman* (from *The Pilgrimage*). Kbd or orch: M:a1-f2. Boosey & Hawkes (1959)

14:1, 32-33 (Job 32:8; Job 33:4, 23, 28)
Cornelius, Peter (ed. M. B. Stearns). *There Is a Spirit in Man,* op. 2, no. 3. Kbd: c♯1-f2. Coburn Press (1971), found in *Lift Up Your Voice*

14:14 (Job 19:25, 26)
Cundick, Robert. *If a Man Die, Shall He Live Again?* (from *The Redeemer*). Kbd: M:b♭1-e♭2. Sonos (Jackman) (1997) 00434, found in *Sabbath Song*

19:25 (Job 19:25; I Corinthians 15:31-52)
Dufford, Bob. *Songs of the Angels* (refrain inspired by the chant *In Paradisum*). Pno, gtr, inst in c, opt duet: b1-d2. NALR (1985) OCP: 5750CC, also found in *The Steadfast Love*

19:25a (Fanny Crosby)
Knapp, Phoebe C. *Open the Gates of the Temple*. Kbd: b♭1-f2. Hal Leonard (n.d.), found in *How Majestic Is Your Name; Soloists Practical Library,* vol. 1

19:25a (Isaiah 25:8; based on)
Soper, Scott. *I Know That My Redeemer Lives*. Kbd, gtr, inst in c, hn: c1-d2. OCP (1990), found in *Return to Me: Music for Funerals and Healing,* vol. 1

19:25-26 SEE: Job 14:14. Cundick, Robert. *If a Man Die, Shall He Live Again?*

19:25-26 (I Corinthians 15:20)
Handel, G. F. *I Know That My Redeemer Liveth* (*Ich weiss, dass mein Erlöser lebet*) (from *Messiah*) (English/German). Kbd: Sop:e1-g♯2; M:d1-f♯2; L:c1-e2. G. Schirmer (1977), found in *20 Distinctive Sacred Songs* (H/L); *52 Sacred Songs; The Church Soloist* (M); *Everybody's Favorite Sacred Songs; Kirchen-Arien und Lieder* (German); *Oratorio Anthology–Sop; Oratorio Repertoire,* vol. 1; *Schirmer's Singer's Library: Sop Arias from Oratorios; Scripture Solos for All Seasons; Vocal Solos for Funeral and Memorial Services* (M); *Sing Solo Sacred* (H/L); *World's Favorite Sacred Songs* (H)

19:25-26 (I Corinthians 15:20)
Handel, G. F. (arr. David Hamilton). *I Know That My Redeemer Liveth* (from *Messiah*) (English/German). Kbd, gtr: b♭1-f2. Birdwing (1993), found in *Steve Green: People Need the Lord*

19:25-26 (I Corinthians 15:20)
Handel, G. F. (arr. James Michael Stevens). *I Know That My Redeemer Liveth* (from *Messiah*). 2-part-Kbd: c1-d2. Integra (1993), found in *Easter MESSIAH for Young Voices*

19:25-26 Peloquin, C. Alexander. *I Believe That My Redeemer Lives*. Org: M:a1-f2. GIA (1971) G-1636

19:25-27 (II Timothy 2:9, 11-12; John 15:13; John 20:18; II Corinthians 4:10)
Hurd, Bob and Dominic MacAller (harm. Craig S. Kingsbury). *I Have Seen the Lord.* U/2-part-Pno, gtr, 2 inst in c: (b1)c1-d2. OCP (1988, 1990), found in *Behold the Cross*

20:8a, 9 SEE: Isaiah 2:22. Barker, Clement W. *Mark the Perfect Man*

22:00 Buck, Dudley. *Acquaint Thyself With Him*. Duet-Org: Sop/Tenor; Alto/Bass. G. Schirmer (1923) (n.v.)

22:21 (I Chronicles 16:29; Psalm 96:8-9; Psalm 99:9; Micah 6:6-8)
Head, Michael. *Acquaint Now Thyself With Him*. Pno/org: H:d1-g2; L:b♭1-e♭2. Boosey & Hawkes (1960)

22:21 (Jeremiah 29:12, 13; Isaiah 65:19; Psalm 90:4)
MacDermid, James G. *Acquaint Now Thyself With Him*. Kbd: H:f1-g2; L:d♭1-e♭2. Forster (1955)

22:21 (Job 11:13, 15, 17, 19; Job 8:5)
Way, Arthur. *Acquaint Now Thyself With Him*. Org: c♯1-f12. Galaxy (1948)

23:3 SEE: Jeremiah 29:11-14. Courtney, Craig. *If You Search With All Your Heart*

23:3 SEE: Deuteronomy 4:29. Mendelssohn, Felix. *If With All Your Hearts*

23:3 SEE: Deuteronomy 4:29. Mendelssohn, Felix (arr. Lynn Hodges). *If With All Your Hearts*

23:3 SEE: Deuteronomy 4:29. Mendelssohn, Felix (ed. Patrick M. Liebergen). *If With All Your Hearts*

23:3 SEE: Deuteronomy 4:29. Mendelssohn, Felix (ed. Lyndell Leatherman). *If With All Your Hearts*

23:3 SEE: Deuteronomy 4:29. Mendelssohn, Felix (arr. Harrison Oxley). *If With All Your Hearts*

23:3 SEE: Deuteronomy 4:29. Roberts, J. E. *If With All Your Hearts*

23:3 (John 20:29)
Rowley, Alec. *O That I Knew Where I Might Find Him.* Kbd: d1-g2. Boosey & Hawkes (1939)

32:8 SEE: Job 14:1, 32-33. Cornelius, Peter. *There Is a Spirit in Man*

33:4, 23, 28
SEE: Job 14:1, 32-33. Cornelius, Peter. *There Is a Spirit in Man*

33:15, 16 SEE: Psalm 27:1, 3, 5-6. Buck, Dudley. *The Lord Is My Light*

36:5, 6, 7 Wooler, Alfred. *Behold, God Is Mighty.* Kbd: H:e1-a3; L:c1-d2. Arthur P. Schmidt (1912)

PSALMS

1:00 Bone, Gene and Howard Fenton. *The First Psalm.* Kbd: M:d♭1-f2; L:b1-d2. Carl Fischer (1945) V 2054

1:00 Bowling, Blanche. *He Shall Be Like a Tree.* Kbd: H:d1-f2; L:c1-e♭2. R. D. Row (1957) H: RS197, L: RS198

1:00 Butt, James. *Psalm 1.* Org: f1-e2. Sphemusations (1958)

1:00 Fromm, Herbert. *Psalm 1* (from *Four Psalms*). Kbd: d1-g2. Transcontinental (1971)

1:00 Karg-Elert, Sigfrid (ed. Johannes M. Michel and Wolfgang Stockmeier). *Der erste Psalm.* Org: M:c1-a3. Breitkopf (1996) 8623

1:00 Lucke, Katharine E. *Blessed Is the Man.* Kbd: c1-f2. Presser (1941)

1:00 Nelhybel, Vaclav. *Blessed Is the Man.* Kbd: c1-e2. Hope (1981)

1:00 Ore, Charles W. *Blessed Is the Man* (from *Lisbon Psalms*). Kbd, vc/ban, 2 vlns, recorder: M:c1-f2. Concordia (1975) Set I - pno: 97-5299; Set II - org: 97-5300

1:00 (Matthew 5:1-12)
Schoenbachler, Tim. *Happy Are They.* Gtr: d1-d2. OCP (1979), found in *All Is Ready*

1:00 Thiman, Eric H. *Happy Is the Man (Psalms)* (from *Two Biblical Songs*). Kbd: b1-e2. Novello (1953), found in *The Church Soloist* (H/L)

1:00 Thornton, William. *Psalm 1 (Happy Are They).* Harp, fl: b1-f2. Southern (1993) V 93

1:1 Roff, Joseph. *He Is Like a Tree.* 2-part-Kbd: c1-e2/b1-d2. Boston Music (1987) 14110

1:1-3 (adapted)
Adler, Samuel. *Happy He Who Walketh Ever* (no. 6 from *Twelve Songs of Praise*). U-Org: c1-d2. Oxford (1988) 94.505

1:1-3 Clements, John. *Blessed Is the Man.* Kbd: b♭1-f2. Lengnick (1982) 4595

1:1-3 (based on)
Cooney, Rory. *Psalm 1 (Roots in the Earth).* U-Kbd, gtr: d1-d2. GIA (1993) G-3969, also found in *Vision*

1:1-3 Schütz, Heinrich. *Wohl dem der nicht wandelt,* SWV 290 *(Blessed Are They)* (from *Kleine geistliche Konzerte* I). Duet-Org: Sop:d1-g2/Alto:a1-c1. GIA (1983) G-2634

1:1-3 (and Alleluia)
Schütz, Heinrich. *Wohl dem der nicht wandelt,* SWV 290 (German) (from *Kleine geistliche Konzerte* I). Duet-Org: Sop:d1-g2/Alto:a1-c1. Hänssler (1982) HE 20.290/02

1:1-3 Schütz, Heinrich. *Wohl dem der nicht wandelt,* SWV 290 (from *Kleine geistliche Konzerte*) (German). Duet-Org: Sop:d1-g2/Alto:a1-c1. Bärenreiter (1982) BA1270

1:1-3 Spies, Claudio. *Blessed Is the Man* (from *Five Psalms*). Fl, fg, hn, mand, vla, vc: Sop: c♯1-a3. Boosey & Hawkes (1962)

1:1-3 Tarsi, Boaz. *Ashrei Ha'Ish* (*Happy Is the Man*) (Hebrew). Transcontinental (1993) (n.v.)

1:1-3 Wagner, Douglas E. *Blessed Is the Man.* 2-part-Kbd: H: b♭1-f2/L:b♭1-d2-d2. Beckenhorst (1979) BP1086

1:1, 4 Greene, Maurice (ed. Marson Martens). *Blessed Is the Man.* Duet-Kbd: Med. Walton (n.v.)

2:1-2 Handel, G. F. *Why Do the Nations* (from *Messiah*). Kbd: Bass:b-e1. C. F. Peters; G. Schirmer; H. W. Gray; Novello (n.d.), found in *Anthology of Sacred Song–Bass; Oratorio Anthology: Baritone/Bass; Oratorio Repertoire,* vol. IV

2:4 Handel, G. F. *He That Dwelleth in Heaven* (from *Messiah*). Kbd: Tenor:e-a2. C. F. Peters; G. Schirmer; H. W. Gray; Novello (n.d.), found in *Oratorio Anthology: Tenor*

2:9 Handel, G. F. *Thou Shalt Break Them* (from *Messiah*). Kbd: Tenor:e-a2. C. F. Peters; G. Schirmer; H. W. Gray; Novello (n.d.), found in *Oratorio Anthology: Tenor*

3:00 Hanson, Jens. *Psalm 3*. Pno: Bar. Canadian Music Centre (1963)

3:00 (based on)
Schoenbachler, Tim. *Here I Am, Send Me*. U/2-part-Gtr, vln or fl: d1-b2. OCP (1979), found in *All Is Ready*

3:1-3 Tapp, Freda. *Thou Art a Shield for Me*. Kbd, gtr (opt orch): b1-d2. Matterhorn Music (1976), found in *Songs for Praise and Worship*

3:1-4 Raksim, David. *Psalm on the Eve of Battle*. Kbd: H:d1-f2; L:a1-c2. Fred Bock Music (1980), found in *The Sanctuary Soloist*

3:3 (based on)
Thomas, Donn and Charles Williams. *A Shield About Me*. Kbd, gtr, (opt orch): d1-a2. Word (1980, 1992), found in *Songs for Praise and Worship*

3:5 SEE: Psalm 103:1. Wesley, Samuel Sebastian. *Praise the Lord, O My Soul (Lead Me, Lord)*

3:6-9 Schütz, Heinrich. *Ich, Liege und Schlafe* SWV 310 (from *Kleine geistliche Konzerte*) (German). Cont: Bass:g-e1. Bärenreiter (1963)

3:8 Greene, Maurice. *Salvation Belongeth Unto the Lord* (from *Lord How Are Thy Increased*). Kbd: H:f1-e♭2; L:e♭1-d♭2. G. Schirmer (1965), found in *The Sunday Solo* (H/L)

3:8 Greene, Maurice. *Salvation Belongeth Unto the Lord* (from *Lord How Are Thy Increased*). Kbd: H:f1- e♭2; L:e♭1-d♭2. G. Schirmer (1994) HL50482071, found in *Second Book of Baritone/Bass Solos*

4:00 Garlick, Anthony. *Psalm 4* (from *A Psalm Cycle*). Pno: Tenor: e♭ 1-f2. Seesaw Music

4:00 Ore, Charles W. *Answer Me When I Call* (from *Lisbon Psalms*). Kbd, vc/bsn, 2 vlns: M:c1-f2. Concordia (1975) Set I - pno: 97-5299; Set II - org: 97-5300

4:1 (Psalm 86:6a, 11a; Psalm 116:3-4)
Gilbert, Harry M. *God of Righteousness*. Kbd: H:e1-a♭ 2; L:b1-e2. Huntzinger (1920), found in *Choice Sacred Songs for Home or Church Services*

4:1 (Psalm 16:1; Psalm 17:10-12; Isaiah 52:1)
Huhn, Bruno S. *Hear Me When I Call*. Pno: H:c♯1-a3; L:a1-f2. G. Schirmer (1904)

4:1 SEE: Psalm 25:4-5. Nelhybel, Vaclav. *Hear Me When I Call*

4:1 (Psalm 5:2)
Schütz, Heinrich (ed. Paul Boepple). *Sacred Concert (Kleines Geistliches Concert)*. Duet-Cont: M/M:d1-e2/L:c♯1-e2. Mercury (1941) 60

4:1 (Psalm 5:2)
Schütz, Heinrich (ed. Don McAfee). *Hear Me, O Lord,* SWV 289 (German/English). Duet-Cont: Equal voices: d1-e2/c♯1-e2. Belwin (1977) CPP131, found in *Eight Sacred Duets*

4:1 (Psalm 5:2)
Schütz, Heinrich (ed. Earnest Murphy). *Hear Me, O Lord,* SWV 289. Duet-Kbd: M:d1-d2/L:b1-a2. McAfee Music (1973), found in *The Baroque Songbook*

4:2 (Psalm 5:2)
Schütz, Heinrich. *Erhöre mich, Wenn ich rufe,* SWV 289 *(Hear Me, O Lord)* (from *Kleine geistliche Konzerte*) (German). Duet-Cont: Equal voices:d1-e2/c♯1-e2. Hänssler (1963)

4:2 (Psalm 5:2)
Schütz, Heinrich. *Erhöre mich, Wenn ich rufe*, SWV 289 (from *Kleine geistliche Konzerte*) (German). Duet-Cont: Sop/Sop:c♯1-e2. Bärenreiter BA1138 (n.v.)

4:6-7 Pasternak, Velvel. *Zivchu Zivché Tsedek (Offer the Sacrifices of Righteousness)* (Hebrew transliterated). Gtr: M:e1-c2. Bloch (1971), found in *Songs of the Chassidim II*

4:8 (Psalm 34:7; Psalm 42:8; Psalm 147:4)
Buck, Dudley (ed. Carl Fredrickson). *I Will Lay Me Down in Peace* (from *Triumph of David*). Kbd: Sop:d1-g2; Tenor:b1-e2. R. D. Row (1963), found in *Church Soloists Favorites,* bk 1

4:8 Greene, Maurice (ed. E. Stanley Roper). *I Will Lay Me Down in Peace*. Kbd: H:e1-f2; L:d1-e2. Bosworth (1910), found in *Seven Sacred Solos of the Early English School*

4:8 SEE: Psalm 5:8. Wesley, Samuel Sebastian. *Lead Me, Lord*

4:8 SEE: Psalm 103:1. Wesley, Samuel Sebastian. *Praise the Lord, O My Soul*

4:9 SEE: Psalm 5:8. Handel, G. F. (arr. Carl Fredrickson). *Lead Me, Lord*

5:1-3 Sprouse, Bill Jr. *Psalm 5.* U-Kbd: e1-d2. BMG Songs (1975), found in *Praise Classics–Lord of Love*

5:1-5, 7 (adapted)
Adler, Samuel. *Hear My Words, O Gracious Lord* (no. 12 from *Twelve Songs of Praise*). U-Org: d1-d2. Oxford (1988) 94.505

5:2 SEE: Psalm 4:1. Schütz, Heinrich. *Hear Me, O Lord*

5:2 SEE: Psalm 4:2. Schütz, Heinrich. *Erhöre mich, Wenn ich rufe*

5:2-3a (Psalm 25:17-18; Psalm 106:1-4; based on)
Foley, John B. *Heed My Call for Help.* Gtr: c♯1-b2. NALR (1974), found in *Neither Silver Nor Gold*

5:3 Corfe, Joseph. *My Voice Shalt Thou Hear.* Kbd: MH:e1-g2. Novello (1961)

5:8 SEE: Numbers 24:5. Gottlieb, Jack. *Ma Tovu*

5:8 (Psalm 119:3; adapted)
Handel, G. F. (arr. Carl Fredrickson). *Lead Me, Lord.* Kbd: e♭1-e♭2. R. D. Row (1959), found in *Sacred Song Masterpieces,* bk 1

5:8 (Psalm 119:3; adapted)
Handel, G. F. (arr. Carl Fredrickson). *Lead Me, Lord.* Duet-Kbd: H/H; H:f1-g2/L:b1-c2; M/L. R. D. Row (1959), found in *Sacred Duet Masterpieces,* bk 1

5:8 (Psalm 23:4)
Molique, Wilhelm Bernhard. *Lead Me, O Lord (Lead Me, Lord)* (from *Abraham*). Kbd: Bass:d-e1. G. Schirmer (1977), found in *Anthology of Sacred Song–Bass; Schirmer's Singer's Library: Bass Arias from Oratorios*

5:8 SEE: Numbers 24:5. Steinberg, Ben. *Mah Tovu*

5:8 SEE: Numbers 24:5. Weiner, Lazar. *Mah Tovu*

5:8 (Psalm 4:8)
Wesley, Samuel Sebastian. *Lead Me, Lord.* U/2-part-Org: d1-d2; H:e1-e2(L:b1-b2). Kevin Mayhew (1992) U-64016 (arr. Manney), also found in *Favorite Anthem,* bk 2

5:8 (Psalm 4:8)
Wesley, Samuel Sebastian (arr. Fred Bock). *Lead Me, Lord.* 2-part mixed-Kbd: c1-d2/d-f1. Fred Bock (1983, 1982) B-G0474

5:8 (Psalm 4:8)
Wesley, Samuel Sebastian (arr. Mary Hamlin). *Lead Me, Lord.* Kbd: M:d1-f2. Boston Music (n.d.)

5:8 SEE: Psalm 103:1. Wesley, Samuel Sebastian. *Praise the Lord, O My Soul*

5:12 SEE: Isaiah 1:18. Barker, Clement W. *The Path of the Just*

5:12 Portugal, Rabbi E. (arr. Velvel Pasternak). *V'yism'chu chol chõsé voch* (*All Those Who Take Refuge in Thee*) (Hebrew transliterated). Gtr: M:a1-d2. Bloch (1971), found in *Songs of the Chassidim II*

6:00 Bernhard, Christoph. *Ach, Herr, strafe mich nicht in deinen Zorn* (German). Duet-Kbd: Sop:a1-g2/Bass:E-d2. Bärenreiter (1972), found in *Geistliche Harmonien*

6:00 Hanson, Howard. *O Lord, Rebuke Me Not in Thine Anger* (from *Four Psalms,* op. 50). Bar-Pno/org: a-f1. Carl Fischer (1972)

6:00 Posch, Isaac (ed. Karl Geiringer). *Domine ne in furore tuo* (from *Harmonia Concertans*) (Latin). Duet-Kbd: Tenor:d1-e2/Bass:G-c2. Ann Arbor: University Microfilm (1968 - 72), found in *Series of Early Music,* vol. 4

6:00 Rubbra, Edmund. *Psalm 6,* op. 61, no. 2 *(O Lord, Rebuke Me Not)* (from *Three Psalms For Low Voice*). Kbd: M:d1-e2. Alfred Lengnick (1947) 3553

6:00 (taken from)
Schalit, Heinrich. *O Lord, Return.* Org or harp: e1-f2. H. Schalit (1952)

6:1-4 Purcell, Henry. *O Lord, Rebuke Me Not.* Kbd: H:c1-g2; L:a1-e2. R. D. Row, found in *Purcell Songs*

6:33-37 Wooler, Alfred. *O Lord, Rebuke Me Not.* Kbd: H:e1-g2; M:c♯1-e2; L:b1-d2. Arthur P. Schmidt (1911)

7:14-15 Laderman, Ezra. *Behold the Wicked Man.* Pno: f1-g2. Oxford (1970), found in *The Psalms*

8:00 Barnes, Milton. *Psalm 8* (from *The Psalms of David*). Duet-Perc, timp, harp or stgs: Mez/Bar. Canadian Music Centre (1973)

8:00 (adapted)
Cesti, Marc Antonio (ed. Gertrude Tingley). *The Wonders of Universe.* Kbd: H:e1-g$^\flat$2; L:b$^\flat$1-d$^\flat$2. G. Schirmer (1965), found in *The Sunday Solo* (H/L)

8:00 Cortese, Luigi. *Salmo VIII,* op. 21 *(Psalm 8)* (Latin). Pno, fl, vc: c1-a3. Edizioni Suvini Zerboni (1949)

8:00 Courtney, Craig. *Psalm VIII (Psalm 8).* Pno: (g)c1-g2(a3). Harold Flammer (1999), found in *Psalm Settings of Craig Courtney*

8:00 Freed, Isadore. *Psalm 8 (O Lord, How Excellent Is Thy Name).* Pno: H or M:c1-f2. Southern (Peer) (1954)

8:00 Frost, Richard. *The Wonder of His Care.* Kbd: d1-f2. MorningStar (1988) MSM-40-900

8:00 Hanson, Howard. *O Lord, Our Lord, How Excellent Is Thy Name* (from *Four Psalms,* op. 50). Kbd: a-c$^\sharp$1. Carl Fischer (1972)

8:00 Lyon, James (ed. Gordon Myers). *Oh, Lord, Our Heavenly King.* Kbd: c1-e$^\flat$2. Eastlane Music Corp., found in *Six Songs of Early America*

8:00 Scott, John Prindle. *When I Consider the Heavens.* Pno: H f1-g2(b3); L:d1-e2(g2). Huntzinger (1921)

8:00 Wright, Norman S. *The Eighth Psalm.* Pno: c1-g2. Huntzinger (1945)

8:1 Lowe, Augustus F. *O Lord How Lovely (Psalm 8).* Org: M. Carl Fischer (1970), found in *Eight Scriptural Solos*

8:1 (paraphrased)
Mozart, W. A. (arr. Hal H. Hopson). *Mighty Are Your Works, O God.* 2-part mixed-Kbd: d1-d2/d-d1. Selah Pub (1992) 410-808

8:1 (based on)
Tunney, Dick (arr. Steven V. Taylor). *How Excellent Is Thy Name.* 2-part-Kbd or Trax: b$^\flat$1-c2. Word (1988), found in *25 Songs for Two-Part Choir*

8:1 (based on)
Tunney, Dick and Melodie; Paul C. Smith. *How Excellent Is Thy Name.* Kbd: H:b$^\flat$1-f$^\sharp$2; MH:a1-f2; M:a1-d2; L:e1-c2. Word (1985, 1988), found in *Glorious Praise: Great Songwriters and Songs* (MH); *GMA Song of the Year,* 3rd edition (MH): *The Song Book,* vol. III (H); *Song of the Year* (M); *Songs for Praise and Worship* (L)

8:1, 3-5, 9
Wetzler, Robert. *How Excellent Is Your Name.* 2-part mixed-Org: M. AMSI (1993) 697

8:1, 3-8 McAfee, Don. *How Excellent Is Thy Name.* Kbd: c1-e$^\flat$2. Sacred Music Press (1969), found in *The Solo Psalmist*

8:1, 3-9 (adapted)
Fettke, Tom. *The Majesty and Glory of Your Name.* Kbd: H:c1-g2(b$^\flat$3); M:c1-e2. Word (1979, 1984), found in *The Lord Is My Light* (H); *Solos from the Word; Songs for Praise and Worship* (M)

8:2-7 (based on; other)
Schutte, Daniel L. and Jim Murray. *All My Days.* U-2-part-Gtr: c1-d2. NALR (1974), found in *Neither Silver Nor Gold*

8:3-4 (Psalm 19:1, other)
Beethoven, Ludwig van (arr. Harrell). *Creation Hymn.* Pno: H:c1-g2; L:a1-e2. Carl Fischer (1939), found in *The Sacred Hour of Song*

8:3-6 SEE: Genesis 1:27. Humphreys, Don. *Man*

8:3-9 SEE: Deuteronomy 6:4-5. Tindall, Adrienne M. *Hear, O Israel*

8:4 SEE: Psalm 45:1-2. Dencke, Jeremiah. *Ich will singen von einem Könige (I Speak of the Things)*

8:4 SEE: Hebrews 2:6. Purcell, Henry. *Lord What Is Man*

8:9 (based on)
Mendelssohn, Felix (arr. Lynn Hodges). *Lord, Our Creator* (from *Elijah*). 2-part-Kbd: c1-f2/b1-e2. Integra (1993), found in *Mendelssohn's ELIJAH for Young Voices*

8:9 Smith, Michael W. *How Majestic Is Your Name.* Kbd: H: (e$^\flat$1-g2(b$^\flat$3); MH: c1-e$^\flat$2(g2); M:(g)c1-d2. Meadowgreen (1981, 1988, 1992) HL00240370, also found in *Bible Songs* (M); *The Big Book of Contemporary Christian Favorites* (M); *Contemporary Christian Classics,* vol. 1*; Glorious Praise: Great Songwriters and Songs; Greatest Songs of Sandi Patty* (H); *How Majestic Is Your Name; Michael W. Smith: Greatest Hits; Our God Reigns; Sandi Patti: Finest Moments & Morning Like This* (MH); *Sandi Patti Medium Voice Collection; Songs for Praise and Worship* (MH); *Very Best of Sandi Patti* (H/M)

8:9 Smith, Michael W. (arr. Tom Fettke). *How Majestic Is Your Name.* Kbd: L:c1-d2. Meadowgreen (1995) MB-545, found in *Low Voice Classics*

8:9 Smith, Michael W. (arr. Steven V. Taylor). *How Majestic Is Your Name* (with *Holy, Holy*). 2-part-Kbd or Trax: c1-d/d-d1. Meadowgreen (1981, 1988) HL00240370, also found in *25 Songs for Two-Part Choir*

9:1-2 (other Psalms)
Horman, John D. *Tell All the World.* U-Kbd, (opt 2-8ve hdbls, Orff): c1-d2(g2). Choristers Guild (1994) CGA681

9:1-2 Spies, Claudio. *I Will Praise Thee, O Lord* (from *Five Psalms*). Duet-Fl, fg, hn, mand, vla, vc: Sop:c♯1-g♯2/Tenor:d-a♭1. Boosey & Hawkes (1962)

9:1-2, 10 Campbell-Tipton, Louis. *I Will Give Thanks Unto the Lord,* op. 25, no. 2. Pno: H:d♭1-a♭3; M:b♭1-f2; L:a♭1-e♭2. G. Schirmer (1936)

9:2-3 Kingsley, Gershon. *I Will Give Thanks Unto the Lord* (from *Three Sacred Songs*). Kbd, vc: c1-f2. Transcontinental (1969)

9:9-10 (paraphrased)
Handel, G. F. *God Is a Constant Sure Defense* (from *Second Chandos Anthem*). Kbd: d1-a3. Boosey & Hawkes, found in *A Collection of Songs*

9:10, 19-20
Hoffmeister, Leon Abbott. *Arise, O Lord.* Pno: H:c1-f2; L:a1-d2. G. Schirmer (1931), found in *52 Sacred Songs*

9:11-12 (adapted)
Schütz, Heinrich (ed. Earnest Murphy). *Praise to the Lord God.* Duet-Kbd: c1-d2/c1-c2. McAfee Music (1973), found in *The Baroque Songbook*

9:11-12 Schütz, Heinrich. *Lobet den Herren, der zu Zion wohnet.* SWV 293 (from *Kleine geistliche Konzerte*) (German). Duet-Cont: Alto/Alto. Bärenreiter (1964) BA 1704 (n.v.)

9:11-12 Schütz, Heinrich (ed. Don McAfee). *Praise to the Lord God,* SWV 293 *(Lobet den Herren, der zu Zion wohnet)* (German/English). Duet-Cont: Equal voices: ML:b♭1-c2; M:c1-d2. Belwin Mills (1977) CPP131, also found in *Eight Sacred Duets* (M)

9:11-12 Schütz, Heinrich (ed. C. Buell Agey). *Praise Ye Jehovah,* SWV 293 *(Lobet den Herren, der zu Zion wohnet).* Duet-Kbd (cont): Unequal voices:c1-d2/c-d1. Abingdon (1962), found in *Kleine Geistliche Concerte,* bk 1, no. 12

9:12-13 Schütz, Heinrich (ed. Don McAfee). *Praise to the Lord God (Lobet den Herren, der zu Zion wohnet)* (German/English). Duet-Kbd: A:b♭1-c2/A:c1-d2. McAfee Music (Belwin), found in *Little Sacred Concertos*

9:13 (Lamentations 3:33; Psalm 34:1, 6; Psalm 103:4; Psalm 116:3a, 6; Psalm 117:2)
Molique, Wilhelm Bernhard. *It Is of the Lord's Great Mercies* (from *Abraham*). Duet-Pno: H:e1-a3/MH:e-e1. Oliver Ditson (1891), found in *Choice Sacred Duets,* vol. 1

9:15 SEE: Psalm 104:5. Laderman, Ezra. *Thou Didst Set the Earth*

10:00 (Psalm 12:00; Psalm 16:00)
Pergolesi, Giovanni B. *O Lord, Have Mercy Upon Me.* Kbd: d1-a3. Abingdon (1964), found in *Select Vocal Solos for the Church Musician*

12:00 Couperin, François. *Usquequo Domine* (Latin). Cont: Tenor:c-b2. Heugel (1972) H32.219, also found in *Neuf motets*

12:00 SEE: Psalm 10:00. Pergolesi, Giovanni B. *O Lord, Have Mercy Upon Me*

12:1-4, 9 Hartley, Walter S. *Allegro* (from *A Psalm Cycle*). Pno, fl: c1-a3. Presser (1970)

12:5 SEE: Exodus 15:3. Anonymous. *The Lord Is a Mighty Warrior*

13:00 Barnes, Milton. *Psalm 13* (from *The Psalms of David*). Duet-Perc, timp, harp or stgs: Mez/Bar. Canadian Music Centre (1973) (n.v.)

13:00 Beech, Robert L. *How Long Will Thou Forget Me, O Lord?* op. 16, no. 1. Kbd: d1-f2. E. Schuberth (1940)

13:00 (adapted)
Card, Michael. *How Long (Psalm 13).* Kbd: M:a1-f♯2. Birdwing (1990), found in *Greatest Songs of Michael Card; The Way of Wisdom*

13:00 Harker, F. Flaxington. *Consider, and Hear Me,* op. 49, no. 1. Pno: H d1-g2; L:b♭1-e2. G. Schirmer (1910)

13:00 Kahn, Erich I. *Psalm 13.* Kbd: b♭1-b3. American Composers Alliance (n.v.)

13:00 (St. Dunstan Psalter)
Lekberg, Sven. *How Long Wilt Thou Forget Me, O Lord?* Kbd: b1-g2. Witmark (1947)

13:00 (adapted)
Ranzzini (ed. Gertrude Tingley). *Lord, How Long Wilt Thou Forget Me?* Kbd: H:e♭1-a♭3; L:c1-f2. G. Schirmer (1965), found in *The Sunday Solo* (H/L)

13:00 Sacco, Peter. *O Lord, How Long Wilt Thou Forget Me* (from *Three Psalms*). Kbd (brass qnt): Tenor or Sop:c1-g♯2. Ostara Press (1973) 110

13:00 (taken from)
Wooler, Alfred. *Consider and Hear Me.* Pno: H:e1-a♭3; M:c1-f2; L:b1-e♭2. Oliver Ditson (1907, 1977), found in *Choice Sacred Songs* (H/L); *Sacred Songs*

13:1 (Psalm 102:7, 9, 12-13)
Rogers, James H. *How Long, O Lord, Wilt Thou Forget Me?* Kbd: d1-e♭2. G. Schirmer (1908)

13:1 (Psalm 22:1)
Schutte, Daniel L. *How Long, O Lord.* Cantor-Kbd, opt duet: d1-d2. OCP (1993) 9918CC

13:1 (Psalm 22:1)
Schutte, Daniel L. (arr. Randall DeBruyn). *How Long, O Lord.* Kbd: d1-d2. OCP (1993), found in *Drawn By a Dream*

13:1-2 (other)
Howard, Tom. *Psalm 13 (When Heaven's Locked in Silence).* Kbd: c1-e♭2. Maranatha! (1982, 1984), found in *The Lord Is My Light*

13:1-3 (Psalm 30:1-3, 11-12)
Archer, Violet. *Miserere et Jubilate* (from *Three Biblical Songs*). Pno: d1-g♯2. Canadian Music Centre (1972)

13:1, 3, 5 Pfleuger, Carl. *How Long Wilt Thou Forget Me? (O Salutaris)* (English/Latin). Kbd: H:d1-g2; M:b♭1-e♭2; L:a♭1-d♭2. Huntzinger (1963)

13:1, 3, 5 Speaks, Oley. *How Long Wilt Thou Forget Me?* Pno: H:e♭1-a♭3; M:c1-f2; L:a1-d2. G. Schirmer (1911)

13:1-5 Brown, Russell J. *How Long Wilt Thou Forget Me?* Duet-Kbd: H:d♭1-g2/L:ab-e♭2. Boston Music (1947)

13:1-5 Buck, Dudley. *How Long, O Lord, Wilt Thou Forget Me?* (from *Triumph of David*). Kbd: H. G. Schirmer (1900) 11102

13:1-5 (adapted)
Hoffmeister, Leon Abbott. *How Long Wilt Thou Forget Me, O Lord?* Pno: H:d1-g2; L: b♭1-e♭2. Huntzinger (1928), found in *Choice Sacred Songs for Home or Church Services*

13:1-6 Powell, Robert J. *How Long Wilt Thou Forget Me?* Kbd: c1-e♭2. Sacred Music Press (1969), found in *The Solo Psalmist*

13:1-6 Sowerby, Leo. *How Long Wilt Thou Forget Me?* Org: a♭-e♭1. H. W. Gray (1929), also found in *Psalms for Bass and O Perfect Love*

13:5-6 Schütz, Heinrich. *Herr, ich hoffe darauf,* SWV 312 *(Lord, My Trust Is in Thee)* (from *Kleine geistliche Konzerte*) (German/English). Duet-Cont: Equal voices:c1-e2/c1-g2. Hänssler (1977) 1138, also found in *Duet Album*

13:5-6 Schütz, Heinrich. *Herr, ich hoffe darauf,* SWV 312 (from *Kliene geistliche Konzert*) (German). Duet-Cont: Sop/Sop: c1-g2. Bärenreiter BA1704 (n.v.)

13:5-6 Schütz, Heinrich (ed. Don McAfee). *Herr, ich hoffe darauf,* SWV 312 *(Lord, My Hope Is in Thee)* (from *Kleine geistliche Konzerte*) (German/English). Duet-Cont: Equal voices: c1-g2. Belwin Mills (1977), found in *Eight Sacred Duets;* also found in *Little Sacred Concertos* (German/English)

14:2, 3 Schütz, Heinrich. *Der Herr schauet vom Himmel auf der Menschen Kinder.* SWV 292 (German). Duet-Cont:Sop, Bass. Hänssler (1981) 20.292

15:00 Bernhard, Christoph. *Herr, wer wird wohnen in deiner Hütten* (German). Duet-Sop:b1-g2/ Bass:E-c1. Bärenreiter (1972), found in *Geistliche Harmonien*

15:1 (Psalm 24:3; Isaiah 58:6-11; based on)
Hurd, Bob (arr. Craig S. Kingsbury). *They Who Do Justice.* Org, gtr, inst in c: f♯1-d2. OCP (1984), found in *In the Breaking of the Bread*

16:00 SEE: Psalm 10:00. Pergolesi, Giovanni B. *O Lord, Have Mercy Upon Me*

16:1 SEE: Psalm 4:1. Huhn, Bruno S. *Hear Me When I Call*

16:1-2, 6-7, 9-11 (based on)
Haugen, Marty. *You Will Show Me the Path of Life.* U/2-part-Kbd, gtr: (g)c♯1-c2. GIA (1988), found in *Psalms for the Church Year,* vol. 2

16:1-2, 7-11 (based on)
Inwood, Paul. *Center of My Life.* Pno or org, gtr, bass, 2 insts in c: L c1-d2. OCP (1985), found in *Come to Set Us Free; United as One,* vol. 2

16:1-5, 7-11
Foley, John B. *Psalm 16 (Keep Me Safe, O God).* Kbd, gtr: b1-d2. GIA (1995), found in *Psalms for the Church Year,* vol. 7

16:2-5, 9, 11 (based on)
Foley, John B. *For You Are My God.* Gtr: b1-a2. NALR (1974), found in *Neither Silver Nor Gold*

16:5-11 Mahnke, Allan. *Psalm 16.* Kbd: c1-e$^{\flat}$2. Concordia (1992) 97-6093, found in *17 Psalms for Cantor and Congregation*

16:10 Handel, G. F. *But Thou Didst Not Leave* (from *Messiah*). Kbd: Tenor:d$^{\sharp}$-g1. G. Schirmer; H. W. Gray; Novello (1959)

16:10 Handel, G. F. *But Thou Didst Not Leave* (from *Messiah*). Kbd: Tenor:d$^{\sharp}$-g1. Hal Leonard (1994), found in *Oratorio Anthology: Tenor*

16:10 (Psalm 31:6; Psalm 91:15; Psalm 116:9; Luke 23:46)
Hurd, Bob (arr. Craig S. Kingsbury). *Be With Me, O God.* U/2-part-Org, gtr, 2 inst in c: (a1)d1-c2. OCP (1986), found in *Each Time I Think of You*

16:10 (Habakkuk 2:4; Acts 13:35; Acts 2:27; Romans 1:17; based on)
Mullins, Rich (arr. Robert Sterling). *The Just Shall Live.* 2-part-Kbd or Trax: c1-c2/c-c1. Edward Grant, Inc. (1992), found in *The Two Part Collection*

16:11a (Psalm 31:19a)
Benedict, Sir Julius. *How Great, O Lord, is Thy Goodness* (from *St. Peter*). Kbd: Bass:c-f1. G. Schirmer, found in *Anthology of Sacred Song–Bass*

17:00 Garlick, Anthony. *Psalm 17* (from *A Psalm Cycle*). Pno: Tenor:f1-g2. Seesaw Music

17:10-12 SEE: Psalm 4:1. Huhn, Bruno S. *Hear Me When I Call*

17:15 (Isaiah 2:4; Isaiah 11:6; Mark 13:33-37; I Corinthians 11:26; Revelation 21:4)
Hurd, Bob and Dominic MacAller (harmony Craig S. Kingsbury). *O, How I Long to See.* U/2-part-Pno, gtr: Cantor:b$^{\flat}$1-e$^{\flat}$2. OCP (1988), also found in *Everlasting Your Love*

18:00 (II Samuel 2:2-3, 7, 18)
Cornelius, Peter (ed. M. B. Stearns). *I Love Thee, Lord, My Strength,* op. 2, no. 2. Kbd:c1-f2. Coburn Press (1971), found in *Lift Up Your Voice*

18:00 Sacco, Peter. *The Sorrows of Death Compassed Me* (from *Three Psalms*). Kbd (brass qnt): Tenor or Sop:d1-c3. Ostara Press (1973) 110

18:1-3, 6 (adapted)
Steele, David (arr. Tom Fettke). *I Love You, Lord.* Kbd: c1-d$^{\sharp}$2(f$^{\sharp}$2). Lillenas (1979), found in *Scripture Solos for All Seasons*

18:1-6, 49
Birch, Robert Fairfax. *I Will Worship the Lord,* op. 35, no. 1. Kbd: H:c1-a$^{\flat}$3; M:a1-f2. Joseph Patelson (1965)

18:2 SEE: II Samuel 22:3. Bach, J. S. *Ever Will I Praise*

18:2 (Psalm 25:2)
Frey, Richard E. *In Thee O Lord Do I Put My Trust.* Kbd: H:d1-f2(g2); L:a1-d2(e2). Oliver Ditson (1903), found in *Solos for Christian Science Services*

18:2 (II Samuel 22:2-3)
Nelhybel, Vaclav. *The Lord Is My Rock.* Org: d1-e2. Agape (1981) 536, also found in *Psalm Settings*

18:2-3, 6, 35
Haas, David (arr. J. Hylton). *You Are My Rock.* U/2-part-Pno, gtr, 2 inst in c: (b1)d1-b2. OCP (1981, 1982, 1987), found in *I Am Yours Today*

18:2-4 SEE: Psalm 27:1, 4, 7-9, 14. Foley, John B. *The Lord Is My Light*

18:2-6 Hammerschmidt, Andreas (ed. Diethard Hellmann). *Herzlich lieb hab' ich dich* (German). Duet-Equal voices:d1-g2/d1-f2. Hänssler (1968), found in *Das geistliche Konzert 79*

18:2-7 Schütz, Heinrich. *Daily Will I Love Thee.* SWV 348 *(Herzlich Lieb hab ich dich)* (from *Symphoniae Sacre* II (German/English). Cont, 2 vlns: g$^{\sharp}$1-b$^{\flat}$2. Associated

18:2-7 Schütz, Heinrich. *Herzlich Lieb hab ich dich.* SWV 348 (from *Symphoniae Sacre* II) (German). Cont, 2 vlns: g$^{\sharp}$1-b$^{\flat}$2. Bärenreiter (1964) BA 1724 (n.v.)

18:3, 46 SEE: Psalm 22:4. O'Shields, Michael. *I Will Call Upon the Lord*

18:28 SEE: Psalm 27:4. Talma, Louise. *Cantata: All the Days of My Life*

18:31 SEE: Psalm 24:7-8, 10. Secchi, Antonio. *Lift Up Your Heads, O Ye Gates!*

18:32, 37 (Psalm 144:1-2; Psalm 91:5; Ephesians 6:11; Revelation 21:7)
Vaughan Williams, Ralph. *The Pilgrim's Psalm* (from *Pilgrim's Progress*). Kbd: d1-f2. Oxford (1952)

19:00 (based on)
Haas, David. *The Stars Declare His Glory.* Cantor-Kbd, gtr: d1-a2. GIA (1986), found in *Light and Peace*

19:00 (based on)
Hanks, Billie, Jr. *The Heavens Declare His Glory.* Kbd: d1-e2. Hope (1971), found in *Everything for the Church Soloist*

19:00 (adapted)
Marcello, Benedetto (ed. Earnest Murphy). *The Heavens Declare God's Glory.* Duet-Kbd: H:f1-f2/L:d1-c2. McAfee Music (1973), found in *The Baroque Songbook*

19:1 SEE: Psalm 8:3-4. Beethoven, Ludwig van. *Creation Hymn*

19:1 (Psalm 136:00, Wisdom 11:00; based on)
Dufford, Bob and John B. Foley. *Praise God.* U/2-part-Gtr: d1-e2(f2). NALR (1976), found in *A Dwelling Place*

19:1 Haydn, F. Joseph (arr. Douglas E. Wagner). *The Heavens Are Telling* (from *The Creation*). 2-part-Kbd: c1-f2/b1-d2. Coronet (n.d.) 392-41488

19:1 (based on)
Selby, William (arr. Barbara Owen). *The Heavens Declare Thy Glory.* U-Org, (opt trpts): c1-e2. Choristers Guild (1981) A-261

19:1a (St. Francis of Assisi)
Haugen, Marty. *Canticle of the Sun.* Pno, gtr, 2 inst in c, opt duet: (c1)e1-e2. GIA (1985), found in *To Be Your Bread*

19:1a (other)
Walker, Tricia. *The Heavens Are Telling.* Kbd, gtr: b♭1-d♭2. Word (1984), found in *Our God Reigns*

19:1-6 (other)
Addison, Joseph. *The Spacious Firmament.* Pno: f1-e2. Oliver Ditson (1906)

19:7-10 (John 6:68)
Haas, David. *Lord, You Have the Words.* Gtr, opt duet: (b1)d1-c2. GIA (1983), found in *We Have Been Told*

19:7-10 (based on Psalm 19; the Grail (England 1968))
Inwood, Paul. *You, Lord, Have the Message.* Cantor-Pno, gtr, inst in c, cl, inst in B♭, opt duet: e1-d2. OCP (1985) 7158CC, also found in *Holy Is God*

19:8 Horowitz, Rabbi M. (arr. Velvel Pasternak). *Tõras Hasem t'mimo* (no. 3) *(The Law of the Lord Is Perfect)* (Hebrew transliterated). Gtr: M:c1-d2. Bloch (1971), found in *Songs of the Chassidim II*

19:8 Mendelowitz, F. (arr. Velvel Pasternak). *Tõras Hasem t'mimo* (no. 1) *(The Law of the Lord Is Perfect)* (Hebrew transliterated). Gtr: M:d1-d2. Bloch (1971), found in *Songs of the Chassidim II*

19:8-9 Pasternak, Velvel. *Tõras Hasem t'mimo* (no. 2) *(The Law of the Lord Is Perfect)* (Hebrew transliterated). Gtr: M:b1-d2. Bloch (1971), found in *Songs of the Chassidim II*

19:8-9 Pasternak, Velvel. *Tõras Hasem t'mimo* (no. 4) *(The Law of the Lord Is Perfect)* (Hebrew transliterated). Gtr: M:c1-d2. Bloch (1971), found in *Songs of the Chassidim II*

19:8-10 Trapp, Lynn. *Psalm 19.* Org: e1-d2. MorningStar (1990) MSM-80-903

19:10 Couperin, François. *Domine Salvum fac regem* (Latin). Duet-Cont: Sop:d1-g2/Bar:f♯-e1. Heugel (1972) H32.219, also found in *Neuf motets*

19:14 SEE: Psalm 46:10a. Bitgood, Roberta. *Be Still and Know That I Am God*

19:14 Humphreys, Don. *My Prayer.* Pno: H:f1-f2; L:e♭1-e♭2. Willis Music (1945), found in *Sing to the Lord*

19:14 Humphreys, Don. *My Praise the Lord, O My Soul.* 2-part-Kbd: e♭1-e♭2/b♭1-c2. Willis Music (1954) W 7195

19:14b Saint-Saëns, Camille. *Thou, O Lord, Art My Protector (Domine, Domine, Adjutor meus)* (English/Latin). Org: H:d1-a3; L:c1-g2. Found in *Album of Sacred Songs* (H/L)

19:15 Davidson, Charles. *Yihyu L'Ratzon* (Hebrew). Unacc: M. Transcontinental (1992)

19:15 Robyn, Alfred G. *Let the Words of My Mouth.* Duet-Kbd: Alto:c1-f2/Tenor:e♭-a♭2. G. Schirmer (1910) 22107

19:15 Weiner, Lazar. *May the Words* (from *Anim Z'Miros*) (Hebrew). Transcontinental (1964) (n.v.)

21:13 (Psalm 55:22; Psalm 57:10, 11)
Huhn, Bruno S. *Be Thou Exalted.* Duet-Kbd: Sop:e♭1-g♭2/Tenor:e♭-g♭1; Alto:c1-e♭2/Bass:c-e♭1. G. Schirmer (1909, 1938), found in *Schirmer's Favorite Sacred Duets*

22:00 Bloch, Ernst. *Psalm 22 (Elohim! Why Hast Thou Forsaken Me?).* Pno: Bar:b-f1. G. Schirmer (n.d.)

22:00 (Psalm 69:00; adapted)
Card, Michael. *Death of a Son (Psalms 22 and 69).* Kbd: M:a1-e2. Birdwing (1990), found in *The Way of Wisdom*

22:00 Cherwien, David. *Psalm 22.* Organ: d1-e2. Augsburg (2001), found in *To God Will I Sing*

22:00 Morawetz, Oskar. *Psalm 22 (My God Why Have You Forsaken Me?).* Pno: M. Canadian Music Centre (1980)

22:00 (adapted)
Talbot, John Michael. *My God, My God.* Gtr: d1-b2. Birdwing (1985), found in *Praise, Praise the Lord, O My Soul and Worship*

22:1 SEE: Psalm 13:1. Schutte, Daniel L. *How Long, O Lord*

22:1-2, 6 (suggested by Isaiah 63:16-19; Isaiah 64:2-7; Psalm 23:1)
Foley, John B. *Redeemer Lord.* Cantor-Gtr, opt duet: e1-e2. NALR (1981) 2pt-gtr: 5744CC; U/org: 5743CC, also found in *Lord of Light*

22:2 Klang, E. (arr. Velvel Pasternak). *Rochõk Mishuosi* (*Thou Art Far From My Help*) (Hebrew transliterated). Gtr: M:c1-d2. Bloch (1971), found in *Songs of the Chassidim II*

22:2 (Matthew 27:46; other)
Schalitt (adapted Kurt Schindler). *Eili, Eili! Invocation* (German/English). Pno: M:g♯-e2; H:c1-f2. G. Schirmer (1917), found in The Free Library of Philadelphia

22:2, 8-11, 17-20, 23, 25 (based on)
Hurd, Bob (acc. Dominic MacAller). *Mi Dios, Mi Dios* (Spanish and English). U/2-part-Pno or org, gtr, 3 inst in c: c1-c2(a2-e2). OCP (1989, 1990), found in *Behold the Cross*

22:2-3, 10-11, 17 (Isaiah 50:5-7; based on)
Hurd, Bob (arr. MacAller and Kingsbury). *From My Mother's Womb.* U/2-part-Pno or Org, gtr, inst in c: a1-c2. OCP (1986), found in *Each Time I Think of You*

22:4-5 Boyce, William. *Our Fathers Hoped in Thee,* (no. 2 from *Lord, Thou Hast Been Our Refuge*). Kbd, orch: Alto:g-g1. Oxford (1977)

22:7 Handel, G. F. *All They That See Him, Laugh Him to Scorn* (from *Messiah*). Kbd: Tenor: f-f1. G. Schirmer; H. W. Gray; Novello (1959)

22:8-9, 17-20, 23-24
Walker, Christopher. *My God, My God.* Kbd, gtr, vc, inst in c: d1-e2. OCP (1989), found in *Out of Darkness*

22:11 Nelhybel, Vaclav. *Be Not Far From Me.* Org: d1-f2. Agape (1981) 536, also found in *Psalm Settings*

22:14 SEE: Psalm 61:1. Laderman, Ezra. *From the End of the Earth*

22:27 SEE: Psalm 57:10. Handel, G. F. *God's Tender Mercy Know No Bounds*

23:00 Adams, Joseph H. *The Lord Is My Shepherd.* Kbd: c1-f2. Paston (1900)

23:00 Adler, Samuel. *Psalm 23* (from *Three Psalms*). Kbd: M:c^{m}1-g2. Southern Music Company (1991) VB-465, also found in *Samuel Adler: Collected Songs for Voice and Piano*

23:00 Allen, David Len. *The King of Love My Shepherd Is.* M-Kbd:g-f2. Jackman Music (1992) S-0180, found in *Scripture Settings for Solo Voice*

23:00 Andrews, Mark. *The Twenty-Third Psalm.* Kbd: b^{b}1-e^{b}2. G. Schirmer (1930)

23:00 Arcadelt, Jacob. *The Lord Is My Shepherd.* Kbd: d1-d2. R. D. Row (1959), found in *Sacred Song Masterpieces,* bk 1

23:00 Archer, Violet. *The Twenty-Third Psalm.* Kbd: b1-f2. BMI (1954) MC2113

23:00 Bach, J. S. *And Though I Wander* (from *The Lord Is My Shepherd,* cantata no. 112). Kbd: Bar:c-e1. Kalmus (1990) 06048

23:00 (based on)
Bain, James Leith Macbeth. *Brother James's Air.* Pno: M:e1-f2; L:c♯1-d2. Oxford (1938, 1951) 345811, also found in *Sing Solo Sacred* (H/L)

23:00 (based on)
Bain, James Leith Macbeth (arr. Malcolm Archer). *Brother James's Air.* Pno: M:e1-f2; L:c♯1-d2. Oxford (1997), found in *Sing Solo Sacred* (H/L)

23:00 Bain, James Leith Macbeth (arr. Walter Rodby). *Air for Brother James.* 2-part-Kbd:c1-d2. Hope (1980) A 518

23:00 Bain, James Leith Macbeth (arr. Phyllis Tate). *Air for Brother James.* Kbd: Med. Oxford (1951) (n.#.)

23:00 Bain, James Leith Macbeth (arr. Arthur Trew). *Air for Brother James.* Kbd: L. Oxford (1938) ISBN 0-19-345835-7

23:00 Barnes, Frederick M. *Psalm 23*. Kbd: H; L:g-e2. JIB Pub (1990, 1989), found in *Great New Solos*

23:00 Barnes, Milton. *Psalm 23* (from *The Psalms of David*). Gtr: Sop. Canadian Music Centre (1973)

23:00 Barnes, Milton. *Psalm 23* (from *The Psalms of David*). Duet-Perc, timp, harp or stgs: Mez/Bar. Canadian Music Centre (1973)

23:00 (Baker)
Beck, John Ness. *The King of Love My Shepherd Is*. Kbd: M:d♭1-g2. Beckenhorst (1991), found in *Hymn Settings of John Ness Beck*

23:00 Bedell, Robert L. *The Twenty-Third Psalm*. Kbd: c1-e2. Edition Le Grand Orgue (1955)

23:00 Ben-Haim, Paul. *Psalm 23* (Hebrew). Kbd: g-g2. Israeli Music (1962)

23:00 Berlinski, Hermann (Hernam). *Psalm XXIII (Psalm 23)*. Fl: c♯1-a3. Transcontinental (1991)

23:00 Betts, Lorne. *Psalm 23*. Org: a♭1-f2. Canadian Music Centre, found in *Six Sacred Songs* (n.v.)

23:00 Binder, Abraham Wolf. *The Lord Is My Shepherd (Psalm 23)*. Org: H:d1-f2; M:c♯1-e2. Transcontinental (1963)

23:00 Blair, Kathleen. *He Restoreth My Soul*. Kbd: H:d1-g2; L:b1-d2. G. Schirmer (1932)

23:00 Bohn, Carl (ed. Wilman Wilmans). *The Lord Is My Shepherd*. Pno: H; L:a♭1-e♭2. Oliver Ditson (1889), found in *Choice Sacred Songs* (H/L)

23:00 Broones, Martin. *David's Psalm*. Pno: H:e1-g2; L:b1-d2. Edwin H. Morris (1950)

23:00 Brown, Keith Crosby. *The Lord Is My Shepherd*. Kbd: H:c1-g2; L:b♭1-f2. R. D. Row (1947) R786D

23:00 Brown, Russell J. *The Twenty-Third Psalm*. Kbd: H:e1-g2; L:c1-e♭2. H. W. Gray (1945)

23:00 (altered)
Burton, Daniel. *The Lord Is My Shepherd,* (no. 1 from *Five Unison Psalms*). U-Kbd: b♭1-e♭2. Kjos (1966) 6189

23:00 Buss, Duane. *Psalm 23*. Pno: d♯1-g2. American Music Centre (1982)

23:00 (Baker)
Butt, James. *The King of Love*. Org: e1-g2. Sphemusations (n.d.)

23:00 (adapted)
Card, Michael. *My Shepherd (Psalm 23)*. Kbd: M:a1-d2. Birdwing (1990), found in *Greatest Songs of Michael Card; The Way of Wisdom*

23:00 Carmichael, Ralph. *The New 23rd Psalm*. Kbd: c1-f2. Lexicon Music (1969), found in *Everything for the Church Soloist; How Majestic Is Your Name; Low Voice Classics; Scripture Solos for All Seasons*

23:00 Carter, John. *The Shepherd Psalm*. Kbd: M:d1-d2. Hope (1984) 1053, also found in *Come With a Singing Heart*

23:00 (Scottish Psalter, 1650)
Childs, Edwin T. *The Lord Is My Shepherd*. Kbd: d1-f2. Ron Harris Music (1990), found in *Art Songs of the Hymnal,* vol. 2

23:00 Clarke, Henry Leland. *The Lord Is My Shepherd*. Fl, stg bass or 3 timp: c1-a3. American Composers Alliance (1974)

23:00 (adapted)
Clatterbuck, Robert C. *A Child's 23rd Psalm*. 2-part-Kbd: e♭1-e♭2/a♭1-d♭2. Carl Fischer (1992) SG153

23:00 (based on)
Colgan, Bro. Tobias (arr. Randall DeBruyn). *Gentle Shepherd (Jesús, pastor tan dulce)* (English/Spanish). U/2-part-Org, 2 inst in c, gtr: e1-c2(a2). OCP (1979, 1983), found in *In Perfect Charity: Contemporary Accomp. Series,* vol. 4

23:00 Collister, Robert. *The Twenty-Third Psalm*. Kbd: d1-g2. Robert Collister (1982) TTP-5

23:00 Courtney, Craig. *The Lord Is My Shepherd*. Pno: b1-f♯2(g2). Beckenhorst (1999), found in *Psalm Settings of Craig Courtney*

23:00 (Baker)
Crawford, John. *The King of Love*. Pno: e1-g2. American Composers Alliance (Ms)

23:00 Creston, Paul. *Psalm XXIII,* op. 37. Kbd: H:f1-a♭3; L:d1-f2. G. Schirmer (1945) L: 50283900, H: 50283910, also found in *Contemporary American Sacred Songs* (L)

23:00 (adapted)
Curran, Pearl G. *The Lord Is My Shepherd*. Kbd: H/L. G. Schirmer (1921) H30229; L30230 (n.v.)

23:00 Davidson, Charles. *The Lord Is My Shepherd (Psalm 23)*. Transcontinental (1966)

23:00 Davye, John J. *The Lord Is My Shepherd* (from *Two Psalms of Mediation*). Org: e1-f2. muSic eSpreSS (1996)

23:00 Deacon, Mary. *Beside Still Waters*. Kbd: b1-f2. H. W. Gray (1956)

23:00 Deutschmann, Gerhard. *Psalm 23* (German). Org, fl: S. W. G. Haas (1999)

23:00 Dvorák, Antonín. *The Lord Is My Shepherd,* op. 99, no. 4 (from *Biblical Songs*) (English/ Chech). Kbd: M:b1-c♯2. Consolidated Music (1960), found in *The Art Song*

23:00 Dvorák, Antonín. *The Lord Is My Shepherd,* op. 99, no. 4 (from *Biblical Songs*). Duet-Org/pno: H/H:e1-e2;g1-e2. R. D. Row (1961), found in *Sacred Duet Masterpieces*

23:00 Edmunds, John. *The Lord Is My Shepherd.* Kbd: H:c1-a3. Dragon's Teeth Press (1975), found in *Fifty Songs by John Edmunds*

23:00 Ellis, James G. *I Shall Not Want.* Kbd: H:d1-g2; M:b21-e♭2; L:a♭1-d♭2. Boston Music (1935)

23:00 Espina, Noni. *Shepherd's Psalm.* Kbd: H:e♭1-g♯2; L:c1-f2. Vita d'Arte (n.d.) (n.#.)

23:00 Eville, Vernon. *I Will Dwell in the House of the Lord.* Kbd: L-a1-d2; M-b1-e2; MH-c1-f2; Hd1-g2. Boosey (1917) 2004-6

23:00 Flowers, Geoffrey E. *The Lord's My Shepherd.* Kbd: M:b♭1-f2(g2). Coburn Press, found in *Eleven Scriptural Songs from the Twentieth Century*

23:00 Flowers, Vernon. *I Will Dwell in the House of the Lord.* Kbd: H:d1-g2; MH:c1-f2; M:b1-e2; L:a1-d2. Boosey & Hawkes (1917)

23:00 (adapted)
Franz, Robert (ed. and arr. K. K. Davis and N. Loring). *The Lord of Love.* Kbd: M:c♯1-e2. Carl Fischer (1948), found in *Sing Unto the Lord,* vol. 2

23:00 Freudenthal, Josef. *The Lord Is My Shepherd.* Kbd: H:c1-g2; L:a1-e2. Transcontinental (1959) TV 497

23:00 Gardner, Aldelaide (arr. Bob Mitchell). *The Lord Is My Shepherd.* Kbd: d1-d2. Robert Brown (1961)

23:00 Garlick, Anthony. *Ps 23* (from *A Psalm Cycle*). Pno: Tenor:e1-f2. Seesaw Music

23:00 Gilbert, N. *The Lord Is My Shepherd.* Duet-Kbd: Med. H. W. Gray

23:00 Goetz, Marty. *Psalm 23.* Kbd: b♭1-c♯2(d2). Meadowgreen (1980), found in *Contemporary Christian Classics,* vol. 1

23:00 Goldman, Edward M. *Psalm 23.* Kbd: b1-e2. World Library (1965)

23:00 Goode, Jack. *Psalm 23.* Kbd: d1-g♯2. Abingdon, found in *Seven Sacred Solos*

23:00 (Baker)
Gounod, Charles. *The King of Love My Shepherd Is.* Kbd: H:f1-g2; M:d1-e2; L:c1-d2. G. Schirmer (1991) HL50481176, also found in *Everbody's Favorite Sacred Songs: The First Book of Baritone/Bass Solos* (L); *Seventeen Sacred Songs For Church and General Use* (H); *Solos for Christian Science Services; Songs of Faith* (M); *Famous Sacred Songs*

23:00 (Isaac Watts)
Graham, Robert. *My Shepherd.* 2-part mixed-Kbd: d1-d2/d-d1. Lorenz (1973) 5781

23:00 (altered)
Grier, Gene and Lowell Everson. *The Lord is My Shepherd.* Duet-Kbd: b1-f♯2/b-d1. Heritage (Lorenz) (1991), found in *Selected Duets for Contest:* Set 1

23:00 Hamblen, Bernard. *Beside Still Waters.* Kbd: H:e♭1-f2; L:c1-d2. Boosey & Hawkes (1925) 5114

23:00 (adapted)
Handel, G. F. (ed. Gertrude Tingley). *My Shepherd.* Kbd: H:f♯1-a3; L:d1-e♭2. G. Schirmer (1965), found in *The Sunday Solo* (H/L)

23:00 Haugen, Marty. *Shepherd Me, O God.* U/2-part-Kbd, gtr, 2 inst in c: c1-d2. GIA (1987), found in *Psalms for the Church Year,* vol. 2; *Shepherd Me, O God*

23:00 (Baker)
Held, Wilbur. *The King of Love.* Kbd: M:d1-d2. Augsburg (1992) 11-10226, found in *Vocal Solos for Funerals and Memorial Services*

23:00 (C. Becker)
Helder, Bartholomaeus (arr. Paul Bunjes). *The Lord Is My Shepherd.* Org: H or M:e1-f2. Concordia (1952), found in *Wedding Blessings*

23:00 (Baker)
Holler, John. *The King of Love My Shepherd Is.* Kbd: c1-f♯2. H. W. Gray (1938, 1966)

23:00 Humphreys, Don. *The Lord Is My Shepherd.* Pno: H:e♭1-g2; L:c1-e2. Willis Music (1945), found in *Sing to the Lord*

23:00 Irvine, Jessie S. (har. Neil Jenkins). *Crimond (The Lord's My Shepherd)*. Kbd: H; L:b♭1-c2. Oxford (1997), found in *Sing Solo Sacred* (H/L)

23:00 Irvine, Jessie S. (descant W. Baird Ross). *Crimond (The Lord's My Shepherd).* Duet-Kbd: H; L:b♭1-c2(b♭1-f2). Paterson's (1947), found in *Sing Solo Sacred* (H/L)

23:00 Irvine, Jessie S. *The Lord's My Shepherd, I'll Not Want*. Kbd, gtr: c1-2. Hal Leonard (1999), found in *The Big Book of Hymns*

23:00 Irvine, Jessie S. (arr. David Grant). *The Lord's My Shepherd, I'll Not Want.* Kbd: c1-d2. Hope (1984), found in *For All the Saints*

23:00 Isaacson, Michael. *Psalm 23* (Hebrew). Pno: d1-a3. Transcontinental (1979)

23:00 (Lyric Psalms)
Joncas, Michael. *Psalm 23*. Cantor-Kbd: e♭1-e♭2. GIA (1985) G-2853, also found in *To Be Your Bread*

23:00 (adapted)
Kalmanoff, Martin. *The Lord Is My Shepherd.* Kbd: b♭1-f2. Carl Fischer (1951)

23:00 (based on)
Kavanaugh, John. *A Banquet Is Prepared.* Gtr: a1-c2. NALR (1974), found in *Neither Silver Nor Gold*

23:00 Kingsley, Gershon. *The Lord Is My Shepherd.* Org: d1-e♭2. Transcontinental (1978) TV 576

23:00 Koch, John. *The Lord Is My Shepherd* (from *Songs of David*). Stg qt, fl: f1-g2. American Music Centre

23:00 (adapted)
Koschat, Thomas (arr. Donald H. Ripplinger). *The Lord Is My Shepherd.* Duet-Pno: H:a1-g2/a1-e2. Jackman Music (1984) JMC-9018, found in *The Duetbook: 14 Duets for Two Equal Voices and Piano*

23:00 LaMontaine, John. *The Lord Is My Shepherd,* op. 36, no. 2. Kbd: b♭1-g♭2. H. W. Gray (1968)

23:00 Lawson, Gordon. *Psalm 23.* Org: Sop:c1-g2. Randall M. Egan (1992) EC92-102

23:00 (paraphrased)
Leavitt, John. *Jesus My Shepherd.* 2-part-Kbd, 2 fl, perc: d1-e2. Augsburg (1993) 11-10447

23:00 Liddle, Samuel. *The Lord Is My Shepherd.* Pno: H:e1-f2; MH:d1-e♭2; M:c♯1-d2; L:b1-c2. Boosey & Hawkes (1929) MH: SGB1014EB; M: SGB1014D, found in *Soloists Practical Library of Sacred Songs,* bk 1

23:00 Liddle, Samuel. *The Lord Is My Shepherd.* Kbd: H:d1-f2. G. Schirmer (1994) HL50482070, found in *The Second Book of Tenor Solos* (H)

23:00 Liddle, Samuel (arr. Neil Jenkins). *The Lord Is My Shepherd.* Kbd: H:d1-f2; L:c1-d2. Oxford (1997), found in *Sing Solo Sacred* (H/L)

23:00 Lowe, Augustus F. *Psalm 23.* Org: e♭-f2. Carl Fischer (1970), found in *Eight Scriptural Solos*

23:00 Mader, Clarence. *The Lord Is My Shepherd* (from *Three Biblical Songs*). Org: c♯1-f♯2. WIM (1975) 128

23:00 Malotte, Albert Hay. *The Twenty-Third Psalm.* Pno: H:d1-g2; M:c1-f2; L:b♭1-e♭2. G. Schirmer (1937), also found in *12 Sacred Songs* (H/L); *Christian Science Service Songs; The Church Soloist; Everything for the Church Soloist* (M); *Seventeen Sacred Songs for Church and General Use* (H/L)

23:00 (altered)
Martin, Gilbert M. *My Shepherd Is Jehovah.* 2-part-Kbd: H:b1-d2/L:a1-b2. Beckenhorst (1990) BP1137

23:00 Martinson, Joel. *The Lord Is My Shepherd.* Org: MH. Concordia (1996) 97-6491

23:00 Matthews, H. Alexander. *The Lord Is My Shepherd.* Duet-Kbd: Sop:d1-g2/Tenor:d-g1. G. Schirmer

23:00 Matthews, Thomas. *The Lord Is My Shepherd.* Org: H:d1-g2; L:a1-d2. H. T. FitzSimons (1965, 1986) H: F0103; L: F0113, also found in *The Communion Soloist*

23:00 Meek, Kenneth. *The Lord Is My Shepherd.* Org: c♯1-a3. H. W. Gray (1959)

23:00 (Baker, adapted)
Mendelssohn, Felix (arr. Carl Fredrickson). *The King of Love My Shepherd Is.* Kbd: H; L:c1-d2. R. D. Row (1964), found in *Sacred Song Masterpieces,* bk 2

23:00 (Baker, adapted)
Mendelssohn, Felix. *The King of Love My Shepherd Is.* Duet-Org/pno: H:e♭1-f2/H:e♭1-g♭2. R. D. Row (1961), found in *Sacred Duet Masterpieces*

23:00 Montgomery, James and Thomas Koshat. *The Lord Is My Shepherd.* Kbd: c1-d2. July (1976), found in *Very Special Sacred Songs*

23:00 (Scottish Psalter, 1650)
Mueller, Carl F. *The Lord Is My Shepherd.* Kbd: H:e♭1-a♭3; M:c1-f2. Carl Fischer (1958)

23:00 (based on)
Norbet, Gregory. *Shepherd Song.* Org, gtr, inst in c: c1-e♭2. OCP (1988), found in *Mountains of My Soul*

23:00 Ore, Charles W. *The Lord Is My Shepherd* (from *Lisbon Psalms*). Kbd, vc/bsn, 2 vlns: M:c1-f2. Concordia (1975) Set I-pno: 97-5299; Set II-org: 97-5300

23:00 Owens, Sam Batt. *Psalm 23 (Dominus regit me).* 2-part-Org, inst in c: d1-f2/b1-f2. Augsburg (1983) 11-4614

23:00 Peery, Rob Roy. *Psalm 23 (Where Pastures Green Invite).* Pno: M. Oliver Ditson, found in *Solos for Christian Science Churches,* vol. 2

23:00 (based on Scottish Psalter, 1950)
Pooler, Marie. *The Lord's My Shepherd.* U/2-part-Kbd: Sop/Alto:c1-d2. Augsburg (1993) 11-10380

23:00 (Isaac Watts)
Pooler, Marie. *My Shepherd Will Supply My Need.* U/2-part-Kbd: (c♯1)d1-f♯2. Augsburg (1963) 11-0609

23:00 Riddle, Peter. *Psalm XXIII (Psalm 23).* Kbd: Mez:c1-g2. Seesaw Music (1976)

23:00 (based on)
Rieth, Mildred F. *Yahweh Is My Shepherd.* Org, gtr, inst in c: c1-b2. OCP (1969), found in *Yahweh Is My Shepherd*

23:00 (paraphrased)
Roth, John. *David's Song.* 2-part-Kbd, inst in c: Sop:a♭1-g♭2/Alto:a♭1-e♭2. Logia (1995) 98-3184

23:00 Rubbra, Edmund. *Psalm XXIII,* op. 61, no. 1 (*The Lord Is My Shepherd*) (from *Three Psalms for Low Voice*). Kbd: M:a♯1-d2. Alfred Lengnick (1947) 3553

23:00 Rusk, Harriet. *The Lord Is My Shepherd* (*Psalm 23*). Kbd: c1-g2. Huntzinger (1946)

23:00 Schack, David. *The Lord Is My Shepherd.* Kbd: f1-e♭2. Augsburg (2001), found in *To God Will I Sing*

23:00 (adapted)
Schubert, Franz (arr. K. K. Davis). *The Lord Is My Shepherd.* Kbd: M:c1-f2. Carl Fischer (1948), found in *Sing Unto the Lord,* vol. 2

23:00 (adapted)
Schubert, Franz (arr. Carl Fredrickson). *The Good Shepherd.* Kbd: L:b1-d2. R. D. Row (1964), found in *Sacred Song Masterpieces,* bk 2

23:00 (based on)
Schutte, Daniel L. *Valleys of Green.* Gtr: g-c2. NALR (1974), found in *Neither Silver Nor Gold*

23:00 Scott, John Prindle. *The Lord Is My Shepherd.* Pno: H:e1-g2; L:c1-e♭2. G. Schirmer (1923)

23:00 (Baker)
Shelley, Harry Rowe. *The King of Love My Shepherd Is.* Org: d1-e2. G. Schirmer (1914) 275400

23:00 (Baker)
Shelley, Harry Rowe. *The King of Love My Shepherd Is.* Duet-Org: H:d1-a♭3/L:b♭1-e2. G. Schirmer (1886, 1914), found in *The Duetbook: 14 Sacred Duets for Two Equal Voices; Schirmer's Favorite Sacred Duets*

23:00 Smart, Henry. *The Lord Is My Shepherd.* Pno: b1-e2(g2). Santorella Publications (1998), found in *22 Sacred Gems*

23:00 (paraphrased)
Smart, Henry. *The Lord Is My Shepherd.* Duet-Pno: Sop:c1-a♭3/Alto:b♭1-e♭2. University Society (1918), found in *Album of Sixteen Sacred Duets; Choice Sacred Duets for All Ages,* vol. 1; *Modern Music & Musician for Vocalists,* vol. III; *Sacred Duets; Sacred Duets,* vol. II (H/L)

23:00 Smith, Gregg. *The Lord Is My Shepherd* (from *Bible Songs for Young Voices*). 2-part-Pno: d1-d2. G. Schirmer (1964) 12325

23:00 Smith, Timothy Whitworth. *The Twenty-Third Psalm.* Pno: M:c1-e♭2. Concordia (1984) 97-5808

23:00 Sowerby, Leo. *The Lord Is My Shepherd.* Kbd: Bass:F-d♭1. H. W. Gray (1929), also found in *Psalms for Bass and O Perfect Love*

23:00 (Baker)
Spence, William. *The King of Love My Shepherd Is.* Kbd: H:e♭1-a♭3; L:b♭1-e♭2. Oliver Ditson (1906)

23:00 Stearns, Peter Pindar (ed. M. B. Stearns). *The Lord Is My Shepherd.* Org: c1-d2. Coburn Press (1971), found in *Lift Up Your Voice*

23:00 Strommen, Carl. *The Lord's Prayer.* U-Pno: b♭1-c2. Boosey & Hawkes (1945, 1972, 1987) OCUB6319; 2pt 6174

23:00 (John 10:3; adapted)
Talbot, John Michael. *I Am the Good Shepherd.* Gtr: d1-d2. Cherry Lane (1982), found in *Praise, Praise the Lord, O My Soul and Worship*

23:00 (adapted)
Talbot, John Michael. *The Lord Is My Shepherd.* Gtr: b1-b2. Cherry Lane (1980), found in *Praise, Praise the Lord, O My Soul and Worship*

23:00 Taylor, Raynor (ed. Gordon Myers). *The Lord Is My Shepherd.* Kbd: b1-e2. Eastlane Music (1970), found in *Six Songs of Early America*

23:00 Tchaikovsky, Peter I. (adapted and arr. Richard Maxwell and Fred Feibel). *The Lord Is My Shepherd.* Kbd: M:c1-d2. G. Schirmer (1939), found in *52 Sacred Songs; First Book of Mezzo-Soprano/Alto Solos*

23:00 (adapted by George Herbert)
Thiman, Eric H. *The God of Love My Shepherd Is* (from *Two Sacred Songs for Low Voice*). Kbd: MH:c1-f2; L:a1-d2. Novello (1926, 1954), found in *The Church Soloist; First Book of Mezzo-Soprano/Alto Solos*

23:00 (Isaac Watts)
Thomson, Virgil. *My Shepherd Will Supply My Need.* Kbd: MH:d1-f♯2. H. W. Gray (1959) 32-414-703, also found in *The Church Soloist*

23:00 Triplett, Robert F. *The Lord Is My Shepherd.* Org: b1-a3. Abingdon (1968)

23:00 VanDeWater, Beardsley. *The Good Shepherd.* Kbd: H:e1-g2; L:c1-e♭2. Oliver Ditson (1892, 1935), found in *Ditson Treasury of Sacred Songs*

23:00 VanDeWater, Beardsley (ed. Carl Fredrickson). *The Good Shepherd.* Kbd: H:e1-g2; L:c1-e♭2. R. D. Row (1963), found in *Church Soloists Favorites,* bk 1

23:00 Vaughan Williams, Ralph. *The Bird's Song* (from *Pilgrim's Progress*). Pno: d♭1-f2. Oxford (1952) 345947

23:00 (Baker)
Vree, Marion. *Psalm 23.* U-Kbd: d2-d2. Schmitt, Hall & McCreary (1969) 2583

23:00 (adapted)
Walker, Christopher. *Because the Lord Is My Shepherd.* Kbd, inst in c, gtr: M:b♭1-c2. OCP (1985), found in *Return to Me: Music for Funerals and Healing,* vol. 1; *Sing of the Lord's Goodness*

23:00 Ward-Stephens. *The Lord Is My Shepherd.* Pno: H:d1-a3; L:b♭1-f2. Chappell (1917), found in *Ward-Stephens Selected Psalms*

23:00 Webb, Charles. *Psalm 23.* U-Kbd: d1-e2. Choristers Guild CGA-252

23:00 Wiemer, Wolfgang. *Der Herr ist meine Hirt* (German). Org: Bar: A-e♭1. Breitkopf & Härtel (1969) 6429

23:00 Wienhorst, Richard. *The King of Love My Shepherd Is.* U/2-part-Org, 2 inst in c: c1-e♭2. Choristers Guild (1992) CGA-602

23:00 Williamson, Malcolm. *King of Love (Psalm 23)* (no. 5 from *Carols of King David*). U-Org: d1-c♯2. Josef Weinberger (1972) OCTW0005

23:00 Winton, Mary. *Psalm 23.* Kbd: M:d1-f2. Carl Fischer (1956), found in *Eight Scriptural Solos*

23:00 Wise, Joe. *The Lord Is My Shepherd.* Cantor-Gtr: c♯1-b2. GIA (1985), found in *To Be Your Bread*

23:00 (William Blake and Scottish metrical paraphrase)
Wolford, Julie Lofgren (ed. Darwin Wolford). *The Shepherd.* Kbd: MH:e1-f2. Harold Flammer (1975), found in *Songs of Praise by Contemporary Composers*

23:00 Zaimont, Judith Lang. *Psalm 24 (23).* Pno, fl, vln, vc: Bar or M. MPL Production (1978)

23:1 (Isaiah 40:11)
Beck, John Ness (trans. Craig Courtney). *He Shall Feed His Flock.* Kbd: M:f1-e2. Beckenhorst (1990), found in *Sacred Songs of John Ness Beck*

23:1 SEE: Psalm 22:1-2, 6. Foley, John B. *Redeemer Lord*

23:1-2 Haan, Raymond H. *The Shepherd Song.* U/2-part-Pno: c1-c2. AMSI (1989) 567

23:1-2 Harris, Ed. *Shepherd Alluluia.* Duet-Pno: Sop/Alto. Kimmel Pub (1987) 1107-019

23:1-2 (Psalm 63:00; adapted; other)
Hummel, Ferdinand. *Alleluia!* Pno: H:e♭1-a♭3; L:a♭1-e♭2. R. D. Row (1964), found in *Sacred Song Masterpieces*

23:1-2 (Psalm 63:00; adapted; other)
Hummel, Ferdinand (arr. Carl Fredrickson). *Alleluia!* Duet-Kbd: H:c1-g2/L:a1-c2. R. D. Row (1960), found in *Sacred Duet Masterpieces*

23:1-2 Lovelace, Austin C. *My Shepherd Will Supply My Need.* 2-part mixed-Kbd: Med. AMSI (1993) G634

23:1-4 (paraphrased)
Dvorák, Antonín. *God Is My Shepherd,* op. 99, no. 4 (from *Biblical Songs*) (English/ Czech/German). Pno: H:e1-f♯2; L:b1-c♯2. Simrock, found in *Dvorák,* op. 99, *Biblical Songs; The Church Year in Song* (L) (German); *First Book of Baritone/Bass Solos* Part II (L); *Soloists Practical Library of Sacred Songs,* bk 1 (H/L)

23:1-4 (English version by Humphrey Procter-Gregg)
Dvorák, Antonín. *God the Lord My Shepherd Is,* op. 99, no. 4 (from *Biblical Songs*) (English only). Pno: H:e1-f♯2; L:b1-c♯2. International (1962), found in *Biblical Songs: A Cycle of Ten Songs,* op. 99

23:1-4 (adapted by K. K. Davis)
Dvorák, Antonín (ed. and arr. K. K. Davis and N. Loring). *God Is My Shepherd,* op. 99, no. 4 (from *Biblical Songs*) (English/ Czech/German). Kbd: M:d1-e2. Carl Fischer (1948), found in *Sing Unto the Lord,* vol. 1

23:1-4 (paraphrased)
Dvorák, Antonín (ed. Otakar Sourek). *Hospokin jest muj pastyr,* op. 99, no. 4 *(Gott der Herr ist Hirte mir; Oh, My Shepherd Is the Lord)* (from *Biblical Songs*) (Czech/ German/English). Pno: H:e1-f♯2. Masters Music (n.d.), found in *Biblical Songs for High Voice and Piano by Antonín Dvorák,* op. 99

23:1-6 Foley, John B. *The Lord Is My Shepherd.* Gtr: c1-d2. NALR (1974), found in *Neither Silver Nor Gold*

23:1-6 Foley, John B. *Psalm 23 (The Lord Is My Shepherd).* Cantor-Kbd: b♭1-d2. GIA (1995), found in *Psalms for the Church Year,* vol. 7

23:1-6 (based on)
Lund, Lynn S. *The Lord Is My Shepherd.* M-Kbd:b1-e♭2. Jackman Music (1992) S-0180, found in *Scripture Settings for Solo Voice*

23:1-6 Tindall, Adrienne M. *Psalm 23 (The Lord's My Shepherd, I'll Not Want).* Kbd: c♯1-e2. Adrienne Tindall (1987), found in *Sacred Solos by Adrienne Tindall,* vol. I

23:2-3 SEE: II Samuel 22:3. Bach, J. S. *Ever Will I Praise*

23:2b (other)
Bach, J. S. *To Living Waters, Bright and Clear* (from *The Lord Is My Shepherd,* cantata no. 112). Kbd: Alto:b1-e2. Carl Fischer (n.d.)

23:3 Halberstam, Rabbi E. (arr. Velvel Pasternak). *Yanchéni (He Guideth Me in the Path of Righteousness)* (Hebrew transliterated). Gtr: H:c1-f2. Bloch (1971), found in *Songs of the Chassidim II*

23:4 Kinscella, Hazel Gertrude. *Yea, Though I Walk Through the Valley.* Kbd: H:d1-g2; M:b♭1-e2; L:g-c♯2. J. Fischer (1936)

23:4 (Isaiah 61:10; Revelation 21:2; paraphrased)
Lovelace, Austin C. *The Love of God.* Kbd: d1-e2. Darcy Press (1993), found in *Sacred Solos by Austin C. Lovelace*

23:4 SEE: Psalm 5:8. Molique, Wilhelm Bernhard. *Lead Me, O Lord*

23:4 (Psalm 139:00; Isaiah 63:00; based on)
O'Connor, Roc (arr. Cotter, Jeanne). *Guide Me, O God.* U-Kbd, gtr: d1-e♭2. NALR (1985) 5705CC, also found in *The Steadfast Love*

23:4 SEE: Psalm 42:5. Reinthaler, C. *Why Art Thou Cast Down, O My Soul?*

23:5 Bach, J. S. *For Me a Table* (from *The Lord Is My Shepherd,* cantata no. 112). Duet-Kbd: Sop:d1-a3/Tenor:d♯-b2. Carl Fischer (n.d.)

23:6 (other)
Gaul, Alfred Robert. *Thou Art the Guide of Our Youth* (from *The Ten Virgins*). Kbd: Alto:b1-e2. G. Schirmer (1977), found in *Anthology of Sacred Song–Alto; Schirmer's Singer's Library: Alto Arias from Oratorios*

23:6 (other)
Peterson, John W. and Alfred B. Smith. *Surely Goodness and Mercy.* Kbd: b♭1-e♭2. Zondervan (Singspiration) (1958), found in *How Majestic Is Your Name*

24:00 (based on)
Tamblyn, William. *King of Glory.* Cantor-Kbd, brass, opt duet. OCP (1981) 7121CC, also found in *Holy Is God*

24:00 Ward-Stephens. *The Earth Is the Lord's.* Pno: H:e♭1-a3; L:c1-f♯2. Chappell (1917), found in *Ward-Stephens Selected Psalms*

24:1a (Georg Weissel)
Freylinghausen, J. A. and Theodore Beck. *Lift Up Your Heads, You Mighty Gates.* 2-part-Org, (opt hdbls): f1-f2/a1-d2. Concordia (1980) 98-2475

24:1, 3-4, 7 (adapted)
Young, Philip M. *Who Shall Come Before the Lord?* U/2-part-Kbd: H:d1-d2(f2) (L:b1-d2). Beckenhorst (1986) BP1256

24:1-4, 7-10 (adapted)
Adler, Samuel. *The Earth With All That Dwell Therein* (no. 8 from *Twelve Songs of Praise*). U-Org: d1-e2. Oxford (1988) 94.505

24:1-5 McAfee, Don. *The Earth Is Lord's.* Kbd: d1-d2. Sacred Music Press (1969), found in *The Solo Psalmist*

24:1-5, 7-9
Lynes, Frank. *The Earth Is the Lord's.* Kbd: H:c1-f2; L:a1-d2. R. D. Row, found in *Soloist's Practical Library,* bk 2

24:1-6 Freudenthal, Josef. *The Earth Is Lord's.* Kbd: H:d1-f2; L:b1-d2. Transcontinental (1955)

24:1-6 Keil, Kevin. *We Long to See Your Face.* 2-part mixed-Kbd: d1-c2/d-d1. GIA (1993) G-3795

24:1-8 Wagner, Douglas E. *The Earth Is the Lord's.* 2-part-Pno: b♭1-e♭2. Beckenhorst (1981) BP1136

24:1-11 SEE: Psalm 130:00. Yardumian, Richard. *Symphony,* no. 2

24:3 SEE: Psalm 15:1. Hurd, Bob. *They Who Do Justice*

24:3 (Jeremiah 31:3)
Joncas, Michael. *I Have Loved You.* Kbd, gtr: d1-d2. NALR (1979), found in *On Eagle's Wings*

24:3-5 (based on)
Rowberry, Robert Lee. *How Beautiful Thy Temples, Lord.* M-Kbd: d1-d2. Sonos (Jackman) (1997) 00434, found in *Sabbath Song*

24:3-5 (Psalm 25:1, 4-9, 20)
Tindall, Adrienne M. *Unto Thee O Lord.* Kbd: c♯1-g2. Adrienne Tindall (1987), found in *Sacred Solos by Adrienne Tindall,* vol. I

24:7 Pasternak, Velvel. *S'u sh'orim (Lift Up Your Heads)* (Hebrew transliterated). Gtr: M:d1-d2. Bloch (1971), found in *Songs of the Chassidim II*

24:7 Young, Carlton. *Processional.* 2-part mixed-Org, hdbls 3-oct: c1-d2/c-d1. Agape (1986) RS 7717

24:7-10 (Matthew 21:9)
Lindh, Jody W. *Lift Up Your Heads.* U/2-part-Pno, opt bass, perc, synth: e1-f2. Choristers Guild (1987) CGA-420

24:7-10 Mahnke, Allan. *Fling Wide the Gates (Psalm 24).* U-Kbd: d1-d2. Concordia (1990) 98-2983, also found in *5 Psalms/Anthems,* set 2

24:7-10 Williamson, Malcolm. *Who Is the King of Glory (Psalm 24)* (no. 4 from *Carols of King David*). 2-part-Org: d1-e♭2. Josef Weinberger (1972) OCTW0004

24:7-8 (The "O" Antiphons)
Joncas, Michael. *Let the King of Glory Come.* Cantors-Pno, gtr: d1-d2. NALR (1979), found in *On Eagle's Wings*

24:7-8, 10 (Psalm 18:31)
Secchi, Antonio. *Lift Up Your Heads, O Ye Gates!* Org: H:c1-g2; L:a1-e2. Huntzinger (1910), found in *Christian Science Service Songs*

24:8 SEE: Psalm 103:1-4. Barett, Joanne and Ron E. Long. *Bless the Lord*

25:00 Fraley, Christopher Lee. *Psalm 25.* Org: Sop:c1-e2. Fraley Music (2002)

25:00 Marzo, Eduardo. *Unto Thee O Lord,* op. 146. Kbd: H:e1-a3; L:c1-f2. Harold Flammer (1917)

25:00 Ore, Charles W. *Turn Thee Unto Me* (from *Lisbon Psalms*). Kbd, vc/bsn, 2 vlns: M:c1-f2. Concordia (1975) Set I-pno: 97-5299; Set II-org: 97-5300

25:1 (Psalm 116:8; other adapted from Psalm 61)
Lynch, Mike (acc. John Strege). *I Believe That I Shall See.* Org, gtr: c1-c2. OCP (1985, 1986), found in *Bread of the World*

25:1 Mahnke, Allan. *Psalm 25.* Cantor-Kbd: d1-d2. Concordia (1992), 97-6093, found in *17 Psalms for Cantor and Congregation*

25:1a, 3-5, 19
Nelson, Ronald A. *To You, O Lord, I Lift Up My Soul.* U-Kbd: d1-e2. Concordia (1989), found in *Psalms/Anthems:* Set 1

25:1, 4-5 (Psalm 28:2)
Malotte, Albert Hay. *Unto Thee, O Lord.* Pno/org: L. G. Schirmer (1942) 39736

25:1, 4-5, 7, 17, 20 (adapted)
Alstott, Owen. *To You, O Lord.* U/2-part-Org, gtr, inst in c: d1-d2. OCP (1984), found in *Jesus, Lord*

25:1, 4-5, 8-10, 14 (based on)
Hurd, Bob (acc. Dominic MacAller). *Psalm 25 (To You, O God, I Lift Up My Soul).* Kbd: c1-d2. OCP (1991), found in *Alleluia! Give the Glory*

25:1, 4-6, 8-9
Manion, Tim. *I Lift Up My Soul.* U/2-part-Gtr: c1-c2. NALR (1976), found in *A Dwelling Place*

25:1, 4-9, 20
SEE: Psalm 24:3-5. Tindall, Adrienne M. *Unto Thee O Lord*

25:1-2, 15-16
Foley, John B. *Look Toward Me.* Gtr: e1-c2. NALR (1974), found in *Neither Silver Nor Gold*

25:1-2, 5, 7 (Psalm 90:16-17; other)
Cornelius, Peter. *Unto Thee I Lift Up My Soul.* Kbd: e♭1-e2. Coburn Press (1971), found in *Lift Up Your Voice*

25:1-2a (Psalm 43:3-4; based on)
Kavanaugh, John. *To You I Lift Up My Soul.* Gtr: b1-c2. NALR (1974), found in *Neither Silver Nor Gold*

25:1-2a, 4-5
Marcello, Benedetto (arr. Barbara Owen). *I Will Lift Up My Soul.* U-Org: c1-c2. Boston Music (1985) 14069

25:1-4 (adapted)
Monroe, Charles F. *Unto Thee, O Lord.* 2-part-Kbd: c1-e2. Charles F. Monroe (1973), found in *Praise Classics–Lord of Hosts*

25:1-4 (adapted)
Monroe, Charles F. *Unto Thee, O Lord.* 2-part-Kbd, gtr, (opt orch): c1-d2. Maranatha! (1971, 1973), found in *Songs for Praise and Worship*

25:1-6, 9, 22
Foley, John B. *Deliver Us, O God of Israel.* Gtr: d1-d2. NALR (1974), found in *Neither Silver Nor Gold*

25:2 SEE: Psalm 18:2. Frey, Richard E. *In Thee O Lord Do I Put My Trust*

25:4 (Psalm 39:6; adapted)
Greene, Maurice (arr. Laurence H. Davies). *Show Me Thy Ways, O Lord* (from *Lord, let my know mine end*). 2-part-Kbd: Sop:e1-e2/Sop:b1-d2. J. Curwen (1966) 11478

25:4-5 (based on)
Fragar, Russell. *Show Me Your Ways.* Kbd, gtr: c1-e♭2. Integrity (1995) HL50313850, found in *Top 25 Heart Seekers*

25:4-5 (Psalm 4:1)
Nelhybel, Vaclav. *Hear Me When I Call.* Org: e1-f2. Agape (1981), found in *Psalm Settings*

25:4-5 (The Psalms for Modern Man, 1970)
Rohlig, Harald. *Teach Me Your Ways, Lord.* U/2-part-Kbd: (c1)d1-e2. Concordia (1973) 98-2358

25:4-5 SEE: Psalm 27:4. Talma, Louise. *Cantata: All the Days of My Life*

25:4-5 (Matthew 6:9-13; Matthew 7:13-15; based on)
Whittemore, Dan (arr. Joseph Linn). *My Lord Is Leading Me On.* Kbd, gtr: e♭1-c♯2. Lillenas (1977, 1978), found in *Scripture Solos for All Seasons*

25:4, 7 (Proverbs 12:28)
Krieg, Melita. *The Way of Righteousness.* Kbd: e♭1-e2. Huntzinger (1958) RH 8203

25:4-7 (adapted)
Pote, Allen. *Praise the Lord, O My Soul for Guidance.* U/2-part-Kbd: (d♭1)f1-d2. Hinshaw (1977) HMC-244

25:4-9 (The Grail)
Inwood, Paul. *Remember Your Mercy, Lord.* Kbd: c1-d2. OCP (1981), found in *Sing of the Lord's Goodness*

25:5 Peter, Johann Friedrich (ed. David). *Leite mich in Deiner Wahrheit (Lead Me in the Truth)* (German/English). Org, stgs: Sop:e♭1-g2. New York Public Library (1954) P6084, also found in *Ten Sacred Songs: Music of the Moravians in America*

25:6 Katz, I. (arr. Velvel Pasternak). *Vaanachnu lõ néda (We Know Not What To Do)* (Hebrew transliterated). Duet-Gtr: M:d1-e2/L:a1-g2. Bloch (1971), found in *Songs of the Chassidim II*

25:8-9, 12-13
Mendelssohn, Felix *For the Lord Will Lead (Doch der Herr, er leitet die Irrenden recht),* op. 112, no. 1, (English/German). Kbd: b♭1-d2. Augsburg (2001), found in *To God Will I Sing*

25:16-18, 20
Dvorák, Antonín. *Turn Thee to Me and Have Mercy,* op. 99, no. 8 (from *Biblical Songs*). Pno: H:f1-f2. G. Schirmer (1994) HL50482070, found in *The Second Book of Tenor Solos* (H)

25:16-18, 20
Dvorák, Antonín. *Turn Thee to Me and Have Mercy,* op. 99, no. 8 (from *Biblical Songs*). Pno: H:f1-f2; L:d♭1-d♭2. Simrock, found in *Dvorák,* op. 99, *Biblical Songs*

25:16-18, 20
Dvorák, Antonín. *Turn Unto Me and Have Mercy,* op. 99, no. 8 (from *Biblical Songs*) (English only). Pno: H:f1-f2; L:d♭1-d♭2. International (1962), found in *Biblical Songs: A Cycle of Ten Songs,* op. 99

25:16-18, 20
Dvorák, Antonín (ed. Sourek, Otakar). *Popatriz na mne A smilujh se nade mnou,* op. 99, no. 8 *(Blikke mich an und erbarme Dich meiner, Herr; Oh, Lord, Have Mercy and Turn Thou Thy Face to Me)* (from *Biblical Songs*) (Czech/German/English). Pno: H:f1-f2. Masters Music (n.d.), found in *Biblical Songs for High Voice and Piano by Antonín Dvorák,* op. 99

25:17-18 SEE: Psalm 5:2-3a. Foley, John B. *Heed My Call for Help*

25:17b SEE: Psalm 42:2-3). Gaul, Alfred Robert. *My Soul Is Athirst for God*

26:8 (Psalm 27:1b, 4-6b; Psalm 96:6)
Baumgartner, H. Leroy. *Lord, I Have Loved the Habitation of Thy House,* op. 48, no. 3 (from *O Lord, My God, Thou Art Very Great*). Kbd: Med. Concordia (1958) 97-5724

26:8 (Psalm 119:89, 105)
Bender, Mark. *O Lord, I Love the Habitation of Your House.* 2-part-Org: e♭1-e♭2/b♭-e♭1. Concordia (1989)

26:8 SEE: Numbers 24:5. Gottlieb, Jack. *Ma Tovu*

26:8 Matthews, H. Alexander. *Lord, I Have Loved the Habitation of Thy House.* Duet-Kbd: Alto/Bass. Oliver Ditson

26:8 SEE: Numbers 24:5. Steinberg, Ben. *Mah Tovu*

26:8 SEE: Numbers 24:5. Weiner, Lazar. *Mah Tovu*

27:00 Edwards, Clara. *The Lord Is My Light.* Kbd: H:d1-g2; L:b♭1-e♭2. G. Schirmer (1938)

27:00 Leavitt, John. *The Lord Is My Light.* Pno: M. John Leavitt (2000) 97-6958U2 w/CD, found in *How Can I Keep from Singing*

27:00 Matthews, H. Alexander. *The Lord Is My Light.* Duet-Kbd: H:d1-g2/Bass:a-e1. G. Schirmer (1939)

27:00 (Jeremiah 9:24; based on)
Schutte, Daniel L. *If the Lord Does Not Build.* U/2-part-Gtr: a1-c2. NALR (1975, 1978), found in *Earthen Vessels*

27:00 Speaks, Oley. *The Lord Is My Light.* Pno: H:d1-g2; M:c-f1; L:b♭1-e♭2. G. Schirmer (1913), also found in *First Book of Tenor Solos* (M)

27:1 (Psalm 98:1; other adapted from Psalm 119)
Lynch, Mike (acc. Bari Colombari). *Sing to the Lord.* Org, gtr, 2 trpt: d1-d2. OCP (1985, 1986), found in *Bread of the World*

27:1 (based on)
Nelson, Jeff. *The Lord Is My Light.* Kbd, gtr, (opt orch): a1-d2. Word (1984, 1989), found in *Songs for Praise and Worship*

27:1 Revicki, Robert. *Dominus Illuminatis Mea (The Lord Is My Light and Salvation)* (from *Songs of Praise*). 2-part-Perc: (c1)f1-f2. Boosey & Hawkes (1965) OC2B5597

27:1 Schütz, Heinrich. *Der Herr ist mein licht und mein heil,* SWV 359 (from *Symphoniae Sacrae* II) (German). Duet-Cont, 2 vlns: Tenor/Tenor:c-g2. Bärenreiter (1968) BA5904 (n.v.)

27:1 Schütz, Heinrich. *Der Herr ist mein licht und mein heil,* SWV 359 (from *Symphoniae Sacrae* II) (German). Duet-Cont: 2 vlns: Tenor:c-g2/Bass:c-e2 or Tenor/Tenor:c-g2. Kalmus (n.d.) P6857

27:1 Sweney, J. *The Lord Is My Light.* Kbd: e♭1-e♭2. Carl Fischer (1965), found in *Hymns From the Crossroads*

27:1 (Lamentations 3:22-27; Psalm 34:22; Psalm 143:7-8)
VanVollenhoven, Hanna. *Hear Me Speedily, O Lord!* Org: H:e1-g2; L:c1-e2. G. Schirmer (1940)

27:1 SEE: Psalm 130:00. Yardumian, Richard. *Symphony,* no. 2

27:1, 2b, 3, 4a, 5
Tindall, Adrienne M. *The Lord Is My Light.* Kbd: d1-g2. Darcy Press (1994), found in *Sacred Solos by Adrienne Tindall,* vol. III

27:1-3 (Book of Common Prayer)
Mahnke, Allan. *Psalm 27.* Cantor-Kbd: d1-d2. Concordia (1992) 97-6093, found in *17 Psalms for Cantor and Congregation*

27:1-3a Wetzler, Robert. *The Lord Is My Light.* U/2-part-Kbd: d1-d2. AMSI (1982) 473

27:1, 3, 5 Allitsen, M. Frances. *The Lord Is My Light.* Pno: H:d1-a$^\flat$3; MH:c1-g2; M:b1-f2; L:a1-e$^\flat$2. Boosey & Hawkes (1925) H: 286670; MH 286680; M 286690; L:286700, also found in *Christian Science Service Songs; The Church Soloist; Everything for the Church Soloist* (M); *The Lord Is My Light* (L); *Soloists Practical Library of Sacred Songs,* bk 1 (H/L); *Solos from the Word; World's Favorite Sacred Songs*

27:1, 3, 5 Allitsen, M. Frances (arr. Neil Jenkins). *The Lord Is My Light.* Kbd: H; L:b1-e2. Oxford (1997), found in *Sing Solo Sacred* (H/L)

27:1, 3, 5 Allitsen, M. Frances (ed. William David Young, arr. Tom Fettke). *The Lord Is My Light.* Kbd: g1-c2. Pilot Point (1999) 083-419-9750, found in *60 Great Solos for Low Voice*

27:1, 3, 5 Allitsen, M. Frances (ed. William David Young, arr. Tom Fettke). *The Lord Is My Light.* Duet-Kbd or Trax: H-c$^\sharp$1-g2; Lc$^\sharp$1-d2. Pilot Point (1993) MB-656, found in *The Sunday Worship Duet Book*

27:1, 3, 5 Allitsen, M. Frances. *The Lord Is My Light.* Duet-Pno: H:c1-g2/L:b1-d2. G. Schirmer (1920)

27:1, 3, 5 Koch, Frederick. *The Lord Is My Light* (from *Violence No More*). Kbd: c1-e$^\flat$2. Carl Fischer (1990), found in *Five Sacred Solos for Worship Service*

27:1-3, 5 Wooler, Alfred. *The Lord Is My Light.* Pno: H:e$^\flat$1-g2; M-H:d$^\flat$1-f2; M:c1-e$^\flat$2; L:b$^\flat$1-d2. Oliver Ditson (1917)

27:1, 3, 5-6
Berthier, Jacques (ed. Brother Robert). *The Lord Is My Light.* U/2-part-Kbd or gtr, inst in c, fl, ob: d1-d2. Taizé (1991, 1984), found in *Music from Taizé,* vol. 2; *Songs and Prayer from Taizé*

27:1, 3, 5-6 (Job 33:15, 16)
Buck, Dudley. *The Lord Is My Light.* Duet-Kbd: Sop:e1-a$^\flat$3/Tenor:e-a$^\flat$2; Alto:b1-e2/Bass:b-d1. G. Schirmer (1889, 1917), found in *Schirmer's Favorite Sacred Duets*

27:1, 3, 5, 7-9, 13-14 (based on)
Dean, Stephen. *One Thing I Ask.* Kbd: b1-d2. OCP (1984), found in *Holy Is God*

27:1, 4-5 (based on)
Joncas, Michael. *The Lord Is Near (May the Angels).* Cantor-Kbd, gtr: c1-e$^\flat$2. NALR (1979) 10758CC, also found in *On Eagle's Wings*

27:1, 4, 6 Charles, Ernest. *Psalm of Exaltation.* Kbd: e1-f2. G. Schirmer (1951)

27:1, 4-6 Humphreys, Don. *The Lord Is My Light.* Kbd: H:c1-f2; L:b$^\flat$1-e$^\flat$2. Boston Music (1947)

27:1b, 4-6b
SEE: Psalm 26:8. Baumgartner, H. Leroy. *Lord, I Have Loved the Habitation of Thy House*

27:1, 4, 6, 14 (based on)
Manion, Tim. *This Alone.* Gtr: d1-b$^\flat$2. NALR (1981), found in *Lord of Light*

27:1, 4, 7, 9, 13 (adapted)
Sands, Ernest. *Song of Farewell.* Cantor-Org, gtr, opt duet: d1-c$^\sharp$2(g2). OCP (1990) 9288CC, also found in *Return to Me: Music for Funerals and Healing,* vol. 1

27:1, 4, 7-9, 13 (based on)
O'Connor, Roc. *In the Shadow of Your Wings.* Cantors-Unacc: d1-d2. NALR (1985) 5712CC, also found in *The Steadfast Love*

27:1, 4, 7-9, 14 (Psalm 18:2-4)
Foley, John B. *The Lord Is My Light.* U/2-part-Gtr: c1-d2(f2). NALR (1976), found in *A Dwelling Place*

27:1-6 Courtney, Craig. *The Lord Is My Light.* Pno:c1-f2. Beckenhorst (1999), found in *Psalm Settings of Craig Courtney*

27:4 (based on)
SEE: Psalm 84:00. Howard, Tom. *Psalm 84 (How Lovely Is Your Dwelling Place)*

27:4 Schütz, Heinrich. *Einbitte ich vom Herren,* SWV 294 (from *Kleine geistliche Konzerte*) (German). Duet-Cont: Tenor/Tenor:d1-f2/a1-f2. Bärenreiter (n.v.)

27:4 Schütz, Heinrich (ed. Don McAfee). *One Thing I Ask of the Lord,* SWV 294 *(Einbitte ich vom Herren)* (German/English). Duet-Cont: Equal Tenors:d1-f2/a1-f2. Belwin Mills (1977) 1138; also found in *Eight Sacred Duets*

27:4 (Deuteronomy 28:67; I Chron 29:15; Job 7:6, 11:17; Psalm 18:28; Psalm 25:4-5; Psalm 30:5; Psalm 39:4-5; Psalm 55:17; Psalm 59:16-17; Psalm 65:8; Psalm 71:15, 17; Psalm 102:11; Psalm 119:62; Mark 13:35; John 9:4; John 12:35; Revelation 22:5)
Talma, Louise. *Cantata: All the Days of My Life.* Pno/celesta, cl, vc, perc: Tenor:c-a2. American Music Centre (n.d.)

27:4, 8 (Psalm 43:4; paraphrased)
Alstott, Owen. *Yes, I Shall Arise.* Kbd: d1-d2. OCP (1988), found in *Return to Me: Music for Funerals and Healing,* vol. 1

27:4, 13-14
Haas, David. *God Is My Light.* Cantor-Kbd, opt duet: c1-f♯2. GIA (1986), found in *Light and Peace*

27:7, 9 Raff, Joseph J. *God, Hear My Voice* (from *The World's End*). Kbd: Bass:d-e♭1. G. Schirmer, found in *Anthology of Sacred Song–Bass*

27:7-9, 11, 13-14
Baumgartner, H. Leroy. *Hear, O Lord, When I Cry With My Voice,* op. 48, no. 4 (from *O Lord, My God, Thou Art Very Great*). Kbd: c1-f2. Concordia (1958) 97-5724

27:7-9, 13-14
Foley, John B. *Psalm 27 (I Believe I Will See).* Cantor-Kbd, gtr: d1-d2. GIA (1995), found in *Psalms for the Church Year,* vol. 7

27:13-14 Roff, Joseph. *Wait for the Lord.* 2-part-Kbd: c1-d2(g♭2). Augsburg (1992) 11-10091

27:13-14 (Ecclesiastes 3:1-8)
Sacco, John. *God's Time.* Pno: d1-f2. G. Schirmer (1944)

28:00 Garlick, Anthony. *Psalm 28* (from *A Psalm Cycle*). Pno: Tenor:f1-f♯2. Seesaw Music

28:1 Purcell, Henry. *Unto Thee Will I Cry* (German/English). Cont, 2 vlns, vla: Bass:d-d1. Bärenreiter (1959)

28:2 SEE: Psalm 25:1, 4-5. Malotte, Albert Hay. *Unto Thee, O Lord*

28:7 SEE: II Samuel 22:3. Bach, J. S. *Ever Will I Praise*

28:7 SEE: Psalm 64:1. Handel, G. F. (arr. Keith W. Bissell). *Supplication*

29:00 Barnes, Milton. *Psalm 29* (from *The Psalms of David*). Duet-Perc, timp, harp or strgs: Mez/Bar. Canadian Music Centre (1973)

29:00 Neumann, Richard, Arr. *Mizmor le David (Psalm 29)* (Hebrew). Transcontinental (1975) (n.v.)

29:00 (adapted)
Talbot, John Michael. *The Lord Will Bless His People.* Gtr: a1-d2. Birdwing (1985), found in *Praise, Prayer and Worship*

29:1-2 (based on)
Chapman, Morris and Greg Massanart. *Come and Sing Praises.* Kbd, gtr: c1-d2. Maranatha! (1984), found in *Our God Reigns*

29:1-2 (Psalm 66:4)
Schütz, Heinrich. *Bringt her dem Herren,* SWV 283 (from *Kleine geistliche Konzerte*) (German). Cont: Sop:e♭1-f2. Bärenreiter (1963) BA1701

29:1-2 (Psalm 66:4)
Schütz, Heinrich. *Bringt her dem Herren,* SWV 283 (from *Kleine geistliche Konzerte*) (German). Cont: Alto:c1-e2. Bärenreiter (1963) BA1702

29:1-2 (Psalm 66:4)
Schütz, Heinrich. *Bringt her dem Herren* (from *Five Short Sacred Concertos*) (German). Kbd or cont: e♭1-f2; c1-e2. Bärenreiter (1963) BA 1701

29:1-2 (Psalm 66:4)
Schütz, Heinrich (ed. Richard T. Gore). *Bring to Jehovah (Bringt her dem Herren)* (from *Five Short Sacred Concertos*) (German/English). Kbd or cont: e♭1-f2; c1-e2. Concordia (1957) 98-1370

29:1-2 Schütz, Heinrich (ed. Lloyd Pfautsch). *Give God, the Father, Praise.* Pno: Hd1-e♭2; L:b1-c2. Lawson Gould (1961), found in *Solos for the Church Soloist*

29:1-2 Schütz, Heinrich (arr. Robert Ross). *To God the Father (Bringt her dem Herren)* (from *Kleine geistliche Konzerte*) (German/English). 2-part-Org: b1-c2(d2). Fortress Press (1985) 3-8504

29:2 SEE: Psalm 96:8. Gay, Roert (arr. Mosie Lister. *No Other Name*

29:2 SEE: I Chronicles 16:29. Handel, G. F. *O Worship the Lord*

29:2 SEE: Psalm 113:3. VanDyke, May. *In the Beauty of Holiness*

29:11 (Psalm 84:12; Psalm 136:1; Psalm 145:6; other)
Pasternak, Velvel. *Yiru Es Adõnoy (Revere the Lord, You, His Holy Ones)* (Hebrew transliterated). Gtr: M:c1-d2. Bloch (1971), found in *Songs of the Chassidim II*

30:00 Cornelius, Peter (ed. M. B. Stearns). *Sing Unto the Lord,* op. 2, no. 4. Kbd: c♯1-d2. Coburn Press (1971), found in *Lift Up Your Voice*

30:1, 3, 4-5, 8-12 (based on; the Grail)
Inwood, Paul. *I Will Praise You, O Lord.* Pno or org, gtr, 2 inst in c: c1-c2. OCP (1985), found in *Come to Set Us Free*

30:1-2, 11
Costa, Michael. *I Will Extol Thee, O Lord!* (from *Eli*). Kbd: Sop:d1-b♭3; L:c1-a♭3.

G. Schirmer (1918, 1977), found in *Anthology of Sacred Song–Sop; Album of Sacred Songs* (H/L); *Oratorio Repertoire,* vol. 1

30:1-3, 10-12 (adapted)
Haas, David. *I Will Praise You, Lord.* U/2-part-Kbd, gtr: d1-e♭2. GIA (1989), found in *Psalms for the Church Year,* vol. 3

30:1-3, 11-12
SEE: Psalm 13:1-3. Archer, Violet. *Miserere et Jubilate*

30:2 (Psalm 34:3; based on)
Mosenthal, Joseph. *I Will Magnify Thee, O God.* Duet-Kbd: Sop:d♭1-a♭3/H:f1-a♭3; Mez:b♭1-f2/Alto:d1-f2. G. Schirmer/ Mosenthal (1892), found in *Album of Sixteen Sacred Duets* (SS)

30:2, 12 SEE: Psalm 69:1. Harris, Cuthbert. *Save Me, O God*

30:5 SEE: Psalm 103:104. Christensen, Chris. *Bless the Lord*

30:5 SEE: Psalm 32:11. Huhn, Bruno S. *Be Glad, O Ye Righteous*

30:5 SEE: Psalm 27:4. Talma, Louise. *Cantata: All the Days of My Life*

30:5-6 Schütz, Heinrich. *Ihr Heiligen, lobsinget dem Herren,* SWV 288 *(O Holy Ones, Sing Praise)* (from *Kleine geistliche Konzerte*) (German/English). Duet-Cont: Equal voices: c♯1-e2/a1-e2. Hänssler (1981) 1138, found in *Eight Sacred Duets*

30:5-6 Schütz, Heinrich. *Ihr Heiligen, lobsinget dem Herren,* SWV 288 (from *Kleine geistliche Konzerte*) (German). Duet-Cont: Sop/Sop: c♯1-e2/a1-e2. Bärenreiter (1963) BA1704

30:5-6 Schütz, Heinrich (ed. Don McAfee). *Praise Ye the Lord,* SWV 288 *(Ihr Heiligen, lobsinget dem Herren)* (German/English). Duet-Cont: Equal voices:c♯1-e2/a1-e2. Belwin Mills (1977) CPP131, found in *Eight Sacred Duets*

31:00 (adapted)
Talbot, John Michael. *Father, I Put My Life in Your Hands.* Gtr: b1-a2. Birdwing (1985), found in *Praise, Prayer and Worship*

31:1-5 (based on)
Vessels, Dennis (arr. Sheryl Soderberg). *My Refuge.* U-Kbd, gtr: b1-c♯2. GIA (1982), found in *And the Light Shines: Joe Wise*

31:1, 9, 15-16
SEE: Psalm 51:1. Starer, Robert. *Have Mercy Upon Me, O Lord*

31:2-3 Schütz, Heinrich. *In Te, Domine, Speravi,* SWV 259 *(Dir, O Herr, gilt all me in Hoffen)* (from *Symphoniae Sacrae* I) (Latin/German). Cont, fl, bas: Alto:c1-d2. Bärenreiter (1965) BA 30

31:2-4 Buxtehude, Dietrich. *Herr, auf dich traue ich* (Geistliche Solokaantaten 2) (German). Sop-2 vlns, cont: d1-a3. Bärenreiter (1949) BA 126

31:2-4 Buxtehude, Dietrich (arr. Clarence Dickinson). *Lord, in Thee Do I Trust.* Org, 2 vlns: d♯1-a3. H. W. Gray (1950) GV 98

31:5 (altered)
Bach, J. S. (ed. Wilbur Held). *Into Thy Hands* (from *God's Time Is Best,* cantata no. 106). Pno/Org: b1-e2. Augsburg (1992) 11-10226, found in *Vocal Solos for Funerals and Memorial Services*

31:5 (Psalm 127:1; Psalm 121:00; Isaiah 14:7)
Vaughan Williams, Ralph. *Watchful's Song* (from *Pilgrim's Progress*). Kbd: c♯1-e2. Oxford (1952)

31:6 SEE: Psalm 16:10. Hurd, Bob. *Be With Me, O God*

31:13-15 Keaggy, Phil. *The Survivor.* Kbd: M:a1-f2. Sparrow (1995), found in *True Believer*

31:19, 24 (Deuteronomy 31:6)
Beaumont, Vivian. *Be of Good Courage.* Pno: H:c1-e♭2; L:a1-d2. G. Schirmer (1957)

31:19a SEE: Psalm 16:11a. Benedict, Sir Julius. *How Great, O Lord, Is Thy Goodness*

32:5-8 (Book of Common Prayer)
Mahnke, Allan. *Psalm 32.* Cantor-Kbd: c1-d♭2. Concordia (1992) 97-6093, found in *17 Psalms for Cantor and Congregation*

32:7 (Psalm 56:3)
Ledner, Michael. *You Are My Hiding Place.* U-Kbd: M:c♯1-b2; L:b1-a2. Maranatha! (1982), found in *Praise Classics–Lord of Peace* (L); *Songs for Praise and Worship* (M)

32:11 (Psalm 30:5; Psalm 55:17; Psalm 145:2; I Timothy 1:17)
Huhn, Bruno S. *Be Glad, O Ye Righteous.* Kbd: H:e1-g2; M:c1-e2; L:b1-d2. Arthur P. Schmidt (1912)

33:00 Posch, Isaac (ed. Karl Geiringer). *Exsultate justi in Domino* (from *Harmonia Concertans*) (Latin). Duet-Sop:c1-f2/Bass:F-b♭1. Ann Arbor: University Microfilm (1968 - 72), found in *Series of Early Music,* vol. 4

33:00 Stewart, Roy James. *Psalm 33.* M-Kbd: d1-e2. Unity (Lorenz) (1997), found in *Wedding Psalms*

33:1-2, 4-5
Schnecker, P. A. *Rejoice in the Lord.* Duet-Pno: Alto:b♭1-e♭2/Bass:F-e♭1. G. Schirmer (1889), found in *Album of Sixteen Sacred Duets*

33:1-2, 4-7, 12-13, 18-22
Foley, John B. *Psalm 33 (God, Let Your Mercy).* Cantor (opt duet)-Kbd: c♯1-d2(e2). GIA (1995), found in *Psalms for the Church Year,* vol. 7

33:3 SEE: Psalm 96:00. Buxtehude, Dietrich (ed. N. Jenne). *Sing to the Lord a New Song (Singet dem Herrn ein neues Leid)*

33:3a (Psalm 98:00; Corinthians 15:00; Revelation 1:00)
Gore, Richard T. *O Sing Unto the Lord a New Song.* Org: H:e1-a♭3; L:b1-e♭2. J. Fischer (1948)

33:4-22 (based on)
Walker, Christopher. *Lord, Be With Us.* Kbd, gtr, inst in c: d♭1-d♭2. OCP (1988, 1989), found in *Out of Darkness*

33:20-21 Portugal, Rabbi E. (arr. Velvel Pasternak). *Nafshénu chik'so (Our Soul Hath Waited for the Lord)* (Hebrew transliterated). Gtr: M:d1-e2. Bloch (1971), found in *Songs of the Chassidim II*

33:20-22 Pelz, Walter L. *Our Soul Waits for the Lord* (from *Three Solos for High Voice*). Org, vc: e1-a3. Augsburg (1979) 11-9477, also found in *Three Solos for High Voice*

33:21 Powell, Robert J. *Our Heart Shall Rejoice in the Lord.* Kbd: d1-e2. Concordia (1974) 97-5278, also found in *Three Wedding Songs*

34:00 Barnard, Mark. *Psalm 34.* Kbd: M:f1-d2. Unity (Lorenz) (1997), found in *Wedding Psalms*

34:00 Honegger, Arthur. *Benedica Dominum In Omni* (from *Trois Psaumes*) (French). Pno: c1-c2. Salabert (1963) 50404590

34:00 Smith, Michael W. (arr. Tom Fettke). *Magnify the Lord.* Kbd: L:b♭1-c2. Lillenas (1985) MB-545, found in *Low Voice Classics*

34:1 (based on)
Rieth, Mildred F. *I Will Bless Yahweh.* U/2-part-Org, gtr, inst in c: b♭1-b♭2. OCP (1969), found in *Yahweh Is My Shepherd*

34:1 (based on)
Schutte, Daniel L. (arr. Bob Harrold). *Ever On My Lips.* Kbd: d1-d2. OCP (1993), found in *Drawn By a Dream*

34:1 Soper, Scott. *I Will Always Thank the Lord.* Cantor-Kbd, gtr, inst in c, opt duet: c1-e♭2. OCP (1988) OCP 9556

34:1, 4, 8 (paraphrased)
Handel, G. F. (arr. Hal H. Hopson). *I Will at All Times Praise the Lord.* U-Kbd: c1-e2. Choristers Guild (1981) CGA-243

34:1-4, 8 Humphreys, Don. *I Sought the Lord.* Pno: H:e1-g2; L:d1-f2. Willis Music (1965), found in *Sing to the Lord*

34:1-5, 8 Schoenbachler, Tim. *Taste and See (I Will Bless the Lord).* Gtr, fl: b1-c♯2. OCP (1979), found in *All Is Ready*

34:1, 6 SEE: Psalm 9:13. Molique, Wilhelm Bernhard. *It Is of the Lord's Great Mercies*

34:1-6 Dietterich, Philip. *Now Will I Praise the Lord.* Kbd: e1-g2. Abingdon (1970)

34:1-6, 8 (based on)
Haas, David. *The Goodness of God.* Duet-Kbd, gtr, 2 inst in c: d1-d2/c-e1. GIA (1993), found in *When Love Is Found*

34:1-6, 8 Walker, Christopher. *Taste and See.* U/2-part-Kbd, gtr, inst in c, cl: b1-e2. OCP (1986), found in *Come to Set Us Free*

34:1-7 Schütz, Heinrich (ed. Richard T. Gore). *Now Will I Praise the Lord With All My Heart,* SWV 306 *(Ich danke dem Herren loben allezeit)* (from *Five Short Sacred Concertos*) (German/English). Kbd or cont: c1-g2. Concordia (1957) 98-1370, also found in *Church Year in Song* (H/L); *Fifty Selected Songs: Five Sacred Song* (H)

34:1-8 (based on)
Cooney, Rory. *Every Morning in Your Eyes.* Cantor-Kbd, gtr, stg qt, fl, opt duet: c1-d2. GIA (1995) G-4112, also found in *Stony Landscapes*

34:1-8 Martinson, Joel. *Taste and See the Goodness of the Lord.* Org: MH. Concordia (1996) 97-6492

34:1-8 (adapted)
Talbot, John Michael. *Taste and See.* Gtr: e1-d2. Birdwing (1985), found in *Praise, Prayer and Worship*

34:1-11 (altered)
Hobby, Robert A. *Psalm 34 (I Will Bless the Lord at All Times).* Cantor/2-part-Org: e♭1-e♭2(g2). MorningStar (1994) MSM-80-707

34:2-4, 9 (Psalm 136:5-6; the Magnificat)
Hurd, Bob (arr. Kingsbury and MacAller).

Taste and See. U/2-part-Kbd, gtr: c1-f2(d2). OCP (1988), found in *Everlasting Your Love; United as One,* vol. 2

34:2-4, 9 (Psalm 136:5-6; the Magnificat)
Hurd, Bob (arr. Craig S. Kingsbury). *Taste and See.* Duet-Kbd, gtr: H:c1-f2/L:c1-d2. OCP (1988), found in *United as One,* vol. 2

34:2-5, 7 Telemann, Georg Philipp (ed. Klaus Hofmann). *Ich will den Herren loben allezeit (The Lord Will I Bless for All My Days)* (German/English). Duet-Cont: H:e1-e2/L:c1-e2. Bärenreiter (1963) 1701; Hänssler (1978) 39.125

34:2-7 (English adaptation by Ruth Michaelis)
Schütz, Heinrich. *I Will Bless the Lord at All Times,* SWV 306 (from *Five Short Sacred Concertos*). Kbd: c1-g2. G. Schirmer (1978), found in *The Church Year in Song*

34:2-7 Schütz, Heinrich. *Ich will den Herren loben allezeit,* SWV 306 (from *Kleine geistliche Konzerte*) (German). Cont: Sop:c1-g2. Bärenreiter (1963) BA1701

34:3 (Psalm 41:1)
Medema, Ken. *Sing to the Lord.* 2-part-Kbd: d1-d2. Word (1974) 301-0334164

34:3 SEE: Psalm 30:2. Mosenthal, Joseph. *I Will Magnify Thee, O God*

34:3 Tunney, Melodie & Dick. *O Magnify the Lord.* Kbd: H:a1-g2(a3); MH:b♭1-f2; L:g-d2. Meadowgreen (1982, 1984, 1988), found in *As Sung By* (MH); *The Big Book of Contemporary Christian Classics,* vol. 2 (L); *Contemporary Christmas Collection; Contemporary Christian Favorites* (H); *Glorious Praise: Great Songwriters & Songs* (H); *Our God Reigns; Sandi Patti: Anthology; Sandi Patti: the Finest Moments; Sandi Patti Medium Voice Collection; Sandi Patti: Morning Like This* (H); *Very Best of Sandi Patti* (H/M)

34:4 (other)
Galbraith, J. Lamont. *I Sought the Lord.* Kbd: M; L. Boston Music (n.v.)

34:4 (Psalm 121:8; Revelation 21:4)
Robyn, Alfred G. *I Sought the Lord.* Duet-Kbd: Alto:c1-f2/Tenor:e♭-a♭2. G. Schirmer (1910)

34:4 (Psalm 121:8; Revelation 21:4)
Stevenson, Frederick (ed. Wilman Wilmans). *I Sought the Lord.* Org: H:d1-f♯2; L:b1-d♯2. Oliver Ditson (1916), found in *Choice Sacred Songs* (H/L)

34:6, 15, 18 (Psalm 36:7; I John 3:10; suggested by)
Foley, John B. *God's Poor Ones.* U-Kbd or gtr, 2 inst in c: c1-c2. NALR (1985), found in *The Steadfast Love*

34:7 SEE: Psalm 4:8. Buck, Dudley. *I Will Lay Me Down in Peace* (n.v.)

34:8 Bach, J. S. *O Taste and See* (from cantata 34). Kbd: M:d1-e2. Paterson (Carl Fischer) (1931)

34:8 Fischer, Irwin. *Taste and See That the Lord Is Good.* Kbd: d1-g2. American Composers Alliance, found in *Composers Facsimile Edition*

34:8 Young, Carlton. *O Taste and See.* U/2-part-Org: d♭1-e♭2. Agape (1987) AG 7282

34:9 (I Corinthians 10:16; John 6:50-51, 58; based on)
Hurd, Bob (accomp. Dominic MacAller). *Fracción Del Pan* (Spanish and English). U/2-part-Kbd, gtr, 2 insts in c: c♯1-c♯2. OCP (1989, 1990), found in *Behold the Cross*

34:9a (Psalm 116:12-13; I Corinthians 11:26)
Joncas, Michael. *Our Blessing Cup.* Cantor-Org, gtr: b1-e2. NALR (1979) 5437CC, also found in *On Eagle's Wings*

34:12-14, 19 (Psalm 42:8; Amos 5:6)
Miller, Merle. *Seek the Lord.* Kbd: Med. R. D. Row (1947)

34:18-19, 21-22
Demarest, C. Agnew. *The Lord Is Nigh Unto Them.* Org: c1-f2. Boston Music (1959)

34:22 SEE: Psalm 27:1. VanVollenhoven, Hanna. *Hear Me Speedily, O Lord!*

35:9 (Psalm 98:4, 6-9)
Bach, J. S. (trans. Hal H. Hopson). *All Hearts Now Be Joyful (Wir müssen durch viel trusal)* (from cantata no. 146). Duet-Kbd: Sop:d1-f2/Alto:a1-c2. Carl Fischer (1983) CM8179

36:5-7, 11
LaForge, Frank. *Thy Mercy, O Lord, Is in the Heavens.* Pno: L:b1-f2. Carl Fischer (1938) H: 1373: L: 1374

36:5-9 MacDermid, James G. *The Shadow of Thy Wings.* Kbd: H:d1-f♯2; L:b1-e2. Forster (1936, 1953)

36:7 SEE: Psalm 34:6, 15, 18; 36:7. Foley, John B. *God's Poor Ones*

36:7-10 Humphreys, Don. *How Excellent Is Thy Loving Kindness.* Pno: H:d1-f2; L:c1-e♭2. Willis Music (1965), found in *Sing to the Lord*

36:7-10 Purcell, Henry (ed. Gertrude Tingley). *Loving Kindness*. Kbd: H:d1-g2; L:b1-e2. G. Schirmer (1965), found in *The Sunday Solo* (H/L)

36:9 SEE: Isaiah 1:18. Barker, Clement W. *The Path of the Just*

37:00 SEE: Psalm 145:00. Fischer, Irwin. *Delight Thyself in the Lord*

37:00 Fyock, Joan A. *Trust in God* (from *Three Psalm Settings*). U-Pno: c1-d2. Hope (1974) JR216

37:1 Medema, Ken (arr. Mark Hayes). *O Rest in the Lord*. Kbd: d1-d2. GlorySound (1982), found in *Songs for the Turning*

37:1, 4-5, 7
Camidge, John (ed. David Patrick). *Put Thou Thy Trust in the Lord* (from *Fret Not Thyself Because of the Ungodly*). Kbd: MH:e1-a3. Boosey & Hawkes (1996), found in *Sacred Songs for the Soloist: 20 Songs on Religious Texts for Medium High Voice*

37:1, 4-5, 7
Mendelssohn, Felix. *O Rest in the Lord* (from *Elijah*). Pno: H:e1-f♯2; MH:e♭1-f2; Alto or L:b1-d2. G. Schirmer (1937), Amsco (1940), found in *20 Distinctive Sacred Solos* (H/L); *52 Sacred Songs; 56 Songs You Like to Sing; Anthology of Sacred Song–Alto; The Church Soloist; Everybody's Favorite Sacred Songs* (L); *Everything for the Church Soloist* (L); *Favorite Sacred Classics* (MH/ML); *Low Voice Classics* (L); *The Oratorio Anthology–Alto; Oratorio Repertoire,* vol. II; *Sing and Worship* (H)

37:1, 4-5, 7
Mendelssohn, Felix. *O Rest in the Lord* (from *Elijah*). Pno: H:e1-f♯2; MH:e♭1-f2; Alto or L:b1-d2. Hal Leonard (1994); Boston Music (1961); R. D. Row (1959), found in *52 Sacred Songs*

37:1, 4-5, 7
Mendelssohn, Felix (arr. Lynn Hodges). *O Rest in the Lord* (from *Elijah*). 2-part-Kbd: b1-c1. Integra (1993), found in *Mendelssohn's ELIJAH for Young Voices*

37:1, 4-5, 7
Mendelssohn, Felix (arr. Hal H. Hopson). *O Rest in the Lord* (from *Elijah*). 2-part mixed-Kbd: Sop/Bass. AMSI (1990) 586

37:1, 4-5, 7
Mendelssohn, Felix (ed. Patrick M. Liebergen). *O Rest in the Lord* (from *Elijah*). Kbd: MH:e♭1-f2. Alfred (1995), found in *Favorite Sacred Classics for Solo Singers*

37:1, 4-5, 7
Mendelssohn, Felix (arr. Leonard Van Camp). *Now Trust in the Lord* (from *Elijah*). Kbd: L:b1-d2. Carl Fischer (1992) w/Cassette: O5183, also found in *Songs for Low Voice in a Comfortable Range*

37:1, 9 SEE: Isaiah 1:18. Barker, Clement W. *The Path of the Just*

37:1-5 Schütz, Heinrich. *Habe deine Lust an dem Herren,* SWV 311 (German). Duet-Cont: Sop/Sop:c1-g2. Bärenreiter (1963) 1138

37:4-7a (adapted)
Humphreys, Don. *Rest In the Lord.* Kbd: H:e1-f2; L:c♯1-d2. R. D. Row (1960); G. Schirmer, found in *Don Humphrey's Song Book* (H/L); *Songs for Christian Science Service,* bk 1

37:7 (Psalm 46:1-2; adapted)
Mozart, W. A. (arr. Carl Fredrickson). *Wait on the Lord.* Kbd: L:c♯1-c♯2. R. D. Row (1964), found in *Sacred Song Masterpieces,* bk 2

37:22a, 23, 31, 33-37
Krieg, Melita. *Behold the Upright.* Kbd: c1-f2. Huntzinger (1950, 1958)

37:25 Schütz, Heinrich. *Ich bin jung gewesen,* SWV 320 (from *Kleine geistliche Konzerte*) (German). Duet-Cont: Bass/Bass:a-e2/f♯-d2. Bärenreiter (1963)

37:25 Schütz, Heinrich. *Ich bin jung gewesen,* SWV 320 *(I Have Been a Young Man and Now am Aged)* (from *Kleine geistliche Konzerte*) (German/English). Duet-Cont: Equal voices: a-e2/f♯-d2. Hänssler (n.d.) 1705

37:37 SEE: Isaiah 2:22. Barker, Clement W. *Mark the Perfect Man*

38:22 SEE: Psalm 64:1. Handel, G. F. (arr. Keith W. Bissell). *Supplication*

39:00 SEE: Psalm 61:1-5, 8. Sowerby, Leo. *Hear My Cry, O God*

39:4-5 SEE: Psalm 27:4. Talma, Louise. *Cantata: All the Days of My Life*

39:4-5 (Isaiah 40:6-8)
Wyner, Yehudi. *Lord, Let Me Know My End.* Fls (2 in C; 1 alto): a1-a3. Associated (1975) AMP 7440, also found in *Memorial Music* II

39:4-7 (Wisdom 3:1)
Brahms, Johannes. *Lord, Make Me to Know* (from *Requiem*) (German/English). Kbd or orch: Bar. G. Schirmer (1963) 1678

39:6 SEE: Psalm 25:4. Greene, Maurice. *Show Me Thy Ways, O Lord*

39:12 SEE: Psalm 55:6. Barnes, A. M. *Oh, That I Had Wings*

39:12b-13a (Psalm 103:13-14)
Laderman, Ezra. *Look Away From Me.* Pno: d♭1-a3. Oxford (1970), found in *The Psalms*

40:00 (adapted)
Beck, John Ness. *Song of Joy.* Pno: b♭1-g2. Carl Fischer (1970) 6840

40:1 Misetich, Marianne. *I Have Waited for the Lord.* Kbd, gtr, bass, inst in c: b♭1-b♭2. OCP (1973, 1982), found in *Comfort My People*

40:1 Saint-Saëns, Camille. *Patiently Have I Waited for the Lord (I Waited for the Lord)* (from *Christmas Oratorio*). Kbd: Alto: b1-f♯2. Presser (1923), found in *Oratorio Repertoire,* vol. II

40:1 Saint-Saëns, Camille. *Patiently I Awaited Christ the Lord* (from *Christmas Oratorio*). Kbd: MH:d1-a3; ML:b♭1-f2. Augsburg (1989) 11-8195, found in *Sing a Song of Joy* (MH/ML)

40:1 Saint-Saëns, Camille (ed. Jerald B. Stone). *Expectans Expectavi Dominum* (from *Christmas Oratorio*). Pno: b1-f♯2. HLH Music (1992), found in *Five Vocal Gems for Mezzo-Soprano and Alto,* vol. 1

40:1 (English version by N. H. Dole)
Saint-Saëns, Camille (arr. K. Lee Scott). *Patiently Have I Waited For the Lord (I Waited For the Lord)* (from *Christmas Oratorio*). Kbd: MH:c1-g2; M:b1-f♯2. Abingdon (1964) APM 308, also found in *Anthology of Sacred Song–Alto* (M); *Second Book of Mezzo-Soprano/Alto Solos* (M); *Select Vocal Solos for the Church Musician* (MH)

40:1-4 (Scottish Psalter, 1929)
Burnett, John Y. *I Waited for the Lord My God.* U-Org: e♭1-f2. Kevin Mayhew (1992), found in *Favorite Anthem,* bk 2

40:1-4 Hartley, Walter S. *Andante con moto* (from *A Psalm Cycle*). Pno, fl: c1-a3. Presser (1970)

40:1-4, 8, 9b, 10b, 11-12, 16
Mader, Clarence. *I Waited Patiently for the Lord* (from *Three Biblical Songs*). Org: M:c1-g2. WIM (1975) 128

40:1-10 (based on)
Rieth, Mildred F. *O Lord, I Have Waited.* Kbd, gtr, inst in c: a1-b♭2. OCP (1969), found in *Yahweh Is My Shepherd*

40:4 Pasternak, Velvel. *Vayitén b'fi shir chodosh (And He Hath Put a New Song in My Mouth)* (Hebrew transliterated). Gtr: M:c1-c2. Bloch (1971), found in *Songs of the Chassidim II*

40:14-18 (Psalm 70:1-5)
Schütz, Heinrich. *Eile, mich Gott, zu erretten,* SWV 282 (from *Kleine geistliche Konzerte*) (German). Cont: Sop:c1-g2. Bärenreiter (1963) BA1701

40:14-18 (Psalm 70:1-5)
Schütz, Heinrich (ed. Richard T. Gore). *Haste Thee, Lord God, Haste to Save Me,* SWV 282 *(Eile, mich Gott, zu erretten)* (from *Five Short Sacred Concertos*) (German/English). Kbd or cont:c1-g2. Concordia (1957) 98-1370, found in *Five Sacred Songs* (H)

40:14-18 (Psalm 70:1-5)
Schütz, Heinrich (ed. Heinrich Spitta). *Haste Thee, Lord God, Haste to Save Me,* SWV 282 *(Eile, mich Gott, zu erretten)* (German/ English). Pno or org: d1-a2. C. F. Peters (n.v.) editions in English and German, found in *5 Short Sacred Concertos*

40:16 (based on)
Ayala, Bob. *The Lord Be Magnified.* 2-part-Kbd: (a1)c1-c2. Intrada (1993), found in *Sing Out With One Voice*

41:1 SEE: Psalm 34:3. Medema, Ken. *Sing to the Lord*

41:1-4 Handel, G. F. *Blessed Are They That Consider the Poor* (from *Foundling Hospital Anthem*). Kbd: Tenor:d1-g2. Novello (n.d.)

42:00 Blair, Kathleen. *As the Hart Panteth.* Kbd: f1-g♭2. H. W. Gray (1953)

42:00 Koprowski, Peter Paul. *Psalm 42.* Perc, stg, picc, alto fl, 2 Eng hn, 2 bass cl, 2 cbsn: Bar. Canadian Music Centre (1980) (n.v.)

42:00 Lansing, A. W. *As Pants the Hart.* Duet-Kbd: Alto/Tenor. White-Smith (1912) (n.v.)

42:00 Liddle, Samuel. *Like as the Hart.* Pno: M. Boosey & Hawkes (1961) (n.v.)

42:00 Marcello, Benedetto. *As Pants the Wearied Hart.* Duet-Kbd: H/H. John Church (1907), found in *Sacred Duets,* vol. I (n.v.)

42:00 Posch, Isaac (ed. Karl Geiringer). *Quemamodum desiderat* (from *Harmonia Concertans*) (Latin). Duet-Equal voices: E-c1. Ann Arbor: University Microfilm (1968-72), found in *Series of Early Music*, vol. 4

42:00 Smith, L. *Psalm 42*. U-Kbd: c1-d2. Marks Music MC 4664 (n.v.)

42:00 Strickland, Lily. *As Pants the Hart*. Kbd: d1-g2. Presser (1919)

42:00 West, John E. *Like as the Hart*. Kbd: H:d1-f2; L:b♭1-d2. Arthur P. Schmidt (1906)

42:1-2 (adapted)
Smart, Henry (arr. L. Kessler). *As Pants the Hart*. Duet-Pno: Sop:e♭1-f2; Alto:c1-d2. Oliver Ditson (1891), found in *Choice Sacred Duets*, vol. 1

42:1-2, 12
Pohle, David (ed. Helmet Winter). *Wie der Hirsch schreyet* (German). Cont, 2 vlns, bass: Tenor:e-g1. Sikorski (1965) 650, score & parts

42:1-3 (Psalm 43:00; based on)
Schutte, Daniel L. *Like the Deer*. U-Pno, gtr: e1-d2. NALR (1985), Gtr: 5714CC; Pno: 5715CC, also found in *The Steadfast Love*

42:1-3, 5 Allitsen, M. Frances. *Like as the Hart Desireth*. Kbd: H:d1-g2; M:c1-f2; L:a1-d2. R. D. Row (1963); Boosey & Hawkes (1925), found in *Soloists Practical Library of Sacred Songs*, bk 2 (H/L)

42:1-4 Derfler, Carl. *As a Deer* (from *Trilogy of Psalms*). Pno: Bar. Canadian Music Centre (1975, 1990)

42:1-4 Gluck, Christoph Von. *As Pants the Hart*. Kbd, vln: M. Boston Music

42:1-4 Harker, F. Flaxington. *Like as the Hart Desireth the Water-Brooks*. Kbd: H; L. G. Schirmer (n.v.)

42:1-4 (based on)
Hurd, Bob (arr. MacAller and Kingsbury). *As the Deer Longs*. Kbd, gtr, inst in c: c1-d2. OCP (1988), found in *Everlasting Your Love*

42:1-4 Misetich, Marianne. *As the Deer Longs*. Kbd, gtr, bass, inst in c: c1-c2. OCP (1973, 1982), found in *Comfort My People*

42:1-4 (Psalm 43:1; adapted)
Young, Ovid (arr. Lyndell Leatherman). *As a Deer Longs So for Water*. Kbd: b1-e2. Lillenas (1985), found in *The Lord Is My Light*

42:1-4a Fromm, Herbert. *Psalm 42* (from *Four Psalms*). Kbd: g1-g2. Transcontinental (1971)

42:1-5, 8 Huijbers, Bernard. *As a Deer*. Org, trpt, gtr: d1-c2. OCP (1987), found in *Stand*

42:1-6, 8 (adapted)
Farrell, Bernadette. *O God, for You I Long*. Kbd, vln: M:d♭1-e♭2. OCP (1988), found in *God, Beyond All Names; Return to Me: Music for Funerals and Healing*, vol. 1

42:1-7 (other)
Nystrom, Martin. *As the Deer*. U-Kbd: b1-d2. Maranatha! (1984), found in *Face to Face; Praise Classics–Lord of Love; Songs for Praise and Worship; WOW Worship Songs*

42:1-7 (other)
Nystrom, Martin. *As the Deer*. Pno: e1-e2. Maranatha! (1984) 301 0327 498, found in *My Utmost for His Highest*

42:1, 8, 11 (based on)
Burton, Daniel. *As the Thirsty Deer at Morning* (no. 3 from *Five Unison Psalms*). U-Kbd: d1-d2. Kjos (1966) 6191

42:2 (Psalm 43:3-4)
Kiel, Friedrich. *For My Soul Is Athirst* (from *The Star of Bethlehem*). Kbd: Alto:c1-f2. G. Schirmer (1977), found in *Anthology of Sacred Song-Alto; Schirmer's Singer's Library: Alto Arias from Oratorios*

42:2 Mendelssohn, Felix. *For My Soul Thirsteth For God* (from *Psalm 42*). Kbd: Sop:e1-a3. G. Schirmer

42:2 Stickles, William. *My Soul Is Athirst for God*. Kbd: H:f1-a3; M:d1-f2; L:c1-e♭2. G. Schirmer (1923)

42:2-3 (Psalm 25:17b)
Gaul, Alfred Robert. *My Soul Is Athirst for God* (from *Holy City*). Kbd: Sop or Tenor: e1-a3. G. Schirmer, found in *52 Sacred Songs; Anthology of Sacred Song–Tenor; Everybody's Favorite Sacred Songs; Oratorio Repertoire*, vol. III

42:2-3, 12 (Psalm 131:00)
Haas, David. *Like a Little Child*. Cantor-Kbd, gtr, opt duet: b1-d2. GIA (1993) G-3956, also found in *No Longer Strangers*

42:3 (Psalm 84:3)
Kehati, Pinchas (arr. Velvel Pasternak). *Tsomo Nafshi (My Soul Thirsteth for God)* (Hebrew transliterated). Gtr: M:c1-d2. Bloch (1971), found in *Songs of the Chassidim II*

42:3-4 Mendelssohn, Felix. *For I Had Gone Forth (My Tears Have Been My Meat)* (from *Psalm 42*). Kbd: Sop:d1-g2. G. Schirmer

42:4b (other)
Handel, G. F. (arr. Hal H. Hopson). *Sing With Songs of Joy*. 2-part-Kbd: c1-c2/C-d1. Harold Flammer (1986) EA-5070

42:5 (Psalm 23:4)
Reinthaler, C. *Why Art Thou Cast Down, O My Soul?* (from *Four Songs of Solomon*). Kbd: Sop:d1-a3. G. Schirmer (1901, 1977), found in *Anthology of Sacred Song-Sop; Schirmer's Singer's Library; Sop Arias from Oratorios*

42:5 Spicker, Max. *Why Art Thou Cast Down, O My Soul?* Pno: c1-f2. G. Schirmer (1902)

42:6 Handel, G. F. *Was betrübst du dich* (German). Duet-2 rec: Sop/Alto. Hänssler (1968), found in *Das geistliche Konzert 67*

42:8 SEE: Psalm 4:8. Buck, Dudley. *I Will Lay Me Down in Peace*

42:8 SEE: Psalm 43:3-5. Mendelssohn, Felix. *Why Art Thou Cast Down, O My Soul?*

42:8 SEE: Psalm 34:12-14, 19. Miller, Merle. *Seek the Lord*

42:11a (Isaiah 62:5b; Zmiros and Sabbath Liturgy)
Talmud, Rabbi Y. (arr. Velvel Pasternak). *Lõ Sevõshi* (*Be Not Ashamed*) (Hebrew transliterated). Gtr: M:a1-e2. Bloch (1971), found in *Songs of the Chassidim II*

43:1 SEE: Psalm 42:1-4. Young, Ovid. *As a Deer Longs So for Water*

43:1-3 Hartley, Walter S. *Adagio Ma non troppo* (from *A Psalm Cycle*). Pno, fl: c1-a3. Presser (1970)

43:1-4 Lynes, Frank. *Send Out Thy Light*. Kbd: H:e1-g2; L:a1-c2. R. D. Row, found in *Soloist's Practical Library,* bk 2

43:1-4 Wooler, Alfred. *Send Out Thy Light*. Pno: H; L:b1-e♭2. Oliver Ditson (1913)

43:3-4 SEE: Psalm 25:1-2a. Kavanaugh, John. *To You I Lift Up My Soul*

43:3-4 SEE: Psalm 42:2. Kiel, Friedrich. *For My Soul Is Athirst*

43:3-5 (Psalm 42:8)
Mendelssohn, Felix. *Why Art Thou Cast Down, O My Soul?* Kbd: c1-e2. Coburn Press (1971), found in *Lift Up Your Voice*

43:4 SEE: Psalm 27:4, 8. Alstott, Owen. *Yes, I Shall Arise*

45:1-2 (Psalm 8:4)
Dencke, Jeremiah (ed. David). *Ich will singen von einem Könige (I Speak of the Things)* (German/English). Org, stgs: Sop:e1-f2. New York Public Library (1954); Carl Fischer P6084, also found in *Ten Sacred Songs: Music of the Moravians in America*

45:2 Jeffreys, George (ed. Peter Aston). *Speciosus forma* (from *Two Devotional Songs*) (Latin). Kbd: Bass:D-c1. Novello (1988) 17 0336

46:00 Dungan, Olive. *Be Still and Know That I Am God*. Pno: c1-g2. Presser (1955)

46:00 Hanson, Howard. *God Is Our Refuge and Strength* (from *Four Psalms,* op. 50). Bar-pno/org: a-f1. Carl Fischer (1972)

46:00 Ward-Stephens. *God Is Our Refuge*. Pno: H:e♭1-a3; L:c1-f♯2. Chappell (1917), found in *Ward-Stephens Selected Psalms*

46:1-2 Montemayor, Judy Horner. *God Is My Refuge*. Kbd, gtr, (opt orch): c1-f2. Intrada (1973, arr. 1992), found in *Songs for Praise and Worship*

46:1-2 SEE: Psalm 37:7. Mozart, W. A. *Wait on the Lord*

46:1-3, 6-7, 9-10
MacDermid, James G. *God Is Our Refuge*. Kbd: d♭1-e♭2. Forster (1915)

46:1-6, 10
Powers, Margaret Westlake. *Be Still, and Know*. Kbd: H:d1-f2; L:b1-d2. G. Schirmer (1941)

46:1-7 (Lutheran Book of Worship 1978, altered)
Luther, Martin (arr. Thomas J. Fleming). *God Is Our Refuge and Our Strength* (from *Three Songs from Martin Luther*). Kbd: c1-e♭2. Concordia (1985) 97-5884

46:8-10 Stanford, Charles Villiers. *O Come Hither* (from *God Is Our Hope and Strength*). Kbd: d1-f2. Novello (1910)

46:9, 10 Chadwick, George Whitefield. *He Maketh Wars to Cease*. Kbd: H:c1-f2; L:a1-d2. Arthur P. Schmidt (1892)

46:10 SEE: Exodus 15:3. Anonymous. *The Lord Is a Mighty Warrior*

46:10 SEE: Exodus 15:26b. Chapman, Steve Curtis (arr. Bryce Inman). *Be Still and Know*

46:10 SEE: Exodus 15:26b. Chapman, Steve Curtis and Tom Fettke (arr. Tom Fettke). *Be Still and Know*

46:10 SEE: Exodus 15:26b. Chapman, Steve Curtis and Tom Fettke (arr. Lee Herrington). *Be Still and Know*

46:10 Franck, César. *Be Thou Still.* Kbd: Med. G. Schirmer, found in *The Church Soloist*

46:10 (Isaiah 30:15; Isaiah 32:17-18)
Lowe, Augustus F. *Be Still.* Org: M. Carl Fischer (1970), found in *Eight Scriptural Solos.*

46:10a (Psalm 145:18; Psalm 62:1; Psalm 19:14; Psalm 85:8)
Bitgood, Roberta. *Be Still and Know That I Am God.* Kbd: H:e1-g2; M:c♯1-e2; L:b1-d2. H. W. Gray (1947)

46:10a (John 11:25; John 14:18; other)
Roma, Caro. *The Silent Voice.* Kbd, vln: e♭1-g2. Witmark (1916)

47:00 (Book of Common Prayer)
Dobry, Wallace. *Psalm 47: Clap Your Hands, All You Peoples (Omnes gentes, plaudite)* (from *A Trio of Psalms*) (English/Latin). 2-part-Kbd: b♭1-e♭2. MorningStar (1994) MSM-80-706

47:00 Hanson, Howard. *O Clap Your Hands, All Ye People* (from *Four Psalms,* op. 50). Bar-pno/org: e♭1-f2. Carl Fischer (1972)

47:00 McDonald, Boyd. *Psalm 47.* Pno: M. Canadian Music Centre (1987) (n.v.)

47:1 (Psalm 66:1; Psalm 88:1)
Burton, Daniel. *Clap Your Hands, All You People* (no. 2 from *Five Unison Psalms*). U-Kbd: d1-e2. Kjos (1966) 6190

47:1 Owens, Jimmy. *Clap Your Hands.* Kbd: c1-c2. Creative Concepts (1993), found in *Very Special Sacred Songs*

47:1 (Psalm 148:1; adapted from the Psalms)
Wagner, Douglas E. *Clap Hands, Be Glad!* 2-part-Pno: H/L:b♭1-e2. Beckenhorst (1982) BP1155

47:1-2 SEE: Psalm 68:4. Horvit, Michael. *Sing to God*

47:1-2, 5-7
Dengler, Lee. *O Clap Your Hands.* Kbd: M:b1-g2. Augsburg (1995) 11-10608, found in *Songs of David*

47:1-2, 5-7 (Book of Common Prayer)
Mahnke, Allan. *Psalm 47.* Cantor-Kbd: b1-e2. Concordia (1992) 97-6093, found in *17 Psalms for Cantor and Congregation*

47:1-2, 5-8
Haugen, Marty. *God Mounts His Throne.* U/2-part-Gtr: d1-e2. GIA (1983), found in *Psalms for the Church Year*

47:1-2, 6-7 (Psalm 48:1-2, 12-14)
Huhn, Bruno S. *Great Is the Lord.* Pno: H:d1-a3; L:b♭1-f2. Boston Music (1923)

47:5 (Psalm 68:17-18)
Bencini, Pietro Paolo (ed. James H. Laster). *Alleluia Ascendit Deus (Alleluia. God Has Gone Up)* (English/Latin). Duet-Kbd: S:d1-g2/S:d1-e2. Treble Clef Press (2002) TC-210

48:1-2, 12-14
SEE: Psalm 47:1-2, 6-7. Huhn, Bruno S. *Great Is the Lord*

47:1, 5-8 McAfee, Don. *O Clap Your Hands.* Kbd: c1-e♭2. Sacred Music Press (1969), found in *The Solo Psalmist*

47:1-6 Schütz, Heinrich. *Frohlocket mit Händen,* SWV 349 (from *Symphoniae Sacrae* II) (German). Cont, 2 vlns: Bass:c-e1. Bärenreiter (1936) BA1088

47:1, 6-7 (based on)
Wilson, Mark. *Lift Every Voice.* 2-Part-Kbd, 4 hndbls: d1-d2. Choristers Guild (1990) CGA-514

47:7 Pasternak, Velvel. *Zamru elõkim* (*Sing Praise to God*) (Hebrew transliterated). Gtr: ML:d1-b♭2. Bloch (1971), found in *Songs of the Chassidim II*

48:1, 4, 9, 11-13 (paraphrased)
Tucker, Margaret R. *Upon Mount Zion Sits Our God (Psalm 48).* U/2-part-Kbd, fc, tamb: c1-e♭2 (f2). MorningStar (1988) MSM-50-9550

49:00 Jones, Kelsey. *Psalm Forty-Nine: (1. Hear This All Ye People; 2. They That Trust in Their Wealth; 3. Death Shall Feed in Them; 4. And the Upright Shall Have Dominion).* Pno: g-g2. Canadian Music Centre (1980) (n.v.)

49:00 Orland, Henry. *From Psalm 49,* op. 18, no. 3 (from *Six Occasional Songs*). Pno: G♯-f1. Seesaw Music (1977)

49:16b SEE: Psalm 127:1. Myers, Gordon. *Except the Lord Build the House*

50:1 SEE: Psalm 113:3. VanDyke, May. *In the Beauty of Holiness*

50:1-3, 5-6 (Hebrews 8:10c; Revelation 21:4)
Case, Henry Lincoln (ed. Carl Fredrickson).

The Mighty God Hath Spoken. Kbd: H:e1-a3; L:a1-e2. R. D. Row (1963), found in *Church Soloists Favorites,* bk 1

50:14 (based on)
Dearman, Kirk. *We Bring the Sacrifice of Praise*. Kbd, gtr, (opt orch): d1-c2(g2). Benson (1984), found in *Songs for Praise and Worship*

50:14 (Psalm 95:1-7)
Pendleton, Emmet. *Sing Unto the Lord,* op. 12, (no. 4 from *The Light of the Lord*). Pno: c1-e♭2. Bruce Humphries (1945)

51:00 Beethoven, Ludwig van (arr. K. Lee Scott). *A Contrite Heart*. Pno: MH:e♭1-f2; ML:c1-d2. Augsburg (1989) 11-8195, found in *Sing a Song of Joy*

51:00 (based on)
Cooney, Rory. *Psalm 51* (*Create Me Again*). Cantor-Kbd, gtr, inst in c, opt duet (opt strg qt): b1-c2 (c1-d2). GIA (1993) G-3975; parts G-3975 INST, also found in *Vision*

51:00 Evans, Vincent. *Create in Me a Clean Heart*. Kbd: e1-g2. Abingdon (1964) APM 308, also found in *Select Vocal Solos for the Church Musician*

51:00 (based on)
Walker, Christopher. *Give Me a New Heart, O God*. Org, gtr, vc, cl, inst in c: c1-e♭2. OCP (1988, 1989), found in *Out of Darkness*

51:00 (metrical)
Wooler, Alfred. *God Be Merciful to Me*. Kbd: He1-f2; L:c♯1-d2. Oliver Ditson (1921)

51:1 (Psalm 31:1, 9, 15-16)
Starer, Robert. *Have Mercy Upon Me, O Lord* (from *Two Sacred Songs*). Kbd: H:d1-g2. Peer (Southern) (1964)

51:1, 10-11, 13, 15, 17
Mendelssohn, Felix. *O God, Have Mercy (Gott sei mir gnädig)* (from *St. Paul*). Pno: H:d1-f2; Bass:B-d1. Lawson Gould (1961), found in *Anthology of Sacred Song–Bass; Oratorio Anthology: Baritone/Bass; Oratorio Repertoire,* vol. IV; *Schirmer's Singer's Library: Bass Arias from Oratorios; Solos for the Church Soloist* (H/L)

51:1, 10-12, 15 (adapted)
Haugen, Marty. *Create in Me*. Cantor-Kbd, gtr: c♯1-d♯2. GIA (1978), found in *I Send My Light*

51:1-4, 10-12 (The Grail Psalter; adapted)
Joncas, Michael. *Be Merciful, O Lord*. Gtr: d1-d2. GIA (1990) G-3433, also found in *Come to Me*

51:1-8 (based on)
Dufford, Bob. *Father, Mercy*. Gtr: c♯1-c♯2. NALR (1974), found in *Neither Silver Nor Gold*

51:1-4, 10-12
Franck, César (arr. Hal H. Hopson). *Lord, Have Mercy (Agnus Dei)* (from *Mass in A*). 2-part-Kbd: H:c1-d2/L:C-c1. GIA (1991) G-3424

51:2 Handel, G. F. (ed. Walter Ehret). *Wash Me Throughly from My Wickedness*. 2-part-Kbd: c♯1-e2/C♯-e1. Walton (1992) WW1169

51:2-3 Bach, J. C. *Amplius lava me ab inquitate mea* (from *Miserere*) (Latin). Kbd: ML:a1-e2. Boosey & Hawkes (1996), found in *Sacred Songs for the Soloist: 20 Songs on Religious Texts for Medium Low Voice*

51:2-3, 10-12, 15 (based on)
O'Connor, Roc. *Psalm Fifty-One (A Prayer for Mercy)*. U/2-part-Pno, gtr: e♭1-c2 (e♭2). NALR (1985), found in *The Steadfast Love*

51:3-4, 9, 12, 14 (based on)
Hurd, Bob (arr. Craig S. Kingsbury). *Create in Me*. Cantor-Kbd, gtr, 2 inst in c, opt duet: (a1)c1-d2. OCP (1986) 8792, also found in *Each Time I Think of You*

51:3-4, 12, 14, 17, 19 (based on)
Hurd, Bob (acc. Dominic MacAller). *Psalm 51 (Create in Me)*. Cantor-Kbd, sax: b1-d2. OCP (1991) 10251CC, also found in *Alleluia! Give the Glory*

51:9-11 Timmings, William. *Turn Thy Face From My Sins*. Kbd: e♭1-f2. Heidelberg Press (1921)

51:10-11 Bernhard, Christoph (ed. David Streetman). *Create in Me a Clean Heart (Schaffe In mir, Gott, ein reines Herz)* (German/English). Org, vc, 2 vlns: b1-a3. Concordia (1972) 97-5041

51:10-12 (based on)
Bannister, Brown. *Create in Me a Clean Heart*. Duet-Kbd: f♯-c♯1/c-e1. Edward Grant, Inc. (1982); Word (1982), found in *42 Songs for All Occasions* (M); *50 Great Songs for All Occasions; The Wedding Collection: 52 Solos* (M/L); *Wedding Duets: 22 Arrangements for Medium Voice*

51:10-12 Buxtehude, Dietrich (ed. James Boeringer). *Create in Me a Clean Heart*. Org, 2 vlns, vc: b♭1-a3. Concordia (1966) 97-9359, score & parts

51:10-12 (adapted)
Green, Keith. *Creat in Me a Clean Heart.* Kbd: c1-b♭2. For the Shepherd (1984) HL00310739, found in *Bible Songs*

51:10-12 Handel, G. F. *Make Me a Clean Heart, O God.* Kbd: c♯1-f♯2. Coburn Press (1971), found in *Lift Up Your Voice*

51:10-12 (other)
Miller, Merle. *Create in Me a Clean Heart.* Kbd: H:d♯1-f♯2; L:b1-d2. R. D. Row (1951)

51:10-12 Schütz, Heinrich. *Lord, Create in Me a Clean Heart,* SWV 291 *(Schaffe In mir, Gott, ein reines Herz)* (from *Kleine geistliche Konzerte*) (German/English). Duet-Cont: H/H:d1-g2. Hänssler (1981) 1707

51:10-12 Schütz, Heinrich (ed. Don McAfee). *Lord, Create in Me a Clean Heart (Schaffe in mir, Gott, ein reines herz)* SWV 291 (from *Kleine geistliche Konzerte*) (German/English). Duet-Cont: M/M:b♭1-e♭2. Belwin Mills (1977) CPP131, found in Eight Sacred Duets; also found in *Little Sacred Concertos* (German/English)

51:10-12 Schütz, Heinrich. *Schaffe in mir, Gott, ein reines herz,* SWV 291 (from *Kleine geistliche konzerte*) (German). Duet-Cont: M/M:b♭1-e♭2; H/H:d1-g2. Bärenreiter (1963)

51:10-12 Willan, Healey. *Create in Me a Clean Heart, O God.* Kbd: e♭1-e♭2. Concordia (1962) 97-6710

51:10-12, 15
Powers, George. *Create in Me.* Org: f1-a3. Abingdon (1966) APM-536

51:10-12, 15 (based on)
Rieth, Mildred F. *God, Make a Heart in Me.* Org, gtr, inst in c:b1-b2. OCP (1969), found in *Yahweh Is My Shepherd*

51:10-13 Barnes, Frederick M. *Create in Me a Clean Heart, O God.* Kbd: H; L:c1-f2. JIB Pub (1990), found in *Great New Solos*

51:10-13 (adapted)
Green, Keith (arr. Bill Svarda). *Create in Me a Clean Heart.* Kbd: d1-f2. Birdwing (1984), found in *Jesus Commands Us to Go*

51:10-13 Mueller, Carl F. *Create in Me a Clean Heart.* Kbd: H:c♯-e2; L:a1-c2. G. Schirmer (1941, 1957), found in *12 Sacred Songs* (H/L); *Christian Science Service Songs*

51:10-13 Mueller, Carl F. *Create in Me a Clean Heart.* Kbd: L:a1-c2. G. Schirmer (1991) HL50481176, found in *The First Book of Baritone/Bass Solos*

51:10-15 Riker, Franklin. *Create in Me a Clean Heart, O Lord.* Org: e1-g-2. Oliver Ditson (1918)

51:12-13 Buxtehude, Dietrich. *Schaffe in mir, Gott, ein rein herz* (Geistliche Solokantaten 11) (German). Cont, 2 vlns: Sop:b♭1-a♭3. Bärenreiter (1968) 1753

51:16-17 (John 4:23-24)
Gounod, Charles (ed. and arr. K. K. Davis. and N. Loring). *God Is Spirit.* Kbd: M:b1-f2. Carl Fischer (1948), found in *Sing Unto the Lord,* vol. 2

51:23 (and other based on)
Moore, Harlan. *Restore the Joy.* Kbd, gtr: b1-f♯2. Lillenas (1978), found in *Scripture Solos for All Seasons*

54:00 Bouman, Paul. *Save Me, O God, By Your Name.* 2-Part-Org: H:c1-f2/L:b♭1-d2. Boosey & Hawkes (1989) OCTB6551

54:00 Clerbois, Roger. *Save Me, O Lord.* Kbd: H:d1-f2; L:c1-e2. Oliver Ditson (1925)

54:00 Wooler, Alfred. *Save Me, O God.* Kbd: H:e1-g2; L:c1-e♭2. Arthur P. Schmidt (1914)

54:1-4 (adapted)
Haas, David. *The Lord Upholds My Life.* Duet-Kbd, 2 inst in c: Sop:d1-f♯2/Bar: d-e1. GIA (1989), found in *Creating God*

55:1-5 Mendelssohn, Felix. *Hear My Prayer* (from *Hear My Prayer*). Kbd: H:d1-g2(a3); L:b1-e2. G. Schirmer (1968, 1907); Kevin Mayhew (1992), found in *Favorite Anthem* bk 2; *Oratorio Repertoire,* vol. 1; *Solos from the Great Oratorios for Soprano*

55:1-8 Dvorák, Antonín. *Give Ear, O God, Unto My Prayer,* op. 99, no. 3 (from *Biblical Songs*) (English only). Pno: H:e♭-a3; L:b♭1-e2. International (1962), found in *Biblical Songs: A Cycle of Ten Songs,* op. 99

55:1-8 Dvorák, Antonín. *Hear My Prayer,* op. 99, no. 3 (from *Biblical Songs*) (English/Czech/German). Pno: H:e♭-a3; L:b♭1-e2. Simrock; G. Schirmer; R. D. Row (1955), found in *Dvorák,* op. 99, *Biblical Songs*

55:1-8 Dvorák, Antonín (ed. Šourek, Otakar). *Slyš, ó Bože! Slyš modlitbu mou,* op. 99, no. 3 (*Gott, o höre, hör' auf mein Gebet; Hear, Oh Hear My Prayer, Lord*) (from *Biblical Songs*) (Czech/German/English). Pno: H:e♭-a3. Masters Music (n.d.), found in *Biblical Songs for High Voice and Piano by Antonín Dvorák,* op. 99

55:6-7 (Psalm 39:12)
Barnes, A. M. *Oh, That I Had Wings.* Pno: b♭1-f2. Oliver Ditson (1903), found in *Sacred Songs*

55:6-7 Mendelssohn, Felix (arr. Harrison Oxley). *O For the Wings of a Dove* (from *Hear My Prayer*). Org: Sop:f♯1-g2. Church (n.d.), found in *Favorite Anthem,* bk 2; *Sacred Songs,* vol. 1

55:6-7 Mendelssohn, Felix (arr. Neil Jenkins). *O For the Wings of a Dove* (from *Hear My Prayer*). Kbd: H; L:b♭2-e♭2. Oxford (1997), found in *Sing Solo Sacred* (H/L)

55:6-7 Roma, Caro. *Oh! For the Wings of a Dove.* Duet-Kbd: H/L. Witmark 166 (n.v.)

55:17 SEE: Psalm 32:11. Huhn, Bruno S. *Be Glad, O Ye Righteous*

55:17 SEE: Psalm 27:4. Talma, Louise. *Cantata: All the Days of My Life*

55:21 (Psalm 57:10; Psalm 108:4; based on)
Mendelssohn, Felix (arr. Lynn Hodges). *Cast Thy Burden on the Lord* (from *Elijah*). U-Kbd: e♭1-e♭2. Integra (1993), found in *Mendelssohn's ELIJAH for Young Voices*

55:22 SEE: Psalm 21:13. Huhn, Bruno S. *Be Thou Exalted*

55:24 Pasternak, Velvel. *Vaani evtach boch (Men of Blood and Deceit)* (Hebrew transliterated). Gtr: H:f1-g2. Bloch (1971), found in *Songs of the Chassidim II*

56:3 SEE: Psalm 32:7. Ledner, Michael. *You Are My Hiding Place*

56:4a (Psalm 61:1-3; Psalm 71:8)
Franck, César. *Hear My Cry, O God.* Kbd: Sop:e♭1-g2; L:b♭1-e♭2. Boston Music (1961), found in *20 Distinctive Sacred Solos* (H/L); *The First Book of Soprano Solos*

56:13 SEE: Isaiah 12:3-4. Calder, Lee. *God Is My Salvation*

57:00 Buxtehude, Dietrich. *Mein Herz ist bereit* (German). Cont, 3 vlns: Bar:F-f1. Bärenreiter (1971) BA 724

57:00 Head, Michael. *Be Merciful Unto Me* (from *Three Psalms*). Kbd: H:c1-b♭3; L:a1-g2. Boosey & Hawkes (1976) H: 186; L: 187

57:00 Schütz, Heinrich. *Mein Herz ist bereit,* SWV 341 (from *Symphoniae Sacrae* II) (German). Cont, 2 vlns: H. Bärenreiter (1964) BA3448

57:lb SEE: Psalm 69:4b. Laderman, Ezra. *What I Did Not Steal*

57:8a, 10, 12
SEE: Psalm 68:4. Horvit, Michael. *Sing to God*

57:9-11 Chambers, Brent. *Be Exalted, O God.* U-Kbd: b♭1-e♭2. Maranatha! (1977, 1986), found in *Face to Face*

57:9-11 (adapted)
Chambers, Brent (arr. Jane Yankitis). *Be Exalted, O God.* Kbd/gtr: b♭1-e2. Lillenas (1980), found in *Scripture Solos for All Seasons; Songs for Praise and Worship*

57:10 (Psalm 22:27)
Handel, G. F. *God's Tender Mercy Knows No Bounds* (from *Sixth Chandos Anthem*). Kbd: d1-a3. Novello (1905)

57:10 SEE: Psalm 55:21. Mendelssohn, Felix. *Cast Thy Burden on the Lord*

57:10, 11 SEE: Psalm 21:13. Huhn, Bruno S. *Be Thou Exalted*

59:16-17 SEE: Psalm 27:4. Talma, Louise. *Cantata: All the Days of My Life*

61:00 Mulligan, Harold Vincent. *Hear My Cry.* Org: c1-e2. G. Schirmer (1943)

61:1 (Psalm 22:14; Psalm 69:3)
Laderman, Ezra. *From the End of the Earth.* Pno: H:b1-g♭2. Oxford (1970), found in *The Psalms*

61:1 (Book of Common Prayer)
Mahnke, Allan. *Psalm 61.* Cantor-Kbd: c♯1-e2. Concordia (1992) 97-6093, found in *17 Psalms for Cantor and Congregation*

61:1 (other)
Wooler, Alfred. *Hear My Cry, O Lord!* Pno: H:d♯1-g2; M:b1-e♭2; L:a1-d♭2. Oliver Ditson (1908), found in *Choice Sacred Songs* (H/L)

61:1-2 (Psalm 64:1)
Nelhybel, Vaclav. *Hear My Voice.* Org: d1-e2. Agape (1981) 536, also found in *Psalm Settings*

61:1-3 SEE: Psalm 56:4a. Franck, César. *Hear My Cry, O God*

61:3 (Psalm 16:00; Luke 13:34; based on)
Hurd, Bob (arr. Craig S. Kingsbury). *Shelter Me, O God.* Cantor-Kbd, gtr, inst in c, opt duet: b1-d2 (a1-b2). OCP (1984) 8836CC, also found in *In the Breaking of the Bread*

61:1, 3-4 (Psalm 63:1, 4-5)
Dvorák, Antonín. *Hear My Crying, O Lord,* op. 99, no. 6 (from *Biblical Songs*) (English/

Czech/German). Pno: H:e1-g2; ML:c♯1-e2; L:b1-d2. Simrock; G. Schirmer (1991); Coburn Press (1971); R. D. Row (1955), found in *Dvorák,* op. 99, *Biblical* Songs (H/L); *Lift Up Your Voice; Sacred Classics* (H/ML); *Second Book of Soprano Solos*

61:1, 3-4 Dvorák, Antonín. *Hear My Prayer,* op. 99, no. 6. Duet-Org/pno:H/H:e1-g2;g1-g2. R. D. Row (1961) found in *Sacred Duet Masterpieces*

61:1, 3-4 (Psalm 63:1, 4-5; English version by Humphrey Procter-Gregg)
Dvorák, Antonín. *Lord, O Harken Unto My Crying,* op. 99, no. 6 (from *Biblical Songs*) (English only). Pno: H:e1-g2; L:b1-d2. International (1962), found in *Biblical Songs: A Cycle of Ten Songs,* op. 99

61:1, 3-4 (Psalm 63:1, 4-5)
Dvorák, Antonín (ed. Šourek, Otakar). *Sly_, ó bože, volání me,* op. 99, no. 6 *(Gott, erhör' mit Langmust mein flehn; Hear, Oh Lord, My Bitter Cry)* (from *Biblical Songs*) (Czech/German/English). Pno: H:e1-g2. Masters Music (n.d.), found in *Biblical Songs for High Voice and Piano by Antonín Dvorák,* op. 99

61:1-5, 8 (Psalm 39:00)
Sowerby, Leo. *Hear My Cry, O God.* Kbd: f-e1. H. W. Gray (1927), also found in *Psalms for Bass and O Perfect Love*

62:00 Kuntz, Michael. *Der 62 Psalm.* Org: Bar:a-d1. Cooppenrath (1992)

62:00 (adapted)
Talbot, John Michael. *Only in God.* Gtr: c1-d2. Cherry Lane (1980), found in *Praise, Prayer and Worship*

62:1 SEE: Psalm 46:10a. Bitgood, Roberta. *Be Still and Know That I Am God*

62:1-2, 8, 11-12
Foley, John B. *Only in God.* Cantor-Gtr, opt duet: b♭1-c2(d2). NALR (1976), 10480CC, also found in *A Dwelling Place*

62:1, 5-7 (Psalm 130:5; Isaiah 40:28-31)
Seaton, Annette. *Those Who Wait on the Lord.* Kbd: b1-e2. Lillenas (1980), found in *Scripture Solos for All Seasons*

62:2 (Psalm 63:1; John 6:67; Amos 8:11; adapted)
Lynch, Mike (acc. Patrick Loomis). *In the Land There Is a Hunger.* Org, gtr, 2 trpts: b1-c2. OCP (1986), found in *Bread of the World*

62:6 (Psalm 131:2; Luke 13:34; based on Psalm 131:00 and 62:00)
Hurd, Bob (arr. Craig S. Kingsbury). *Like a Weaned Child.* Org, gtr, inst in c: e1-d2. OCP (1984), found in *In the Breaking of the Bread*

63:00 Goode, Jack. *Thou Art My God.* Kbd: Med. Abingdon, found in *Seven Sacred Solos*

63:00 SEE: Psalm 23:1-2. Hummel, Ferdinand. *Alleluia!*

63:00 SEE: Psalm 23:1-2. Hummel, Ferdinand (arr. Carl Fredrickson). *Alleluia!*

63:1, 4-5 SEE: Psalm 61:1, 3-4. Dvorák, Antonín. *Hear My Crying, O Lord*

63:1 SEE: Psalm 62:2. Lynch, Mike. *In the Land There Is a Hunger*

63:1-4 (based on)
Conry, Tom (acc. Patrick Loomis). *I Will Lift Up My Eyes.* U-Kbd, trpt, timp, susp cym: c1-d2. OCP (1984), found in *Jesus, Lord; Justice, Like a River*

63:1-5 Hartley, Walter S. *Andante molto* (from *A Psalm Cycle*). Pno, fl: c1-a3. Presser (1970)

63:1-5 (based on)
Rieth, Mildred F. *O God, You Are My God.* U/2-part-Org, gtr, inst in c: c1-c2. OCP (1969), found in *Yahweh Is My Shepherd*

63:1-5, 7-8 (altered)
Cooney, Rory. *Psalm 63* (*My Soul Is Longing*). Cantor-Kbd, gtr, ob or vln, vc or bsn, opt duet: b1-f♯2. GIA (1990), found in *Psalms for the Church Year,* vol. 4; *Safety Harbor*

63:1-7 (adapted)
Schutte, Daniel L. (acc. Thomas Kendzia). *My Soul Thirsts.* Kbd: c1-d2. OCP (1978, 1989), found in *Lover of Us All*

63:1-8 (adapted)
Haas, David. *In the Shadow of Your Wings.* Cantor-Kbd, gtr, 2 inst in c, opt duet: b1-f2. GIA (1986), found in *Light and Peace*

63:1-8 (based on)
Hurd, Bob (acc. Dominic MacAller). *My Soul Is Thirsting.* U/2-part-Pno, gtr, inst in c: (b♭1)c1-c2. OCP (1990), found in *Behold the Cross*

63:1-8 (alternative verses based on)
Walker, Christopher. *O Lord, I Will Sing.* U-Kbd, gtr, inst in c, cl: a1-d2. OCP (1989), found in *Out of Darkness*

63:1-9 Foley, John B. *Psalm 63 (My Soul Is Thirsting For You).* Cantor-Kbd, gtr, opt duet: e♭1-d2(e♭2). GIA (1995), found in *Psalms for the Church Year,* vol. 7

63:1b-9 Haugen, Marty. *In the Morning I Will Sing (My Soul Is Thirsting).* Cantor-Kbd, inst in c, gtr, opt duet: (a1)c1-d2. GIA (1995) G-4276

63:2-3 Pasternak, Velvel. *Kén bakõdesh (So I Have Looked for Thee)* (Hebrew transliterated). Gtr: H:g1-f2. Bloch (1971), found in *Songs of the Chassidim II*

63:2-6 Moore, Bob. *In the Shadow of Your Wings.* Cantor-Kbd, gtr:. GIA (1993) G-3857

63:3-4 (based on)
Mitchell, Hugh. *Thy Loving Kindness.* Kbd, gtr, (opt orch): d1-b2. Singspiration (1956), found in *Songs for Praise and Worship*

63:5-6 Scott, Charles P. *When I Remember Thee.* 2-part-Org: Sop/Alto. Carl Fischer 108 (n.v.)

63:6 (Matthew 5:11; I Peter 4:13-14; other)
Elgar, Edward (ed. Bernard Taylor). *The Sun Goeth Down* (from *Kingdom*). Kbd:Sop:e♭1-b♭3. Novello; G. Schirmer (1968), found in *Solos from the Great Oratorios for Soprano*

64:1 (Psalm 28:7; Psalm 38:22; other Scripture)
Handel, G. F. (arr. Keith W. Bissell). *Supplication.* Kbd-e♭1-g2. Waterloo (1971)

64:1 SEE: Psalm 61:1-2. Nelhybel, Vaclav. *Hear My Voice*

65:00 (Adrienne Tindall)
Lovelace, Austin C. *You Crown the Year with Goodness.* Kbd: c1-f2. Darcy Press (1993), found in *Sacred Solos by Austin C. Lovelace*

65:00 (Psalm 66:4-5, 10, 15, 16; based on)
Schutte, Daniel L. *Glory and Praise to Our God.* U/2-part-Gtr: (c1)d1-c2(f♯2). NALR (1976), found in *A Dwelling Place*

65:8, 11 SEE: Psalm 27:4. Talma, Louise. *Cantata: All the Days of My Life*

65:9 Parker, Harold. *Thou Visitest the Earth* (from *The Sower*). Kbd: H:e♭1-a3. Oxford (n.v.)

65:9, 11, 13
Cowen, Frederic Hymen. *How Excellent Is Thy Loving Kindness* (from *Ruth*). Kbd: Tenor:f1-b♭3. G. Schirmer, found in *Anthology of Sacred Song–Tenor; Oratorio Repertoire,* vol. III

66:00 Wyner, Yehudi. *Halleluya.* Kbd: a1-f♯2. Associated (1957), found in *Psalms and Early Songs*

66:1 SEE: Psalm 47:1. Burton, Daniel. *Clap Your Hands, All You People,* no. 2

66:1-2 (Psalm 98:4-5; Acts 17:28a; based on)
Speir, Randy. *In Him We Live.* Kbd, gtr, (opt orch): c1-d2. Intrada (1981, arr. 1992), found in *Songs for Praise and Worship*

66:1-3, 5-6, 9, 19-20 (based on)
Hurd, Bob (acc. Dominic MacAller). *Let All the Earth Cry Out.* U/2-part-Pno, gtr, trpt: c1-d2(e2). OCP (1990), found in *Behold the Cross*

66:1-4 Wyner, Yehudi. *Psalm 66* (from *Psalms and Early Songs*). Kbd: a1-f♯2. Associated (1972) AMP 7123

66:1-6 (based on)
O'Connor, Roc. *Lift Up Your Hearts.* U/2-part-Gtr: d1-c2. NALR (1981), found in *Lord of Light*

66:1-7, 16-20
Cooney, Rory. *Psalm 66 (Let All the Earth Cry Out).* Cantor-Kbd, gtr, opt duet. OCP 10466CC

66:1-7, 16-20
Foley, John B. *Psalm 66 (Let All the Earth).* Cantor-Kbd, gtr, opt duet: c♯1-e2(f♯2). GIA (1995), found in *Psalms for the Church Year,* vol. 7

66:1-8 (altered)
Walker, Tricia. *Sing the Glory of His Name.* Kbd, gtr: b♭1-c2(e♭2). Word (1984), found in *The Song Book,* vol. III

66:2 (Psalm 147:1; Psalm 150:00; Revelation 5:13)
Wolaver, Bill and Robin (choral arr. Steven V. Taylor). *Make His Praise Glorious.* 2-part-Kbd or Trax: a1-f♯2/d-e1(f♯1). Word (1988), found in *25 Songs for Two-Part Choir,* vol. II

66:2 (Psalm 147:1; Psalm 150:00; Revelation 5:13)
Wolaver, Bill and Robin. *Make His Praise Glorious.* Kbd or Trax: H:b1-g2; L:e1-c♯2. Word (1988), found in *40 Contemporary Hits; Fifty Contemporary Favorites for Low Voice; Sandi Patti: Anthology; Sandi Patti Medium Voice Collection; Very Best of Sandi Patti* (H/M)

66:4 SEE: Psalm 29:1-2. Schütz, Heinrich. *Bringt her dem Herren*

66:4 SEE: Psalm 29:1-2. Schütz, Heinrich (ed. Richard T. Gore). *Bring to Jehovah (Bringt her dem Herren)*

66:4-5, 10, 15, 16
SEE: Psalm 65:00. Schutte, Daniel L. *Glory and Praise to Our God*

66:9 Krugman, E. M. (arr. Velvel Pasternak). *Hasom nafshénu (He Kept Us Alive)* (Hebrew transliterated). Gtr: M:d1-d2. Bloch (1971), found in *Songs of the Chassidim II*

66:14-15 Gordigiani, L. *O Come Hither, and Hearken.* Kbd: Sop:e1-e2. Church (n.d.), found in *Sacred Songs,* vol. 1

67:00 Barker, Clement W. *Bless the Lord, O My Soul.* Kbd: MH:f1-f2; ML:d1-d2. R. D. Row (1948)

67:00 Edwards, Leo. *Psalm no. 67 (God Be Merciful Unto Us).* Kbd: Bar:a-d1. Willis Music (1983) 10621

67:00 Freudenthal, Josef. *The Lord's Blessing.* Kbd: H:d1-g2; L:b^{b}1-e^{b}2. Transcontinental (1962) TV 480

67:00 Fryxell, Regina H. *Psalm 67.* Kbd: Med. G. Schirmer

67:00 Godard, Benjamin. *Be Merciful, O Lord.* 2-part-Org:Sop/Alto. Carl Fischer 109

67:00 Koch, John. *God Be Merciful Unto Us* (from *Songs of David*). Stg qt, fl: g1-g2. American Music Centre (n.v.)

67:00 (Book of Common Prayer)
Mahnke, Allan. *Psalm 67.* Cantor-Kbd: c1-e2. Concordia (1992) 97-6093, found in *17 Psalms for Cantor and Congregation*

67:00 (adapted)
Talbot, John Michael. *May God Bless Us.* Gtr: b1-c2. Birdwing (1985), found in *Praise, Prayer and Worship*

67:00 Wolfe, Jacques. *Psalm LXVII (Joy for All the Ages)* (from *Hebrew Trilogy*). Org/pno: L:a1-g2. American Composers Alliance (1969)

67:3-7 Hammerschmidt, Andreas (rel. Fritz Oberdoerffer). *Es danken dir, Gott, die Voelker (Let the People Praise Thee, O God)* (from *Musicalische Andachten*) (German/English). U-Org, orch, cont, 2 vlns or fl: c$^{\sharp}$1-e2. Bärenreiter (n.d.) 459

68:00 Handel, G. F. *Like as the Smoke Vanisheth (Gleich wie der Rauch schnell verweh)* (English/German). Duet-Kbd: Alto/Bass. John Church (1902), found in *Sacred Duets,* vol. II (H/L)

68:00 Rogers, Bernard. *Psalm 68.* Pno, orch: a-g. Peer-Southern (1955)

68:1-3 Wooler, Alfred. *Let God Arise.* Kbd: H:e1-g2. Oliver Ditson (1929), found in *Ditson Treasury of Sacred Songs*

68:1-6, 17-18
Couperin, François. *Salvum me fac Deus* (Latin). Cont, 2 vlns: b$^{\flat}$-e$^{\flat}$1. Heugel (1972) H32.219

68:4 Handel, G. F. *O Sing Unto God (O singt unserm Gott)* (English/German). Duet-Kbd: Alto/Bass. John Church (1902), found in *Sacred Duets,* vol. II (H/L)

68:4 (Psalm 47:1-2; Psalm 57:8a, 10, 12)
Horvit, Michael. *Sing to God.* Pno: f1-b$^{\flat}$3. Transcontinental (1977)

68:17-18 SEE: Psalm 47:5. Bencini, Pietro Paolo (ed. James H. Laster). *Alleluia. Ascendit Deus (Alleluia. God Has Gone Up)*

68:18 Handel, G. F. *Thou Art Gone Up On High* (from *Messiah*). Kbd: H:f1-a2; M:a1-e$^{\flat}$2; L:c1-e2. Carl Fischer; G. Schirmer (1994); Novello (1959), found in *Oratorio Anthology: Alto/Mezzo–Soprano* (M)

68:19 Greene, Maurice. *Praised Be the Lord.* Kbd: c1-f2. Oxford (1925)

68:19 Greene, Maurice (ed. E. Stanley Roper). *Praised Be the Lord.* Kbd: c1-f2. Bosworth (1910), found in *Seven Sacred Solos of the Early English School*

69:00 (adapted)
SEE: Psalm 22:00. Card, Michael. *Death of a Son*

69:00 (adapted)
Charles, Ernest. *Save Me, O God.* Pno: H:d1-a3; L:b1-f$^{\sharp}$2. G. Schirmer (1947), also found in *Songs of Ernest Charles*

69:00 Tornioli, Marcantonio (ed. Karl Gustav Fellerer). *Salvum me fac deus (1617)* (Latin). Unacc Duet: Tenor:d1-g2/Tenor:b1-e2. Arno Volk Verlag (1958 - 1976), found in *Anthology of Music,* vol. 31: *The Monody*

69:1, 3 Randegger, Alberto. *Save Me, O God!* Pno: H:d1-b$^{\flat}$3; L:b1-g2. G. Schirmer (1988), found in *Album of Sacred Songs* (H/L); *Oratorio Repertoire,* vol. 1

69:1, 3, 29 (Psalm 30:2, 12)
Harris, Cuthbert. *Save Me, O God.* Kbd: H: d1-g2; L:b$^{\flat}$1-e$^{\flat}$2. Arthur P. Schmidt (1925)

69:1-3, 5, 16-17, 29-30
Butler, Eugene. *Save Me, O God.* Kbd: b1-

e2. Sacred Music Press (1969), found in *The Solo Psalmist*

69:1-3, 14-17, 20
Floyd, Carlisle. *Save Me, O God, for the Waters Are Come in Unto My Soul* (from *The Pilgrimage*). Kbd or orch: M:g1-f2. Boosey & Hawkes (1959)

69:3 SEE: Psalm 61:1. Laderman, Ezra. *From the End of the Earth*

69:4b (Psalm 57:1b; Psalm 119:148, 150)
Laderman, Ezra. *What I Did Not Steal.* Pno: d1-g2. Oxford (1970), found in *The Psalms*

69:5-6 Dengler, Lee. *You Know My Folly*. Kbd: M:c1-f2. Augsburg (1995) 11-10608, found in *Songs of David*

69:8 SEE: Psalm 104:5. Laderman, Ezra. *Thou Didst Set the Earth*

69:14 Davidowitz, M. (arr. Velvle Pasternak). *Vaani s'filosi (Let My Prayer Be Unto Thee)* (Hebrew transliterated). Gtr: H:b♭1-f2. Bloch (1971), found in *Songs of the Chassidim II*

69:14 SEE: Numbers 24:5. Gottlieb, Jack. *Ma Tovu*

69:14 SEE: Numbers 24:5. Steinberg, Ben. *Mah Tovu*

69:14 SEE: Numbers 24:5. Weiner, Lazar. *Mah Tovu*

69:20 Handel, G. F. *Thy Rebuke Hath Broken His Heart* (from *Messiah*). Kbd: Tenor:d♯-g1. Carl Fischer; G. Schirmer; Hal Leonard (1994); Novello (1959), found in *Oratorio Anthology: Tenor*

69:24 SEE: Exodus 32:10. Mendelssohn, Felix. *Consume Them All, Lord Sabaoth*

70:00 Schütz, Heinrich (ed. Lloyd Pfautsch). *A Psalm of David.* Pno: H:c1-g2; L:a♭1-d♭2. Lawson Gould (1961), found in *The Church Soloist; Solos for the Church Soloist*

70:00 (Psalm 86:00)
Sutermeisster, Heinrich. *Der 70 und 86 Psalm* (German). Org: M:g♯-f2. Schott (1951) 4049

70:1-5 (Psalm 71:2)
Himmel, F. H. *Incline Thine Ear to Me.* Org: Alto:c1-d2. Augsburg (n.d.) 1040

70:1-5 SEE: Psalm 40:14-18. Schütz, Heinrich. *Haste Thee, Lord God, Haste to Save Me*

70:2-6 Hammerschmidt, Andreas (ed. Diethard Hellmann). *Eile mich, Gott, zu erretten* (German). Duet-Cont: Equal voices:d1-g2/c♯1-g2. Hänssler (n.d.), found in *Das geistliche Konzert 78*

Psalm 70:2-6
Wiemer, Wolfgang. *Eile, Gott, mich zu erretten.* Org: H. Breitkopf & Härtel (1966) 6524 (n.v.)

71:1, 5, 8, 15 (adapted)
Haas, David. *I Will Sing*. U/2-part-Kbd, gtr: b1-e2. GIA (1989), found in *Psalms for the Church Year,* vol. 3

71:1, 9, 12, 18
Spicker, Max. *In Thee, O God, Do I Put My Trust,* op. 48. Pno/stg qt, org: b1-f2. G. Schirmer (1899)

71:2 SEE: Psalm 70:1. Himmel, F. H. *Incline Thine Ear to Me*

71:8 SEE: Psalm 56:4a. Franck, César. *Hear My Cry, O God*

71:9, 12 SEE: Isaiah 45:1-2, 22. VanWoert, Rutger. *Be Not Far From Me, Oh God*

71:14 Peter, Johann Friedrich (ed. and arr. Karl Kroeger). *I Will Always Trust the Lord (I will immer Harren).* Pno/org: S:f1-g2, found in *Moravian Music Foundation Publications* (1974) no. 7

71:15, 17 SEE: Psalm 27:4. Talma, Louise. *Cantata: All the Days of My Life*

71:16a Herbst, Johannes (ed. Donald M. McCorkle). *I Will Go in the Strength of the Lord* (from *Three Sacred Songs of Johannes Herbst*) (German/English). Kbd or stg qt: H:e1-g2. Boosey & Hawkes; Carl Fischer

72:00 (adapted)
Talbot, John Michael. *Lord, Every Nation on Earth Shall Adore You.* Gtr: b1-a3. Birdwing (1985), found in *Praise, Prayer and Worship*

72:1-2, 7-8, 10-11, 12-13 (adapted)
Joncas, Michael. *Every Nation on Earth.* Gtr: d1-d2. GIA (1990) G-3340, also found in *Come to Me*

72:2-3, 6-11
LaForge, Frank. *He Shall Judge Thy People.* Kbd: Med. G. Schirmer (n.v.)

73:25-26 (other)
Buxtehude, Dietrich. *Herr, wenn ich nur dich Habe* (Geistliche Solokataten 12) (German). Cont, 2 vlns: Sop:d1-g2. Bärenreiter (1970) BA 1139

74:20 SEE: Exodus 15:3. Anonymous. *The Lord Is a Mighty Warrior*

75:1 (Isaiah 9:6)
Hancock, Vicki. *Unto Thee, O Lord, Do We Give Thanks*. 2-part-Kbd: e♭1-e♭2. Broadman Press (1979) 4559-18

76:6 SEE: Exodus 15:3. Anonymous. *The Lord Is a Mighty Warrior*

78:1-3 Schütz, Heinrich. *Attendite, popule meus,* SWV 270 *(So höre doch, meine Gemeinde)* (from *Symphoniae Sacrae* I) (Latin/German). Cont, 4 tbns: Bass:F-c1. Bärenreiter (1967) BA37 (n.v.)

78:1-3 Schütz, Heinrich. *Attendite, popule meus, legem meam,* SWV 270 (from *Symphoniae Sacrae* I) (Latin). Cont, 4 tbns: Bass:F-c1. Musica Rara (1962)

80:00 Pinkham, Daniel. *Psalm 79*. Kbd: f1-g2. American Composers Alliance, found in *Composers Facsimile Edition*

80:1-3, 7, 15-16 (based on)
Dufford, Bob. *Save Us, O Lord*. Cantor-Gtr, opt duet: d1-d2. NALR (1981); OCP: 9495CC, also found in *Lord of Light*

81:1-3 Handel, G. F. (ed. Hal H. Hopson). *Sing Out Your Joy to God*. 2-part mixed-Kbd: c1-d2/ c-b♭1. Hope (1990) AA 1688

81:1-4 Childs, David. *Psalm 81*. Org: e1-f2. Abingdon (1966) H: APM 390; L: APM 385, also found in *Seven Psalms for Voice and Organ*

81:9-11 (Isaiah 43:1, 25)
Stevenson, Frederick. *Hear, O My People*. Org: c1-b3. Oliver Ditson (1921)

82:1-5, 8 Cohen, Gerald. *Ad Matai (How Long?)*. (Hebrew transliterated). Pno: M:c1-f2. Oxford (2001), found in *Come Before God with Joyous Song*

83:00 Sacco, Peter. *Keep Not Thou Silence, O God* (from *Three Psalms*). Kbd (brass qnt): H:c♯1-g♯2. Ostara Press (1973) 110

83:1-4, 13, 18
Childs, David. *Psalm 83*. Org: c1-f2. Abingdon (1966) H: APM 390; L: APM 385, also found in *Seven Psalms for Voice and Organ*

83:1-5, 13-15, 18
Siegel, Arsene. *Keep Thou Not Silence, O God*. Pno: H:b1-a2; L:a1-g2. Galaxy (1944)

84:00 Coombs, Charles Whitney. *O How Amiable Are Thy Dwellings* (from *The Ancient of Days*). Duet-Kbd: Mez/Bass. G. Schirmer (n.v.)

84:00 (The Psalms of David in Prose and Meeter, 1650)
Grantham, Donald. *How Lovely Is Thy Dwelling Place*. U/2-part-Pno: H:d1-e2;L: c♯1-d2. Fostco (Mark Foster) (1992) MF 818

84:00 Greenbaum, Matthew. *Psalm 84*. Pno, fl, cl, vn: c1-a3. American Music Centre (n.v.)

84:00 Hopson, Hal H. *Psalm 84*. 2-part-Kbd: d1-d2. Hope (1989) HH 3935

84:00 (Psalm 27:4; based on)
Howard, Tom. *Psalm 84* (*How Lovely Is Your Dwelling Place*). Kbd: a1-e2. Maranatha! (1982), found in *The Lord Is My Light*

84:1-2, 4 Haydn, F. Joseph (arr. Carl Fredrickson). *How Lovely Is Thy Dwelling Place*. Kbd: c1-e♭2. R. D. Row (1959), found in *Sacred Song Masterpieces,* bk 1

84:1-2, 4 Haydn, F. Joseph. *How Lovely Is Thy Dwelling Place.* Duet-Org/pno:H:e1-f♯2; H:e1-e2. R. D. Row (1961) found in *Sacred Duet Masterpieces*

84:1-2, 4 SEE: Luke 2:48-49. Schütz, Heinrich. *Meine Seele, Warum Hast du uns das getan?*

84:1-2, 4 SEE: Luke 2:48-49. Schütz, Heinrich. *My Son, Wherefore Hast Thou Done This to Us? (Meine seele, warum hast du uns das getan?)*

84:1-2, 10-11
deLange, S. (ed. Max Spicker). *How Beautiful Are Thy Dwellings* (from *Moses*). Pno: Sop:d1-a♭3. G. Schirmer (1902, 1977), found in *Anthology of Sacred Song–Soprano; Schirmer's Singer's Library: Soprano Arias from Oratorios*

84:1-3 Davis, Katherine K. *How Lovely Are Thy Dwellings*. Kbd: d1-g2. Galaxy (1952) 1.1872.7

84:1-3, 8, 10
Liddle, Samuel. *How Lovely Are Thy Dwellings*. Kbd: H:e♭1-a♭3; MH:d♭1-g♭2; M:c1-f2; L:b♭1-e♭2. Boosey & Hawkes (1908, 1936), found in *60 Great Solos for Low Voice; First Book of Soprano Solos Part II; How Majestic Is Your Name*

84:1-4 Carter, John. *How Lovely Is Thy Dwelling Place*. Kbd: M:c1-f2. Hope (1987) 1053, also found in *The Church Soloist; Come With a Singing Heart*

84:1-4, 8, 11
Alstott, Owen. *How Lovely Is Your Dwelling Place.* Duet-Org, inst in c: c1-d2. OCP (1983, 1988) 8813

84:1-7, 9 Hurd, David. *Psalm 84 (How Dear to Me Is Your Dwelling).* 2-part-Kbd: c1-d2. Augsburg (1991) 11-10106

84:1-8, 10-11
Joncas, Michael. *How Lovely Is Your Dwelling Place.* Org, gtr: b1-d2. NALR (1979), found in *On Eagle's Wings*

84:1-8, 10-11
Joncas, Michael. *How Lovely Is Your Dwelling Place.* 2 Cantors-Org, gtr. OCP (1991) 10756CC

84:2 SEE: Psalm 135:1-2. Handel, G. F. *Praise Him, All Ye That in His House Attend*

84:3 SEE: Psalm 42:3. Kehati, Pinchas. *Tsomo Nafshi*

84:3-4 (based on)
Foley, John B. *The Sparrow Finds a Home.* Gtr: d1-c2. NALR (1974), found in *Neither Silver Nor Gold*

84:3-4, 10-12 (Book of Common Prayer)
Pelz, Walter L. *Happy Are They Who Dwell in Your House* (from *Three Solos for High Voice*). Org, ob: e1-e2. Augsburg (1979) 11-9477

84:4-5 Greene, Maurice (ed. E. Stanley Roper). *Blessed Are They That Dwell in Thy House.* Kbd: H:e1-g2; L:d1-f♯2. Bosworth (1910), found in *Seven Sacred Solos of the Early English School*

84:10 SEE: Psalm 92:1. Costa, Michael. *This Night I Lift My Heart to Thee (It Is a Good Thing To Give Thanks Unto the Lord)*

84:10 (other)
Redman, Matt. *Better Is One Day.* Kbd, gtr: b1-c♯2. Found in *Top 25 Heart Seekers; WOW Worship Orange*

84:12 (other)
Bach, J. S. *Gott ist unser Sonn' und Schild (Gott, der Herr, ist Sonn' und Schild)* (from *Kantate* Nr. 79) (German). Pno, ob or fl: Alto:c♯-e2. Kalmus, found in *Arias from Church Cantatas for Contralto,* vol. II

84:12 (other)
Handel, G. F. *Powerful Guardian* (arr. Carl Frederickson). Duet-Org/pno:H:g1-g2; H:f1-f2. R. D. Row (1961) found in *Sacred Duet Masterpieces;* also found in *Sacred Song Masterpieces,* bk 2

84:12 SEE: Psalm 29:11. Pasternak, Velvel. *Yiru Es Adõnoy*

85:1-2, 10-13
Oxley, Harrison. *Lord, How Gracious.* 2-part-Org: H:c1-f2/L:b♭1-f2. Kevin Mayhew (1992), found in *Favorite Anthem,* bk 2

85:6-11 Robyn, Alfred G. *Wilt Thou Not Receive Us Again.* Duet-Kbd: Alto/Tenor. Oliver Ditson (1913)

85:7 (Psalm 86:5)
Boyce, William. *Shew Us Thy Mercy, O Lord* (no. 3 from *Lord, Thou Hast Been Our Refuge*). Duet-Kbd, orch: Alto:g-e2/Tenor: d-f1. Oxford (1977)

85:8 SEE: Psalm 46:10a. Bitgood, Roberta. *Be Still and Know That I Am God*

85:8 Tindall, Adrienne M. *Lord, Make Me an Instrument.* Kbd: c1-e2. Darcy Press (1994), found in *Sacred Solos by Adrienne Tindall,* vol. III

85:8-9 SEE: Ezekiel 13:3. Barker, Clement W. *Woe Unto the Foolish Prophets*

85:8-9, 11-14 (based on)
Hurd, Bob (accomp. Dominic MacAller). *Psalm 85 (Show Us Your Kindness).* Cantor-Kbd: d1-c2. OCP (1991), found in *Alleluia! Give the Glory*

85:8-13 SEE: Psalm 46:10a. Bitgood, Roberta. *Be Still and Know That I Am God*

85:8-13 (Book of Common Prayer)
Mahnke, Allan. *Psalm 85.* Cantor-Kbd: e♭1-e♭2. Concordia (1992) 97-6093, found in *17 Psalms for Cantor and Congregation*

85:9, 12 (based on)
Bennett, Sir William Sterndale. *His Salvation Is Nigh Them That Fear Him* (from *The Woman of Samaria*). Pno: Tenor:f♯1-g♯2; L:d1-e2. Found in *Album of Sacred Songs* (H/L); *Oratorio Repertoire,* vol. III

85:9-14 Martinson, Joel. *Psalm 85.* Org, fl: e♭1-f2. Concordia (1996) 97-6587

86:00 SEE: Psalm 70:00. Sutermeisster, Heinrich. *Der 70 und 86 Psalm*

86:1-3, 5 Frey, Richard E. *Bow Down Thine Ear, O Lord.* Kbd: H; L:b1-e2. Oliver Ditson (1913), found in *Solos for Christian Science Services*

86:1-3, 5-6, 11 (adapted)
Gardner, Irene Justine. *Bow Down Thine Ear*. Kbd: H:c1-f♯2; L:a♭1-d2. Huntzinger (1958)

86:1a, 4a, 6-7, 13 (adapted)
Hamblen, Bernard. *Hear Thou My Prayer*. Pno: H:c1-g2; L:a1-e2. Huntzinger (1923), found in *Selected Sacred Songs for General Use*

86:1-4, 6-7, 11-12
MacFadyen, Alexander. *Bow Down Thine Ear, O Lord*. Kbd: H:d♯1-g2; L:b1-e♭2. John Church (1912)

86:1-5 (adapted)
Adler, Samuel. *Bow Down Thine Ear,* (no. 5 from *Twelve Songs of Praise*). U-Org: c1-d2. Oxford (1988) 94.505

86:4-6, 12 (adapted)
Vivaldi, Antonio (ed. Lloyd Pfautsch). *Lord, to Thee Do I Lift My Soul*. Kbd: H:d1-g2; L:a1-d2. Lawson - Gould (1957), found in *Solos for the Church Year* (H/L)

86:5 SEE: Psalm 85:7. Boyce, William. *Shew Us Thy Mercy, O Lord*

86:5-6, 9-10, 15-16
Trapp, Lynn. *Psalm 86* (from *Four Psalm Settings*). Cantor-Org: d1-d2. MorningStar (1989) MSM-80-701

86:6a, 11a
SEE: Psalm 4:1. Gilbert, Harry M. *God of Righteousness*

86:10-12, 15 (Book of Common Prayer)
Mahnke, Allan. *Psalm 86*. Cantor-Kbd: c1-d2. Concordia (1992) 97-6093, found in *17 Psalms for Cantor and Congregation*

86:11 (paraphrased)
Sedio, Mark. *Teach Me Your Way, O Lord*. 2-part-Kbd: (c1)e1-d2. AMSI (1995) 711

86:11-13 Kingsley, Gershon. *Teach Me, O Lord*. Kbd: H; M. Transcontinental (1959) 553

86:12-13 Mendelssohn, Felix. *I Praise Thee, O Lord, My God* (from *St. Paul*). Kbd: Bar or Bass:c-c1. G. Schirmer

86:17 Shapiro, Rabbi Y. (arr. Velvel Pasternak). *Asé imonu õs (Work in Our Behalf a Sign For Good)* (Hebrew transliterated). Gtr: M:b1-e2. Bloch (1971), found in *Songs of the Chassidim II*

88:1 SEE: Psalm 47:1. Burton, Daniel. *Clap Your Hands, All You People*

89:00 (Psalm 145:00; Magnificat)
Schoenbachler, Tim. *Forever I Will Sing*. Gtr, inst in c: d1-d2. OCP (1979), found in *All Is Ready*

89:00 (adapted)
Talbot, John Michael. *Forever Will I Sing*. Gtr: e1-d2. Cherry Lane (1982), found in *Praise, Prayer and Worship*

89:1 (adapted)
Fillmore, James H. and Tom Fettke, Tom (arr. Lee Herrington). *I Will Sing of the Mercies*. Kbd, gtr, (opt orch): d1-d2. Word (1986, 1992), found in *Bible Songs; Songs for Praise and Worship*

89:1 Mendelssohn, Felix. *I Will Sing of Thy Great Mercies* (from *St. Paul*). Kbd: H:e1-f2; ML:c1-d♭2. Augsburg (1989) 11-8195, found in *Sing a Song of Joy* (H/L)

89:1 Mendelssohn, Felix. *I Will Sing of Thy Great Mercies* (from *St. Paul*). Kbd: H:e1-f2; ML:c1-d♭2. Lawson Gould (1961), found in *Oratorio Repertoire,* vol. 1; *Soloist's Practical Library,* bk 2; *Solos for the Church Soloist* (H/ML)

89:1 Mendelssohn, Felix (ed. Gordon Young). *I Will Sing of Thy Mercies* (from *St. Paul*). 2-part-Kbd: e♭1-e♭2/b♭1-d♭2. Agape (1978) AG7228.

89:1 (adapted)
Paris, Twila. *You Have Been Good*. Kbd, gtr, (opt orch): d1-b2. Star Song/Mountain Spring Music (1988, 1900), found in *Songs for Praise and Worship*

89:1 (Psalm 100:5; Jeremiah 33:11)
Wienhorst, Richard. *I Will Sing the Story of Thy Love*. Org, fl: c♯1-e2. Chantry (1980) 8012

89:1, 5, 8-9, 11, 14-15
Powell, Robert J. *I Will Sing of the Mercies of the Lord*. Kbd: c1-f2. Sacred Music Press (1969), found in *The Solo Psalmist*

89:1-2, 15-16 (adapted)
Lynch, Mike (acc. John Strege). *Forever I Will Sing*. U/2-part-Org, gtr: a1-e2 (a1-f♯2). OCP (1985, 1986), found in *Bread of the World*

89:1-4, 15-18 (Book of Common Prayer)
Mahnke, Allan. *Psalm 89*. Cantor-Kbd: c1-d2. Concordia (1992) 97-6093, found in *17 Psalms for Cantor and Congregation*

89:1-5, 15-18, 52
Triplett, Robert F. *I Will Sing of Thy Steadfast Love*. Org: d1-a3. Abingdon (1968) APM 603

89:1-5, 6, 9, 14
Diemer, Emma Lou. *I Will Sing of Your Steadfast Love*. Org: H:e1-a2. Arisa Press (1987) 153

89:1-6, 16-19, 21-22, 25, 27
Foley, John B. *Psalm 89 (Forever I Will Sing)*. Cantor-Kbd, gtr: f1-d2. GIA (1995), found in *Psalms for the Church Year,* vol. 7

89:1, 15-16 (Psalm 119:105)
Parker, Clifton. *Blessed Is the People*. Kbd: d1-f♯2. Carl Fischer (1934)

89:2-3, 16-19
Trapp, Lynn. *Psalm 89* (from *Four Psalm Settings*). U/Cantor-Org: d1-d2. MorningStar (1989) MSM-80-701

89:15 Handel, G. F. *Righteous and Equity* (from *Chandos Anthem*). U-Kbd: c♯1-d2. H 5967

89:15, 18 (based on)
Schutte, Daniel L. *Happy Are the Ones*. Gtr: d1-d2. NALR (1974), found in *Neither Silver Nor Gold*

89:26 SEE: Isaiah 2:22. Barker, Clement W. *Mark the Perfect Man*

90:00 Barnes, Milton. *Psalm 90* (from *The Psalms of David*). Duet-Perc, timp, harp or stgs: Mez/Bar. Canadian Music Centre (1973)

90:00 Humphreys, Don. *Lord, Thou Hast Been Our Dwelling Place*. Kbd: H:b♭1-f2; L:g-d2. R. D. Row (1952)

90:00 Phillips, Louis Baker. *Lord, Thou Hast Been Our Dwelling Place*. Pno: b1-g♭2. Boosey & Hawkes (1923)

90:00 Wenzel, Eberhard. *Psalm 90* (German). Spoken-Org: M. Merseburger (1973) 895

90:1, 16-17 (Psalm 92:1, 2, 4-5)
Fischer, Irwin. *Let the Beauty of the Lord*. Org: H or M:e1-f♯2. Coburn Press, found in *Eleven Scriptural Songs from the Twentieth Century*

90:1-2, 4 (Isaac Watts)
Croft, William (arr. Jerry Ray). *O God, Our Help in Ages Past*. Pno, gtr: e1-d2. Alfred (1993), found in *World's Greatest Hymns*

90:1-2, 4 (Isaac Watts)
Davies, Henry Walford. *O God, Our Help in Ages Past*. Kbd, gtr: e1-d2. Hal Leonard (1991), found in *The Big Book of Hymns; Favorite Hymns; Great Hymns Treasury*

90:1-2, 4 (Isaac Watts)
Davies, Henry Walford (arr. Harrison Oxley). *O God, Our Help in Ages Past*. U/2-part-Org: (g)b♭1-e♭2(g2). Kevin Mayhew (1992), found in *Favorite Anthem,* bk 2

90:1-2, 4, 10, 12, 14, 17
Kellermeyer, David M. *A Prayer of Moses*. Org: M:a1-e2. MorningStar (1993) MSM-40-908

90:1-2, 4, 16-17
Butt, James. *Psalm 90*. Org: e1-e2. Sphemusations (n.d.)

90:2-6 (adapted)
Dick, Colleen R. (arr. Craig S. Kingsbury). *We Are the Earth*. Duet-Kbd, gtr: MH:b-f♯2; M:b-c♯2. OCP (1990, 1992), found in *Return to Me: Music for Funerals and Healing,* vol. 1

90:4 SEE: Job 22:21. MacDermid, James G. *Acquaint Now Thyself With Him*

90:12 SEE: Acts 17:28. Gieseke, Richard W. *God's Own Time*

90:12-17 Stewart, Roy James. *Fill Us With Your Love, O Lord*. Cantor-Kbd, inst in c, gtr, opt duet: c1-b2(g2). GIA (1993) G-3746 INST, also found in *Psalms for the Church Year,* vol. 5

90:14 Halberstam, Rabbi S. (arr. Velvel Pasternak). *Sah'énu (Satisfy Us in the Morning)* (Hebrew transliterated). Gtr: M:a1-f2. Bloch (1971), found in *Songs of the Chassidim II*

90:16-17 SEE: Psalm 25:1-2, 5, 7. Cornelius, Peter. *Unto Thee I Lift Up My Soul*

90:16-17a
Nelson, Ronald A. *Let Thy Work Appear* (from *Four Anthems for Young Choirs*). U-Kbd: e1-e♭2. Boosey & Hawkes (1965) 5576

90:17 Lovelace, Austin C. *The Beauty of the Lord*. Kbd: d1-f♯2. Darcy Press (1993), found in *Sacred Solos by Austin C. Lovelace*

91:00 Davye, John J. *He That Dwelleth in the Secret Place* (from *Two Psalms of Meditation*). Org: f1-f2. muSic eSpreSS (1978)

91:00 (adapted)
Mendelssohn, Felix (arr. Carl Fredrickson). *Thy Secret Place*. Kbd: c1-c2. R. D. Row (1959), found in *Sacred Song Masterpieces,* bk 1

91:00 (adapted)
Mendelssohn, Felix. *Thy Secret Place.* Duet-Org/pno:H:e♭1-e♭2; H:e♭1-g♭2. R. D. Row (1961) found in *Sacred Duet Masterpieces*

91:00 O'Connor-Morris, Geoffrey. *Psalm 91.* Kbd: Med. Carl Fischer (1949) V 1988

91:00 Sowerby, Leo. *Whoso Dwelleth (Psalm 91)* (from *Three Psalms*). Org: M:a1-f♯2. H. W. Gray (1949)

91:1-2 Shelley, Harry Rowe. *He That Dwelleth in the Secret Place* (from *Psalm XCI*). Org: H:e1-g2; L:c1-e♭2. G. Schirmer (1921), found in *Seventeen Sacred Songs for Church and General Use*

91:1-2 (based on)
Wexelberg, Shannon. *You Are My Refuge.* Kbd, gtr: a1-a2. Marantha! (1999), found in *Top 25 Heart Seekers*

91:1-2, 4-5, 11
Humphreys, Don. *He That Dwelleth in the Secret Place.* Kbd: e♭1-f2. Willis Music (1950)

91:1-2, 4, 9, 11
Lowe, Augustus F. *Sanctuary.* Org: M. Carl Fischer (1951), found in *Eight Scriptural Solos*

91:1-2, 5-6, 9-10, 14-16
Baumgartner, H. Leroy. *He That Dwelleth in the Secret Place,* op. 48, no. 2 (from *O Lord, My God, Thou Art Very Great*). Kbd: e1-a3. Concordia (1958) 97-5724

91:1-2, 5-7, 11-12
Scott, John Prindle. *He Shall Give His Angel Charge.* Pno: H:f1-a♭3; L:d1-f2. Huntzinger (1918)

91:1-2, 10-12, 14-15 (based on)
Hurd, Bob (arr. Craig S. Kingsbury). *Psalm 91 (Be With Me).* Cantor-Kbd: c1-d2. OCP (1991) OCP 10250CC, also found in *Alleluia! Give the Glory*

91:1-4 Childs, David. *Psalm 91.* Org: f1-f2. Abingdon (1966) H: APM 390; L: APM 385, found in *Seven Psalms for Voice and Organ*

91:1-4, 11 (adapted)
Liszt, Franz (arr. Carl Fredrickson). *Ninety-First Psalm.* Kbd: H; L: d1-d2. R. D. Row (1964), found in *Sacred Song Masterpieces,* bk 2

91:1, 4-5, 11
Bukvich. *Four Phrases From Psalm 91.* Pno: Sop:b♭1-c3. ChoralWeb Publishing (1998) CWP-V8121-SG1

91:1, 4, 7, 10-11
Fisher, William Arms (ed. Wilman Wilmans). *He That Dwelleth in the Secret Place.* Kbd: H:d1-g2(a♭3); L:c1-e♭2(g2). Oliver Ditson (1910), found in *Solos for Christian Science Churches*

91:1, 5, 9-12
Davis, M. *Ninety First Psalm.* Kbd: H:d1-f2; L:b♭1-d2. R. D. Row, found in *Soloist's Practical Library,* bk 2

91:1, 5-6, 9, 10-12
MacDermid, James G. *The Ninety-First Psalm (He That Dwelleth In the Secret Place of the Most High).* Pno: H:e♭1-a♭3; M:c1-f2; L:b♭1-e♭2. Forster (1908, 1935)

91:1, 5-7, 11-12
Rogers, Faith Helen. *Whoso Dwelleth in the Secret Place.* Kbd: d♭1-b♭3. G. Schirmer (1919)

91:1, 9-11, 14, 16
Neidlinger, W.H. *He That Dwelleth in the Secret Place.* Kbd: c1-g2. John Church (1919)

91:1-7, 11-12
Joncas, Michael. *On Eagle's Wings.* Cantors-Kbd, vc, inst in c, gtr: a1-d2. NALR (1979) JO-0

91:1-7, 11-12
Joncas, Michael. *On Eagle's Wings.* Pno: c1-f2. New Dawn (1998) Hope, H: 8055; M: 459; L: 460, found in *Michael Crawford–On Eagle's Wings;* also found in *The Church Soloist; Everything for the Church Soloist*

91:1-7, 11-12
Joncas, Michael. *On Eagle's Wings.* Cantors-Kbd, vc, inst in c, gtr: a1-d2. OCP (1979) 9493, also found in *On Eagle's Wings; Return to Me: Music for Funerals and Healing,* vol. 1

91:1-7, 11-12
Joncas, Michael (arr. Mark Hayes). *On Eagle's Wings.* Cantor-Kbd, 2 fl/ob, 2 cl hn, bs, syn, timp, perc, orchbls or Trax, opt duet: a1-d2(g2). Alfred (1997) 16106

91:1-7, 11-12
Joncas, Michael (arr. Mark Hayes). *On Eagle's Wings.* Cantor-Kbd: MH:c1-f2; ML:b♭1-e♭2. New Dawn (1979, 1991) MH 19100; ML 19103, found in *10 Hymns and Gospel Songs for Solo Voice: For Concerts, Contests, Recitals and Worship*

91:1-7, 11-12
Joncas, Michael (arr. Lloyd Larson). *On Eagle's Wings*. Duet-Kbd: H:d1-a♭3/L: G-c2. Hope (2000) 8065, found in *Sacred Vocal Duets for High and Low Voice*

91:1-7, 9-12
Courtney, Craig. *Psalm 91*. Pno, fl, & opt stg qt: d1-f2. Beckenhorst (1996, 1999) flute: BP1500A; string parts: BP1500B, found in *Psalm Settings of Craig Courtney*

91:1-12 Ward-Stephens. *He That Dwelleth in the Secret Place*. Pno: H:c♯1-g2; L:a1-e♭2. Chappell (1917), found in *Ward-Stephens Selected Psalms*

91:2, 5, 10-12, 14-15
Foley, John B. *To His Angels*. Gtr: e1-d2. NALR (1974), found in *Neither Silver Nor Gold*

91:2-7, 10 (based on)
Schutte, Daniel L. *Blest Be the Lord*. Gtr: b♭1-c2. NALR (1976), found in *A Dwelling Place*

91:3-7 (based on)
Schutte, Daniel L. *Blest Be the Lord*. 2-part-Pno, gtr, 2 inst in c: c1-d2. OCP (1976) 9488

91:4, 11-12
Busarow, Donald. *He Shall Give His Angels Charge Over Thee*. Org, fl: H:c1-a♭3. Concordia (1981) H: 97-5633; L: 97-5634

91:4, 11-12
Busarow, Donald. *He Shall Give His Angels Charge Over Thee*. 2-part-Org, (opt inst in C or B♭): S:b♭1-e♭2/A:b♭1-c♯2. Concordia (1994) 98-3168

91:5 SEE: Genesis 1:3. MacDermid, James G. *Love*

91:5 SEE: Genesis 1:3. Roberts, John Varley and Mary Baker Eddy. *Love*

91:5 SEE: Genesis 1:3. Root, Frederic W. *Love*

91:5 SEE: Psalm 18:32, 37. Vaughan Williams, Ralph. *The Pilgrim's Psalm*

91:8-12 Malotte, Albert Hay. *Only With Thine Eyes*. Pno/org: L. G. Schirmer (1940) 39191

91:9-12, 15-16
Hillert, Richard. *He Shall Give His Angels Charge Over You*. U-Org, ob, opt stg qt: c1-e♭2. GIA (1993) G-3983

91:11 (Psalm 121:4)
Schlösser, Adolphe. *He That Keepeth Israel*. Kbd: M:d1-d2. Found in *52 Sacred Songs; Album of Sacred Songs; First Book of Tenor Solos; The Sacred Collection* (H/L)

91:11-12 (based on)
Kosche, Kenneth T. *God's Angels*. 2-part-Kbd: d1-d2/b1-d2. MorningStar (1988) MSM-50-9401

91:11-12 (Luke 2:9-14; Luke 24:1-5; Psalm 103:20)
Nelson, Ronald A. *Angels*. 2-part-Kbd: b1-e2. AMSI (1996) 726

91:15 SEE: Psalm 16:10. Hurd, Bob. *Be With Me, O God*

92:00 Adler, Samuel. *Psalm 92* (from *Three Psalms*) (Hebrew). Kbd: M:c1-f♯2. Southern (1991) VB-465, also found in *Samuel Adler: Collected Songs for Voice and Piano*

92:00 Fromm, Herbert. *Praise Ye the Lord* (from *Two Psalm Settings*). U-Kbd: f1-d2. Transcontinental; Hope (1970) SA 1400, also found in *The Singing People*

92:00 Lagourgue, Charles. *Psalm 92*. Kbd: Med. H. C. L. Publishing

92:00 (adapted)
Talbot, John Michael. *Lord, it Is Good*. Gtr: d1-c2. Birdwing (1985), found in *Praise, Prayer and Worship*

92:1 (Psalm 84:10; Psalm 103:1)
Costa, Michael. *This Night I Lift My Heart to Thee (It Is a Good Thing to Give Thanks Unto the Lord)* (from *Eli*). Kbd: Alto:a1-c♯2. G. Schirmer, found in *Anthology of Sacred Song–Alto; Oratorio Repertoire,* vol. II

92:1, 2, 4-5
SEE: Psalm 90:1, 16-17. Fischer, Irwin. *Let the Beauty of the Lord*

92:1-2 (other)
Weber, Jim and Niles Borop. *It Is Good*. Kbd, gtr: e1-f♯2. Meadowgreen (1984), found in *Our God Reigns*

92:1-2, 5, 12-13 (Psalm 118:8)
Berthier, Jacques (ed. Brother Robert). *Bonum Est Confidere (It Is Good to Trust and Hope in the Lord)*. U/2-part-Kbd or gtr, ob, trpt, vc or bsn: (a1)d1-d2. Taizé (1991, 1984), found in *Music From Taizé,* vol. 2; *Songs and Prayer from Taizé*

92:1-3 Distler, Hugo. *It Is a Precious Thing to Thank Our God,* op. 17, no. 1 (from *Three Sacred Concertos*). Org: H:b1-g2. Concordia (1969) 97-4925

92:1-3 Kent, James (ed. David Patrick). *It Is a Good Thing to Give Thanks to the Lord.* Kbd: ML:d1-e2. Boosey & Hawkes (1996), found in *Sacred Songs for the Soloist: 20 Songs on Religious Texts for Medium Low Voice*

92:1-3, 7, 10, 12-13 (based on)
Schutte, Daniel L. (arr. Randall DeBruyn). *Like Cedars.* Kbd: a1-d2. OCP (1993), found in *Drawn By a Dream*

92:1-5 Childs, David. *Psalm 92.* Org: c1-g2. Abingdon (1966) H: APM 390; L: APM 385, also found in *Seven Psalms for Voice and Organ*

92:1-5 (adapted)
Schweizer, Rolf. *How Good to Offer Thanks.* Kbd: f1-e♭2. Hänssler (1968, 1973), found in *Choirbook for Saints and Singers*

92:1-5, 9, 12-15 (adapted)
Adler, Samuel. *It Is Good to Sing Thy Praises* (no. 11 from *Twelve Songs of Praise*). U-Org: d1-g2. Oxford (1988) 94.505

92:1-6 Foley, John B. *How Good it Is to Give Thanks to God.* Gtr: b1-c2. NALR (1974), found in *Neither Silver Nor Gold*

92:1-7, 10, 12-13 (based on)
Schutte, Daniel L. *Like Cedars They Shall Stand.* Gtr: a1-d2. NALR (1974), found in *Neither Silver Nor Gold*

92:2-5 Bernhard, Christoph. *Das ist ein köstlich ding, dem Herren danden* (German). Duet-Equal voices: c1-g2/d1-g2. Bärenreiter (1972), found in *Geistliche Harmonien*

92:2-5, 13-16
Foley, John B. *Psalm 92* (*Lord it Is Good to Give Thanks to You*). Kbd, gtr: c1-c2. GIA (1995), found in *Psalms for the Church Year,* vol. 7

92:2-16 Rebbi of Kalev (arr. Velvel Pasternak). *Tõ l'hõdõs (It Is Good to Give Thanks)* (Hebrew transliterated). Gtr: H:d1-f2. Bloch (1971), found in *Songs of the Chassidim II*

92:2-16 Weiner, Lazar. *Tov L'Hodos* (from *Anim Z'Miros*) (Hebrew). Transcontinental (1964) (n.v.)

92:12 (Psalm 128:2-4)
Felciano, Richard. *Benedicto Nuptialis.* Kbd: e♭1-e♭2. G. Schirmer (1972) 2318

93:00 Penn, Marilyn. *Psalm 93.* Pno: Bar:a-d♯1. American Music Centre (1982)

93:4 Handel, G. F. (ed. Jerald B. Stone). *Waves of the Sea* (from *O Sing Unto the Lord, Chandos Anthem,* no. 4). Pno: f1-g2. HLH Music (1992), found in *Five Vocal Gems for Tenor,* vol. 1

93:4 Pasternak, Velvel. *Mikõlõs mayim (Above the Voices of Many Waters)* (Hebrew transliterated). Gtr: M:c1-c2. Bloch (1971), found in *Songs of the Chassidim II*

94:1-2 Pasternak, Velvel. *El n'komõs (God of Vengeance)* (Hebrew transliterated). Gtr: MH:c1-f2. Bloch (1971), found in *Songs of the Chassidim II*

94:18 Lowenbraun, S. (arr. Velvel Pasternak). *Im omarti* (no. 1, *If I say, "My foot slippeth")* (Hebrew transliterated). Gtr: H:b♭1-f2. Bloch (1971), found in *Songs of the Chassidim II*

94:18 Shapiro, Rabbi N. (arr. Velvel Pasternak). *Im omarti* (no. 2, *If I say, "My Foot Slippeth")* (Hebrew transliterated). Gtr: M:a1-d2. Bloch (1971), found in *Songs of the Chassidim II*

95:00 Freudenthal, Josef. *Let Us Sing Unto the Lord.* Kbd: H:d1-g2; L:b1-e2. Transcontinental (1949)

95:00 (adapted)
Handel, G. F. (arr. Carl Fredrickson). *Come, Let Us Make a Joyful Noise.* Duet-Kbd: H:e1-g2/L:b1-c2. R. D. Row (1960), found in *Sacred Duet Masterpieces,* bk 1

95:00 Handel, G. F. *For Look as High as the Heaven* (from *Chandos Anthem I*). U-Kbd: f1-a3. Novello (1925)

95:00 Mendelssohn, Felix. *O Come, Let Us Worship.* 2-part-Org: Sop/Alto. Carl Fischer 117

95:1 (other)
Marcello, Benedetto (ed. Earnest Murphy). *O Sing Unto the Lord.* Duet-Kbd: H:d1-f2/M:d1-e2. McAfee Music (1973), found in *The Baroque Songbook.*

95:1 Zimmermann, Heinz Werner. *Come, Let Us Praise (Christmas Carol).* U-Kbd: e♭1-e♭2. Carl Fischer (1976) CM7986

95:1-2 Handel, G. F. *For This Our Truest Interest.* Kbd: f1-a3. Novello

95:1-2, 6-9
Haas, David. *If Today You Hear His Voice.* U/2-part-Gtr, 2 inst in c: d♭1-e♭2. GIA (1983), found in *We Have Been Told*

95:1-2, 6-9
Haugen, Marty. *Come, O Come, Let Us Sing*. 2-part mixed-Kbd, inst in c, gtr: d1-d2/d-d1. GIA (1995) G-4275

95:1-2, 6-9 (adapted; based on)
Hurd, Bob (acc. Dominic MacAller). *Psalm 95 (If Today)*. Kbd, fl: e1-c2. OCP (1991), found in *Alleluia! Give the Glory*

95:1-2, 6-9 (adapted; based on)
Hurd, Bob (arr. Bellamy). *Psalm 95 (If Today)*. Cantor-Kbd, fl: e1-c2. OCP (1991) 10249CC

95:1-3 (Thomas Ken)
Liebergen, Patrick M. *Psalm 95* (incorporates *Tallis Canon*). 2-part-Kbd: c1-c2(f2). Alfred (1992) 4276

95:1-6 (adapted)
Larson, Lloyd. *O Come, Let Us Sing to the Lord*. 2-part-Kbd: c1-c2(d2). Beckenhorst (1993) BP1415

95:1-6 SEE: Psalm 130:00. Yardumian, Richard. *Symphony,* no. 2

95:1-7 Cooper, Lowell. *Come, Sing to the Lord*. U/2-part-Kbd, gtr, bass: c1-e2. Hope (1975) CF 172

95:1-7 (Book of Common Prayer)
Dobry, Wallace. *Psalm 95: Come, Let Us Sing to the Lord (Venite, exultemus)* (from *A Trio of Psalms*) (English/Latin). 2-part-Kbd: c1-d2. MorningStar (1994) MSM-80-706

95:1-7 Lekberg, Sven. *O Come, Let Us Sing Unto the Lord*. Kbd: MH:d♯1-g2. Galaxy (1963)

95:1-7 SEE: Psalm 50:14. Pendleton, Emmet. *Sing Unto the Lord,* op. 12, no. 4

95:1-8 (based on)
Inwood, Paul. *Ring Out Your Joy*. Pno, gtr, inst in c: d1-d2. OCP (1985), found in *Come to Set Us Free*

95:2 (Psalm 100:4)
Baird, Lynn. *Come into His Presence*. Kbd, gtr, (opt orch): d1-d2. Intrada (1992), found in *Songs for Praise and Worship*

95:3-6 (Psalm 96:4)
Mendelssohn, Felix (arr. James McKelvy). *For the Lord Is a Mighty God*. 2-Part-Org: H:c1-e♭2/L:C-e♭1. Mark Foster (1982) MF 233

95:3-6 (Psalm 96:4)
Mendelssohn, Felix (arr. Hal H. Hopson). *For the Lord Is a Mighty God*. 2-Part-Org: H:c1-e♭2/L:C-e♭1. Hope (1982) A 540

95:4 Mendelssohn, Felix. *In His Hands Are All the Corners of the Earth* (German/English). Duet-Kbd: Equal high voices. Church (1907), found in *Choice Sacred Duets,* vol. II; *Sacred Duets,* vol. I

95:4, 6 Schnecker, P. A. *In His Hands Are All the Corners of the Earth*. Duet-Kbd: Sop:d1-a3/Alto:c1-d2. G. Schirmer (1888, 1916), found in *Album of Sixteen Sacred Duets*

95:6 SEE: Numbers 24:5. Pasternak, Velvel. *Ma Tõvu*

95:6-7 (based on)
Doherty, Dave. *Come, Let Us Worship and Bow Down*. Kbd, gtr, (opt orch): d1-g2. Word (1992), found in *Songs for Praise and Worship; WOW Worship Blue*

95:6-8 Handel, G. F. (ed. M. B. Stearns). *O Come Let Us Worship*. Kbd: H:e1-a3; MH:d-g2. Coburn Press (1971), found in *Lift Up Your Voice*

96:00 (Psalm 33:3)
Buxtehude, Dietrich (ed. N. Jenne). *Sing to the Lord a New Song (Singet dem Herrn ein neues leid)* (German/English). Cont, vln: Sop:c1-g2. Concordia (1969) 97-4897

96:00 (paraphrased)
Hassler, Hans Leo (arr. Kenny Williams). *Cantate Domino*. 2-Part-Kbd: c1-d2/b1-a2. Sunburst Music (1987) S 116

96:00 (adapted)
Herbert, Muriel. *Sing Unto the Lord All the Earth*. Pno: d1-f2. Presser (1957)

96:00 Whikehart, Lewis E. *O Sing Unto the Lord*. Org: d1-a♭3. H. W. Gray (1959)

96:1 (Psalm 98:00; Psalm 100:00)
Courtney, Craig. *Sing to the Lord a New Song*. Pno, opt hn: b♭1-f2(g2). Beckenhorst (1999), found in *Psalm Settings of Craig Courtney*

96:1-2, 6, 9, 13
LaForge, Frank. *Let the Heavens Rejoice*. Kbd: Med. G. Schirmer, found in *Christian Science Service Songs*

96:1, 4 Unknown (arr. Tom Fettke). *Sing Unto the Lord*. Kbd, gtr, (opt orch): d1-f2. Word (1992), found in *Songs for Praise and Worship*

96:1-3 Spies, Claudio. *O Sing Unto the Lord* (from *Five Psalms*). Duet-Fl, fg, hn, mand, vla, vc: Sop:d1-g♯2/Tenor:e-g1. Boosey & Hawkes (1962)

96:1-3 (adapted)
Talbot, John Michael. *Today Is Born Our Savior*. Gtr: d1-e2. Birdwing (1985), found in *Praise, Prayer and Worship*

96:1-3, 11-12 (based on)
Martin, Joseph M. *Come, Sing Unto the Lord*. 2-part mixed-Kbd: Sop:c1-c2/Bass: c-d1. Timespann Music (1994) 10/1236T

96:1-4 (based on; and other)
Handel, G. F. *Sing Unto the Lord.* Duet-Org/pno: H:e1-g2;H:g1-f2. R. D. Row (1961) found in *Sacred Duet Masterpieces*

96:1-4 Patillo, Leon (arr. Tom Fettke). *Sing Unto the Lord*. Kbd, gtr, (opt orch): c1-d2. Word (1992), found in *Songs for Praise and Worship*

96:1-4 Pergolesi, Giovanni B. (ed. and arr. Michael Burkhardt). *Sing to the Lord God* (from *Stabat Mater*). U-Kbd, inst in c: d1-f2. MorningStar (1993) MSM-50-9451

96:1-4 Schütz, Heinrich (ed. Fritz Ricco). *Singet dem Herrn ein neues leid,* SWV 342 (from *Symphoniae Sacrae* II) (German). Cont, 2 vlns: c1-f2. Bornart (1949) BA 3669

96:1-4, 7-9
Reeves, Jeff. *Sing Unto the Lord*. U/2-part-Kbd, hdbls: M. Broadman Press (1989) 44566-55 (Code C)

96:1-4, 9-10 (adapted)
Haas, David and Marty Haugen. *Proclaim to All the Nations*. U/2-part-Kbd, gtr: b1-d2(e2). GIA (1989), found in *Psalms for the Church Year,* vol. 3

96:1-5, 7-13
Foley, John B. *Psalm 96 (Give to God).* Kbd, gtr: c1-d2. GIA (1995), found in *Psalms for the Church Year,* vol. 7

96:1-6, 9-13 (adapted)
Adler, Samuel. *Psalm 96* (from *Three Psalms*). Kbd: M:d1-g2. Southern (1991) VB-465, also found in *Samuel Adler: Collected Songs for Voice and Piano*

96:2-5, 7-9
Foley, John B. *Sing to the Lord*. Gtr: c♯1-c♯2. NALR (1974), found in *Neither Silver Nor Gold*

96:4 SEE: Psalm 95:3-6. Mendelssohn, Felix (arr. James McKelvy). *For the Lord Is a Mighty God*

96:4 SEE: Psalm 95:3-6. Mendelssohn, Felix (arr. Hal H. Hopson). *For the Lord Is a Mighty God*

96:6 SEE: Psalm 26:8. Baumgartner, H. Leroy. *Lord, I Have Loved the Habitation of Thy House*

96:6 SEE: Psalm 113:3. VanDyke, May. *In the Beauty of Holiness*

96:7-8 Gaul, Alfred Robert. *Ascribe Unto the Lord Worship and Power* (from *The Ten Virgins*). Kbd: Tenor:f1-a3. G. Schirmer, found in *Anthology of Sacred Song–Tenor; Oratorio Repertoire,* vol. III

96:7-9 Travers, John (arr. Harrison Oxley). *Ascribe Unto the Lord (O Worship the Lord).* Org: d1-e2. Kevin Mayhew (1992), found in *Favorite Anthem,* bk 2

96:8 (Psalm 29:2; other)
Gay, Roert (arr. Mosie Lister). *No Other Name*. Kbd, gtr: c1-c2. Integrity (1988) 083-417-2615, found in *Bring Us Back*

96:8-9 SEE: Job 22:21. Head, Michael. *Acquaint Now Thyself With Him*

96:8, 10 Giovanni, Bassani (ed. Gertrude Tingley). *Ascribe to the Lord*. Kbd: H:d1-f♯2; L:b♭1-d2. G. Schirmer (1965), found in *The Sunday Solo*

96:9 SEE: I Chronicles 16:29. Handel, G. F. *O Worship the Lord*

96:11 (other based on Psalms)
Baloche, Paul and Gary Sadler. *Rise Up and Praise Him*. Kbd, gtr: g-g1. Integrity (1996) 19556, found in *WOW Worship Songbook Green*

96:12 SEE: Psalm 98:1, 7-8. Dvorák, Antonín. *O Sing Unto the Lord*

97:1-2, 4-6, 8, 11
Butler, Eugene. *The Lord Reigns*. Kbd: c1-e♭2. Sacred Music Press (1969), found in *The Solo Psalmist*

97:2-6 Dvorák, Antonín. *Clouds and Darkness,* op. 99, no. 1 (from *Biblical Songs*). Pno: H:d♯1-f♯1; L:b1-d2. Simrock; G. Schirmer; R. D. Row (1955), also found in *Dvorák,* op. 99, *Biblical Songs*

97:2-6 (English version by Humphrey Procter-Gregg)
Dvorák, Antonín. *Clouds and Darkness,* op. 99, no. 1 (from *Biblical Songs*) (English only). Pno: H:d♯1-f♯1; L:b1-d2.

International (1962), found in *Biblical Songs: A Cycle of Ten Songs,* op. 99

97:2-6 Dvorák, Antonín (ed. Otakar Sourek). *Oblak A mrokotá jest vukol Neho,* op. 99, no. 1 *(Wolken und Finsternis hullen Sein Antlitz; Darkness and Thunderclouds Are Round About Him)* (from *Biblical Songs*) (Czech/German/English). Pno: H:d♯1-f♯1. Masters Music (n.d.), found in *Biblical Songs for High Voice and Piano by Antonín Dvorák,* op. 99

97:10 (Psalm 103:11)
Handel, G. F. *The Lord Preserveth Souls* (from *For Look as High as Heaven is, Chandos Anthem,* no. 5). U-Kbd: G♯-d1. Novello

98:00 (based on)
Dufford, Bob. *All the Ends of the Earth.* Cantor-Gtr: c♯1-d2. NALR (1981), 10475CC, also found in *Lord of Light*

98:00 (based on)
Dufford, Bob. All the Ends of the Earth. Duet-Gtr: 2 Cantors: c♯1-d2. OCP 9970CC

98:00 Goldman, Edward M. *Psalm 97 (O Sing Unto the Lord a New Song).* U-Kbd: b1-f♯2. World Library (1965)

98:00 SEE: Psalm 33:3a. Gore, Richard T. *O Sing Unto the Lord a New Song*

98:00 Telemann, Georg Philipp (ed. Klaus Hofmann). *Singet dem Herrn (Sing Now To God)* (German/English). Duet-Cont: Mez:a1-d2/Tenor:d1-f♯2. Hänssler (1977), found in *Singet dem Herrn ein neues Lied*

98:00 (Isaac Watts)
Weaver, Powell. *Joy to the World.* Kbd: f♯1-g2. Galaxy (1941)

98:1 SEE: Psalm 96:12. Dvorák, Antonín. *O Sing Unto the Lord,* op. 99, no. 10

98:1 SEE: Psalm 96:1. Courtney, Craig. *Sing to the Lord a New Song*

98:1 SEE: Psalm 27:1. Lynch, Mike. *Sing to the Lord*

98:1-2, 4, 7, 9 (Psalm 100:2-4; based on)
Tecson, Andrew. *Sing Unto the Lord.* Pno: H:c♯1-f♯2. Concordia (1990) 97-6042

98:1-3 (verses by Adrienne Tindall)
Lovelace, Austin C. *Sing a New Song!* Kbd: c♯1-e2. Darcy Press (1993), found in *Sacred Solos by Austin C. Lovelace*

98:1, 3-6 Hurd, Bob (arr. Craig S. Kingsbury). *All the Ends of the Earth.* Org, gtr, c-trpt, 2 insts in c: c♯1-c2. OCP (1988), found in *Everlasting Your Love*

98:1-3, 9 Pachelbel, Johann. *Sing to the Lord a New Song.* 2-part mixed-Kbd: d1-f2/E-f1. Concordia (1994) 98-3151

98:1-4 Buxtehude, Dietrich. *Singet dem Herrn (Geitliche Solokantaten 1)* (German). Cont, vln: Sop:d1-g2. Bärenreiter (1966) BA 121

98:1a, 4-6 (adapted; other)
Sleeth, Natalie. *Sing a New Song to the Lord.* 2-part-Kbd, opt trpt: e1-d2. Sacred Music Press (1987) S-400

98:1-6 Haas, David and Marty Haugen. *All the Ends of the Earth.* U/2-part-Gtr, 2 inst in c: (a1)d1-d2. GIA (1983), found in *We Have Been Told*

98:1-6 Joncas, Michael. *All the Ends of the Earth.* U-Gtr: b♭1-d2. GIA (1990) G-3431, also found in *Come to Me*

98:1a, 6 (based on)
Schutte, Daniel L. *Sing a New Song.* Gtr: c♯1-d2. NALR (1974), found in *Neither Silver Nor Gold*

98:1, 7-8 (Psalm 96:12)
Dvorák, Antonín. *O Sing Unto the Lord,* op. 99, no. 10 (from *Biblical Songs*). Pno: H:f1-g2; L:c1-d2. Simrock; G. Schirmer; R. D. Row (1955), found in *Dvorák,* op. 99, *Biblical Songs*

98:1, 7-8 (Psalm 96:12)
Dvorák, Antonín. *Sing a New Song,* op. 99, no. 10 (from *Biblical Songs*) (English only). Pno: H:f1-g2; L:c1-d2. International (1962), found in *Biblical Songs: A Cycle of Ten Songs,* op. 99

98:1, 7-8 (Psalm 96:12)
Dvorák, Antonín (ed. Otakar Sourek). *Zpívetje Hospodinu píen novou,* op. 99, no. 10 (*Singt, singet Gott, dem Herren, neue Lieder; Oh, Sing Unto the Lord a Joyful Song*) (from *Biblical Songs*) (Czech/German/English). Pno: H:f1-g2. Masters Music (n.d.), found in *Biblical Songs for High Voice and Piano by Antonín Dvorák,* op. 99

98:1, 7-8 (Psalm 96:12)
Dvorák, Antonín (arr. Leonard Van Camp). *Sing Ye a Joyful Song!* (from *Biblical Songs*). Pno: L:b♭1-c2. Carl Fischer (1992) O5183, also found in *Songs for Low Voice in a Comfortable Range*

98:4-5 SEE: Psalm 66:1-2. Speir, Randy. *In Him We Live*

98:4-6 Buxtehude, Dietrich. *Jubilate Domino* (Geistliche Solokantaten 7) (Latin). Cont: Alto. Bärenreiter (1970) 6462

98:4-6 Roff, Joseph. *Make a Joyful Noise to the Lord.* 2-part-Kbd: f1-f2/f1-d2. Concordia (1991) 98-2957

99:1-5 (Book of Common Prayer)
Mahnke, Allan. *Psalm 99.* U/2-part-Kbd: d1-d2(f2). Concordia (1992) 97-6093, found in *17 Psalms for Cantor and Congregation*

99:2-3 (other)
Paris, Twila (choral arr. Taylor, Steven V.). *Exalt the Name* (with *He Is Exalted*). 2-part-Kbd or Trax: a♭1-d2/b♭-d1. Straight Way Music (1990), found in *25 Songs for Two-Part Choir,* vol. II

99:2-3 (based on)
Paris, Twila. *He Is Exalted.* Kbd, gtr, (opt orch): d1-e2. Straight Way Music (1985), found in *Inspirational Selections; Songs for Praise and Worship; WOW Worship Songbook Green*

99:3 (Psalm 119:144a; Isaiah 6:3a; 2 Peter 1:17; Revelation 5:12-13)
Paris, Twila. *Holy Is the Lord.* Kbd or Trax: c1-g2. Ariose Music (1987) VST87 1030

99:9 (based on)
Gardner, Daniel. *Exalt the Lord Our God.* Kbd, gtr, (opt orch): c1-c2. Intrada (1992), found in *Songs for Praise and Worship*

99:9 Handel, G. F. *O Magnify the Lord (O Come, Let Us Sing)* (from *Eighth Chandos Anthem*). U-Kbd: e1-g♯2. Novello

99:9 SEE: Job 22:21. Head, Michael. *Acquaint Now Thyself With Him*

100:00 Bernhard, Christoph (ed. Bruno Grusnick). *Psalm 100 (Jauchzet dem Herrn, alle Welt)* (German). Duet-equal voices: c1-g2. Bärenreiter (1972), found in *Geistliche Harmonien*

100:00 Britton, D. Guyver. *Know Ye That the Lord He Is God.* Org: a1-e♭2. Boston Music (1963)

100:00 Campra, André. *Jubilate Deo (Psalm 99).* Cont: e1-g♯2. Verlag Edmund Bieler (1960)

100:00 Cohen, Gerald. *Hariu Ladonai kolhaarets (Acclaim Adonai, All People on Earth).* (Hebrew transliterated). M-pno: f1-f2. Oxford (2001), found in *Come Before God with Joyous Song*

100:00 Head, Michael. *Make a Joyful Noise* (from *Three Psalms*). Kbd: H:d1-g2; L:b1-e2. Boosey & Hawkes (1976) H:186; L:187

100:00 Koch, John. *Make a Joyful Noise Unto the Lord* (from *Songs of David*). Stg qt, fl: e♭1-a3. American Music Centre

100:00 LaForge, Frank. *Make a Joyful Noise.* Pno: b1-d2. Carl Fischer (1938) V1370

100:00 MacDermid, James G. *Make a Joyful Noise.* Pno: H:e♭1-g2; L:b1-e♭2. Forster (1918, 1946)

100:00 (adapted)
McFeeters, Raymond. *A Psalm of Praise.* Pno: d1-f2. Carl Fischer (1940)

100:00 Mueller, Carl F. *The One Hundredth Psalm.* Kbd: c1-e2. Harold Flammer (1935)

100:00 Robison, P. *Make a Joyful Noise.* Kbd: c1-e♭2. White Harvest

100:00 Rorem, Ned. *A Psalm of Praise.* Kbd: H:c1-g2. Associated (1946) AMP 19468-4

100:00 Roth, Robert N. *Psalm 100 (Jubilate Deo).* U/2-part-Kbd: e♭1-f♯2. E. C. Kerby Ltd. (1972) HL50481027

100:00 Schütz, Heinrich. *Jubilate deo omnis terra,* SWV 262 *(Lobt den Herren)* (from *Symphoniae Sacrae* I) (German/Latin). Cont, 2 fls or vlns: F♯-d1. Bärenreiter (1949) BA33

100:00 Sowerby, Leo. *O Be Joyful in the Lord (Psalm 100)* (from *Three Psalms*). Org: M:c1-e♭2. H. W. Gray (1949) GV 390

100:00 (Psalm 101:00; Psalm 103:00)
Strandberg, Newton. *De David* (French). Perc ensemble: celesta, gong, chimes, bass drum, opt chorus: b♭1-f2. American Music Centre (1979)

100:00 Suben, Joel. *Make a Joyful Noise.* Kbd: c♯1-a3. Belwin Mills (1971)

100:00 Tappe, Stephen. *Psalm 100.* U-Org: c1-g2. Concordia (1985) 98-2702

100:00 Telemann, Georg Philipp. *Jauchzet dem Herrn, alle Welt* (German/English). Cont, trpt, vln, vla: Bass. Hänssler (1974) 39.106

100:00 (Isaiah 29:00 and 30:00)
Ziegenhals, Harriet. *You Shall Have a Song.* 2-part-Kbd, fl: d1-e♭2. Hope (1985) A 577

100:1 SEE: Psalm 96:1. Courtney, Craig. *Sing to the Lord a New Song*

100:1 Schalk, Carl. *Be Joyful in the Lord, All You Lands*. Org: MH. Concordia (1996) 97-6493

100:1-2, 4-5
SEE: Isaiah 63:7. Fischer, Irwin. *Psalm of Praise*

100:2 (Psalm 117:1; other from the Psalms)
Caldara, Antonio (ed. and arr. Michael Burkhardt). *Bless the Lord, All Nations*. U/2-part-Kbd, 2 inst in c: e1-c2(e2). MorningStar (1993) MSM-50-9506; parts MSM-50-9506A

100:2-4 SEE: Psalm 98:1-2, 4, 7, 9. Tecson, Andrew. *Sing Unto the Lord*

100:3 Handel, G. F. (ed. Stan Pethel). *Be Ye Sure*. 2-part mixed-Kbd: d1-d2/b-e1. Hope (1986) MW 1231

100:3 Jadassohn, Solomon. *Arioso from 100th Psalm (Erkennet, erkennt, dass der Herr ist Gott)* (English/German). Kbd: H:d1-g2; L:c1-f2. Found in *Album of Sacred Songs* (H/L)

100:3 Jadassohn, Solomon (ed. and arr. K. K. Davis and N. Loring). *God Hath Made Us All*. Kbd: M:b1-f2. Carl Fischer (1948), found in *Sing Unto the Lord,* vol. 2

100:4 SEE: Psalm 95:2. Baird, Lynn. *Come Into His Presence*

100:4 (Psalm 118:24)
Brethorst, Leona Von. *He Has Made Me Glad (I Will Enter His Gates)*. U-Kbd: e♭1-c2. Maranatha! (1976), found in *Face to Face*

100:4 (Psalm 118:24)
Brethorst, Leona Von. *I Will Enter His Gates (He Has Made Me Glad)*. Kbd, gtr, (opt orch): c♯1-c2. Maranatha! (1976), found in *Songs for Praise and Worship*

100:4 (Psalm 148:3-5, 12-13; based on)
O'Connor, Roc. *In Praise of His Name*. U/2-part-Gtr: d1-d2 (g2). NALR (1976), found in *A Dwelling Place*

100:5 (John 8:32; Ephesians 6:14)
Humphreys, Don. *Truth*. Kbd: H:f1-f2; L:d1-d2. R. D. Row (1956), found in *Don Humphrey's Song Book* (H/L)

100:5 SEE: Psalm 89:1. Wienhorst, Richard. *I Will Sing the Story of Thy Love*

100:12 Mozart, W. A. (arr. Hal H. Hopson). *Come, Be Joyful*. 2-part mixed-Kbd: c1-e2/b-c1. MorningStar MSM-50-7302

101:00 SEE: Psalm 100:00. Strandberg, Newton. *De David*

102:1-2, 6-7, 11 (based on)
Foley, John B. *Answer When I Call*. U/2-part-Gtr, ob: d1-c♯2(f♯2). NALR (1981), found in *Lord of Light*

102:7, 9, 12-13
SEE: Psalm 13:1. Rogers, James H. *How Long, O Lord, Wilt Thou Forget Me?*

102:11 SEE: Psalm 27:4. Talma, Louise. *Cantata: All the Days of My Life*

103:00 (adapted)
Benati (ed. Gertrude Tingley). *Bless Thou the Lord*. Kbd: H:f♯1-g2; L:c1-d2. G. Schirmer (1965), found in *The Sunday Solo*

103:00 (Henry F. Lyte)
Cassler, G. Winston. *Praise, My Soul, the King of Heaven*. Duet-Org: Equal voices: c♯1-f♯2/c♯1-g2. Augsburg (1968) 11-9272, also found in *Sacred Duets for Equal Voices*

103:00 Geisler, Johann Christian (ed. Ewald Nolte). *Bless the Lord, O My Soul (Lobe den Herrn, meine Seele)*. Duet-Pno(stgs): SS. Boosey & Hawkes (1968) (n.v.)

103:00 Jordan, Alice. *Bless the Lord, O My Soul*. Kbd: c1-e♭2. Abingdon (1970) APM-800

103:00 LaForge, Frank. *Bless the Lord*. Kbd: d1-f♯2. Carl Fischer (1933)

103:00 Schockman, Gregg. *Psalm 103*. M-Kbd: c1-d2. Unity (Lorenz) (1997), found in *Wedding Psalms*

103:00 SEE: Psalm 100:00. Strandberg, Newton. *De David*

103:00 Wiemer, Wolfgang. *Lobe den Herrn, meine Seele* (German). Org, perc: Bar. Breitkopf & Härtel (n.v.)

103:1 SEE: Psalm 92:1. Costa, Michael. *This Night I Lift My Heart to Thee*

103:1 Courch, Andraé. *Bless His Holy Name*. Kbd: Md1-d♭2; ML:e1-c2. Sparrow (1979) HL00310739, found in *Bible Songs* (M); *Songs for Praise and Worship* (M); *Very Special Sacred Songs* (ML)

103:1 Mason, Babbie. *Bless the Lord*. Kbd, gtr: a♭1-b♭2. Word (1988), found in *With All My Heart*

103:1 Unknown (arr. Tom Fettke). *Bless the Lord, O My Soul.* Kbd, gtr, (opt orch): e♭1-d2. Word (1992), found in *Songs for Praise and Worship*

103:1 (Psalm 3:5; Psalm 4:8; Psalm 5:8)
Wesley, Samuel Sebastian. *Praise the Lord, O My Soul (Lead Me, Lord).* Kbd: H:c1-g2; M:a1-e2. Carl Fischer (1939), found in *The Sacred Hour of Song*

103:1-2 Mendelssohn, Felix. *Praise Thou the Lord, O My Spirit* (from *Hymn of Praise*). Kbd: Sop:f1-b♭3. G. Schirmer (1970)

103:1-2 Mendelssohn, Felix (ed. Robert Shaw). *Praise Thou the Lord, O My Spirit* (from *Lobgesang*) (German). Kbd: Sop:f1-b♭3. Available from Atlanta Symphony Orchestra (1986)

103:1, 2-4
Greene, Maurice (ed. E. Stanley Roper). *Praise the Lord, O My Soul.* Kbd: H:e1-g2; L:d1-f2. Bosworth (1910), found in *Seven Sacred Solos of the Early English School*

103:1-2, 8, 14-15, 21 (based on)
Foley, John B. *Praise the Lord, My Soul.* U/2-part-Gtr: e1-b2(g1-e2). NALR (1975, 1978), found in *Earthen Vessels*

103:1-3 McArthur, Edwin. *Bless the Lord, O My Soul.* Pno: c♯1-f2. Chappell (1959)

103:1-4 (Psalm 24:8; other)
Barrett, Joanne and Ron E. Long. *Bless the Lord.* Kbd: c1-e♭2. Lillenas (1983), found in *The Lord Is My Light; Low Voice Classics*

103:1-4 (Psalm 30:5)
Christensen, Chris. *Bless the Lord.* Kbd, gtr, (opt orch): b1-d2. Intrada (1984, 1992), found in *Bible Songs; Songs for Praise and Worship*

103:1-4 Ippolitof-Ivanof, Mikhail (arr. William Stickles). *Bless the Lord, O My Soul.* Kbd: L:c1-c2. Boston Music (1961), found in *20 Distinctive Sacred Solos* (H/L)

103:1-4 Larson, Sonia. *Psalm 103.* 2-part-Kbd, fl: M. AMSI (1993) 636

103:1-4 (based on)
Walker, Christopher. *O My Soul, Bless the Lord.* U/2-part-Kbd, gtr, inst in c, cl: d1-c2(e2). OCP (1985), found in *Come to Set Us Free*

103:1-4, 11, 13
Davis, Katherine K. *Bless the Lord, O My Soul.* Kbd: c♭1-e♭2. Galaxy (1952) 1.1924.7

103:1-4, 19 (adapted)
Fauré, Gabriel. *Bless the Lord, O My Soul.* Kbd: e♭1-g2. Boston Music (1921)

103:1-5, 8, 13
Stephenson, Richard T. *Psalm 103.* Kbd: c1-e2. Carl Fischer (1949), found in The Free Library of Philadelphia

103:1-5, 11, 17a
Smith, Jeffrey. *Psalm 103.* 2-part-Kbd: b1-e2(g♯2). Concordia (1992) 98-3025

103:1-5, 13, 17a, 20-22 (adapted)
Fredrickson, Carl. *Bless the Lord.* Kbd: c1-f2. Harmony Music (1957)

103:1-5, 19
O'Connor-Morris, Geoffrey. *Thanksgiving.* Kbd: Med. Carl Fischer (1970), found in *Eight Scriptural Solos*

103:2-4 Hammerschmidt, Andreas (ed. Johannes Günther Kraner). *Lobe den Herren, meine Seele* (German). Duet-Equal voices: c♯1-e2. Hänssler (1972) HE 5.168, also found in *Das geistliche Konzert 174*

103:2-4 Hammerschmidt, Andreas (ed. Martin Striebel). *Lobe den herren, meine seele* (German). Duet-2 vn or 2 alto recorders: Equal voices: d1-e2/c1-d2. Hänssler (1972), found in *Das geistliche konzert 168/02*

103:2-4, 19 (Psalm 104:5)
Franck, César (ed. and arr. K. K. Davis and N. Loring). *Bless the Lord, O My Soul.* Kbd: M:d1-f♯2. Carl Fischer (1947), found in *Sing Unto the Lord,* vol. 2

103:2-4, 6, 8-11, 13, 19-20
Foley, John B. *Psalm 103 (The Lord Is Kind and Merciful).* U/2-part-Kbd, gtr: d1-d2(f2). GIA (1995), found in *Psalms for the Church Year,* vol. 7

103:4 SEE: Psalm 9:13. Molique, Wilhelm Bernhard. *It Is of the Lord's Great Mercies*

103:8 (other)
Parry, C. H. H. *The Lord Is Long-suffering* (from *Judith*). Kbd: Alto:d1-e2. Presser (1923), found in *Oratorio Repertoire,* vol. II

103:11 SEE: Psalm 97:10. Handel, G. F. *The Lord Preserveth Souls (For Look as High as Heaven Is)*

103:11-17
Doig, Don. *So Great Is His Mercy.* Kbd: c1-e2. Hope (1980), found in *Everything for the Church Soloist*

103:13 Boyce, William. *Yea, Like as a Father Pitieth His Own Children,* no. 4 (from *Lord, Thou hast been our refuge*). Kbd, orch: Tenor:f-a2. Oxford (1977)

103:13-14
Cowen, Frederic Hymen. *Like as a Father* (from *Ruth*). Kbd: Alto:a1-d2. G. Schirmer (1929), found in *Anthology of Sacred Song–Alto; Oratorio Repertoire,* vol. II

103:13-14
SEE: Daniel 9:9. Gaul, Alfred Robert. *To the Lord Our God Belong Mercies*

103:13-14
SEE: Psalm 39:12b, 13a. Laderman, Ezra. *Look Away From Me*

103:13-17
Scott, John Prindle. *Like as a Father.* Kbd: H:f♯1-g2; L:d1-e♭2. G. Schirmer (1922)

103:20 Greene, Maurice (ed. E. Stanley Roper). *O Praise the Lord.* Kbd: H:f♯1-a3; L:e♭1-g♭2. Bosworth (1910), found in *Seven Sacred Solos of the Early English School*

103:20 SEE: Psalm 91:11-12. Nelson, Ronald A. *Angels*

103:21 Handel, G. F. *O Praise the Lord* (from *Twelfth Chandos Anthem*). Kbd: Bass:b-e1. Novello

104:00 Lederer, Charles. *Psalm 104.* Kbd: Med. Carl Fischer

104:00 Schoenbachler, Tim (arr. Sheryl Soderberg). *Send Out Your Spirit.* Cantor-Kbd, hdbls: c1-b♭2(f1-f2). OCP (1979), 8874CC; also found in *All Is Ready*

104:00 VanDyke, May. *God Is a Spirit.* Kbd: H:d1-a♭3; L:d1-e♭2. Boosey & Hawkes (1922)

104:1 SEE: I Chronicles 16:29. Schubert, Franz. *The Grand Alleluia*

104:1, 2, 5, 24, 30
Fischer, Irwin. *O Lord, How Manifold Are Thy Works.* Kbd: e♭1-g2. American Composers Alliance (1957)

104:1, 2, 33-34
Jefferies, George. *Praise the Lord, O My Soul.* Kbd: Bass:E-d1. Norton (1973), found in *The Solo Song*

104:1-3 Schütz, Heinrich. *Cantabo Domino in vita mea,* SWV 260 *(Ich singe dem Herrn)* (from *Geistliches Konzert*) (Latin/German). Cont, 2 vlns: Tenor. Bärenreiter (1949) BA31 (n.v.)

104:1, 3a, 19, 29 (based on)
Rieth, Mildred F. *Bless Yahweh, O My Soul.* Org, gtr, inst in c: c♯1-b2. OCP (1969), found in *Yahweh Is My Shepherd*

104:1-3b, 5-6, 10-14, 24, 27-28, 30-31, 33-34
Foley, John B. *Psalm 104 (God, Send Out Your Spirit).* U/2-part-Kbd, gtr: d1-d2. GIA (1995), found in *Psalms for the Church Year,* vol. 7

104:1-3, 24 (Psalm 145:9; Psalm 147:3-4; Romans 11:33-36)
Baumgartner, H. Leroy. *O Lord, My God, Thou Art Very Great* (from *O Lord, My God, Thou Art Very Great,* op. 48). Kbd: d1-g2. Concordia (1958) 97-5724

104:1a-4 Bavicchi, John Alexander. *Thou Art Clothed With Honor* (from *Psalm 104: Bless the Lord, O My Soul*). Kbd, inst: Sop:d1-a3. Oxford (1982)

104:1, 5-6, 10-12, 24, 29-31, 34 (based on)
Walker, Christopher. *Send Forth Your Spirit, O Lord (Bless the Lord, O My Soul).* U/2-part-Kbd, gtr, 2 inst in c, cl: d1-e2. OCP (1984, 1985), found in *Come to Set Us Free*

104:1, 24 Stearns, Peter Pindar. *Bless the Lord, O My Soul.* Vc, ob, hn: c1-b♭3. American Composers Alliance (1965), found in *Three Sacred Songs*

104:1, 24, 29-31 (adapted from the New American Bible)
Connolly, Michael. *Lord Send Out Your Spirit.* Kbd: c1-c2. GIA (1988), found in *We Live a Mystery*

104:1, 24, 29-33 (adapted)
Joncas, Michael. *Send Forth Your Spirit.* U-Gtr: d1-g2. GIA (1990) G-3436, also found in *Come to Me*

104:1, 24, 30-31, 34
Haas, David. *Lord, Send Out Your Spirit.* U/2-part-Kbd, gtr: d1-e2. GIA (1983), found in *Psalms for the Church Yea*

104:5 SEE: Psalm 103:2-4, 19. Franck, César. *Bless the Lord, O My Soul*

104:5 (Psalm 9:15; Psalm 69:8)
Laderman, Ezra. *Thou Didst Set the Earth.* Pno: d♭1-a♭3. Oxford (1970), found in *The Psalms*

104:10-16
Bavicchi, John Alexander. *Thou Makest the Spring Gush Forth* (from *Psalm 104: Bless the Lord, O My Soul*). Org: Tenor:e-a2. Oxford (1982)

104:19-23
Bavicchi, John Alexander. *Thou Hast Made the Moon* (from *Psalm 104: Bless the Lord, O My Soul*). Org: Bass:A-e♭1. Oxford (1982)

104:24, 28a, 30
Vieker, Jon D. *Come, Holy Spirit.* U-Kbd: d1-c2. Concordia (1992) 98-3061

104:30 (Luke 1:47; 2 Timothy 1:10)
Bach, J. S. (arr. Dolores Hruby). *My Spirit Rejoice*. U-Kbd, inst in c: c1-e2. Augsburg (1978) 11-0335

104:30 (other)
Hurd, Bob. *Envía Tu Espíritu* (Spanish and English). U/2-part-Org, gtr, inst in c: b1-d2. OCP (1988), found in *Everlasting Your Love*

104:31-34
Archer, Violet. *Te Deum* (from *Three Biblical Songs*). Pno: d1-g2. Canadian Music Centre (1972)

104:33 SEE: Isaiah 52:7. Harker, F. Flaxington. *How Beautiful Upon the Mountains*

104:33 SEE: Isaiah 52:7. Harker, F. Flaxington. *How Beautiful Upon the Mountains* (duet)

104:34 (based on)
Nibley, Reid. *Jesus, the Very Thought of Thee.* M-Kbd: c1-c2. Sonos (Jackman) (1997) 00434, found in *Sabbath Song*

105:1-3 Smith, Michael W. *Sing Unto Him.* Pno: c1-g2. Meadowgreen (1988), found in *Michael W. Smith: Greatest Hits*

106:1 (Psalm 107:1; Psalm 118:1-4, 29; Psalm 136:1; based on)
Paris, Twila. *Come Worship the Lord.* Kbd: g1-g2. Star Song (1991)

106:1, 2 (paraphrased)
Hopson, Hal H. *Give Thanks to the Lord.* Kbd: c1-d♭2. Lorenz (2001), found in *Simple Songs for Young Singers*

106:1, 47-48 (Psalm 108:3-5)
Barrus, Lemar. *Praise.* Kbd: d1-e2. Harold Flammer (1975), found in *Songs of Praise by Contemporary Composers*

106:1-4 SEE: Psalm 5:2-3a. Foley, John B. *Heed My Call For Help*

106:1-4 Humphreys, Don. *Praise Ye the Lord.* Pno: H:e♭1-a♭2; L:c1-f2. Willis Music (1956), found in *Sing to the Lord*

107:1 SEE: Psalm 106:1. Paris, Twila. *Come Worship the Lord*

107:1 (adapted)
Talbot, John Michael. *Give Thanks to the Lord.* Gtr: c1-c2. Cherry Lane (1982), found in *Praise, Prayer and Worship*

107:1-2, 43
Powell, Robert J. *O Give Thanks.* Kbd: d1-e2. Sacred Music Press (1969), found in *The Solo Psalmist*

107:2a Ellis, Ward L. *Let the Redeemed.* Kbd, gtr, (opt orch): d1-d2. Ward L. Ellis (1978), found in *Songs for Praise and Worship*

107:2, 14-15, 19
Mendelssohn, Felix. *He Counteth All Your Sorrows* (*Sing Ye Praise*) (from *Hymn of Praise*). Kbd: Tenor:d1-g2. G. Schirmer; Novello, found in *Anthology of Sacred Song–Tenor*

107:2, 14-15, 19
Mendelssohn, Felix (ed. Robert Shaw). *Saget es, die ihr erlöst seid* (from *Lobgesang*) (German). Kbd: Tenor:d1-g2. Available from Atlanta Symphony Orchestra (1986)

107:2-4 Schütz, Heinrich. *Paratum cor meum,* SWV 257 *(Mein Herz ist gerüstet)* (from *Symphoniae* Sacrae I) (Latin/German). Cont, 2 vlns: H. Bärenreiter (1949) BA28 (n.v.)

107:2-4 Schütz, Heinrich (ed. Stantum). *Paratum cor meum*, SWV 257 (from *Symphoniae* Sacrae I) (Latin). Kbd, 2 vlns: c1-e2. Hinrichsen (1952) 181

107:6, 9 (Psalm 100:1-2, 4)
Adair, Hazel Ferrell. *Praise and Give Thanks.* Kbd: H:d1-g2; L:b♭1-e♭2. Huntzinger (1927)

107:20 (taken from)
Humphreys, Don. *He Sent His Word and Healed Them.* Pno: H:e1-f2; L:c♯1-d2. R. D. Row (1956), G. Schirmer, found in *Don Humphrey's Song Book* (H/L); *Songs for Christian Science Service,* bk 1

107:20 SEE: John 1:1. MacDermid, James G. *He Sent His Word*

107:20 Olds, W. B. *He Sent His Word and Healed Them.* Kbd: Med. Carl Fischer

108:00 (adapted)
Ferris, William. *My Heart Is Ready, O God.* Kbd: e♭1-a♭3. Belwin Mills (1974)

108:00 (adapted)
Talbot, John Michael. *My Heart Is Ready.* Gtr: f♯1-c2. Birdwing (1985), found in *Praise, Prayer and Worship*

108:1-4 Roff, Joseph. *My Heart Is Steadfast (A Psalm of David).* 2-part-Kbd: c1-f♯2/b1-d2. Boston Music (1989) 14136

108:1-5 Edmunds, John. *O Lord, My Heart Is Fixed.* Kbd: H:e1-a3. Dragon's Teeth Press (1975), found in *Fifty Songs by John Edmunds*

108:3-5 SEE: Psalm 106:1, 47-48. Barrus, Lemar. *Praise*

108:4 SEE: Psalm 55:21. Mendelssohn, Felix. *Cast Thy Burden on the Lord*

110:00 Bellini, Vincenzo. *Tecum principium* (Latin). Sop-Orch: d1-g2. Carus (1984) CV 40.062

111:00 Paer, Ferdinando (ed. Himie Voxman). *Beatus vir* (Latin). Pno, cl: Sop:e♭1-b♭3. Nova Music (1980) Score and parts for rental; N.M. 125

111:00 Posch, Isaac (ed. Karl Geiringer). *Confitebor tibi Domine* (from *Harmonia Concertans*) (Latin). Duet-Sop:e1-g2/Bass:G-d2. Ann Arbor: University Microfilm (1968-72), found in *Series of Early Music,* vol. 4

111:00 Schütz, Heinrich. *Ich danke dem Herren,* SWV 284 (from *Kleine geistliche Konzerte*) (German). Cont: Alto:c1-f2. Bärenreiter (n.v.) BA1702

111:00 Schütz, Heinrich. *O God, I Will Praise Thee,* SWV 284 *(Ich danke dem Herren)* (from *Five Short Sacred Concertos*) (German/English). Kbd or cont: c1-f2. Concordia (1957), found in *Church Year in Song* (H/L); *Fifty Selected Songs; Five Sacred Songs* (H)

111:2, 4, 5-9
Gast, Lothar. *Wir rühmen uns allein des Kreuzes.* Org: M:c1-e2. Hänssler (1971) HE 12.218

112:00 Englert, Eugene. *Psalm 112.* Kbd: M:d1-d2. Unity (Lorenz) (1997), found in *Wedding Psalms*

112:1b-3 Telemann, Georg Philipp (ed. Klaus Hofmann). *Wohl dem, der den Herrn fürchtet (O Blest Is He Who Reveres the Lord)* (German/English). Duet-Cont: Equal voices. Hänssler (1980) 39.126, found in *Singet dem Herrn ein neues Lied*

112:1-4, 6-7, 9
Haas, David. *God's Command.* U/2-part-Kbd, gtr: c1-e2. GIA (1993), found in *When Love Is Found*

112:10 Vivaldi, Antonio. *Peccator videbit* (from *Beatus Vir,* RV597) (Latin). Kbd: Tenor: c-f1. Hal Leonard (1994), found in *Oratorio Anthology: Tenor*

113:00 (adapted)
Adler, Samuel. *Praise God, Ye Servants of the Lord,* (no. 10 from *Twelve Songs of Praise*). U-Org: c1-e2. Oxford (1988) 94.505

113:00 (text from Lyric Psalms)
Haas, David. *Nations and Heavens (Psalm 113).* U/2-part-Kbd, gtr: e1-e2. GIA (1985), found in *To Be Your Bread*

113:00 Zelenka, Jan Dismas. *Laudate pueri* (Latin). Cont, stgs, trpt: Tenor:g-a2. Deutscher Verlag (1982) score and parts

113:1-2, 4-8
Buxtehude, Dietrich (ed Gottlieb Harms and Helmar Trede). *Laudate, Pueri* (Latin). Duet-Vc, 2 vla, violone: Equal voices:c♯1-g2/c1-a3. Klecken: Ugrino, Abteilung Verlag (1925 - 1958), found in *Dreizehn Kirchenkantaten für zwei Singstimmen*

113:1-4 Telemann, Georg Philipp. *Laudate pueri Dominum* (Latin). Cont, 2 vlns: H:d1-g2. Hänssler (1981) HE 39.123

113:1-5 Edmunds, John. *Praise We the Lord.* Pno: c1-a3. Dragon's Teeth Press (1975), found in *Fifty Songs by John Edmunds*

113:1-5 (Psalm 135:1; based on)
Traditional Folk Song - Hasidic (arr. Samuel Adler). *Praise the Lord.* 2-part-Pno: d1-d2/b♭1-b♭2. Oxford (1970) 94.401

113:1-5, 7-9
Ridge, M. D. *Praise the Lord (Psalm 113).* Cantor-Kbd, gtr, inst in c, opt duet: (g)b1-c2(e2). OCP (1989, 1992) 9273CC, found in *In Every Age*

113:2 SEE: Job 1:21a. Rogers, Dawn and Tricia Walker. *Baruch Hashem Adonai*

113:3 (I Chronicles 16:29; Psalm 29:2; Psalm 50:1; Psalm 96:6)
VanDyke, May. *In the Beauty of Holiness.* Kbd: H:e1-g2; L:b1-d2. Boosey & Hawkes (1937)

113:3-4 (Malachi 1:11)
Greene, Maurice (ed. E. Stanley Roper). *The Lord's Name Is Praised.* Kbd: H:e1-g2; L:c♯1-e2. Bosworth (1910), found in *Seven Sacred Solos of the Early English School*

114:00 Bloch, Ernst. *Psalm 114 (Snatched Away by Jehovah)* (from *Deux Psaumes*) (English/French). Orch: M:a2-a3. G. Schirmer (1919)

114:1 Edmunds, John. *When Israel Went Out of Egypt.* M:d1-f2. Dragon's Teeth Press (1975), found in *Fifty Songs by John Edmunds*

114:12-14
SEE: Acts 9:2. Mendelssohn, Felix. *But the Lord Is Mindful of His Own*

115:3 SEE: I Corinthians 3:16-17. Mendelssohn, Felix. *For Know Ye Not That Ye Are His Temple (O Wherefore Do Ye These Things?)*

115:12 Walfish, H. (arr. Velvel Pasternak). *Y'Voréch (He Will Bless the House of Israel)* (Hebrew transliterated). Duet-Gtr: H:a1-d2/M:a1-c2. Bloch (1971), found in *Songs of the Chassidim II*

115:13-15
Bach, J. S. *Der Herr segne euch (The Lord Bless You)* (from *Der Herr denket an un,* cantata no. 196) (German/English). Duet-Org: H:f♯1-g2/L:c1-b2. Concordia (1959) 97-9240, also found in *Sing Unto the Lord; Wedding Blessing*

115:14-15
Mendelssohn, Felix. *The Lord Shall Bless Thee With Abundance* (from *Psalm 115*). Kbd: Bar or Bass:b♭-e♭1. G. Schirmer

116:00 (paraphrased)
Haas, David. *The Name of God.* U/3-part-Kbd, gtr, inst in c: d1-d2(f2). GIA (1987), found in *As Water to the Thirsty; Psalms for the Church Year,* vol. 3

116:00 Stewart, Roy James. *I Will Walk in the Presence of the Lord.* U/2-part-Kbd, inst in c, gtr: c1-c2(g2). GIA (1993) G-3746 INST, also found in *Psalms for the Church Year,* vol. 5

116:1, 3, 5, 12-13, 15-18 (I Corinthians 10:16)
Hurd, Bob (arr. Craig S. Kingsbury). *Our Blessing Cup.* U/2-part-Org, gtr, 3 inst in c: c1-c2. OCP (1988), found in *Everlasting Your Love*

116:1-5, 7-8
Duke, John. *I Love the Lord.* Kbd: b♭1-e2. Boosey & Hawkes (1962)

116:1-8, 12-16, 17 (based on)
Dean, Stephen. *How Can I Repay the Lord.* Kbd, cl: b♭1-d2. OCP (1981, 1987), found in *Holy Is God*

116:1-8, 15, 18 (In Paradisum, the Grail)
Dean, Stephen. *May Choirs of Angels Welcome You.* Kbd: c♯1-d2. OCP (1991), found in *Return to Me: Music for Funerals and Healing,* vol. 1

116:1-19 Foley, John B. *Psalm 116 (I Will Walk in the Presence of God).* U/2-part-Kbd, gtr: c♯1-d2(e2). GIA (1995), found in *Psalms for the Church Year,* vol. 7

116:3 (Ephesians 5:14; adapted)
Mendelssohn, Felix. *Strikke des Todes (The Sorrows of Death)* (from *Hymn of Praise*) (German/English). Kbd: Tenor:e♭-a♭2. Hal Leonard (1994), found in *Oratorio Anthology: Tenor*

116:3 (Ephesians 5:14; adapted)
Mendelssohn, Felix (ed. Robert Shaw). *Strikke des Todes* (from *Lobgesang*) (German). Kbd: Tenor:e♭-a♭2. Available from Atlanta Symphony Orchestra (1986)

116:3-4 SEE: Psalm 4:1. Gilbert, Harry M. *God of Righteousness*

116:3a, 6 SEE: Psalm 9:13. Molique, Wilhelm Bernhard. *It Is of the Lord's Great Mercies*

116:5-9 (Book of Common Prayer)
Mahnke, Allan. *Psalm 116.* Kbd: d1-d2. Concordia (1992) 97-6093, found in *17 Psalms for Cantor and Congregation*

116:7-8 Kiel, Friedrich. *Turn Again to Thy Rest* (from *The Star of Bethlehem*). Kbd: Alto:b1-f2. G. Schirmer (1977), found in *Anthology of Sacred Song–Alto; Schirmer's Singer's Library: Alto Arias from Oratorios*

116:7-8, 12-14, 18-19
Courtney, Craig. *What Shall I Render to the Lord?* Pno: M:b♭1-f2. Beckenhorst (1999), found in *Psalm Settings of Craig Courtney*

116:8 SEE: Psalm 25:1-2a. Lynch, Mike. *I Believe That I Shall See*

116:9 SEE: Psalm 16:10. Hurd, Bob. *Be With Me, O God*

116:10-17 (Book of Common Prayer)
Mahnke, Allan. *Psalm 116:10-17.* Kbd: U/parts: M:c1-d2. Concordia (1992) 97-6093, found in *17 Psalms for Cantor and Congregation*

116:12 (I John 4:18)
Dean, Stephen. *Lord, Your Love Has Drawn Us Near.* Kbd, 2 insts in c: d1-d2. St. Thomas Moore Group (1992), found in *United as One,* vol. 2

116:12-13
SEE: Psalm 34:9a. Joncas, Michael. *Our Blessing Cup*

116:12-14 (adapted)
Talbot, John Michael. *Our Blessing Cup.* Gtr: e1-c♯2. Cherry Lane (1982), found in *Praise, Prayer and Worship*

116:12-14, 17-19
LaForge, Frank. *What Shall I Render Unto the Lord.* Kbd: H:f1-g2; L:c1-d2. G. Schirmer (1942)

116:17 Kranzler, E. (arr. Velvel Pasternak). *L'Cho Ezbach,* no. 2 *(To Thee I Offer Thanksgiving)* (Hebrew transliterated). Duet-Gtr: M:d1-e2/M:b1-c2. Bloch (1971), found in *Songs of the Chassidim II*

116:17 Pasternak, Velvel. *L'Cho Ezbach,* no. 1) *(To Thee I Offer Thanksgiving)* (Hebrew transliterated). Duet-Gtr: M:a1-d2/L:a1-b2. Bloch (1971), found in *Songs of the Chassidim II*

117:00 Buxtehude, Dietrich. *Laudate Dominum* (Geistliche Solokantaten 9) (Latin). Cont, 2vlns: Sop. Bärenreiter BA 1092 (n.v.)

117:00 SEE: Ecclesiasticus 47:2. Ferris, William. *I Have Seen Water*

117:00 (Mark 16:15; altered)
Haas, David. *Go Out to All the World.* Duet-Kbd, 2 inst in c: c♯1-d2. GIA (1988), found in *Who Calls You by Name,* vol. 2

117:00 (based on)
Inwood, Paul. *Holy Is God.* Cantor-Kbd, gtr, 2 trpts, opt duet: d1-d2. OCP/ Paul Inwood (1984), found in *Holy Is God*

117:00 (English; adapted by Neil Jenkins)
Mozart, W. A. *Laudate Dominum* (from *Vesperae Solemnes de Confessore*) (Latin/ English). Kbd: L:b1-e2. Oxford (1997), found in *Sing Solo Sacred* (H/L)

117:00 Mozart, W. A. (arr. Doreen Rao). *Laudate Dominum* (from *Vesperae Solemnes de Confessore*) (Latin). 2-Part-Kbd: Opt Mez, MH:a1-f2/L:a1-b♭2. Boosey & Hawkes (1990) OCTB6537

117:00 Mozart, W. A. *Laudate Dominum* (from *Vesperae Solemnes de Confessore*) (Latin). Kbd: Mez:a1-f2. Kalmus; Breitkopf (n.d.) BA 4894a, found in *Five Vocal Gems for Soprano; Oratorio Anthology: Soprano; Singer's Wedding Anthology*

117:00 Powell, Robert J. *Praise the Lord, All Ye Nations* (from *Surely the Lord Is in This Place*). Kbd: M:d1-g2. Augsburg (1995) 11-10607

117:00 (metrical version)
Slater, Jean. *From All That Dwell Below the Skies.* U/2-part-Org: e♭1-e♭2. Concordia (1989) 98-2931, also found in *Psalms/ Anthems:* set 1

117:00 (Shafferman and Thomas Ken; adapted)
Traditional English (arr. Anna Laura Page). *Thanksgiving Canon (Praise God, From Whom All Blessings Flow).* U/2-part-Kbd, fl. Med. Alfred (1997) 16147

117:1 SEE: Psalm 100:2. Caldara, Antonio. *Bless the Lord, All Nations*

117:1 Chait, B. (arr. Velvel Pasternak). *Hal'lu (O Praise the Lord, All Ye Nations)* (Hebrew transliterated). Gtr: M:c1-e♭2. Bloch (1971), found in *Songs of the Chassidim II*

117:1 (based on)
Larson, Lloyd. *O Praise the Lord!* 2-part-Kbd: H:c1-e2/L:c1-d2. Beckenhorst (1983) BP1190

117:2 SEE: Psalm 9:13. Molique, Wilhelm Bernhard. *It Is of the Lord's Great Mercies*

118:1, 10, 14-17, 19, 21
LaForge, Frank. *Hymn of Thanks and Praise.* Kbd: MH; L. G. Schirmer (n.v.)

118:1, 16-17, 19 (adapted)
Conry, Tom (acc. Dominic MacAller). *Now Comes the Day.* Kbd, trpt, tb, gtr: d1-f♯2. OCP/Team (1987), found in *Stand*

118:1-2, 16-17, 22-23 (based on)
Hurd, Bob (acc. Dominic MacAller). *This Is the Day.* U/2-part-Pno, gtr, 2 trpt: c1-d2(e2). OCP (1990), found in *Behold the Cross*

118:1-4, 29
SEE: Psalm 106:1. Paris, Twila. *Come Worship the Lord*

118:1-4, 8-9, 13-17, 21-24, 26
Foley, John B. *Psalm 118 (This Is the Day).* U/2-part-Kbd, gtr: d1-c2(e2). GIA (1995), found in *Psalms for the Church Year,* vol. 7

118:1-7, 19-22 (The Grail)
Farrell, Bernadette. *The Stone Which the Builders Rejected.* Kbd, 2 inst in c, gtr: M: b1-d2. GIA (1990), found in *God, Beyond All Names*

118:4, 14, 18, 21, 24 (based on)
Dufford, Bob. *Sing to the Mountains.* U-Gtr: d1-e2. NALR (1975), found in *Earthen Vessels*

118:8 SEE: Psalm 92:1-2, 5-12-13. Berthier, Jacques. *Bonum Est Confidere*

118:14 SEE: Isaiah 12:3-4. Calder, Lee. *God Is My Salvation*

118:14, 19-24 (adapted)
Walker, Christopher. *This Day Was Made by the Lord.* Org, gtr, brass, timp: d1-d2. OCP (1989), found in *Out of Darkness*

118:14, 24, 26, 28-29
Huhn, Bruno S. *The Lord Is My Strength.* Kbd: H:f1-f2; L. G. Schirmer (1909), found in *Seventeen Sacred Songs for Church and General Use*

118:14-15 (Psalm 141:3-4)
Scott, Charles P. *The Voice of Joy.* Kbd: H:f1-g2; L:d1-e2. Oliver Ditson (1935)

118:22 Chait, B. (arr. Velvel Pasternak). *Even Moasu (The Stone Which the Builders Rejected)* (Hebrew transliterated). Duet-Gtr: H:b♭1-f2/M:b♭1-c2. Bloch (1971), found in *Songs of the Chassidim II*

118:22 (John 1:1-4, 29; John 8:12; John 14:6; Revelation 1:8; adapted)
Joncas, Michael. *Take and Eat.* Gtr: f1-d♭2. GIA (1990) G-3435, also found in *Come to Me*

118:24 SEE: Psalm 100:4. Brethorst, Leona Von. *I Will Enter His Gates*

118:24a (other)
Brown, Scott Wesley. *This Is the Day.* Pno: d1-d2. Chappell (1966), found in *10 Wedding Solos*

118:24a (other)
Brown, Scott Wesley. *This Is the Day.* Pno: c1-d2. Hal Leonard (1979), found in *The Bride's Guide to Wedding Music*

118:24 (other)
Garrett, Les. *This Is the Day.* U-Kbd: e1-e2. Maranatha! (1967, 1986), found in *Bible Songs; Face to Face; Praise Classics–Lord of Peace; Songs for Praise and Worship*

118:24 (other)
Misetich, Marianne. *This Is the Day.* Kbd, gtr, bass, inst in c: c1-c2. OCP (1973, 1982), found in *Comfort My People*

118:24 Portugal, Rabbi E. (arr. Velvel Pasternak). *Ze Hayõm (This Is the Day Which the Lord Has Made)* (Hebrew transliterated). Gtr: M:c1-d2. Bloch (1971), found in *Songs of the Chassidim II*

118:24 (other)
Schoenbachler, Tim. *This Is the Day.* U/2-part-Kbd, gtr: e1-b2 (f♯2). OCP (1979), found in *All Is Ready*

118:24 Vejvanovsky, Pavel Josef (ed. Konrad Ruhland). *Haec Dies quam fecit Dominus* Duet-Cont, stg qnt: SI:d1-f♯2; SII:b1-d2. Coppenrath (1993)

118:24 (Romans 5:8; I Corinthians 9:24-27; I Corinthians 10:16)
Warren, Clara. *Let Us Keep the Feast.* Kbd: H:d1-f2; L:b♭1-d2. R. D. Row (1948)

119:00 (taken from)
Hamblen, Bernard. *Teach Me, O Lord.* Pno: H:e♭1-f2; L:c1-d2. Harms (1925)

119:00 Jackson, Stanley. *Teach Me, O Lord.* Kbd: Med. Carl Fischer (1959)

119:00 (based on)
Uszler, Marienne (arr. Tim Schoenbachler). *Speak Lord.* U/2-part-Gtr: d1-d2(e1-f♯2). OCP (1979), found in *All Is Ready*

119:1-5, 8
Reger, Max. *Wohl denen, die ohne tadel leben* (German). Org: e1-g2. Bote and Bock (1975)

119:1-7 Tindall, Adrienne M. *Aleph (Blessed Are the Undefiled in the Way).* Kbd: d1-g2. Adrienne Tindall (1987), found in *Sacred Solos by Adrienne Tindall,* vol. I

119:3 SEE: Psalm 5:8. Handel, G. F. (arr. Carl Fredrickson). *Lead Me, Lord*

119:4-5, 18
Greene, Maurice (ed. E. Stanley Roper). *Thou Hast Charged (O That My Ways).* Kbd: H:f1-a♭3; L:e♭1-e♭2. Bosworth (1910), found in *Seven Sacred Solos of the Early English School*

119:10-13, 15
Tindall, Adrienne M. *Beth (With My Whole Heart Have I Sought Thee).* Kbd: d1-f2. Adrienne Tindall (1987), found in *Sacred Solos by Adrienne Tindall,* vol. I

119:12, 18, 28, 35, 59, 68
Fischer, Irwin. *Lord, Teach Me Thy Statues.* Kbd: d1-f♯2. American Composers Alliance (1957)

119:25-32
Wyner, Yehudi. *Psalm 119.* Kbd: b♭1-f2. Associated (1973), found in *Psalms and Early Songs*

119:30-37
Courtney, Craig. *I Have Chosen the Way of Truth.* Pno: M:a1-f2. Beckenhorst (1999), found in *Psalm Settings of Craig Courtney*

119:33-34, 37
LaForge, Frank. *Teach Me, O Lord.* Pno: H:e♭1-g2; L:c1-e2. Carl Fischer (1938)

119:33-34, 37
Manney, Charles F. *Teach Me, O Lord.* Kbd: H:e1-g2; M:d1-f2; L:c1-e♭2. Arthur P. Schmidt (1908)

119:33-35, 44-45, 171-172
Nystedt, Knut. *Teach Me, O Lord.* 2-part-Pno, perc: Treble:d1-g2/d1-d2. MorningStar (1988) MSM-50-9400

119:33-36, 38, 40
Tindall, Adrienne M. *He (Teach Me, O Lord, the Way of Thy Statutes).* Kbd: d1-g2. Adrienne Tindall (1987), found in *Sacred Solos by Adrienne Tindall,* vol. I

119:49-50, 54-56
Otte, Paul R. *Your Decrees Are My Song.* U-Kbd: d1-d2. Concordia (1987) 98-2779

119:49-52, 54-55
Tindall, Adrienne M. *Zain* (*Remember the Word Unto Thy Servant*). Kbd: b♭1-g♭2. Adrienne Tindall (1987), found in *Sacred Solos by Adrienne Tindall,* vol. I

119:50 Freudenthal, Josef. *A Lamp Unto My Feet.* Kbd: H:e♭1-g2; L:c1-e2. Transcontinental (1957) TV 499

119:54, 55, 97, 103, 105, 125
Bone, Gene and Howard Fenton. *Thy Word Is a Lamp.* Kbd: H:c1-f2; L:b♭1-e♭2. Carl Fischer (1948) H:R579; R. D. Row: R-750B

119:62 SEE: Psalm 27:4. Talma, Louise. *Cantata: All the Days of My Life*

119:73-74, 76-77, 80
Tindall, Adrienne M. *Jod (Thy Hands Have Made Me and Fashioned Me).* Kbd: b1-f♯2. Adrienne Tindall (1987), found in *Sacred Solos by Adrienne Tindall,* vol. I

119:89, 105
SEE: Psalm 26:8. Bender, Mark. *O Lord, I Love the Habitation of Your House*

119:97, 99, 101-103
Tindall, Adrienne M. *Mem* (from *Song of the Law*). Kbd: b1-e2. Augsburg (1983, 1987), found in *Sacred Solos by Adrienne Tindall,* vol. I

119:105 Englert, Andrew Lloyd. *Thy Word Is a Lamp.* Pno: H:d1-e2; L:c1-d2. R. D. Row (1962)

119:105 (Psalm 145:00)
MacDermid, James G. *Thy Word Is a Lamp.* Kbd: H:d♭1-g♭2; L:b♭1-e♭2. Forster (1948)

119:105 SEE: Psalm 89:1, 15-16. Parker, Clifton. *Blessed Is the People*

119:105 (other)
Smith, Michael W. and Amy Grant. *Thy Word.* Pno: b♭1-a♭2. Meadowgreen (1984, 1988), found in *Amy Grant: The Collection; The Best Contemporary Christian Songs Ever; Bible Songs; The Big Book of Contemporary Christian Favorites; The Big Book of Contemporary Christian Favorites, 2nd ed; Glorious Praise; Michael W. Smith: Greatest Hits; Our God Reigns; Praise Classics–Lord of Peace; the Song Book,* vol. III; *Songs for Praise and Worship*

119:105 (other)
Smith, Michael W. (arr. Steven V. Taylor). *Thy Word.* 2-part-Pno or Trax: b♭1-b♭2(c2). Meadowgreen (1988), found in *25 Songs for Two-Part Choir,* vol. II

119:105-106, 108, 110-112
Tindall, Adrienne M. *Nun* (from *Song of the Law*). Kbd: c♯1-g♯2. Augsburg (1983, 1987), found in *Sacred Solos by Adrienne Tindall,* vol. I

119:114-115, 117, 120
Dvorák, Antonín. *Lord, Thou Art My Refuge,* op. 99, no. 2 (from *Biblical Songs*) (English only). Pno: H:e1-f2; L:b1-c2. International (1962), found in *Biblical Songs: A Cycle of Ten Songs,* op. 99

119:114-115, 117, 120
Dvorák, Antonín. *Lord, Thou Art My Refuge,* op. 99, no. 2 (from *Biblical Songs*). Pno: H:e1-f2; L:b1-c2. Simrock; G. Schirmer (1991); R. D. Row (1955), found in *Dvorák,* op. 99, *Biblical Songs*

119:114-115, 117, 120
Dvorák, Antonín (ed. Sourek, Otakar). *Skryse ma A paveza má Ty jsi,* op. 99, no. 2 (*Du, Du bist mire ein Schirm und Schild; Lord My Shield, My Refuge)* (from *Biblical*

Songs) (Czech/German/English). Pno: H:e1-f2. Masters Music (n.d.), found in *Biblical Songs for High Voice and Piano by Antonín Dvorák,* op. 99

119:135, 165 (other)
Lully, Jean Baptiste. *Great Peace Have They*. Kbd: c1-e♭2. R. D. Row (1959), found in *Sacred Song Masterpieces,* bk 1

119:144a SEE: Psalm 99:3. Paris, Twila. *Holy Is the Lord*

119:148, 150
SEE: Psalm 69:4b. Laderman, Ezra. *What I Did Not Steal*

119:165, 174-176
Rogers, James H. *Great Peace Have They Which Love Thy Law*. Org: H:f1-g2; M:d1-e♭2; L:b1-c2. G. Schirmer (1936), found in *Christian Science Service Songs*

119:165-166, 175-176
Brown, Allanson G. Y. *Great Peace Have They*. Pno: c1-e♭2. Oliver Ditson (1945)

120:00 Rorem, Ned. *A Song of David (Psalm 120)*. Pno: d1-g2. Associated (1946) AMP 19469-3; 7742, also found in *American Art Songs*

121:00 (adapted)
Adler, Samuel. *I Lift Mine Eyes,* (no. 7 from *Twelve Songs of Praise*). U-Org: b1-e2. Oxford (1988) 94.505

121:00 Barnes, Frederick M. *I Will Lift Up Mine Eyes*. Kbd: H; L:f-c2. JIB Pub (1990) (1981), found in *Great New Solos*

121:00 Barnes, Milton. *Psalm 121* (from *The Psalms of David*). Duet-Perc, timp, harp or stgs: Mez/Bar. Canadian Music Centre (1973)

121:00 Barta, Daniel. *Psalm 121*. 2-part-Kbd: (b1)c1-d2. Logia (1994) 98-3158

121:00 Bartlett, Floy Little. *I Will Lift Up My Eyes*. Kbd: H:d1-g2; M:c♯1-f♯2; L:b1-c2. Arthur P. Schmidt (1947), found in The Free Library of Philadelphia

121:00 Burns, William K. *Psalm 121* (from *Four Meditative Songs*). Kbd: f1-g2. Abingdon (1972) APM-515

121:00 Childs, David. *Psalm 121*. Org: d1-g2. Abingdon (1966) H: APM-390; L: APM-385, also found in *Seven Psalms for Voice and Organ*

121:00 (paraphrased)
Cornelius, Peter. *I Will Lift Mine Eyes*. Duet-Pno: d1-f2/f-e♭1. E. C. Schirmer (1941, 1970), found in *Sacred Duets*

121:00 Crowe, B. *One Hundred Twenty-First Psalm*. Kbd: H:d1-g2; L:b♭1-e♭2. Pro Art/Royal Palm Music (1937)

121:00 David, Ferdinand. *Mein Aug' erheb' ich (Unto the Hills)* (German/English). Duet-Sop/Alto; Alto/Tenor; Sop/Bass: f1-a♭2/c1-f2. Church (1907), found in *Sacred Duets*

121:00 David, Ferdinand. *Unto the Hills,* op. 33 *(Mein Aug' erheb' ich)*. Duet-Kbd: H:f1-a♭3/L:c1-f2

121:00 Derfler, Carl. *I Lift Up My Eyes* (from *Trilogy of Psalms*). Pno: Bar. Canadian Music Centre (1975, 1990)

121:00 Eaton, Chris. *Psalm 121*. Kbd, gtr: g-b♭2. Word (1996), found in *Contemporary Chart Toppers; the Praise Collection,* vol. 1

121:00 Eville, Vernon. *I Will Lift Up Mine Eyes*. Pno: H:f1-g2; M:e♭1-f2; L:c1-d2. Boosey & Hawkes (1943)

121:00 Fromm, Herbert. *Psalm 121* (from *Four Psalms*). Kbd: d♯-d2. Transcontinental (1971)

121:00 Fromm, Herbert. *Unto the Hills* (from *Two Psalm Settings*). Kbd: d1-e2. Hope (n.d.) SA 1400

121:00 Fyock, Joan A. *Look to the Mountains* (from *Three Psalm Settings*). U-Pno: c1-d2. Hope (1974) JR216

121:00 Gellman, Steven. *Psalm 121*. Pno, fl: Sop. Canadian Music Centre (1977)

121:00 Gober, Belle Biard. *I Will Lift Up Mine Eyes*. Kbd: d♭1-f2. FitzSimmons (1941)

121:00 (from Lyric Psalms)
Haas, David. *The Mountain I See (Psalm 121)*. U/2-part-Kbd: c♯1-d2. GIA (1985), found in *To Be Your Bread*

121:00 SEE: Ephesians 4:7. Harker, F. Flaxington. *I Will Lift Up Mine Eyes to the Hills*

121:00 Head, Michael. *I Will Lift Up Mine Eyes* (from *Three Psalms*). Kbd: H:e1-a3; L:b1-e2. Boosey & Hawkes (1976) H:186; L:187

121:00 Hoffmeister, Leon Abbott. *I Will Lift Up Mine Eyes*. Pno: H:c1-g2; L:a1-e2. Huntzinger (1930)

121:00 Hopson, Hal H. *I Lift Up My Eyes to the Hills*. Kbd, inst in c: c1-d2. GIA (1980) G-2239

121:00 Horwood, Michael S. *Psalm 121*. Pno: Sop or A. Canadian Music Centre (1980)

121:00 Humphreys, Don. *I Will Lift Up Mine Eyes Unto the Hills*. Kbd: H:d1-f2; L:b1-d2. Boston Music (1947)

121:00 Jennings, Kenneth. *I Lift Up My Eyes to the Hills*. Kbd: H:d1-g2; L:d1-f2. Augsburg (1967)

121:00 (taken from)
Jensen, Adolf (arr. Carl Fredrickson). *Lift Up Thine Eyes*. Kbd: d$^{\flat}$1-d$^{\flat}$2. R. D. Row (1959), found in *Sacred Song Masterpieces,* bk 1

121:00 (adapted)
Joncas, Michael. *Guiding Me*. Gtr: d1-c2. GIA (1990) G-3438, also found in *Come to Me*

121:00 Kayden, Mildred. *Psalm 121*. Pno: d1-b$^{\flat}$3. Mercury (1956)

121:00 Kendrick, Virginia. *I Will Lift Up Mine Eyes*. Kbd: e1-f2. Schmitt (1975)

121:00 Koch, John. *I Will Lift Up Mine Eyes* (from *Songs of David*). Stg qt, fl: e1-f2. American Music Centre

121:00 (St. Dunstan Psalter)
Lekberg, Sven. *I Will Lift Up Mine Eyes*. Kbd: d1-f$^{\sharp}$2. Witmark (1947)

121:00 (adapted)
Lynch, Mike (arr. Dennis Richardson). *I Lift Up My Eyes*. Org, gtr, inst in c: b1-c2. OCP (1986), found in *Bread of the World*

121:00 MacDermid, James G. *I Will Lift Up Mine Eyes*. Kbd: H:e1-a$^{\flat}$3; M:c1-f2; L:b1-e$^{\flat}$2. Forster (1942)

121:00 Mendelssohn, Felix (ed. Hal H. Hopson). *I to the Hills Will Lift My Eyes*. 2-part mixed-Org: d1-d2/c-d1. Agape (1978) HH 3910

121:00 Parker, Clifton. *I Will Lift Up Mine Eyes Unto the Hills*. Kbd: M:c1-e2. Carl Fischer (1934) V2064

121:00 Proulx, Richard. *Psalm 121 (From Whence Shall Come My Help?)*. Cantor-Kbd: Med. GIA (1993) G-3637

121:00 Raigorodsky, Natalie. *I Will Lift Up Mine Eyes*. Kbd: H or M:c1-f$^{\sharp}$2. Coburn Press, found in *Eleven Scriptural Songs from the Twentieth Century*

121:00 Repp, Ray. *I Lift Up My Eyes*. Kbd, gtr: c1-d2. FEL Publications (1970) 70-500

121:00 Rutenber, C. B. *I Will Lift Up Mine Eyes*. Org: c1-a$^{\flat}$3. G. Schirmer (1921)

121:00 Sowerby, Leo. *I Will Lift Up Mine Eyes (Psalm 121)* (from *Three Psalms*). Org: M:b1-e2. H. W. Gray (1949) GV 390

121:00 Sowerby, Leo (arr. John Delorey and Ronald Stalford). *I Will Lift Up Mine Eyes* (a solo version of SATB anthem). Org: M:a$^{\flat}$-e$^{\flat}$2. The Leo Sowerby Foundation (1996), found in *Psalms for Bass and O Perfect Love*

121:00 Stanford, Charles Villiers. *A Song of Trust* (from *Bible Songs*). Org: a$^{\flat}$1-g2. Stainer & Bell (1909)

121:00 Stearns, Peter Pindar. *I Will Lift Up Mine Eyes*. Org: d$^{\sharp}$1-d2. Coburn Press (1971), found in *Lift Up Your Voice*

121:00 Steinberg, Ben. *Esa Einai (I Will Lift Up Mine Eyes)* (Hebrew). Unacc: M. Transcontinental (1984)

121:00 Telemann, Georg Philipp. *Ich habe meine Augen auf zu den Bergen* (German/English). Kbd: H. Hänssler (1978) 39.111

121:00 Twinn, Sydney. *I Will Lift Up Mine Eyes*. Kbd: d1-a3. Carl Fischer (1948)

121:00 SEE: Psalm 31:5. Vaughan Williams, Ralph. *Watchful's Song*

121:00 Ward-Stephens. *I Will Lift Up Mine Eyes*. Pno: H:e$^{\flat}$1-b$^{\flat}$3; L:c1-g2. Chappell (1917), found in *Ward-Stephens Selected Psalms*

121:00 Watkins, Margery (ed. Wilman Wilmans). *I Will Lift Up Mine Eyes*. Pno: H:c1-f2(a3); L:b$^{\flat}$1-e$^{\flat}$2(g2). Oliver Ditson (1935), found in *Choice Sacred Songs* (H/L); *Solos for Christian Science Services*

121:00 SEE: Psalm 130:00. Yardumian, Richard. *Symphony,* no. 2

121:1-2 (additional text by Burnam)
Burnam, Edna Mae. *I Will Lift Up Mine Eyes Unto the Hills*. Kbd: c1-f2. Willis Music (1977)

121:1-2 Golde, W. *I Will Lift Up Mine Eyes*. Kbd: H:f1-f2; L:d1-d2. Brodt (1961)

121:1-2 Horowitz, Rabbi M. (arr. Velvel Pasternak). *Eso énai* (no. 1) *(I Will Lift Up Mine Eyes)* (Hebrew transliterated). Gtr: M:d1-c2. Bloch (1971), found in *Songs of the Chassidim II*

121:1-2 Kehati, Pinchas (arr. Velvel Pasternak). *Mé-aylin yovõ ezri (From Whence Shall Come My Help?)* (Hebrew transliterated). Gtr: M:a1-e♭2. Bloch (1971), found in *Songs of the Chassidim II*

121:1-2 (other)
Norbet, Gregory. *Mountains of My Soul.* Pno, gtr, fr hn, inst in c: e♭1-d2. OCP (1988), found in *Mountains of My Soul*

121:1-2 (paraphrased)
Sleeth, Natalie. *Psalm.* U/2-part-Kbd: c1-e♭2. AMSI (1983) 441

121:1-3, 7-8
Dengler, Lee. *I Will Lift Up My Eyes.* Kbd: M:c1-g2. Augsburg (1995) 11-10608, found in *Songs of David*

121:1-4 Dvorák, Antonín. *I Will Lift Up Mine Eyes,* op. 99, no. 9 (from *Biblical Songs*) (English only). Pno: H:f♯1-g2; L:d1-e♭2. International (1962), found in *Biblical Songs: A Cycle of Ten Songs,* op. 99

121:1-4 Dvorák, Antonín. *I Will Lift Up Mine Eyes,* op. 99, no. 9 (from *Biblical Songs*) (English/ Czech/ German). Pno: H:f♯1-g2; L:d1-e♭2. Simrock; G. Schirmer; Carl Fischer (1948), R. D. Row (1955), found in *Dvorák,* op. 99, *Biblical Songs; Sing Unto the Lord,* vol. 2

121:1-4 Dvorák, Antonín (ed. Otakar Sourek). *Pozdvihuji ocí svych k horám,* op. 99, no. 9 *(Ich hebe den blick zum berg empor; My Eyes Will I to the Hills Lift Up)* (from *Biblical Songs*) (Czech/German/ English). Pno: H:f♯1-g2. Masters Music (n.d.), found in *Biblical Songs for High Voice and Piano by Antonín Dvorák,* op. 99

121:1-4 (altered from the Psalter 1912)
Lovelace, Austin C. *I Lift Mine Eyes Unto the Hills.* Kbd: d♭1-f2. Darcy Press (1993), found in *Sacred Solos by Austin C. Lovelace*

121:1-4 Mendelssohn, Felix (adapted Carl Deis). *Lift Thine Eyes to the Mountains* (from *Elijah*). 2-part-Pno: Sop:g1-f2/Sop:c1-c2. G. Schirmer (1954) 10221

121:1-4 Mendelssohn, Felix (arr. Carl Fredrickson). *Lift Thine Eyes* (from *Elijah*). Duet-Kbd: H:a1-g2/L:c♯1-c♯2; M/L. R. D. Row (1960), found in *Sacred Duet Masterpieces,* bk 1

121:1-4 Rebbi of Chernowitzer (arr. Velvel Pasternak). *Eso énai* (no. 2) *(I Will Lift Up Mine Eyes)* (Hebrew transliterated). Gtr: M:b♭1-c2. Bloch (1971), found in *Songs of the Chassidim II*

121:1-4 Stearns, Theodore. *I Lift Up Mine Eyes.* Kbd: H or M:c1-f2. Coburn Press

121:1-8 Spies, Claudio. *I Will Lift Up Mine Eyes Unto the Hills* (from *Five Psalms*). Fl, fg, hn, mand, vla, vc: Tenor:c♯1-g♯1. Boosey & Hawkes (1962)

121:3 (based on)
Mendelssohn, Felix (arr. Lynn Hodges). *He, Watching Over Israel* (from *Elijah*). 2-part-Kbd: (b♭1)d1-e♭2. Integra (1993), found in *Classic Choruses for Young Voices; Mendelssohn's ELIJAH for Young Voices*

121:3 Weldon, John (ed. David Patrick). *He Will Not Suffer Thy Foot to be Moved* (from *I Will Lift Up Mine Eyes*). Kbd: MH:c♯1-e2. Boosey & Hawkes (1996), found in *Sacred Songs for the Soloist: 20 Songs on Religious Texts for Medium High Voice*

121:4 SEE: Psalm 91:11. Schlösser, Adolphe. *He That Keepeth Israel*

121:6 SEE: Isaiah 60:19. Greence, Maurice (ed. E. Stanley Roper). *The Sun Shall Be No More Thy Light*

121:8 SEE: Psalm 34:4. Robyn, Alfred G. *I Sought the Lord*

121:8 SEE: Psalm 34:4. Stevenson, Frederick. *I Sought the Lord*

121:8 Weldon, John (ed. David Patrick). *The Lord Shall Preserve Thee from All Evil* (from *I Will Lift Up Mine Eyes*). Kbd: MH:e1-f♯2. Boosey & Hawkes (1996), found in *Sacred Songs for the Soloist: 20 Songs on Religious Texts for Medium High Voice*

122:00 Couperin, François. *Ad te levavi occulos meus* (Latin). Cont, 2 vlns: F-d1. Heugel (1972) H32.219, also found in *Neuf motets*

122:00 Haas, David. *I Was Glad.* Cantor-Kbd, gtr. GIA (1995) G-4133

122:00 (adapted)
Joncas, Michael. *Let Us Go Rejoicing.* Gtr: b1-b2. GIA (1990) G-3437, also found in *Come to Me*

122:00 Proulx, Richard. *Psalm 122 (I Rejoiced).* Cantor-Kbd: Med. GIA (1993) G-3897

122:00 (adapted)
Talbot, John Michael. *I Rejoiced When I Heard Them Say.* Gtr: d1-d2. Cherry Lane (1982), found in *Praise, Prayer and Worship*

122:00 (based on)
Walker, Christopher. *I Rejoiced.* U/2-part-Kbd, gtr, inst in c, inst in B$^\flat$: c1-e$^\flat$2. OCP (1988) OCP 7185, also found in *Out of Darkness*

122:1 (Luke 4:18-19; Proverbs 9:1; Pia Moriarty)
Hurd, Bob. *Pueblo De Dios* (Spanish and English). Pno, gtr, inst in c: a1-d2. OCP (1990), found in *Behold the Cross*

122:2-3, 6-8
Wernick, Richard F. *A Prayer for Jerusalem* (Hebrew). Perc ensemble: vibes, glcknspl, crotales, fc: g-a3. Presser (1975) 110-40083

122:7 SEE: Psalm 127:1. Myers, Gordon. *Except the Lord Build the House*

123:1-5 Childs, David. *Psalm 123.* Org: c1-a3. Abingdon (1966) H: APM 390; L: APM 385, found in *Seven Psalms for Voice and Organ*

124:00 Stanford, Charles Villiers. *A Song of Battle* (from *Bible Songs*). Org: e$^\flat$1-g2. Stainer & Bell (1909)

126:00 Bobb, Barry L. *The Lord Has Done Great Things for Them.* U-Kbd, inst in c, cymbal: c1-f2. Concordia (1982) 98-2556

126:00 Brod, Max. *Psalm CXXVI (Psalm 126)* (Hebrew/English). Pno: d1-g2. Israeli Music Pub. (1953)

126:00 Courtney, Craig. *We Are Glad.* Pno, opt Inst in c: c1-g2. Beckenhorst (1992, 1999), found in *Psalm Settings of Craig Courtney*

126:00 Kahn, Erich I. *Psalm 126.* Kbd: a1-b3. American Composers Alliance, found in *Composers Facsimile Edition*

126:1-2, 5-6
Handy, William Christopher. *They That Sow in Tears.* Pno: e$^\flat$1-a$^\flat$3. Handy Bros. (1950)

126:1-3 Rosenblatt, Yossele (arr. Velvel Pasternak). *Shir hamaalõs (When the Lord Turned Again the Captivity of Zion)* (Hebrew transliterated). Gtr: M:c1-e$^\flat$2. Bloch (1971), found in *Songs of the Chassidim II*

126:1-6 Foley, John B. *Psalm 126 (Our God Has Done Great Things for Us).* U/2-part-Kbd, gtr: e1-d$^\sharp$2(e2). GIA (1995), found in *Psalms for the Church Year,* vol. 7

126:1-6 (Book of Common Prayer)
Mahnke, Allan. *Psalm 126.* Kbd: c1-c2. Concordia (1992) 97-6093, found in *17 Psalms for Cantor and Congregation*

126:5-6 Harker, F. Flaxington. *They That Sow in Tears Shall Reap in Joy.* Kbd: G. Schirmer

126:5-6 Rogers, James H. *They That Sow in Tears.* Pno: d1-f2. G. Schirmer (1908)

127:00 Biber, Heinrich Ignaz Franz (ed. Wolfram Stude). *Nisi Dominus aedificaverit domum* (Latin). Vln, vc: Bass. Broude (1972) 9516

127:00 Dinn, Freda. *Psalm 127.* Kbd: c1-f2. Schott

127:00 Gideon, Miriam. *The Labor of Thy Hands* (no. 1 from *A Woman of Valor*) (Hebrew/English). Pno: f$^\sharp$1-g2. American Composers Alliance

127:1 Humphreys, Don. *The House of God.* Pno: H:d1-f2; M:b1-d2. R. D. Row (1953)

127:1 (Isaiah 2:2; Malachi 3:10)
MacDermid, James G. *Bring Ye All the Tithes into the Storehouse.* Kbd: H:d1-a$^\flat$3; L:b$^\flat$1-f2. Forster (1960)

127:1 (Psalm 49:16b; Psalm 122:7)
Myers, Gordon. *Except the Lord Build the House.* Kbd: d1-e$^\flat$2. Eastlane Music (1968)

127:1 SEE: Psalm 31:5. Vaughan Williams, Ralph. *Watchful's Song*

127:2 Benedict, Sir Julius. *He Giveth His Beloved Sheep.* Kbd: Sop:e1-e2(f2). John Church (n.d.), found in *Sacred Songs,* vol. 1

128:00 Barnes, Milton. *Psalm 128* (from *The Psalms of David*). Duet-Perc, timp, harp or stgs: Mez/Bar. Canadian Music Centre (1973)

128:00 (adapted)
Dailey, William. *Psalm 128.* Kbd, gtr:c1-d2. Lillenas (1979) 11-0714

128:00 Gideon, Miriam. *The Labor of Thy Hands* (no. 3 from *A Woman of Valor*) (Hebrew/English). Pno: e1-a3. American Composers Alliance

128:00 Haas, David. *Happy Are They Who Honor the Lord.* U/2-part-Kbd, gtr: c1-e2. GIA (1993), found in *When Love Is Found*

128:00 Jongen, Joseph (ed. Tom Cunningham). *Deux Abraham (God of Abraham)* (English/Latin). Org, vln or vc: M:d$^\sharp$1-f2. Oxford (1998) 96.009

128:00 Keil, Kevin. *Psalm 128.* Kbd: M:d1-c2. Unity (Lorenz) (1997), found in *Wedding Psalms*

128:00 (I Corinthians 13:1-2, 4a; adapted)
McCray, James. *Love Is…* (from *Rites of Love*) (Latin and English). Pno: M:c1-e2. Leyerle (1989)

128:00 SEE: Psalm 129:00. Milhaud, Darius. *Cantate de Psaume*

128:00 Schiavone, John. *Happy Are You Who Fear the Lord.* Kbd: H:g1-f2; L:e1-d2. Concordia (1980) H: 97-5582; L: 97-5583, found in *Seven Wedding Songs*

128:00 Sinzheimer, Max. *Blessed Are Those Who Fear the Lord.* Org: Alto or Bar:d1-f2. Concordia (1974) 97-4893

128:00 Stewart, Roy James. *Happy Are Those Who Fear the Lord.* U/2-part-Kbd, inst in c, gtr: c1-c2(f2). GIA (1993) G-3746 INST, also found in *Psalms for the Church Year,* vol. 5

128:00 (adapted)
Talbot, John Michael. *Happy Are Those Who Fear the Lord.* Gtr: c1-c2. Birdwing (1985), found in *Praise, Prayer and Worship*

128:00 Wetzler, Robert. *Psalm 128 (A Wedding Song).* Org: M:c1-e2. Augsburg (1964) 11-0714; also AMSI (1996) V19

128:1 Powell, Robert J. *Blessed Are Those Who Fear the Lord.* Kbd: d1-e2. Concordia (1974) 97-5278, also found in *Three Wedding Songs*

128:1-2 Handel, G. F. *Blessed Are They That Fear the Lord* (from *Wedding Anthem* (1736)). Kbd: H; L:c1-e2(f2). Oxford (1997), found in *Sing Solo Sacred* (H/L)

128:1-4 Bender, Jan. *Wedding Song.* Org: c1-d2. Concordia (1968) 97-4887

128:1-5 (The Grail)
Inwood, Paul. *O Blessed Are Those.* Kbd, gtr, inst in c: d1-d2. GIA (1981), found in *United as One,* vol. 2

128:1-6 Foley, John B. *Psalm 128 (Happy Are They).* U/2-part-Kbd: f1-d♭2(f2). GIA (1995), found in *Psalms for the Church Year,* vol. 7

128:2-4 SEE: Psalm 92:12. Felciano, Richard. *Benedicto Nuptialis*

128:4-6 Ferris, William. *Behold, Thus Is the Man Blessed.* Org: c1-f2. GIA (1968) G-1475

128:5 Taub, Rabbi S. E. (arr. Velvel Pasternak). *Y'vorech'cho Hasem (The Lord Bless You From Zion)* (Hebrew transliterated). Gtr: H:f1-f2. Bloch (1971), found in *Songs of the Chassidim II*

129:00 (Psalm 122:00; Psalm 136:00; Psalm 145:00; Psalm 147:00)
Milhaud, Darius. *Cantate de Psaume* (French/German). Orch: Bar. Universal (1970)

129:1-4 Foley, John B. *Rescue Me From My Enemies.* Gtr: a♭1-c2. NALR (1974), found in *Neither Silver Nor Gold*

130:00 Bantock, Granville. *Out of the Depths.* Kbd: c1-f2. Alexander Broude

130:00 Bedell, Robert L. *Out of the Deep Have I Called Unto Thee.* Kbd: H:e♭1-f2; L:c1-d2. G. Schirmer (1938), found in *52 Sacred Songs*

130:00 Bernhard, Christoph. *Aus der Tiefen* (German). Vc, 2 vlns: a1-a3. Bärenreiter (1957) 3425

130:00 Burns, William K. *Out of the Depths* (from *Four Meditative Songs*). Kbd: a1-e♭2. Abingdon (1972) APM-515

130:00 (based on; metrical text)
Campion, Thomas. *Out of My Soul's Depth.* Lute: f♯1-f2. Roger Dean (1974) CMC 103, also found in *First Booke of Ayres,* vol. 1–*English Lute Songs*

130:00 (paraphrase by Martin Luther)
English Tune, 17th c. (ed. K. Lee Scott). *Out of the Depths I Cry to Thee.* Kbd: MH: e1-f2; ML:d♯1-e2. Augsburg (1987, 1992) 11-10228, found in *Rejoice, Now My Spirit*

130:00 Marks, J. Christopher. *Out of the Deep.* Kbd: H:d1-g2; L:a♭1-d♭2. Novello (1905)

130:00 Rogers, James H. *Out of the Depths.* Kbd: H:c1-f2; L:g-c2. Arthur P. Schmidt (1905)

130:00 Scott, John Prindle. *Out of the Depths.* Pno: H:e1-g2; L:c1-e♭2. Huntzinger (1918), found in *Choice Sacred Songs for Home or Church Services*

130:00 Selle, Thomas (ed. Klaus Vetter). *Aus der tiefe* (German). Duet-Sop:e1-f2/Bass:G♯-c1. Hänssler (n.d.), found in *Das geistliche konzert 89*

130:00 Sifler, Paul. *De Profundis* (Latin). Org: b♭1-f2. H. W. Gray (1953)

130:00 Stanford, Charles Villiers. *A Song of Hope* (from *Bible Songs*). Org: e♭1-g2. Stainer & Bell (1909)

130:00 (adapted)
Talbot, John Michael. *With the Lord There Is Mercy*. Gtr: d1-c2. Birdwing (1985), found in *Praise, Prayer and Worship*

130:00 Weiner, Lazar. *Mimaamakim (Out of the Depths)* (Hebrew). Pno: c1-f2. Transcontinental (1973)

130:00 Wooler, Alfred. *Out of the Depths*. Kbd: H:f♯1-g2; L:c♯1-d2. Summy Birchard (1913)

130:00 (Psalm 24:1-11; Psalm 27:1; Psalm 95:1-6; Psalm 121)
Yardumian, Richard. *Symphony,* no. 2. Orch: M. Elkan Vogel (1965)

130:1-3 (other)
Krismann, Bob (arr. Craig S. Kingsbury). *His Mercy Endures*. U/2-part-Org, gtr: b1-b2 (d2). OCP (1984), found in *Jesus, Lord*

130:1-3, 5-6
Butler, Eugene. *Out of the Depths*. Kbd: c♯1-e2. Sacred Music Press (1969), found in *The Solo Psalmist*

130:1-4 Hopson, Hal H. *Lord, From the Depths I Call to You*. 2-part mixed-Kbd: c♯1-d2/d-c1. Alfred (1990) 7862

130:1-4, 6-8
Foley, John B. *Psalm 130 (If You, O God)*. U/2-part-Kbd: (c1)d1-c2. GIA (1995), found in *Psalms for the Church Year,* vol. 7

130:1, 6 SEE: Job 19:25. Dufford, Bob. *Songs of the Angels*

130:1-6 Hovhaness, Alan. *Out of the Depths,* op. 142, no. 3. Kbd: H:e1-a3. Carl Fischer (1958)

130:3-4 Bach, J. S. *So du willst, so du willst* (from cantata no. 131). Duet-Kbd: Sop:d1-d2/Bass:a-e♭1

130:4-6 Cowen, Frederic Hymen. *With Thee There Is Forgiveness*. Kbd: Sop:a1-f2. John Church (n.d.), found in *Sacred Songs,* vol. 1

130:5 SEE: Psalm 62:1, 5-7. Seaton, Annette. *Those Who Wait on the Lord*

130:6 Bach, J. S. *Meine Seele wartet auf den Herrn* (from cantata no. 131, *Aus der Tiefer rufe ich*). Duet-Kbd: Alto:b1-g2/Tenor:c-a♭2. Breitkopf and Härtel (1960) 7131, also other editions

131:00 SEE: Psalm 42:2-3, 12. Haas, David. *Like a Little Child*

131:00 Haas, David. *My Soul Is Still*. Kbd, gtr: d1-d2. GIA (1985), found in *To Be Your Bread*

131:00 (Book of Common Prayer)
Mahnke, Allan. *Psalm 131*. Kbd: c1-d♯2. Concordia (1992) 97-6093, found in *17 Psalms for Cantor and Congregation*

131:00 (based on)
Walker, Christopher. *Like a Child Rests*. Org, gtr, inst in c, cl, vc: c1-a2. OCP (1989), found in *Out of Darkness*

131:2 SEE: Psalm 62:6. Hurd, Bob. *Like a Weaned Child*

133:00 Edmunds, John. *Behold, How Good*. M:c1-f2. Dragon's Teeth Press (1975), found in *Fifty Songs by John Edmunds*

133:00 Matesky, Thelma. *Behold, How Good and How Pleasant*. Kbd: d1-g2. Mercury (1964)

133:1 Kosche, Kenneth T. *How Good and Pleasant it is*. U-Kbd: Med. Concordia 98-3060

133:1 Naplan, Allan E. *Hine Ma Tov*. 2-part-Pno: c1-d2. Boosey & Hawkes (1995) OCTB6782

133:1 Talmud, Rabbi Y. (arr. Velvel Pasternak). *Hiné ma tõv* (no. 1) *(Behold How Good and How Pleasant It Is)* (Hebrew transliterated). Duet-Gtr: H:a1-e2/M:a1-d2. Bloch (1971), found in *Songs of the Chassidim II*

133:1 (paraphrased)
Tindall, Adrienne M. *Psalm 133 (How Good and How Pleasant it is)*. Kbd: d1-e2. Augsburg (1983, based on anthem 11-4619), found in *Sacred Solos by Adrienne Tindall,* vol. I

134:00 Chajes, Julius. *Old Jerusalem*. Pno: e1-g2. Transcontinental (1975)

134:00 SEE: Genesis 28:16-17. Powell, Robert J. *Surely the Lord Is in This Place*

134:00 Rorem, Ned. *Behold, Bless Ye the Lord* (from *A Cycle of Holy Songs*). Pno: H:d1-d♯2. Peer-Southern (1955)

134:00 (Milton)
Thiman, Eric H. *How Lovely Are Thy Dwellings Fair*. Duet-Org: Equal high voices. Novello (1939) 78

134:1-4 Rosenmüller, Johann. *Der 134th Psalm (Psalm 134)* (Latin/German). Cont, 2 vlns: a1-c2. Schott (1957) 81

135:00 Cassler, G. Winston. *Laudate nomen (Oh Praise the Lord)*. Org: b1-e2. Augsburg (1965)

135:00 (metrical)
Handel, G. F. *Thy Mercy, Lord* (from *Sixth Chandos Anthem*). Kbd: Sop:d1-g2. Paterson (1935)

135:1 SEE: Psalm 113:1-5. Traditional Folk Song–Hasidic. *Praise the Lord*

135:1-2 (Psalm 84:2)
Handel, G. F. *Praise Him, All Ye That in His House Attend* (from *Sixth Chandos Anthem*). Kbd: f1-a♭3. Novello (1969)

135:5 Handel, G. F. *That God Is Great (O Praise the Lord)* (from *Sixth Chandos Anthem*). Kbd: Bass or Bar:a-f1. Novello (1969)

136:00 (based on)
Haugen, Marty. *Your Love Is Never Ending.* Kbd, gtr, inst in c: b1-b2. GIA (1987), found in *Psalms for the Church Year,* vol. 2; *Shepherd Me, O God*

136:00 (based on)
Joncas, Michael. *Eternal Is His Mercy.* U/2-part-Kbd, gtr: d1-d2. OCP 5420CC, also found in *On Eagle's Wings*

136:00 SEE: Psalm 129:00. Milhaud, Darius. *Cantate de Psaume*

136:1 SEE: Psalm 19:1. Dufford, Bob and John B. Foley. *Praise God*

136:1 SEE: Psalm 106:1. Paris, Twila. *Come Worship the Lord*

136:1 SEE: Psalm 29:11. Pasternak, Velvel. *Yiru Es Adõnoy*

136:1, 2 (and other)
Boito, A. *Give Thanks Unto God.* Duet-Org/pno: H:e♭1-f2; H:f1-a♭3. R. D. Row (1960), found in *Sacred Duet Masterpieces,* bk 1

136:1, 4-6, 8-9 (The Magnificat)
Hurd, Bob (arr. Craig S. Kingsbury). *Everlasting Your Love.* U/2-part-Org, gtr, inst in c: (a1)b1-e2. OCP (1988), found in *Everlasting Your Love*

136:1-4 (based on)
Schutte, Daniel L. (arr. Randall DeBruyn). *Give Thanks to the Lord.* Kbd: b1-b2. OCP (1993), found in *Drawn by a Dream*

136:1-9 Starer, Robert. *Give Thanks Unto the Lord* (from *Two Sacred Songs*). Kbd: H:c1-a3. Peer-Southern (1964)

136:1-9, 24-26
Haas, David and Marty Haugen. *His Love Is Everlasting.* U/2-part-Kbd, gtr: e1-e2. GIA (1983), found in *Psalms for the Church Year*

136:5-6 SEE: Psalm 34:2-4, 9. Hurd, Bob. *Taste and See*

136:23 Pasternak, Velvel. *Sheb'shiflénu (Who Remembered Us When We Were Downcast)* (Hebrew transliterated). Gtr: M:a1-d2. Bloch (1971), found in *Songs of the Chassidim II*

137:00 (paraphrased)
Bach, J. S. *By Waters of Babylon.* Org, vln (fl or ob):d1-e2. H. W. Gray (1967)

137:00 Bloch, Ernst. *Psalm 137 (By the Waters of Babylon)* (from *Deux Psaumes*) (English/French). M-orch: g♭1-a3. G. Schirmer (1919)

137:00 Chajes, Julius. *By the Rivers of Babylon.* Org (or pno, vc): g1-a3. Transcontinental (1942)

137:00 Eville, Vernon. *By the Waters of Babylon.* Kbd: H:e1-g2; M:d1-f2; L:c1-e2. Boosey & Hawkes (1928)

137:00 Freedman, Harry. *Psalm 137.* Unaccompanied. Canadian Music Centre (1985)

137:00 Goldman, Edward M. *By the Rivers of Babylon.* Kbd: Med. World Library (1965)

137:00 Richards, Stephen. *Psalm 137 (By the Waters of Babylon).* Org: d1-g2. Transcontinental (1971) TV 578

137:00 Schein, Johann Hermann (ed. Paul Horn). *An wasserflüsswen Babylon* (German). Duet-Equal voices: d1-f2. Hänssler (n.d.), found in *Das geistliche Konzert 115*

137:00 Schoenbachler, Tim. *Babylon.* U/2-part-Kbd, gtr, ob: e1-c♯2. OCP (1979), found in *All Is Ready*

137:00 Seeger, Charles. *Psalm 137.* Unacc: b1-a3. American Music Centre (1954)

137:00 Wilder, Alec. *By the Rivers of Babylon.* Kbd: b1-g2. Edwin H. Morris (1944)

137:1 Watson, Michael. *Babylon.* Pno: H:c1-f2; L:b♭1-e♭2. Found in *Album of Sacred Songs* (H/L)

137:1-4, 6 (adapted)
Lynch, Mike (acc. Patrick Loomis). *Let My Tongue Be Silenced.* Cantor-Org, gtr, inst in c, opt duet: (b1)c1-d2. OCP (1986) 9456CC, also found in *Bread of the World*

137:1-5 Dvorák, Antonín. *By the Still Waters of Babylon,* op. 99, no. 7 (from *Biblical Songs*) (English only). Pno: H:d1-g2. International (1962), found in *Biblical Songs: A Cycle of Ten Songs,* op. 99

137:1-5 Dvorák, Antonín. *By the Waters of Babylon,* op. 99, no. 7 (from *Biblical Songs*). Pno: H:d1-g2; L:b♭1-e♭2. Simrock; G. Schirmer; R. D. Row (1955) vol. 1824, also found in *Dvorák,* op. 99, *Biblical Songs*

137:1-5 Dvorák, Antonín (ed. Otakar Sourek). *Pri rekách babylonskych,* op. 99, no. 7 *(Als wir dort an den Wassern der Stadt Baylon sassen; By the Shore of the River Babylon) (from Biblical Songs)* (Czech/German/ English). Pno: H:d1-g2. Masters Music (n.d.), found in *Biblical Songs for High Voice and Piano by Antonín Dvorák,* op. 99

137:1-5 Howell, Charles T. (ed. Wilman Wilmans). *By the Waters of Babylon.* Pno: H:b1-g2; M:a1-f2; L:g-e♭2. Oliver Ditson (1918), found in *Choice Sacred Songs* (H/L); *Ditson Treasury of Sacred Songs*

137:1-5 Speaks, Oley. *By Waters of Babylon.* Kbd: H:g1-g2; M:d1-d2. G. Schirmer (1935), found in The Free Library of Philadelphia

137:1-6 (adapted)
Cooney, Rory. *If I Forget You, Jerusalem.* Kbd, gtr, sop sax: b1-d2. GIA (1990) G-3411, also found in *Safety Harbor*

137:1-6 Stewart, Roy James. *Let My Tongue Be Silenced.* 2-part mixed-Kbd, inst in c, gtr: d1-c2/f-e♭1. GIA (1993) G-3746 INST, also found in *Psalms for the Church Year,* vol. 5

137:3 Pasternak, Velvel. *Shiru Lonu (Sing Us One of the Songs of Zion)* (Hebrew transliterated). Gtr: M:d1-d2. Bloch (1971), found in *Songs of the Chassidim II*

138:00 Honegger, Arthur. *Confitebor tibi, Domine* (from *Trois Psaumes*) (French). Pno: d1-f2. Salabert (1963)

138:00 Marot, Clement. *Il faut que de tour mes espirits* (from *Trois Psaumes*) (French). Pno: f1-g2. Salabert (1963)

138:00 Matesky, Thelma. *I Will Praise Thee With My Whole Heart.* Pno: d1-a3. Mercury (1964)

138:00 (Psalm 139:00)
Row, Richard D. *Thy Right Hand Shall Hold Me.* Kbd: H:c1-g2; L:b♭1-f2. R. D. Row (1945)

139:00 Burgess, Dan and Harold Decou (arr. Bob Krogstad). *You Are There* (*Jane's Song*). Pno: b1-g2. Belwin Mills (1983), found in *Gospel & Inspirational Showstoppers*

139:00 (adapted)
Card, Michael. *Search Me and Know Me (Psalm 139).* Kbd: M:d1-d2. Birdwing (1990), found in *The Way of Wisdom*

139:00 (adapted)
Demarest, Alison. *Whither Shall I Go From Thy Spirit.* Pno: c1-e2. Canyon (1950)

139:00 (paraphrased)
McAfee, Don. *Psalm 139.* Kbd, inst in c: H:c1-g2; L:c1-e2. Abingdon (1973)

139:00 Mueller, Carl F. *Whither Shall I Go From Thy Spirit.* Kbd: H:f1-f♯2; L:d♯1-e2. Carl Fischer (1951)

139:00 SEE: Psalm 138:88. Row, Richard D. *Thy Right Hand Shall Hold Me*

139:00 Schinhan, Jan Philip. *Whither Shall I Go From Thy Spirit.* Pno: c♯1-g2. Brodt (1956)

139:00 Scrivener, Joseph. *Psalm 139.* M-Pno: c1-f2. Cormorant Press (1985)

139:00 Ward-Stephens. *Search Me, O God, and Know My Heart.* Pno: H:d1-a♭3; L:b1-f2. Chappell (1917), found in *Ward-Stephens Selected Psalms*

139:1 St. James, Rebecca (arr. Dennis Allen). *Psalm 139.* Kbd, gtr: a1-b2. Bibbitsong Music (1996), found in *25 Contemporary Solos*

139:1, 4, 8
Lekberg, Sven. *O Lord, Thou Hast Searched Me.* Org: b♭1-g2. G. Schirmer (1972)

139:1-18, 23 (adapted)
Joncas, Michael. *You Have Searched Me.* U-Kbd: c1-e♭2. GIA (1990) G-3241, also found in *Come to Me*

139:1-2, 5, 7-9, 11-18, 23-24
Cooney, Rory. *Psalm 139 (Wings of Dawn).* Gtr, fl: a1-d2. GIA (1990) G-3419, also found in *Safety Harbor*

139:1-2, 7-10 (based on)
Haas, David. *You've Searched Me.* Kbd, vc or bsn: d1-e2. GIA (1987), found in *As Water to the Thirsty*

139:1-4 Bennett, Sir William Sterndale. *O Lord, Thou Hast Searched Me Out* (from *The Woman of Samaria*). Kbd: Alto:c1-d2. Presser (1923), found in *Oratorio Repertoire,* vol. II

139:1-4 Bennett, Sir William Sterndale (ed. Heinrich Kiehl). *O Lord, Thou Hast Searched Me Out* (from *The Woman of Samaria*). Kbd: H:e♭1-f2; L or Alto:c1-d2. G. Schirmer (1913), found in *Anthology of Sacred Song–Alto*

139:1-4, 6-10, 23-24
Floyd, Carlisle. *O Lord, Thou Hast Searched Me and Known Me* (from *The Pilgrimage*). Kbd or orch: M:b1-g♭2. Boosey & Hawkes (1959), found in *Pilgrimage*

139:2-8, 13-15, 17-18 (based on)
Schutte, Daniel L. (pno acc. Randall DeBruyn). *You Are Near.* Cantor-Pno, gtr inst in c: c1-d2. NALR (1974); OCP 9503, also found in *Neither Silver Nor Gold*

139:4, 23-24
Dvorák, Antonín (ed. M. B. Stearns). *Search Me, O God (Sing Ye a Joyful Song!).* Pno: d1-d2. Coburn Press (1971), found in *Lift Up Your Voice*

139:7, 9-10
SEE: Psalm 23:4. O'Connor, Roc. *Guide Me, O God*

139:7-10 (based on; other)
Bach, J. S. *Erbarme dich (Ich armer Mensch)* (from Kantate Nr. 55) (German). Pno: Tenor:d-b♭2. Kalmus, found in *Arias from Church Cantatas for Tenor,* vol. II

139:7-10 (Book of Common Prayer)
Mahnke, Allan. *Psalm 139.* Kbd: c♯1-d2. Concordia (1992) 97-6093, found in *17 Psalms for Cantor and Congregation*

139:7-10 (Romans 8:38-39)
Winton, Mary. *Whither Shall I Go From Thy Spirit.* Kbd: M:d1-f2. Carl Fischer (1956), found in *Eight Scriptural Solos*

139:7-10, 12, 14, 23-24
VanNuys, Rena. *Whither Shall I Go.* Kbd: d♭1-g♭2. G. Schirmer (1950)

139:7-12 MacDermid, James G. *Whither Shall I Go From Thy Spirit.* Kbd: H:d1-g2; L:b♭1-e♭2. Forster (1937)

139:7-12 Selle, Thomas (ed. Klaus Vetter). *Herr, wo soll ich hingehen* (German). Duet-2 vlns: Sop:d1-e♭2/Tenor:d1-g2. Hänssler (n.d.), found in *Das geistliche konzert 87*

139:7-8 Beall, Mary Kay. *He Is There.* 2-part-Kbd: b1-c2. Hope (1990) PP 123

139:9-11, 14, 17
Fischer, Irwin. *If I Take the Wings of the Morning.* Kbd: d1-g2. American Composers Alliance (1964)

139:11 SEE: Isaiah 26:3. Speaks, Oley. *Thou Wilt Keep Him in Perfect Peace*

140:00 DeBese, Theodore. *O Dieu donne moi deliverance* (from *Trois Psaumes*) (French). Pno: c1-a♭3. Salabert (1963)

140:00 Honegger, Arthur. *Eripe Me Domine, ab homine malo* (from *Trois Psaumes*) (French). Pno: c1-a♭3. Salabert (1963)

140:00 Sessions, Roger. *Psalm 140.* Org: d♭1-b♭3. Marks Music (1964)

141:1-5, 8-9
Inwood, Paul. *Evening Psalm (Let My Prayer Rise Before You).* Kbd, gtr: c1-c2. OCP (1985), found in *Come to Set Us Free*

141:1-5, 8-9
Trapp, Lynn. *Psalm 141* (from *Four Psalm Settings*). U/Cantor-Org: e1-d2. MorningStar (1989) MSM-80-701

141:2 (other)
Archer, Malcolm. *Let Our Praise to You.* U/2-part-Org, (opt inst in c): c1-d2(f2). Kevin Mayhew (1991), found in *Our Praise To You*

141:3-4 SEE: Psalm 118:14-15. Scott, Charles P. *The Voice of Joy*

142:00 Rorem, Ned. *I Cried to the Lord* (from *A Cycle of Holy Songs*). Pno: H:b1-g2. Peer-Southern (1955)

142:00 Sowerby, Leo. *Psalm 142.* Org: e1-a3. H. W. Gray (1966)

142:1, 6 Dengler, Lee. *I Cried Unto the Lord.* Kbd: M:d1-g2. Augsburg (1995) 11-10608, found in *Songs of David*

143:6, 7 Bradshaw, Daniel. *Abide With Me; 'tis Eventide.* Kbd: M:d1-d2. Sonos (Jackman) (1997) 00434, found in *Sabbath Song*

143:7-8 SEE: Psalm 27:1. VanVollenhoven, Hanna. *Hear Me Speedily, O Lord!*

144:1-2 SEE: Psalm 18:32, 37. Vaughan Williams, Ralph. *The Pilgrim's Psalm*

144:9 (Psalm 145:1-6)
Dvorák, Antonín. *I Will Sing New Songs of Gladness,* op. 99, no. 5 (from *Biblical Songs*) (English/Czech/German). Pno: H or MH:g1-g2; ML or L:e♭1-e♭2; Bass:c-c1. Simrock; G. Schirmer (1991); R. D. Row (1955), found in *Dvorák,* op. 99, *Biblical Songs; Favorite Sacred Classics for Solo Singers* (MH/ML); *Sacred Classics* (H/L); *Second Book of Baritone/Bass Solos* (L); *Songs for Bass in a Comfortable* (Bass) *Range*

144:9 (Psalm 145:1-6)
Dvorák, Antonín (arr. Carl Fredrickson). *I Will Sing New Songs of Gladness,* op. 99, no. 5 (from *Biblical Songs*). Duet-Pno H: g1-g2/L:a1-d♭2. Simrock; G. Schirmer; R. D. Row (1955), found in *Sacred Duet Masterpieces,* bk 1

144:9 (Psalm 145:1-6)
Dvorák, Antonín (ed. Otaker Sourek). *Boze! Boze! Písen novou,* op. 99, no. 5 *(Herr, mein Gott, ich sing' en neues Lied; Song of Gladness Will I Sing Thee)* (from *Biblical Songs*) (Czech/German/ English). Pno: H:g1-g2. Masters Music (n.d.), found in *Biblical Songs for High Voice and Piano by Antonín Dvorák,* op. 99

144:9 (Psalm 145:1-6)
Dvorák, Antonín. *Lord, a New Song I Would Fashion,* op. 99, no. 5 (from *Biblical Songs*) (English only). Pno: H:g1-g2; L:e♭1-e♭2. International (1962), found in *Biblical Songs: A Cycle of Ten Songs,* op. 99

145:00 Canedo, Ken. *Psalm 145.* Kbd: M:c1-d2. Unity (Lorenz) (1997), found in *Wedding Psalms*

145:00 (based on)
Farrell, Jim (arr. Craig S. Kingsbury). *Sing a Joyful Song.* Cantor-Org, gtr, hbells, inst in c, opt duet: d1-d2(c1-e2). OCP (1984) 9292CC, also found in *Jesus, Lord*

145:00 (Psalm 37:00)
Fischer, Irwin. *Delight Thyself in the Lord.* Kbd: e1-f2. American Composers Alliance (1959)

145:00 LaForge, Frank. *I Will Extol Thee.* Kbd: Med. Carl Fischer (1943) V1679

145:00 SEE: Psalm 119:105. MacDermid, James G. *Thy Word Is a Lamp*

145:00 SEE: Psalm 129:00. Milhaud, Darius. *Cantate de Psaume*

145:00 Schmutz, Albert D. *I Will Extol Thee.* Kbd: d1-e2. Abingdon (1976) APM 633, also found in *Sacred Songs*

145:00 SEE: Psalm 89:00. Schoenbachler, Tim. *Forever I Will Sing*

145:1-2 Bach, J. S. (ed. Graham Batable). *Laudamus Te* (from *Mass in b minor*) (Latin). Cont, vln: Sop:c1-e2. International (1999) 3473, found in *12 Arias*

145:1-2 (based on)
Brixi, Franz Xaver (ed. David Patrick). *Laudamus Te* (from *Missa Integra in D*) (English/Latin). Kbd: b1-f2. Boosey & Hawkes (1996), found in *Sacred Songs for the Soloist: 20 Songs on Religious Texts for Medium Low Voice*

145:1-2 Mozart, W. A. *Laudamus Te* (from *Grand Mass in c minor*). Kbd, trpt, timp: Sop. Roger Dean (2001) 30/1676R, found in *Festival Arias for soprano, mezzo–soprano and trumpet*

145:1-2 (based on)
Vivaldi, Antonio (arr. Vernon M. Whaley). *We Praise You God (Laudamus Te)* (from *Gloria,* R. 589) (English/Latin). 2-part-Kbd: f♯1-f♯2/d1-e2. Integra (1993), found in *Classic Choruses for Young Voices*

145:1-2, 8-11, 13-14
Trapp, Lynn. *Psalm 145* (from *Four Psalm Settings*). U-Org: d1-c2. MorningStar (1989) MSM-80-701

145:1-3, 8-9 (Psalm 150:1-2, 6; Doxology)
Courtney, Craig. *Praise Him!* Duet-Kbd: H:d1-f2(a3)/L:d1-e2. Beckenhorst (1989) BP1350, also found in *Duets for the Master*

145:1-3, 8-9, 13b-14, 17-18, 21
Folkemer, Stephen P. *Psalm 145.* Duet-Org, trpt. GIA (1980) G-2337

145:1-3, 8-10, 21
Hartley, Walter S. *Allegro con brio* (from *A Psalm Cycle*). Pno, fl: c1-a3. Presser (1970)

145:1, 3, 16, 18-20
Molique, Wilhelm Bernhard. *I Will Extol Thee, My God* (from *Abraham*). Kbd: Sop:f1-b♭3. G. Schirmer (1901), found in *Anthology of Sacred Song–Soprano; Schirmer's Singer's Library: Soprano Arias from Oratorios*

145:1-6 SEE: Psalm 144:9. Dvorák, Antonín. *I Will Sing New Songs of Gladness,* op. 99, no. 5

145:1-13 (Isaiah 9:6; Luke 19:37-40; Philippians 2:9-11)
Lyles, Dwight and Niles Borop. *Proclaim the Glory of the Lord.* Kbd: M:a1-e2; MH:c1-f2. Word (1984), found in *The Lord Is My Light* (M); *Low Voice Classics; Our God Reigns* (MH)

145:1-13 (Luke 2:1-20; adapted)
Smiley, Billy and Bill George. *Worship the King.* Kbd or Trax: d1-f♯2. Paragon (1984), found in *The Lord Is My Light*

145:1, 15-18
Kaufmann, Julius (arr. Carl Fredrickson). *I Will Magnify Thee* (adapted to the first prelude of J. S. Bach). Pno: H:e♭1-g2; L:c1-e2. G. Schirmer (1957)

145:2 SEE: Psalm 32:11. Huhn, Bruno S. *Be Glad, O Ye Righteous*

145:2, 9 Handel, G. F. *Every day Will I Give Thanks.* Org: d1-f♯2. Coburn Press (1971), found in *Lift Up Your Voice*

145:3a (based on)
Gollner, Ronald E. *Great Is the Lord.* Kbd, gtr: c1-c2. Lorenz (1999), found in *Take the Nations*

145:3a (based on)
Smith, Michael W. and Deborah D. Smith. *Great Is the Lord.* Kbd: H:c♯1-f♯2; MH:b1-f♯2(g2); L:b1-d2. Meadowgreen (1983), found in *The Big Book of Contemporary Christian Favorites* (MH); *The Big Book of Contemporary Christian Favorites,* 2nd Edition (MH); *Contemporary Christian Classics,* vol. 2 (H); *Face to Face* (L); *Low Voice Classics; Our God Reigns* (MH); *Ray Boltz: The Classics* (MH); *The Song Book,* vol. III (M); *Songs for Praise and Worship* (MH); *WOW Worship Songbook Green*

145:3a (based on)
Smith, Michael W. and Deborah D. Smith. *Great Is the Lord.* Duet-Kbd: H:d1-a3/L:c1-d2. Meadowgreen (2000) Hope 8065, found in *Sacred Vocal Duets for High and Low Voice*

145:3a (based on)
Smith, Michael W. and Deborah D. Smith. (arr. Steven V. Taylor). *Great Is the Lord.* 2-part-Kbd, gtr or Trax: b1-d2. Meadowgreen (1982, this arr. 1988), found in *25 Songs for Two-Part Choir*

145:3, 4 (and Alleluia)
Schütz, Heinrich. *Der Herr ist gross und sehr löblich,* SWV 286 (German). Duet-Cont: S/S. Hänssler (1981) HE 20.286

145:3-4 Schütz, Heinrich. *Der Herr ist gross,* SWV 286 (from *Kleine geistliche konzerte*) (German). Duet-Cont: Sop/Sop:c1-f2. Bärenreiter (n.v.)

145:3-4 Schütz, Heinrich (ed. Bradley L. Almquist). *Der Herr ist gross,* SWV 286 (from *Kleine geistliche konzerte*) (German/English). Duet-Cont or kbd and bass inst: S/A:c1-f2. Alliance Music (1996) AMP 0126

145:3-4 Schütz, Heinrich (arr. Don McAfee). *Great Is the Lord,* SWV 286 *(Der Herr ist gross)* (from *Kleine geistliche Konzerte*) (German/English). Duet-Cont: Equal voices:d1-f♯2/d1-g2. Belwin Mills (1977) CP131, also found in *Eight Sacred Duets*

145:6 SEE: Psalm 29:11. Pasternak, Velvel. *Yiru Es Adõnoy*

145:8-10, 17-18 (adapted)
Cotter, Jeanne. *Our God Is Compassion.* U/2-part-Kbd, gtr, vc: c♯1-c♯2(c♯-e1). GIA (1993), found in *When Love Is Found*

145:9 SEE: Psalm 104:1-3, 24. Baumgartner, H. Leroy. *O Lord, My God, Thou Art Very Great*

145:10 (Revelation 4:8b)
Dykes, John Bacchus (choral arr. Steven V. Taylor). *Holy, Holy, Holy.* U/2-part-Kbd or Trax: d♯1-f2/c-e♭1. O'Ryan Music (1990), found in *25 Songs for Two-Part Choir,* vol. II

145:10-12, 17-18
Benati. *All Thy Works Shall Praise Thee.* Kbd: H:e1-f♯2; L:c1-d2. R. D. Row (1963), found in *Church Soloists Favorites,* bk 1

145:13 SEE: I Chronicles 16:29. Schubert, Franz. *The Grand Alleluia*

145:13b-16
Wienhorst, Richard. *The Lord Is Faithful.* U-Org, fl: c1-d2. Mark Foster (1985) MF 705

145:15-16
Boyce, William. *The Eyes of All Wait Upon Thee, O Lord,* (no. 6 from *Lord, Thou Hast Been Our Refuge*). Kbd or orch: Alto:a1-c2. Oxford (1977)

145:15-16, 18
Kirk, Theron. *The Eyes of All Wait Upon Thee.* 2-part mixed-Pno: c1-c2/c-d1. G. Schirmer (1982) 12445

145:18 SEE: Psalm 46:10a. Bitgood, Roberta. *Be Still and Know That I Am God*

146:00 (Book of Common Prayer)
Dobry, Wallace. *Psalm 146: Praise the Lord, O My Soul (Lauda, anima mea)* (from *A Trio of Psalms*) (English/Latin). 2-part-Kbd: d1-f2. MorningStar (1994) MSM-80-706

146:1 Stockhommer, A. (arr. Velvel Pasternak). *Hal'lu nafshi (Praise the Lord, O My Soul)* (Hebrew transliterated). Gtr: M:a1-d2. Bloch (1971), found in *Songs of the Chassidim II*

146:1-2 (Psalm 148:1-3)
Floyd, Carlisle. *Praise the Lord, O My Soul* (from *The Pilgrimage*). Kbd or orch: M:d1-f$\sharp$2. Boosey & Hawkes (1959), found in *Pilgrimage*

146:1-2 Spies, Claudio. *Praise the Lord, O My Soul* (from *Five Psalms*). Duet-Fl, fg, hn, mand, vla, vc: Sop:f1-b3/Tenor:d$\flat$-g$\sharp$1. Boosey & Hawkes (1962)

146:1-6 (based on)
Rieth, Mildred F. *Praise the Lord.* U/2-part-Kbd, gtr, inst in c: b$\flat$1-b$\flat$2(d1-c2). OCP (1969), found in *Yahweh Is My Shepherd*

146:2 Greene, Maurice (ed. Earnest Murphy). *I Will Sing Unto the Lord.* Duet-Kbd: H:e1-f2/M:b1-b2. McAfee Music (1973), found in *The Baroque Songbook.*

146:2-10 (adapted)
Joncas, Michael. *I Will Praise the Lord.* Gtr: c1-b$\flat$2. GIA (1990) G-3434, also found in *Come to Me*

147:00 Goode, Jack. *Psalm 147.* Kbd: c$\sharp$1-f2. Abingdon (1967), found in *Seven Sacred Solos*

147:00 SEE: Psalm 129:00. Milhaud, Darius. *Cantate de Psaume*

147:1 SEE: Psalm 66:2. Wolaver, Bill and Robin. *Make His Praise Glorious*

147:1, 5a, 7a, 12a
Powell, Robert J. *Sing Praises to Our God.* 2-part-Org: Treble:(b1)d1-e2. Concordia (1988) 98-2813

147:1, 15 (based on)
Telemann, Georg Philipp (arr. Hal H. Hopson). *Sing to the Lord, Rejoice!* 2-part-Kbd: b1-d2/b$\flat$-c1. Alfred (1992) 4246

147:3-4 SEE: Psalm 104:1-3, 24. Baumgartner, H. Leroy. *O Lord, My God, Thou Art Very Great*

147:3-7a, 8-9, 18a
Cartwright, Marion L. *Great Is Our Lord.* Pno: d1-g2. Huntzinger (1948), found in *Choice Sacred Songs for Home or Church Services*

147:4 SEE: Psalm 4:8. Buck, Dudley. *I Will Lay Me Down in Peace*

148:00 Delaney, Maureen. *Psalm 148.* Kbd: H: c1-f2. Abingdon (1991), found in *O Sing to the Lord!*

148:00 Hoy, Dawn Riske. *Psalm 148.* Kbd: M:c1-d2. Unity (Lorenz) (1997), found in *Wedding Psalms*

148:00 (Psalm 149:00, 150:00; based on)
Hurd, Bob (arr. Craig S. Kingsbury). *I Want to Praise Your Name.* U/2-part-Org, gtr, inst in c: (b1)e1-d2. OCP (1984), found in *In the Breaking of the Bread*

148:00 Rorem, Ned. *Praise Ye the Lord* (from *A Cycle of Holy Songs*). Pno: H:d1-g2. Peer-Southern (1955)

148:00 Stainer, John (arr. Austin C. Lovelace). *Praise the Lord Ye Heavens.* U-Kbd: Med. Choristers Guild (1988) CGA-453

148:00 (other)
Talbot, John Michael. *Word of God Became Man.* Gtr: e1-e2. Birdwing (1985), found in *Praise, Prayer and Worship*

148:00 (other)
Weber, Carl M. von (ed. Dorothy Allan Park). *Praise the Lord, Ye Heavens.* Kbd: M:c1-a3. Waterloo Music (1960)

148:1 SEE: Psalm 47:1. Wagner, Douglas E. *Clap Hands, Be Glad!*

148:1-3 SEE: Psalm 146:1-2. Floyd, Carlisle. *Praise the Lord, O My Soul*

148:1, 3, 7, 9, 11-13 (Psalm 150:1, 3-6)
Fischer, Irwin. *Praise Ye the Lord.* Kbd: c1-g2. American Composers Alliance (1966)

148:1-3, 7, 9-10, 12-13 (adapted)
Michaels, John (arr. Craig S. Kingsbury). *O Bless the Lord.* U-Org, inst in c: a1-d2. OCP (1984), found in *Jesus, Lord*

148:1-4, 12-13 (adapted)
Cotter, Jeanne. *Let All Praise the Name of the Lord.* U/2-part-Kbd, gtr: d$\sharp$1-e2(a1-e1). GIA (1993), found in *When Love Is Found*

148:1-6 Childs, David. *Psalm 148.* Org: f$\sharp$1-a3. Abingdon (1966) H: APM 390; L: APM 385, found in *Seven Psalms for Voice and Organ*

148:1-6, 9, 11 (Psalm 149:1)
MacDermid, James G. *Sing Unto the Lord a New Song.* Kbd: H:d1-a3; L:b1-f2. Forster (1939)

148:3-5, 12-13
SEE: Psalm 100:4. O'Connor, Roc. *In Praise of His Name*

149:00 SEE: Psalm 148:00. Hurd, Bob. *I Want to Praise Your Name*

149:1 SEE: Psalm 148:1-6, 9, 11. MacDermid, James G. *Sing Unto the Lord a New Song*

149:1-3 Roff, Joseph. *Sing Praise to the Lord.* Cantor-Org, opt duet: MH:d1-e2/M:b1-c2. OCP (1989) OCP 9146

149:1-4 Fromm, Herbert. *Psalm 149* (from *Four Psalms*). Kbd: e♭1-g2. Transcontinental (1971)

149:1-4 (Book of Common Prayer)
Mahnke, Allan. *Psalm 149.* Cantor-Kbd: c1-c2. Concordia (1992) 97-6093, found in *17 Psalms for Cantor and Congregation*

149:3 (based on)
Pethel, Stan. *Sing a New Song.* 2-part mixed-Kbd: c1-d2/c-d1. Triune (1988) TUM 327

150:00 (adapted)
Adler, Samuel. *Praise the Lord,* (no. 1 from *Twelve Songs of Praise*). U-Org: d1-e2. Oxford (1988) 94.505

150:00 (adapted)
Anderson, Ronald. *Psalm of Joy.* 2-part-Kbd: c1-e2. AMSI (1982) 423

150:00 Bantock, Granville. *Praise Ye the Lord.* Kbd: d1-f2. Cramer (1924)

150:00 Butt, James. *Psalm 150.* Org: e1-f2. Sphemusations (1961)

150:00 Goldman, Edward M. *Psalm 150.* Kbd: Med. World Library (1965)

150:00 Koch, John. *Praise the Lord* (from *Songs of David*). Stg qt, fl: e♭1-g2. American Music Centre

150:00 Rorem, Ned. *Praise Ye the Lord* (from *A Cycle of Holy Songs*). Pno: H:d1-a3. Peer-Southern (1955)

150:00 Rubbra, Edmund. *Psalm 150,* op. 61, no. 3 *(Praise Ye the Lord)* (from *Three Psalms for Low Voice*). Kbd: M:b1-f2. Alfred Lengnick (1947) 3553

150:00 Schilling, Hans Ludwig. *Psalm 150 in the Form of a Ciacona.* Kbd: H. Breitkopf & Härtel (1964) 6445

150:00 (based on)
Schutte, Daniel L. *Psalm 150.* U/2-part-Gtr: d1-e2. NALR (1974), found in *Neither Silver Nor Gold*

150:00 (paraphrased)
Weaver, Powell. *Praise the Lord His Glories Show (Alleluia).* Kbd: e1-g2. Galaxy (1948) 1.666.7

150:00 Weinberger, Jaromir. *Psalm 150.* Org: H:c1-b♭3. H. W. Gray (1940)

150:00 SEE: Psalm 66:2. Wolaver, Bill and Robin. *Make His Praise Glorious*

150:1 (Colossians 3:1-2; adapted)
Borneman, Bruce and Judi. *It's Time to Praise the Lord (Don't You Know).* Kbd: a1-a2. Maranatha! (1981), found in *The Lord Is My Light*

150:1-2, 6
SEE: Psalm 145:1-3, 8-9. Courtney, Craig. *Praise Him!*

150:1-3, 5-6 (paraphrased)
Perry, Dave and Jean Perry. *Psalm 150.* 2-part-Kbd: e1-f2/b♭1-d2. Alfred (1991) 7976

150:1, 3-6
SEE: Psalm 148:1, 3, 7, 9, 11-13. Fischer, Irwin. *Praise Ye the Lord*

150:1, 4, 7, 14-15 (Isaac Watts)
Croft, William (arr. K. K. Davis). *The Mighty God Hath Spoken.* Kbd: M:d1-f2. Carl Fischer (1948), found in *Sing Unto the Lord,* vol. 1

150:1-5 Misetich, Marianne. *A Joyful Sound.* Kbd, gtr, bass, inst in c: b♭1-c2. OCP (1973, 1982), found in *Comfort My People*

150:1-5 Schutte, Daniel L. *With Merry Dancing.* Gtr: b1-e2. NALR (1974), found in *Neither Silver Nor Gold*

150:2-6 Page, Anna Laura. *Hallelujah! Praise Ye the Lord.* U-Kbd, 2-octave hdbls, perc: c1-e2. Kirkland House (1988) K 102

150:3-4, 6
SEE: Psalm 148:00. Hurd, Bob. *I Want to Praise Your Name*

150:6 (Isaiah 55:12; other)
Tunney, Melodie (arr. Joseph Linn). *Sound His Praise.* Kbd (Trax or orch): c1-f♯2. Laurel Press (1984) Orch: AN-2562a, also found in *The Lord Is My Light*

PROVERBS

1:7-9 Leichtling, Alan. *The Fear of the Lord* (from *Two Proverbs*). Cl trio: Mez:b1-g2. Seesaw Music (1969)

1:20-21 SEE: Proverbs 22:17-18. Beale, James. *On Wisdom*

2:1-5 (Proverbs 3:1-6, 23-24)
Tindall, Adrienne M. *Trust in the Lord.* Kbd: e1-g2. Darcy Press (1994), found in *Sacred Solos by Adrienne Tindall,* vol. III

2:19-22 Leichtling, Alan. *The Lord By Wisdom Founded Earth* (from *Two Proverbs*). Cl trio: Mez:c1-a3. Seesaw Music (1969)

3:1, 5-6 Haydn, F. Joseph (arr. Carl Fredrickson). *Trust in the Lord.* Kbd: c♯1-e2. R. D. Row (1959), found in *Sacred Song Masterpieces,* bk 1

3:1-6 Isaacson, Michael. *B'Ni* (*My Son*) (Hebrew). Transcontinental (1991), found in *Seasons in Time,* vol. 1

3:1-6, 23-24
SEE: Proverbs 2:1-5. Tindall, Adrienne M. *Trust in the Lord*

3:5-6 Davis, Katherine K. *Trust in the Lord.* Kbd: H:c1-g2; L:b1-f2. Galaxy (1946) H: 1.1551.7; L: 1.552.7

3:5-6 Meyers, Don (arr. Mark Barnard). *Trust in the Lord.* Kbd: d1-d2. Lorenz (1995), found in *Reflections and Meditations*

3:5-6 (Proverbs 4:18)
Sullivan, Sir Arthur. *Trust in the Lord* (from *The Light of the World*). Kbd: c1-d2. Coburn Press (1971), found in *Lift Up Your Voice*

3:5-6 (Proverbs 4:18)
Sullivan, Sir Arthur. *Trust in the Lord* (from *The Prodigal Son*). Kbd: a-f♯1. Presser (1923), found in *Oratorio Reperoitre,* vol. IV

3:5-6, 19-20, 25-26 (Proverbs 4:18-19)
MacDermid, James G. *Trust in the Lord With All Thine Heart.* Kbd: H:e♭1-a♭3; L:c1-f2. Forster (1940)

3:13, 15-18
Thiman, Eric H. *Happy Is the Man (Proverbs)* (from *Two Biblical Songs*). Org: b1-e2. Novello (1953, 1981), found in *The Church Soloist*

3:13, 16, 17, 19, 21
Fischer, Irwin. *The Lord By Wisdom Hath Founded Earth.* Kbd: e1-f2. American Composers Alliance (1967)

3:13-23 Mader, Clarence. *Happy Is the Man* (from *Three Biblical Songs*). Org: M:d1-e2. WIM (1975) 128

3:17-18 Weiner, Lazar. *Etz Chayim* (from *Anim Z'Miros*) (Hebrew). Transcontinental (1964) (n.v.)

3:24 (Isaiah 42:6; Jeremiah 31:3)
Wolf, Hugo. *With an Everlasting Love.* Kbd: Med. Coburn Press (1971), found in *Lift Up Your Voice*

4:18 SEE: Isaiah 1:18. Barker, Clement W. *The Path of the Just*

4:18 SEE: Proverbs 3:5-6. Sullivan, Sir Arthur. *Trust in the Lord*

4:18-19 SEE: Proverbs 3:5-6, 19-20, 25-26. MacDermid, James G. *Trust in the Lord With All Thine Heart*

8:00 (taken from)
MacDermid, James G. *Doth Not Wisdom Cry?* Kbd: H:e♭1-a♭3; L:c1-f2. Forster (1945)

8:32, 35-36
SEE: Proverbs 22:17-18. Beale, James. *On Wisdom.*

9:1 SEE: Psalm 122:1. Hurd, Bob. *Pueblo De Dios*

12:19 Beale, James. *On Truth* (from *Proverbs*). Pno/celeste, Eng hn, vibraphone: Bass:F♯-a1. Composers Facsimilie Edition (1960)

12:28 SEE: Psalm 25:4, 7. Krieg, Melita. *The Way of Righteousness*

22:17-18 (Proverbs 1:20-21; Proverbs 8:32, 35-36; Proverbs 26:7)
Beale, James. *On Wisdom* (from *Proverbs*). Pno/celeste, Eng hn, vibraphone: Bass:a-c1. Composers Facsimilie Edition (1960)

24:19 SEE: Isaiah 1:18. Barker, Clement W. *The Path of the Just*

24:30-31, 33-34
Beale, James. *On Laziness* (from *Proverbs*). Pno/celeste, Eng hn, vibraphone: Bass:g♭-e♭1. Composers Facsimilie Edition (1960)

26:7 SEE: Proverbs 22:17-18. Beale, James. *On Wisdom*

26:21-23 Beale, James. *On Slander* (from *Proverbs*). Pno/celeste, Eng hn, vibraphone: Bass:c-b1. Composers Facsimilie Edition (1960)

31:10-11, 17, 20, 26, 28, 30
Zaimont, Judith Lang. *A Woman of Valor* (Hebrew/English). Stg qt: c1-g♯2. American Composers Alliance (n.d.)

31:10-17 Pasternak, Velvel. *Eshes Chayil (A Woman of Worth)* (Hebrew transliterated). Gtr: M:a1-a2. Bloch (1971), found in *Songs of the Chassidim II*

31:10, 25, 28, 31
Gideon, Miriam. *Woman of Valor* (from *A Woman of Valor*). Stg qt: f1-g♯2. American Composers Alliance (n.d.)

31:10-31 (based on)
Fettke, Tom. *Far Above Riches.* Kbd, gtr:e1-f2. Pilot Point (1998) MB-825, found in *Solos from the Word*

31:20, 28-30
Adler, Samuel. *A Woman of Valor*. Kbd: g1-g2. Transcontinental (1965) T.V. 568

31:25-28 Pasternak, Velvel. *Oz V'Hodor (Dignity and Honor Are Her Garb)* (Hebrew transliterated). Gtr: M:f1-d2. Bloch (1971), found in *Songs of the Chassidim II*

31:25-31 (based on)
Wilson, John Floyd. *A Worthy Woman.* Kbd: d1-d2. Hope (1974), found in *Everything for the Church Soloist*

ECCLESIASTES

1:2 (Ecclesiastes 2:22-23; Ecclesiastes 8:15)
Pinkham, Daniel. *Vanity of Vanities* (no. 1 from *Three Songs from Ecclesiastes*). Pno/stg qt: H:b1-a3. E. C. Schirmer (1963)

2:22-23 SEE: Ecclesiastes 1:2. Pinkham, Daniel. *Vanity of Vanities*

3:1-3 Steinberg, Ben. *Lakol Z'Man (To Everything There Is a Season)* (Hebrew/English). Transcontinental (1979) (n.v.)

3:1-8 Courtney, Craig. *There Is a Time.* Kbd: M:c1-f2. Beckenhorst (1995, 1997) BP1463, also found in *Sacred Solos of Craig Courtney*

3:1-8 (based on)
Goemanne, Noel. *A Time for Everything.* Org: d1-e2. GIA (1980) G-2380

3:1-8 (based on)
Kavanaugh, John. *All Things Have Their Time.* Unison (2-part)-Gtr: d1-g2. NALR (1974), found in *Neither Silver Nor Gold*

3:1-8 Koch, Frederick. *For Everything Its Season.* Kbd: c1-e2. Carl Fischer (1990), found in *Five Sacred Solos for Worship Service*

3:1-8 Pinkham, Daniel. *To Everything There Is a Season* (no. 3 from *Three Songs from Ecclesiastes*). Pno/stg qt: H:b1-a3. E. C. Schirmer (1963)

3:1-8 SEE: Psalm 27:13-14. Sacco, John. *God's Time*

3:1-8 Toch, Ernst. *There Is a Season to Everything.* Fl, vln, cl, vc: d1-a2. Affiliated Musicians (1953) 6003

3:1-9 Kirkland, Terry. *God's Good Time.* U/2-part-Kbd, perc: c1-d2. Triune (1986) TUM 292

3:1-9 (Matthew 13:4-8; based on)
Ridge, M. D. (acc. Patrick Loomis). *Parable.* U/2-part-Kbd, gtr, inst in c: b1-d2(e2). OCP (1987, 1991), found in *In Every Age; Return to Me: Music for Funerals and Healing,* vol. 1

3:19-22 Brahms, Johannes (ed. Carl Deis). *Denn es gehet dem menschen (One Thing Befalleth the Beasts)* (from *Vier ernste gesang*) (German/English). Pno: M:a-f1. G. Schirmer (1964) 1678; Abindgon (1964)

4:1-3 Brahms, Johannes (ed. Carl Deis). *Ich wandte mich und sahe an (I Journeyed on My Way)* (from *Vier ernste Gesang*) (German/English). Pno: M:a-f1. G. Schirmer (1964) 1678; Abindgon (1964)

8:15 SEE: Ecclesiastes 1:2. Pinkham, Daniel. *Vanity of Vanities*

9:7-9 Pinkham, Daniel. *Go Thy Way, Eat Thy Bread With Joy* (no. 3 from *Three Songs from Ecclesiastes*). Pno/stg qt: H:b1-a3. E. C. Schirmer (1963)

12:1-7 Scott, John Prindle. *Remember Now Thy Creator.* Pno: H:f1-g2; L:d1-e2. Harold Flammer (1920)

12:1-8 Eggert, Fred E. *Remember Now Thy Creator.* Pno: H:c♯1-e2; L:b1-d2. Heidelberg Press (1919)

SONG OF SONGS

1:1-2 (Song of Songs 3:2; Song of Songs 8:14)
Sharlin, William. *Shir Hashirim (Song of Songs)* (Hebrew). Kbd: H; M. Transcontinental (1985) (n.v.)

1:2 Saltzman, Peter. *Kiss Me, Make Me Drunk With Your Kisses* (from *A 'Song of Songs' Cycle*). Pno: M:c1-e2. Oxford (2000)

1:00 - 8:14
Glick, Srul Irving. *Seven Tableaux from the Song of Songs.* Pno, vc, vln: S. Canadian Music Centre (1992)

2:00 Blackford, Richard. *From the Song of Songs.* M-Pno: b♭1-b♭3. Oxford (1985) ISBN 0 19 345164 6

2:1 Saltzman, Peter. *I Am the Rose of Sharon* (from *A 'Song of Songs' Cycle*). Pno: M:e1-f2. Oxford (2000)

2:1-3a LaMontaine, John. *I Am the Rose of Sharon and the Lily of the Valley* (from *Songs of the Rose of Sharon,* op. 6). Pno (orch red.): d1-a3. Broude (1962)

2:1-5 Bugatch, Samuel. *Ani Chavatselet Hasharon (I am the Rose of Sharon)* (Hebrew/English). Pno: d1-g2. Transcontinental (1967)

2:2-3 Richards, Stephen. *A Lily Among Thorns.* H; M. Transcontinental (1983)

2:3-6 Thornton, William. *As the Apple Tree* (from *Solomon Songs*). Pno: M:b♭1-f2. Southern (1989) V-82

2:3b-5 LaMontaine, John. *I Sat Down Under the Shadow* (from *Songs of the Rose of Sharon,* op. 6). Pno (orch red.): f♯1-g2. Broude (1962)

2:4 Saltzman, Peter. *I Am in the Fever of Love* (from *A 'Song of Songs' Cycle*). Pno: M:b1-f♯2. Oxford (2000)

2:6 LaMontaine, John. *His Left Hand Is Under My Head, and His Right Hand Doth Embrace Me* (from *Songs of the Rose of Sharon,* op. 6). Pno (orch red.): f1-d2. Broude (1962)

2:8 (other; based on the Song of Songs)
Manion, Tim. *Lord of Glory.* U/2-part-Gtr: d1-c2(e2). NALR (1976), found in *A Dwelling Place*

2:8-10a LaMontaine, John. *The Voice of My Beloved! Behold, He Cometh* (from *Songs of the Rose of Sharon,* op. 6). Pno (orch red.): c♯1-b♭3. Broude (1962)

2:8-13 Barkan, Emanuel. *Hark, My Beloved.* Pno: e♭1-b2. Transcontinental (1966)

2:10 (Song of Songs 8:6)
Card, Michael and Scott Brasher *Arise, My Love.* Kbd, gtr: a1-c2. Birdwing (1990) found in *Greatest Songs of Michael Card*

2:10-11 Nelson, Rachelle. *Ana Dodi* (Hebrew). Transcontinental (1987)

2:10-12 SEE: Ruth 1:16-17. Haas, David. *Whereever You Go*

2:10-12 Kingsley, Gershon. *Rise Up My Love* (from *Three Sacred Songs*). Kbd, vc: b♭1-f2. Transcontinental (1969)

2:10-13 (Song of Songs 6:3)
Goldman, Maurice. *I Am My Beloved's.* H; M. Transcontinental (1984)

2:10b-13 LaMontaine, John. *Rise Up, My Love, My Fair One, and Come Away* (from *Songs of the Rose of Sharon,* op. 6). Pno (orch red.): d♯1-a3. Broude (1962)

2:10-13b Rochberg, George. *Rise Up My Love* (from *Four Songs of Solomon*). Pno: H:d1-a3. E. C. Schirmer (1949), found in *The Sacred Collection* (H/L)

2:10-13 Samama, Leo. *My Beloved Spake* (from *Wedding Cantata*). Org: Tenor:f1-a3. WIM (1974) 118

2:10-13 Thornton, William. *Rise Up, My Love* (from *Solomon Songs*). Pno: M:b1-g2. Southern (1989) V-82

2:10-13 Ultan, Lloyd. *Wedding Song.* Unacc: d1-f2. American Composers Alliance (1990)

2:10-18 Helfman, Max. *The Voice of My Beloved.* Kbd: c1-a♭3. Transcontinental (1969) TV 529, also found in *Song of Songs / 95*

2:11-13 Bilchick, Ruth Coleman. *The Song of Songs.* Kbd: Med. American Music Centre (1972)

2:13 SEE: Hosea 2:21, 22. Adler, Samuel. *I Will Betroth Her Unto Me*

2:14 LaMontaine, John. *O My Dove, That Art in the Clefts of the Rock* (from *Songs of the Rose of Sharon,* op. 6). Pno (orch red.): e♯1-g♯2. Broude (1962)

2:14 Thomson, Virgil. *O My Dove,* (no. 3 from *Five Phrases Song of Solomon*). Perc: e♭1-a3. American Music Edition (1953) 96 / Song of Songs

2:16 (based on)
Britten, Benjamin. *Canticle I–My Beloved Is Mine and I am His,* op. 40 *(My Beloved is Mine and I am His).* Pno: H:d♭2-g2. Boosey & Hawkes (1949)

2:16 (Song of Songs 7:00; Song of Songs 8:6)
McCray, James. *Set Me as a Seal* (from *Rites of Love*). Pno: M:c♯1-g2. Leyerle (1989)

2:16-17 LaMontaine, John. *My Beloved Is Mine and I am His* (from *Songs of the Rose of Sharon,* op. 6). Pno (orch red.): b1-a♭3. Broude (1962)

3:1-2 Saltzman, Peter. *I Longed For My Love Sharon* (from *A 'Song of Songs' Cycle*). Pno: M:d1-a♭2. Oxford (2000)

3:1-2 Thomson, Virgil. *By Night,* (no. 5 from *Five Phrases Song of Solomon*). Perc: g1-a3. American Music Edition (1953) 96 / Song of Song

3:1, 3 Foss, Lukas. *By Night on My Bed* (from *The Song of Songs*). Pno or orch: d♭1-a3. Carl Fischer (1950) 3661

3:1-3 Archer, Violet. *Requiem* (from *Three Biblical Songs*). Pno: d1-g2. Canadian Music Centre (1972)

3:1-3 (Song of Songs 4:16; Song of Songs 5:7) Thornton, William. *I Sought Him* (from *Solomon Songs*). Pno: M:a1-g2. Southern (1989) V-82

3:2 SEE: Song of Songs 1:1-2. Sharlin, William. *Shir Hashirim*

3:9-11 Samama, Leo. *Thou Hast Ravished My Heart* (from *Wedding Cantata*). Org: e1-a3. WIM (1974) 118

4:1 Rochberg, George. *Behold! Thou Art Fair* (from *Four Songs of Solomon*). Pno: H:f1-b♭3. Presser (1975), found in *The Sacred Collection* (H/L)

4:9-10, 16
Cohen, Gerald. *Libavtini achoti chala (You Have Captured My Heart, My Own, My Bride).* (Hebrew transliterated). M-Pno: d1-g2. Oxford (2001), found in *Come Before God with Joyous Song*

4:9-11 Samama, Leo. *Wedding Cantata,* mvt. 2. Org: Tenor:a-a2. WIM (1974) 118

4:16 Foss, Lukas. *Awake, O North Wind* (from *The Song of Songs*). Pno or orch: d♭1-a3. Carl Fischer (1950) 366

4:16 SEE: Song of Songs 3:1-3. Thornton, William. *I Sought Him*

5:7 SEE: Song of Songs 3:1-3. Thornton, William. *I Sought Him*

5:16 Schiller, Benjie Ellen. *Zeh Dodi* (Hebrew). Transcontinental (1992)

6:3 SEE: Song of Songs 2:10-13. Goldman, Maurice. *I am My Beloved's*

6:3 Thomson, Virgil. *I am My Beloved's* (no. 4 from *Five Phrases Song of Solomon*). Perc: g1-a3. American Music Edition (1953)

6:12 SEE: Ruth 1:16-17. Hurd, Bob. *Where You Go*

6:13 Thomson, Virgil. *Return, O Shulamite!,* (no. 2 from *Five Phrases Song of Solomon*). Perc: e1-a3. American Music Edition (1953)

7:6 Vogel, Howard. *Behold, How Fair and Pleasant*. Org: c1-f2. Belwin Mills (1969), found in *Song of Songs / 97*

7:6-7 SEE: Ruth 1:16-17. Haas, David. *Whereever You Go*

7:10-14 Gottlieb, Jack. *Come, My Beloved.* Pno, fl: H. Transcontinental (1991) 983051

7:11 Foss, Lukas. *Come My Beloved* (from *The Song of Songs*). Pno or orch: d♭1-a3. Carl Fischer (1950) 3661

7:11 Rochberg, George. *Come, My Beloved* (from *Four Songs of Solomon*). Pno: H:c♯1-a3. Presser (1975), found in *The Sacred Collection* (H/L)

7:11-13 Overby, Rolf Peter. *Come, My Beloved.* Kbd: c1-g2. Augsburg (1961)

8:6 SEE: Song 2:10. Card, Michael and Scott Brasher. *Arise, My Love*

8:6 Saltzman, Peter. *Bind Me as a Seal Upon Your Heart* (from *A 'Song of Songs' Cycle*). Pno: M:a1-g2. Oxford (2000)

8:6-7 Berman, Judith M. *Set Me as a Seal*. Kbd: H:b1-e2. Transcontinental (1978)

8:6-7 Betts, Lorne. *Set Me as a Seal*. Org: b1-d2. Canadian Music Centre 98 / Song of Songs/ Isaiah, also found in *Six Sacred Songs*

8:6-7 Birch, Robert Fairfax. *Love*. Kbd: d1-g2. Presser (n.v.)

8:6-7 Castelnuovo-Tedesco, Maro. *Seal My Heart*. Transcontinental (1951) 601003 (n.v.)

8:6-7 Clokey, Joseph W. *Set Me as a Seal* (from *A Wedding Suite*). Org: e♭1-e♭2. J. Fischer (1951) 8607

8:6-7 DeLong, Richard. *Set Me as a Seal* (from *Three Wedding Songs*). Kbd: M:d1-f2. E. C. Schirmer (1993) 4758

8:6-7 Foss, Lukas. *Set Me as a Seal* (from *The Song of Songs*). Pno or orch: d♭1-a3. Carl Fischer (1950)

8:6-7 Helfman, Max. *Set Me as a Seal Upon Thy Heart*. Pno: d1-f♯2. Transcontinental (1973)

8:6-7 (adapted)
Landry, Rev. Carey (arr. Margaret Pizzuti). *Like a Seal on Your Heart*. Org: d1-c2. NALR (1979)

8:6-7 Pinkham, Daniel. *Wedding Song* (from *Wedding Cantata*). Org: d♯1-g2. C. F. Peters (1975) 66565

8:6-7 Reznick, Hyman. *A Seal Upon Thy Heart*. Pno: c1-f2. Transcontinental (1958)

8:6-7 Rochberg, George. *Set Me as a Seal* (from *Four Songs of Solomon*). Pno: H:g1-a3. G. Schirmer (1958); Presser (1975), found in *A Wedding Garland; The Sacred Collection* (H/L); *Wedding Bouquet* (H/L)

8:6-7 (and other)
Scholz, Robert. *Set Me as a Seal.* Kbd, vln: M:c1-a3. MorningStar (1995) MSM-40-879

8:6-7 Scott, K. Lee. *Set Me as a Seal*. Kbd: MH:f1-g2; ML:d♭1-e♭2. Augsburg (1989) 11-8195, found in *Sing a Song of Joy*

8:6-7 Wallach, Joelle. *Simëni kachotam al libbecha (Set Me as a Seal Upon Your Heart)* (Hebrew transliterated). Chamber orch: b1-g2. Joelle Wallach (1987)

8:6-7 Willis, Michelle. *Set Me as a Seal*. Duet-Pno: Mez:c1-e2/Bar:c-f1. ChoralWebb Publishing (2000) CWP-V8133-SG2

8:6-7a, 10
Thornton, William. *Wear Me as a Seal* (from *Solomon Songs*). Pno: M:b♭1-f2. Southern (1989) V-82

8:6, 8 McConnell, Doug. *Set Me as a Seal*. Fl or org: Sop:d1-f2. Chantry (1987) VOS 8714

8:13 Thomson, Virgil. *Thou That Dwellest in the Garden* (no. 1 from *Five Phrases Song of Solomon*). Perc: e1-a3. American Music Edition (1953)

8:14 SEE: Song 1:1-2. Sharlin, William. *Shir Hashirim*

ISAIAH

1:2, 4, 18-19
Riker, Franklin. *Hear, O Heavens, and Give Ear O Earth*. Pno: H:e♭1-g♭2; L:b♭1-e♭2. G. Schirmer (1922)

1:6, 10 Young, Walter E. *The Wilderness*. Kbd: H:d1-g2; L:b♭1-e♭2. Arthur P. Schmidt (1919)

1:18 (Isaiah 44:22; Proverbs 4:18; Proverbs 24:19; Psalm 36:9; Psalm 5:12; Psalm 37:1, 9)
Barker, Clement W. *The Path of the Just*. Kbd: H:d1-f2; L:b1-d2. R. D. Row (1951)

1:18 (Jeremiah 31:3; other)
Protheroe, Daniel. *A Song of Redemption*. Kbd: H:e♭1-g2. Oliver Ditson (1926), found in *Ditson Treasury of Sacred Songs*

1:18, 20, 28
Stebbins, G. Waring. *Come Now and Let Us Reason Together*. Org: d1-a3. Oliver Ditson (1923)

2:1-4 (Micah 4:1-4; paraphrase)
Hopson, Hal H. *Neath Vine and Fig Tree*. U/2-part-Kbd: b1-c2. MorningStar (1992) MSM-50-0300

2:2 SEE: Psalm 127:1. MacDermid, James G. *Bring Ye All the Tithes into the Storehouse*

2:3-4 (Isaiah 11:9; I Corinthians 12:4-31; based on)
Hurd, Bob (acc. Dominic MacAller). *Gather Your People*. Pno: c1-d2. OCP (1991), found in *Alleluia! Give the Glory*

2:4 SEE: Psalm 17:15. Hurd, Bob. *O, How I Long to See*

2:4 Scott, John Prindle. *He Maketh Wars to Cease*. Org: f♯1-g2. Flammer (1918)

2:4 (Isaiah 11:9; Micah 4:4)
Steinberg, Ben. *Lo Yareiu (They Shall Not Hurt Nor Destroy)* (Hebrew). Transcontinental (1988), found in *A Ben Steinberg Solo Collection* (n.v.)

2:5 (Isaiah 30:19)
Butler, Eugene. *Walk in the Way of the Lord*. 2-part-Kbd: d1-f2. Sacred Music Press (1986)

2:11 Portugal, Rabbi E. (arr. Velvel Pasternak). *V'nisgov (And the Lord Alone)* (Hebrew transliterated). Gtr: a1-f2. Bloch (1971), found in *Songs of the Chassidim II*

2:22 (Job 20:8a, 9; Psalm 37:37; Psalm 89:26)
Barker, Clement W. *Mark the Perfect Man*. Kbd: H:e♭1-f2; L:d1-e♭2. R. D. Row (1946)

6:1-4 (based on)
Chisum, John and Don Moen (arr. Carl Seal). *I See the Lord.* Kbd, gtr: c1-f2. Integrity (1994) MB-825, found in *Solos from the Word*

6:3a SEE: Psalm 99:3. Paris, Twila. *Holy Is the Lord*

6:3 Prince, Nolene. *Holy, Holy, Holy Is the Lord of Hosts*. Kbd, gtr, (opt orch): c1-d2. Maranatha! (1976), found in *Songs for Praise and Worship*

6:3 (Mark 10:10a; Matthew 21:9c)
Scholtes, Peter. *Holy, Holy, Holy* (*Hosanna*). Kbd, gtr, (opt orch): d♭1-e♭2. Lorenz (1991), found in *Songs for Praise and Worship*

6:3 (other)
Smith, Michael W.; Deborah D. Smith; Debbie and Brown Bannister. *Holy, Holy*. Kbd, gtr: b1-d2. Meadowgreen (1984), found in *The Song Book,* vol. III

6:3b (Matthew 21:9b)
Wold, Wayne L. *Sanctus and Benedictus*. U-Kbd: d♯1-f♯2. MorningStar (1994) MSM-80-779

6:8 (John 4:34-35; based on)
Manuel, Ralph. *Hark, the Voice of Jesus Calling*. Duet-Kbd: b♭1-b♭2/d1-e♭2. Beckenhorst (1993) VC5; also found in *We Come Before You, O Lord*

6:8 (based on)
Schutte, Daniel L. *Here I Am, Lord*. Kbd, inst in c: M:d♭2-f2. New Dawn Music (1981), also found in *Everything for the Church Soloist; Sacred Solos of Craig Courtney; I Will Sing of My Redeemer*

6:8 (based on)
Schutte, Daniel L. *Here I Am, Lord*. U/2-part-Gtr: c1-c2(d2). NALR (1981), found in *Lord of Light*

6:8 (based on)
Schutte, Daniel L. *Here I Am, Lord*. Duet-Kbd: H:g1-a♭3/L:c1-c2. New Hope (2000) 8065, found in *Sacred Vocal Duets For High and Low Voice*

7:14 (Luke 1:31-36; Luke 2:10-11; other)
Fettke, Tom. *Jesus–He Shall Be Great*. Kbd: c1-g2. Lillenas (1980), found in *The Lord Is My Light*

7:14 (Matthew 1:23)
Handel, G. F. *Behold, a Virgin Shall Conceive* (from *Messiah*). Kbd: Alto:a1-b2. Carl Fischer; G. Schirmer; Novello (1959)

8:31 SEE: Romans 8:31. Cark, Michael (arr. Marty Parks). *Immanuel*

9:1 Klass, Leon V. *The People Who Walked in Darkness* (Hebrew). Kbd: b1-e2. Transcontinental (1978) 991035

9:2 SEE: Isaiah 61:1-2. MacDermid, James G. *The Spirit of the Lord God Is Upon Me*

9:2-3 Handel, G. F. *The People That Walked in Darkness* (from *Messiah*). Kbd: Bass:G-e1. Carl Fischer; G. Schirmer; Novello (1959), found in *Anthology of Sacred Song–Bass; Oratorio Anthology: Baritone/Bass; Oratorio Repertoire,* vol. IV

9:2, 6-7 SEE: Philippians 4:4. Distler, Hugo. *O Rejoice in the Lord at All Times*

9:2-7 Bryant, Larry and Lesa Bryant. *Unto Us (Isaiah 9)*. Kbd or Trax: H:e♭1-g2; M:g-d2. Stonebrook Music (1987, 1991), found in *42 Songs for All Occasions; 50 Great Songs for All Occasions; Contemporary Christmas Collection; Very Best of Sandi Patti–Medium Voice*

9:2-7 Bryant, Larry and Lesa Bryant (arr. Robbie Buchanan). *Unto Us (Isaiah 9) with "Thema" (Thema)*. Kbd:b♭1-f2; M:g-d2. Stonebrook Music Co. (1987), found in *42 Songs for All Occasions; Contemporary Christmas Collection; Greatest Songs of Sandi Patty; Very Best of Sandi Patti–Medium Voice*

9:2a (Isaiah 60:1; and other)
Burton, Wendell and Marty Goetz. *Arise, Shine*. Kbd: c1-g2. Meadowgreen (1985), found in *The Song Book,* vol. III

9:6a (and other based on)
Chapman, Morris. *Bethlehem Morning*. Kbd or Trax: a1-e2. Word (1982), found in *Sandi Patti: Anthology; Sandi Patti Medium Voice Collection; Very Best of Sandi Patti* (H/M)

9:6c Goss, Lari. *Cornerstone*. Kbd: a1-c♯2. Heartwarming Music (1976), found in *Gospel & Inspirational Showstoppers; Low Voice Treasury*

9:6 SEE: Psalm 75:1. Hancock, Vicki. *Unto Thee, O Lord, Do We Give Thanks*

9:6 Handel, G. F. (ed. James Michael Stevens; arr. W. Daniel Landes). *For Unto Us a Child Is Born* (from *Messiah*). 2-part-Kbd: c1-d2(f2). Integra (1991), found in *Christmas MESSIAH for Young Voices; Classic Choruses for Young Voices*

9:6 SEE: Psalm 145:1-13. Lyles, Dwight. *Proclaim the Glory of the Lord*

9:6 (Philippians 2:5-11)
Pendleton, Emmet. *Christ Is Lord,* op. 12, no. 3 (from *The Light of the Lord*). Bruce Humphries (1945)

9:6c (Isaiah 28:16)
Patillo, Leon. *Cornerstone.* Kbd: b1-e♭2. Word (1983), found in *Bible Songs; Our God Reigns; The Song Book,* vol. III; *Songs for Praise and Worship*

9:6c (Isaiah 28:16)
Patillo, Leon (arr. Steven V. Taylor). *Cornerstone.* 2-part-Kbd or Trax: b1-e♭2. Word (1988), found in *25 Songs for Two-Part Choir*

9:6 (I John 1; based on)
Schutte, Daniel L. *City of God.* U/2-part-Gtr: e1-c♯2(f♯2). NALR (1981), found in *Lord of Light*

9:6 Tunney, Melodie and Dick Tunney. *For Unto Us.* Pno: g-c2. Lorenz (1986), found in *Contemporary Low Voice*

11:1-4 Bernhard, Christoph. *Es wird eine rute aufgehen vom stamm Isai* (German). Duet-Sop:c1-g2/Alto:g-a2. Bärenreiter (1972), found in *Geistliche Harmonien*

11:6 SEE: Psalm 17:15. Hurd, Bob. *O, How I Long to See*

11:6-9 (adapted)
Page, Anna Laura. *Creation Will be at Peace.* 2-part mixed-Kbd: a1-e2/c-d1. Alfred (1992) 5899

11:7 (based on)
Kalmanoff, Martin. *The Lion and Lamb.* Pno: b1-g2. Elkan Vogel (1970)

11:9 SEE: Isaiah 2:3-4. Hurd, Bob. *Gather Your People*

11:9 SEE: Isaiah 2:4. Steinberg, Ben. *Lo Yareiu*

12:00 Krapf, Gerhard. *O Lord, I Will Praise Thee (Confitebor Tibi).* Kbd: c1-f2. Concordia (1966) 98-1853

12:00 Schmutz, Albert D. *And in That Day Thou Shalt Say.* Kbd: d1-e2. Abingdon (1976) APM 633, also found in *Sacred Songs*

12:2, 4b-5
Lindh, Jody W. *Behold, God Is My Salvation.* U/2-part-Org: g1-e2. Concordia (1993) 98-3193, also found in *6 Scripture Anthems,* set 1

12:3 Horowitz, Rabbi M. (arr. Velvel Pasternak). *Ushavtem Mayim (Joyfully Shall You Draw)* (Hebrew transliterated). Gtr: M:b1-d2. Bloch (1971), found in *Songs of the Chassidim II*

12:3-4 (Psalm 56:13; Psalm 118:14; and other)
Calder, Lee. *God Is My Salvation.* Kbd: c1-d2. Galaxy (1961)

14:7 SEE: Psalm 31:5. Vaughan Williams, Ralph. *Watchful's Song*

25:8 SEE: Job 19:25a. Soper, Scott. *I Know That My Redeemer Lives*

25:8 SEE: Revelation 21:3-5. Sullivan, Sir Arthur. *The Lord Is Risen*

25:8-9 (Revelation 21:3-4; adapted)
Liszt, Franz (arr. Carl Fredrickson). *God Shall Wipe Away All Tears.* Pno: H:b♭1-e♭2. R. D. Row (1959), found in *Sacred Song Masterpieces,* bk 1

26:2-3 Bischoff, John W. (ed. Richard D. Row). *Open to Me the Gates.* Pno: Med. R. D. Row (1963), found in *Soloists Practical Library of Sacred Songs,* bk 2 (H/L)

26:3 (Philippians 4:7; John 20:19, 21, 26)
Schubert, Franz. *Peace Be Unto You.* Kbd: Med. Coburn Press (1971), found in *Lift Up Your Voice*

26:3 (Psalm 139:11)
Speaks, Oley. *Thou Wilt Keep Him in Perfect Peace.* Pno: H:e1-g2; M:d1-f2; L:c1-d2. G. Schirmer (1941)

26:3-4 Beck, Theodore. *Thou Wilt Keep Him in Perfect Peace.* Kbd: H:e♭1-f2. MorningStar (1988) MSM-40-890

26:3-4 (John 14:27; other)
Kretz, Vivian A. *Thou Wilt Keep Him in Perfect Peace.* Kbd: c1-e♭2. Lillenas (1960, 1980), found in *Music for Solemn Moments; Scripture Solos for All Seasons*

26:3-4 Shawn, Allen. *Thou Wilt Keep Him in Perfect Peace.* Kbd: b♭1-f2. Coburn Press, found in *Eleven Scriptural Songs from the Twentieth Century*

26:3-4 Thiman, Eric H. *Thou Wilt Keep Him in Perfect Peace.* Org: H:d1-g2; L:b1-e♭2. H. W. Gray (1962), H: GV410; L: GV411

26:3-4 Wienhorst, Richard. *Thou Wilt Keep Him in Perfect Peace.* Kbd: H:d1-f2; L:b1-d2. Concordia (1980) H: 97-5584; L: 97-5585, also found in *Seven Wedding Songs*

26:3-4, 11-12
Scott, John Prindle. *Trust Ye in the Lord.* Kbd: H:c1-g2; L:a♭1-e♭2. Huntzinger (1917), found in *Selected Sacred Songs for General Us*

26:3-4, 13-14
MacDermid, James G. *Thou Wilt Keep Him in Perfect Peace*. Kbd: H:d♭1-a♭2; M:b♭1-f2; L:a♭1-e♭2. Forster (1921)

27:1-5 (based on)
Ruston, Kevin and Vince Nichols (arr. Malcolm Archer). *I am the Keeper*. U/2-part-Org: opt descant or inst: c1-c2(g2). Kevin Mayhew (1991), found in *Our Praise to You*

28:16 SEE: Isaiah 9:6c. Patillo, Leon. *Cornerstone*

29:00 SEE: Psalm 100:00. Ziegenhals, Harriet. *You Shall Have a Song*

30:00 SEE: Psalm 100:00. Ziegenhals, Harriet. *You Shall Have a Song*

30:15 SEE: Psalm 46:10. Lowe, Augustus F. *Be Still*

30:15, 18, 27 (Lamentations 3:22-23, 25-26; based on)
Foley, John B. *The Steadfast Love*. U/2-part-Kbd, gtr, 2 inst in c: d1-c2. NALR (1985), found in *The Steadfast Love*

30:19 SEE: Isaiah 2:5. Butler, Eugene. *Walk in the Way of the Lord*

32:15-17 (adapted)
MacKenzie, Alexander C. (comp. Irving Brown). *The Wilderness Shall Be* (from *The Rose of Sharon*). Kbd: Bass:E-d1. G. Schirmer (1977), found in *Schirmer's Singer's Library: Bass Arias from Oratorios*

32:17-18 SEE: Psalm 46:10. Lowe, Augustus F. *Be Still*

33:24 (based on)
Graff, Leta Bishop. *The Inhabitants Shall Not Say I am Sick*. Kbd: c1-c2. Jenkins Music (1926)

34:1 LaForge, Frank. *Come Near Ye Nations*. Kbd: d1-a♭3. Carl Fischer (1946) V-1828

35:00 Humphreys, Don. *The Ransomed of the Lord*. Pno: H:d1-f2; L:b♭1-e♭2. Willis Music (1957), found in *Sing to the Lord*

35:00 MacDermid, James G. *The Ransomed of the Lord*. Kbd: H:d1-g2; L:b♭1-e♭2. Forster (1917, 1945)

35:1-2, 6-8, 10 (Isaiah 51:11)
Thiman, Eric H. *The Wilderness*. Kbd: M or L:b♭1-e2. Novello (1953), also found in *The Church Soloist* (H/L)

35:1-6 (Ezekiel 11:19-20; John 4:7-15; based on)
Hurd, Bob (arr. MacAller and Kingsbury). *Flow River Flow*. U/2-part-Pno or org, gtr, inst in c: b1-c2. OCP (1986), found in *Each Time I Think of You*

35:1-6 (Isaiah 40:1-5; Ezekiel 11:19-20; based on)
Hurd, Bob (arr. Craig S. Kingsbury). *Ready the Way*. U/2-part-Org, gtr, inst in c: b1-c2. OCP (1986), found in *Each Time I Think of You*

35:4 Wesley, Samuel Sebastian (arr. Harrison Oxley). *Say to Them of a Fearful Heart*. U-Org: d1-g2. Kevin Mayhew (1992), found in *Favorite Anthem,* bk 2

35:5-6 (Isaiah 40:1, 3-4, 9; based on)
Dufford, Bob. *Every Valley*. Cantor-Gtr, opt duet: a1-d2. NALR (1974); OCP 10476CC, also found in *Neither Silver Nor Gold*

35:5-6 SEE: Isaiah 40:11. Handel, G. F. *He Shall Feed His Flock* (from *Messiah*)

35:5-6 SEE: Isaiah 40:11. Handel, G. F. (ed. Jay Althouse). *He Shall Feed His Flock* (from *Messiah*)

35:5-6 SEE: Isaiah 40:11. Handel, G. F. (ed. Carl Deis). *He Shall Feed His Flock* (from *Messiah*)

35:5-6 Handel, G. F. *Then Shall the Eyes of the Blind* (from *Messiah*). Kbd: H:e♭1-f2; Alto or L:c1-d2. R. D. Row (1959); G. Schirmer; Novello (1959); Boston Music (1961), found in *20 Distinctive Sacred Solos* (H/L); *Soloists Practical Library of Sacred Songs,* bk 1 (H/L)

35:6-7 Misetich, Marianne. *Here Is Your God*. Kbd, gtr, bass, inst in c: a1-a2. OCP (1982), found in *Comfort My People*

35:10 (Revelation 21:3-4)
Ambrose, Paul. *God Shall Wipe Away All Tears*. Kbd: H:e♭1-a♭3; L:b♭1-e♭2. R. D. Row (1963), found in *Soloists Practical Library,* bk 2 (H/L)

35:10 SEE: I Corinthians 15:20, 22. Bach, J. S. *Now Christ Is Risen*

40:00 (based on)
Kosche, Kenneth T. *Comfort, My People*. 2-part-Kbd, inst in c. Augsburg (2001) 0-8006-7408-1

40:1 Dvorák, Antonín. *Comfort Ye, My People*. Kbd: f1-a♭3. Abingdon (1964) APM-308

40:1 (adapted)
Mendelssohn, Felix (arr. William Stickles). *I Waited for the Lord* (from *Hymn of Praise*). Pno: M:c1-e2. Boston Music (1961), found in *20 Distinctive Sacred Solos* (H/L)

40:1 Mendelssohn, Felix. *I Waited for the Lord (Ich harrete des Herrn)* (from *Hymn of Praise*). Duet-Pno: Sop:e♭1-a♭3/Mez:d1-f2. Jacksman Music (1985); Oliver Ditson (1936); G. Schirmer (n.d.); University Society (1918); John Church (1907) HL50264630, also found in *Album of Sixteen Sacred Duets; Choice Sacred Duets for All Voices; Duetbook: 14 Duets for Two Equal Voices and Piano; Modern Music & Musicians for the Vocalist,* vol. III; *Sacred Duets,* vol. 1 (H/H), vol. 2 (H/L)

40:1 Mendelssohn, Felix (ed. Robert Shaw). *Ich harrete des Herrn* (from *Lobgesang*) (German). Duet-Pno: Sop:e♭1-a♭3/Alto:d1-f2. Available from Atlanta Symphony Orchestra (1986)

40:1 (Revelation 21:9-10)
Parker, Horatio W. *Glorious Jerusalem.* Org: Tenor:c1-g2. Coburn Press (1971), found in *Lift Up Your Voice*

40:1, 3-4, 9
SEE: Isaiah 35:5-6. Dufford, Bob. *Every Valley*

40:1-3 Handel, G. F. *Comfort Ye* (from *Messiah*). Kbd: Tenor:e-g1; M:d-f2. Carl Fischer; G. Schirmer; Novello, found in *Oratorio Anthology: Tenor; Oratorio Repertoire,* vol. III; *Sing Unto the Lord,* vol. 1

40:1-3 Rubenstein, Anton (arr. Carl Fredrickson). *Comfort Ye My People.* Kbd: Bar:B1-d2. R. D. Row (1959), found in *Sacred Song Masterpieces,* bk 1

40:1-3 Rubenstein, Anton (arr. Carl Fredrickson). *Comfort Ye My People.* Duet-Kbd: H:f♯1-f♯2/L:b1-b2. R. D. Row (1960), found in *Sacred Duet Masterpieces,* bk 1

40:1-5 SEE: Isaiah 35:1-6. Hurd, Bob. *Ready the Way*

40:3-5 Thorne, Francis. *Prepare Ye the Way of the Lord* (from *Joshua*). Org or pno: d1-f2. G. Schirmer (1972)

40:3-5 (Willard F. Jabusch)
Traditional Folk Song – Hasidic (pno trans. Lyndell Leatherman). *Enter in the Wilderness.* Kbd: d1-e2. Lillenas (1980), found in *Scripture Solos for All Seasons*

40:3, 6, 7, 8
Scott, John Prindle. *The Voice in Wilderness.* Pno: H:e1-a♭3; M:d1-g2; L:c1-f2. Huntzinger (1916), also found in *Selected Sacred Songs for General Use*

40:4 (Matthew 2:8; Mark 11:8; Luke 3:5; Lutheran Book of Worship)
Ferguson, John. *Prepare the Royal Highway.* Kbd: f1-f2. Augsburg (1990) 11-5360, also found in *Three Swedish Folk Hymns*

40:4 Handel, G. F. *Every Valley* (from *Messiah*). Kbd: Tenor:d-g1. Carl Fischer; G. Schirmer; Novello, found in *Oratorio Anthology–Tenor; Oratorio Repertoire,* vol. III

40:4 Misetich, Marianne. *Comfort My People.* Duet-Kbd, gtr, bass, inst in c: M:d1-c2;M:b1-b2. OCP (1982), found in *Comfort My People*

40:4-5 Beck, John Ness (trans. Craig Courtney). *Every Valley.* Kbd: M:d♭1-g2. Beckenhorst (1990), found in *Sacred Songs of John Ness Beck*

40:4-5 Rowan, William. *Prepare the Way of the Lord.* 2-part/SATB-Kbd: b♭1-e♭2. Hope (1987) A 596

40:5 Handel, G. F. (ed. James Michael Stevens, arr. W. Daniel Landes). *And the Glory of the Lord* (from *Messiah*). 2-part-Kbd: c1-d2. Integra (1991), found in *Christmas MESSIAH for Young Voices*

40:6-8 Picket, Frederick. *All Flesh Is Grass* (from *Three Biblical Songs*). Kbd: f1-a♭3. Transcontinental (1968)

40:6-8 SEE: Psalm 39:4-5. Wyner, Yehudi. *Lord, Let Me Know My End*

40:6, 8, 28-31
MacDermid, James G. *They Shall Run and Not Be Weary.* Kbd: H:d1-g2; L:b1-e2. Forster (1923)

40:9 (Matthew 11:28-30; Ezekiel 34:11)
Dufford, Bob. *Like a Shepherd.* U/2-part-Gtr: b♭1-e♭2. NALR (1976), found in *A Dwelling Place*

40:9 (Isaiah 60:1)
Handel, G. F. *O Thou That Tellest Good Tidings To Zion* (from *Messiah*). Kbd, trpt: Mez:a1-b2. Roger Dean (2001) 30/1676R, found in *Festival Arias for soprano, mezzo-soprano and trumpet*

40:9 (Isaiah 60:1)
Handel, G. F. *O Thou That Tellest Good Tidings to Zion* (from *Messiah*). Kbd: Alto:a1-b2. Carl Fischer; G. Schirmer; Novello (1959), found in *Oratorio Anthology: Alto/Mezzo-Soprano; Oratorio Repertoire,* vol. II

40:9 (Isaiah 60:1)
Handel, G. F. (ed. James Michael Stevens, arr. W. Daniel Landes). *O Thou That Tellest Good Tidings To Zion* (from *Messiah*). U-Kbd: c1-d2. Integra (1991), found in *Christmas MESSIAH for Young Voices; Classic Choruses for Young Voices*

40:11 SEE: Psalm 23:1. Beck, John Ness. *He Shall Feed His Flock*

40:11 Caldwell, Mary E. *The Shepherd.* Kbd, fl: M:b1-e2. Fred Bock (1971), found in *A Celebration of Melody*

40:11 Handel, G. F. *Er weidet seine Herde (He Shall Feed His Flock)* (from *Messiah*) (German/English). Kbd: Sop:f1-g2. Carl Fischer 2451, also found in *Kirchen-Arien und Lieder*

40:11 (Isaiah 35:5-6)
Handel, G. F. *He Shall Feed His Flock* (from *Messiah*). Kbd or CD: Mez: c1-d2. Hal Leonard (1997) HL000740074, found in *Classical Contest Solos: Mezzo-Soprano*

40:11(Isaiah 35:5-6)
Handel, G. F. *He Shall Feed His Flock* (from *Messiah*). U-Kbd, 2 inst in c: d1-e2. MorningStar (1991) MSM-50-9404

40:11(Isaiah 35:5-6)
Handel, G. F. *He Shall Feed His Flock* (from *Messiah*). Kbd: H:f1-g2; MH:e♭1-f2; Alto or M:c1-d2; L:b♭1-c2. R. D. Row (1959); G. Schirmer; Boston Music (1961); Novello (1959), found in *20 Distinctive Sacred Solos* (H/L); *52 Sacred Songs; Christmas Solos for Singers; Classical Contest Solos: Mezzo-Soprano; Christmas Songs for Solo Singers* (MH/ML); *Everything for the Church Soloist* (M); *Everybody's Favorite Sacred Songs* (M); *Oratorio Repertoire,* vol. II; *Scripture Solos for All Seasons; Seventeen Sacred Songs* (M/H); *Soloists Practical Library of Sacred Songs,* bk 1 (MH/L); *Solos from the Word*

40:11 (Isaiah 35:5-6)
Handel, G. F. (ed. Carl Deis). *He Shall Feed His Flock* (from *Messiah*). Kbd: H:f1-g2; Alto:c1-d2 G. Schirmer (1937) H:HL50286360; Alto:HL50280650

40:11 Harker, F. Flaxington. *He Shall Feed His Flock,* op. 24, no. 2. Duet-Kbd: Sop:c1-a3/ Alto:a1-d2 (f2), Sop:e♭1-a♭3/Tenor:e♭-a♭2. G. Schirmer (1944)

40:11 (John 10:11)
Misetich, Marianne. *Like a Shepherd.* Kbd, gtr, bass, inst in c: d1-d2. OCP (1982), found in *Comfort My People*

40:11 (John 11:52; based on)
VanDyke, May. *As a Shepherd.* Kbd: H:f1-f2; M:d1-d2. Boosey & Hawkes (1933)

40:11, 26, 29-30 (Isaiah 41:10)
Haas, David. *We Will Rise Again.* Cantors-Kbd, inst in c, gtr: (d1-f2) c1-d2. GIA (1985) G-3454; 8731CC

40:28-31 (based on)
Hamblen, Bernard. *On Eagle's Wings.* Kbd: b1-d2. Chappell (1919)

40:28-31 (Habakkuk 3:17-18; based on)
Harlan, Benjamin (arr. Tom Fettke). *With Wings as Eagles.* Duet-Kbd or Trax: H:b♭1-f2; L:b♭1-e♭2. Pilot Point (1993) MB-656, found in *The Sunday Worship Duet Book*

40:28-31 LaForge, Frank. *Hast Thou Not Known.* Pno: H:d1-g2; L:b1-d2. G. Schirmer (1939)

40:28-31 Lovelace, Austin C. *Have You Not Known?* Kbd: d1-a3. Darcy Press (1993), found in *Sacred Solos by Austin C. Lovelace*

40:28-31 Malotte, Albert Hay. *Hast Thou Not Known?* Kbd: H. M. G. Schirmer (n.v.)

40:28-31 (based on)
O'Connor, Roc. *Trust in the Lord.* U/2-part-Gtr: b♭1-d2(f2). NALR (1976), found in *A Dwelling Place*

40:28-31 Schmutz, Albert D. *Hast Thou Not Known.* Kbd: c1-c2. Abingdon (1976) APM 633, also found in *Sacred Songs*

40:28-31 SEE: Psalm 62:1, 5-7. Seaton, Annette. *Those Who Wait on the Lord*

40:28-31 Swift, Robert F. *Hast Thou Not Known?* Kbd: M:c1-f2. Coburn Press, found in *Eleven Scriptural Songs from the Twentieth Century*

40:29-31 Manzo, Laura (arr. Mac Lynch). *They Shall Soar Like Eagles.* Duet-Kbd, inst in c: H:c1-d2; L:c-f1. Fred Bock (1986) MB 112, found in *We Will Serve the Lord*

40:31-32 (Isaiah 49:15; Isaiah 54:6-10; based on)
Schutte, Daniel L. *Though the Mountains May Fall.* U/2-part-Gtr: b♭1-c2(f2). NALR (1975), found in *Earthen Vessels*

41:10 (based on)
Boren, Murry. *How Firm A Foundation.* M-Kbd: b♭1-e♭2. Sonos (Jackman) (1997) 00434, found in *Sabbath Song*

41:10 SEE: Isaiah 40:11, 26, 29-30. Haas, David. *We Will Rise Again*

41:10 SEE: Isaiah 49:7. Mendelssohn, Felix. *Hear Ye, Israel*

41:10 Schütz, Heinrich. *Feurchte dich nicht,* SWV 296 (from *Kleine geistliche Konzerte*) (German). Duet-Cont: Bass/Bass:e-d2; f♯-a♭2. Bärenreiter (1963) BA 1705

41:10 Schütz, Heinrich. *Fürchte dich nicht,* SWV 296 (from *Kleine geistliche Konzerte*) (German). Duet-Cont: Equal Voices:e-d2/ fsharp-aflat2. Hänssler (1981)

41:10 (Ezekiel 34:11, 15-16, 25-26)
Tindall, Adrienne M. *Fear Not!* Kbd: d1-e♭2. Darcy Press (1994), found in *Sacred Solos by Adrienne Tindall,* vol. III

41:10, 13 SEE: II Chronicles 20:15b, 17. Koch, Frederick. *Be Not Afraid*

41:13 (Isaiah 51:12; Isaiah 54:10; Isaiah 50:13)
Foley, John B. *Let All Who Fear the Lord.* Gtr: d2-c1. NALR (1974), found in *Neither Silver Nor Gold*

41:18-19 (other)
Misetich, Marianne. *Holy One of Israel.* Kbd, gtr, bass, inst in c: d1-c2. OCP (1982), found in *Comfort My People*

42:1-17 (adapted)
Hurd, Bob (arr. Craig S. Kingsbury). *Roll Down the Ages.* U/2-part-Gtr: e1-c2/e1-e2. OCP (1979), found in *Roll Down the Ages*

42:6 SEE: Proverbs 3:24. Wolf, Hugo. *With An Everlasting Love*

42:6-7 (I Corinthians 6:11)
Brown, Allanson G. Y. *Behold! The Former Things Are Come to Pass.* Kbd: H:d1-f♯2; L:c♯1-e2. R. D. Row (1951)

42:6-7 SEE: I Corinthians 6:11. Telemann, Georg Philipp. *Ein jeder Lauft, der In den Schranken kauft*

43:1-4 Courtney, Craig. *Be Not Afraid.* Pno, inst in c: M:c1-f♯2. Beckenhorst (1992, 1997) also found in *Sacred Solos of Craig Courtney*

43:1, 25 SEE: Psalm 81:9-11. Stevenson, Frederick. *Hear, O My People*

43:2-3 (Luke 6:20; based on)
Dufford, Bob. *Be Not Afraid.* U/2-part-Org, gtr: b1-c2(e2). OCP (1975, 1991) A683

43:2-3 (Luke 6:20; based on)
Dufford, Bob (arr. Theophane Hytreak). *Be Not Afraid.* Cantors-Org, gtr: b1-c2(d1-e2). OCP (1975, 1991), also found in *Earthen Vessels*

43:2-3 (Luke 6:20; based on)
Dufford, Bob (arr. Jack Schrader). *Be Not Afraid.* Kbd: M:b1-c2. Hope (1977) 461

44:22 SEE: Isaiah 1:18. Barker, Clement W. *The Path of the Just*

45:1-2, 22 (Psalm 71:9, 12)
VanWoert, Rutger. *Be Not Far From Me, Oh God.* Pno: c1-f2. Chappell

45:4-6, 11-13
Kendrick, Virginia. *Look Unto Me, Saith Our God.* Pno: c♯1-d2. Coburn Press, found in *Eleven Scriptural Songs from the Twentieth Century*

45:22-23 (Isaiah 51:4, 6, 12; based on)
Foley, John B. *Turn to Me.* Cantor-Gtr, opt duet: b1-b2(c♯2). NALR (1978), also found in *Earthen Vessels*

45:22-23, 28
SEE: Acts 27:22, 24, 28. MacDermid, James G. *God That Made the World*

45:23 (Romans 14:11; Philippians 2:10-11; based on)
Driskell, Gary and Marty Hennis. *Kings Shall Bow.* Kbd: L:f-b♭2. Word (1994), found in *50 Great Low Voice Solos*

45:23b (Philippians 2:10-11; based on)
Nelson, Greg and Phil McHugh. *Power in Jesus Name.* Kbd, gtr: f♯1-e2. Hal Leonard (1984), found in *Our God Reigns*

46:3-5 (Isaiah 49:15; Jeremiah 31:15-22; based on)
Hurd, Bob (arr. Craig S. Kingsbury). *Each Time I Think of You.* Pno: M. OCP (1987)

48:1, 18 SEE: Isaiah 49:7. Mendelssohn, Felix. *Hear Ye, Israel*

48:20 Shaw, Martin. *With A Voice of Singing.* 2-part-Org: Sop:c1-g2/Alto:a1-e2. G. Schirmer (1953) 10227

48:20 Shaw, Martin (arr. Maurice Jacobson). *With a Voice of Singing.* U-Kbd: c1-g2 (opt 2pt). J. Curwen & Sons, Ltd. (1958) 11765

49:1-7 (based on)
Schutte, Daniel L. *Servant Song.* Gtr: c♯1-e2. NALR (1974), found in *Neither Silver Nor Gold*

49:7 (Isaiah 41:10; Isaiah 48:1, 18; Isaiah 51:12-13; Isaiah 53:1)
Mendelssohn, Felix. *Hear Ye, Israel* (*Höre, Israel*) (from *Elijah*) (English/German). Kbd: Sop:d♯1-a♯3. G. Schirmer; H. W. Gray; Novello, found in *Oratorio Anthology: Soprano; Oratorio Repertoire,* vol. 1; *Schirmer's Singer's Library: Soprano Arias from Oratorios*

49:15 SEE: Isaiah 49:15. Hurd, Bob. *Each Time I Think of You*

49:15 SEE: Isaiah 40:31-32. Schutte, Daniel L. *Though the Mountains May Fall*

50:5-7 SEE: Psalm 22:2-3, 10-11, 17. Hurd, Bob. *From My Mother's Womb*

50:6 SEE: Isaiah 53:3. Handel, G. F. *He Was Despised*

50:6 SEE: Isaiah 53:3. Handel, G. F. (arr. James Michael Stevens). *He Was Despised*

50:13 SEE: Isaiah 41:13. Foley, John B. *Let All Who Fear the Lord*

51:3 Benet, Ch. (arr. Velvel Pasternak). *Ki Nicham* (no. 1) *(For the Lord Has Comforted Zion)* (Hebrew transliterated). Gtr: M:d1-d2. Bloch (1971), found in *Songs of the Chassidim II*

51:3 Horowitz, Rabbi M. (arr. Velvel Pasternak). *Ki Nicham* (no. 2) *(For the Lord Has Comforted Zion)* (Hebrew transliterated). Gtr: M:d1-d2. Bloch (1971), found in *Songs of the Chassidim II*

51:4, 6, 12
SEE: Isaiah 45:22-23. Foley, John B. *Turn to Me*

51:6 (I John 2:15, 17; Revelation 21:1-2, 5-6)
MacDermid, James G. *Lift Up Your Eyes to the Heavens.* Kbd: Med. Forster (1942)

51:7-8 (adapted)
Tchaikovsky, Peter I. (arr. Carl Fredrickson). *Lift Up Your Eyes.* Kbd: L:b♭1-e♭2. R. D. Row (1964), found in *Sacred Song Masterpieces,* bk 2

51:11 Lake, Ruth. *Therefore the Redeemed.* U-Kbd: d1-d2. Maranatha! (1986), found in *Praise Classics–Lord of Hosts; Songs for Praise and Worship*

51:11 SEE: Isaiah 35:1-2, 6-8, 10. Thiman, Eric H. *The Wilderness*

51:11b SEE: Matthew 13:43. Mendelssohn, Felix. *Then Shall the Righteous Shine*

51:11b SEE: Matthew 13:43. Mendelssohn, Felix (arr. Wilbur Held). *Then Shall the Righteous Shine*

51:12 SEE: Isaiah 41:13. Foley, John B. *Let All Who Fear the Lord*

51:12-13 SEE: Isaiah 49:7. Mendelssohn, Felix. *Hear Ye, Israel*

52:00 (taken from)
Scott, John Prindle. *The Messenger of Peace.* Kbd: e♭1-a♭3. Harold Flammer (1920)

52:1 SEE: Psalm 4:1. Huhn, Bruno S. *Hear Me When I Call*

52:7 (Psalm 104:33; other)
Harker, F. Flaxington. *How Beautiful Upon the Mountains,* op. 41, no. 3. Pno: H:e1-a3; M:d1-g2; L:b1-e2. G. Schirmer (1910, 1938) H: HL50276820

52:7 (Psalm 104:33; other)
Harker, F. Flaxington (arr. J. Lamont Galbraith). *How Beautiful Upon the Mountains,* op. 41, no. 3. Duet-Pno: H:d1-a3/ M:b♭1-f2. G. Schirmer (1923), found in *The Duetbook: 14 Sacred Duets for Two Equal Voices; Schirmer's Favorite Sacred Duets*

52:7 SEE: Psalm 104:33. Harker, F. Flaxington. *How Beautiful Upon the Mountains,* op. 41, no. 3

52:7 (other)
Mendelssohn, Felix (arr. Carl Fredrickson). *How Beautiful on the Mountains.* Kbd: H:d♭1-g♭2; L:b♭1-e♭2. R. D. Row (1960), found in *Sacred Song Masterpieces*

52:7 (other)
Mendelssohn, Felix (arr. Fredrickson, Carl). *How Beautiful on the Mountains.* Duet-Kbd: H:d♭1-g♭2/L:a1-c2. R. D. Row (1960), found in *Sacred Duet Masterpieces,* bk 1

52:7 Perry, Julian. *How Beautiful Are the Feet.* Pno: e♭1-f2. Galaxy (1954)

52:7 (other)
Smith, Leonard E. Jr. *Our God Reigns.* Kbd, gtr, (opt orch): c1-d2. New Jerusalem Music (1978), found in *Songs for Praise and Worship*

52:7 (Isaiah 61:1-4)
Toolan, Sr. Suzanne (arr. Randall DeBruyn). *Great Is the Lord.* U/2-part-Org, 2 trpts, inst in c, gtr: d1-e2. GIA (1974, 1983), found in *In Perfect Charity: Contemporary Accomp. Series,* vol. 4

52:7-8 (Zechariah 9:9; Matthew 21:9; based on)
Manion, Tim. *Blessings on the King*. U/2-part-Gtr: e1-d2. NALR (1974), found in *Neither Silver Nor Gold*

52:7, 9 Fischer, Irwin. *How Beautiful Upon the Mountains*. Kbd: d1-f♯2. American Composers Alliance (1951)

52:7-9 Lovelace, Austin C. *How Beautiful Upon the Mountains*. Kbd: e♭1-g2. Darcy Press (1993), found in *Sacred Solos by Austin C. Lovelace*

52:7-9 (based on)
Paris, Twila. *How Beautiful*. Kbd, gtr: HH: g1-e2; H: f1-e2; MH: d1-c♯2; M:c1-b2: L:f♯-d1. Ariose Music (1990) HL00351562 (MH), also found in *24 Songs for Solo Ministry; 50 Great Wedding Favorites* (M); *60 Great Low Voice Solos* (L); *The Best Contemporary Christian Songs Ever* (M); *Christian Wedding Songbook* (MH); *Christian Wedding Songs; Cry For the Desert* (M); *High Voice Treasury; The Low Voice Book; Singer's Christian Wedding Collection* (H/M); *Songs For a Christian Wedding* (HH); *Wedding Music: 49 Solos and Duets* (M/L)

52:7-9 (based on)
Paris, Twila. *How Beautiful*. Duet-Kbd, gtr: MH/L:c1-f2/a1-a2. Ariose Music/Mountain Spring Music (1990), found in *Christian Wedding Duets*

52:8 (Matthew 25:7; based on)
Bach, J. S. *Zion hört die wächter singen (Zion Hears Her Watchman Crying)* (from *Wachet auf,* (cantata no. 140). Kbd: Tenor:e♭-g2. Carl Fischer

52:8-9 (Matthew 12:18-21)
Elgar, Edward (ed. Bernard Taylor). *The Voice of Thy Watchman* (from *The Apostle*). Kbd: Sop:e♭1-g2. G. Schirmer (1968), found in *Solos from the Great Oratorios for Soprano*

53:1 SEE: Isaiah 49:7. Mendelssohn, Felix. *Hear Ye, Israel*

53:1-11 (adapted)
Dauermann, Stuart (trans. Lyndell Leatherman). *Who Hath Believed Our Report?* Kbd, gtr: b♭1-e2. Lillenas (1980), found in *Scripture Solos for All Seasons*

53:3 (Isaiah 50:6)
Handel, G. F. *He Was Despised* (from *Messiah*). Kbd: Alto:b♭1-c2. Carl Fischer; G. Schirmer (1986, 1994); Novello; Boston Music (1961), found in *20 Distinctive Sacred Solos* (H/L); *Anthology of Sacred Song–Alto; Oratorio Anthology: Alto/Mezzo-Soprano; Oratorio Repertoire,* vol. II

53:3 (Isaiah 50:6)
Handel, G. F. (arr. James Michael Stevens). *He Was Despised* (from *Messiah*). 2-part-Kbd: c1-c2. Integra (1993), found in *Easter MESSIAH for Young Voices*

53:3 (John 19:5; I John 4:9; based on)
Owens, Jimmy. *Behold the Man*. Kbd, gtr: b♭-g2. Lexicon (1973), found in *Scripture Solos for All Seasons*

53:3 (John 19:5; I John 4:9; based on)
Owens, Jimmy (arr. Tom Fettke). *Behold the Man*. Duet-Kbd, gtr: b♭1-f2/b♭1-d2. BudJohn Songs (1973), found in *Duets for All Seasons*

53:3-6 Courtney, Craig. *He Was Wounded.* Kbd: M:c1-f2. Beckenhorst (1986, 1997), also found in *Sacred Solos of Craig Courtney*

53:3-7 (Luke 23:11-25; based on; other)
Baroni, David and Niles Borop. *Behold the Man*. Kbd: c♯1-f♯2. Word (1983), found in *The Lord Is My Light*

53:4-5 (John 1:29; Luke 23-24; Revelation 11:15)
Dufford, Bob (arr. John B. Foley). *Behold the Lamb of God.* Cantor-Pno, gtr, 2 insts in c, opt duet: c1-e♭2(g2). NALR (1985); OCP 5696CC, also found in *The Steadfast Love*

53:4-5 Lully, Jean Baptiste (ed. Earnest Murphy). *Our God Has Borne Our Troubles*. Duet-Kbd: H:e1-e2/M:c1-e2. McAfee Music (1973), found in *The Baroque Songbook*

53:4, 5 (based on)
Rowberry, Robert Lee. *I Stand All Amazed.* M-Kbd: c1-e♭2. Sonos (Jackman) (1997) 00434, found in *Sabbath Song*

53:4-6 DeVidal, David. *Surely He Bore Our Griefs.* Kbd: c1-d2. Fred Bock (1970, 1989), found in *The Communion Soloist*

53:5 SEE: Lamentations 1:12. Foster, Myles B. *Is it Nothing to You?*

53:6 Handel, G. F. (arr. James Michael Stevens). *All We Like Sheep Have Gone Astray* (from *Messiah*). 2-part-Kbd: c1-d2. Integra (1993), found in *Easter MESSIAH for Young Voices*

53:6 (based on)
Moen, Don. *All We Like Sheep*. Kbd, gtr: d1-d2. Intrada (1988), found in *God Will Make a Way*

53:7 (other)
Kiel, Friedrich. *He Was Oppress'd* (from *Christus*). Kbd: Alto:c♭1-f2. G. Schirmer (1977), found in *Anthology of Sacred Song–Alto; Schirmer's Singer's Library: Alto Arias from Oratorios*

53:8 Handel, G. F. *He Was Cut Off* (from *Messiah*). Kbd: Tenor:d♯-g1. Carl Fischer; G. Schirmer (1994); Novello (1959), found in *Oratorio Anthology: Tenor*

54:6-10 SEE: Isaiah 40:31-32. Schutte, Daniel L. *Though the Mountains May Fall*

54:10 SEE: Isaiah 41:13. Foley, John B. *Let All Who Fear the Lord*

54:10 SEE: Isaiah 55:6. MacDermid, James G. *For the Mountains Shall Depart*

54:10 Mendelssohn, Felix. *For the Mountains Shall Depart* (*Ja, es sollen wohl berge weichen*) (from *Elijah*) (English/German). Kbd: M or Bar:b-e1. G. Schirmer; Carl Fischer (1948); H. W. Gray; Novello, found in *Oratorio Anthology: Baritone/Bass* (German); *Sing Unto the Lord,* vol. 2

54:10, 13 Bowling, Blanche. *For the Mountains Shall Depart.* Kbd: H:e♭1-g2; L:c1-e2. R. D. Row (1958)

54:11, 14 Benedict, Sir Julius. *O Thou Afflicted, and Tossed With Tempest* (from *St. Peter*). Kbd: Alto:a♭1-d2. G. Schirmer (1929), found in *Anthology of Sacred Song–Alto*

54:13 Wagner, Douglas E. *For the Mountains Shall Depart.* U-Kbd: c1-e♭2. Augsburg 11-1962

55:00 Secchi, Antonio (tran. William Reddick). *Bow Down Your Ear.* Org: H:c1-f2; L:a♭1-d♭2. Huntzinger (1919), found in *Choice Sacred Songs for Home or Church Services*

55:1 SEE: John 6:51. Kieserling, Richard. *I Am the Bread of Life*

55:1 (Revelation 22:1)
Klein, Manuel. *Ho! Everyone That Thirsteth.* Pno: Sop:e1-a3(b♭3). Witmark & Sons (1909)

55:1 (based on)
Rider, Lucy J. (arr. Gene Thomas and Tom Fettke). *Come, Every One Who Is Thirsty.* Duet-Kbd or Trax: H:b♭1-f2; L:b♭1-c♯2. Pilot Point (1993) MB-656, found in *The Sunday Worship Duet Book*

55:1 (based on)
Ross, Barbara. *You Who Are Thirsty.* Kbd, gtr, (opt orch): c1-d2. Word (1992), found in *Songs for Praise and Worship*

55:1, 3 Charles, Ernest. *Incline Thine Ear.* Kbd: H:d♭1-f2(g♭2); L:b♭1-d2(e♭2). G. Schirmer (1948), found in *First Book of Tenor Solos Part II* (H)

55:1, 3 (Matthew 5:6; adapted)
Cherubini, Luigi (ed. and arr. K. K. Davis and N. Loring). *Come to the Waters.* Kbd: M:d1-g2. Carl Fischer (1948), found in *Sing Unto the Lord,* vol. 1

55:1, 3 Handel, G. F. (arr. Carl Fredrickson). *Come to the Waters.* Kbd: d1-e♭2. R. D. Row (1959), found in *Sacred Song Masterpieces,* bk 1

55:1, 3 Handel, G. F. (arr. Carl Fredrickson). *Come to the Waters.* Duet-Kbd: H:f1-g2/L:b1-d2. R. D. Row (1960), found in *Sacred Duet Masterpieces,* bk 1

55:1, 3, 10-11
MacDermid, James G. *As the Rain Cometh Down.* Pno: H:f1-f2(a3); L:d♭1-d♭2(f2). Forster (1948, 1920)

55:1, 3, 12
Strickland, Lily. *Incline Your Ear.* Kbd: H:f1-f2; L:d1-d2. G. Schirmer (1958)

55:1-3 (Romans 6:8-9; Joel 2:13)
Dean, Stephen. *Water of Life.* U/2-part-Kbd, gtr, inst in c, cl: b1-c2. OCP (1983), found in *Come to Set Us Free*

55:1-3 Frey, Richard E. *Incline Your Ear.* Kbd: H:e1-g2; L:c1-e♭2. Oliver Ditson (1910), found in *Solos for Christian Science Services*

55:3 Peter, Johann Friedrich (ed. and arr. Thor Johnson and Donald M. McCorkle). *I Will Make an Everlasting Covenant (Ich will mit euch einen ewigen bund machen)* (from *Three Sacred Songs for Soprano*) (English/German). Kbd: Sop:d1-f2. Boosey & Hawkes (1958) VAB-31H

55:6 Humphreys, Don. *Seek Ye the Lord.* Pno: H:e1-g2; L:c1-d2. Willis Music (1953), found in *Sing to the Lord*

55:6 SEE: Matthew 11:28. LaForge, Frank. *Come Unto Me*

55:6 Lynes, Frank. *Seek Ye the Lord.* Kbd: H:f1-g2; L:d♭1-e♭2. Arthur P. Schmidt (1909)

55:6 (Isaiah 54:10)
MacDermid, James G. *For the Mountains Shall Depart*. Kbd: H:e1-g2; M:c♯1-e2; L:b1-d2. Forster (1908)

55:6-7 Campion, Thomas. *Seek the Lord*. Lute: d1-d2. Roger Dean (1974), found in *First Booke of Ayres*, vol. 1–*English Lute Songs*, 2nd series

55:6-7 Carter, John. *Seek the Lord*. Kbd: M:d1-f2. Hope (1984) 1053, also found in *The Church Soloist; Come With a Singing Heart*

55:6-7 Lansing, A. W. *Seek Ye the Lord*. Duet-Kbd: Sop/Alto. Oliver Ditson (1923)

55:6-7 Lovelace, Austin C. *Seek Ye the Lord*. Kbd: c1-g2. Darcy Press (1993), found in *Sacred Solos by Austin C. Lovelace*

55:6-7 Roberts, John Varley (adapted Carl Deis). *Seek Ye the Lord*. Kbd: H:e♭1-f2; L:c1-d2. G. Schirmer (1919, 1946 and 1948) H: HL50284510

55:6-7 Roberts, John Varley (adapted Richard D. Row). *Seek Ye the Lord*. Kbd: H:e♭1-f2; L:c1-d2. R. D. Row (1959), found in *Christian Science Service Songs; Soloists Practical Library of Sacred Songs*, bk 1 (H/L)

55:6-7 (Isaiah 58:8-9)
VanDyke, May. *Seek Ye the Lord*. Kbd: H:e♭1-f2; L:c1-d2. Michael Keane (1937)

55:6-9 DeLong, Richard. *Seek Ye the Lord* (from *Five Sacred Songs*). M-kbd: d1-g2. E. C. Schirmer (1993) 4759

55:12 (based on)
Dauermann, Stuart. *The Trees of the Field*. Kbd, gtr, (opt orch): b1-e2. Lillenas (1975), found in *Songs for Praise and Worship*

55:12 SEE: Psalm 150:6. Tunney, Melodie. *Sound His Praise*

58:1, 3-6, 8-9
MacDermid, James G. *Is Not This the Fast*. Kbd: Med. Forster (n.d.)

58:6-11 SEE: Psalm 15:1. Hurd, Bob. *They Who Do Justice*

58:8-9 SEE: Isaiah 55:6-7. VanDyke, May. *Seek Ye the Lord*

59:1, 19 SEE: Revelation 3:20. MacDermid, James G. *Arise, Shine for Thy Light Is Come*

60:00 Scott, John Prindle. *Arise, Shine*. Kbd: H:e♭1-g2; L:c1-e2. Huntzinger (1923)

60:1 SEE: Isaiah 9:2a. Burton, Wendell/Goetz, Marty. *Arise, Shine*

60:1 Franck, Melchior (ed. Nitsche, Herbert and Stern, Hermann). *Mache dich auf, werde licht* (German). Duet-2 vlns: Sop:c1-g2/Tenor:c♯1-g2. Hänssler (1961), found in *Das geistliche konzert 71*

60:1 SEE: Isaiah 40:9. Handel, G. F. *O Thou That Tellest Good Tidings to Zion*

60:1 SEE: Isaiah 40:9. Handel, G. F. (ed. James Michael Stevens, arr. W. Daniel Landes). *O Thou That Tellest Good Tidings to Zion*

60:1 Humphreys, Don. *Arise, Shine for Thy Light Is Come*. Pno: H:e1-g2; L:c1-e2. Willis Music (1965), found in *Sing to the Lord*

60:1 SEE: Revelation 3:20. MacDermid, James G. *Arise, Shine for Thy Light Is Come*

60:1 Urspringer, Steven and Jay Robinson. *Arise Shine*. Kbd, gtr, (opt orch): c1-c2. Priesthood Pub. (1983), found in *Songs for Praise and Worship*

60:1-3 Koch, Frederick. *Arise, Shine*. Kbd: a1-e2. Carl Fischer (1990), found in *Five Sacred Solos for Worship Service*

60:1-3, 13, 21
Harker, F. Flaxington. *Arise, Shine, for Thy Light Is Come*, op. 56, no. 6. Kbd: d1-a3. Presser (1930)

60:1-3, 18-19
Schmutz, Albert D. *Arise, Shine, for Thy Light Is Come*. Kbd: b♭1 -d2. Abingdon (1976) APM 633, also found in *Sacred Songs*

60:1-4 (suggested by)
Foley, John B. *Awake, Arise*. U/2-part-Pno, 2 inst in c: d1-d2(g2). NALR (1985), found in *The Steadfast Love*

60:1-4 (based on)
Foley, John B. *Rise Up, Jerusalem*. Org or gtr: c1-d2. NALR (1974), found in *Neither Silver Nor Gold*

60:1-4 Wallbridge, Richard L. A. *Glory of the Lord*. Kbd: H:e1-f♯2; L:c1-d2. R. D. Row (1946)

60:1-6 Telemann, Georg Philipp. *Ihr Volkers, Hört* (from *A Solo Cantata for Epiphany*) (German). Cont, fl: d1-e2. Bärenreiter (1961) 387

60:2-3 Handel, G. F. *For Behold, Darkness Shall Cover the Earth* (from *Messiah*). Kbd:

Bass:f♯-e1. Carl Fischer; G. Schirmer; Novello, found in *Anthology of Sacred Song–Bass; Oratorio Anthology: Baritone/Bass*

60:16 Herbst, Johannes (arr. Karl Kroeger). *And Thou Shalt Know it (Du solst erfahren)* (German/English). Kbd or stg qt: H:d1-g2. Boosey & Hawkes (1978), found in *Three Sacred Songs of Johannes Herbst*

60:19 (Psalm 121:6)
Greene, Maurice (ed. E. Stanley Roper). *The Sun Shall Be No More Thy Light*. Kbd: H:e1-g2; L:d1-f2. Bosworth (1910), found in *Seven Sacred Solos of the Early English School*

60:20 Peter, Johann Frederich (ed. and arr. Thor Johnson and Donald M. McCorkle). *The Days of All Thy Sorrow (Die Tage Deines Leides)* (from *Three Sacred Songs for Soprano*) (German/English). Kbd: Sop:d1-a3. Boosey & Hawkes (1958) VAB-31H

61:1 (adapted)
Talbot, John Michael. *The Spirit of the Lord*. Gtr: d1-c2. Birdwing (1985), found in *Praise, Prayer and Worship*

61:1, 2 (Isaiah 9:2; Malachi 3:2, 3)
MacDermid, James G. *The Spirit of the Lord God Is Upon Me*. Kbd: H:e♭1-a♭3; L:b1-f♯2. Forster (1938)

61:1-3 Fredrickson, Carl. *Garment of Praise*. Kbd: H:d1-g2; L:b♭1-e♭2. R. D. Row (1958)

61:1-3 Wetzler, Robert. *Good Tidings*. Org, ob or vln: b1-e2. Augsburg (1974) 11-0740; also AMSI (1996) V-20

61:1-3 (Luke 4:18-19)
Wiant, Bliss. *The Great Commission*. Pno: H:c1-g2; L:a1-e2. Abingdon (1967)

61:1-3, 10
Young, Philip M. *I Will Greatly Rejoice in the Lord*. U/2-part-Kbd: c1-e2(f♯2). Concordia (1993) 98-3093

61:1-4 SEE: Isaiah 52:7. Toolan, Sr. Suzanne. *Great Is the Lord*

61:3b (based on)
Ingles, David. *Garment of Praise*. Kbd, gtr, (opt orch): c1-c2. D. I. Music (1976), found in *Songs for Praise and Worship*

61:10 (Isaiah 62:1)
Coryell, Marion. *The Robe of Righteousness*. Kbd: H: d♭1-a♭3; M:c1-f2. Carl Fischer (1947) V1887

61:10 SEE: Psalm 23:4. Lovelace, Austin C. *The Love of God*

61:10-11 Burton, Patti and Wendell Burton. *Greatly Rejoice*. Kbd: f1-g2. Meadowgreen (1984), found in *Our God Reigns*

62:1 SEE: Isaiah 61:10. Coryell, Marion. *The Robe of Righteousness*

62:3 (based on; Matthew 11:28)
Hurd, Bob (arr. Craig S. Kingsbury). *Come Unto Me*. U/2-part-Org, gtr, inst in c: d1-c2 (b1-g1). OCP (1984), found in *In the Breaking of the Bread*

62:5b SEE: Psalm 42:11a. Talmud, Rabbi Y. *Lõ Sevõshi*

63:00 SEE: Psalm 23:4. O'Connor, Roc. *Guide Me, O God*

63:5 (Hebrews 3:7-8; II Corinthians 6:2)
Rogers, James H. (ed. Carl Fredrickson). *Today If Ye Will Hear His Voice*. Kbd: H:d1-f♯2; L:ab-d♯2. R. D. Row (1963), found in *Church Soloists Favorites,* bk 1

63:7 (Psalm 100:1-2, 4-5; James 1:17)
Fischer, Irwin. *Psalm of Praise*. Kbd: e1-f2. American Composers Alliance (1951)

63:16-19 SEE: Psalm 22:1-2, 6. Foley, John B. *Redeemer Lord*

64:1, 8-11 (Isaiah 63; based on)
Dufford, Bob. *Return to Your People, O Lord*. Gtr: b1-d2. NALR (1974), found in *Neither Silver Nor Gold*

64:2-7 SEE: Psalm 22:1-2, 6. Foley, John B. *Redeemer Lord*

64:4 (Hebrews 4:9; 11:10; I Corinthians 2:9)
Gaul, Alfred Robert. *Eye Hath Not Seen* (from *Holy City*). Kbd: H:d1-f2; A/L:b1-d2. G. Schirmer (1939); Oliver Ditson (1903); Amsco (1940); Boston Music (1961), found in *20 Distinctive Sacred Solos* (H/L); *52 Sacred Songs; Anthology of Sacred Song–Alto; Choice Sacred Songs* (H/L); *Ditson Treasury of Sacred Songs; Everybody's Favorite Sacred Songs* (H); *Favorite Sacred Classics for Solo Singers* (MH/ML); *Five Solos from the Holy City; Oratorio Repertoire,* vol. II; *Sacred Songs; Schirmer's Singer's Library: Alto Arias from Oratorios* (L); *Second Book of Mezzo-Soprano/Alto Solos; Seventeen Sacred Songs For Church and General Use; Sing and Worship* (H/L); *Solo Singer; World's Favorite Sacred Songs* (H)

65:13, 25 (based on; the Magnificat)
Hurd, Bob (arr. Barbara Bridge and Dominic MacAller). *Arise, O Jerusalem.* U/2-part-Kbd, gtr, inst in c: (d1)g1-f2. OCP (1984) 8714CC, also found in *In the Breaking of the Bread*

65:17-22a, 25
Wolpe, Stefan. *Isaiah* (from *Six Songs from the Hebrew*). Pno: b♭-e♭1. McGinnis & Marks (1962)

65:19 SEE: Job 22:21. MacDermid, James G. *Acquaint Now Thyself With Him*

66:1 SEE: Joel 2:12. Harker, F. Flaxington. *Turn Ye Even to Me With All Your Heart*

66:10 Shapiro, Rabbi Y. (arr. Velvel Pasternak). *Simchu es y'rusholayim (Rejoice Ye With Jerusalem)* (Hebrew transliterated). Gtr: M:e1-d2. Bloch (1971), found in *Songs of the Chassidim II*

66:13 SEE: Wisdom 51:35. Brahms, Johannes. *Ye Now Are Sorrowful*

JEREMIAH

1:00 (based on)
Lundy, Damian (arr. Malcolm Archer). *Song For a Young Prophet.* U/2-part-Org, inst in c; c1-d2. Kevin Mayhew (1991), found in *Our Praise to You*

1:1-5 (Jeremiah 2:8-11)
Rosenmüller, Johann. *Lamentationes Jeremiae Prophetae* (Latin/German). Cont: M. Nagel (1929) (n.v.)

1:4-10 (based on)
Schutte, Daniel L. *Before the Sun Burned Bright.* U/2-part-Gtr: e1-d2. NALR (1974), found in *Neither Silver Nor Gold*

1:5 Lynch, Mike (acc. Patrick Loomis). *We Are Called.* Org, gtr: d1-c2. OCP (1986), found in *Bread of the World*

1:8 SEE: Revelation 2:10. Mendelssohn, Felix. *Be Thou Faithful Unto Death*

2:2 Applebaum, Louis. *Cry of the Prophet.* Pno: L. Canadian Music Centre (1952) (n.v.)

2:8-11 SEE: Jeremiah 1:1-5. Rosenmüller, Johann. *Lamentationes Jeremiae Prophetae*

5:3 (other)
Bach, J. S. *Weh der Seele (Herr, deine Augen sehen nach dem Glauben)* (from Kantate nr. 102) (German). Pno, ob: Alto: b1-e2. Kalmus, found in *Arias from Church Cantatas for Contralto,* vol. II

5:3 (other)
Bach, J. S. (ed. Max Schneider). *Weh der Seele* (from Kantate nr. 102 *Herr, deine Augen sehen nach dem Glauben*) (German). Kbd: Alto:b1-e♭2. C. F. Peters (n.d.), found in *J. S. Bach–Alt-Arien aus Kantaten*

5:15-22 Pisk, Paul A. *Lamentation.* Org/pno: b♭1-f2. American Composers Alliance

8:22 (based on)
Spiritual (arr. Harry T. Burleigh). *Balm in Gilead.* Kbd: H:b♭2-f2; L:g1-d2. Belwin Mills (1919), found in *The Spirituals of Harry T. Burleigh;* also found in *The Sacred Collection* (H/L)

8:22 (based on)
Spiritual (arr. William Dawson). *There Is a Balm in Gilead (Balm in Gilead).* Kbd: Tuskegee (Kjos) (1939), H:TH105; L:TL105

8:22 (based on)
Spiritual (arr. Mark Hayes). *There Is a Balm in Gilead (Balm in Gilead).* Kbd: MH:g1-e2; ML:e1-c2. Alfred (1998) MH: 17954; ML: 17959, found in *The Mark Hayes Vocal Solo Collection: 10 Spirituals* (MH/ML)

8:22 (based on)
Spiritual (arr. Bruce Greer). *There Is a Balm in Gilead (Balm in Gilead).* Kbd: M:d1-d2; L:g-g1. Word (1994), found in *The Sunday Soloist,* vol. III (M/L)

8:22 (based on)
Spiritual (arr. Hall Johnson). *There Is a Balm in Gilead (Balm in Gilead).* Kbd: H:b♭1-f2. G. Schirmer (1949), found in *Thirty Spirituals*

9:23-24 SEE: Jeremiah 31:31, 33-34. MacDermid, James G. *Let Not the Wise Man Glory in His Wisdom*

9:24 SEE: Psalm 27:00. Schutte, Daniel L. *If the Lord Does Not Build*

15:16 (based on)
Gates, Crawford. *For I am Called by Thy Name* (from *Three Songs for the Young Heart,* op. 49). Kbd: M:d♭1-f2. Jackman Music (1992) S-0180, found in *Scripture Settings for Solo Voice*

22:10 (based on)
Spiritual (arr. Harry T. Burleigh). *Don't You Weep When I'm Gone*. Pno: $d^{\flat}$1-$e^{\flat}$2. Belwin Mills (1919), found in *The Spirituals of Harry T. Burleigh*

23:29 Mendelssohn, Felix. *Is Not His Word Like a Fire? (Ist nicht des Herrn Wort wie ein Feuer?)* (from *Elijah*) (English/German). Kbd: Bass:b-f1. G. Schirmer; H. W. Gray; Novello, found in *Anthology of Sacred Song–Bass; Oratorio Anthology: Baritone/Bass; Schirmer's Singer's Library: Bass Arias from Oratorios*

29:10-14 Foley, John B. *A Song of Hope*. U-Pno, gtr: $e^{\flat}$1-c2. NALR (1985), found in *The Steadfast Love*

29:11-14 (Deuteronomy 4:29; Job 23:3; Joel 2:13)
Courtney, Craig. *If You Search With All Your Heart*. Pno: M:d1-e2. Beckenhorst (1997) VCC8, also found in *Sacred Solos of Craig Courtney*

29:12-13 SEE: Job 22:21. MacDermid, James G. *Acquaint Now Thyself With Him*

29:13 Mendelssohn, Felix. *Ye People Rend Your Hearts (Zerreisseteure Herzen)* (from *Elijah*). Kbd: Tenor:f♯1-$a^{\flat}$3; L:c♯1-$e^{\flat}$2. Hal Leonard (1994); G. Schirmer; H. W. Gray; Novello; Amsco (1940); Oxford (1985) *17 Sacred Songs For Church & General Use* (H/L); *52 Sacred Songs; Anthology of Sacred Songs–Tenor; Everybody's Favorite Sacred Songs; Everything for the Church Soloist; Solo Singer; Oratorio Anthology: Tenor*; *World's Best Sacred Songs; Sing Solo Tenor* (H)

29:13 Mendelssohn, Felix (arr. Lynn Hodges). *Ye People Rend Your Hearts* (from *Elijah*). Kbd: c♯1-d2. Integra (1993), found in *Mendelssohn's ELIJAH for Young Voices*

31:3 SEE: Exodus 15:26b. Chapman, Steve Curtis (arr. Bryce Inman). *Be Still and Know*

31:3 SEE: Exodus 15:26b. Chapman, Steve Curtis and Tom Fettke (arr. Tom Fettke). *Be Still and Know*

31:3 SEE: Exodus 15:26b. Chapman, Steve Curtis and Tom Fettke (arr. Lee Herrington). *Be Still and Know*

31:3 SEE: Psalm 24:3. Joncas, Michael. *I Have Loved You*

31:3 SEE: Isaiah 1:18. Protheroe, Daniel. *A Song of Redemption*

31:3 SEE: Proverbs 3:24. Wolf, Hugo. *With an Everlasting Love*

31:6, 16 (other)
Buck, Dudley. *Fear Not Ye, O Israel*. Kbd: H:f♯1-a3; MH:e1-g2; L:c♯1-e2. G. Schirmer (1917); R. D. Row (1959), found in *Seventeen Sacred Songs For Church and General Use* (H/L); *Soloists Practical Library of Sacred Songs,* bk 1 (H/L)

31:12 SEE: Revelation 21:4. Joy, Jeanne Alden. *Ye Shall Not Sorrow Any More*

31:15-22 SEE: Isaiah 49:15. Hurd, Bob. *Each Time I Think of You*

31:31, 33-34 (Jeremiah 9:23-24)
MacDermid, James G. *Let Not the Wise Man Glory in His Wisdom*. Kbd: H:d1-g2; L:b1-e2. Forster (1924)

31:33 (Ezekiel 36:26; Joel 2:12)
Haas, David (pno arr. Jeanne Cotter). *Deep Within*. U/2-part-Gtr: d1-d2/d-c1. GIA (1987), found in *Who Calls You By Name,* vol. 1

31:33 (Ezekiel 36:26; Joel 2:12)
Haas, David. *Deep Within*. Gtr: d1-d2. GIA (1987), found in *As Water to the Thirsty*

33:11 SEE: Psalm 89:1. Wienhorst, Richard. *I Will Sing the Story of Thy Love*

LAMENTATIONS

1:1 (Luke 23:24, 28, 43; Matthew 27:46; Mark 15:34)
Berthier, Jacques (ed. Brother Robert). *All You Who Pass This Way*. U-Kbd: c1-d2. Taizé (1984), found in *Music From Taizé,* vol. 2

1:12 Dubois, Theodore (ed. Nicholas Douty). *All Ye People* (from *Seven Last Words*) (Latin/English). Kbd: Sop:f1-g2. Presser (1923), found in *Oratorio Repertoire,* vol. 1

1:12 Dubois, Theodore (ed. David Patrick). *O vos omnes* (from *Seven Last Words of Christ*) (Latin/English). Kbd: Sop:f1-g2. Boosey & Hawkes (1996), found in *Sacred Songs for the Soloist: 20 Songs on Religious Texts for Medium High Voice*

1:12 (Baker)
Dubois, Theodore (ed. Bernard Taylor). *O vos omnes (O All Ye Who Travel)* (from *Seven Last Words of Christ*) (Latin/English). Kbd: Sop:f1-g2. G. Schirmer (1968), found in *Solos from the Great Oratorios for Soprano*

1:12 (Isaiah 53:35; John 3:16)
Foster, Myles B. *Is it Nothing to You?* Duet-Kbd: H:d1-f2/L:a1-c2. John Church (1907), found in *Sacred Duets,* vol. 2

1:12 Handel, G. F. *Behold and See* (from *Messiah*). Kbd: Tenor:d♯-g1. Carl Fischer; G. Schirmer; Novello (1959)

1:12 Handel, G. F. *Behold and See* (from *Messiah*). Kbd: Tenor:d♯-g1. Hal Leonard (1994), found in *Oratorio Anthology: Tenor*

3:22-23 McNeil, Edith. *The Steadfast Love of the Lord.* Kbd, gtr, (opt orch): b♭1-c2. Maranatha! (1975), found in *Bible Songs; Songs for Praise and Worship*

3:22-23, 25-26
SEE: Isaiah 30:15, 18, 27. Foley, John B. *The Steadfast Love*

3:22-37 SEE: Psalm 27:1. VanVollenhoven, Hanna. *Hear Me Speedily, O Lord!*

3:33 SEE: Psalm 9:13. Molique, Wilhelm Bernhard. *It Is of the Lord's Great Mercies*

EZEKIEL

1:15 (based on)
Spiritual (arr. Margaret Bonds). *Ezek'el Saw the Wheel.* Pno: M:c1-c2. Mercury (1959) 151-00334

11:19-20 SEE: Isaiah 35:1-6. Hurd, Bob. *Ready the Way*

13:3 (Psalm 85:8-9)
Barker, Clement W. *Woe Unto the Foolish Prophets*. Pno: H:d♭1-g♭2; L:g-e♭2. G. Schirmer (1943)

34:11 SEE: Isaiah 40:9. Dufford, Bob. *Like a Shepherd*

34:11, 15-16, 25-26
SEE: Isaiah 41:10. Tindall, Adrienne M. *Fear Not!*

36:26 SEE: Jeremiah 31:33. Haas, David. *Deep Within*

37:00 (based on)
Wolfe, Jacques. *Bone Come A-knittin'*. Pno: H:d1-g2; L:b♭1-e♭2. Harold Flammer (1933)

DANIEL

3:00 (based on)
MacGimsey, Robert. *Shadrach.* Pno: H:d1-a3; L:c1-g2. Carl Fischer (1937)

3:51-90 (based on)
Schutte, Daniel L. *Meadows and Mountains.* Kbd: b1-c♯2. OCP (1989), found in *Lover of Us All*

6:22 (based on)
Spiritual. *Didn't My Lord Deliver Daniel?* Kbd or CD: Sop. Hal Leonard (1997) HL 00740073, found in *Classical Contest Solos–Soprano*

6:22 (based on)
Spiritual (arr. Edward Boatner). *Didn't My Lord Deliver Daniel?* Pno, gtr: a♭1-f2. Belwin Mills (1973), found in *The Story of the Spirituals*

6:22 (based on)
Spiritual (arr. Harry T. Burleigh). *Didn't My Lord Deliver Daniel?* Pno, gtr: a♭1-f2. Hal Leonard (2001), found in *The Sacred Collection* (H/L)

9:9 (Psalm 103:13)
Gaul, Alfred Robert. *To the Lord Our God Belong Mercies* (from *Holy City*). Kbd: Tenor:e1-g2. G. Schirmer

HOSEA

2:16-22 Wallach, Joelle. *V'erastich li l'olam* (Hebrew transliterated). Duet-Unacc: Sop:c1-g2/T or Bar:d-e1. Joelle Wallach (1990)

2:21, 22 (Song of Songs 2:13)
Adler, Samuel. *I Will Betroth Her Unto Me.* Kbd: d1-a3. Transcontinental (1985)

2:21-22 Castelnuovo-Tedesco, Maro. *V'Erstich (Eternal Love).* Transcontinental (1951) 601001 (n.v.)

2:21-23 DeLong, Richard. *I Will Espouse You to Me Forever* (from *Three Wedding Songs*). Kbd: M:d1-f2. E. C. Schirmer (1993) 4758

7:13 Mendelssohn, Felix. *Woe, Woe Unto Them Who Forsake Him!* (from *Elijah*). Kbd: M:b1-e2. Presser (1923), found in *Oratorio Repertoire,* vol. II

7:13 Mendelssohn, Felix. *Woe Unto Them Who Forsake Him!* (from *Elijah*). Kbd: M:b1-e2. G. Schirmer (1994); H. W. Gray; Novello, found in *Oratorio Anthology: Alto/Mezzo-Soprano*

11:00 (Matthew 18:10-14; based on)
Hurd, Bob (arr. Craig S. Kingsbury). *Return to Me*. U/2-part-Org, gtr, inst in c: d1-d2 (g2). OCP (1984), found in *In the Breaking of the Bread; Return to Me: Music for Funerals and Healing,* vol. 1

13:14 (based on)
Zaabriskie, David A. *Pioneer Lullaby.* M-Kbd: c1-f2. Sonos (Jackman) (1997) 00434, found in *Sabbath Song*

JOEL

2:1 (based on)
Terndrup, Craig. *Blow the Trumpet in Zion.* Kbd, gtr, (opt orch): b1-c♯2. Intrada (1983, arr. 1992), found in *Songs for Praise and Worship*

2:12 SEE: Jeremiah 31:33. Haas, David. *Deep Within*

2:12 (II Corinthians 6:2; based on)
Haas, David. *Now, the Acceptable Time.* U/2-part-Kbd, gtr, inst in c: (a1)c1-c2. GIA (1988), found in *Who Calls You By Name,* vol. 2

2:12 (Isaiah 66:1; Matthew 13:4-43)
Harker, F. Flaxington. *Turn Ye Even to Me With All Your Heart.* Kbd: Med. G. Schirmer (1932)

2:12-13, 15-17
Andrews, Mark. *Blow Ye the Trumpet.* Org: f1-g2. G. Schirmer (1906)

2:13 SEE: Jeremiah 29:11-14. Courtney, Craig. *If You Search With All Your Heart*

2:13 SEE: Isaiah 55:1-3. Dean, Stephen. *Water of Life*

2:13 SEE: Deuteronomy 4:29. Mendelssohn, Felix. *If With All Your Hearts*

2:13 SEE: Deuteronomy 4:29. Mendelssohn, Felix (arr. Lynn Hodges). *If With All Your Hearts*

2:13 SEE: Deuteronomy 4:29. Mendelssohn, Felix (arr. Harrison Oxley). *If With All Your Hearts*

2:15 (Matthew 11:29)
Purcell, Henry. *Blow Ye the Trumpet.* Kbd: a1-d2. R. D. Row (1959), found in *Sacred Song Masterpieces,* bk 1

2:15 (Matthew 11:29)
Purcell, Henry. *Blow Ye the Trumpet.* Duet-Org/Pno: H:d1-f2(b♭3);H:g1-g2. R. D. Row (1961), found in *Sacred Duet Masterpieces*

2:28 (John 1:5; other)
Wise, Joe. *And the Light Shines.* Kbd: d1-b2. GIA (1982), found in *And the Light Shines: Joe Wise*

2:28-32 Foley, John B. *Never Shall A Soul.* Gtr: c1-c2. NALR (1974), found in *Neither Silver Nor Gold*

AMOS

5:6 SEE: Psalm 34:12-14, 19. Miller, Merle. *Seek the Lord*

5:15 Barnby, J. *O Ye, That Love the Lord* (from *The Lord Is King*). Kbd: Alto: a1-e♭2. Presser (1923), found in *Oratorio Repertoire,* vol. II

5:24 Kingsley, Gershon. *Prepare to Meet Thy God* (from *Three Sacred Songs*). Kbd, vc: b1-f2. Transcontinental (1969)

8:11 SEE: Psalm 62:2. Lynch, Mike. *In the Land There Is a Hunger*

9:7-15 Horvit, Michael. *The Prophecy of Amos.* Org: H:e1-a2. Southern (1990) V-87

9:13, 15 Steinberg, Ben. *Hinei Yamin Ba-Im (Behold, the Days Come)* (Hebrew). Transcontinental (1988), found in *A Ben Steinberg Solo* (n.v.)

MICAH

4:1-4 SEE: Isaiah 2:1-4. Hopson, Hal H. *Neath Vine and Fig Tree*

4:4 SEE: Isaiah 2:4. Steinberg, Ben. *Lo Yareiu*

6:6-8 Freudenthal, Josef. *The Precepts of Micah.* Kbd: H:e1-g2; L:c1-e♭2. Transcontinental (1961) TV 559

6:6-8 SEE: Job 22:21. Head, Michael. *Acquaint Now Thyself With Him*

6:7-8 Banks, Harry C. *He Hath Shewed Thee O Man.* Kbd: H:f1-g♭2; L:d1-e2. Heidelberg Press (1923)

6:8 Haas, David. *We Are Called.* U/2-part-Kbd, gtr: (c♯1)e1-e2. GIA (1988), found in *Who Calls You By Name,* vol. 1

HABAKKUK

2:4 SEE: Psalm 16:10. Mullins, Rich. *The Just Shall Live*

2:20 Peter, Johann Friedrich (ed. David). *Herr ist in seinem heiligen Temple, Der* (*The Lord Is in His Holy Temple*) (German/English). Org, stgs: Sop:e♭1-e♭2. New York Public Library (1954) P6084, also found in *Ten Sacred Songs: Music of the Moravians in America*

3:17-18 SEE: Isaiah 40:28-31. Harlan, Benjamin (arr. Tom Fettke). *With Wings as Eagles*

ZEPHANIAH

1:00 - 3:20 (based on)
Archer, Violet. *God Sings in Pleasure.* Pno: Bass/Bar. Canadian Music Centre (1990) (n.v.)

3:00 MacDermid, James G. *Sing, O Daughters of Zion.* Kbd: H:e♭1-a♭3; L:c1-f2. Forster (1952)

3:17 Butler-Moore, Nylea L. *The Lord Your God Is with You.* Kbd: a1-e2. Abingdon (1991), found in *O Sing to the Lord!*

HAGGAI

2:6, 7 (Malachi 3:1, 2)
Handel, G. F. *Thus Saith the Lord* (from *Messiah*). Kbd: Bass:a-d1; H:c1-g2. Carl Fischer; G. Schirmer; Novello (1959), found in *Anthology of Sacred Song–Bass; Oratorio Anthology: Baritone/Bass*

ZECHARIAH

4:6 (other)
Phillips, Leslie. *By My Spirit.* Kbd: f♯-g♭2. Word (1984), found in *The Song Book,* vol. III

9:9 SEE: Isaiah 52:7-8. Manion, Tim. *Blessings on the King*

9:9 (Matthew 21:9; Mark 11:9-10)
Posch, Isaac (ed. Karl Geiringer). *Ecco Dominus veniet* (from *Harmonia Concertans*) (Latin). Duet-Equal voices:c1-f2. Ann Arbor: University Microfilm (1968-72), found in *Series of Early Music,* vol. 4

9:9-10 Handel, G. F. *Rejoice Greatly, O Daughter of Zion* (from *Messiah*). Kbd: Sop:e1-a♭3. Carl Fischer; G. Schirmer (1977); Novello, also found in *Anthology of Sacred Song–Soprano; Festival Arias for soprano, mezzo-soprano and trumpet; Oratorio Anthology–Soprano; Oratorio Repertoire,* vol. 1; *Schirmer's Singer's Library: Soprano Arias from Oratorios,* vol. 2

9:9-10 Willan, Healey. *Rejoice Greatly, O Daughter of Zion.* 2-part-Kbd: Sop/Alto. Concordia 98-1113

MALACHI

1:11 SEE: Psalm 113:3-4. Greene, Maurice. *The Lord's Name Is Praised*

3:1, 2 SEE: Haggai 2:6, 7. Handel, G. F. *Thus Saith the Lord*

3:2 Handel, G. F. *But Who May Abide* (from *Messiah*). Kbd: Alto:g-e2; Bass:a-f1. Carl Fischer; G. Schirmer; Novello (1959), found in *Anthology of Sacred Song–Bass; Oratorio Anthology: Baritone/Bass; Oratorio Anthology: Alto/Mezzo-Soprano; Oratorio Repertoire,* vol. IV

3:2, 3 SEE: Isaiah 61:1, 2. MacDermid, James G. *The Spirit of the Lord God Is Upon Me*

3:4 Pasternak, Velvel. *V'or'vo lashem (The Offering of Judah and Jerusalem)* (Hebrew transliterated). Gtr: MH:d1-f2. Bloch (1971), found in *Songs of the Chassidim II*

3:10 SEE: Psalm 127:1. MacDermid, James G. *Bring Ye All the Tithes into the Storehouse*

4:1-2 SEE: II Timothy 1:12. Scott, John Prindle. *I Know in Whom I Have Believed*

4:2 (Wesley)
Butt, James. *Christ Whose Glory.* Kbd: f1-f2. Sphemusations (n.d.)

The Apocrypha

TOBIT

8:5-7 DeLong, Richard. *Bless Are You, O God of Our Fathers* (from *Three Wedding Songs*). M-Kbd: e1-f2. E. C. Schirmer (1993) 4758

ECCLESIASTICUS
OR SIRACH

24:3-7, 12-14
Stanford, Charles Villiers. *A Song of Wisdom* (from *Bible Songs*). Org: H:e♭1-g2; L:c1-e2. Stainer & Bell (1909)

41:1-2 Brahms, Johannes (ed. Carl Deis). *O Tod, wie bitter bist du (O Death How Bitter)* (from *Vier ernste Gesang*) (German/English). Pno: M:b-f♯1; L. Abingdon (1964) G. Schirmer (1964) vol. 1678

44:00 Vaughan Williams, Ralph. *Let Us Now Praise Famous Men* (from *Pilgrim's Progress*). Org: e1-g♯2. Curwen (1959) 71619

47:2 (Psalm 117:00)
Ferris, William. *I Have Seen Water*. Org: M:d1-d2. GIA (1980) G-2352

I MACABEES

3:58 Handel, G. F. (arr. Richard Walters). *Arm, Arm, Ye Brave!* (from *Judas Maccabeus*). Kbd: Bass:c-e1. Hal Leonard (1994), found in *Oratorio Anthology: Baritone/Bass; Oratorio Repertoire*, vol. IV

The New Testament

MATTHEW

1:21 Burroughs, Bob. *Christmas Prophecy*. Kbd: d1-c2. Hope (1970) 501, also found in *New Testament Songs*

1:23 (Luke 2:14)
Franck, Melchior (ed. Herbert Nitsche and Hermann Stern). *Siehe, eine Jungfrau ist schwanger* (German). Duet-Equal voices: c1-g2/b1-f2. Hänssler (n.d.), found in *Das geistliche Konzert 72*

1:23 SEE: Isaiah 7:14. Handel, G. F. *Behold, a Virgin Shall Conceive*

1:23 (Luke 2:14)
LaMontaine, John. *Behold, A Virgin Shall Be With Child.* Kbd: b$^{\flat}$1-e$^{\flat}$2. H. W. Gray, found in *Songs of the Nativity*

2:1-2, 11 (adapted)
Handel, G. F. (arr. Carl Fredrickson). *There Upon a Manger Bed.* Kbd: L:b$^{\flat}$1-e$^{\flat}$2. R. D. Row (1964), found in *Sacred Song Masterpieces,* bk 2

2:1-12 (based on)
Wolaver, Bill (arr. Tom Fettke and Bill Wolaver). *Rejoice With Exceeding Great Joy.* Kbd: g-g2. Pilot Point (1998) MB-825, found in *Solos from the Word*

2:8 SEE: Isaiah 40:4. Ferguson, John. *Prepare the Royal Highway*

2:10-11 Cornelius, Peter. *The Kings*. Kbd: Med. G. Schirmer, found in *The Church Soloist*

3:1-2, 7, 8, 11, 12
Scott, John Prindle. *Repent Ye*. Pno: H:d1-g2; M:b1-e2; L:a1-d2. G. Schirmer (1917), found in *Christian Science Service Songs*

3:16 (poem by Luce)
Barker, Clement W. *Behold the Lamb of God*. Org: H:e1-g2; L:c1-e2. Carl Fischer (1969) L: V-2394; H: V-2395

4:4 (I John 3:1)
Fichthoin, Claude. *Behold What Manner of Love*. Org: d1-g$^{\sharp}$2. Church (1942)

4:4 (Luke 9:25; Romans 10:8-13; based on)
Hurd, Bob (arr. Craig S. Kingsbury). *The Word is in Your Heart.* U/2-part-Org, gtr, inst in c: d1-d2 (b1-a2). OCP (1985), found in *Each Time I Think of You*

4:4 (Luke 9:25; Romans 10:8-13; based on)
Hurd, Bob. *The Word is in Your Heart*. Org, gtr, inst in c: Cantor: d1-d2. OCP (1986) OCP 8617CC

4:10 Bender, Jan. *Begone Satan,* op. 32, no. 10. Org/pno: M:c1-d2. Concordia (1966) 98-1848

4:18 (Matthew 14:24-33; Matthew 26:69-75; Acts 2:3-4; based on)
Freud, Joyce (arr. Lyndell Leatherman). *Peter Was a Fisherman*. Kbd: a$^{\flat}$1-d2. Lillenas (1980), found in *Scripture Solos for All Seasons*

4:23 SEE: James 5:16. Curran, Pearl G. *Prayer*

5:1-2 SEE: James 5:16. Curran, Pearl G. *Prayer*

5:1-10 Humphreys, Don. *The Beatitudes*. Kbd: H:e$^{\flat}$1-g2; L:c1-e2. R. D. Row (1953)

5:1-10, 12
Wood, Don. *The Beatitudes*. Kbd: H:e$^{\flat}$1-f2; L:c1-d2. G. Schirmer (1959)

5:1-12 Browning, Mortimer. *The Beatitudes*. Org: H:e1-a3; L:c1-f2. Carl Fischer (1939)

5:1-12 Kavanaugh, Patrick. *The Beatitudes*. Duet-Vc: Sop/Alto. American Music Centre (n.d.)

5:1-12 SEE: Psalm 1:00. Schoenbachler, Tim. *Happy Are They*

5:1-16 Jones, Hilton Kean. *Happy Are the Lowly Poor*. 2-part mixed-Kbd: Med. Concordia (1994) 98-3154

5:3 (based on)
Ward-Stephens. *Blessed Are the Poor In Spirit* (from *The Beatitudes*). Pno: H:e$^{\flat}$1-f2; L:(n.v.). G. Schirmer (1921), found in *The Ward-Stephens Musical Settings of Poems by Anne Campbell Stark based on the Beatitudes*

5:3-4, 6, 8 (Matthew 11:28; adapted)
Gounod, Charles (ed. and arr. K. K. Davis and N. Loring). *O Come to Me*. Kbd: M:d1-f2. Carl Fischer (1948), found in *Sing Unto the Lord,* vol. 1

5:3-6 Malotte, Albert Hay. *The Beatitudes*. Pno: H:e1-g2; M:c1-e$^{\flat}$2;L:d1-f2. G. Schirmer (1938) HL50280840, found in *12 Sacred Songs* (H/M); *Christian Science Service Songs; The Church Soloist* (L); *The First Book of Soprano Solos*

5:3-10 Foley, John B. *The Beatitudes.* U-Pno, gtr: $e^{\flat}1$-$d^{\flat}2$. NALR (1985), found in *The Steadfast Love*

5:3-10, 16 (adapted)
Greif, Jean Anthony (arr. Randall DeBruyn). *We Are the Light of the World.* U/2-part-Org, gtr, inst in c: c1-c2(a1-f2). OCP (1966, 1983), found in *In Perfect Charity: Contemporary Accomp. Series,* vol. 4

5:3-11 (based on)
Wolfe, Jacques. *The Blessed.* Pno: H:e1-f♯2; L:b1-d2. G. Schirmer (1954)

5:3-12 Haas, David (vocal arr. Michael Joncas). *Blest Are They.* U/2-part-Kbd, gtr, 2 insts in c: c1-d2(f2). GIA (1985), also found in *Come and Journey; To Be Your Bread; When Love is Found*

5:4, 5 (based on)
Ward-Stephens. *Blessed Are They That Mourn* (from *The Beatitudes*). Pno: H; L:b1-d2. G. Schirmer (1921), found in *The Ward-Stephens Musical Settings of Poems by Anne Campbell Stark based on the Beatitudes*

5:5 (based on)
Ward-Stephens. *Blessed Are the Meek* (from *The Beatitudes*). Pno: M:b1-d2. G. Schirmer (1921), found in *The Ward-Stephens Musical Settings of Poems by Anne Campbell Stark based on the Beatitudes*

5:6 SEE: Isaiah 55:1, 3. Cherubini, Luigi. *Come to the Waters*

5:6 (based on)
Ward-Stephens. *Blessed Are They Which Do Hunger* (from *The Beatitudes*). Pno: H:d1-a3; L:(n.v.). G. Schirmer (1921), found in *The Ward-Stephens Musical Settings of Poems by Anne Campbell Stark based on the Beatitudes*

5:7 (based on)
Ward-Stephens. *Blessed Are the Merciful* (from *The Beatitudes*). Pno: H:(n.v.); L:$b^{\flat}1$-$e^{\flat}2$. G. Schirmer (1921), found in *The Ward-Stephens Musical Settings of Poems by Anne Campbell Stark based on the Beatitudes*

5:8 (Keble)
Harker, F. Flaxington. *Blest Are the Pure in Heart.* Kbd: H:f1-a3; L:d1-f2. Huntzinger (1916, 1952), found in *Sacred Songs Especially Suitable for Christian Science Services* (H/L)

5:8 (based on)
Ward-Stephens. *Blessed Are the Pure in Heart* (from *The Beatitudes*). Pno: H; L. G. Schirmer (1921), found in *The Ward-Stephens Musical Settings of Poems by Anne Campbell Stark based on the Beatitudes*

5:9 (based on)
Ward-Stephens. *Blessed Are the Peacemakers* (from *The Beatitudes*). Pno: H; L:a1-e2. G. Schirmer (1921), found in *The Ward-Stephens Musical Settings of Poems by Anne Campbell Stark based on the Beatitudes*

5:9-10 Sacco, Peter. *Blessed Are the Peacemakers.* Kbd: $d^{\flat}1$-$a^{\flat}3$. Ostara Press (n.d.)

5:10 (based on)
Ward-Stephens. *Blessed Are They Which Are Persecuted* (from *The Beatitudes*). Pno: H:$e^{\flat}1$-f2; L. G. Schirmer (1921), found in *The Ward-Stephens Musical Settings of Poems by Anne Campbell Stark based on the Beatitudes*

5:11 SEE: Psalm 63:6. Elgar, Edward. *The Sun Goeth Down*

5:13-14 (Matthew 10:26-27; based on)
Schutte, Daniel L. *What You Hear in the Dark.* U/2-part-Gtr: b1-c♯2(b1-d2). NALR (1975), found in *Earthen Vessels*

5:13-16 (based on)
Avery, Richard and Donald Marsh. *You Are the Salt of the Earth.* U/2-part-Kbd, gtr: b1-b2. Proclamation (1973), found in *Exodus Songbook*

5:14-16, 43-45, 48
LaForge, Frank. *Ye Are the Light of the World.* Kbd: d1-f2. G. Schirmer (1944)

6:6-13 SEE: James 5:16. Curran, Pearl G. *Prayer*

6:9-12 Flowers, Geoffrey E. *The Lord's Prayer.* Kbd: H or M:f1-f2. Coburn Press, found in *Eleven Scriptural Songs from the Twentieth Century*

6:9-13 Aäddissen, Erol. *The Lord's Prayer.* Pno: H:$d^{\flat}1$-$a^{\flat}3$; M:$b^{\flat}1$-f2; L:$a^{\flat}1$-$e^{\flat}2$. Presser (1997) 491-00458

6:9-13 Albrecht, M. *The Lord's Prayer.* Kbd: c1-e2. GIA

6:9-13 Anderson, Leroy and Alfred Heller. *The Lord's Prayer.* Org: f1-g2. Mercury (1967) A406

6:9-13 Bach, J. S. *The Lord's Prayer.* Kbd: M:$e^{\flat}1$-$e^{\flat}2$. Carl Fischer (1948), found in *Sing Unto the Lord,* vol. 1

6:9-13 Bantock, Granville. *The Lord's Prayer.* Kbd: d1-e♭2. Paxton (1943)

6:9-13 Barnes, Milton. *The Lord's Prayer.* Kbd: f♯1-d2. Canadian Music Centre (1954)

6:9-13 Bottenberg, Henry. *Our Father Who Art in Heaven.* Pno/org: M:c♯1-f2. Fritz Spies (1967)

6:9-13 Cadzow, Dorothy. *The Lord's Prayer.* Kbd: d1-d2. Century Music (1949)

6:9-13 Chausson, Ernest (ed. Patrick, David). *Pater Noster.* Kbd: MH:c♯1-g2. Boosey & Hawkes (1996), found in *Sacred Songs for the Soloist: 20 Songs on Religious Texts for Medium High Voice*

6:9-13 Cory, George. *The Lord's Prayer.* Kbd: e♭1-e♭2. G. Schirmer (1964)

6:9-13 Daigle, Gary. *The Lord's Prayer (Chant Mode II).* U-Kbd: f1-b♭2. GIA (1994) G-4022, also found in *Praise the Maker's Love*

6:9-13 Dame, William. *Our Father.* Kbd: d1-f♯2. Carl Fischer (1955)

6:9-13 Dennis, Randall. *Our Father.* Kbd, gtr: c1-d2. Pilot Point (1994) MB-825, found in *Solos from the Word*

6:9-13 Earls, Paul. *The Lord's Prayer.* Org or brass sextet: d♭1-e♭2. Stainer (1970) 2162

6:9-13 (other)
Eilers, Joyce. *Thy Will Be Done.* Pno: M:c1-d2. HMP (1975, 1980) SM 43

6:9-13 Forsyth, Josephine. *The Lord's Prayer.* Pno: a1-e♭2. G. Schirmer (1929)

6:9-13 Franco, Johan. *The Lord's Prayer.* Kbd: c1-f♯2. American Composers Alliance, found in *Composers Facsimile Edition*

6:9-13 Gaskill, Clarence. *Our Father.* Kbd: c1-d2. Bergman (1946)

6:9-13 Gates, B. Cecil. *The Lord's Prayer.* Pno, vln: L:b♭1-e♭2; M:c1-f2; H:d1-g2. Choir Publishing (1937)

6:9-13 Haas, David. *The Lord's Prayer I.* Kbd, gtr: c1-d2. GIA (1986), found in *Light and Peace*

6:9-13 Hamblen, Bernard. *The Lord's Prayer.* Kbd: d♭1-f2. Belwin Mills (1946), octavo available

6:9-13 Head, Michael. *The Lord's Prayer.* Kbd: b♭1-e♭2. Boosey & Hawkes (1956)

6:9-13 Head, Michael. *The Lord's Prayer.* Kbd: L:a1-d2. Boosey & Hawkes (1996), found in *Sing Solo Sacred* (H/L)

6:9-13 Heiller, Anton. *Pater Noster* (Latin). Kbd: c1-c♯2. Doblinger (1963)

6:9-13 Henschel, George. *The Lord's Prayer.* Kbd: H:c1-f♯2; M:b♭1-e2. Bayley & Ferguson (1919), found in *The Sacred Hour of Song*

6:9-13 Hines, Jerome. *The Lord's Prayer* (from *I am the Way*). Pno: H. Carl Fischer (1965) V2369

6:9-13 Hoffmeister, Leon Abbott. *The Lord's Prayer.* Pno: H:e♭1-f2; L:c1-d2. Huntzinger (1929), found in *Selected Sacred Songs for General Use*

6:9-13 Hurd, Bob and Paul Ford (arr. Craig S. Kingsbury). *Our Father.* U-Gtr: e1-c2. OCP (1979), found in *Roll Down the Ages*

6:9-13 Isensee, Paul R. *The Lord's Prayer.* Kbd: b1-d2. Hope (1981) 911, also found in *Everything for the Wedding Soloist*

6:9-13 Johnson, David N. *The Lord's Prayer* (uses traditional as well as ICET text). Kbd (opt bass): c1-d2. Augsburg (1974) 11-074

6:9-13 Jorgensen, Philip. *The Lord's Prayer.* Kbd: f1-g2. Calumet (1941)

6:9-13 Kirkland, Terry. *The Lord's Prayer.* U/2-part-Kbd: b1-e2(g♯2). Broadman Press (1977) 4172-86

6:9-13 Krebs, Karl August. *Vater unser (The Lord's Prayer)* (German/English). Org: H:d♭1-g♭2; L:b♭1-e♭2. G. Schirmer (1907) 2451, also found in *Album of Sacred Songs* (H/L); *Kirchen-Arien und Lieder* (H)

6:9-13 (adapted)
Lee, John. *Thine Be the Glory.* Pno, gtr: b1-g2. Word (1974), found in *Time for Joy*

6:9-13 MacGimsey, Robert. *Our Father.* Pno: c1-f2. Carl Fischer (1950), found in *Contemporary American Sacred Songs* (MH)

6:9-13 Malotte, Albert Hay. *The Lord's Prayer.* Org/Pno: H:e♭1-b♭3; MH:d♭-a♭2; M:c1-g2; ML:b♭1-f2; L:a♭1-e♭2; LL:g-c1. G. Schirmer (1935), found in *12 Sacred Songs* (MH/ML); *Bible Songs* (M); *The Bride's Guide to Wedding Music* (L); *Christian Science Service Songs; Christian Wedding Songbook* (L); *The Church Soloist* (ML); *Contemporary*

American Sacred Songs (M); *The Complete Lord's Prayer; O My Soul; For All the Saints; Everything for the Church Soloist* (M/L); *Hymns & Voices; The Joy of Wedding Music* (ML); *Sandi Patti Anthology; Singers Christian Wedding Collection* (M/L); *Wedding & Love* (M); *Wedding Songs of Love & Friendship* (M)

6:9-13 Malotte, Albert Hay (arr. Steve Green). *The Lord's Prayer (Padre Nuestro).* Kbd: b♭1-f2. Sparrow (1992), found in *Steve Green: Hymns–A Portrait of Christ*

6:9-13 Malotte, Albert Hay. *The Lord's Prayer.* Duet-Org/Pno: S:d♭2-a♭2/Alto:e♭-d♭2; S:d♭1-a♭2/Tenor:e♭-d♭2; Alto:a1-e♭2/Bass:b♭-e♭1. G. Schirmer (1935, 1946), also found in *Schirmer's Favorite Sacred Duets*

6:9-13 Mayfield, Larry. *O Father in Heaven.* Kbd: c1-f2. Lillenas (1977) 911, also found in *Everything for the Church Soloist; Everything for the Wedding Soloist*

6:9-13 Mead, Sr. Janet. *The Lord's Prayer.* U/2-part-Kbd, gtr: b1-d2. DuMonde/Almo (1974), found in *Exodus Songbook*

6:9-13 Mendelssohn, Felix. *The Lord's Prayer.* Kbd: d1-e♭2. July (1976), found in *Very Special Sacred Songs*

6:9-13 Mendelssohn, Felix (arr. Michael Johnson). *The Lord's Prayer.* Kbd: b♭1-e♭2. Portside Music (1996), found in *All-American Gospel*

6:9-13 Merbecke, John (arr. Everett Jay Hilty). *The Lord's Prayer.* Pno/Org: D-a2. Oxford (1971) 96.202

6:9-13 Myers, Gordon. *The Lord's Prayer.* Kbd: e♭1-e♭2. Eastlane Music Corp.

6:9-13 Nagy, Russell. *The Lord's Prayer.* U-Kbd: d1-b2. Beckenhorst (1990) JH511

6:9-13 Peeters, Flor. *Pater Noster,* op. 102 *(The Lord's Prayer)* (Latin/English). Org: H:e1-f2; M:c1-d2; L:b♭1-d2. C. F. Peters (1962) H:P6342a; M:P6342b; L:P6342c

6:9-13 Peeters, Flor. *Pater Noster,* op. 102 *(The Lord's Prayer)* (Latin/English). Duet-Org: Unequal voices. C. F. Peters (1962) P6341

6:9-13 Penn, Marilyn. *Thy Will Be Done.* Duet-Kbd: H/L. Witmark 166

6:9-13 Proulx, Richard. *The Lord's Prayer (Ar nathir)* (uses Ancient Gaelic folk hymn). Org: M:d1-e2. GIA (1972) G-1705

6:9-13 Roma, Caro. *The Lord's Prayer.* Duet-Kbd: H/L. Witmark (n.v.)

6:9-13 (adapted)
Romer, Charles B. *Praise the Lord, O My Soul.* Kbd: b♭1-e♭2. Lillenas (1982), found in *The Lord is My Light*

6:9-13 Rorem, Ned. *The Lord's Prayer.* Kbd: d1-g2. Henmar (C. F. Peters) (1957) 6371

6:9-13 (paraphrased)
Roth, John. *God of Love Beyond All Wonder.* Kbd: g-c2. Augsburg (1993) 11-10432

6:9-13 Sheatz, Elizabeth Q. *The Lord's Prayer.* Kbd: H:d1-g2; L:b1-e2. Oliver Ditson (1913), found in *Songs for Christian Science Services*

6:9-13 Shenk, Louis. *The Lord's Prayer.* Kbd: H:d1-g2; L:b1-e2. Presser (1951)

6:9-13 (adapted)
Sibelius, Jean (arr. Richard D. Row). *The Lord's Prayer.* Kbd: H:a♭1-f2; L:f1-d2. R. D. Row (1959), found in *Soloists Practical Library of Sacred Songs,* bk 1 (H/L)

6:9-13 Smith, Michael W. *As it is in Heaven (The Lord's Prayer).* Kbd: M:c1-c2. O'Ryan Music (1995), found in *I'll Lead You Home*

6:9-13 Strals, Arnold (arr. Les Sands). *The Lord's Prayer.* Pno, gtr: d1-d2. Du Monde Music (1973) 4993LSMX, found in *Gospel & Inspirational Showstoppers*

6:9-13 SEE: Psalm 25:4-5. Whittemore, Dan. *My Lord is Leading Me On*

6:9-13 Willan, Healey. *The Lord's Prayer.* U-Org: d♭1-b♭2. Concordia, found in *A Third Morning Star Choir Book*

6:9-13 Williamson, Inez McC. *The Lord's Prayer.* Kbd: f1-a3. Intrada (1972), found in *Whom God Hath Joined Together*

6:9-13 Young, Carlton. *The Lord's Prayer.* U-Kbd: b♭1-b♭2. Agape (1973), found in *The Genesis Songbook*

6:12 Fettke, Tom. *Forgive Our Sins as We Forgive.* Kbd: (b♭1)c1-e♭2. Lillenas (1980), found in *Scripture Solos for All Seasons*

6:19-21, 24, 33 (Isaiah 40:7)
Krieg, Melita. *The World of Our God Shall Stand.* Kbd: e♭1-e♭2. Huntzinger (1963) RH 8204

6:25-26, 28-29
Topliff, Robert. *Consider the Lilies.* Pno: H:c♯1-f♯2; ML:b♭1-e♭2; L:a1-d2. G. Schirmer

(1924); Church (n.d.), found in *Sacred Songs,* vol. 1–*Soprano; Seventeen Sacred Songs For Church and General Use* (H/L); *Songs for Christian Science Services* (H/ML)

6:25-26, 28-29
Topliff, Robert. *Consider the Lilies.* Duet-Pno: c1-f2/b♭1-e♭2. G. Schirmer (1924); John Church (1907), found in *Sacred Duets,* vol. II (H/L)

6:25-29 Bischoff, John W. *If God So Clothe the Grass.* Kbd: c♯1-e2. Boston Music (1929, 1943)

6:25-32 (based on)
Sleeth, Natalie. *Consider the Lilies.* U-Kbd, fl or vln: e1-c2. Choristers Guild (1978) CGA-195

6:25-33 Fisher, William Arms (ed. Wilman Wilmans). *Seek Ye First the Kingdom of God,* op. 16, no. 2. Org: H:d1-g2(b♭3); MH:c♯1-f♯2(a3); L:b1-e2(g2). Oliver Ditson (1913), found in *Solos for Christian Science Churches*

6:25-34 SEE: Job 11:16. Hurd, Bob. *God's Eye is on the Sparrow*

6:25c-26, 28b-30
Bischoff, John W. (ed. Carl Fredrickson). *Consider the Lilies.* Kbd: H:d1-g2; L:a1-d2. R. D. Row (1963), found in *Church Soloists Favorites,* bk 1

6:28, 31 (Luke 12:24-31; adapted)
Talbot, John Michael. *The Lilies of the Field.* Gtr: c1-c2. Birdwing (1985), found in *Praise, Praise the Lord, O My Soul and Worship*

6:28-29 (Luke 12:24, 27; Matthew 7:9; other)
Thurman, Geoffrey P. *Jehovah.* Kbd, gtr: a1-a2. Meadowgreen (1984), found in *The Song Book,* vol. III

6:28-32 (Matthew 11:28-30; Matthew 7:7-8; adapted)
Haas, David (pno arr. Jeanne Cotter). *Seek First the Kingdom.* Duet-Kbd, gtr, 2 inst in c: b1-d2. GIA (1993) G-3955, also found in *No Longer Strangers; When Love is Found*

6:28-32 (Matthew 11:28-30; Matthew 7:7-8; adapted)
Haugen, Marty. *Come Unto Me.* 2-part-Gtr, ob, fl: a1-d2. GIA (1978), found in *I Send My Light*

6:28-34 Carter, John. *Surely He Will Care for Me.* Kbd: M:b1-d♭2. Hope (1984) 1053, also found in *Come With a Singing Heart*

6:28-34 Scott, John Prindle. *Consider the Lilies.* Kbd: H:e♭1-g2; L:c1-e2. G. Schirmer (1921, 1949), found in *Christian Science Service Songs*

6:28-34 (Luke 12:27-31; Matthew 7:9; based on)
Thurman, Geoffrey P. *Jehovah.* Duet-Kbd: a1-b2. Meadowgreen (1984, 1983), found in *Our God Reigns*

6:28-34 (Luke 12:27-31; Matthew 7:9; based on)
Thurman, Geoffrey P. (ed. Steven V. Taylor). *Jehovah.* 2-part-Kbd or Trax: a1-a2/c♯-c♯1. Meadowgreen (1988), found in *25 Songs for Two-Part Choir*

6:31-33 Foster, Myles B. *Seek Ye First the Kingdom of God* (from *Seed Time and Harvest).* Kbd: Tenor:f1-g2. G. Schirmer, found in *Anthology of Sacred Song–Tenor*

6:33 Grant, Amy and Wes King. *Seek First.* Kbd, gtr: ML:a1-b2. Age to Age Music (1992), found in *Songs from the Loft*

6:33 (Matthew 7:7; Deuteronomy 8:3b)
Lafferty, Karen. *Seek Ye First.* Kbd: M:d1-a2. Hope (1980), found in *Everything for the Church Soloist* (ML)

6:33 (Matthew 7:7; Deuteronomy 8:3b)
Lafferty, Karen. *Seek Ye First.* U/2-part: M: c1-b♭2(e♭2); ML:b1-a2(d2). Maranatha! (1989), found in *Bible Book; Everything for the Church Soloist* (ML); *Praise Classics-Lord of Peace* (ML); *Songs for Praise and Worship* (M); *WOW Worship Songbook Green*

6:33 (Matthew 7:7, Deuteronomy 8:3b)
Lafferty, Karen. *Seek Ye First.* Duet-Kbd: b1-a2(d2). Marantha! (2000) 2145, also found in *WOW Worship Songbook Green*

6:33 (Deuteronomy 6:1-5)
Pendleton, Emmet. *The Kingdom of God,* op. 12, no. 1 (from *The Light of the Lord*). Pno: c1-a♯3. Bruce Humphries (1945)

7:7-8 SEE: Matthew 6:33. Lafferty, Karen. *Seek Ye First*

7:7-8 SEE: Matthew 6:28-32. Haas, David. *Seek First the Kingdom*

7:7-8 SEE: Matthew 6:28-32. Haugen, Marty. *Come Unto Me*

7:7-8 (Matthew 11:28-30; Luke 11:9-10)
Scarlatti, Alessandro. *Come Unto Me.* Kbd: H:e♯1-f♯2; M:d♯1-e2. Carl Fischer (1939), found in *The Sacred Hour of Song* (H/M)

7:9 SEE: Matthew 6:28-29. Thurman, Geoffrey P. *Jehovah*

7:13-15 SEE: Psalm 25:4-5. Whittemore, Dan. *My Lord is Leading Me On*

8:8 Aichinger, Gregor (ed. William E. Hettick). *Domine, non sum dignus* (Latin). Duet-Cont: Tenor:c1-f2/Tenor:c1-d2. A-R Editions (1986), found in Aichinger's *The Vocal Concertos*

8:20 (Matthew 24:21; based on)
Spiritual (arr. Harry T. Burleigh). *Hard Trials.* Pno: e♭1-e♭2. Belwin Mills (1927), found in *The Spirituals of Harry T. Burleigh*

9:11-13 (Matthew 11:25, 28; Matthew 18:1-4; based on)
Schutte, Daniel L. *Come to Me All Who Are Weary.* Gtr: c1-c2. NALR (1974), found in *Neither Silver Nor Gold*

9:20-22 SEE: Mark 5:24-29, 34. Hart, Theron Wolcott. *The Healing of the Woman*

9:36b-37 Burroughs, Bob. *The Commission.* Kbd: e♭1-f2. Hope (1970) 501, also found in *New Testament Songs*

9:39 (John 4:35-38; based on)
Schutte, Daniel L. *Come With Me Into the Fields.* Gtr: c1-d2. NALR (1974), found in *Neither Silver Nor Gold*

10:8 (based on)
Owens, Carol. *Freely, Freely.* Kbd: a1-c2. Communiqué Music (1972), found in *Very Special Sacred Songs*

10:26-27 SEE: Matthew 5:13-14. Schutte, Daniel L. *What You Hear in the Dark*

10:29-31 (W. S. Passmore)
Abt, Franz. *Not a Sparrow Falleth.* Kbd: c1-f2. Amsco (1940), found in *Everybody's Favorite Sacred Songs*

10:29-31 (John 14:1; based on)
Gabriel, Charles H. *His Eye is on the Sparrow.* Kbd: H:c1-f2; M: a♭1-d2; L:g-c♯2. Lillenas (1980), found in *The Low Voice Book* (L); *Scripture Solos for All Seasons* (M); *Solos from the Word* (H)

11:4-5 (Luke 24:5-6; Matthew 28:2-7, 19; Revelation 21:4-5)
Haas, David. *Song of the Risen One.* U/2-part-Kbd, gtr: (b1)f♯1-e2. GIA (1988), found in *Who Calls You By Name,* vol. 1

11:25, 28 SEE: Matthew 9:11-13. Schutte, Daniel L. *Come to Me All Who Are Weary*

11:27-28 SEE: Revelation 3:20. Bryant, Verna Mae. *Behold, I Stand at the Door*

11:28 SEE: Isaiah 62:3. Hurd, Bob. *Come Unto Me*

11:28 (Isaiah 55:6)
LaForge, Frank. *Come Unto Me.* Pno: e♭1-e2. Carl Fischer (1942)

11:28 (John 1:29; other)
Lyon, A. Laurence. *Behold the Lamb of God.* Kbd: M:d1-f2. Jackman Music (1992) S-0180, found in *Scripture Settings for Solo Voice*

11:28-29 Cady, Gertrude. *Come Unto Me.* Org: Hc1-g2(a2); L:a1-e2(f♯2). Harold Flammer (1929)

11:28-29 Handel, G. F. *Come Unto Him (Kommt her zu ihm)* (from *Messiah*). Kbd: Sop or H:f1-g2; L:d1-e2. Carl Fischer; G. Schirmer; Novello (1959), found in *52 Sacred Songs; The Church Soloist* (L); *The Church Soloist—A Collection* (H); *Everybody's Favorite Sacred Songs; Kirchen-Arien und Lieder* (German)*; Oratorio Repertoire,* vol. 1; *Schirmer's Singer's Library: Soprano Arias from Oratorios; Scripture Solos for All Seasons; Seventeen Sacred Songs for Church and General Use* (L); *Sing Solo Sacred* (H/L); *Singer's Repertoire: Songs of Faith; World's Favorite Sacred Songs*

11:28-29 Handel, G. F. (ed. James Michael Stevens; arr. W. Daniel Landes). *Come Unto Him* (from *Messiah*). Kbd: c1-d2. Integra (1991), found in *Christmas MESSIAH for Young Voices*

11:28-30 (adapted)
Bach, J. S. *Come Unto Him.* Kbd: H:c1-g2; L:a1-e2. R. D. Row (1959), found in *Soloists Practical Library of Sacred Songs,* bk 1 (H/L)

11:28-30 Beethoven, Ludwig van (adapted Alexander Aslanoff). *Come to Me,* op. 27, no. 2. Pno: H:d1-g2; L:b1-e2. G. Schirmer (1933), found in *52 Sacred Songs*

11:28-30 Chadwick, George Whitefield. *Come Unto Me.* Duet-Kbd: Sop:c♯1-a3/Tenor:d-a2. G. Schirmer (1957) 43927

11:28-30 (John 4:10; poem)
Coenen, William. *Come Unto Me.* Pno: H:e♭1-f2; L:c1-d2. G. Schirmer (1918,

1924); John Church (n.d.); Carl Fischer (1942), found in *Album of Sacred Songs* (H/L); *Sacred Songs,* vol. 1–*Soprano* (H); *Seventeen Sacred Songs for Church and General Use*

11:28-30 SEE: Isaiah 40:9. Dufford, Bob. *Like a Shepherd*

11:28-30 (adapted)
Dvorák, Antonín. *Come Unto Me (Ihr Alle)* (English/German). Kbd: Sop:e1-f2. John Church (n.d.), found in *Sacred Songs,* vol. 1–Soprano

11:28-30 SEE: Matthew 5:3-4, 6, 8. Gounod, Charles. *O Come to Me*

11:28-30 SEE: Matthew 6:28-32. Haas, David. *Seek First the Kingdom*

11:28-30 (John 14:6)
Handel, G. F. *Come Unto Me.* Kbd: H:e♭1-f2; L:c1-d2. R. D. Row (1960), found in *Soloist's Practical Library,* bk 2

11:28-30 SEE: Matthew 6:28-32. Haugen, Marty. *Come Unto Me*

11:28-30 (adapted)
Joncas, Michael. *Come to Me.* Gtr: c1-e♭2. GIA (1990) G-3432, also found in *Come to Me*

11:28-30 Leslie, Henry. *Come Unto Him.* Kbd: Sop:f1-g2. Presser (n.d.), found in *Sacred Songs,* vol. 1–Soprano

11:28-30 Rutenber, C. B. *Come Unto Me.* Org: e1-f2. G. Schirmer (1921)

11:28-30 SEE: Matthew 7:7-8. Scarlatti, Alessandro. *Come Unto Me*

11:28-30 Schütz, Heinrich. *Venite ad me,* SWV 261 *(Kommt alle zu mir)* (from *Symphoniae Sacrae* I) (Latin/German). Cont, 2 vlns: Tenor:c-g1. Bärenreiter (1949) BA32

11:28-30 (adapted)
Talbot, John Michael. *My Yoke is Easy.* Gtr: c1-d2. Birdwing (1987), found in *Praise, Praise the Lord, O My Soul and Worship*

11:28-30 Willan, Healey. *Come Unto Me, All Ye That Labor.* U-Org: e1-e2. Concordia, found in *A Third Morning Star Choir Book*

11:29 SEE: Joel 2:15. Purcell, Henry. *Blow Ye the Trumpet*

12:18-21 SEE: Isaiah 52:8-9. Elgar, Edward. *The Voice of Thy Watchman*

13:4-8 SEE: Ecclesiastes 3:1-9. Ridge, M. D. *Parable*

13:4-43 SEE: Joel 2:12. Harker, F. Flaxington. *Turn Ye Even to Me With All Your Heart*

13:43 (Isaiah 51:11b)
Mendelssohn, Felix. *Then Shall the Righteous Shine (Dann werden die Gerechten leuchten)* (from *Elijah*) (English/German). Kbd: Tenor:e♭-a♭2; H:d1-g2; M:c1-f2. Carl Fischer (1939), found in *Anthology of Sacred Song–Tenor; Everything for the Church Soloist* (M); *The Oratorio Anthology–Tenor; Oratorio Repertoire,* vol. III; *Sacred Hour of Song* (H/M); *Vocal Solos for Funerals and Memorial Services* (M)

13:44-45 Hopson, Hal H. *The Treasure and Pearl.* U/2-part-Kbd: d1-d2. AMSI (1984) 462

13:44-45 (John 6:68; based on)
Schutte, Daniel L. *I Found the Treasure.* Cantor-Pno, gtr, inst in c, opt duet: c1-c2(f2). NALR (1985) Gtr: 5709CC; Pno: 5710CC, also found in *The Steadfast Love*

14:13-21 (Mark 6:35-41; Mark 8:1-10; Luke 9:12-17; John 6:1-14)
Hopson, Hal H. *Jesus Fed the Hungry Thousands.* Kbd: d1-d2. Hope (1985)

14:17-21 (based on)
Smith, Michael W. and Deborah D. Smith. *Could He Be the Messiah.* Pno: a1-e2. Meadowgreen (1988), found in *Michael W. Smith: Greatest Hits*

14:24-33 SEE: Matthew 4:18. Freud, Joyce. *Peter Was a Fisherman*

16:13-18, 25 (II Corinthians 5:7; other)
McGuire, Dony. *Upon This Rock.* Kbd: Original:c1-c3; H:c1-e♭2(a♭3); M:a1-f2; L:a♭1-e2. Gaither Music (1984), found in *The Best Gospel Songs Ever* (H); *The Big Book of Contemporary Christian Favorites* (L); *GMA Song of the Year* (H); *Greatest Songs of Sandi Patty; The Lord is My Light; Sandi Patti: Anthology* (L); *Sandi Patti: The Finest Moments; Sandi Patti Medium Voice Collection; Song of the Year* (H); *Very Best of Sandi Patty* (H/M); *Very Special Sacred Songs* (M)

16:25 (based on)
Smith, Marcus. *Evening Song.* Kbd: M:b♭1-d2. Sonos (Jackman) (1997) 00434, found in *Sabbath Song*

16:26 (other)
Anthony, Dick. *Where is the Profit?* Kbd: c1-d2. Lillenas (1970, 1976), found in *Scripture Solos for All Seasons*

18:1-4 (Mark 10:14; Luke 18:17)
Day, Stanley A. *Suffer the Little Children.* Pno:d♭1-f2. Boston (1951)

18:1-4 SEE: Matthew 9:11-13. Schutte, Daniel L. *Come to Me All Who Are Weary*

18:2-5 (Linda Rebuck)
Fettke, Tom. *Jesus Has Time.* Kbd: b1-d2. Lillenas (1983), found in *The Lord is My Light*

18:10 SEE: Mark 10:13-14. Underhill, Charles D. *Suffer the Little Children*

18:10-14 SEE: Hosea 11:00. Hurd, Bob. *Return to Me*

18:13 (based on)
Spiritual (arr. Edward Boatner). *Lost Sheep.* Pno, gtr: c1-e2. Belwin Mills (1973), found in *The Story of the Spirituals*

19:1-2, 13-15 (Luke 18:17)
LaForge, Frank. *Suffer the Little Children.* Kbd: H:e♭1-g2; L:c1-e2. Carl Fishcer (1950)

19:6 (Mark 10:8-9; William Vaughan Jenkins)
Lovelace, Austin C. *Wedding Song.* Kbd: e1-e2. Darcy Press (1993), found in *Sacred Solos by Austin C. Lovelace*

19:6 (Ephesians 5:25; I John 4:12; adapted)
Nelson, Ronald A. *Not Two, But One.* Kbd or Gtr: a1-d2. Augsburg (1985) 11-7475

19:13-14 (based on)
Kirkland, Terry. *Jesus and the Children.* U/2-part-Kbd, hdbls: b♭1-e♭2. Triune (1987) TUM 314

19:14 (Luke 18:17)
Fischer, Irwin. *Suffer the Children to Come Unto Me.* Kbd: d1-g2. American Composers Alliance, found in *Composers Facsimile Edition*

19:14 (Mark 10:15; Luke 18:17)
Schultz, A. L. *Suffer the Little Children.* Kbd: e♭1-e♭2. Tullan-Meredith (1902)

19:15 (Acts 8:17; Acts 19:6; based on)
Spiritual (arr. Harry T. Burleigh). *I Know de Lord's Laid His Hands on Me.* Pno: H:c1-f2; L:b♭1-e♭2. Belwin Mills (1925), found in *The Spirituals of Harry T. Burleigh* (H/L)

21:8, 9 Lekberg, Sven. *And a Very Great Multitude.* Kbd: c1-e2. Witmark (1947) 20608-3

21:9 Bach, J. S. *Benedictus* (from *Mass in b minor*) (Latin). Kbd: Tenor:e-a2. Hal Leonard (1994), found in *Oratorio Anthology: Tenor*

21:9 Carr, Arthur. *Hosanna to the Son of David.* Kbd: Med. G. Schirmer (1947) 91565

21:9 Grimm, Heinrich. *Hosianna, dem Sohne David* (from *Zwei Kleine Weihnachtskonzerte*) (German). Duet-Cont: Equal voices: c1-g2/c1-f2. Bärenreiter (1974) 6460

21:9 (Mark 11:9-10)
Haydn, F. Joseph. *Benedictus* (from *Eine Kleine Orgen Messe*) (Latin). Kbd: Sop:e♭2-b♭3. HLH Music (1992), found in *Five Vocal Gems for Soprano*

21:9 (Mark 11:9-10)
Haydn, F. Joseph (ed. H. C. Robbins Landon). *Benedictus* (from *Missa Brevis Sancti Joannis de Deo*) (Latin). Org, cont., 2 vlns: Sop:e♭2-b♭3. G. Schirmer (1974) 2923

21:9 (based on; other)
Helvering, Sandi Patti; Phil McHugh and Gloria Gaither. *In the Name of the Lord.* Pno/Trax: H:a♭1-a3; M:g♭-g2; ML:e-d2(f2); L:b1-d♭2. Meadowgreen (1986, 1988, 1990) Trax: 301 7165 205, found in *50 EZ Inspirational Favorites; The Best Contemporary Christian Songs Ever* (H); *Contemporary Low Voice; Fifty Contemporary Favorites for Low Voice* (ML); *Glorious Praise: Great Songwriters and Songs* (H); *GMA Song of the Year* (H); *Greatest Songs of Sandi Patty* (H); *Inspirational Selections; Sandi Patti: Anthology* (M); *Sandi Patti: the Finest Moments; Sandi Patti: Morning Like This* (H); *Sandi Patti Medium Voice Collection; Song of the Year* (H); *Songs for Praise and Worship* (L); *Very Best of Sandi Patti* (H/M)

21:9 SEE: Psalm 24:7-10. Lindh, Jody W. *Lift Up Your Heads*

21:9 SEE: Isaiah 52:7-8. Manion, Tim. *Blessings on the King*

21:9 Nelson, Ronald A. *Hosanna!* 2-part-Kbd: Sop:e1-e2/Alto:c1-c2. AMSI (1993)

21:9 (Mark 11:9-10)
Pergolesi, Giovanni B. (ed. Francesco Cafarelli). *Benedictus qui vent* (Latin). Duet-Sop:d1-g2/Alto:b♭1-b♭2. Gli amici della musica da camera (1939), found in *Opera Omnia,* vol. 16

21:9 SEE: Zechariah 9:9. Posch, Isaac. *Ecco Dominus veniet*

21:9 (Parks)
Rogers, Sharon Elery. *Song of Hosanna.* Kbd: d1-g2. Hope (1970) 501, also found in *New Testament Songs*

21:9 (Mark 11:9-10)
Silvia, Giulio. *Benedictus* (from *Mass in Honor of the Sacred Heart*) (Latin). Duet-Unequal voices: H:d1-f2/L:d1-d2. Birchard (1934)

21:9 (Luke 19:40)
Smith, G. Alan. *The Lord Comes.* U/2-part-Kbd: b♭1-d2. Agape (1989) AG 7286

21:9 (based on; other)
Smith, Michael W. and Deborah D. Smith. *Hosanna.* Pno: c♯1-e2. Meadowgreen (1984, 1988), found in *42 Songs for All Occasions; Michael W. Smith: Greatest Hits; The Song Book,* vol. III

21:9 (based on; other)
Smith, Michael W. and Deborah D. Smith (arr. Steven V. Taylor). *Hosanna.* 2-part-Pno or Trax: g♯-c♯2/c♯-d1. Meadowgreen (1988), found in *25 Songs for Two-Part Choir*

21:9c SEE: Isaiah 6:3. Scholtes, Peter. *Holy, Holy, Holy*

21:9b SEE: Isaiah 6:3b. Wold, Wayne L. *Sanctus and Benedictus*

22:37-39 McAfee, Don. *The Two Commandments.* Kbd: e1-f2. Hope (1970) 501, also found in *New Testament Songs*

22:37-39 (Mark 12:30-31; I Corinthians 13:4-5, 13)
VanDyke, May. *Love.* Kbd: H:f1-g2; L:d1-e♭2. Boosey & Hawkes (1932)

23:37a (Mark 15:39)
Klughardt, August (comp. Irving Brown). *Truly, This Man Was the Son of God!* (from *The Burial of Christ*). Kbd: Bass:a-f1. G. Schirmer (1977), found in *Schirmer's Singer's Library: Bass Arias from Oratorios*

23:37 Manookin, Robert P. *Prayer of Dedication.* Kbd: M:d1-d2. Sonos (Jackman) (1997) 00434, found in *Sabbath Song*

23:37 (Luke 13:34)
Mendelssohn, Felix. *Jerusalem! Jerusalem! Thou That Killest the Prophets* (from *St. Paul*). Kbd: Sop:f1-f2; L:d1-d2. G. Schirmer (1977); Lawson Gould (1957), found in *52 Sacred Songs; Anthology of Sacred Song–Soprano; Oratorio Repertoire,* vol. 1; *Schirmer's Singer's Library: Soprano Arias from Oratorios; Solos for the Church Year* (H/L)

23:37 Mendelssohn, Felix (ed. Lloyd Pfautsch). *Jerusalem.* Kbd:d1-f2. Lawson Gould (1955), found in *Solos for the Church Year*

24:21 SEE: Matthew 8:20 (based on). Spiritual (arr. Harry T. Burleigh). *Hard Trials*

24:27 (based on)
Smith, Marcus. *Softly Beams the Sacred Dawning.* Kbd: M:c1-e2, found in *Sabbath Song*

24:42 (I Peter 4:7; based on)
Marsh, Donald. *Beloved.* Kbd: c1-f♯2. ASCAP (1983), found in *The Lord Is My Light*

25:1-6 (Matthew 45:11; Philippians 4:7)
Dencke, Jeremiah. *Go Ye Forth In His Name* (German/English). Org, stgs: Sop:f1-f2. New York Public Library (1954) P6084, also found in *Ten Sacred Songs: Music of the Moravians in America*

25:1-13 Bender, Jan. *Lord, Lord Open to Us.* Kbd: f1-e2. Concordia (1966) 98-1833

25:7 SEE: Isaiah 52:8. Bach, J. S. *Zion hört die Wächter singen*

25:34 Gaul, Alfred Robert. *Come Ye Blessed* (from *Holy City*). Kbd: H:f1-g2; M:d1-e2; L:b♭1-c2. Amsco (1940), G. Schirmer; Boston Music (1961), found in *20 Distinctive Sacred Solos* (H/L); *Everybody's Favorite Sacred Songs* (H); *First Book of Mezzo-Soprano/Alto Solos* part II (M); *Oratorio Repertoire,* vol. II

25:34-36 Scott, John Prindle. *Come Ye Blessed.* Pno: H:e♭1-a♭3; M:c1-f2. G. Schirmer (1940), found in *Seventeen Sacred Songs for Church and General Use*

25:34-36 Scott, John Prindle. *Come Ye Blessed.* Pno: L:b♭1-e♭2. G. Schirmer (1994) HL50482071, found in *Second Book of Baritone/Bass Solo*

25:41-45 Scott, John Prindle. *Depart From Me.* Pno: H:e1-g2; L:c1-e2. Harold Flammer (1919)

26:26 SEE: John 6:35. Mendelssohn, Felix (ed. M. B. Stearns). *Beard of Life*

26:26-28 Bock, Fred. *Take, Eat (Communion Meditation).* Kbd: a2-f2. Fred Bock (2001), found in *The Sanctuary Soloist,* vol. 3

26:26-29 (other hymn text)
Bach, J. S. *Sacrament* (from *St. Matthew Passion*). Kbd: H:d1-g2; L:b1-e2. Carl Fischer (1939), found in *The Sacred Hour of Song*

26:30, 39-41
Berthier, Jacques (ed. Brother Robert). *The Spirit is Willing*. U-Kbd: d1-d2. Taizé (1984), found in *Music From Taizé,* vol. 2

26:36-39, 42 (adapted)
Shafferman, Jean Anne and George C. Strattner. *A Lenten Lesson*. U/2-part-Kbd, (opt hdbls): c1-d♭2. Alfred (1991) 4216

26:38-39a, 45
Berthier, Jacques (ed. Brother Robert). *My Heart is Breaking With Grief.* U-Kbd: f1-e♭2. Taizé (1984), found in *Music From Taizé,* vol. 2

26:42 (other)
Handel, G. F. *My Father, My Father, Look Upon My Anguish* (from *The Passion*). Kbd: Bass:b♭-e♭1. G. Schirmer, found in *Anthology of Sacred Song–Bass*

26:47 through 27:50; paraphrased)
Overholt, Ray (arr. Tom Fettke). *Ten Thousand Angels*. Kbd (Trax): H: d♭1-f♯2; L: g-b♭2; M: c1-d2; L: g-b♭2. Lillenas (1959, 1981), found in *The Church Soloist; The Lord is My Light; The Low Voice Book; Solos from the Word*

26:69-75 SEE: Matthew 4:18. Freud, Joyce. *Peter Was a Fisherman*

27:1-50 SEE: Matthew 26:47. Overholt, Ray. *Ten Thousand Angels*

27:28, 62-66
Rorem, Ned. *Resurrection.* Pno: b♭1-a♭3. Peer - Southern (1956)

27:30 (Mark 15:22; Luke 23:33; John 19:17; based on)
Card, Michael. *This Must Be the Lamb.* Kbd, gtr: d1-c2. Mole End Music (1983), found in *Greatest Songs of Michael Card*

27:45-46 Nystedt, Knut. *Tenebrae factae sunt* (Latin). Org: Bass: A-f1. Norsk Musikforlag (1978) NMO 9021

27:46 SEE: Lamentations 1:1. Berthier, Jacques. *All You Who Pass This Way*

27:46 (other)
Dubois, Theodore. *God, My Father* (from *Seven Last Words of Christ*) (Latin/English). Kbd: Bass:d-f1. G. Schirmer (1926) 186, also found in *Anthology of Sacred Song–Bass*

27:46 (other)
Dubois, Theodore. *O My Father* (from *Seven Last Words of Christ*). Kbd: Bass:d-f1. Presser (1923), found in *Oratorio Repertoire,* vol. IV

27:46 SEE: Psalm 22:2. Schalitt. *Eili, Eili! Invocation*

28:1-6 Coombs, Charles Whitney. *As it Began to Dawn*. Kbd: f♯1-f2. G. Schirmer (1914)

28:1-6 Speaks, Oley. *In the End of the Sabbath* (*Easter Song*). Kbd: H:c1-a3; L:a1-f2. G. Schirmer (1918), found in *Christian Science Service Songs*

28:1-7 (other)
Barnes, Frederick M. *He is Risen!* Kbd: L:a1-f2. JIB Pub (1990)/F. M. Barnes (1981), found in *Great New Solos*

28:1-7 (hymn)
Harker, F. Flaxington. *As it Began to Dawn.* Pno: H:e1-f♯2; L:c1-d2. G. Schirmer (1905)

28:1-8 (Mark 16:107; Luke 24:1-15; John 20:1-18; paraphrased)
Croegaret, Jim. *Was it a Morning Like This?* Pno: c1-c2. Meadowgreen (1990), found in *Sandi Patti Anthology; Sandi Patti: Morning Like This; Sandi Patty Medium Voice*

28:1-10 (other)
Larson, Sonia. *Sing Allelu, Alleluia!* U/2-part-Kbd: d1-g2. AMSI (1991) 617

28:1-10 (Revelation 19:16; based on)
Nelson, Grey and Bob Farrell (Sandi Patti Helvering). *Who Will Call Him Kings of Kings*. Kbd, gtr: c1-f2. Word (1990), found in *42 Songs for All Occasions*

28:2, 5-6 Ferguson, Michael. *Angelus Domini*. Org, vc: Sop. Paraclete Press (1992) PPMO 9226

28:2-7, 19 SEE: Matthew 11:4-5. Haas, David. *Song of the Risen One*

28:5-6 (hymn)
Scott, John Prindle. *Angels Roll the Rock Away*. Pno: H:e1-a3; L:c1-g2. Huntzinger (1918)

28:5-7 (John 20:13, 15)
Phillips, Madalyn. *He is Risen, As He Said.* Kbd: d1-f2. Witmark

28:18-20 (Mark 16:15; James O. Teel)
Hart, Don. *Go to All the World.* Kbd, gtr: e1-a♭3. Lillenas (1979), found in *Scripture Solos for All Seasons*

28:18-20 (Luke 10:1-7; adapted)
Talbot, John Michael. *Send Us Out*. Gtr: c1-c2. Cherry Lane (1984), found in *Praise, Praise the Lord, O My Soul and Worship*

28:19-20 SEE: Luke 24:36c, 49. Elgar, Edward. *Peace Be Unto You*

28:19-20 Joncas, Michael. *Go Out to the World.* Cantor-Org: b1-d2. NALR (1979); 5868CC, also found in *On Eagle's Wings*

28:19-20 Schalk, Carl. *Go Therefore and Make Disciples of All Nations.* 2-part mixed-Org: d-e1/d1-d2. MorningStar (1990) MSM-50-6200

45:11 SEE: Matthew 25:1-6. Dencke, Jeremiah. *Go Ye Forth in His Name*

MARK

4:1-34 (based on; other)
Huijbers, Bernard. *Song of All Seed.* Org, gtr: e1-b2. OCP (1987), found in *Stand*

4:30 (based on)
Rowberry, Robert Lee. *O Galilee.* Kbd: M:d1-d2. Sonos (Jackman) (1997) 00434, found in *Sabbath Song*

4:37-39 (and other)
Bennett, Roger (arr. Russell Mauldin). *Don't Be Afraid.* Kbd, gtr: b1-g2. Onward Bound (1994) MB-825, found in *Solos from the Word*

5:24-29, 34 (Matthew 9:20-22)
Hart, Theron Wolcott. *The Healing of the Woman.* Kbd: e♭1-a3. G. Schirmer (1947), also found in *Christian Science Services Songs*

5:39-41 Haas, David. *Who Can This Be?* U/2-part-Kbd, gtr, vc or bsn, inst in c: (b♭1)f1-e♭2. GIA (1987), found in *As Water to the Thirsty*

6:35-41 SEE: Matthew 14:13-21. Hopson, Hal H. *Jesus Fed the Hungry Thousands*

6:50 Bertrand, Lucy and Brown Bertrand. *Be Not Afraid.* Pno: e♭1-f2. Boston Music (1923)

7:37 Bach, J. S. (arr. David Stocker). *God Does All Things Well (Gott hat Alles)* (from cantata no. 35). 2-part-Kbd or cont, 2 ob: c1-e2/b1-e2. ChoralWeb Publishing (1996) CWP-1125-SG2: full score and parts

8:1-10 SEE: Matthew 14:13-21. Hopson, Hal H. *Jesus Fed the Hungry Thousands*

10:8-9 SEE: Matthew 19:6. Lovelace, Austin C. *Wedding Song*

10:10a SEE: Isaiah 6:3. Scholtes, Peter. *Holy, Holy, Holy*

10:13-14 (Matthew 18:10; Luke 18:17)
Underhill, Charles D. *Suffer the Little Children.* Pno: H:c1-g2; M:b♭1-f2; L:a♭1-e♭2. White-Smith (1900)

10:13-16 (Luke 18:17)
Hausman, Ruth L. *Suffer the Little Children.* Pno: c1-f2. G. Schirmer (1931), found in *52 Sacred Songs*

10:13-16 (adapted)
Johnson, Gary (arr. Joseph Linn). *Does Anybody Love the Children?* Kbd: b♭1-c2. Lillenas (1977, 1980), found in *The Lord is My Light*

10:14 Bender, Jan. *Let the Children Come Unto Me* (from *Two Solos for Baptism*). Org, opt inst in c: M:e1-f♯2. Chantry (1973), score: EK12-907360; part: EK12-907361

10:14-15 Bender, Jan. *Whosoever Does Not Receive the Kingdom* (from *Two Solos for Baptism*). Org, fl: e1-g2. Chantry (1973), score: EK12-907360; part: EK12-907361; also found in *To God Will I Sing*

10:14-15 SEE: Matthew 18:1-4. Day, Stanley A. *Suffer the Little Children*

10:15 SEE: Matthew 19:14. Schultz, A. L. *Suffer the Little Children*

10:15-16 (Ephesians 1:3-4; based on)
Cox, Joe. *Blessed to Be a Blessing.* U/2-part)-Pno: d1-e2. MorningStar (1993) MSM-50-9409

10:17-24 Davis, Katherine K. *Treasure in Heaven.* Kbd: H:d1-g2; L:b♭1-e♭2. R. D. Row (1951); Galaxy (1946) GM1552-5

10:21 SEE: John 3:13-15, 17-18. Mozart, W. A. (ed. M. B. Stearns). *Behold the Son of God*

10:46, 52 (based on)
Spiritual (arr. Harry T. Burleigh). *De Blin' Man Stood on de Road an' Cried.* Pno: H:f1-f2; L:d♭1-d♭2. Belwin Mills (1928), found in *Album of Negro Spirituals* (H/L); *The Spirituals of Harry T. Burleigh* (H/L)

10:46-52 Hart, Theron Wolcott. *The Healing of Blind Bartimaeus.* Kbd: Medium. G. Schirmer, found in *Christian Science Services Songs*

11:8 SEE: Isaiah 40:4. Ferguson, John. *Prepare the Royal Highway*

11:9-10 Beall, Mary Kay. *Hosanna! Hosanna!* 2-part-Pno: b1-d2(f2). Hope (1990) PP 121

11:9-10 SEE: Matthew 21:9. Haydn, F. Joseph. *Benedictus*

11:9-10 SEE: Matthew 21:9. Haydn, F. Joseph (ed. H. C. Robbins Landon). *Benedictus*

11:9-10 Mercadante, S. *Blessed Is He That Cometh* (*Salve Maria*). Kbd: Sop:d1-g2. Church (n.d.), found in *Sacred Songs,* vol. 1–*Soprano*

11:9-10 SEE: Matthew 21:9. Pergolesi, Giovanni B. *Benedictus qui vent*

11:9-10 SEE: Zechariah 9:9. Posch, Isaac. *Ecco Dominus veniet*

11:9-10 SEE: Matthew 21:9. Silvia, Giulio. *Benedictus*

11:9-10 Wilson, John Floyd. *Hosanna! Blessed is He.* 2-part-Kbd: d1-d♯2. Hope (1986) A587

12:28-31 Clifford, Beatrice. *The First Commandment.* Kbd: b1-e2. Summy (1919)

12:30-31 SEE: Matthew 22:37-39. VanDyke, May. *Love*

12:30-33 (based on)
Whitehouse, Jan. *You Must Love the Lord.* Kbd: a1-c2. Lorenz (1995), found in *Reflections and Meditations*

12:31 SEE: Deuteronomy 6:4-5. Haas, David. *Hear, O Israel*

13:33-37 SEE: Psalm 17:15. Hurd, Bob. *O, How I Long to See*

13:35 SEE: Psalm 27:4. Talma, Louise. *Cantata: All the Days of My Life*

14:24 Demarest, Victoria (ed. Wilman Wilmans). *Hymn of the Last Supper.* Kbd: H:e♭1-g♯2; L:b♭1-d♯2. Oliver Ditson (1927), found in *Choice Sacred Songs* (H/L)

15:22 (based on)
SEE: Matthew 27:30. Card, Michael. *This Must Be the Lamb*

15:34 SEE: Lamentations 1:1. Berthier, Jacques. *All You Who Pass This Way*

15:39 SEE: Matthew 23:37a. Klughardt, August. *Truly, This Man Was the Son of God!*

16:1-7 (paraphrased)
SEE: Matthew 28:1-8. Croegaret, Jim. *Was it a Morning Like This?*

16:15 SEE: Psalm 117:00. Haas, David. *Go Out to All the World*

16:15 SEE: Matthew 28:18-20. Hart, Don. *Go to All the World*

LUKE

1:26-28 Hurd, Bob (arr. Craig S. Kingsbury). *Be it Done Unto Me.* U/2-part-Kbd, gtr, inst in c: b1-d2. OCP (1986), found in *Each Time I Think of You*

1:27-31 (Luke 2:11-12, adapted)
Nagy, Russell. *And the Angel Said.* 2-part-Kbd: c1-d2. Beckenhorst (1994) JH536-2

1:28 (expanded)
Kantor, Daniel (arr. Rob Glover). *Ave Maria.* U-Pno, gtr, inst in c, cello: e1-c♯2. GIA (1993) G-3958, also found in *No Longer Strangers*

1:28-30-31
Dorff, Daniel. *Ave Maria.* Pno/org: Mez:d1-e2. Presser (1986) 111-40104

1:28, 30-31 (expanded)
Mascagni, Pietro (arr. Eduardo Marzo). *Ave Maria.* Pno: H:d1-a3. Oliver Ditson (1907), found in *Ditson Treasury of Sacred Songs*

1:28, 30-31 (expanded)
Mascagni, Pietro (arr. Steven Mercurio). *Ave Maria.* Pno: H:a1-a3. Subito Music (1998), found in *Andrea Bocelli-Arie Sacre*

1:28, 30-31
Soler, Hanns. *Ave Maria* (Latin). H-vln, org: d♭1-a3. Doblinger (1990) D 17 709

1:28, 30-31, 42 (expanded)
Abt, Franz. *Ave Maria,* op. 438 *(O Lord, Most Holy)* (Latin/English). Kbd: Sop:e♭-g2. G. Schirmer (n.d.), found in *First Book of Soprano Solos,* part II; *Sacred Songs,* vol. 1–*Soprano*

1:28, 30-31, 42 (expanded)
Amedeo, Leone. *Ave Maria* (Latin). Kbd: d1-a♭3. Santorella Publications (n.d.)

1:28, 30-31, 42 (expanded)
Bizet, Georges. *Ave Maria* (Latin). Kbd: Sop:e1-a3. G. Schirmer; Oxford, found in *Sing Solo Sacred* (H/L)

1:28, 30-31, 42
Caccini, Giulio (arr. Steven Mercurio). *Ave Maria* (Latin). Pno or orch: c1-f2. Subito Music (1998) 491-00478, found in *Andrea Bocelli-Arie Sacre*

1:28, 30-31, 42 (expanded)
Cherubini, Luigi. *Ave Maria (Holy, Holy, Lord God of Hosts).* Kbd: Sop:d1-g2; M. John Church (n.d.); G. Schirmer, found in *Sacred Songs,* vol. 1–*Soprano*

1:28, 30-31, 42 (based on)
Dupré, Marcel. *Ave Maria,* op. 9 (from *Lyra Sacra*). Kbd: Med. Leduc (1917) 15, 974

1:28, 30-31, 42
Franck, César (arr. Neil Jenkins). *Ave Maria.* Kbd: L:d1-e$^{\flat}$2. Oxford (1977), found in *Sing Solo Sacred* (H/L)

1:28, 30-31, 42
Franck, César. *Ave Maria.* Kbd: L:d1-e$^{\flat}$2. Hal Leonard (2001), found in *The Sacred Collection* (H/L)

1:28, 30-31, 42 (based on)
Gounod, Charles. *Ave Maria* (adapted to the first prelude of J. S. Bach) (Latin/English/oriental characters). Kbd: H:d1-b3; MH:c1-a3; M:b$^{\flat}$1-g2; ML:a1-f$^{\sharp}$2; L:g-e2. Hal Leonard (1992) H:HL50272110; M:HL50272840; L:HL50272850, also found in *32 Wedding Songs* (MH); *A Wedding Garland* (H); *Andrea Bocelli-Arie Sacre* (H); *Big Book of Love & Wedding Songs; The Bride's Guide to Wedding Music; Complete Ave Maria* (ML, M, MH); *The Essential Wedding Book; Everybody's Favorite Sacred Songs* (M); *Everything for the Wedding Soloist; For All the Saints* (M); *Favorite Sacred Classics for Solo Singers; Favorite Wedding Classics for Solo Singers; Michael Crawford–On Eagle's Wings* (MH); *The Perfect Wedding Songbook; Sacred Classics* (ML/MH); *The Sacred Collection* (H/L); *Sing Solo Sacred* (H/L); *Singer's Wedding Anthology* (H/L); *Wedding Bouquet* (H/L); *Wedding Classics* (MH/ML); *World's Favorite Sacred Songs*

1:28, 30-31, 42 (based on)
Gounod, Charles. *Ave Maria* (adapted to the first prelude of J. S. Bach) (Latin/English). Kbd, gtr: d1-b3. Belwin-Mills (1980), found in *The Best of Popular Wedding Music; Traditional & Popular Wedding Music*

1:28, 30-31, 42 (based on)
Gounod, Charles (arr. Robert Schultz). *Ave Maria* (adapted to the first prelude of J. S. Bach) (Latin/English). Kbd: d1-b3. Belwin Mills (1980), found in *The Complete Wedding Music Collection*

1:28, 30-31, 42 (alternative text based on)
Gounod, Charles. *Cross of Calvary* (sacred text) *(Ave Maria)* (English/Latin). Kbd: a1-e2. Amsco (1940) 40189, found in *Everybody's Favorite Sacred Songs*

1:28, 30-31, 42 (expanded)
Hamblen, Bernard. *Ave Maria* (Latin). Kbd: H; L. Boston Music (n.v.)

1:28, 30-31, 42 (expanded)
Head, Michael. *Ave Maria* (from *Three Sacred Songs*) (Latin/English). Pno (stg qt and orch parts available for hire): H:c1-g2; L:a1-e2. Boosey & Hawkes (1954) 17868

1:28, 30-31, 42 (expanded)
Luzzi, Luigi. *Ave Maria,* op. 80 *(Sing Hallelujah With Glad Rejoicing)* (Italian/English). Pno: H:c$^{\sharp}$1-g$^{\flat}$2; L:b$^{\flat}$1-e$^{\flat}$2. John Church (n.d.); G. Schirmer (1911), found in *Sacred Songs,* vol. 1

1:28, 30-31, 42 (expanded; English adaptation by Charles Lange)
Meininger, F. C. *Ave Maria* (Latin/English). Kbd, vln: Mez or Bar:g-f1. Balmer & Weber Music House (1892)

1:28, 30-31, 42 (expanded)
Millard, H. *Ave Maria (Hear Us, O Father).* Kbd: H:c1-a3; M:b$^{\flat}$1-g2. Century Music (1908) H:1367; M:1368

1:28, 30-31, 42 (expanded)
Millard, H. (arr. Gottlieb Harms). *Ave Maria.* Duet-Kbd: H/L. Witmark 166 (n.v.)

1:28, 30-31, 42 (expanded)
Peeters, Flor. *Ave Maria,* op. 104 *(Hail Mary)* (Latin/English). Kbd: H:e$^{\flat}$1-g2; M:d$^{\flat}$1-f2; L:b1-e$^{\flat}$2. Carl Fischer (1962) H:P6345a; M:P6345b; L:P6345c

1:28, 30-31, 42 (expanded)
Peeters, Flor. *Ave Maria,* op. 104 *(Hail Mary)* (Latin/English). Duet-Kbd: Med. Carl Fischer (1962) P6343

1:28, 30-31, 42 (expanded)
Pinkham, Daniel. *Ave Maria* (from *Three Canticles From Luke*) (Latin). Org: Sop/Tenor:d1-g2. E. C. Schirmer (1993)

1:28, 30-31, 42 (based on)
Rameau, J. P. *Ave Maria (Hear Us, O Savior).* Duet-Kbd: H:c1-f2/L:a1-d2

1:28, 30-31, 42 (based on)
Rheinberger, Josef (ed. David Patrick). *Ave Maria,* op. 171, no. 1 (from *Marianische Hymnen*). Kbd: d1-g2. Boosey & Hawkes (1996), found in *Sacred Songs for the Soloist: 20 Songs on Religious Texts for Medium High Voice*

1:28, 30-31, 42 (expanded)
Rodríguez, Bernardo (arr. Rick Modlin). *Ave Maria.* 2-part-Kbd, gtr: c1-c2. OCP (1993) OCP 9880

1:28, 30-31, 42 (expanded)
Saint-Saëns, Camille. *Ave Maria* (Latin/English). Kbd: H:e$^{\flat}$1-a3. Durand (1957) 2666

1:28, 30-31, 42 (expanded)
Saint-Saëns, Camille. *Ave Maria* (Latin/English). Kbd: Sop:e$^{\flat}$1-a3. John Church (1907), found in *Sacred Songs,* vol. 1

1:28, 30-31, 42 (expanded)
Saint-Saëns, Camille. *Ave Maria (Come Blessed Savior)* (Latin/English). Duet-Pno: Sop:d♯1-f♯2/Alto:b1-c♯2. John Church (1907); Oliver Ditson (1891), found in *Choice Sacred Duets,* vol. 1; *Sacred Duets,* vol. 1 (H/H), vol. 2 (H/L)

1:28, 30-31, 42 (expanded)
Schubert, Franz. *Ave Maria* (English/German/Latin). Kbd: H: g1-g2; MH:f1-f2; ML:e$^{\flat}$1-e$^{\flat}$2; L:d1-d2. Carl Fischer S4955, also found in *50 Great Wedding Favorites* (ML); *52 Sacred Songs* (MH); *56 Songs* (H); *Andrea Bocelli-Arie Sacre* (H); *Art Songs for School & Studio,* 2nd yr (M); *The Best of Popular Wedding Music* (ML); *The Big Book of Love & Wedding Songs; The Bride's Guide to Wedding Music* (L); *Complete Ave Maria* (M/M; H/H); *The Complete Wedding Music Collection* (ML); *Complete Wedding Songbook for Organ* (MH); *Everybody's Favorite Sacred Songs* (MH); *Famous Sacred Songs; Favorite Christmas Classics for Solo Singers* (MH/ML); *Favorite Sacred Classics for Solo Singers; Favorite Wedding Classics for Solo Singer; For All the Saints* (ML); *The Joy of Wedding Music* (L); *Joy, Joy, Joy* (L); *Marion Anderson Album* (MH); *The Perfect Wedding Songbook* (ML); *Singer's Wedding Anthology* (H/L); *The Sacred Collection* (H/L); *Sing Solo Sacred* (H/L); *Traditional & Popular Wedding Music* (ML); *Wedding & Love* (H); *Wedding Bouquet* (H/MH); *Wedding Classics* (M/H); *Wedding Collection* (M); *Wedding Collection: 52 Solos* (L/M); *Wedding Songbook* (H); *World's Favorite Sacred Songs*

1:28, 30-31, 42
Schubert, Franz. *Ave Maria* (Latin/English). Pno, vc: f1-f2. Resort Music (1997)

1:28, 30-31, 42
Schubert, Franz. *Ave Maria* (Latin/English). Duet: Pno, gtr: MH:e$^{\flat}$1-e$^{\flat}$2; LL:b$^{\flat}$1-b$^{\flat}$2. Word (1991), found in *Wedding Music: 49 Solos and Duets*

1:28, 30-31, 42 (expanded)
Whitaker, James. *Ave Maria* (from *Songs of Supplication*) (Latin). Pno or gtr: M:e1-e2. Leyerle (1992)

1:28, 31 (Liber Usualis)
Pinkham, Daniel. *Ave Maria.* 2-part-Sop:d1-g$^{\flat}$2/Alto:a$^{\flat}$1-b$^{\flat}$2. Associated Music (1962) A-367

1:28, 31, 34-35, 38 (trans. by Paul R. Ladd, Jr.)
Kulla, Hans (ed. Paul R. Ladd, Jr.). *Ave Maria.* U-Kbd: d1-d2. Found in *A Choir Book for Advent*

1:28, 32 (adapted)
Arcadelt, Jacob. *Ave Maria (O Savior, Lord of Heaven).* Kbd: Sop:f1-f2. John Church (n.d.), found in *Sacred Songs,* vol. 1

1:28, 42 Atkinson, René. *Ave Maria (Hail Holy Mary)* (Latin). Kbd: H:e1-g2; L:c1-e$^{\flat}$2. Oxford (1987), found in *Sing Solo Christmas* (H/L)

1:30-32 (Luke 2:8-11, 13-14)
Hoffmeister, Leon Abbott. *The Birth of Christ.* Kbd: H:e$^{\flat}$-g2(b$^{\flat}$2); L:c1-e2(g2). Huntzinger (1929)

1:31-36 SEE: Isaiah 7:14. Fettke, Tom. *Jesus–He Shall Be Great*

1:45-55 Couperin, François (ed. Paul Brunold). *Magnificat* (Latin). Duet-Equal voices:d1-g2/c1-g2. L'Oiseau Lyre (1932) 33, found in *Musique vocale II*

1:46 Bach, J. S. *Et exultavit spiritus meus* (from *Magnificat in D*) (Latin). Pno: Sop:d1-f♯2. Oxford (1928, 1956) 45.276

1:46 Bach, J. S. (ed. Graham Batable). *Et exultavit spiritus meus* (from *Magnificat in D*) (Latin). Cont: Sop: c♯1-f♯2. International (1999) 3473, found in *12 Arias*

1:46 Bach, J. S. (ed. Alfred Dürr). *Et exultavit spiritus meus* (from *Magnificat in D*) (Latin). Cont: Sop: c♯1-f♯2. Kassel (1956) BA 5103a

1:46-47 Bambino, Annemarie. *My Soul Magnifies the Lord.* Kbd, gtr: c1-c2. Integrity (1990) MB-856, found in *All the Best Songs*

1:46-47 Bernardi, Steffano. *Magnificat* (Latin). Cont: H:f1-f2. Coppenrath (1994) 16

1:46-47 Burkhard, Willy. *Magnificat* (Latin). Org: e♭1-a3. Bärenreiter (1973) 6476

1:46-47 Gaslini, Giorgio. *Magnificat (1963)* (Latin). Pno, sax, bass: d1-f♯2. Universal (1970) 13589

1:46-47 Sandresky, Margaret. *My Soul Doth Magnify*. Kbd: e1-a3. H. W. Gray (1959)

1:46-47 Savioni, Mario. *Magnificat*. Cont: d1-a3. Smith College (1972) found in *Thirteen Motets for Solo Voice*

1:46-47 Schein, Johann Hermann (ed. Paul Horn). *Magnificat anima mea Dominum* (Latin). Duet-Bass tromb: Sop:c♯1-g2/Tenor:c1-g2. Hänssler (1975), found in *Das geistliche Konzert 151*

1:46-47 Schütz, Heinrich. *Meine Seele erhebt den Herren,* SWV 344 (from *Symphoniae Sacrae* II) (German). Cont, 2 vlns: Sop. Bärenreiter (n.v.) 4335

1:46-47 Telemann, Georg Philip. *Kleines Magnificat* (German). Cont, fl, vln: Sop:d1-g2. Hänssler (1978) HE 10.139

1:46-47 Thompson, Randall. *My Soul Doth Magnify the Lord!* (from *The Nativity According to St. Luke*). Pno: b1-g2. Stainer (1962) 124

1:46-47 Thorne, Francis. *Magnificat*. Kbd: a1-a3. Boston Music (1972)

1:46-49 Burns, William K. *My Soul Doth Magnify the Lord* (from *Two Sacred Songs*). Kbd: H:d1-g2; L:b1-e2. Abingdon (1967)

1:46-49, 76-77
SEE: Genesis 48:16. Schutte, Daniel L. *Blessed Are You*

1:46-50 Dencke, Jeremiah (ed. David). *Meine Seele erhebet den Herrn (My Soul Doth Magnify the Lord)* (German/English). Org, stgs: Sop:f1-f2. New York Public Library (1947) P6084, also found in *Ten Sacred Songs: Music of the Moravians in America*

1:46-55 (based on)
Dufford, Bob (arr. John B. Foley). *My Spirit Takes Joy*. Cantor-Pno, gtr, inst in c: c1-c2. NALR (1985) OCP 5733CC, also found in *The Steadfast Love*

1:46-55 Duke, John. *Magnificat*. Org: c1-f2. Boston Music (1970)

1:46-55 Foley, John B. *Magnificat*. Gtr: c1-b2. NALR (1974), found in *Neither Silver Nor Gold*

1:46-55 Haas, David. *Magnificat*. 2-part-Kbd, gtr, inst in c: d1-c2/e-d1. GIA (1990), found in *I Shall See God*

1:46-55 Haas, David. *Tell Out, My Soul (The Magnificat)*. Kbd, gtr, 2 insts in c: d1-d2. GIA (1986, words Hope 1962), found in *Light and Peace*

1:46-55 Hatch, Verna. *My Soul Doth Magnify the Lord!* Kbd: H:e1-g2. Harold Flammer (1975), found in *Songs of Praise by Contemporary Composers*

1:46-55 Hovland, Egil. *Magnificat* (Latin). Fl, harp: Med:g-f2. Norsk Musikforlag (1966)

1:46-55 (Doxology)
Pinkham, Daniel. *Magnificat* (from *Three Canticles From Luke*) (Latin). Org: Sop/Tenor:c1-g2. E. C. Schirmer (1993)

1:46-55 Posch, Isaac (ed. Karl Geiringer). *Magnificat* (from *Harmonia Concertans*) (Latin). Duet-Equal voices:c1-f2/d1-f2. Ann Arbor: University Microfilm (1968–72), found in *Series of Early Music,* vol. 6

1:46-55 Poterack, Kurt. *Magnificat*. Org: Med:d1-e2. Concordia (1991) 97-6097

1:46-55 (based on)
Rieth, Mildred F. *Mary's Song*. Org, gtr, inst in c: c♯1-b2. OCP (1969), found in *Yahweh is My Shepherd*

1:46-55 (paraphrased)
Roth, John. *Magnificat*. Cantor-Kbd, inst in c. Concordia 98-3236

1:46-55 Schein, Johann Hermann. *Magnificat anima mea Dominum* (Latin). Duet-Cont: Sop:c1-g2; T:c-g1. Hänssler (1975) HE 5.151

1:46-55 Schwarz, May. *Magnificat*. U-Org: d1-b♭2. MorningStar (1993) MSM-80-075

1:46-55 (adapted)
Skillings, Otis. *Mary's Magnificat (Canticle of the Virgin)*. Kbd: c1-(f2)b♭3. Lillenas (1966), found in *The Lord is My Light; Solos from the Word*

1:46-55 Zentner, Johannes. *Lobegesang der Maria* (Latin). Org: Alto:c1-e2. Hänssler (1960) 3705

1:47 Bach, J. S. *Et exultavit (My Soul Rejoice)* (from *Magnificat*). Pno: Sop:d1-f♯2. Oxford (1928, 1956) 45.276

1:47 SEE: Psalm 104:30. Bach, J. S. (arr. Dolores Hruby). *My Spirit Rejoice*

1:48 (English text; Henry S. Drinker) Bach, C. P. E. *Quia respexit (Lo, He Regarded)* (from *Magnificat*) (Latin/English). Kbd: Sop:f♯1-a3. G. Schirmer (1968), found in *Solos From the Great Oratorios for Soprano*

1:48 Bach, J. S. *Quia respexit* (*For He Hath Regarded*) (from *Magnificat in D*) (Latin/English). Kbd: Sop:d1-f♯2. G. Schirmer (1968), found in *Solos from the Great Oratorios for Soprano*

1:48 Bach, J. S. *Quia respexit* (from *Magnificat in D*) (Latin). Kbd: Sop:d1-f♯2. Hal Leonard (1994), found in *Oratorio Anthology: Soprano*

1:48 Bach, J. S. (ed. Graham Batable). *Quia respexit humilitatem* (from *Magnificat in D*) (Latin). Kbd, obd: Sop:d1-f♯2. International (1999) 3473, found in *12 Arias*

1:49 Bach, C. P. E. *Quia fecit mihi magna* (from *Magnificat*) (Latin). Kbd: Tenor:d-a2. Hal Leonard (1994), found in *Oratorio Anthology: Tenor*

1:49 Bach, J. S. *Quia fecit mihi magna* (from *Magnificat in D*) (Latin). Kbd: Bass:g♯-d1. Hal Leonard (1994), found in *Oratorio Anthology: Baritone/Bass*

1:49 Bach, J. S. *Quia fecit mihi magna (For He That Is Mighty)* (from *Magnificat in D*) (Latin/English). Kbd: Bass:g♯-d1. Hal Leonard (1994)/G. Schirmer (1977), found in *Schirmer's Singer's Library: Baritone Arias from Oratorios*

1:50 Charpentier, Marc-Antoine (ed. M. Alfred Bichsel). *Sicut locutus est ad patres* (from *Magnificat in G*) (Latin). Duet-Tenor:a1-f1/Bass:f♯-d1. Concordia (1960)

1:51 Bach, C. P. E. *Fecit potentiam* (from *Magnificat*) (Latin). Kbd: Bass:a-f♯1. Hal Leonard (1994), found in *Oratorio Anthology: Baritone/Bass*

1:52 Bach, J. S. *Deposuit potentes* (from *Magnificat in D*) (Latin). Kbd: Tenor:c♯-a2. Hal Leonard (1994), found in *Oratorio Anthology: Tenor*

1:52 Pachelbel, Johann (arr. Jerald B. Stone). *Deposuit potentes* (from *Magnificat in C*) (Latin). Pno: Bass:G-d1. HLH Music (1992), found in *Five Vocal Gems for Bass,* vol. 1

1:53 Charpentier, Marc-Antoine (ed. M. Alfred Bichsel). *Et misericordia ejus* (from *Magnificat in G*) (Latin). Tenor:g-a2. Concordia (1960) 97-6343

1:53 Pachelbel, Johann (arr. Jerald B. Stone). *Esurientes* (from *Magnificat in C*) (Latin). Pno: Tenor:e1-f♯2. HLH Music (1992), found in *Five Vocal Gems for Tenor,* vol. 1

1:53 Pachelbel, Johann (arr. Jerald B. Stone). *Et misericordia* (from *Magnificat in C*) (Latin). Kbd: c1-c2. HLH Music (1992), found in *Five Vocal Gems for Mezzo-Soprano and Alto,* vol. 1

1:53 Vivaldi, Antonio (ed. Günter Graulich). *Esurientes (Behold, the Hungry He Fills)* (from *Magnificat,* TV 610) (Latin). Duet-Equal voices:f1-g2/e1-f2. Carus Verlag (1978)

1:53 Vivaldi, Antonio. *Esurientes implevit* (from *Magnificat* RV610a-611) (Latin). Kbd: M:a1-c2. Hal Leonard (1994), found in *Oratorio Anthology: Alto/Mezzo-Soprano*

1:54 Charpentier, Marc-Antoine (ed. M. Alfred Bichsel). *Suscepit Israel* (from *Magnificat in G*) (Latin). Kbd: B:d1-d2. Concordia (1960)

1:68-79 Foley, John B. *Blessed Be the Lord.* Kbd: c1-d2. NALR (1974), found in *Neither Silver Nor Gold*

2:1, 4-7 Vaughan Williams, Ralph. *And it Came to Pass in Those Days* (from *Hodie*). U-Org: Treble:d1-e♭2. Oxford (1954)

2:1-20 SEE: Psalm 145:1-13. Smiley, Billy and Bill George. *Worship the King*

2:8 Handel, G. F. *There Were Shepherds (And Lo! The Angel of the Lord)* (from *Messiah*). Kbd: Sop:a2-a3. Carl Fischer; G. Schirmer; Novello (1959)

2:8 Handel, G. F. (ed. James Michael Stevens, arr. W. Daniel Landes). *There Were Shepherds (And Lo! the Angel of the Lord)* (from *Messiah*). 2-part-Kbd: c1-d2. Integra (1991), found in *Christmas MESSIAH for Young Voices*

2:8-11, 13-14 SEE: Luke 1:30-32. Hoffmeister, Leon Abbott. *The Birth of Christ*

2:8-11, 14 Foster, Myles B. *There Were Shepherds.* Duet-Kbd: H:c1-g2/L:g-a1. John Church (1907), found in *Sacred Duets,* vol. 2

2:8-13 Cornelius, Peter. *The Shepherds*. Kbd: Med. G. Schirmer, found in *The Church Soloist*

2:8-13 Cornelius, Peter. *The Shepherds*. Duet-Org/Pno: H:e1-g2/H:a1-g2. R. D. Row (1961) found in *Sacred Duet Masterpieces*

2:8-13 Schütz, Heinrich. *Angel's Message to the Shepherds* (from *The Christmas Story*). Kbd: d1-e2. Coburn Press (1971), found in *Lift Up Your Voice*

2:8-14 LaForge, Frank. *And There Were Shepherds Abiding in the Fields*. Pno: d1-g2. Carl Fischer (1938) V-1367

2:8-14 Schütz, Heinrich (ed. M. B. Stearns). *Recitative and Angel's Message to the Shepherds* (from *The Christmas Story*). Kbd: c♯1-f♯2. Coburn Press (1971), found in *Lift Up Your Voice*

2:8-15 (metrical version by Tate)
Belcher, Supply (ed. Gordon Myers). *There Were Shepherds*. Pno: b1-e2. Abingdon (1964) APM-372

2:8-15 Boex, Andrew J. *And There Were Shepherds*. Kbd: e1-f2. George B. Jennings (1902)

2:8-15 Scott, John Prindle. *There Were Shepherds*. Org: H:f1-a♭3; L:d1-f2. Harold Flammer (1917)

2:9 Handel, G. F. *And Lo! The Angel of the Lord* (from *Messiah*). Kbd: Sop:a2-a3. Carl Fischer; G. Schirmer; Novello (1959)

2:9 Handel, G. F. (ed. James Michael Stevens, arr. W. Daniel Landes). *And Lo! The Angel of the Lord* (from *Messiah*). 2-part-Kbd: c1-d2. Integra (1991), found in *Christmas MESSIAH for Young Voices*

2:9-11 Handel, G. F. *And Lo! The Angel of the Lord Came Upon Them* (from *Messiah*). Kbd: Sop:f1-g2. Carl Fischer; G. Schirmer; Novello (1959)

2:9-14 SEE: Psalm 91:11-12. Nelson, Ronald A. *Angels*

2:9-15 Rorem, Ned. *An Angel Speaks to the Shepherd*. Pno: a1-a♭3. Peer-Southern (1956)

2:10-11 SEE: Isaiah 7:14. Fettke, Tom. *Jesus–He Shall Be Great*

2:10-11 Hammerschmidt, Andreas (ed. Johannes Günther Kraner). *Fürchte euch nicht* (German). Duet-Equal voices. Hänssler (1975) HE 5.173, also found in *Das geistliche Konzert 173*

2:10-11 Handel, G. F. *And the Angel Said Unto Them* (from *Messiah*). Kbd: Sop:g♯1-f♯2. Carl Fischer; G. Schirmer; Novello (1959)

2:10-12 Schütz, Heinrich. *Be Not Afraid* (from *The Christmas Story*). Kbd: d1-e2. G. Schirmer

2:10-14 Harker, F. Flaxington. *Glory to God in the Highest*. Pno: H:e♭1-f2; L:b♭1-c2. G. Schirmer (1910) 134 / Luke

2:11 Schütz, Heinrich. *Hodie Christus natus est*, SWV 315 (from *Kleine geistliche Konzerte*) (Latin). Duet-Cont: Sop/Tenor. Bärenreiter BA3665 (n.v.)

2:11 Valentini, Giovani. *Hodie Christus Natus Est*. Org, 2 vlns: L:g-a2. Coppenrath (1992) 6

2:11-12 SEE: Luke 1:27-31. Nagy, Russell. *And the Angel Said*

2:13 Handel, G. F. *And Suddenly There Was With the Angel* (from *Messiah*). Kbd: Sop:a2-a3. Carl Fischer; G. Schirmer; Novello (1959)

2:13-14 (other)
Boex, Andrew J. *Now Let All Christian Men Rejoice*. Kbd: d1-g2. J. Church (1896)

2:14 Daigle, Gary. *Glory to God (Rite of Blessing and Sprinkling of Water)*. U/2-part-Kbd, gtr, fl: g-d2. GIA (1994) G-4020, also found in *Praise the Maker's Love*

2:14 SEE: Matthew 1:23. Franck, Melchior. *Siehe, eine Jungfrau ist schwanger*

2:14 Handel, G. F. *Gloria*. Orch: Sop:c1-a3. Bärenreiter (2001) 4248

2:14 SEE: Matthew 1:23. LaMontaine, John. *Behold, a Virgin Shall Be With Child*

2:14 (adapted)
Pergolesi, Giovanni B. (ed. and arr. Michael Burkhardt). *Glory to God (Inflammatus et accensus)* (from *Stabat Mater*) (English only). 2-part-Kbd, 2 insts in c: d1-d2. MorningStar (1990) MSM-50-1450

2:14 Rorem, Ned. *Gloria*. Duet-Sop:b♭1-c3/Mez:g1-b♭3. Boosey & Hawkes (1972)

2:14 Schoenbachler, Tim (arr. Sheryl Soderberg). *Glory To God*. U-Kbd, gtr, hndbls: d1-c2. OCP (1979), found in *All is Ready*

2:14 Vierdanck, Johann (ed. and arr. Michael Burkhardt). *Gloria* (from *Lo, I Bring Tidings*). 2-part-Cont: Treble:f1-f2/d1-d2. MorningStar (1994) MSM-50-1452

2:14 Vivaldi, Antonio (arr. W. Daniel Landes). *Glory To God* (from *Gloria,* R. 589). 2-part-Kbd: c1-c2. Integra (1993), found in *Classic Choruses for Young Voices; Vivaldi's GLORIA for Young Voices*

2:14a Vivaldi, Antonio (arr. Vernon M. Whaley). *Gloria* (from *Gloria,* R. 589). 2-part-Kbd: b1-e2/d1-b2. Integra (1993), found in *Classic Choruses for Young Voices; Vivaldi's GLORIA for Young Voices.*

2:14b Vivaldi, Antonio (arr. Vernon M. Whaley). *And to All Goodwill (Et In Terra Pax Hominibus)* (from *Gloria,* R. 589) (English/Latin). 2-part-Kbd: (b1)a2-c♯2. Integra (1993), found in *Classic Choruses for Young Voices*

2:14 Wold, Wayne L. *Gloria in Excelsis Deo.* U-Kbd: d1-e2. MorningStar (1993) MSM-80-101

2:14 Zentner, Johannes. *Gloria* (Latin). Duet-Org: Sop:f1-a3/Alto:c1-d2. Hänssler (1966) 4160

2:21-22, 29-33 (based on)
Cornelius, Peter. *Simeon,* op. 8, no. 4. Pno: L:b1-e2. R. D. Row (1959), found in *Solos for the Church Year* (H/L)

2:22-35 (Exodus 13:2, 12-13; based on)
Card, Michael. *Now That I've Held Him in My Arms (Simeon's Song).* Kbd, gtr: g-c2(g2). Mole End Music (2001), found in *Greatest Songs of Michael Card*

2:25-30 (based on)
Berkig, Luarey and Jon Lugo. *My Eyes Have Seen Your Salvation* (Latin). Pno: f-d2. Lillenas (1990), found in *Contemporary Low Voice*

2:29-30 Schütz, Heinrich. *Herr, nun lassert du deinen, Diener im Friede fahren,* SWV 352 (German). Cont, 2 vlns: Bass:D-d1. Bärenreiter (1968) BA 630

2:29-32 Burgon, Geoffrey. *Nunc Dimittis.* Org (opt trpt): e1-e2. J & W Chester (1979) JWC 55243

2:29-32 Buxtehude, Dietrich. *Herr, nun lassert du deinen diener* (Geistlicher Solokataten 10) (German). Cont, 2 vlns: Tenor:c-g1. Bärenreiter (1969) BA 1752

2:29-32 (Doxology)
Pinkham, Daniel. *Nunc Dimittis* (from *Three Canticles From Luke*) (Latin). Org: S/T:c1-g2. E. C. Schirmer (1993)

2:29-32 Thorne, Francis. *Nunc Dimittis* (from *Joshua).* Org/pno: g1-a♭3. G. Schirmer (1972)

2:29-32 Trapp, Lynn. *Nunc Dimittis.* Cantor-Kbd, fl: f♯1-d2. MorningStar (1991) MSM-80-777

2:29-32 Walker, Christopher. *Nunc Dimittis.* U/2-part-Pno, vln/fl, inst in c: c1-e♭2(g2). OCP (1989), found in *Out of Darkness*

2:29-32 Young, Carlton. *Nunc Dimittis (We Have Seen Your Salvation)* (Latin/English). 2-part-Kbd: b♭1-b♭2. Agape (1973), found in *Choirbook for Saints and Singers*

2:29-35 Walker, W. (arr. Max V. Exner). *Song of Simeon (Farewell, Dear Companion)* (optional text from *Southern Harmony,* 1835). Kbd: M:d1-d2. Augsburg (1993) 11-10047

2:42 (Nahum Tate)
Purcell, Henry. *The Blessed Virgin's Expostulation* (from *Harmonia Sacra*). Pno: H:d♭1-g2; L:b♭1-e♭2. Boosey & Hawkes (1947), found in *40 Songs–Purcell*

2:48-49 (Psalms 84:1-2, 4)
Schütz, Heinrich (ed. Richard T. Gore). *My Son, Wherefore Hast Thou Done This to Us? (Meine Seele, Warum Hast du uns das getan?)* (German/English). Cont, 2 vlns: Med. Concordia (1962) 97-9347, also found in *Luke / 135*

3:5 SEE: Isaiah 40:4. Ferguson, John. *Prepare the Royal Highway*

4:18, 21 (John 12:33, 40, 44)
Sullivan, Sir Arthur (ed. M. B. Stearns). *The Spirit of the Lord is Upon Me* (from *The Light of the World*). Kbd: e1-e2. Coburn Press (1971), found in *Lift Up Your Voice*

4:18-19 SEE: Psalm 122:1. Hurd, Bob. *Pueblo De Dios*

4:18-19 SEE: Isaiah 61:1-3. Wiant, Bliss. *The Great Commission*

4:40 (based on)
Spiritual (arr. Edward Boatner). *I Know the Lord Laid His Hands on Me.* Pno, gtr: c1-f2(a3). Belwin Mills (1973), found in *The Story of the Spirituals*

5:1-11 Krapf, Gerhard. *Master, We Toiled All Night.* Kbd: b1-e2. Concordia (1969) 98-1980

5:5 Schütz, Heinrich. *Meister, wir habe die ganze Nacht gearbeitet,* SWV 317 *(Master, Though Laboring All the Night and Toiling*

Here) (German). Duet-Cont: Tenor:d1-e2/Tenor:c1-f2. Hänssler (1983) HE 20.317

6:13 (adapted)
Talbot, John Michael. *The Lord's Prayer.* Pno: d1-d2. Cherry Lane (1979), found in *The Perfect Wedding Songbook*

6:20 SEE: Isaiah 43:2-3. Dufford, Bob (arr. Theophane Hytreak). *Be Not Afraid*

6:20 SEE: Isaiah 43:2-3. Dufford, Bob. *Be Not Afraid*

6:20 SEE: Isaiah 43:2-3. Dufford, Bob (arr. Schraeder). *Be Not Afraid*

6:36-42 Krapf, Gerhard. *Be Merciful, Even as Your Father is Merciful.* Kbd: e1-e2. Concordia (1969) 98-1979

7:11-16 Hart, Theron Wolcott. *Raising the Son of the Widow.* Kbd: Med. G. Schirmer, found in *Christian Science Services Songs*

7:11-17 Krapf, Gerhard. *Jesus Said to the Widow, 'Do Not Weep'.* Kbd: e♭1-e2. Concordia (1969) 98-2031

7:22 SEE: John 14:6, 8-9. Warren, Clara. *Hast Thou Not Known Me?*

7:36-40, 47-48
Warren, Raymond. *Drop, Drop Slow Tears.* Pno, fl: b♭1-f2. Novello (1961) 19037

9:12-17 SEE: Matthew 14:13-21. Hopson, Hal H. *Jesus Fed the Hungry Thousands*

9:20-24 (Revelation 22:13; based on)
Foley, John B. *The Christ of God.* U-Kbd, gtr: d1-d2. NALR (1985), found in *The Steadfast Love*

9:23-27 (adapted)
Talbot, John Michael. *Take Up Your Cross.* Gtr: c1-b2. Birdwing (1985), found in *Praise, Praise the Lord, O My Soul and Worship*

9:25 SEE: Matthew 4:4. Hurd, Bob. *The Word is in Your Heart*

9:28-29, 35 (other)
Ellis, James G. *Transfiguration.* Kbd: d1-f2. Boston Music (1939) 9190; 136 / Luke

10:1-7 SEE: Matthew 28:18-20. Talbot, John Michael. *Send Us Out*

10:23-24 SEE: Genesis 48:16. Schutte, Daniel L. *Blessed Are You*

11:9-10 SEE: Matthew 7:7-8. Scarlatti, Alessandro. *Come Unto Me*

12:15-20 (Matthew 6:19)
Barnes, Edward Shippen. *Treasure in Heaven.* Duet-Org: Sop:c1-a3/Tenor:c-g2. G. Schirmer (1953)

12:24, 27, 29, 32
Bach, J. S. *Fear Not, Little Flock.* Kbd: b♭1-e♭2. Coburn Press (1971), found in *Lift Up Your Voice*

12:24, 27-31
SEE: Matthew 6:28-34. Thurman, Geoffrey P. *Jehovah*

12:24-31 SEE: Matthew 6:28, 31. Talbot, John Michael. *The Lilies of the Field*

13:34 SEE: Psalm 62:6. Hurd, Bob. *Like a Weaned Child*

13:34 SEE: Psalm 61:3. Hurd, Bob. *Shelter Me, O God*

13:34 SEE: Matthew 23:37. Mendelssohn, Felix. *Jerusalem! Jerusalem! Thou That Killest the Prophets*

14:16-24 Krapf, Gerhard. *At the Time of the Banquet.* Kbd: d1-e2. Concordia (1969) 98-1977

15:3-10 Hopson, Hal H. *Gentle Shepherd, Kind and True.* U-Kbd, 2 hbls: d1-d2. Choristers Guild (1994) CGA687

15:4-7 (other)
Campion, Edward. *The Ninety and Nine.* Kbd: H:f1-a3; M:e1-g2; L:c1-e2. G. Schirmer (1906), also found in *Solos from the Word* (L)

15:4-7 (other)
Sankey, Ira D. (arr. O. D. Hall, Jr.). *The Ninety and Nine.* Kbd: b♭1-c2(f2). Lillenas (1975), found in *The Lord is My Light*

15:11-24 Cornelius, Peter. *Our Loving Father.* Kbd: Med. Coburn Press (1971), found in *Lift Up Your Voice*

15:11-25 VanDewater, Beardsley. *The Penitent.* Kbd: H:d1-a3; M:b1-f2 L:a1-e♭2. R. D. Row (1959); Oliver Ditson (1892), found in *Choice Sacred Songs* (H/M); *Soloists Practical Library of Sacred Songs,* bk 1 (H/L)

15:11-32 (based on)
Dufford, Bob. *My Son Has Gone Away.* Gtr: b1-d2. NALR (1975), found in *Earthen Vessels*

15:17-19 Sullivan, Sir Arthur. *How Many Hired Servants* (from *The Prodigal Son*). Pno: g1-g2. Oliver Ditson (n.d.)

16:19-31 Krapf, Gerhard. *Father Abraham, Have Mercy on Me*. Kbd: d1-e2. Concordia (1969) 98-1976

18:10-14 VanDewater, Beardsley. *Praise the Lord, O My Soul*. Kbd: H:(b♭1)e♭1-g2; L:(g)c1-e2. Oliver Ditson (1920, 1936), found in *Choice Sacred Songs* (H/L); *How Majestic is Your Name* (L); *Sacred Songs*

18:15-16 Scott, Charles P. *Suffer the Little Children*. Kbd: H:e♭1-g2; L:b♭1-d2. Lorenz (1924)

18:17 SEE: Matthew 18:1-4. Day, Stanley A. *Suffer the Little Children*

18:17 SEE: Matthew 19:14. Fischer, Irwin. *Suffer the Children to Come Unto Me*

18:17 SEE: Mark 10:13-16. Hausman, Ruth L. *Suffer the Little Children*

18:17 SEE: Matthew 19:1-2, 13-15. LaForge, Frank. *Suffer the Little Children*

18:17 SEE: Matthew 19:14. Schultz, A. L. *Suffer the Little Children*

18:17 SEE: Mark 10:13-14. Underhill, Charles D. *Suffer the Little Children*

18:22 (John 15:16; 16:20-22; based on)
Hurd, Bob (arr. Craig S. Kingsbury). *If You Belong to Me*. U/2-part-Kbd, gtr, inst in c: (a1)c♯1-d2. OCP/Bob Hurd (1984), found in *In the Breaking of the Bread*

19:28-39 Vance, Margaret. *God Bless the King*. Pno: d1-g2. Charles Hansen (1973) 75083

19:37-40 SEE: Psalm 145:1-13. Lyles, Dwight. *Proclaim the Glory of the Lord*

19:40 SEE: Matthew 21:9. Smith, G. Alan. *The Lord Comes*

21:25-26, 33
Bender, Jan. *And There Will Be Signs,* op. 32, no. 21. Kbd: M:c1-f♯2. Concordia (1971) 97-5947

21:34-36 Schütz, Heinrich. *Heutet euch* (German). Cont, 2 vlns: E-e1. Bärenreiter (1936) 1088; Luke/John / 137

22:14-15 Aichinger, Gregor (ed. William E. Hettick). *Discubuit Jesus* (Latin). Duet-Cont: Tenor:c1-e2/Tenor:c1-f2. A-R Editions (1986), found in Aichinger's *The Vocal Concertos*

22:14-30 (adapted)
Kufferschmid, Steve. *Come to the Table*. 2-part-Kbd: c1-d2. Alfred (1992) 4203

22:17-20 McGuire, Bobby. *Communion Song*. Kbd: b♭1-c2. Lillenas (1980), found in *Scripture Solos for All Seasons*

22:19 (other)
English Folk Melody (arr. Bruce Greer). *Lord, From Your Hand* (uses tune *Waly, Waly*). Kbd: c1-f2. Pilot Point (1999) MB-825, found in *Solos from the Word*

22:19 (I Corinthians 11:24; and other)
Wood, Dale. *In This Moment of Remembrance*. Kbd: MH:e1-f♯2. Sacred Music Press (1995), found in *Songs of Reflection*

22:54 (based on)
Spiritual (arr. Edward Boatner). *They Led My Lord Away*. Pno, gtr: g1-e2. Belwin Mills (1973), found in *The Story of the Spirituals*

23:00 SEE: Isaiah 53:4-5. Dufford, Bob. *Behold the Lamb of God*

23:24, 28, 43
SEE: Lamentations 1:1. Berthier, Jacques. *All You Who Pass This Way*

23:28-29a (John 16:33)
Sullivan, Sir Arthur. *Daughters of Jerusalem* (from *The Light of Life*). Kbd: Bass:d-f♯1. G. Schirmer (1929), found in *Anthology of Sacred Song–Bass; Oratorio Repertoire,* vol. IV

23:33 (based on)
SEE: Matthew 27:30. Card, Michael. *This Must Be the Lamb*

23:46 SEE: Psalm 16:10. Hurd, Bob. *Be With Me, O God*

24:00 (Wesley)
Scott, John Prindle. *The First Easter Morn*. Org: H:f1-g2; L:d1-e2. G. Schirmer (1950)

24:1-5 SEE: Psalm 91:11-12. Nelson, Ronald A. *Angels*

24:1-15 SEE: Matthew 28:1-8. Croegaret, Jim. *Was it a Morning Like This?*

24:5 (John 11:25; Funeral Liturgy)
Schutte, Daniel L. *May the Angels*. U/2-part-Gtr: c♯1-d2. NALR (1974), found in *Neither Silver Nor Gold*

24:5-6 SEE: Matthew 11:4-5. Haas, David. *Song of the Risen One*

24:5-6a Foster, Myles B. *Why Seek Ye the Living Among the Dead?* Duet-Kbd: H:e1-f2/L:a1-c2. John Church (1907), found in *Sacred Duets,* vol. 2

24:13 (John 4:40; other)
Bennett, Sir William Sterndale. *Abide With Me* (from *The Woman of Samaria*). Pno: H:f1-$g^{\flat}$2; M:a1-e2. Carl Fischer (1939), found in *The Sacred Hour of Song*

24:13-31 Weinberger, Jaromir. *The Way to Emmaus*. Org: d1-a3. H. W. Gray (1940)

24:32 (other)
Conry, Tom. *Were Not Our Hearts Burning Within Us*. Pno, gtr: e1-c2. OCP (1987), found in *Stand*

24:36 SEE: John 20:25. Pethel, Stan. *We Have Seen the Risen Lord*

24:36c, 49 (Matthew 28:19-20)
Elgar, Edward. *Peace Be Unto You* (from *The Apostle*). Kbd: Bass or Bar:c-f1. Novello

JOHN

1:1 (Psalm 107:20; Hebrews 4:12; Hebrews 11:3)
MacDermid, James G. *He Sent His Word*. Kbd: H:e1-g2; L:b1-$e^{\flat}$2. Forster (1921)

1:1, 3, 7-8, 14 (Linda Lee Johnson)
Fettke, Tom. *Words of Love*. Kbd: $b^{\flat}$1-$e^{\flat}$2. Lillenas (1980), found in *Scripture Solos for All Seasons*

1:1-4, 29 SEE: Psalm 118:22. Joncas, Michael. *Take and Eat*

1:1-14 Robinson, McNeil. *In the Beginning Was the Word*. Kbd: H or M:c1-g2. Coburn Press (1975), found in *Eleven Scriptural Songs from the Twentieth Century*

1:5 McAfee, Don. *When All Things Began* (from *Two Songs for Medium Voice*). Kbd: d1-f2. Abingdon (1968)

1:5 SEE: Joel 2:28. Wise, Joe. *And the Light Shines*

1:14 Aichinger, Gregor (ed. William E. Hettick). *Angelus Domini* (Latin). Duet-Cont: Sop:c1-e2; Bass:$F^{\sharp}$-a1. A-R Editions (1986), found in Aichinger's *The Vocal Concertos*

1:26-27 Selle, Thomas (ed. Klaud Vetter). *Ich taufe mit Wasser* (German). Duet-Tenor:e1-g2/Bass:E-c1. Hänssler (n.d.), found in *Das geistliche Konzert 88*

1:29 (Revelation 5:12; other)
Rambo, Dottie. *Behold the Lamb*. Kbd: $b^{\flat}$1-$e^{\flat}$2. John T. Benson Company (1979), found in *More Than Wonderful; Praise: A Collection of Worship and Praise*

1:29 Bach, J. S. *Agnus Dei* (from *Mass in B minor*) (Latin/English). Kbd: Alto:a1-d2. Presser (1923), found in *Oratorio Repertoire*, vol. II

1:29 Bizet, Georges. *Agnus Dei (Lamb of God)* (from *L'Arlésienne Suite*, no. 2) (Latin/English/German). Pno: H:d1-$b^{\flat}$3; MH:c1-$a^{\flat}$3; M:b1-g2; L:a1-f2. G. Schirmer (n.d.) H: HL50266960; M: HL50266970, found in *52 Sacred Songs; Album of Sacred Songs* (H/M); *Everybody's Favorite Sacred Songs* (MH); *Famous Sacred Songs; Favorite Sacred Classics for Solo Singers* (MH); *Sacred Classics* (MH/L); *The Sacred Collection* (H/L); *Sacred Songs–Soprano*, vol. 1; *Sacred Songs for Easter; Sing Solo Sacred* (H/L); *World's Favorite Sacred Songs* (MH)

1:29 SEE: Isaiah 53:4-5. Dufford, Bob. *Behold the Lamb of God*

1:29 (other)
Fettke, Tom and Phillip P. Bliss (arr. Tom Fettke). *He Takes Away the Sins of the World*. Duet-Kbd or Trax: H:c1-g2; L:c1-$e^{\flat}$2. Pilot Point (1983) MB-656, found in *The Sunday Worship Duet Book*

1:29 Handel, G. F. (arr. James Michael Stevens). *Behold the Lamb of God* (from *Messiah*). 2-part-Kbd: c1-d2. Integra (1993), found in *Easter MESSIAH for Young Voices*

1:29 Herbst, Johannes (arr. Karl Kroeger). *See Him, He is the Lamb of God (Siehe das ist Gottes Lamm)* (German/English). Kbd or stg qt: H:d1-f2. Boosey & Hawkes (1978), found in *Three Sacred Songs of Johannes Herbst*

1:29 SEE: Matthew 11:28. Lyon, A. Laurence. *Behold the Lamb of God*

1:29 Mozart, W. A. (arr. Neil Jenkins). *Agnus Dei* (from *Coronation Mass*). Kbd: H; L:a1-d2. Oxford (1977), found in *Sing Solo Sacred* (H/L)

1:29 Pergolesi, Giovanni B. (ed. and arr. Michael Burkhardt). *Agnus Dei* (from *Stabat Mater*). U-Cont: b1-$e^{\flat}$2. MorningStar (1993) MSM-50-3752

1:29 (John 21:16-17)
Wold, Wayne L. *Agnus Dei, Lamb of God*. U-Org: d1-e2. MorningStar (1989) MSM-80-830

2:1-10 (based on)
Buxtehude, Dietrich. *Lord Who at Cana's Wedding*. Kbd: Med. Concordia (1952), found in *Wedding Blessings*

3:5-7, 16 (John 14:6)
MacDermid, James G. *God So Loved the World.* Kbd: H:e♭1-a♭3; M:c1-f2; L:b♭1-e♭2. Forster (1924)

3:13-15, 17-18 (Mark 10:21; John 18:34-35; Romans 8:1-2)
Mozart, W. A. (ed. M. B. Stearns). *Behold the Son of God,* K.146. Kbd: d1-e2. Coburn Press (1971), found in *Lift Up Your Voice*

3:14-15 Buxtehude, Dietrich. *Sicut Moses* (Geistliche Solokatаten 3) (Latin). Cont, 2 vlns: Sop:d1-b3. Bärenreiter (1927) 127

3:16 Buxtehude, Dietrich. *Also hat Gott die Welt geliebt* (Geistliche Solokataten 5) (German). Cont, 2 vlns: Sop:d1-g2. Bärenreiter (n.d.) 288

3:16 Dauermann, Stuart. *For God So Loved.* Duet-Pno: b1-d2(g2)/b1-d2. Lillenas (1988), found in *Duets For All Seasons*

3:16 (other)
Eaton, Chris. *God So Loved.* Kbd: a1-b2. SGO Music (1997) 301 7251 233, found in *25 Inspirational Easter Favorites; Contemporary Christian Hits; Inspirational Chart Toppers; The Jaci Velasquez Songbook; WOW the 90's Songbook; WOW 1998/1999 Songbook*

3:16 SEE: Lamentations 1:12. Foster, Myles B. *Is it Nothing to You?*

3:16 (I John 3:16; based on)
Scruggs, Randy. *Tell the World that Jesus Loves You.* Kbd, gtr: c1-c2. Mole End Music (1983), found in *Greatest Songs of Michael Card*

3:16-17 Burroughs, Bob. *God's Love.* Kbd: d1-g2. Hope (1970) 501, also found in *New Testament Songs*

3:16-17 Fearis, John S. *God So Loved the World.* Kbd: H:e♭-g2; L:b♭1-d2. Boston Music (1925) H:7311; L:7312

3:16-17 Fischer, Irwin. *God So Loved the World.* Kbd: c1-g2. American Composers Alliance, found in *Composers Facsimile Edition*

3:16-17 (based on)
Handel, G. F. (ed. Earnest Murphy). *God Sent His Son Into the World.* Duet-Kbd: H:c1-f2/Med:c1-d2. McAfee Music (1973), found in *The Baroque Songbook*

3:16-17 (adapted)
Handel, G. F. (ed. and arr. K. K. Davis and N. Loring). *God So Loved the World.* Kbd: Med:c♯1-e2. Carl Fischer (1948), found in *Sing Unto the Lord,* vol. 2

3:16-17 Martinson, Joel. *God So Loved the World.* 2-part-Org: d1-f♯2/b1-e2. Concordia (1993) 98-3098

3:16-17 Stainer, John. *God So Loved the World* (from *The Crucifixion*). Kbd: H:d1-g2; MH:d♭1-g♭2; L:b♭1-e♭2. G. Schirmer (1960), found in *Bible Songs; Sacred Songs for Easter; Church Soloists Favorites,* bk 1 (M/H); *Songs for the Easter Season* (MH)

3:16-17 Stainer, John (arr. Carl Fredrickson). *God So Loved the World* (from *The Crucifixion*). Duet-Kbd: H:d1-g2/L:f-d2. R. D. Row (1960), found in *Sacred Duet Masterpieces*

3:16-17 Stainer, John (arr. Carol McClure). *God So Loved the World* (from *The Crucifixion*). U-Kbd, inst in c: c1-e2. Integra (1993), found in *Classic Choruses for Young Voices*

3:16-17 (Romans 8:16-17, 38-39)
Tindall, Adrienne M. *I Am Persuaded.* Kbd: d♯1-f2. Darcy Press (1994), found in *Sacred Solos by Adrienne Tindall,* vol. III

3:16-21 (adapted)
Debruyn, Randall. *Jesus, Lord.* U-Org, gtr, inst in c: c1-c2. OCP (1984), found in *Jesus, Lord*

4:7-15 SEE: Isaiah 35:1-6. Hurd, Bob. *Flow River Flow*

4:10 SEE: Matthew 11:28-30. Coenen, William. *Come Unto Me*

4:14 (I John 4:18; Horatius Bonar, alt.)
Lovelace, Austin C. *O Love That Casts Out Fear.* Kbd: d1-e2. Darcy Press (1993), found in *Sacred Solos by Austin C. Lovelace*

4:14-15 Haas, David. *The Water I Give.* U/2-part-Kbd, gtr, inst in c: (a1)c♯1-d2. GIA (1988), found in *Who Calls You By Name,* vol. 1

4:23-24 SEE: Psalm 51:16-17. Gounod, Charles. *God is Spirit*

4:23-24 Hopekirk, Helen. *God is a Spirit.* Pno: d1-f2. Boston Music (1917)

4:23-24 McArthur, Edwin. *God is a Spirit.* Kbd: c1-f2. R. D. Row (1956)

4:23-24 Mourant, Walter. *The Hour Cometh.* Pno: G-d1. American Composers Alliance (1970)

4:23-24 (Revelation 20:17)
Roberts, J. E. *God is a Spirit.* Kbd: H:f1-g2; M:d1-e2; L:c1-d2. Arthur P. Schmidt (1928)

4:23-24 Scott, Charles P. (ed. Wilman Wilmans). *God is a Spirit.* Kbd: H:e1-f2; L:c1-d♭2. Oliver Ditson (1919), found in *Choice Sacred Songs* (H/L); *Ditson Treasury of Sacred Songs*

4:23-24 Scott, John Prindle. *God is a Spirit.* Kbd: Med. Oliver Ditson

4:23-24, 35-36
LaForge, Frank. *But the Hour Cometh.* Kbd: Med. G. Schirmer

4:34-35 SEE: Isaiah 6:8. Manuel, Ralph. *Hark, the Voice of Jesus Calling*

4:35-38 SEE: Matthew 9:38. Schutte, Daniel L. *Come With Me Into the Fields*

4:40 SEE: Luke 24:13; other. Bennett, Sir William Sterndale. *Abide With Me*

5:5-7, 9 Clark, Palmer John. *This is My Commandment.* Kbd: H:e1-f2; L:c♯1-d2. Remick (1915)

6:00 (paraphrased; adapted)
Koch, Frederick. *The Bread of Life.* Kbd: e1-f2. Carl Fischer (1990), found in *Five Sacred Solos for Worship Service*

6:00 Olds, W. B. *The Bread of Life.* Kbd: d♯1-g2. Carl Fischer (1946)

6:1-14 SEE: Matthew 14:13-21. Hopson, Hal H. *Jesus Fed the Hungry Thousands*

6:35 (Matthew 26:26)
Mendelssohn, Felix (ed. M. B. Stearns). *Bread of Life* (from *Lauda Sion,* op. 73). Org: c1-f2. Coburn Press (1971) 140 / John, also found in *Lift Up Your Voice*

6:35 (other)
Talbot, John Michael. *I Am the Bread of Life.* Pno: e1-c2. Cherry Lane (1983), found in *Contemporary Christian Today*

6:35, 51, 53 (John 11:25, 27)
Toolan, Sr. Suzanne. *I Am the Bread of Life.* Kbd, gtr: M:a1-e2. GIA (1976) G-2054

6:50-51, 58
SEE: Psalm 34:9. Hurd, Bob. *Fracción Del Pan*

6:51 (Isaiah 55:1; adapted)
Kieserling, Richard. *I Am the Bread of Life.* Pno: H:f♯1-g2; L:d1-e♭2. Huntzinger (1930), found in *Selected Sacred Songs for General Use*

6:51-58 (adapted)
Talbot, John Michael. *I Am the Bread of Life.* Gtr: e1-c2. Cherry Lane (1982), found in *Praise, Praise the Lord, O My Soul and Worship*

6:54 Aichinger, Gregor (ed. William E. Hettick). *Amen, amen dico vobis* (Latin). Duet-Cont: Tenor:c1-f2/Tenor:c1-f2. A-R Editions (1986), found in Aichinger's *The Vocal Concertos*

6:59 Aichinger, Gregor (ed. William E. Hettick). *Hic est panis* (Latin). Duet-Cont: Tenor:c1-d2/Tenor:c1-e♭2. A-R Editions (1986), found in Aichinger's *The Vocal Concertos*

6:67 SEE: Psalm 62:2. Lynch, Mike. *In the Land There is a Hunger*

6:68 SEE: Psalm 19:7-10. Haas, David. *Lord, You Have the Words*

6:68 Haas, David. *You Alone Are the Word.* Kbd, vc or bsn, gtr: e1-e2. GIA (1988), found in *Who Calls You By Name,* vol. 2

6:68 (John 8:12; other)
Haugen, Marty. *Speak, O Lord.* U/2-part-Kbd, gtr, 2 insts in c: c1-d2. GIA (1987), found in *Shepherd Me, O God*

6:68 Joncas, Michael. *Lord, to Whom Shall We Go?* U/2-part-Kbd, gtr: (c1)e1-d2. NALR (1979); OCP 5429CC, also found in *On Eagle's Wings*

6:68 (adapted)
Nazareth, Aniceto. *Without Seeing You.* U/2-part-Org: c1-d2. Kevin Mayhew (1984), found in *Our Praise to You*

6:68 SEE: Matthew 13:44-45. Schutte, Daniel L. *I Found the Treasure*

8:2, 12, 31-32, 36
Fischer, Irwin. *Ye Shall Know the Truth.* Kbd: H:c1-g♭2; Medium. Coburn Press, found in *Eleven Scriptural Songs from the Twentieth Century*

8:12 SEE: John 6:68. Haugen, Marty. *Speak, O Lord*

8:12 SEE: Ephesians 5:14. Humphreys, Don. *Light of the World*

8:12 SEE: Psalm 118:22. Joncas, Michael. *Take and Eat*

8:12 SEE: Revelation 3:20. MacDermid, James G. *Arise, Shine for Thy Light is Come*

8:32 SEE: Psalm 100:5. Humphreys, Don. *Truth*

8:32 (John 14:6)
Mendelssohn, Felix. *O Christ the Way.* Kbd: Med. Coburn Press (1971), found in *Lift Up Your Voice*

9:3-5 Elgar, Edward. *Neither Hath This Man Sinned* (from *The Light of Life*). Kbd: Bass or Bar:c♯-d1. Novello (1989)

9:4 SEE: Psalm 27:4. Talma, Louise. *Cantata: All the Days of My Life*

10:3 SEE: Psalm 23:00. Talbot, John Michael. *I Am the Good Shepherd*

10:10, 14 (John 17:17, 24)
Elgar, Edward. *I Am the Good Shepherd* (from *The Light of Life*). Kbd: Bass or Bar:c-f1. Novello (n.d.) John / 141

10:11 SEE: Isaiah 40:11. Misetich, Marianne. *Like a Shepherd*

10:11-16 (Scottish Psalter 1650)
Nevin, George. *I Am the Good Shepherd.* Org: b♭1-e2. Oliver Ditson (1920)

10:12 (other)
Bach, J. S. *Jesus ist ein guter Hirt (Ich bin ein guter Hirt)* (from Kantate nr. 85) (German). Pno, vln: Alto:c1-e♭2. Kalmus, found in *Arias from Church Cantatas for Contralto,* vol. II

10:14, 16a
Burroughs, Bob. *I Am the Good Shepherd.* Kbd: d1-d2. Hope (1970) 501, also found in *New Testament Songs*

11:1, 3-4, 15, 17, 41-44
Davis, Katherine K. *The Raising of Lazarus.* Kbd: b1-e2. Carl Fischer (1947)

11:1-44 (taken from)
Barker, Clement W. *The Raising of Lazarus.* Kbd: H:d1-g2; L:b1-e2. R. D. Row (1946) H: RS46

11:25 Anderson, Jim. *I Am the Resurrection.* U/2-part-Org, gtr: b1-d2(e1-e2). OCP (1982), found in *In Perfect Charity: Contemporary Accomp. Series,* vol. 4

11:25 SEE: Psalm 46:10a. Roma, Caro. *The Silent Voice*

11:25 SEE: Luke 24:5. Schutte, Daniel L. *May the Angels*

11:25 (Revelation 1:8)
Smith, Michael W. *I Am.* Kbd: c1-f2. Sesac (1980), found in *The Lord is My Light*

11:25, 27 SEE: John 6:35, 51, 53. Toolan, Sr. Suzanne. *I Am the Bread of Life*

11:25-26 Buxtehude, Dietrich. *I Am the Resurrection* (German/English). Cont, 2 vlns: Bass:E-d1. Concordia (1967) 97-4821

11:25-26 Haas, David. *I Am the Resurrection.* Kbd, gtr, 2 inst in c: b1-d2. GIA (1988), found in *Who Calls You By Name,* vol. 1

11:25-26 Hammerschmidt, Andreas (ed. Harold Mueller). *I Am the Resurrection (Ich bin die Auferstehung)* (German/English). Stg qt, cont: Tenor:d1-f2. Concordia (1960) 97-6317

11:25-26 Rotermund, Melvin. *I Am the Resurrection and the Life.* U/2-part-Org (opt inst in c): d1-g2. Concordia (1993) 98-3271, also found in *6 Scripture Anthems,* set 1

11:25-26 (adapted)
Talbot, John Michael. *I Am the Resurrection.* Gtr: c1-c2. Birdwing (1985), found in *Praise, Praise the Lord, O My Soul and Worship*

11:43 (other)
Petree, Larry and Arlie Petree. *Lazarus, Come Forth.* Kbd, gtr: d1-c2. Timber Wind Music (1989) HB 9104, found in *Homeland Harmony,* vol. 2

11:52 SEE: Isaiah 40:11. VanDyke, May. *As A Shepherd*

12:23-24, 26 (John 15:4-5, 7-8, 27; II Timothy 2:11-12)
Farrell, Bernadette. *Unless a Grain of Wheat.* Org, cl, inst in c, gtr: a1-d2. OCP (1983), found in *Return to Me: Music for Funerals and Healing,* vol. 1

12:24 (George Herbert; adapted)
Hurd, Bob (arr. Craig S. Kingsbury). *Unless a Grain of Wheat.* Org, gtr, inst in c: c1-d♭2. OCP (1984), found in *In the Breaking of the Bread*

12:24, 32 (John 15:13, based on Good Friday Liturgy)
Schutte, Daniel L. *Behold the Wood.* Gtr: c1-b2. NALR (1976), found in *A Dwelling Place*

12:24, 32, 35 (John 13:34-35; based on)
Norbet, Gregory. *Those Who Hear My Words.* Org, inst in c: c1-c2. OCP (1988), found in *Mountains of My Soul*

12:24-25 Anthony, Dick. *Living By Dying.* Kbd: c1-g♭2. Lillenas (1977), found in *Scripture Solos for All Seasons*

12:33, 40, 44
SEE: Luke 4:18, 21. Sullivan, Sir Arthur. *The Spirit of the Lord is Upon Me*

12:35 SEE: Psalm 27:4. Talma, Louise. *Cantata: All the Days of My Life*

13:5-7 (I Corinthians 13:13; other)
Walker, Christopher. *Faith, Hope and Love.* U/2-part-Org: b1-d2(f♯2). OCP (1987), found in *Out of Darkness*

13:34-35 SEE: John 12:24, 32, 35. Norbet, Gregory. *Those Who Hear My Words*

13:35 SEE: John 15:12. Hustad, Donald. *This is My Commandment*

14:1 SEE: Matthew 10:29-31. Gabriel, Charles H. *His Eye is on the Sparrow*

14:1-2 Chadwick, George Whitefield. *Let Not Your Heart Be Troubled.* Kbd: H:c1-g2; L:a1-e2. Arthur P. Schmidt (1915)

14:1-2 (and other)
Franz, Robert. *Let Not Your Hearts Be Troubled.* Duet-Org/pno: H:d1-e2/H:d1-f2. R. D. Row (1961) found in *Sacred Duet Masterpieces*

14:1-2, 27
Haeussler, Paul. *Let Not Your Heart Be Troubled.* Pno: H:d1-f♯2; L:c1-e2. Boosey & Hawkes (1928)

14:1-2, 27
Reese, Dorothy Dasch. *Let Not Your Heart Be Troubled.* Kbd: H:d1-g2. FitzSimons

14:1-3 Reiff, Stanley T. (ed. Wilman Wilmans). *Let Not Your Heart Be Troubled.* Kbd: H:d1-g2; L:b1-e2. Oliver Ditson (1934), found in *Choice Sacred Songs* (H/L); *Solos for Christian Science Services*

14:1-3 Snyder, Virginia. *Let Not Your Heart Be Troubled.* Kbd: c♯1-g2. Elkan-Vogel (1947)

14:1-3, 6a
Jewell, Lucina (ed. Wilman Wilmans). *In My Father's House Are Many Mansions.* Pno: H:e1-g♯2; L:c1-e2. Oliver Ditson (1902, 1930), found in *Choice Sacred Songs* (H/L); *Sacred Songs; Solos for Christian Science Services; Solos for Christian Science Services,* bk 2

14:1-3, 6, 14
Misetich, Marianne. *Let Not Your Hearts.* Duet-Kbd, gtr, bass, inst in c: M:d1-c2/M:b1-b2. OCP (1982), found in *Comfort My People*

14:1-3, 19, 20
Rutenber, C. B. *Let Not Your Heart Be Troubled.* Org: M:c1-d2. G. Schirmer (1921)

14:1-6 (other)
Mullins, Rich. *That Where I Am, There You . . .* Kbd, gtr: e1-d2. Word (1998), found in *WOW 1998/1999 Songbook*

14:1, 27 Speaks, Oley. *Let Not Your Heart Be Troubled.* Kbd: H:d1-a3; M:c1-g2; L:a1-e2. G. Schirmer (1919) choral octavo 6915

14:1, 27 (John 16:33)
Thompson, William H. *Peace I Leave With You.* Pno: b1-d2. Oliver Ditson (1948)

14:2-3 (Revelation 21:18, 21)
Lewis Jr., Ross (arr. Bo Williams). *In My Father's House.* U/2-part-Pno: b♭1-f2. Lewis Ross, Jr. (1996)

14:2-4, 27
MacDermid, James G. *In My Father's House Are Many Mansions.* Kbd: H:d1-g2; M:b1-e2; L:a1-d2. Forster (1937) John / 143

14:2-4, 27
Ward-Stephens. *In My Father's House Are Many Mansions.* Pno: H:d1-g2; L:b1-e2. Chappell (1917), found in *The Ward-Stephens Musical Settings of Sacred Words*

14:6 SEE: Matthew 11:28-30. Handel, G. F. *Come Unto Me*

14:6 SEE: Psalm 118:22. Joncas, Michael. *Take and Eat*

14:6 SEE: John 3:5-7, 16. MacDermid, James G. *God So Loved the World*

14:6 SEE: John 8:32. Mendelssohn, Felix. *O Christ the Way*

14:6a (I John 2:15a, 17)
Sullivan, Sir Arthur. *Love Not the World* (from *The Prodigal Son*). Pno: H:c1-g2: L:b♭1-f2. R. D. Row (1959); Oliver Ditson (n.d.), found in *Anthology of Sacred Song–Alto; Oratorio Repertoire,* vol. II; *Soloists Practical Library of Sacred Songs,* bk 1 (H/L); *Songs for Christian Science Services*

14:6, 8-9 (Luke 7:22)
Warren, Clara. *Hast Thou Not Known Me?* Kbd: M:c1-f2; L:b♭1-e♭2. R. D. Row (1948), found in The Free Library of Philadelphia

14:15 (I Corinthians 2:9)
Foster, Myles B. *Eye Hath Not Seen, Nor Ear Heard.* Duet-Kbd: d1-e2/b1-b2. John Church (1907), found in *Sacred Duets,* vol. 2

14:16 Fischer, Irwin. *If Ye Love Me, Keep My Commandments.* Kbd: d1-f2. American Composers Alliance, found in *Composers Facsimile Edition*

14:18 SEE: Job 11:16. Hurd, Bob. *God's Eye is on the Sparrow*

14:18 Nelson, Ronald A. *I Will Not Leave You Comfortless* (from *Four Anthems for Young Choirs*). 2-part-Kbd: e1-d2. Boosey & Hawkes (1965) 5576

14:18 SEE: Psalm 46:10a. Roma, Caro. *The Silent Voice*

14:18-21 Row, Richard D. *I Will Not Leave You Comfortless.* Pno: H:c1-f2; L:b♭1-e♭2. R. D. Row (1959), found in *Soloists Practical Library of Sacred Songs,* bk 1 (H/L)

14:18, 28 Pinkham, Daniel. *I Will Not Leave You Comfortless* (from *Two Motets)* (Latin/English). Fl, gtr: c1-b♭3. Stainer (1971)

14:23 Bender, Jan. *If a Man Loves Me,* op. 32, no. 11. Kbd: e1-e2. Concordia (1963) 98-1697

14:27 Dichmont, William. *Peace I Leave With You.* Kbd: H:e♭1-g2. Oliver Ditson (1928), found in *Ditson Treasury of Sacred Songs*

14:27 Gounod, Charles. *The Peace of God.* Kbd: H:e♭1-f2; L:b♭1-d2. Oliver Ditson (1903), found in *Album of Sacred Songs; Sacred Songs* (L)

14:27 SEE: Isaiah 26:3-4. Kretz, Vivian A. *Thou Wilt Keep Him in Perfect Peace*

14:27 (John 16:6, 33)
Roberts, John Varley (ed. Carl Deis). *Peace I Leave With You.* Org: H:c1-f2; L:a1-d♯2. G. Schirmer (1936), found in *Christian Science Service Songs*

14:27 (based on)
Whitehouse, Jan. *Peace I Leave You.* Kbd: c1-a2. Lorenz (1995), found in *Reflections and Meditations*

15:00 (based on)
Atkins, Jean (arr. Mark Barnard). *Abide in Christ.* Kbd: c♯1-b2. Lorenz (1995), found in *Reflections and Meditations*

15:00 Hamblen, Bernard. *This is My Commandment.* Kbd: H:f1-f2; L:c1-c2. R. D. Row (1946)

15:1, 2, 4-6
Isham, Royce. *I Am the Vine.* Kbd: M:d1-f2. Sonos (Jackman) (1997) 00434, found in *Sabbath Song*

15:1-3, 5-7
MacDermid, James G. *I Am the True Vine.* Kbd: H:d1-g2; L:b1-e2. Forster (1946)

15:1-6 Doig, Don. *I Am the Vine.* Kbd: c1-f2. Hope (1980), found in *Everything for the Church Soloist*

15:1-8 (adapted)
Talbot, John Michael. *I Am the Vine.* Gtr: b1-b2. Cherry Lane (1982), found in *Praise, Praise the Lord, O My Soul and Worship*

15:4 (Romans 6:4; Galatians 2:20)
Coleman. *Christ is With Me.* 2-part-Kbd, inst in c: Sop/Alto. Concordia (1992) 98-3120, (opt SATB, 98-3051)

15:4 Herbst, Johannes (arr. Karl Kroeger). *Abide in Me (Bleibet in mir)* (German/English). Kbd or stg qt: H:e1-f2. Boosey & Hawkes (1978), found in *Three Sacred Songs of Johannes Herbst*

15:4-5, 7-8, 27
SEE: John 12:23-24, 26. Farrell, Bernadette. *Unless a Grain of Wheat*

15:5-6, 12
Pote, Allen (arr. Dale Wood). *I Am the Vine* (from *A Reason to Rejoice*). Kbd: M:c1-d2. Sacred Music Press (1988), found in *Sacred Songs: Nine Solos for Medium Voice*

15:7, 9-10, 12
LaForge, Frank. *If Ye Abide in Me.* Kbd: H:g1-g2; L:d1-d2. G. Schirmer (1942)

15:9-10 (based on; other)
Bach, J. S. *Komm, mein Herze steht dir offen (Wer mich liebet, der wird mein Wort halten)* (from Kantate Nr. 74) (German). Kbd, 2 inst (Eng hn): Sop:f1-g2. Kalmus, found in *Arias from Church Cantatas for Soprano,* vol. III

15:9-10 (based on; other)
Bach, J. S. (ed. Max Schneider). *Wer mich liebet, der wird mein Wort halten* (from Kantate nr. 74) (German). Kbd: Alto:b1-e2. C. F. Peters (n.d.), found in *J. S. Bach-Alt-Arien aus Kantaten*

15:12 (John 13:35; James 5:16)
Hustad, Donald. *This is My Commandment*. Kbd: d1-e2. Hope (1980), found in *Everything for the Church Soloist*

15:13 SEE: Job 19:25-27. Hurd, Bob. *I Have Seen the Lord*

15:13 SEE: John 12:24, 32. Schutte, Dan L. *Behold the Wood*

15:16 Gates, Crawford. *A New Commandment I Give Unto You* (from *Three Songs for the Young Heart,* op. 49). Kbd: M:d1-e2. Jackman Music (1992) S-0180, found in *Scripture Settings for Solo Voice*

15:16 SEE: Luke 18:22. Hurd, Bob. *If You Belong to Me*

16:6, 33 SEE: John 14:27. Roberts, John Varley. *Peace I Leave With You*

16:20-22 SEE: Luke 18:22. Hurd, Bob. *If You Belong to Me*

16:22 SEE: Wisdom 51:35. Brahms, Johannes. *Ye Now Are Sorrowful*

16:33 SEE: Luke 23:28-29a. Sullivan, Sir Arthur. *Daughters of Jerusalem*

16:33 SEE: John 14:1, 27. Thompson, William H. *Peace I Leave With You*

17:1, 11 (chorale text by K. K. Davis)
Bach, J. S. *God and Man*. Kbd: M:c1-e♭2. Carl Fischer (1948), found in *Sing Unto the Lord,* vol. 1

17:1, 5, 11, 21, 23
Head, Michael. *Thus Spake Jesus*. Org: H:(b1)d♯1-g♯2; L:(g)b1-e2. Boosey & Hawkes (1955)

17:3-4, 21-23
Foley, John B. *Father, May They All Be One*. Gtr: b1-b2. NALR (1974), found in *Neither Silver Nor Gold*

17:11, 15 SEE: Genesis 48:16. Schutte, Daniel L. *Blessed Are You*

17:17, 24 SEE: John 10:10, 14. Elgar, Edward. *I Am the Good Shepherd*

18:34-35 SEE: John: 3:13-15, 17-18. Mozart, W. A. *Behold the Son of God*

19:5 SEE: Isaiah 53:3. Owens, Jimmy. *Behold the Man*

19:17 (based on)
SEE: Matthew 27:30. Card, Michael. *This Must Be the Lamb*

19:26-27 Spiritual (arr. Hall Johnson). *Take My Mother Home*. Pno: M. Carl Fischer (1940) V-1473

19:30 Antes, John. *And Jesus Said: It is Finished.* Kbd: b♭1-g2. Boosey & Hawkes (1963)

20:1, 11, 14-15, 17-20, 26, 30-31 (John 11:25-27; John 21:1, John 25; Revelation 20:12)
Curran, Pearl G. *The Resurrection*. Kbd: H:e♭1-a2; L:c1-f♯2. G. Schirmer (1924), found in *Seventeen Sacred Songs for Church and General Use*

20:1-18 SEE: Matthew 28:1-8. Croegaret, Jim. *Was it a Morning Like This?*

20:11 (based on)
Spiritual (arr. Harry T. Burleigh). *Weepin' Mary*. Pno: H:f1-f2; L:d1-d2. Belwin Mills (1917), found in *The Spirituals of Harry T. Burleigh* (H/L)

20:11 (based on)
Spiritual (arr. Harry T. Burleigh). *Weepin' Mary*. Pno: H:f1-f2; L:d1-d2. Belwin (1969), found in *Album of Negro Spirituals* (H/L); Hal Leonard (2001), found in *The Sacred Collection* (H/L)

20:13 Mendelssohn, Felix. *Ye Have Taken Away My Lord* (German/English). Duet-Kbd: H/H. John Church (1907), found in *Sacred Duets,* vol. I

20:13, 15 SEE: Matthew 28:5-7. Phillips, Madalyn. *He is Risen, as He Said*

20:13-15 Mendelssohn, Felix. *They Have Taken Away My Lord (Tulerunt Dominum meum)* (English/Latin). Duet-Pno: H:e1-f2; L:c♯1-d2. E. C. Schirmer (1970), found in *Forty Eight Duets of the 17th–19th Centuries*

20:13-17 Bernhard, Christoph. *Dialogus auf Ostern: Sie Haben meinen Herrn hinweggenommen* (German). Duet-2 vlns, 2 vla: Sop:c1-a3/ Bass:E-d2. Bärenreiter (1972), found in *Geistliche Harmonien*

20:18 SEE: Job 19:25-27. Hurd, Bob. *I Have Seen the Lord*

20:19, 21, 26
SEE: Isaiah 26:3. Schubert, Franz. *Peace Be Unto You*

20:25 (Luke 24:36; other based on John 21:4-5)
Pethel, Stan. *We Have Seen the Risen Lord.* Kbd: b♭2-f2. Hope (1995) 801, found in *The Church Soloist*

20:26-29 (adapted)
Balchmetev, Nikolai. *Despite Locked Doors.* 2-part-Kbd: Sop/Alto, Sop/Tenor, Sop/Bass or Tenor/Bass: g1-c2/c-g1. Found in *A Choir Book for Advent*

20:29 (based on)
Haas, David. *Happy Are They Who Believe.* Kbd, gtr, vc or bsn: d1-c2. GIA (1987), found in *As Water to the Thirsty*

20:29 SEE: Job 23:3, 8-9. Rowley, Alec. *O That I Knew Where I Might Find Him*

21:00 (paraphrased; adapted)
Koch, Frederick. *Feed My Lambs.* Kbd: b1-e2. Carl Fischer (1990), found in *Five Sacred Solos for Worship Service*

21:1, 25 SEE: John 20:1, 11, 14-15, 17-20, 26, 30-31. Curran, Pearl G. *The Resurrection*

21:4-5 SEE: John 20:25. Pethel, Stan. *We Have Seen the Risen Lord*

21:15 Faulkner, George. *Feed My Sheep.* Org: H:e1-g♯2; L:c1-e2. Carl Fischer (1957) H:V-2113; L:V-2114

21:16-17 SEE: John 1:29. Wold, Wayne L. *Agnus Dei, Lamb of God*

21:17 (based on)
Spiritual (arr. Edward Boatner). *You Hear the Lambs A-Crying.* Pno, gtr: f1-f2. Belwin Mills (1973), found in *The Story of the Spirituals*

ACTS

1:8 (Acts 2:1-47; Romans 1:6-17; other)
Peterson, John W. (arr. Tom Fettke). *Come, Holy Spirit.* Kbd: d1-f2. John W. Peterson Music (1971), found in *The Lord is My Light*

2:00 (Revelation 21:16; based on)
Spiritual (arr. Harry T. Burleigh). *I Want to Be Ready.* Pno: c1-e♭2. Belwin Mills (1917), found in *Spirituals for Church and Concert; The Sacred Collection* (H/L)

2:00 (Revelation 21:16; based on)
Spiritual (arr. Phillip McIntyre). *I Want to Be Ready.* Pno: H:e1-g2(b3). FitzSimons (1990), found in *The Spirituals of Harry T. Burleigh*

2:1-47 SEE: Acts 1:8. Peterson, John W. *Come, Holy Spirit*

2:3-4 SEE: Matthew 4:18. Freud, Joyce. *Peter Was a Fisherman*

2:14b, 16-17, 21-23, 32-33, 36
Elgar, Edward. *I Have Prayed to Thee* (from *The Kingdom*). Kbd: Bass or Bar:c-f1. Novello (1906, 1984) 73 0009 03

2:27 SEE: Psalm 16:10. Mullins, Rich. *The Just Shall Live*

3:1-3 Richner, Thomas. *Rise Up and Walk.* Kbd: H:c1-g2. Harold Flammer (1975), found in *Songs of Praise by Contemporary Composers*

3:1-8 Warren, Clara. *Rise and Walk.* Kbd: H:d1-e2; L:b♭1-c2. R. D. Row (1963)

7:48 SEE: I Corinthians 3:16-17. Mendelssohn, Felix. *For Know Ye Not That Ye Are His Temple (O Wherefore Do Ye These Things?)*

8:17 SEE: Matthew 19:15. Spiritual (arr. Harry T. Burleigh). *I Know De Lord's Laid His Hands on Me*

9:2 (Psalm 114:12-14; Philippians 4:5; II Timothy 2:19)
Mendelssohn, Felix. *But the Lord is Mindful of His Own* (from *St. Paul*). Kbd: H:c1-f2; L or Alto:a1-d2. G. Schirmer (n.d.); Boston Music (1961), also found in *20 Distinctive Sacred Solos* (H/L); *Anthology of Sacred Song–Alto; Everybody's Favorite Sacred Songs; Sacred Hour of Song* (H/M); *Oratorio Repertoire,* vol. II

13:35 SEE: Psalm 16:10. Mullins, Rich. *The Just Shall Live*

17:24 SEE: I Corinthians 3:16-17. Mendelssohn, Felix. *For Know Ye Not That Ye Are His Temple (O Wherefore Do Ye These Things?)*

17:28 (Psalm 90:12)
Gieseke, Richard W. *God's Own Time.* Kbd: M:d1-e2. MorningStar (1992) 40-860

17:28 (Philippians 2:5-11; based on)
O'Connor, Roc. *Jesus the Lord.* U/2-part-Gtr: b1-d2(e2). NALR (1981), found in *Lord of Light*

17:28a SEE: Psalm 66:1-2. Speir, Randy. *In Him We Live*

19:6 SEE: Matthew 19:15. Spiritual (arr. Harry T. Burleigh). *I Know de Lord's Laid His Hands on Me*

26:26 SEE: Romans 8:38-39. Floyd, Carlisle. *For I Am Persuaded*

27:22, 24, 28 (Isaiah 45:22-23, 28; Philippians 2:1)
MacDermid, James G. *God That Made the World.* Kbd: H:e1-g2; L:c1-e$^{\flat}$2. Forster (1958)

ROMANS

1:6-17 SEE: Acts 1:8. Peterson, John W. *Come, Holy Spirit*

1:17 SEE: Psalm 16:10. Mullins, Rich. *The Just Shall Live*

5:8 SEE: Psalm 118:24. Warren, Clara. *Let Us Keep the Feast*

6:00 (based on)
Green, Steve and Jon Mohr. *Other Side of the Grave.* Kbd: d$^{\flat}$1-a$^{\flat}$3. Birdwing (1984), found in *The Lord is My Light*

6:3-4 Soler, Joseph. *An ignoratis quia quicumque* (from *Two Songs*) (Latin). Pno: g-g1. Peer-Southern (1972) Romans / 147

6:4 SEE: John 15:4. Coleman. *Christ is With Me*

6:8-9 SEE: Isaiah 55:1-3. Dean, Stephen. *Water of Life*

6:14 SEE: Romans 14:11. Barker, Clement W. *Draw Nigh to God*

8:1-2 SEE: John 3:13-15, 17-18. Mozart, W. A. *Behold the Son of God*

8:2, 6 (I Corinthians 15:22, 51-52a, 55, 57)
Joy, Jeanne Alden. *Thanks Be to God.* Kbd: H:e1-f2; L:d1-e$^{\flat}$2. R. D. Row (1947)

8:16-17, 38-39
SEE: John 3:16. Tindall, Adrienne M. *I Am Persuaded*

8:28 Carter, John. *All Things Work Together for Good.* 2-part mixed-Kbd: b$^{\flat}$1-d2/d-d1. Hope (1990) PP 117

8:31, 33-34
Handel, G. F. *If God Be for Us* (from *Messiah*). Kbd: Equal voices:H:e$^{\flat}$1-a$^{\flat}$3/L:a$^{\flat}$1-d$^{\flat}$2. Carl Fischer; G. Schirmer; Novello (1959), found in *Oratorio Anthology: Soprano; Solos from the Great Oratorios for Soprano*

8:31, 35, 37-39
Burns, William K. *If God Be for Us* (from *Two Sacred Songs*). Kbd: H:f1-a3; L:d1-f2. Abingdon (1967)

8:31-39 (based on)
Foley, John B. *If God is for Us.* U/2-part-Gtr: c1-b$^{\flat}$2(d2). NALR (1975), found in *Earthen Vessels*

8:35, 37-39
Pinkham, Daniel. *Who Shall Separate Us From the Love of Christ,* (no. 2 from *Letters from St. Paul*). Kbd or Stg Qt: c$^{\sharp}$1-a$^{\flat}$3. Stainer (1971)

8:35, 38-39
Doig, Don. *Who Shall Separate Us?* Kbd: d1-f2. Hope (1976), found in *Everything for the Church Soloist*

8:35, 38-39
Haas, David (kbd acc. Marty Haugen). *The Love of the Lord.* U/2-part-Kbd, gtr: c1-e2. GIA (1983), found in *We Have Been Told*

8:35-39 (Ephesians 1:4-5; other)
Dolck, Doug and Tom Fettke. *He Loved Me.* Kbd: b$^{\flat}$1-f2(a$^{\flat}$3). Lillenas (1982), found in *The Lord is My Light*

8:38, 39 (Numbers 6:24-26; Acts 26:26)
Floyd, Carlisle. *For I Am Persuaded* (from *The Pilgrimage*). Kbd or orch: M:g1-f2(a3). Boosey & Hawkes (1959)

8:38-39 SEE: Psalm 139:7-10. Winton, Mary. *Whither Shall I Go From Thy Spirit*

9:2 (Isaiah 7:14; other)
Card, Michael (arr. Marty Parks). *Immanuel.* Kbd: d1-e2. Lillenas (1999), found in *Solos from the Word*

10:8-13 SEE: Matthew 4:4. Hurd, Bob. *The Word is in Your Heart*

10:13-15 Bock, Fred. *Diving Calling.* Kbd: d1-e2. Fred Bock (2001), found in *The Sanctuary Soloist*, vol. 3

10:15 Handel, G. F. *How Beautiful Are the Feet* (from *Messiah*). Kbd: Sop:f$^{\sharp}$1-g2. Carl Fischer; G. Schirmer (1994); Novello (1959), found in *Anthology of Sacred Song–Soprano; Schirmer's Singer's Library: Soprano Arias from Oratorios,* vol. 2; *Sing Unto the Lord,* vol. 2; *the Singer's Repertoire: Songs of Faith*

10:15 Handel, G. F. (arr. Harrison Oxley). *How Beautiful Are the Feet* (from *Messiah*). U-Kbd: H:f$^{\sharp}$1-g2. Kevin Mayhew (1992), found in *Favorite Anthem,* bk 2

10:15 Handel, G. F. (arr. Richard Peek). *How Beautiful Are the Feet* (from *Messiah*). U-Kbd: Med:d♯1-e2. MorningStar (1989) MSM-50-9505

10:15 Handel, G. F. (arr. Doreen Rao). *How Beautiful Are the Feet* (from *Messiah*). U-Kbd: H:f♯1-g2. Boosey & Hawkes (1992) OCTB6702

10:15 Handel, G. F. (arr. James Michael Stevens). *How Beautiful Are the Feet* (from *Messiah*). Kbd: c1-d2. Intrada (1993), found in *Easter MESSIAH for Young Voices*

10:15 Handel, G. F. (arr. Richard Peek). *How Beautiful Are the Feet* (from *Messiah*). U-Kbd: M:d♯1-e2. MorningStar (1989) MSM-50-9505

10:15 Wooler, Alfred. *How Beautiful on the Mountains*. Kbd, vln: M:g1-a♭2; L:e1-f2. Oliver Ditson (1927)

10:18 Handel, G. F. *Their Sound is Gone Out* (from *Messiah*). Kbd: f1-g2. Carl Fischer; G. Schirmer; Novello

11:33-36 SEE: Psalm 104:1-3, 24. Baumgartner, H. Leroy. *O Lord, My God, Thou Art Very Great*

11:33, 36 Elliott, John G. *Romans Doxology*. Cantor-Kbd: c1-e2. BMG Songs (1993), found in *American Worships: Songs From the Heart of the Church*

11:33-36 Powell, Robert J. *The Wisdom, Riches and Knowledge of God* (from *Surely the Lord is in This Place*). Kbd: M:c1-f2. Augsburg (1995) 11-10607

12:1-2 McAfee, Don. *A Living Sacrifice*. Kbd: c1-g2. Hope (1970) 501, also found in *New Testament Songs*

12:11-12, 18
Distler, Hugo. *My Dear Brethren, Meet the Demands of This Time,* op. 17, no. 3 (from *Three Sacred Concertos*) (German/English). Org: H:c1-a3. Concordia (1969) 97-4925, also found in *Three Sacred Concertos*

13:8-10 Telemann, Georg Philipp. *Hemmet den Eifer, verbannet die Rache* (German). Cont, fl or rec: e1-g2. Bärenreiter (1973), found in *Harmonische Gottesdienst* (1925/26)

13:11-12 Pinkham, Daniel. *Now it is High Time to Awake* (no. 6 from *Letters from St. Paul*). Kbd/stg qt: b1-a♭3. Stainer (1971) 142

14:11 (Romans 6:14; I Corinthians 15:34; I Thessalonians 5:5; James 4:8)
Barker, Clement W. *Draw Nigh to God.* Kbd: H:f1-g♭2; L:d1-e♭2. Carl Fischer (1935)

14:11 SEE: Isaiah 45:23. Driskell, Gary and Marty Hennis. *Kings Shall Bow*

I CORINTHIANS

1:22-25 (based on)
Bennard, George. *The Old Rugged Cross.* Kbd: d1-e♭2. Beam Me Up Music (1991), found in *Gospel & Inspirational Showstoppers*

1:22-25 (based on)
Bennard, George. *The Old Rugged Cross.* Kbd: d1-e♭2. Hal Leonard (1991), found in *The Best Gospel Songs Ever; Smoky Mountain Gospel Favorites*

1:27-29 (II Corinthians 4:6-7; based on)
Foley, John B. *Earthen Vessels.* Cantor-Org, gtr, 2 inst in c, opt duet: c♯1-c♯2(e2). NALR (1991) OCP 9490, also found in *Earthen Vessels*

2:9 (Hebrews 11:10)
Faulkner, William M. *Eye Hath Not Seen.* Kbd: e1-f2. Carl Fischer (1956)

2:9 SEE: John 14:15. Foster, Myles B. *Eye Hath Not Seen, Nor Ear Heard*

2:9 SEE: Isaiah 64:4. Gaul, Alfred Robert. *Eye Hath Not Seen*

2:9 Stearns, Peter Pindar. *Eye Hath Not Seen* (from *Three Sacred Songs*). Vc, ob, hn: b1-g2. American Composers Alliance

2:9-10 Lovelace, Austin C. *Than Eye Hath Seen.* Kbd: e1-e2. Darcy Press (1993), found in *Sacred Solos by Austin C. Lovelace*

2:9-12 Wolf, Hugo. *Man the Child of God*. Kbd: Med. Coburn Press (1971), found in *Lift Up Your Voice*

3:16-17 (Psalm 115:3; Acts 7:48; Acts 17:24; based on)
Mendelssohn, Felix. *For Know Ye Not That Ye Are His Temple (O Wherefore Do Ye These Things?)* (from *St. Paul*). Kbd: Bass:a-d1. G. Schirmer (1977), found in *Anthology of Sacred Song–Bass; Oratorio Anthology: Baritone/Bass; Schirmer's Singer's Library: Bass Arias from Oratorios*

5:7-8 (I Corinthians 15:20-22)
Scott, John Prindle. *Christ is Risen*. Kbd: H:f1-g2; Med:d1-e2. Harold Flammer (1920)

6:11 SEE: Isaiah 42:6-7. Brown, Allanson G. Y. *Behold! The Former Things Are Come to Pass*

6:11 (Isaiah 42:6-7)
Telemann, Georg Philipp. *Ein jeder Lauft, der In den Schranken kauft* (German). Cont, ob: f1-g2. Bärenreiter (1957) 3627

9:24-27 SEE: Psalm 118:24. Warren, Clara. *Let Us Keep the Feast*

10:11 SEE: Exodus 13:14. Hayford, Jack. *Tell Ye This Story*

10:13-15 Bock, Fred. *Divine Calling*. Kbd: d1-e2. Fred Bock (2001), found in *The Sanctuary Soloist*, vol. 3

10:16 SEE: Psalm 34:9. Hurd, Bob. *Fracción Del Pan*

10:16 SEE: Psalm 118:24. Warren, Clara. *Let Us Keep the Feast*

10:16-17 (I Corinthians 11:24-26; other)
Dean, Stephen. *The Bread That We Break*. Org, B♭-cl: c1-d2. OCP (1982), found in *Sing of the Lord's Goodness*

10:16-17 (I Corinthians 12:4; Galatians 3:28; other)
Foley, John B. *One Bread, One Body*. Cantors-Org, gtr: b1-c2(d2). NALR (1978), found in *Vision for Mission*

10:16-17 SEE: Psalm 116:1, 3, 5, 12-13, 15-18. Hurd, Bob. *Our Blessing Cup*

10:16-17 SEE: Psalm 34:9a. Joncas, Michael. *Our Blessing Cup*

11:23-26 (adapted)
Dolck, Doug. *Remember Me*. Kbd: e♭1-d2. Lillenas (1982), found in *The Lord is My Light*

11:23-26 (adapted)
Hayford, Jack (arr. Lyndell Leatherman). *Until He Comes Again*. Kbd: c1-e♭2. Lillenas (1980), found in *Scripture Solos for All Seasons*

11:23-26 Johnson, Gary (arr. Joseph Linn). *In Remembrance of Me*. Kbd: M:c1-d2. Lillenas (1980), found in *Scripture Solos for All Seasons*

11:23-26 Johnson, Gary (arr. Cheri Keaggy). *In Remembrance of Me*. Kbd or Trax: H:f♯1-g2; L:a1-b2. Sparrow (1966), found in *My Faith Will Stay*

11:24 SEE: Luke 22:19. Wood, Dale. *In This Moment of Remembrance*

11:24-25 (based on)
Foley, John B. *This is My Body*. Gtr: c1-d2. NALR (1974), found in *Neither Silver Nor Gold*

11:24-26 SEE: I Corinthians 10:16-17. Dean, Stephen. *The Bread That We Break*

11:26 SEE: Psalm 17:15. Hurd, Bob. *O, How I Long to See*

12:4 SEE: I Corinthians 10:16-17. Foley, John B. *One Bread, One Body*

12:4-31 SEE: Isaiah 2:3-4. Hurd, Bob. *Gather Your People*

12:5, 12, 26 (based on)
Hurd, Bob (acc. Dominic MacAller). *We Are All Parts of One Body*. U-Kbd: c1-c2. OCP (1991), found in *Alleluia! Give the Glory*

12:13, 27 (Ephesians 2:21-22; I John 4:12; other)
Hurd, Bob (acc. Dominic MacAller). *Let Us Share This Bread of Life*. U-Kbd: e1-e2. OCP (1991), found in *Alleluia! Give the Glory*

13:00 Behrens, Jack. *I Corinthians 13,* op. 20. Org: Sop:e♭1-a3. Canadian Music Centre (1962)

13:00 Bitgood, Roberta. *The Greatest of These is Love*. Kbd: H:e♭1-f2; L:c1-d2. H. W. Gray (1936)

13:00 Haskins, V. *Love Never Faileth*. Kbd: d1-g2. G. Schirmer

13:00 Penhorwood, Edwin. *The Greatest of These is Love*. Org: b♭1-e♭2. Hinshaw (1976) HMV 104

13:00 Read, Gardner. *Epistle to the Corinthians,* op. 144b. Org: H:c♯2-a3(b3). Media Press (1999)

13:00 Root, Frederic. *Love Never Faileth*. Kbd: f1-g2. Summy Birchard (1907)

13:00 Ward-Stephens. *Love Never Faileth*. Pno: H:d1-g2; L:b1-e2. Chappell (1917), found in *The Ward-Stephens Musical Settings of Sacred Words*

13:00 Ware, Harriet. *The Greatest of These*. Pno: H:e♭1-a♭3; L:d1-f♯2. Boston Music (1947)

13:00 Wetzler, Robert. *The Greatest of These is Love* (from *Two Scriptural Songs)*. Org, fl: c1-e2. AMSI (1979) V-4

13:1 (based on)
Leech, Bryan Jeffrey (arr. Ruth Morris Bray). *The Greatest of These is Love.* Kbd, gtr: b♭1-c2. Fred Bock (1992), found in *A Joyous Wedding Celebration*

13:1-2, 4a (adapted)
SEE: Psalm 128:00. McCray, James. *Love Is . . .*

13:1-2, 4-8
Clausen, René. *The Greatest of These is Love* (from *A New Creation*). Org: H:e1-g2; M:d1-f2. Mark Foster (1990) H:MF 2047; Med:MF 247

13:1, 3 (based on)
Hopson, Hal H. *The Gift of Love.* Kbd: d1-d2. Hope (1972, 1981) 911; CF 148 (U/2-part), also found in *The Church Soloist; Everything for the Church Soloist; Everything for the Wedding Soloist; I Will Sing of My Redeemer*

13:1, 3 (based on)
Hopson, Hal H. *The Gift of Love.* Duet-Kbd: d1-d2. Hope (1972) Hope 911; CF 148, also found in *Choirbook for Saints and Singers; Folk Songs for Weddings*

13:1, 3 (based on)
Hopson, Hal H. (arr. Lloyd Larson). *The Gift of Love.* Duet-Kbd: H:f1-g2/L:b♭1-d2. Hope (1972, 2000) Hope 8065, found in *Sacred Vocal Duets For High and Low Voice*

13:1, 3 (based on)
Hopson, Hal H. (arr. Lyndell Leatherman). *The Gift of Love.* Kbd: d1-e♭2. Hope (1972), found in *The Lord is My Light*

13:1-3 (other)
St. James, Rebecca and Matt Bronleewe. *For the Love of God.* Kbd, gtr: b1-c2. Hal Leonard (2000) HL 00306418, also found in *Rebecca St. James: Transformed*

13:1-3, 12-13
Brahms, Johannes (ed. Carl Deis). *Wenn ich mit Menschen und mit Engelszungen (Though I Speak With the Tongues of Men)* (from *Vier ernste Gesang*) (German/English). Pno: M:a1-g2; L. G. Schirmer (1964), Abingdon (1964) APM 308, also found in *Select Vocal Solos for the Church Musician*

13:1-6, 8, 13
Hartley, Evaline. *Charity.* Kbd: H:f1-g2; M:d♭1-e♭2. Huntzinger (1939), found in *Sacred Songs Especially Suitable for Christian Science Services* (H/L)

13:1-7 McAfee, Don. *If I Am Without Love.* Kbd: d1-g♯2. Hope (1970) 501, also found in *New Testament Songs*

13:1-7 Moe, Daniel. *The Greatest of These is Love.* Kbd: H:d♭1-f♯2;L:b♭1-d♯2. Augsburg (1958) H:11-0702; L:11-0703

13:1-7 (adapted)
Talbot, John Michael. *1 Corinthians 13.* Gtr: g-b2. Birdwing (1987), found in *Praise, Praise the Lord, O My Soul and Worship*

13:1-7, 11-13 (other)
Gulliksen, Kenn. *Charity.* Kbd, gtr: c1-c2. Maranatha! (1971, 1978), found in *How Majestic is Your Name*

13:1-7, 13 (based on)
Johnson, Paul. *Love Theme.* Kbd, gtr: b♭1-e♭2. Sonlife Music (1975), found in *Together*

13:1-8 Archer, Violet. *1 Corinthians 13.* Pno: Mez. Canadian Music Centre (1976)

13:1-8 (adapted)
Fauré, Gabriel (arr. Carl Fredrickson). *Love Never Faileth.* Kbd: H; L:d1-f2. R. D. Row (1964), found in *Sacred Song Masterpieces,* bk 2

13:1-8 (based on)
Ridge, M. D. (acc. Patrick Loomis). *The Greatest of These is Love.* Cantor-Pno, gtr, 2 insts in c, opt duet: c1-c2. OCP (1985, 1988) 8893, also found in *In Every Age; United as One,* vol. 2

13:1-11, 13
Griffin, Charles B. *Soggetto Cavato.* Pno: H:d1-f♯2. Charles B. Griffin (1996)

13:3 (I John 4:7-8; based on)
Wolford, Darwin. *For Love is of God.* Kbd: M:d1-f♯2. Jackman Music (1992) S-0180, found in *Scripture Settings for Solo Voice*

13:4 Cotter, Jeanne. *In Love We Choose to Live.* U/2-part-Kbd, gtr: b1-b2(f♯-d1). GIA (1993), found in *When Love Is Found*

13:4-5, 13
SEE: Matthew 22:37-39. VanDyke, May. *Love*

13:4-7, 10, 13 (I John 4:16)
Haas, David (arr. Craig S. Kingsbury). *Where There is Love.* Pno or org, inst in c, gtr: MH:c1-f2. OCP (1985), found in *United As One,* vol. 1

13:4-7, 10, 13 (I John 4:16)
Haas, David. *Where There is Love.* Kbd, gtr: MH:c1-f2. OCP (1985), found in *When Love Is Found*

13:4-7, 13 (paraphrased)
Lynn, Lorna. *The Greatest of These is Love.* Pno or gtr: a1-a2. Golden Music (1980)

13:4-8, 13 (adapted)
Tindall, Adrienne M. *Love Never Fails.* Kbd, fl: c$^\sharp$1-g2. Adrienne Tindall (1987), found in *Sacred Solos by Adrienne Tindall,* vol. I

13:9, 12 (Frederick Lucien Hosmer, alt.)
Lovelace, Austin C. *O God, in All Thy Might.* Kbd: e1-g$^\flat$2. Darcy Press (1993), found in *Sacred Solos by Austin C. Lovelace*

13:13 SEE: John 13:5-7. Walker, Christopher. *Faith, Hope and Love*

15:00 SEE: Psalm 33:3a. Gore, Richard T. *O Sing Unto the Lord a New Song*

15:20 SEE: Job 19:25-26. Handel, G. F. *I Know That My Redeemer Liveth*

15:20 SEE: Job 19:25-26. Handel, G. F. (arr. David Hamilton). *I Know That My Redeemer Liveth*

15:20, 22 (Isaiah 35:10; other)
Bach, J. S. *Now Christ Is Risen.* Duet-Kbd: H:d1-g2/L:a1-b2. R. D. Row (1960), found in *Sacred Duet Masterpieces,* bk 1

15:20-22 SEE: I Corinthians 5:7-8. Scott, John Prindle. *Christ is Risen*

15:20, 23 (Ephesians 5:14; adapted)
Handel, G. F. (arr. Carl Fredrickson). *Awake Thou That Sleepest.* Kbd: d$^\flat$1-e$^\flat$2. R. D. Row (1959), found in *Sacred Song Masterpieces,* bk 1

15:20, 26-28 (Colossians 3:1-3)
Bach, J. S. *Awake, All Ye People* (from cantata no. 15). Kbd: g-e2. Coburn Press (1971), found in *Lift Up Your Voice*

15:22, 51-52a, 55, 57
SEE: Romans 8:2, 6. Joy, Jeanne Alden. *Thanks Be to God*

15:29 SEE: I Peter 3:18, 19. Galbraith, Robert. *I Wait Upon Thee*

15:31-52 SEE: Job 19:25. Dufford, Bob. *Songs of the Angels*

15:34 SEE: Romans 14:11. Barker, Clement W. *Draw Nigh to God*

15:45, 53, 49
Tindall, Adrienne M. *The Mists of Adam Dreaming.* Kbd: e1-f2. Darcy Press (1994), found in *Sacred Solos by Adrienne Tindall,* vol. III

15:50-58 Telemann, Georg Philipp. *Jauchzt, ihr Christen, seid vergnügt* (German). Cont, vln: d1-g2. Bärenreiter (1971) 720

15:51-52 (I Thessalonians 4:17)
Fettke, Tom and Bob Ashton. *We Shall All Be Changed.* Kbd: c1-a3. Pilot Point (1991) MB-825, found in *Solos from the Word*

15:51-52 (I Thessalonians 4:17)
Fettke, Tom and Bob Ashton. *We Shall All Be Changed.* Duet-Kbd or Trax: H:c1-a3; L:c1-e2. Pilot Point (1993) MB-656, found in *The Sunday Worship Duet Book*

15:51-52a
Handel, G. F. *Behold, I Tell You a Mystery* (from *Messiah*). Kbd: Bass:a-e1. Carl Fischer; G. Schirmer; Novello (1959), found in *Anthology of Sacred Song–Bass; Oratorio Anthology: Baritone/Bass*

15:51-52a
Handel, G. F. (arr. James Michael Stevens). *Behold, I Tell You a Mystery* (from *Messiah*). Kbd:c1-c2. Integra (1993), found in *Easter MESSIAH for Young Voices*

15:51-52, 54b-55 (Hebrews 13:14)
Brahms, Johannes. *Lo, I Unfold Unto You a Mystery* (from *Requiem*) (German/English). Kbd or orch: Bar. G. Schirmer 1678

15:51-52, 55, 57 (based on)
Larson, Lloyd. *Death, Where is Your Sting?* 2-part mixed-Kbd: H:c1-c2/L:c-d$^\flat$1. Beckenhorst (1989) BP1339

15:51-55 (other)
Fettke, Tom. *Changed.* Kbd: a1-f2(g2). Lillenas (1980), found in *Scripture Solos for All Seasons*

15:52 (Revelation 4:1; based on)
Rambo, Dottie. *We Shall Behold Him.* Kbd: MH:a$^\flat$1-e2(a3); M:c1-d2(g2). Benson (1980, 1985), found in *Greatest Songs of Sandi Patty* (H); *GMA Song of the Year* (H); *How Majestic Is Your Name; Low Voice Treasury; Sandi Patti: Anthology; More Than Wonderful* (M); *Sandi Patti Medium Voice Collection; Sandi Patti: The Finest Moments; Song of the Year; Very Best of Sandi Patty* (H/M)

15:52 (based on)
Spiritual (arr. Harry T. Burleigh). *You May Bury Me in de Eas'.* Pno: f1-g2. Belwin Mills (1917), found in *The Spirituals of Harry T. Burleigh*

15:52 (Philippians 2:10; Hebrews 1:7; based on)
Tunney, Dick & Melodie. *In Majesty He Will Come with Majesty* (*Majesty*). Kbd or Trax: M:g-g2. Pamela Kay Music (1988) Sparrow trax: 5535, also found in *Sandi Patti: Anthology; Sandi Patti Medium Voice Collection; Very Best of Sandi Patti* (H/M)

15:52b-53
Handel, G. F. *The Trumpet Shall Sound* (from *Messiah*). Kbd: Bass:A-e1. Carl Fischer; G. Schirmer; Novello (1959); also found in *Oratorio Repertoire,* vol. IV

15:52b-53
Handel, G. F. (arr. James Michael Stevens). *The Trumpet Shall Sound* (from *Messiah*). U-Kbd: c1-d2. Integra (1993), found in *Easter MESSIAH for Young Voices*

15:54 Handel, G. F. *Then Shall Be Brought to Pass* (from *Messiah*). Kbd: Alto:d1-a2. Carl Fischer; G. Schirmer; Novello (1959)

15:55-56 Handel, G. F. (ed. Colin Pemberton). *O Death, Where is Thy Sting?* Duet-Kbd: d1-d2/g-a1. HMP (1991), found in *Selected Duets for Contest:* set 1

15:55-56 Handel, G. F. *O Death, Where is Thy Sting?* (from *Messiah*). Duet-Kbd: Alto:b♭1-b♭2/ Tenor:f-g1. Carl Fischer; G. Schirmer; Novello (1959)

15:57 (other)
Gluck, Christoph von (arr. Carl Fredrickson). *Thanks Be to God.* Kbd: H; L:b♭1-e♭2. R. D. Row (1964), found in *Sacred Song Masterpieces,* bk 2

15:57 (other)
Gluck, Christoph von (arr. Carl Fredrickson). *Thanks Be to God.* Duet-Kbd: H:e1-g2/L:a1-d2. R. D. Row (1960), found in *Sacred Duet Masterpieces,* bk 1

II CORINTHIANS

3:9-12 Pisk, Paul A. *The Spirit of God.* Kbd: c1-f2. American Composers Alliance

3:17 SEE: Galations 5:1, 25. Barker, Clement W. *If We Live in the Spirit*

4:6-7 SEE: I Corinthians 1:27-29. Foley, John B. *Earthen Vessels*

4:10 SEE: Job 19:25-27. Hurd, Bob. *I Have Seen the Lord*

5:1 (based on)
Smith, Marcus. *Home, Dost Thou Beckon?* Kbd: Med:c♯1-d2. Sonos (Jackman) (1997) 00434, found in *Sabbath Song*

5:7 SEE: Matthew 16:13-18, 25. McGuire, Dony. *Upon This Rock*

5:17 (based on)
Wilson, John Floyd. *A New Creature.* U/2-part-Kbd, gtr: b1-e2(f2). Hope (1972, 1973), found in *The Genesis Songbook; Man Alive*

6:2 SEE: Joel 2:12. Haas, David. *Now, the Acceptable Time*

6:2 SEE: Isaiah 63:5. Rogers, James H. *Today If Ye Will Hear His Voice*

6:16 Barker, Clement W. *Temple of Glory.* Kbd: H:e♭1-g2; L:c1-e2. R. D. Row (1963)

10:5 (based on)
Searcy, George. *Making War in the Heavenlies.* Kbd, gtr, (opt orch): e1-d♭2. Justin Peters/Tourmaline Music (1989), found in *Songs for Praise and Worship*

12:7-10 (based on)
Fettke, Tom (arr. Dick Bolks). *Three Times I Asked Him.* Kbd: e♭1-f2. Lillenas (1980), found in *Scripture Solos for All Seasons; Solos from the Word*

GALATIANS

2:19-20 (Galatians 3:27; Galatians 6:17; based on)
Hurd, Bob and Dominic MacAller (har. Craig S. Kingsbury). *No Longer I.* U/2-part-Kbd, gtr, inst in c: (a1)c1-c2. OCP (1990), found in *Behold the Cross*

2:20 SEE: John 15:4. Coleman. *Christ is With Me*

3:20 (based on)
Elliott, John G. *I Am Crucified with Christ.* Kbd, gtr, (opt orch): e1-b2. BMG Sons, Inc. (1990), found in *Songs for Praise and Worship*

3:27 SEE: Galatians 2:19-20. Hurd, Bob. *No Longer I*

3:28 SEE: I Corinthians 10:16-17. Foley, John B. *One Bread, One Body*

5:1, 25 (II Corinthians 3:17; II Timothy 1:7)
Barker, Clement W. *If We Live in the Spirit.* Kbd: MH:e♭1-g2; ML:c1-e2. Carl Fischer (1935)

5:25 (based on)
Hustad, Donald. *Spirit of God.* Pno: H:c1-d2; L:b$^{\flat}$1-c2. Fred Bock (1964), found in *Everything for the Church Soloist; The Sanctuary Soloist*

6:9a (other)
Harris, Don and Martin J. Nystrom (arr. Carl Seal). *Don't Grow Weary.* Kbd, gtr: b$^{\flat}$1-c2. Integrity (1993) MB-825, found in *Solos from the Word*

6:14 (Isaac Watts)
Hope, Lawrence. *When I Survey the Wondrous Cross.* Kbd: d1-f2. Turner & Phillips (1904)

6:14 (Isaac Watts)
Lorenz, Ellen Jane. *When I Survey the Wondrous Cross.* Kbd: c1-f2. Lorenz (1896)

6:14 (Isaac Watts)
Murray, Lyn. *When I Survey the Wondrous Cross.* Kbd: H:e1-f2; L:c1-d2. Intrada (1964), found in *The Sanctuary Soloist*

6:14 (Ephesians 2:8-9)
Rambo, Dottie (arr. Linn and Lyndell Leatherman). *I Will Glory in the Cross.* Kbd: b$^{\flat}$1-e$^{\flat}$2. ASCAP (1978), found in *The Lord is My Light*

6:14 (Isaac Watts)
Thomson, Sydney. *When I Survey the Wondrous Cross.* Org: f1-f2. G. Schirmer (1922) 154 / Ephesians GALATIANS

6:17 SEE: Galatians 2:19-20. Hurd, Bob. *No Longer I*

EPHESIANS

1:2 (Ephesians 3:14-17; based on)
Foley, John B. *Dwelling Place.* Gtr: a1-d2. NALR (1976), found in *A Dwelling Place*

1:3-4 SEE: Mark 10:15-16. Cox, Joe. *Blessed to Be a Blessing*

1:3-6, 11-13, 17-18 (Ephesians 2:4-6)
Foley, John B. *Bless Our God.* U/2-part-Gtr, inst in c: c1-c2(e2). NALR (1976), found in *A Dwelling Place*

1:4-5 SEE: Romans 8:35-39. Dolck, Doug and Tom Fettke. *He Loved Me*

2:4-6 SEE: Ephesians 1:3-6, 11-13, 17-18. Foley, John B. *Bless Our God*

2:7-18 (Ephesians 5:19-28; inspired by)
Schutte, Daniel L. *Lover of Us All.* Kbd: c1-d2. OCP (1987, 1989), found in *Lover of Us All*

2:8-9 SEE: Galatians 6:14. Rambo, Dottie. *I Will Glory in the Cross*

2:10 Haas, David. *You Are God's Work of Art.* Kbd, gtr: d1-d2. GIA (1988), found in *Who Calls You By Name,* vol. 1

2:14 (I Peter 5:7; based on)
Groves, Kandela. *He Is Our Peace.* Kbd, gtr, (opt orch): b$^{\flat}$1-c2. Word (1998) 27454, also found in *Songs for Praise and Worship*

2:21-22 SEE: I Corinthians 12:13, 27. Hurd, Bob. *Let Us Share This Bread of Life*

3:14-15 Schütz, Heinrich. *Ich beuge meine knie,* SWV 319 *(I Bow and Bend the Knee)* (German). Duet-Cont: Equal voices: Bass:F-c1. Hänssler (1983); Bärenreiter (1963) 1705

3:14-17 SEE: Ephesians 1:2. Foley, John B. *Dwelling Place*

3:18 (other)
Parks, Marty. *The Love of Christ.* Kbd: d$^{\flat}$1-c2. PsalmSinger (1999) MB-825, found in *Solos from the Word*

4:5-6 Haas, David. *Initiation Acclamation (There is One Lord).* Kbd, gtr: d1-b2. GIA (1988), found in *Who Calls You By Name,* vol. 1

4:6-10 (based on)
Cotter, Jeanne. *There is One Body.* Kbd, gtr: c1-d2. GIA (1993), found in *When Love is Found*

4:7 (Psalm 121:00)
Harker, F. Flaxington. *I Will Lift Up Mine Eyes to the Hills,* op. 34, no. 2. Pno: H:e$^{\flat}$1-a$^{\flat}$3; L:c1-f2. Harold Flammer (1923) 496

4:7 (Psalm 121:00)
Harker, F. Flaxington. *I Will Lift Up Mine Eyes to the Hills,* op. 34, no. 2. Duet-Pno. Harold Flammer (1928) 932

4:31-32 Davis, Katherine K. *Be Ye Kind, One to Another.* Kbd: c1-e$^{\flat}$2. Galaxy (1948) 1.1696.7

5:2 (adapted)
Handel, G. F. (arr. Carl Fredrickson). *Walk Humbly With Thy God.* Kbd: H; L:c1-d2. R. D. Row (1964), found in *Sacred Song Masterpieces,* bk 2

5:2, 8, 11, 15, 19
Powell, Robert J. *Walk in Love.* Kbd: H:d1-f2; L:b1-d2. Concordia (1980) H:97-5578; L:97-5579, also found in *Seven Wedding Songs*

5:8-15 (Revelation 21:5)
Haas, David (arr. Jeanne Cotter). *Christ Will Be Your Light.* Cantor-Kbd, gtr, opt duet: e♭1-d♭2(f2). GIA (1988), found in *Who Calls You By Name,* vol. 1

5:14 SEE: I Corinthians 15:20, 23. Handel, G. F. *Awake Thou That Sleepest*

5:14 (John 8:12)
Humphreys, Don. *Light of the World.* Kbd: H:e♭1-g2; L:b♭1-e2. R. D. Row (1960); G. Schirmer, found in *Don Humphrey's Song Book* (H/L); *Songs for Christian Science Service,* bk 1

5:14 SEE: Psalm 116:3. Mendelssohn, Felix. *Strikke des Todes*

5:14 (I Thessalonians 5:5, 16-23)
Ward-Stephens. *Awake Thou That Sleepest.* Pno: H:d♭1-a♭3; L:b1-f♯2. Chappell (1917), found in *The Ward-Stephens Musical Settings of Sacred Words*

5:19-28 SEE: Ephesians 2:7-18. Schutte, Daniel L. *Lover of Us All*

5:25 SEE: Matthew 19:6. Nelson, Ronald A. *Not Two, But One*

6:10-13 (other)
Humphreys, Don. *Put on the Whole Armour of God.* Kbd: H:d1-f2; L:c1-e♭2. R. D. Row (1956); G. Schirmer, found in *Don Humphrey's Song Book* (H/L); *Songs for Christian Science Service,* bk 1

6:11 SEE: Psalm 18:32, 37. Vaughan Williams, Ralph. *The Pilgrim's Psalm*

6:14 SEE: Psalm 100:5. Humphreys, Don. *Truth*

6:16-17 (adapted)
Bach, J. S. *Be Strong In the Lord.* Kbd: d1-e♭2. R. D. Row (1959), found in *Sacred Song Masterpieces,* bk 1

PHILIPPIANS

1:3-11 (adapted)
Beck, John Ness. *Song of Devotion.* Pno: H:e1-a3; L:c♯1-f♯2. G. Schirmer (1968), found in *12 Sacred Songs* (H/L)

1:6 Mohr, Jon. *He Who Began a Good Work in You.* Kbd, gtr: L:a1-c2. Birdwing (1987), found in *40 Contemporary Hits; Bible Songs; The Big Book of Contemporary Christian Favorites; Contemporary Low Voice; Fifty Contemporary Favorites for Low Voice; The Solo Book; Songs for Praise and Worship*

1:6 Mohr, Jon (arr. Steven V. Taylor). *He Who Began a Good Work in You.* Duet-Kbd, gtr or Trax: M/MH:a1-d♭2(e♭2); M/M:b1-d♭2/d-d♭1. Birdwing (1987), found in *25 More Contemporary Favorites for Duet* (M/M); *25 Songs for Two-Part Choir,* vol. II (M/MH); *The Church Soloist*

2:1-2, 5 (II Timothy 1:7)
Humphreys, Don. *Let This Mind Be in You.* Pno: H:d1-g2; L:c1-e♭2. Willis Music (1965), found in *Sing to the Lord*

2:5-11 (adapted)
Fettke, Tom. *God Exalted Him.* Kbd: b1-f2. Lillenas (1984), found in *The Lord is My Light*

2:5-11 (adapted)
Fettke, Tom. *God Exalted Him.* Duet-Kbd or Trax: H:b1-f2/L:b1-d2. Lillenas (1993), found in *The Sunday Worship Duet Book*

2:5-11 SEE: Acts 17:28. O'Connor, Roc. *Jesus the Lord*

2:5-11 SEE: Isaiah 9:6. Pendleton, Emmet. *Christ is Lord,* op. 12, no. 3

2:6-11 (adapted)
Berry, Cindy (arr. Richard Huggins). *At the Name of Jesus.* 2-part-Kbd, gtr or Trax or Orch: c1-f2/c-d♭1. Word (1985) orch: 301 0185 251, also found in *The Best of Times*

2:6-11 (other)
Mason, Babbie. *Jesus the One and Only.* U/2-part-Kbd, gtr. Word (1988), found in *With All My Heart*

2:8-9, 11 Foley, John B. *I Will Sing of the Lord.* U/2-part-Gtr: d1-b2. NALR (1974), found in *Neither Silver Nor Gold*

2:9-10 Jeffreys, George (ed. Peter Aston). *O quam suave* (from *Two Devotional Songs*) (Latin). Kbd: Bass:F-d1. Novello (1988) 17 0336

2:9-11 SEE: Psalm 145:1-13. Lyles, Dwight. *Proclaim the Glory of the Lord*

2:10 SEE: I Corinthians 15:52. Tunney, Dick & Melodie. *In Majesty He Will Come with Majesty*

2:10-11 SEE: Isaiah 45:23. Driskell, Gary and Marty Hennis. *Kings Shall Bow*

2:10-11 (based on)
Jernigan, Dennis L. *At the Name of Jesus.* Kbd, gtr, (opt orch): f1-e2(g2). Shepherd's Heart Music (1989), found in *Songs for Praise and Worship*

2:10-11 SEE: Isaiah 45:23b. Nelson, Greg and Phil McHugh. *Power in Jesus Name*

2:11 SEE: Acts 27:22, 24, 28. MacDermid, James G. *God That Made the World*

2:15, 18 (Philippians 3:7-16)
Schutte, Daniel L. (arr. John B. Foley). *Only This I Want.* Pno, gtr: d1-d2. NALR (1981), found in *Lord of Light*

3:7-16 SEE: Philippians 2:15, 18. Schutte, Daniel L. *Only This I Want*

4:4 (Isaiah 9:2, 6-7)
Distler, Hugo. *O Rejoice in the Lord at All Times,* op. 17, no. 2 (from *Three Sacred Concertos*). Org: H:c1-g2. Concordia (1969) 97-4925

4:4 Miller, Merle. *Think on These Things.* Kbd: H:c1-e♭2; L:b♭1-d♭2. R. D. Row (1947)

4:4-5 Kosche, Kenneth T. *Rejoice in the Lord Always.* 2-part-Kbd: Sop/Alto:d1-d2. Concordia (1993) 98-3091

4:4-5, 7-8
Humphreys, Don. *Rejoice in the Lord.* Kbd: d1-f2. Willis Music (1962)

4:4-7 Gieseke, Richard W. *Rejoice in the Lord Always.* Kbd: M:b♭1-d♭2. MorningStar (1992) MSM-40-1

4:4-7 Pinkham, Daniel. *Rejoice in the Lord Always* (no. 5 from *Letters from St. Paul*). Kbd: d1-g2. Stainer (1971) 142

4:4, 8 Lane, Richard. *Rejoice in the Lord.* Kbd: H or M:e1-f2(g2). Coburn Press (1975), found in *Eleven Scriptural Songs from the Twentieth Century*

4:5 SEE: Acts 9:2. Mendelssohn, Felix. *But the Lord is Mindful of His Own*

4:7 SEE: Matthew 25:1-6. Dencke, Jeremiah. *Go Ye Forth In His Name*

4:7 SEE: Isaiah 26:3. Schubert, Franz. *Peace Be Unto You*

4:8-9 (adapted)
MacGimsey, Robert. *Think on These Things.* Kbd: H:e1-g2; L:b♭1-e♭2. Carl Fischer (1956)

4:8-9 (adapted)
Skillings, Otis. *Whatever is True.* Kbd: c1-f2. Lillenas (1980), found in *Scripture Solos for All Seasons; Solos from the Word*

4:13 (other)
Chapman, Steven Curtis and Jerry Salley. *His Strength is Perfect.* Kbd, gtr: d1-a♭2. Sparrow (1988), found in *Twenty Favorites of Steven Curtis Chapman*

4:13 (other)
Chapman, Steven Curtis and Jerry Salley (choral arr. Steven V. Taylor). *His Strength is Perfect.* 2-part-Kbd or Trax: c1-e♭2/c-e♭1. Sparrow (1988, this arr. 1990), found in *25 Songs for Two-Part Choir,* vol. II

COLOSSIANS

3:1-2 SEE: Psalm 150:1. Borneman, Bruce and Judi. *It's Time to Praise the Lord*

3:1-2 Foster, Myles B. *If Ye Then Be Risen With Christ.* Duet-Kbd: H:e1-g2/L:a1-c2. John Church (1907), found in *Sacred Duets,* vol. 2

3:1-3 SEE: I Corinthians 15:20, 26-28. Bach, J. S. *Awake, All Ye People*

3:1-4 Soler, Joseph. *Fraters: Si Consurrexistis cum Christo* (from *Two Songs*) (Latin). Pno: f-e2. Peer-Southern (1972)

3:12-14, 17
Becker, Gerhardt C. *You Are the People of God.* Org: d1-e2. Concordia (1983) 98-2603

3:12-15 (based on)
Moore, Bob. *We Are a Chosen People.* U/2-part-Kbd, trpt, sax, gtr: d1-d2. GIA (1993) G-3875, also found in *When the Lord In Glory Comes*

3:12-17 (adapted)
Fedak, Alfred V. *You Are the Chosen of the Lord.* Org: e♭1-f2. AMSI (1987) V-10

3:12-17 (adapted)
Smith, G. Alan. *Because You Are God's Chosen Ones*. Kbd: d1-f2. Hope (1980) 911, 804, also found in *Everything for the Church Soloist; Everything for the Wedding Soloist*

3:15 Cagle, Denny (arr. Ken Barker). *Let the Peace of Christ Rule in Your Heart*. Kbd, gtr, (opt orch): d1-d2. Between the Lines Music (1981), found in *Songs for Praise and Worship*

3:15-17 Proulx, Richard. *Wedding Song From Colossians*. Org: Med:e1-f2. GIA (1993) G-3784

3:16 Pinkham, Daniel. *Let the Word of Christ Dwell in You* (no. 3 from *Letters from St. Paul*). Kbd (or stg qt): c1-g2. Stainer (1971) 142

I THESSALONIANS

4:17 SEE: I Corinthians 15:51-52. Fettke, Tom and Bob Ashton. *We Shall All Be Changed*

5:1-6 Pinkham, Daniel. *But of the Times and the Seasons* (no. 4 from *Letters from St. Paul*). Kbd (or stg qt): c♯1-a3. Stainer (1971) 142

5:5 SEE: Romans 14:11. Barker, Clement W. *Draw Nigh to God*

5:5, 16-23
SEE: Ephesians 5:14. Ward-Stephens. *Awake Thou That Sleepest*

I TIMOTHY

1:17 SEE: Psalm 32:11. Huhn, Bruno S. *Be Glad, O Ye Righteous*

1:17 Sonnenberg, Lorraine. *Now Unto the King Eternal*. Kbd, gtr, (opt orch): d1-d2. Sesac (1972), found in *Bible Songs; Songs for Praise and Worship*

II TIMOTHY

1:7 SEE: Galations 5:1, 25. Barker, Clement W. *If We Live in the Spirit*

1:7 SEE: Philippians 2:1-2, 5. Humphreys, Don. *Let This Mind Be in You*

1:7 SEE: II Chronicles 20:15b, 17. Koch, Frederick. *Be Not Afraid*

1:10 SEE: Psalm 104:30. Bach, J. S. (arr. Hruby, Dolores). *My Spirit Rejoice*

1:12 (Malachi 4:1-2)
Scott, John Prindle. *I Know in Whom I Have Believed.* Kbd: H:d1-g2; L:a1-d2. Presser (1914) 158 / II Timothy/Hebrews

2:9 SEE: Job 19:25-27. Hurd, Bob. *I Have Seen the Lord*

2:11-12 SEE: John 12:23-24, 26. Farrell, Bernadette. *Unless a Grain of Wheat*

2:19 (Wisdom of Solomon 3:1)
DeLong, Richard. *But the Lord is Mindful of His Own* (from *Five Sacred Songs*). Kbd: Med:c1-g2. E. C. Schirmer (1993) 4759

2:19 SEE: Acts 9:2. Mendelssohn, Felix. *But the Lord is Mindful of His*

HEBREWS

1:5 Handel, G. F. *Unto Which of the Angels Said He at Any Time* (from *Messiah*). Kbd: Tenor:a1-g2. Novello; G. Schirmer; Carl Fischer

1:7 SEE: I Corinthians 15:52. Tunney, Dick & Melodie. *In Majesty He Will Come With Majesty*

2:6 (Psalm 8:4)
Purcell, Henry. *Lord, What is Man* (from *Harmonia Sacra, Four Sacred Songs*). Pno: H:d1-a3; L:b♭1-f2. Boosey & Hawkes (1947); International Music, found in *40 Sacred Songs*

3:7-8 SEE: Isaiah 63:5. Rogers, James H. *Today If Ye Will Hear His Voice*

4:9 SEE: Isaiah 64:4. Gaul, Alfred Robert. *Eye Hath Not Seen*

4:12 SEE: John 1:1. MacDermid, James G. *He Sent His Word*

8:10c SEE: Psalm 50:1-3, 5-6. Case, Henry Lincoln. *The Mighty God Hath Spoken*

8:10 SEE: Deuteronomy 32:11. Mendelssohn, Felix. *God Hath Led His People On*

10:22-23 SEE: I John 3:1. Burns, William K. *His Children*

11:1-2, 13, 16b (Hebrews 12:1-2a; adapted)
Lovelace, Austin C. *Faith Is*. Kbd: d1-a3. Augsburg (1979) 11-9497, found in *Three Solos for High Voice*

11:3 SEE: John 1:1. MacDermid, James G. *He Sent His Word*

11:10 SEE: I Corinthians 2:9. Faulkner, William M. *Eye Hath Not Seen*

11:10 SEE: Isaiah 64:4. Gaul, Alfred Robert. *Eye Hath Not Seen*

11:13-16 (Revelation 21; based on)
Harrah, Walt. *No More Night*. Kbd, gtr: b♭1-e2. Word (1984), found in *Our God Reigns; The Song Book,* vol. III

11:14 (based on)
Spiritual (arr. Harry T. Burleigh). *I Don't Feel No-Ways Tired.* Pno: a1-e2. Belwin Mills (1917), found in *The Spirituals of Harry T. Burleigh*

12:1-2 Allen, Dennis and Nan Allen. *Look Unto Jesus.* Kbd, gtr: b1-f2. Pilot Point (1995) MB-825, found in *Solos from the Word*

12:1-2a SEE: Hebrews 11:1-2, 13, 16b. Lovelace, Austin C. *Faith Is*

12:1-2 Pinkham, Daniel. *Wherefore Seeing* (no. 1 from *Letters from St. Paul*). Kbd or stg qt: f♯1-a♭3. E. C. Schirmer (1971) 142

12:2 Kosche, Kenneth T. *Come, Let Us Fix Our Eyes on Jesus.* 2-part-Kbd, opt inst in c, opt vc or bsn: d1-e2/b1-d2. Concordia (1995) 98-3198

12:6, 11 Sullivan, Sir Arthur. *Come Ye Children* (from *The Prodigal Son*). Pno: H:d1-g2; L:b♭1-e♭2. R. D. Row (1963), found in *The Church Soloists Favorites* (H/L); *Oratorio Repertoire,* vol. III

13:8 (other)
Whitsett, Eleanor (arr. Gene Thomas). *Jesus Christ, the Same.* Kbd: e1-e2. Lillenas (1974, 1979), found in *Scripture Solos for All Seasons; Solos from the Word*

13:14 SEE: I Corinthians 15:51-52, 54b-55. Brahms, Johannes. *Lo, I Unfold Unto You a Mystery*

JAMES

1:16-17, 19-20, 22, 25, 27
Sisler, Hampson, A. *Every Good and Perfect Gift.* 2-part mixed-Kbd: H:b1-e2/L:b♭-e1. Laurendale (1992) CH-1023

1:17 SEE: Isaiah 63:7. Fischer, Irwin. *Psalm of Praise*

1:17-22 Rider, Dale G. *Every Good and Perfect Gift.* Kbd: d1-g2. Augsburg 12-974100

1:17-22 Telemann, Georg Philipp. *Ew'ge Qwelle, milder Strom* (German). Cont, fl: d♯1-e2. Bärenreiter (1953) 3629

4:8 SEE: Romans 14:11. Barker, Clement W. *Draw Nigh to God*

4:14 (adapted)
Schram, Ruth Elaine. *Vanished Like a Vapor.* 2-part-Kbd, fl: b1-c2. Alfred (1990) 7833

5:16 (Matthew 4:23; Matthew 5:1-2; Matthew 6:6-13)
Curran, Pearl G. *Prayer.* Kbd: H or M:d1-g2; L:b1-e2. G. Schirmer (1927) 33376

5:16 SEE: John 15:12. Hustad, Donald. *This is My Commandment*

I PETER

2:9 Clattenburg, Jeannie and Rick Powell. *Chosen Generation.* Kbd, gtr, (opt orch): d1-d2. Sound III (1978), found in *Songs for Praise and Worship*

3:18, 19 (I Peter 4:6; I Corinthians 15:29; based on)
Galbraith, Robert. *I Wait Upon Thee.* Kbd: Med:c1-d2. Sonos (Jackman) (1997) 00434, found in *Sabbath Song*

4:6 SEE: I Peter 3:18, 19. Galbraith, Robert. *I Wait Upon Thee*

4:7 SEE: Matthew 24:42. Marsh, Donald. *Beloved*

4:13-14 SEE: Psalm 63:6. Elgar, Edward. *The Sun Goeth Down*

5:6 (based on)
Hudson, Bob. *Humble Thyself in the Sight of the Lord.* 2-part mixed-Kbd, gtr, (opt orch): d1-b2. Singspiration (1956), found in *Songs for Praise and Worship*

5:7 SEE: Ephesians 2:14. Groves, Kandela. *He is Our Peace*

5:7 (based on)
Willard, Kelly. *Cares Chorus (I Cast All My Cares Upon You).* Kbd, gtr, (opt orch): c1-d2. Word (1988), found in *Songs for Praise and Worship*

II PETER

1:17 SEE: Psalm 99:3. Paris, Twila. *Holy is the Lord*

I JOHN

1:00 SEE: Isaiah 9:6. Schutte, Daniel L. *City of God*

1:1-3 (other)
Brown, Keith Crosby. *When From the Lips of Truth.* Kbd: H:e1-g2; L:c♯1-e2. R. D. Row (1951) 771

1:1, 5-7, 9
Baumgartner, H. Leroy. *This We Declare Unto You*, op. 49, no. 1 (from *Behold What Manner of Love*). Kbd: d1-g2. Concordia (1955) 97-5725

2:15, 17 SEE: Isaiah 51:6. MacDermid, James G. *Lift Up Your Eyes to the Heavens*

2:15a, 17 SEE: John 14:6a. Sullivan, Sir Arthur. *Love Not the World*

2:15a, 17 Ward-Stephens. *Love Not the World.* Pno: H:e♭1-a♭3; L:c1-f2. Chappell (1917, 1947), found in *The Ward-Stephens Musical Settings of Sacred Words*

2:25 (I John 3:1-2)
Cruikshank, Helen M. *Behold What Names of Love.* Kbd: H:d1-f2; L:c1-e♭2. R. D. Row (1958)

3:1 (Hebrews 10:22-23)
Burns, William K. *His Children* (from *Four Meditative Songs*). Kbd: e1-g2. Abingdon (1972) APM 515

3:1 SEE: Matthew 4:4. Fichthoin, Claude. *Behold What Manner of Love*

3:1 Vantine, Patricia. *Behold What Manner of Love.* Kbd, gtr, (opt orch): b♭1-c2. Maranatha! (1981), found in *Songs for Praise and Worship*

3:1 Vantine, Patricia. *Behold What Manner of Love.* 2-part-Kbd: b♭1-c2. Maranatha! (1981), found in *Kids Praise!*

3:1-2 SEE: I John 2:25. Cruikshank, Helen M. *Behold What Names of Love*

3:1-2 Dubois, Theodore. *Behold What Manner of Love.* Kbd: H:d1-g2; L:b♭1-e♭2. R. D. Row (1963), found in *Soloists Practical Library of Sacred Songs,* bk 2 (H/L)

3:1-3 (other)
Bach, J. S. *Von der Welt verlang' ich nichts (Sehet, welch eine Liebe)* (from Kantate nr. 64) (German). Pno, obd, vln or vla: Alto:b1-e♭2. Kalmus, found in *Arias from Church Cantatas for Contralto,* vol. II

3:1-3 Baumgartner, H. Leroy. *Behold What Manner of Love,* op. 49, no. 2 (from *Behold What Manner of Love*). Kbd: d1-g2. Concordia (1955) 97-5725

3:1-3 Hatch, Wilbur. *Behold! What Manner of Love.* Kbd: c1-a♭3. Shawnee (1955) A-5046, also found in *I John / 161*

3:1-3 Humphreys, Don. *Behold What Manner of Love.* Kbd: H:d1-f2; L:b1-d2. R. D. Row (1951); G. Schirmer (1941), found in *Christian Science Service Songs; Don Humphrey's Song Book* (H/L)

3:1, 3 SEE: Genesis 1:26-27. MacDermid, James G. *Behold What Manner of Love*

3:1-3 Paris, Harry Allen. *Behold, What Manner of Love.* Kbd: H:d1-g2; L:b♭1-e♭2. Huntzinger (1938), found in *Sacred Songs Especially Suitable for Christian Science Services* (H/L)

3:2 (other)
Cross, Phil and Carolyn Cross. *We Shall Be Like Him.* Kbd, gtr: d1-c2. Welcome Home Press (1988) HB9104, found in *Homeland Harmony,* vol. 2

3:2 (and other; based on)
Gersmehl, Mark and Scott Douglas. *We Will See Him as He Is.* Kbd, gtr or Trax: H:b♭1-a♯3; M:g-g2. Yellow House Music and Paragon Music (1984), found in *Greatest Songs of Sandi Patty* (H)*; More Than Wonderful* (H); *Sandi Patti Medium Voice Collection; The Song Book,* vol. III; *Very Best of Sandi Patti* (H/M)

3:2a (other)
Hall, Pam Mark. *The Now and the Not Yet.* Kbd: e-b2. Meadowgreen (1984, 1981), found in *Our God Reigns*

3:2 Stearns, Peter Pindar. *Beloved, Now Are We the Sons of God*. Vc, ob, hn: f1-e♭2. American Composers Alliance

3:8b (other)
Kendrick, Graham. *For This Purpose*. Kbd, gtr, (opt orch): d1-e2. Maranatha! (1985), found in *Songs for Praise and Worship*

3:10 SEE: Psalm 34:6, 15, 18. Foley, John B. *God's Poor Ones*

3:16 SEE: John 3:16. Scruggs, Randy. *Tell the World That Jesus Loves You*

4:7 Head, Michael. *Beloved, Let Us Love One Another*. Kbd: a1-d2. Boosey & Hawkes (1964) S 2635

4:7-8 (based on)
Busarow, Donald. *Beloved, Let Us Love*. Org, opt fl: H:d♭1-a♭3. MorningStar (1991) MSM-40-882

4:7-8 Myers, Gordon. *Beloved, Let Us Love One Another*. Kbd: e♭1-e♭2. Eastlane Music

4:7-8 (based on)
Proulx, Richard. *Beloved, Let Us Love*. Org: d1-f2. Augsburg (1970) 11-0715

4:7-8 Ryder, Dennis. *First John 4:7 and 8*. 2-part-Kbd: c1-c2. Maranatha! (1981), found in *Kids Praise!*

4:7, 8, 11, 14, 16, 20-21
Fischer, Irwin. *Love One Another*. Kbd: e1-f2. American Composers Alliance (1952)

4:7-11 Sherman, Arnold B. (arr. Dale Wood). *Let Us Love One Another*. Kbd: M:d1-d2. Sacred Music Press (1988), found in *Sacred Songs: Nine Solos for Medium Voice*

4:7-12, 18-19, 21
Baumgartner, H. Leroy. *Love is of God*, op. 49, no. 3 (from *Behold What Manner of Love*). Kbd: d1-f2. Concordia (1955) 97-5725

4:8, 11-12, 16
O'Carroll, Fintan and Christopher Walker. *Celtic Alleluia*. U/2-part-Kbd, gtr, inst in c, inst in b♭: e1-d2(f♯2). OCP (1985, 1992), found in *United As One*, vol. 2

4:9 SEE: Isaiah 53:3. Owens, Jimmy. *Behold the Man*

4:12 SEE: I Corinthians 12:13, 27. Hurd, Bob. *Let Us Share This Bread of Life*

4:12 SEE: Matthew 19:6. Nelson, Ronald A. *Not Two, But One*

4:16 SEE: I Corinthians 13:4-7, 10, 13. Haas, David. *Where There is Love*

4:16 Humphreys, Don. *God is Love*. Kbd: H:d1-f2; L:c1-e2. R. D. Row (1951); G. Schirmer, found in *Don Humphrey's Song Book* (H/L); *Songs for Christian Science Service*, bk 1

4:16 (based on)
Kavanaugh, John. *God is Love*. Gtr: c1-d2. NALR (1974), found in *Neither Silver Nor Gold*

4:16, 20, 21 (based on)
Hurd, Bob (acc. Dominic MacAller). *Where There is Love*. U-Kbd: Cantor:c1-d2. OCP (1991) 9798CC, also found in *Alleluia! Give the Glory*

4:18 SEE: Psalm 116:12. Dean, Stephen. *Lord, Your Love Has Drawn Us Near*

4:18 SEE: John 4:14. Lovelace, Austin C. *O Love That Casts Out Fear*

5:4-5, 7, 11, 14, 15
Baumgartner, H. Leroy. *This is the Victory, Even Our Faith* (from *Behold What Manner of Love*). Kbd: d1-g2. Concordia (1955) 97-5725

JUDE

1:24-25 (based on)
Morris, David. *Now Unto Him*. Kbd, gtr, (opt orch): c1-d2. Intrada (1986, arr. 1992), found in *Bible Songs; Songs for Praise and Worship*

1:24-25 Smith, Michael W. *Jude Doxology*. Pno: a1-f2. Meadowgreen (1988), found in *Michael W. Smith: Greatest Hits*

REVELATION

1:00 SEE: Psalm 33:3a. Gore, Richard T. *O Sing Unto the Lord a New Song*

1:00 (based on)
Spiritual (arr. Harry T. Burleigh). *John's Gone Down On De Island*. Pno: e♭1-f2. Belwin Mills (1917), found in *The Spirituals of Harry T. Burleigh*

1:8 SEE: Psalm 118:22. Joncas, Michael. *Take and Eat*

1:8 Shelley, Harry Rowe. *I am Alpha and Omega*. Kbd: H; L. G. Schirmer

1:8 Trowbridge, J. Eliot. *I am Alpha and Omega.* Kbd: H. Evans (1902) 172 (n.v.)

1:8 SEE: John 11:25. Smith, Michael W. *I Am*

2:7 (Revelation 22:1-2, 18)
Vaughan Williams, Ralph. *The Song of Leaves of Life and Water of Life* (from *Pilgrim's Progress*). Pno: d1-e2. Oxford (1952)

2:10 (Jeremiah 1:8)
Mendelssohn, Felix. *Be Thou Faithful Unto Death* (from *St. Paul*). Kbd: Tenor:d1-g2. G. Schirmer (1994) HL50482070, found in *Oratorio Repertoire,* vol. III; *Second Book of Tenor Solos* (H)

2:10 (Jeremiah 1:8)
Mendelssohn, Felix. *Be Thou Faithful Unto Death* (from *St. Paul*). Kbd: T or H:d1-g2; M:a1-d2. G. Schirmer; Carl Fischer, found in *Anthology of Sacred Song–Tenor; Sacred Hour of Song* (H/M)

3:10-12 MacDermid, James G. *My New Name.* Kbd: b1-f2. Forster (1923)

3:20 (Matthew 11:27-28)
Bryant, Verna Mae. *Behold, I Stand at the Door.* Kbd: H:d1-f♯2; L:b♭1-d2. G. Schirmer (1955)

3:20 (Isaiah 59:1, 19; Isaiah 60:1; John 8:12)
MacDermid, James G. *Arise, Shine For Thy Light is Come.* Kbd: H:d1-g2; M:b♭1-e♭2; L:a♭1-d♭2. Forster (1936)

4:1 SEE: I Corinthians 15:52. Rambo, Dottie. *We Shall Behold Him*

4:8b SEE: Psalm 145:10. Dykes, John Bacchus. *Holy, Holy, Holy*

4:8 SEE: Revelation 5:12-13. Smith, Michael W. *Agnus Dei*

4:10-11 (Revelation 5:9; based on)
Mills, Pauline Michael. *Thou Art Worthy.* Kbd, gtr, (opt orch): H:c1-f2; L:b♭1-c2. Fred Bock (1963, 1975), renewed (1991), found in *Gospel & Inspirational Showstoppers* (H); *Songs for Praise and* Worship (L)

4:10-11 (Revelation 5:9; based on)
Mills, Pauline Michael (arr. Fred Bock). *Thou Art Worthy.* Kbd: c1-f2. Fred Bock (1979), found in *Bible Songs; How Majestic is Your Name*

5:2-5, 9, 12-13 (based on)
Dufford, Bob. *Worthy is the Lamb.* Gtr: d1-d2. NALR (1974), found in *Neither Silver Nor Gold*

5:8-10 (based on)
Rogers, Sharon Elery. *Song of the Redeemed.* Kbd: e1-g2. Hope (1970) 501, also found in *New Testament Songs*

5:9 SEE: Revelation 4:10-11. Mills, Pauline Michael. *Thou Art Worthy*

5:12 (based on)
Wyrtzen, Don. *Worthy is the Lamb.* Kbd: L:b1-b2. Singspiration (1973) MB-545, found in *Low Voice Classics*

5:12-13 (adapted)
Chapman, Morris. *Worthy is the Lamb.* Kbd: d1-e2. Word (1984), found in *Our God Reigns*

5:12-13 Handel, G. F. (arr. James Michael Stevens). *Worthy is the Lamb That Was Slain* (from *Messiah*). 2-part-Kbd: c1-d2. Integra (1993), found in *Easter MESSIAH for Young Voices*

5:12-13 Harlan, Benjamin. *Worthy is the Lamb.* Kbd, gtr: b1-g2(a3). Pilot Point (1988) MB-825, found in *Solos from the Word*

5:12-13 Harlan, Benjamin. *Worthy is the Lamb.* Duet-Kbd or Trax: H:b1-a3; L:b♭1-f♯2. Pilot Point (1993) MB-656, found in *The Sunday Worship Duet Book*

5:12-13 (based on)
Moen, Don. *Worthy the Lamb That Was Slain.* Kbd, gtr: c1-d2. Intrada (1986), found in *Bible Songs; God Will Make a Way; Songs for Praise and Worship*

5:12-13 SEE: Psalm 99:3. Paris, Twila. *Holy is the Lord*

5:12-13 (based on)
Smith, Michael W. *Agnus Dei.* Kbd, gtr: f1-e2. Milene Music (1990), found in *Exodus; I Can Only Imagine; WOW 1998/1999*

5:12-13 (Revelation 4:8; Revelation 19:6)
Smith, Michael W. *Agnus Dei.* Kbd, gtr: c♯1-d2. Milene Music (1990) 19556, found in *All the Best Songs; WOW Worship Songs Green*

5:12-13 (based on)
Wyrtzen, Don. *Worthy is the Lamb.* Kbd, gtr, (opt orch): d1-d2. Singspiration (1973), found in *Songs for Praise and Worship*

5:13 Graafsma, Debbye. *To Him Who Sits on the Throne.* Kbd, gtr, (opt orch): c1-g2. Intrada (1984, arr. 1992), found in *Songs for Praise and Worship; WOW Worship Songbook Green*

5:13 (Revelation 22:1; Revelation 21:11; adapted)
Smith, Michael W. and Gary Moore (choral arr. Steven V. Taylor). *The Throne*. 2-part-Kbd or Trax: c1-d2/e-d1. O'Ryan Music (1990), found in *25 Songs for Two-Part Choir,* vol. II

5:13 SEE: Psalm 66:2. Wolaver, Bill and Robin. *Make His Praise Glorious*

5:13b (Psalm 95:1-2, 7; Psalm 96:13)
Myers, Gordon. *Thanksgiving*. Kbd: M:d1-f2. Eastlane Music

6:2 (based on)
Spiritual (arr. Harry T. Burleigh). *Ride On, King Jesus*. Pno: d1-d2(f2). Belwin Mills (1929), found in *The Spirituals of Harry T. Burleigh*

6:2 (based on)
Spiritual (arr. Hall Johnson). *Ride On, King Jesus*. Pno: H:c1-a3; M:b♭1-g2; L: a♭1-f2. Carl Fischer (1951) H: V2223; M: V2131; L: V2224

7:9-10, 13-16
Lovelace, Austin C. *The Great White Host*. Kbd: e♭1-a♭3. Darcy Press (1993), found in *Sacred Solos by Austin C. Lovelace*

7:9-15 (other)
Pearce, Almeda J. (arr. Paul Mickelson). *When He Shall Come*. Kbd: c1-g2. Almeda J. Pearce (1934, 1971), found in *The Lord is My Light*

7:12 SEE: I Samuel 17:47. Owens, Jimmy and Jamie Collins. *The Battle Belongs to the Lord*

7:13-17 Manookin, Robert P. *Who Are These Arrayed in White Robes?* Kbd: Med:c1-c2. Sonos (Jackman) (1997) 00434, found in *Sabbath Song*

7:14-15 Gaul, Alfred Robert. *These Are They Which Came Out of Great Tribulation* (from *The Holy City*). Kbd: Sop:e1-g♯2; L:c1-e2. G. Schirmer (1977); Boston Music (1961); Amsco (1940), found in *20 Distinctive Sacred Solos* (H/L); *52 Sacred Songs; Anthology of Sacred Song–Soprano; Everybody's Favorite Sacred Songs; Oratorio Repertoire,* vol. 1; *Schirmer's Singer's Library: Soprano Arias from Oratorios,* vol. 2

7:16 (Revelation 21:3-4, 6)
Roma, Caro. *God Shall Wipe Away All Tears*. Kbd: H:d♯1-f♯2; M:b1-c♯2; L:g-c2. Witmark (1913)

7:16 (Revelation 21:3-4, 6)
Roma, Caro. *God Shall Wipe Away All Tears*. Duet-Pno: Sop:d♯1-f♯2(a3)/Bar:e-e1; Sop:d♯1-f♯2/Alto:a♯1-d2. Witmark (1913)

8:10 (paraphrased)
Spiritual. *My Lord, What a Morning*. Kbd or CD: M:d1-d2. Hal Leonard (1997) HL00740074, found in *Classical Contest Solos–Mezzo-Soprano*

8:10 (paraphrased)
Spiritual (ed. Jay Althouse). *My Lord, What a Morning*. Kbd or CD: MH; ML. Alfred (1997) MH: 11696 or w/CD 16915; ML: 11698 or w/CD 11916, found in *Spirituals for Solo Singers* (MH/ML)

8:10 (paraphrased)
Spiritual (arr. Harry T. Burleigh). *My Lord, What a Morning*. Pno: H:f1-f2; L:d♭1-d♭2. Belwin Mills (1918), found in *The Spirituals of Harry T. Burleigh* (H/L); *The Sacred Collection* (H/L)

8:10 (paraphrased)
Spiritual (arr. Harry T. Burleigh). *My Lord, What a Morning*. Kbd: H:f1-f2; MH:e♭1-e♭2; M:d1-d2; L:c1-c2

8:10 (paraphrased)
Spiritual (arr. William Dawson). *My Lord, What a Morning*. Kbd: H:f1-f2; MH:e♭1-e♭2; M:d1-d2; L:c1-c2. FitzSimons

8:10 (paraphrased)
Spiritual (arr. Mark Hayes). *My Lord, What a Morning*. Pno: MH: d1-g2; ML:b♭1-d♯2. Alfred (1998) MH 17954; ML 17959, found in *The Mark Hayes Vocal Solo Collection: 10 Spirituals* (MH/ML)

8:10 (paraphrased)
Spiritual (arr. Hall Johnson). *My Lord, What a Morning*. Pno: a♭1-f2. G. Schirmer (1949), found in *Thirty Spirituals*

8:12 SEE: John 3:13-15, 17-18. Mozart, W. A. (ed. M. B. Stearns). *Behold the Son of God*

11:15 SEE: Isaiah 53:4-5. Dufford, Bob. *Behold the Lamb of God*

14:3 (Revelation 15:3)
Rogers, Sharon Elery. *A Song of Victory*. Kbd: d1-g2. Hope (1970) 501, also found in *New Testament Songs*

14:15-18 (Revelation 15:3-4)
Raff, Joseph J. *Thrust in Thy Sickle and Reap* (from *The World's End*). Kbd: Alto:b♭1-f♯2. G. Schirmer (1977), found in *Schirmer's Singer's Library: Alto Arias from Oratorios*

15:1 Lepke, Charma Davies. *Great and Marvelous Are Thy Works*. Kbd: H:c1-g2(a3). Coburn Press (1975), found in *Eleven Scriptural Songs from the Twentieth Century*

15:3 SEE: Revelation 14:3. Rogers, Sharon Elery. *A Song of Victory*

15:3-4 Humphreys, Don. *Great and Marvelous*. Kbd: H:(c1)e♭1-f2; L:a1-d2. R. D. Row (1951)

15:3-4 Raff, Joseph J. *Great and Wonderful Are All Thy Works* (from *The World's End*). Kbd: Alto:b♭1-f♯2. G. Schirmer (1977), found in *Anthology of Sacred Song–Alto; Schirmer's Singer's Library: Alto Arias from Oratorios*

15:3-4 SEE: Revelation 14:15-18. Raff, Joseph J. *Thrust in Thy Sickle and Reap*

18:10-13 Walton, William. *Babylon Was a Great City* (from *Belshazzar's Feast*). Kbd: Bar:A-d♭1. Oxford (1931, 1959)

19:6 SEE: Revelation 5:12-13. Smith, Michael W. *Agnus Dei*

19:16 SEE: Matthew 28:1-10. Nelson, Grey and Bob Farrell. *Who Will Call Him Kings of Kings*

20:12 SEE: John 20:1, 11, 14-15, 17-20, 26, 30-31. Curran, Pearl G. *The Resurrection*

20:17 SEE: John 4:23-24. Roberts, J. E. *God is a Spirit*

21:00 Harker, F. Flaxington. *God Shall Wipe Away All Tears,* op. 49, no. 2. Pno: H:c1-a3; L:a♭1-f2. G. Schirmer (1938)

21:00 Harker, F. Flaxington (arr. Wallingford Riegger). *God Shall Wipe Away All Tears,* op. 49, no. 2. Duet-Pno: Sop:c1-a3/Alto:a1-f2. G. Schirmer (1910, 1931, 1938)

21:1 SEE: Hebrews 11:13-16. Harrah, Walt. *No More Night*

21:1, 2 Gounod, Charles. *The Vision of St. John* (from *Mors et Vita*). Kbd: Bass: f♯-e1. Presser (1923), found in *Oratorio Repertoire,* vol. IV

21:1-2, 5-6
SEE: Isaiah 51:6. MacDermid, James G. *Lift Up Your Eyes to the Heavens*

21:1-3 Shelley, Harry Rowe. *And I, John, Saw the Holy City* (from *The Inheritance Divine*). Org: e1-a♭3. G. Schirmer (1895)

21:1-4 (based on)
Card, Michael and Scott Brasher *The New Jerusalem*. Kbd, gtr: (f)a1-d2. Word (1996), found in *Greatest Songs of Michael Card*

21:1, 4, 5, 6
Mitchell, Raymond Earle. *The Tabernacle of God is With Men*. Pno: H:d1-f♯2; L:b♭1-d2. Huntzinger (1929), found in *Sacred Songs Especially Suitable for Christian Science Services* (H/L); *Selected Sacred Songs for General Use*

21:1-5 Tindall, Adrienne M. *And I Saw a New Heaven*. Kbd: d1-f♯2(g2). Darcy Press (1994), found in *Sacred Solos by Adrienne Tindall,* vol. III

21:1-7 Romer, Charles B. (arr. Lyndell Leatherman). *New Heaven-New Earth*. Kbd (opt inst in c): b1-d2. Lillenas (1980) 164 / Revelation, also found in *Scripture Solos for All Seasons*

21:1-7 (based on)
Rubin, Steffi. *A New Heaven and a New Earth*. Kbd, gtr: g1-b♭2. Lillenas (1990), found in *Contemporary Low Voice*

21:2 SEE: Psalm 23:4. Lovelace, Austin C. *The Love of God*

21:3-4 SEE: Isaiah 35:10. Ambrose, Paul. *God Shall Wipe Away All Tears*

21:3-4 (adapted)
Hoffmeister, Leon Abbott. *Behold the Tabernacle of God*. Kbd: H:f1-e♭2; L:c1-d2. G. Schirmer (1932), found in *Seventeen Sacred Songs for Church and General Use*

21:3-4 SEE: Isaiah 25:8-9. Liszt, Franz. *God Shall Wipe Away All Tears*

21:3-4 Peery, Rob Roy. *God Shall Wipe Away All Tears*. Pno: b♭1-e♭2. G. Schirmer (1939), found in *52 Sacred Songs*

21:3-4 Raff, Joseph J. *Behold, the House of God is With Men* (from *The World's End*). Kbd: Alto:b1-e2. G. Schirmer (1977), found in *Anthology of Sacred Song–Alto; Schirmer's Singer's Library: Alto Arias from Oratorios*

21:3-4, 6 SEE: Revelation 7:16. Roma, Caro. *God Shall Wipe Away All Tears*

21:3-5 (Isaiah 25:8)
Sullivan, Sir Arthur. *The Lord is Risen* (from *The Light of Life*). Kbd: Alto:b1-e2. G. Schirmer (1929), found in *Anthology of Sacred Song–Alto*

21:3-5 (Isaiah 25:8)
Sullivan, Sir Arthur. *The Lord is Risen.* Duet-Org/Pno: H:d1-g2/H:d1-f2. R. D. Row (1961), found in *Sacred Duet Masterpieces*

21:4 SEE: Psalm 50:1-3, 5-6. Case, Henry Lincoln. *The Mighty God Hath Spoken*

21:4 Field, J. T. *God Shall Wipe Away All Tears.* Org: b1-d2. G. Schirmer (1907); Boston Music, found in *Album of 12 Sacred Solos*

21:4 SEE: Psalm 17:15. Hurd, Bob. *O, How I Long to See*

21:4 Joy, Jeanne Alden. *Ye Shall Not Sorrow Any More.* Kbd: H; L. R. D. Row (1951) RDR 768-5 (n.v.)

21:4 SEE: Psalm 34:4. Robyn, Alfred G. *I Sought the Lord*

21:4 SEE: Psalm 34:4. Stevenson, Frederick. *I Sought the Lord*

21:4-5 SEE: Matthew 11:4-5. Haas, David. *Song of the Risen One*

21:4-5a Sullivan, Sir Arthur. *And God Shall Wipe Away All Tears* (from *The Light of the World*). Pno: H:d1-g2; M:b1-e2; L:b♭1-e♭2. Boston Music (1961), found in *20 Distinctive Sacred Solos* (H/L); *52 Sacred Songs* (M); *Choice Sacred Songs* (H/L); *Oratorio Repertoire,* vol. II

21:4-5a Sullivan, Sir Arthur (arr. Neil Jenkins). *And God Shall Wipe Away All Tears* (from *The Light of the World*). Kbd: L:b1-e2. Oxford (1997), found in *Sing Solo Sacred* (H/L)

21:5 SEE: Ephesians 5:8-15. Haas, David. *Christ Will Be Your Light*

21:5 Whitehouse, Jan. *He Makes All Things New.* Kbd: b♭1-e♭2. Lorenz (1995), found in *Reflections and Meditations*

21:7 SEE: Psalm 18:32, 37. Vaughan Williams, Ralph. *The Pilgrim's Psalm*

21:9-10 SEE: Isaiah 40:1. Parker, Horatio W. *Glorious Jerusalem*

21:9-10 (adapted)
Wolf, Hugo (arr. K. K. Davis). *Revelation.* Kbd: M:c1-f2. Carl Fischer (1948), found in *Sing Unto the Lord,* vol. 1

21:11 SEE: Revelation 5:13. Smith, Michael W. and Gary Moore. *The Throne*

21:12-13, 22 (traditional)
Spiritual (arr. Hal H. Hopson). *Twelve Gates Into the City.* U/2-part-Kbd: c1-c2. Mark Foster (1987) MF 812

21:16 SEE: Acts 2:00. Spiritual (arr. Harry T. Burleigh). *I Want to Be Ready*

21:16 SEE: Acts 2:00. Spiritual (arr. Phillip McIntyre). *I Want to Be Ready*

21:18, 21 SEE: John 14:2-3. Lewis Jr., Ross. *In My Father's House*

22:1 SEE: Isaiah 55:1. Klein, Manuel. *Ho! Everyone That Thirsteth*

22:1 SEE: Revelation 5:13. Smith, Michael W. and Gary Moore. *The Throne*

22:1-2, 18
SEE: Revelation 2:7. Vaughan Williams, Ralph. *The Song of Leaves of Life and Water of Life*

22:1-4 Butt, James. *River of Life.* Kbd: c♯1-e2. Sphemusations (1965), found in *Revelation / 165*

22:1, 14, 17
Fischer, Irwin. *Come, Take the Water of Life.* Kbd: e1-g2. American Composers Alliance (1960)

22:1, 14, 17
Joy, Jeanne Alden. *The River of Water of Life.* Kbd: H:e♭1-f2; L:b♭1-e♭2. R. D. Row (1947) 724

22:5 SEE: Psalm 27:4. Talma, Louise. *Cantata: All the Days of My Life*

22:13 SEE: Luke 9:20-24. Foley, John B. *The Christ of God*

22:14, 16 Shelley, Harry Rowe. *I Jesus, Have Sent Mine Angel.* Org: b♭-d♭1. G. Schirmer (1895)

Composer Index

Aäddissen, Erol.
The Lord's Prayer. Matthew 6:9-13.
Abt, Franz.
Ave Maria, op. 438. Luke 1:28, 30-31, 42.
Not a Sparrow Falleth. Matthew 10:29-31.
O Lord, Most Holy. Luke 1:28, 30-31, 42.
Adair, Hazel Ferrell.
Praise and Give Thanks. Psalm 107:6, 9.
Adams, Joseph H.
The Lord Is My Shepherd. Psalm 23:00.
Addison, Joseph.
The Spacious Firmament. Psalm 19:1-6.
Adler, Samuel.
Bow Down Thine Ear. Psalm 86:1-5.
The Earth With All That Dwell Therein. Psalm 24:1-4, 7-10.
Happy He Who Walketh Ever. Psalm 1:1-3.
Hear My Words, O Gracious Lord. Psalm 5:1-5, 7.
I Lift Mine Eyes. Psalm 121:00.
I Will Betroth Her Unto Me. Hosea 2:21, 22.
It Is Good to Sing Thy Praises. Psalm 92:1-5, 9, 12-15.
Laments. II Samuel 1:19-27.
Praise God, Ye Servants of the Lord, no. 10. Psalm 113:00.
Praise the Lord. Psalm 113:1-5.
Praise the Lord, no. 1. Psalm 150:00.
Psalm 23. Psalm 23:00.
Psalm 92. Psalm 92:00.
Psalm 96. Psalm 96:1-6, 9-13.
A Woman of Valor. Proverbs 31:20, 28-30.
Aichinger, Gregor.
Amen, amen dico vobis. John 6:54.
Angelus Domini. John 1:14.
Discubuit Jesus. Luke 22:14-15.
Domine, non sum dignus. Matthew 8:8
His est panis. John 6:59
Albrecht, M.
The Lord's Prayer. Matthew 6:9-13.
Allen, David Len.
The King of Love My Shepherd Is. Psalm 23:00.
Allen, Dennis and Nan Allen.
Look Unto Jesus. Hebrews 12:1-2.
Allitsen, M. Frances.
Like as the Hart Desireth. Psalm 42:1-3, 5.
The Lord Is My Light. Psalm 27:1, 3, 5.
The Lord Is My Light (arr. William David Young and Tom Fettke). Psalm 27:1, 3, 5.
Alstott, Owen.
How Lovely Is Your Dwelling Place. Psalm 84:1-4, 8, 11.
To You, O Lord. Psalm 25:1, 4-5, 7, 17, 20.
Yes, I Shall Arise. Psalm 27:4, 8.
Ambrose, Paul.
God Shall Wipe Away All Tears. Isaiah 35:10.
Amedeo, Leone.
Ave Maria. Luke 1:28, 30-31, 42.
Anderson, Jim.
I am the Resurrection. John 11:25.
Anderson, Leroy and Alfred Heller.
The Lord's Prayer. Matthew 6:9-13.
Anderson, Ronald.
Psalm of Joy. Psalm 150:00.
Andrews, Mark.
Blow Ye the Trumpet. Joel 2:12-13, 15-17.
The Twenty-Third Psalm. Psalm 23:00.
Anonymous.
The Lord Is a Mighty Warrior. Exodus 15:3.
Antes, John.
And Jesus Said: It Is Finished. John 19:30.
Anthony, Dick.
Living By Dying. John 12:24-25.
Where Is the Profit? Matthew 16:26.
Applebaum, Louis.
Cry of the Prophet. Jeremiah 2:2.
Arcadelt, Jacob.
Ave Maria. Luke 1:28, 32.
The Lord Is My Shepherd. Psalm 23:00.
O Savior, Lord of Heaven. Luke 1:28, 32.
Archer, Malcolm.
Let Our Praise to You. Psalm 141:2.
Archer, Violet.
1 Corinthians 13. I Corinthians 13:1-8.
God Sings in Pleasure. Zephaniah 1:00 - 3:20.
Miserere et Jubilate. Psalm 13:1-3.
Requiem. Song of Songs 3:1-3.
Te Deum. Psalm 104:31-34.
The Twenty-Third Psalm. Psalm 23:00.
Atkins, Jean.
Abide in Christ. John 15:00.
Atkinson, René.
Ave Maria. Luke 1:28, 42.
Hail Holy Mary (1985). Luke 1:28, 42.
Avery, Lawrence.
Al Tifigi vi Le-Ozveich. Ruth 1:16-17.
Entreat Me Not to Leave Thee. Ruth 1:16-17.
Avery, Richard and Donald Marsh.
I Will Follow. Ruth 1:16, 17.
You Are the Salt of the Earth. Matthew 5:13-16.
Ayala, Bob.
The Lord Be Magnified. Psalm 40:16.

Bach, C. P. E.
Fecit potentiam. Luke 1:51.
Lo, He Regarded. Luke 1:48.
Quia fecit mihi magna. Luke 1:49.
Quia respexit. Luke 1:48.
Bach, J. C. F.
Amplius lava me ab inquitate mea. Psalm 51:2-3.
Bach, J. S.
Agnus Dei. John 1:29.
All Hearts Now Be Joyful (trans. Hal H. Hopson). Psalm 35:9.
Awake, All Ye People. I Corinthians 15:20, 26-28.
Be Strong in the Lord. Ephesians 6:16-17.
Benedictus. Matthew 21:9.
By Waters of Babylon. Psalm 137:00.
Come Unto Him. Matthew 11:28-30.
Deposuit potentes. Luke 1:52.
Erbarme dich. Psalm 139:7-10.
Et exultavit. Luke 1:47.
Et exultavit spiritus meus. Luke 1:46.
Ever Will I Praise. II Samuel 22:3.

Fear Not, Little Flock. Luke 12:24, 27, 29, 32.
For He Hath Regarded. Luke 1:48.
For He That is Mighty. Luke 1:49.
For Me a Table. Psalm 23:5.
God and Man. John 17:1, 11.
God Does All Things Well (arr. David Stocker). Mark 7:37.
Gott ist unser Sonn' und Schild. Psalm 84:12.
Gott, der Herr, ist Sonn' und Schild. Psalm 84:12.
Gott hat Alles (arr. David Stocker). Mark 7:37.
Herr segne euch, Der. Psalm 115:13-15.
Herr, deine Augen sehen nach dem Glauben. Jeremiah 5:3.
Ich armer Mensch. Psalm 139:7-10.
Ich bin ein guter Hirt. John 10:12.
Into Thy Hands. Psalm 31:5.
Jesus ist ein guter Hirt. John 10:12.
Komm, mein Herze steht dir offen. John 15:9-10.
Laudamus Te. Psalm 145:1-2.
The Lord Bless You. Psalm 115:13-15.
The Lord's Prayer. Matthew 6:9-13.
Meine Seele wartet auf den Herrn. Psalm 130:6.
My Spirit Rejoice (arr. Dolores Hruby). Psalm 104:30.
Now Christ Is Risen. I Corinthians 15:20, 22.
O Taste and See. Psalm 34:8.
Quia fecit mihi magna. Luke 1:49.
Quia respexit. Luke 1:48.
Quia respexit humilitatem. Luke 1:48.
Sacrament. Matthew 26:26-29.
Sehet, welch eine Liebe. I John 3:1-3.
So du willst, so du willst. Psalm 130:3-4.
And Though I Wander. Psalm 23:00.
To Living Waters, Bright and Clear. Psalm 23:2b.
Von der Welt verlang' ich nichts. I John 3:1-3.
Weh der Seele. Jeremiah 5:3.
Wer mich liebet, der wird mein Wort halten. John 15:9-10.
Wir müssen durch viel Trusal (trans. Hal H. Hopson). Psalm 35:9.
Zion Hears Her Watchman Crying. Isaiah 52:8.
Zion hört die Wächter singen. Isaiah 52:8.

Bain, James Leith Macbeth.
Air for Brother James (arr. Walter Rodby). Psalm 23:00.
Air for Brother James (arr. Phyllis Tate). Psalm 23:00.
Air for Brother James (arr. Arthur Trew). Psalm 23:00.
Brother James's Air. Psalm 23:00.
Brother James's Air (arr. Malcolm Archer). Psalm 23:00.

Baird, Lynn.
Come into His Presence. Psalm 95:2.

Balchmetev, Nikolai.
Despite Locked Doors. John 20:26-29.

Baloche, Paul and Gary Sadler.
Rise Up and Praise Him. Psalm 96:11.

Bambino, Annemarie.
My Soul Magnifies the Lord. Luke 1:46-47.

Banks, Harry C.
He Hath Shewed Thee O Man. Micah 6:7-8.

Bannister, Brown.
Create in Me a Clean Heart. Psalm 51:10-12.

Bannister, Debbie and Brown; Michael W. and Deborah D. Smith.
Holy, Holy. Isaiah 6:3.

Bantock, Granville.
The Lord's Prayer. Matthew 6:9-13.
Out of the Depths. Psalm 130:00.
Praise Ye the Lord. Psalm 150:00.

Barkan, Emanuel.
Hark, My Beloved. Song of Songs 2:8-13.

Barker, Clement W.
Behold the Lamb of God. Matthew 3:16.
Bless the Lord, O My Soul. Psalm 67:00.
Draw Nigh to God. Romans 14:11.
If We Live in the Spirit. Galatians 5:1, 25.
Mark the Perfect Man. Isaiah 2:22.
The Path of the Just. Isaiah 1:18.
The Raising of Lazarus. John 11:1-44.
Temple of Glory. II Corinthians 6:16.
Woe Unto the Foolish Prophets. Ezekiel 13:3.

Barnard, Mark.
Psalm 34. Psalm 34:00.

Barnby, J.
O Ye, That Love the Lord. Amos 5:15.

Barnes, A. M.
Oh, That I Had Wings. Psalm 55:6-7.

Barnes, Edward Shippen.
Treasure in Heaven. Luke 12:15-20.

Barnes, Frederick M.
Create in Me a Clean Heart, O God. Psalm 51:10-13.
He is Risen! Matthew 28:1-7.
I Will Lift Up Mine Eyes. Psalm 121:00.
Psalm 23. Psalm 23:00.

Barnes, Milton.
The Lord's Prayer. Matthew 6:9-13.
Psalm 8. Psalm 8:00.
Psalm 13. Psalm 13:00.
Psalm 23. Psalm 23:00.
Psalm 29. Psalm 29:00.
Psalm 90. Psalm 90:00.
Psalm 121. Psalm 121:00.
Psalm 128. Psalm 128:00.

Baroni, David and Niles Borop.
Behold the Man. Isaiah 53:3-7.

Barrett, Joanne and Ron E. Long.
Bless the Lord. Psalm 103:1-4.

Barrett-Ayres, Reginald.
Am I My Brother's Keeper? Genesis 4:9.

Barrus, Lemar.
Praise. Psalm 106:1, 47-48.

Barta, Daniel.
Psalm 121. Psalm 121:00.

Bartlett, Floy Little.
I Will Lift Up My Eyes. Psalm 121:00.

Baumgartner, H. Leroy.
Behold What Manner of Love. I John 3:1-3.
He That Dwelleth in the Secret Place. Psalm 91:1-2, 5-6, 9-10, 14-16.
Hear, O Lord, When I Cry With My Voice. Psalm 27:7-9, 11, 13-14.
Lord, I Have Loved the Habitation of Thy House. Psalm 26:8.
Love Is of God. I John 4:7-12, 18-19, 21.
O Lord, My God, Thou Art Very Great. Psalm 104:1-3, 24.
This Is the Victory, Even Our Faith. I John 5:4-5, 7, 11, 14, 15.
This We Declare Unto You. I John 1:1, 5-7, 9.

Bavicchi, John Alexander.
Thou Art Clothed With Honor. Psalm 104:1a-4.
Thou Hast Made the Moon. Psalm 104:19-23.
Thou Makest the Spring Gush Forth. Psalm 104:10-16.

Beale, James.
On Laziness. Proverbs 24:30-31, 33-34.
On Slander. Proverbs 26:21-23.
On Truth. Proverbs 12:19.
On Wisdom. Proverbs 22:17-18.

Beall, Mary Kay.
He Is There. Psalm 139:7-8.
Hosanna! Hosanna! Mark 11:9-10.
Beaumont, Vivian.
Be of Good Courage. Psalm 31:19, 24.
Beck, Joe and Tom Lane.
The Prayer of Jabez. I Chronicles 4:10.
Beck, John Ness.
Every Valley (trans. Craig Courtney). Isaiah 40:4-5.
He Shall Feed His Flock (trans. Craig Courtney). Psalm 23:1.
The King of Love My Shepherd Is. Psalm 23:00.
Song of Devotion. Philippians 1:3-11.
Song of Joy. Psalm 40:00.
Beck, Theodore and J. A. Freylinghausen.
Lift Up Your Heads, You Mighty Gates. Psalm 24:1a.
Thou Wilt Keep Him in Perfect Peace. Isaiah 26:3-4.
Becker, Gerhardt C.
You Are the People of God. Colossians 3:12-14, 17.
Bedell, Robert L.
Out of the Deep Have I Called unto Thee. Psalm 130:00.
The Twenty-Third Psalm. Psalm 23:00.
How Long Will Thou Forget Me, O Lord? op. 16, no. 1. Psalm 13:00.
Beethoven, Ludwig van.
Come to Me (adapted Alexander Aslanoff). Matthew 11:28-30.
A Contrite Heart (arr. K. Lee Scott). Psalm 51:00.
Creation Hymn (arr. Harrell). Psalm 8:3-4.
Behrens, Jack.
1 Corinthians 13. I Corinthians 13:00.
Belcher, Supply.
There Were Shepherds (ed. Myers, Gordon). Luke 2:8-15.
Bellini, Vencenzo.
Tecum principium. Psalm 110:00.
Benati.
All Thy Works Shall Praise Thee. Psalm 145:10-12, 17-18.
Bless Thou the Lord (arr. Gertrude Tingley). Psalm 103:00.
Bencini, Pietro Paolo.
Alleluia. Ascendit Deus (Alleluia. God Has Gone Up) (ed. James H. Laster). Psalm 47:5.
Bender, Jan.
Begone Satan. Matthew 4:10.
If a Man Loves Me. John 14:23.
Let the Children Come unto Me. Mark 10:14.
Lord, Lord Open to Us. Matthew 25:1-13.
And There Will Be Signs. Luke 21:25-26, 33.
Wedding Song. Psalm 128:1-4.
Whosoever Does Not Receive the Kingdom. Mark 10:14-15.
Bender, Mark.
O Lord, I Love the Habitation of Your House. Psalm 26:8.
Benedict, Sir Julius.
He Giveth His Beloved Sheep. Psalm 127:2.
How Great, O Lord, Is Thy Goodness. Psalm 16:11a.
O Thou Afflicted, and Tossed With Tempest. Isaiah 54:11, 14.
Benet, Ch.
For the Lord Has Comforted Zion. Isaiah 51:3.
It Was Turned to the Contrary. Esther 9:1.
Ki Nicham, no. 1 (arr. Velvel Pasternak). Isaiah 51:3.
V'nahafõch, no. 2 (arr. Velvel Pasternak). Esther 9:1.
Ben-Haim, Paul.
Psalm 23. Psalm 23:00.
Bennard, George.
The Old Rugged Cross. I Corinthians 1:22-25.
Bennett, Roger.
Don't Be Afraid. Mark 4:37-39.
Bennett, Sir William Sterndale.
O Lord, Thou Hast Searched Me Out. Psalm 139:1-4.
Abide With Me. Luke 24:13.
His Salvation Is Nigh Them That Fear Him. Psalm 85:9, 12.
Berkig, Laurey and Jon Lugo.
My Eyes Have Seen Your Salvation. Luke 2:25-30.
Berlinski, Hermann (Hernam).
Psalm 23. Psalm 23:00.
Berman, Judith M.
Set Me as a Seal. Song of Songs 8:6-7.
Ach, Herr, strafe mich nicht in deinen Zorn. Psalm 6:00.
Aus der Tiefen. Psalm 130:00.
Create in Me a Clean Heart. Psalm 51:10-11.
Das ist ein köstlich ding, dem Herren danden. Psalm 92:2-5.
Dialogus auf Ostern: Sie Haben meinen Herrn hinweggenommen. John 20:13-17.
Es wird eine rute aufgehen vom stamm Isai. Isaiah 11:1-4.
Herr, wer wird wohnen in deiner Hütten. Psalm 15:00.
Bernardi, Steffano.
Magnificat. Luke 1:46-47.
Bernhard, Christoph.
Jauchzet dem Herrn, alle Welt. Psalm 100:00.
Psalm 100. Psalm 100:00.
Schaffe in mir, Gott, ein reines Herz. Psalm 51:10-11.
Berry, Cindy.
At the Name of Jesus (arr. Richard Huggins). Philippians 2:6-11.
Berthier, Jacques.
All You Who Pass This Way (ed. Brother Robert). Lamentations 1:1.
Bonum Est Confidere (ed. Brother Robert). Psalm 92:1-2, 5, 12-13.
It is Good to Trust and Hope in the Lord (ed. Brother Robert). Psalm 92:1-2, 5-12-13.
The Lord is My Light (ed. Brother Robert). Psalm 27:1, 3, 5-6.
My Heart is Breaking with Grief (ed. Brother Robert). Matthew 26:38-39a, 45.
The Spirit is Willing (ed. Brother Robert). Matthew 26:30, 39-41.
Bertrand, Lucy and Brown Bertrand.
Be Not Afraid. Mark 6:50.
Betts, Lorne.
Psalm 23. Psalm 23:00.
Set Me as a Seal. Song of Songs 8:6-7.
Biber, Heinrich Ignaz Franz.
Nisi Dominus aedificaverit domum (ed. Wolfram Stude). Psalm 127:00.
Bilchick, Ruth Coleman.
The Song of Songs. Song of Songs 2:11-13.
Binder, Abraham Wolf.
The Lord Is My Shepherd. Psalm 23:00.
Psalm 23. Psalm 23:00.
Birch, Robert Fairfax.
Entreat Me Not to Leave Thee. Ruth 1:16-17.
I Will Worship the Lord. Psalm 18:1-6, 49.
Love. Song of Songs 8:6-7.
Bischoff, John W.
Consider the Lilies (ed. Carl Fredrickson). Matthew 6:25c-26, 28b-30.
If God So Clothe the Grass. Matthew 6:25-29.
Open to Me the Gates (ed. Richard D. Row). Isaiah 26:2-3.

Bitgood, Roberta.
Be Still and Know That I Am God. Psalm 46:10a.
The Greatest of These Is Love. I Corinthians 13:00.
Bizet, Georges.
Agnus Dei. John 1:29.
Ave Maria. Luke 1:28, 30-31, 42.
Lamb of God. John 1:29.
Lord and Savior (ed. Patrick M. Liebergen). John 1:29.
Black, Jennie Prince.
The Pledge. Ruth 1:16-17.
Blackford, Richard.
From the Song of Songs. Song of Songs 2:00.
Blair, Kathleen.
As the Hart Panteth. Psalm 42:00.
He Restoreth My Soul. Psalm 23:00.
Bloch, Ernst.
By the Waters of Babylon. Psalm 137:00.
Elohim! Why Hast Thou Forsaken Me? Psalm 22:00.
Psalm 22. Psalm 22:00.
Psalm 114. Psalm 114:00.
Psalm 137. Psalm 137:00.
Snatched Away by Jehovah. Psalm 114:00.
Bobb, Barry L.
The Lord Has Done Great Things for Them. Psalm 126:00.
Bock, Fred.
Divine Calling. Romans 10:13-15.
Take Eat (Communion Meditation). Matthew 26:26-28.
Boex, Andrew J.
Now Let All Christian Men Rejoice. Luke 2:13-14.
And There Were Shepherds. Luke 2:8-15.
Bohn, Carl.
The Lord is My Shepherd. Psalm 23:00.
Boito, A.
Give Thanks Unto God. Psalm 136:1, 2 (and other).
Bone, Gene and Howard Fenton.
The First Psalm. Psalm 1:00.
Thy Word is a Lamp. Psalm 119:54, 55, 97, 103, 105, 125.
Boren, Murry.
How Firm a Foundation. Isaiah 41:10 (based on).
Borneman, Bruce and Judi.
Don't You Know. Psalm 150:1.
It's Time to Praise the Lord. Psalm 150:1.
Borop, Niles and David Baroni.
Behold the Man. Isaiah 53:3-7.
Borop, Niles and Dwight Lyles.
Proclaim the Glory of the Lord. Psalm 145:1-13.
Borop, Niles and Jim Weber.
It is Good. Psalm 92:1-2.
Bottenberg, Henry.
Our Father Who Art in Heaven. Matthew 6:9-13.
Bouman, Paul.
Save Me, O God, By Your Name. Psalm 54:00.
Bowling, Blanche.
For the Mountains Shall Depart. Isaiah 54:10, 13.
He Shall Be Like a Tree. Psalm 1:00.
Boyce, William.
The Eyes of All Wait upon Thee, O Lord. Psalm 145:15-16.
Our Fathers Hoped in Thee. Psalm 22:4-5.
Shew Us Thy Mercy, O Lord. Psalm 85:7.
Yea, Like as a Father Pitieth His Own Children. Psalm 103:13.
Bradshaw, Daniel.
Abide With Me; 'tis Eventide. Psalm 143:6, 7.
Brahms, Johannes.
Lo, I Unfold Unto You a Mystery. I Corinthians 15:51-52, 54b-55.
Lord, Make Me to Know. Psalm 39:4-7.
Ye Now Are Sorrowful. Wisdom of Solomon 51:35.
Denn es gehet dem Menschen. Ecclesiastes 3:19-22.
I Journeyed On My Way. Ecclesiastes 4:1-3.
Ich wandte mich und sahe an. Ecclesiastes 4:1-3.
O Death How Bitter. Ecclesiasticus 41:1-2.
O Tod, wie bitter bist du. Ecclesiasticus 41:1-2.
One Thing Befalleth the Beasts. Ecclesiastes 3:19-22.
Though I Speak with the Tongues of Men. I Corinthians 13:1-3, 12-13.
Wenn ich mit Menschen und mit Engelszungen. I Corinthians 13:1-3, 12-13.
Brasher, Scott and Michael Card.
Arise, My Love. Song of Songs 2:10.
The New Jerusalem. Revelation 21:1-4.
Brethorst, Leona Von.
He Has Made Me Glad. Psalm 100:4.
I Will Enter His Gates. Psalm 100:4.
Britten, Benjamin.
Abraham and Issac. Genesis 22:2-19.
Canticle I–My Beloved Is Mine and I Am His. Song of Songs 2:16.
Canticle II–Abraham and Isaac. Genesis 22:2-19.
My Beloved is Mine and I Am His. Song of Songs 2:16.
Britton, D. Guyver.
Know Ye That the Lord He Is God. Psalm 100:00.
Brixi, Franz Xaver.
Laudamus Te (ed. David Patrick). Psalm 145:1-2.
Brod, Max.
Psalm CXXVI. Psalm 126:00.
Bronleewe, Matt and Rebecca St. James.
For the Love of God. I Corinthians 13:1-3.
Brooks, Tom and Robin Brooks.
Heal Our Land. II Chronicles 7:14.
Broones, Martin.
David's Psalm. Psalm 23:00.
Brown, Allanson G. Y.
Behold! The Former Things Are Come to Pass. Isaiah 42:6-7.
Great Peace Have They. Psalm 119:165-166, 175-176.
Brown, Bertrand and Lucy Brown.
Be Not Afraid. Mark 6:50.
Brown, Keith Crosby.
The Lord is My Shepherd. Psalm 23:00.
When From the Lips of Truth. I John 1:1-3.
Brown, Russell J.
How Long Wilt Thou Forget Me? Psalm 13:1-5.
The Twenty-Third Psalm. Psalm 23:00.
Brown, Scott Wesley.
This Is the Day. Psalm 118:24a.
Browning, Mortimer.
The Beatitudes. Matthew 5:1-12.
Bryant, Larry and Lesa Bryant.
Unto Us (Isaiah 9) with "Thema" (arr. Robbie Buchanan). Isaiah 9:2-7.
Bryant, Verna Mae.
Behold, I Stand at the Door. Revelation 3:20.
Unto Us (Isaiah 9) with "Thema". Isaiah 9:2-7.
Buck, Dudley.
I Will Lay Me Down in Peace. Psalm 4:8.
Acquaint Thyself With Him. Job 22:00.

Fear Not Ye, O Israel. Jeremiah 31:6, 16.
How Long, O Lord, Wilt Thou Forget Me? Psalm 13:1-5.
The Lord is My Light. Psalm 27:1, 3, 5-6.
Bugatch, Samuel.
Ani Chavatselet Hasharon. Song of Songs 2:1-5.
Sharon. Song of Songs 2:1-5.
Bukvich.
Four Phrases From Psalm 91. Psalm 91:1, 4-5, 11.
Burgess, Dan and Harold Decou.
Jane's Song (arr. Bob Krogstad). Psalm 139:00.
Burgon, Geoffrey.
Nunc Dimittis. Luke 2:29-32.
Burkhard, Willy.
Magnificat. Luke 1:46-47.
Burnam, Edna Mae.
I Will Lift Up Mine Eyes unto the Hills. Psalm 121:1-2.
Burnett, John Y.
I Waited for the Lord My God. Psalm 40:1-4.
Burns, William K.
His Children. I John 3:1.
If God Be for Us. Romans 8:31, 35, 37-39.
My Soul Doth Magnify the Lord. Luke 1:46-49.
Out of the Depths. Psalm 130:00.
Psalm 121. Psalm 121:00.
Burroughs, Bob.
Christmas Prophecy. Matthew 1:21.
The Commission. Matthew 9:36b-37.
God's Love. John 3:16-17.
I Am the Good Shepherd. John 10:14, 16a.
Burton, Daniel.
As the Thirsty Deer at Morning. Psalm 42:1, 8, 11.
Clap Your Hands, All You People. Psalm 47:1.
The Lord Is My Shepherd. Psalm 23:00.
Burton, Wendell and Patti Burton.
Greatly Rejoice. Isaiah 61:10-11.
Burton, Wendell and Marty Goetz.
Arise, Shine. Isaiah 9:2a.
Busarow, Donald.
Beloved, Let Us Love. I John 4:7-8.
He Shall Give His Angels Charge Over Thee. Psalm 91:4,11-12.
Buss, Duane.
Psalm 23. Psalm 23:00.
Butler, Eugene.
The Lord Reigns. Psalm 97:1-2, 4-6, 8, 11.
Out of the Depths. Psalm 130:1-3, 5-6.
Save Me, O God. Psalm 69:1-3, 5, 16-17, 29-30.
Walk in the Way of the Lord. Isaiah 2:5.
Butler-Moore, Nylea L.
The Lord Your God Is with You. Zephaniah 3:17.
Butt, James.
Christ Whose Glory. Malachi 4:2.
Courage. Joshua 1:5-7.
The King of Love. Psalm 23:00.
Psalm 1. Psalm 1:00.
Psalm 90. Psalm 90:1-2, 4, 16-17.
Psalm 150. Psalm 150:00.
River of Life. Revelation 22:1-4.
Buxtehude, Dietrich.
Also hat Gott die Welt geliebt. John 3:16.
Create in Me a Clean Heart. Psalm 51:10-12.
Herr, auf dich traue ich. Psalm 31:2-4.
Herr, nun lassert du deinen diener. Luke 2:29-32.
Herr, wenn ich nur dich Habe. Psalm 73:25-26.
I Am the Resurrection. John 11:25-26.
Jubilate Domino. Psalm 98:4-6.
Laudata Dominum. Psalm 117:00.
Laudate, Pueri. Psalm 113:1-2, 4-8.
Lord, in Thee Do I Trust (arr. Clarence Dickinson). Psalm 31:2-4.
Lord Who at Cana's Wedding. John 2:1-10.
Mein Herz ist bereit. Psalm 57:00.
Schaffe in mir, Gott, ein rein Herz. Psalm 51:12-13.
Sicut Moses. John 3:14-15.
Sing to the Lord a New Song. Psalm 96:00.
Singet dem Herrn. Psalm 98:1-4.

Caccini, Giulio.
Ave Maria (arr. Steven Mercurio). Luke 1:28, 30-31, 42.
Cady, Gertrude.
Come Unto Me. Matthew 11:28-29.
Cadzow, Dorothy.
The Lord's Prayer. Matthew 6:9-13.
Cagle, Denny.
Let the Peace of Christ Rule in Your Heart (arr. Ken Barker). Colossians 3:15.
Caldara, Antonio.
Bless the Lord, All Nations (ed. and arr. Michael Burkhardt). Psalm 100:2.
Calder, Lee.
God Is My Salvation. Isaiah 12:3-4.
Caldwell, Mary E.
The Shepherd. Isaiah 40:11.
Camidge, John.
Put Thou Thy Trust in the Lord (ed. David Patrick). Psalm 37:1, 4-5, 7.
Campbell-Tipton, Louis.
I Will Give Thanks unto the Lord. Psalm 9:1-2, 10.
Campion, Edward.
The Ninety and Nine. Luke 15:4-7.
Campion, Thomas.
Out of My Soul's Depth. Psalm 130:00.
Seek the Lord. Isaiah 55:6-7.
Campra, André.
Jubilate Deo. Psalm 100:00.
Psalm 99. Psalm 100:00.
Canedo, Ken.
Psalm 145. Psalm 145:00.
Card, Michael.
Barocha. Numbers 6:24.
Death of a Son. Psalm 22:00.
How Long. Psalm 13:00.
Immanuel (arr. Marty Parks). Romans 9:2.
My Shepherd. Psalm 23:00.
Now That I've Held Him in My Arms. Luke 2:22-35.
Psalm 13. Psalm 13:00.
Psalm 23. Psalm 23:00.
Psalm 139. Psalm 139:00.
Psalms 22 and 69. Psalm 22:00.
Search Me and Know Me. Psalm 139:00.
Simeon's Song. Luke 2:22-35.
This Must Be the Lamb. Matthew 27:30.
Card, Michael and Scott Brasher.
Arise, My Love. Song of Songs 2:10.
The New Jerusalem. Revelation 21:1-4.
Carmichael, Ralph.
The New 23rd Psalm. Psalm 23:00.

Carr, Arthur.
Hosanna to the Son of David. Matthew 21:9.
Carswell, Eddie and Oliver Wells.
Come Let's Worship Him. I Chronicles 16:8-9.
Carter, John.
All Things Work Together for Good. Romans 8:28.
How Lovely Is Thy Dwelling Place. Psalm 84:1-4.
Seek the Lord. Isaiah 55:6-7.
The Shepherd Psalm. Psalm 23:00.
Surely He Will Care for Me. Matthew 6:28-34.
Cartwright, Marion L.
Great Is Our Lord. Psalm 147:3-7a, 8-9, 18a.
Case, Henry Lincoln.
The Mighty God Hath Spoken. Psalm 50:1-3, 5-6.
Cassler, G. Winston.
Laudate nomen. Psalm 135:00.
Oh Praise the Lord. Psalm 135:00.
Praise, My Soul, the King of Heaven. Psalm 103:00.
Whither Thou Goest. Ruth 1:16-17.
Castelnuovo-Tedesco, Maro.
Eternal Love. Hosea 2:21-22.
Seal My Heart. Song of Songs 8:6-7.
V'Erstich. Hosea 2:21-22.
Cesti, Marcantonio.
The Wonders of Universe. Psalm 8:00.
Chadwick, George Whitefield.
Come Unto Me. Matthew 11:28-30.
He Maketh Wars to Cease. Psalm 46:9, 10.
Let Not Your Heart Be Troubled. John 14:1-2.
Chait, B.
Even Moasu (arr. Velvel Pasternak). Psalm 118:22.
Hal'lu (arr. Velvel Pasternak). Psalm 117:1.
O Praise the Lord, All Ye Nations (arr. Velvel Pasternak). Psalm 117:1.
The Stone Which the Builders Rejected (arr. Velvel Pasternak). Psalm 118:22.
Chajes, Julius.
By the Rivers of Babylon. Psalm 137:00.
Old Jerusalem. Psalm 134:00.
Chambers, Brent.
Be Exalted, O God. Psalm 57:9-11.
Be Exalted, O God (arr. Jane Yankitis). Psalm 57:9-11.
Chapman, Morris.
Be Bold, Be Strong. Joshua 1:9.
Bethlehem Morning. Isaiah 9:6a.
Worthy Is the Lamb. Revelation 5:12-13.
Chapman, Morris and Greg Massanart.
Come and Sing Praises. Psalm 29:1-2.
Chapman, Steven Curtis.
Be Still and Know (arr. Bryce Inman). Exodus 15:26b.
Chapman, Steven Curtis and Tom Fettke.
Be Still and Know (arr. Tom Fettke). Exodus 15:26b.
Be Still and Know (arr. Lee Herrington). Exodus 15:26b.
Chapman, Steven Curtis and Jerry Salley.
His Strength Is Perfect. Philippians 4:13.
Charles, Ernest.
Incline Thine Ear. Isaiah 55:1, 3.
Psalm of Exaltation. Psalm 27:1, 4, 6.
Save Me, O God. Psalm 69:00.
Charpentier, Marc-Antoine.
Et misericordia ejus. Luke 1:53.
Sicut locutus est ad patres. Luke 1:50.
Suscepit Israel. Luke 1:54.
Chausson, Ernest.
Pater Noster. Matthew 6:9-13.
Cherubini, Luigi.
Ave Maria. Luke 1:28, 30-31, 42.
Come to the Waters (ed. and arr. K. K. Davis and N. Loring). Isaiah 55:1, 3.
Holy, Holy, Lord God of Hosts. Luke 1:28, 30-31, 42.
Cherwin, David.
Psalm 22. Psalm 22:00.
Chiasson, Basil.
Be Strong and Take Courage (arr. Carl Seal). Joshua 1:9.
Childs, David.
Psalm 81. Psalm 81:1-4.
Psalm 83. Psalm 83:1-4, 13, 18.
Psalm 91. Psalm 91:1-4.
Psalm 92. Psalm 92:1-5.
Psalm 121. Psalm 121:00.
Psalm 123. Psalm 123:1-5.
Psalm 148. Psalm 148:1-6.
Childs, Edwin T.
The Lord Is My Shepherd. Psalm 23:00.
Chisum, John and Don Moen.
I See the Lord. Isaiah 6:1-4.
Christensen, Chris.
Bless the Lord. Psalm 103:1-4.
Clark, Palmer John.
This Is My Commandment. John 5:5-7, 9.
Clarke, Henry Leland.
The Lord Is My Shepherd. Psalm 23:00.
Clattenburg, Jeannie and Rick Powell.
Chosen Generation. I Peter 2:9.
Clatterbuck, Robert C.
A Child's 23rd Psalm. Psalm 23:00.
Clausen, René.
The Greatest of These Is Love. I Corinthians 13:1-2, 4-8.
Clements, John.
Blessed Is the Man. Psalm 1:1-3.
Clerbois, Roger.
Save Me, O Lord. Psalm 54:00.
Clifford, Beatrice.
The First Commandment. Mark 12:28-31.
Clokey, Joseph Waddel.
Set Me as a Seal. Song of Songs 8:6-7.
Coenen, William.
Come unto Me. Matthew 11:28-30.
Cohen, Gerald.
Acclaim Adonai, All People on Earth. Psalm 100:00.
Ad Matai. Psalm 82:1-5, 8.
Hariu Ladonai kol Haarets. Psalm 100:00.
How Long? Psalm 82:1-5, 8.
Libavtini achoti chala. Song of Songs 4:9-10, 16.
May Adonai Bless You. Numbers 6:24-26.
Y'varech'cha. Numbers 6:24-26.
You Have Captured My Heart, My own, My Bride. Song of Songs 4:9-10, 16.
Coleman.
Christ Is With Me. John 15:4.
Colgan, Bro. Tobias.
Gentle Shepherd (arr. Randall DeBruyn). Psalm 23:00.
Jesús, pastor tan dulce (arr. Randall DeBruyn). Psalm 23:00.
Collister, Robert.
The Twenty-Third Psalm. Psalm 23:00.

Colvin, Herbert.
Surely the Lord Is in This Place (arr. Richard Huggins). Genesis 28:16-17.
Connolly, Michael.
Lord Send Out Your Spirit. Psalm 104:1, 24, 29-31.
Conry, Tom.
I Will Lift Up My Eyes. Psalm 63:1-4.
Now Comes the Day. Psalm 118:1, 16-17, 19.
Were Not Our Hearts Burning Within Us. Luke 24:32.
Cook, Gerald.
Ruth (to Naomi). Ruth 1:16-17.
Coombs, Charles Whitney.
As it Began to Dawn. Matthew 28:1-6.
O How Amiable Are Thy Dwellings. Psalm 84:00.
Cooney, Rory.
Create Me Again. Psalm 51:00.
Every Morning in Your Eyes. Psalm 34:1-8.
If I Forget You, Jerusalem. Psalm 137:1-6.
Let All the Earth Cry Out. Psalm 66:1-7, 16-20.
My Soul Is Longing. Psalm 63:1-5, 7-8.
Psalm 1. Psalm 1:1-3.
Psalm 51. Psalm 51:00.
Psalm 63. Psalm 63:1-5, 7-8.
Psalm 66. Psalm 66:1-7, 16-20.
Psalm 139. Psalm 139:1-2, 5, 7-9, 11-18, 23-24.
Roots in the Earth. Psalm 1:1-3.
Wings of Dawn. Psalm 139:1-2, 5, 7-9, 11-18, 23-24.
Cooper, Jim and Regie Hamm.
Beyond the Borders. I Chronicles 4:10.
Cooper, Lowell.
Come, Sing to the Lord. Psalm 95:1-7.
Corfe, Joseph.
My Voice Shalt Thou Hear. Psalm 5:3.
Cornelius, Peter.
I Love Thee, Lord, My Strength. Psalm 18:00.
I Will Lift Mine Eyes. Psalm 121:00.
The Kings. Matthew 2:10-11.
Our Loving Father. Luke 15:11-24.
The Shepherds. Luke 2:8-13.
Simeon. Luke 2:21-22, 29-33.
Sing unto the Lord. Psalm 30:00.
There Is a Spirit in Man. Job 14:1, 32-33.
Unto Thee I Lift Up My Soul. Psalm 25:1-2, 5, 7.
Cortese, Luigi.
Salmo VIII. Psalm 8:00.
Cory, George.
The Lord's Prayer. Matthew 6:9-13.
Coryell, Marion.
The Robe of Righteousness. Isaiah 61:10.
Costa, Michael.
I Will Extol Thee, O Lord! Psalm 30:1-2, 11.
It Is a Good Thing to Give Thanks unto the Lord. Psalm 92:1.
Cotter, Jeanne.
In Love We Choose to Live. I Corinthians 13:4.
Let All Praise the Name of the Lord. Psalm 148:1-4, 12-13.
Our God Is Compassion. Psalm 145:8-10, 17-18.
There Is One Body. Ephesians 4:6-10.
This Night I Lift My Heart to Thee. Psalm 84:4, 10.
Couperin, François.
Ad te levavi occulos meus. Psalm 122:00.
Domine Salvum fac regem. Psalm 19:10.
Magnificat. Luke 1:45-55.
Salvum me fac Deus. Psalm 68:1-6, 17-18.
Usquequo Domine. Psalm 12:00.
Courtney, Craig.
Be Not Afraid. Isaiah 43:1-4.
He Was Wounded. Isaiah 53:3-6.
I Have Chosen the Way of Truth. Psalm 119:30-37.
If You Search With All Your Heart. Jeremiah 29:11-14.
The Lord Is My Light. Psalm 27:1-6.
The Lord Is My Shepherd. Psalm 23:00.
Praise Him! Psalm 145:1-3, 8-9.
Psalm VIII. Psalm 8:00.
Psalm 91. Psalm 91:1-7, 9-12.
Sing to the Lord a New Song. Psalm 96:1.
There Is a Time. Ecclesiastes 3:1-8.
We Are Glad. Psalm 126:00.
What Shall I Render to the Lord? Psalm 116:7-8, 12-14, 18-19.
Cowen, Frederic Hymen.
How Excellent Is Thy Loving Kindness. Psalm 65:9, 11, 13.
Like as a Father. Psalm 103:13-14.
With Thee There is Forgiveness. Psalm 130:4-6.
Cox, Joe.
Blessed to Be a Blessing. Mark 10:15-16.
Crawford, John.
The King of Love. Psalm 23:00.
Creston, Paul.
Psalm XXIII, op. 37. Psalm 23:00.
Croegaret, Jim.
Was It a Morning Like This? Matthew 28:1-8.
Croft, William.
The Mighty God Hath Spoken (arr. K. K. Davis). Psalm 150:1, 4, 7, 14-15.
Croft, William.
O God, Our Help in Ages Past (arr. Jerry Ray). Psalm 90:1-2, 4.
Cross, Phil and Carolyn Cross.
We Shall Be Like Him. I John 3:2.
Crouch, Andraé.
Bless His Holy Name. Psalm 103:1.
Crowe, B.
One Hundred Twenty-First Psalm. Psalm 121:00.
Cruikshank, Helen M.
Behold What Names of Love. I John 2:25.
Cumming, Richard.
The Song of Moses. Exodus 15:00.
Cundick, Robert.
If a Man Die, Shall He Live Again? Job 14:14.
Curran, Pearl G.
Prayer. James 5:16.
The Lord Is My Shepherd. Psalm 23:00.
The Resurrection. John 20:1, 11, 14-15, 17-20, 26, 30-31.

Daigle, Gary.
Chant Mode II. Matthew 6:9-13.
Covenant Hymn. Ruth 1:16.
Glory to God. Luke 2:14.
The Lord's Prayer. Matthew 6:9-13.
Rite of Blessing and Sprinkling of Water. Luke 2:14.
Dailey, William.
Psalm 128. Psalm 128:00.
Dame, William.
Our Father. Matthew 6:9-13.
Damrosch, Leopold.
Entreat Me Not to Leave Thee. Ruth 1:16-17.

Dauermann, Stuart.
For God So Loved. John 3:16.
The Trees of the Field. Isaiah 55:12.
Who Hath Believed Our Report? Isaiah 53:1-11.
David, Ferdinand.
Mein Aug' erheb' ich. Psalm 121:00.
Unto the Hills. Psalm 121:00.
Davidowitz, M.
Let My Prayer Be unto Thee (arr. Velvel Pasternak). Psalm 69:14.
Vaani s'filosi (arr. Velvel Pasternak). Psalm 69:14.
Davidson, Charles.
The Lord Is My Shepherd. Psalm 23:00.
Psalm 23. Psalm 23:00.
Yihyu L'Ratzon. Psalm 19:15.
Davies, Henry Walford.
O God, Our Help in Ages Past. Psalm 90:1-2, 4.
Davis, Katherine K.
Be Ye Kind, One to Another. Ephesians 4:31-32.
Bless the Lord, O My Soul. Psalm 103:1-4, 11, 13.
How Lovely Are Thy Dwellings. Psalm 84:1-3.
The Raising of Lazarus. John 11:1, 3-4, 15, 17, 41-44.
Treasure in Heaven. Mark 10:17-24.
Trust in the Lord. Proverbs 3:5-6.
Davis, M.
Ninety First Psalm. Psalm 91:1, 5, 9-12.
Davye, John J.
He That Dwelleth in the Secret Place. Psalm 91:00.
The Lord is My Shepherd. Psalm 23:00.
Day, Stanley A.
Suffer the Little Children. Matthew 18:1-4.
Deacon, Mary.
Beside Still Waters. Psalm 23:00.
Dean, Stephen.
The Bread That We Break. I Corinthians 10:16-17.
How Can I Repay the Lord. Psalm 116:1-8, 12-16, 17.
Lord, Your Love Has Drawn Us Near. Psalm 116:12.
May Choirs of Angels Welcome You. Psalm 116:1-8, 15, 18.
One Thing I Ask. Psalm 27:1, 3, 5, 7-9, 13-14.
Water of Life. Isaiah 55:1-3.
Dearman, Kirk.
We Bring the Sacrifice of Praise. Psalm 50:14.
DeBese, Theodore.
O Dieu donne moi deliverance. Psalm 140:00.
DeBruyn, Randall.
Jesus, Lord. John 3:16-21.
Delaney, Maureen.
Psalm 148. Psalm 148:00.
deLange, S.
How Beautiful Are Thy Dwellings. Psalm 84:1-2, 10-11.
DeLong, Richard.
Absalom. II Samuel 18:33.
Blessed Are You, O God of Our Fathers. Tobit 8:5-7.
But the Lord is Mindful of His Own. II Timothy 2:19.
I Will Espouse You to Me Forever. Hosea 2:21-23.
Seek Ye the Lord. Isaiah 55:6-9.
Set Me as a Seal. Song of Songs 8:6-7.
Demarest, Alison.
Whither Shall I Go from Thy Spirit. Psalm 139:00.
Demarest, C. Agnew.
The Lord Is Nigh unto Them. Psalm 34:18-19, 21-22.
Demarest, Victoria.
Hymn of the Last Supper. Mark 14:24.
Dencke, Jeremiah.
Go Ye Forth in His Name. Matthew 25:1-6.
I Speak of the Things. Psalm 45:1-2.
Ich will singen von einem Könige. Psalm 45:1-2.
Meine Seele erhebet den Herrn. Luke 1:46-50.
My Soul Doth Magnify the Lord. Luke 1:46-50.
Dengler, Lee.
I Cried unto the Lord. Psalm 142:1, 6.
I Will Lift Up My Eyes. Psalm 121:1-3, 7-8.
O Clap Your Hands. Psalm 47:1-2, 5-7.
Sing unto the Lord. I Chronicles 16:23-25, 27, 31.
You Know My Folly. Psalm 69:5-6.
Dennis, Randall.
Our Fathers. Matthew 6:9-13.
Derfler, Carl.
As a Deer. Psalm 42:1-4.
I Lift Up My Eyes. Psalm 121:00.
Deutschmann, Gerhard.
Psalm 23. Psalm 23:00.
DeVidal, David.
Surely He Bore Our Griefs. Isaiah 53:4-6.
Dewey, Richard A.
Whither Thou Goest. Ruth 1:16-17.
Diamond, David.
David Mourns for Absalom. II Samuel 18:33.
Dichmont, William.
Peace I Leave with You. John 14:27.
Dick, Colleen R.
We Are the Earth (arr. Craig S. Kingsbury). Psalm 90:2-6.
Diemer, Emma Lou.
I Will Sing of Your Steadfast Love. Psalm 89:1-5, 6, 9, 14.
Dietterich, Philip.
Now Will I Praise the Lord. Psalm 34:1-6.
Dinn, Freda.
Psalm 127. Psalm 127:00.
Distler, Hugo.
It Is a Precious Thing to Thank Our God. Psalm 92:1-3.
My Dear Brethren, Meet the Demands of This Time. Romans 12:11-12, 18.
O Rejoice in the Lord at All Times. Philippians 4:4.
Dobry, Wallace.
Lauda, anima mea. Psalm 146:00.
Omnes gentes, plaudite. Psalm 47:00.
Psalm 47: Clap Your Hands, All You Peoples. Psalm 47:00.
Psalm 95: Come, Let Us Sing to the Lord. Psalm 95:1-7.
Psalm 146: Praise the Lord, O My Soul. Psalm 146:00.
Venite, exultemus. Psalm 95:1-7.
Doherty, Dave.
Come, Let Us Worship and Bow Down. Psalm 95:6-7.
Doig, Don.
I am the Vine. John 15:1-6.
So Great is His Mercy. Psalm 103:11-17.
Who Shall Separate Us? Romans 8:35, 38-39.
Dolck, Doug and Tom Fettke.
He Loved Me. Romans 8:35-39.
Remember Me. I Corinthians 11:23-26.
Dorff, Daniel.
Ave Maria. Luke 1:28, 30-31.
Douglas, Scott and Mark Gersmehl.
We Will See Him as He Is. I John 3:2.
Driskell, Gary and Marty Hennis.
Kings Shall Bow. Isaiah 45:23.

Dubois, Theodore.
Behold What Manner of Love. I John 3:1-2.
God, My Father. Matthew 27:46.
O All Ye Who Travel. Lamentations 1:12.
O My Father. Matthew 27:46.
O vos omnes. Lamentations 1:12.
Dufford, Bob.
All the Ends of the Earth. Psalm 98:00.
Be Not Afraid. Isaiah 43:2-3.
Be Not Afraid (arr. Theophane Hytreak). Isaiah 43:2-3.
Be Not Afraid (arr. Jack Schrader). Isaiah 43:2-3.
Behold the Lamb of God (arr. John B. Foley). Isaiah 53:4-5.
Every Valley. Isaiah 35:5-6.
Father, Mercy. Psalm 51:1-8.
Like a Shepherd. Isaiah 40:9.
My Son Has Gone Away. Luke 15:11-32.
My Spirit Takes Joy (arr. John B. Foley). Luke 1:46-55.
Return to Your People, O Lord. Isaiah 64:1, 8-11.
Save Us, O Lord. Psalm 80:1-3, 7, 15-16.
Sing to the Mountains. Psalm 118:4, 14, 18, 21, 24.
Songs of the Angels. Job 19:25.
Worthy is the Lamb. Revelation 5:2-5, 9, 12-13.
Dufford, Bob and John B. Foley.
Praise God. Psalm 19:1.
Duke, John.
I Love the Lord. Psalm 116:1-5, 7-8.
Magnificat. Luke 1:46-55.
Dungan, Olive.
Be Still and Know That I Am God. Psalm 46:00.
Dupré, Marcel.
Ave Maria, op. 9. Luke 1:28, 30-31, 42.
Dvorák, Antonín.
Als wir dort an den Wassern der Stadt Baylon sassen. Psalm 137:1-5.
Blikke mich an und erbarme Dich meiner, Herr. Psalm 25:16-18, 20.
Bože! Bože! Písen novou. Psalm 144:9.
By the Shore of the River Babylon. Psalm 137:1-5.
By the Still Waters of Babylon. Psalm 137:1-5.
By the Waters of Babylon. Psalm 137:1-5.
Clouds and Darkness. Psalm 97:2-6.
Come unto Me. Matthew 11:28-30.
Comfort Ye, My People. Isaiah 40:1.
Darkness and Thunderclouds Are Round About Him. Psalm 97:2-6.
Du, Du bist mire ein Schirm und Schild. Psalm 119:114-115, 117, 120.
Give Ear, O God, Unto My Prayer. Psalm 55:1-8.
God is My Shepherd. Psalm 23:1-4.
God the Lord My Shepherd Is. Psalm 23:1-4.
Gott der Herr ist Hirte mir. Psalm 23:1-4.
Gott, erhör' mit Langmust mein Flehn. Psalm 61:1, 3-4.
Gott, o höre, hör' auf mein Gebet. Psalm 55:1-8.
Hear My Crying, O Lord. Psalm 61:1, 3-4.
Hear My Prayer. Psalm 55:1-8.
Hear My Prayer (duet). Psalm 61:1, 3-4.
Hear, Oh Hear My Prayer, Lord. Psalm 55:1-8.
Hear, Oh Lord, My Bitter Cry. Psalm 61:1, 3-4.
Herr, mein Gott, ich sing' en neues Lied. Psalm 144:9.
Hospokin jest muj pastyr. Psalm 23:1-4.
I Will Lift Up Mine Eyes. Psalm 121:1-4.
I Will Sing New Songs of Gladness (arr. Carl Fredrickson). Psalm 144:9.
Ich hebe den Blick zum Berg empor. Psalm 121:1-4.
Ihr Alle. Matthew 11:28-30.
Lord Is My Shepherd. Psalm 23:00.
Lord My Shield, My Refuge. Psalm 119:114-115, 117, 120.
Lord, a New Song I Would Fashion. Psalm 144:9.
Lord, O Harken Unto My Crying. Psalm 61:1, 3-4.
Lord, Thou Art My Refuge. Psalm 119:114-115, 117, 120.
My Eyes Will I to the Hills Lift Up. Psalm 121:1-4.
O Sing unto the Lord. Psalm 98:1, 7-8.
Oblak a mrokotá jest vukol Neho. Psalm 97:2-6.
Oh, Lord, Have Mercy and Turn Thou Thy Face to Me. Psalm 25:16-18, 20.
Oh, My Shepherd Is the Lord. Psalm 23:1-4.
Oh, Sing unto the Lord a Joyful Song. Psalm 98:1, 7-8.
Popatriz na mne a smilujh se nade mnou. Psalm 25:16-18, 20.
Pozdvihuji ocí svych k horám. Psalm 121:1-4.
Pri rekách babylonskych. Psalm 137:1-5.
Search Me, O God. Psalm 139:4, 23-24.
Sing a New Song. Psalm 98:1, 7-8.
Sing Ye a Joyful Song! Psalm 98:1, 7-8.
Sing Ye a Joyful Song! Psalm 139:4, 23-24.
Singt, singet Gott, dem Herren, neue Lieder. Psalm 98:1, 7-8.
Skryse ma a paveza má Ty jsi. Psalm 119:114-115, 117, 120.
Slyš, ó Bože! Slyš modlitbu mou. Psalm 55:1-8.
Slyš, ó bože, volání me. Psalm 61:1, 3-4.
Song of Gladness Will I Sing Thee. Psalm 144:9.
Turn Thee to Me and Have Mercy. Psalm 25:16-18, 20.
Wolken und Finsternis hullen Sein Antlitz. Psalm 97:2-6.
Zpívetje Hospodinu píen novou. Psalm 98:1, 7-8.
Dykes, John Bacchus.
Holy, Holy, Holy. Psalm 145:10.

Earls, Paul.
The Lord's Prayer. Matthew 6:9-13.
Eaton, Chris.
God So Loved. John 3:16.
Psalm 121. Psalm 121:00.
Eben, Petr.
Lied der Ruth. Ruth 1:16-17.
Song of Ruth. Ruth 1:16-17.
Edmunds, John.
Behold, How Good. Psalm 133:00.
The Lord Is My Shepherd. Psalm 23:00.
O Lord, My Heart Is Fixed. Psalm 108:1-5.
Praise We the Lord. Psalm 113:1-5.
When Israel Went Out of Egypt. Psalm 114:1.
Edwards, Clara.
The Lord Is My Light. Psalm 27:00.
Edwards, Leo.
God Be Merciful Unto Us. Psalm 67:00.
Psalm No. 67. Psalm 67:00.
Eggert, Fred E.
Remember Now Thy Creator. Ecclesiastes 12:1-8.
Eilers, Joyce.
Thy Will Be Done. Matthew 6:9-13.
Elgar, Edward.
I am the Good Shepherd. John 10:10, 14.
I Have Prayed to Thee. Acts 2:14b, 16-17, 21-23, 32-33, 36.
Neither Hath This Man Sinned. John 9:3-5.
Peace Be unto You. Luke 24:36c, 49.
The Sun Goeth Down. Psalm 63:6.
The Voice of Thy Watchman. Isaiah 52:8-9.
Elliott, John G.
I Am Crucified with Christ. Galatians 3:20.
Romans Doxology. Romans 11:33, 36.

Ellis, James G.
I Shall Not Want. Psalm 23:00.
Transfiguration. Luke 9:28-29, 35.
Ellis, Ward L.
Let the Redeemed. Psalm 107:2a.
Engel, James.
Whither Thou Goest. Ruth 1:16-17.
Englert, Andrew Lloyd.
Thy Word Is a Lamp. Psalm 119:105.
Englert, Eugene.
Psalm 112. Psalm 112:00.
English Folk Melody.
Lord, From Your Hand (arr. Bruce Greer). Luke 22:19.
English Tune, 17th c.
Out of the Depths I Cry to Thee. Psalm 130:00.
Espina, Noni.
Shepherd's Psalm. Psalm 23:00.
Evans, Vincent.
Create in Me a Clean Heart. Psalm 51:00.
Eville, Vernon.
By the Waters of Babylon. Psalm 137:00.
I Will Dwell in the House of the Lord. Psalm 23:00.
I Will Lift Up Mine Eyes. Psalm 121:00.

Farrell, Bernadette.
O God, for You I Long. Psalm 42:1-6, 8.
The Stone Which the Builders Rejected. Psalm 118:1-7, 19-22.
Unless a Grain of Wheat. John 12:23-24, 26.
Farrell, Bob and Grey Nelson.
Who Will Call Him Kings of Kings. Matthew 28:1-10.
Farrell, Jim.
Sing a Joyful Song (arr. Craig S. Kingsbury). Psalm 145:00.
Faulkner, George.
Feed My Sheep. John 21:15.
Faulkner, William M.
Eye Hath Not Seen. I Corinthians 2:9.
Fauré, Gabriel.
Bless the Lord, O My Soul. Psalm 103:1-4, 19.
Love Never Faileth. I Corinthians 13:1-8.
Fearis, John S.
God So Loved the World. John 3:16-17.
Fedak, Alfred V.
You Are the Chosen of the Lord. Colossians 3:12-17.
Felciano, Richard.
Benedicto Nuptialis. Psalm 92:12.
Ferguson, John.
Prepare the Royal Highway. Isaiah 40:4.
Ferguson, Michael.
Angelus Domini. Matthew 28:2, 5-6.
Ferris, William
Behold, Thus Is the Man Blessed. Psalm 128:4-6.
I Have Seen Water. Ecclesiasticus 47:2.
My Heart is Ready, O God. Psalm 108:00.
Fettke, Tom.
Be Still and Know. Exodus 15:26b.
Behold the Man. Isaiah 53:3.
Bless the Lord, O My Soul. Psalm 103:1.
Changed. I Corinthians 15:51-55.
Come, Holy Spirit. Acts 1:8.
Far Above Riches. Proverbs 31:10-31.
Forgive Our Sins as We Forgive. Matthew 6:12.
God Exalted Him. Philippians 2:5-11.
I Love You, Lord. Psalm 18:1-3, 6.
Jesus Has Time. Matthew 18:2-5.
Jesus–He Shall Be Great. Isaiah 7:14.
The Majesty and Glory of Your Name. Psalm 8:1, 3-9.
Sing unto the Lord. Psalm 96:1-4.
Ten Thousand Angels. Matthew 26:47-27:50.
Three Times I Asked Him. II Corinthians 12:7-10.
Words of Love. John 1:1, 3, 7-8, 14.
Fettke, Tom and Bob Ashton.
We Shall All Be Changed. I Corinthians 15:51-52.
Fettke, Tom and Phillip Bliss.
He Takes Away the Sins of the World. John 1:29.
Fettke, Tom and Doug Dolck.
He Loved Me. Romans 8:35-39.
Fichthoin, Claude.
Behold What Manner of Love. Matthew 4:4.
Field, J. T.
God Shall Wipe Away All Tears. Revelation 21:4.
Fillmore, James H. and Tom Fettke.
I Will Sing of the Mercies. Psalm 89:1.
Fischer, Irwin.
Come, Take the Water of Life. Revelation 22:1, 14, 17.
Delight Thyself in the Lord. Psalm 145:00.
God So Loved the World. John 3:16-17.
How Beautiful Upon the Mountains. Isaiah 52:7, 9.
If I Take the Wings of the Morning. Psalm 139:9-11, 14, 17.
If Ye Love Me, Keep My Commandments. John 14:16.
Let the Beauty of the Lord. Psalm 90:1, 16-17.
The Lord By Wisdom Hath Founded Earth. Proverbs 3:13, 16, 17, 19, 21.
Lord, Teach Me Thy Statues. Psalm 119:12, 18, 28, 35, 59, 68.
Love One Another. I John 4:7, 8, 11, 14, 16, 20-21.
O Lord, How Manifold Are Thy Works. Psalm 104:1, 2, 5, 24, 30.
Praise Ye the Lord. Psalm 148:1, 3, 7, 9, 11-13.
Psalm of Praise. Isaiah 63:7.
Suffer the Children to Come Unto Me. Matthew 19:14.
Taste and See That the Lord is Good. Psalm 34:8.
Ye Shall Know the Truth. John 8:2, 12, 31-32, 36.
Fisher, William Arms.
He That Dwelleth in the Secret Place. Psalm 91:1, 4, 7, 10-11.
Seek Ye First the Kingdom of God. Matthew 6:25-33.
Flowers, Geoffrey E.
The Lord's My Shepherd. Psalm 23:00.
The Lord's Prayer. Matthew 6:9-12.
Flowers, Vernon.
I Will Dwell in the House of the Lord. Psalm 23:00.
Floyd, Carlisle.
For I Am Persuaded. Romans 8:38, 39.
Man That is Born of a Woman. Job 14:1, 2, 7-12.
O Lord, Thou Hast Searched Me and Known Me. Psalm 139:1-4, 6-10, 23-24.
Praise the Lord, O My Soul. Psalm 146:1-2.
Save Me, O God, for the Waters Are Come in unto My Soul. Psalm 69:1-3, 14-17, 20.
Foley, John B.
Answer When I Call. Psalm 102:1-2, 6-7, 11.
Awake, Arise. Isaiah 60:1-4.
The Beatitudes. Matthew 5:3-10.
Bless Our God. Ephesians 1:3-6, 11-13, 17-18.
Blessed Be the Lord. Luke 1:68-79.
The Christ of God. Luke 9:20-24.
Deliver Us, O God of Israel. Psalm 25:1-6, 9, 22.
Dwelling Place. Ephesians 1:2.

Earthen Vessels. I Corinthians 1:27-29.
Father, May They All Be One. John 17:3-4, 21-23.
For You Are My God. Psalm 16:2-5, 9, 11.
Forever I Will Sing. Psalm 89:1-6, 16-19, 21-22, 25, 27.
Give to God. Psalm 96:1-5, 7-13.
God, Let Your Mercy. Psalm 33:1-2, 4-7, 12-13, 18-22.
God, Send Out Your Spirit. Psalm 104:1-3b, 5-6, 10-14, 24, 27-28, 30-31, 33-34.
God's Poor Ones. Psalm 34:6, 15, 18.
Happy Are They. Psalm 128:1-6.
Heed My Call for Help. Psalm 5:2-3a.
How Good It Is to Give Thanks to God. Psalm 92:1-6.
I Believe I Will See. Psalm 27:7-9, 13-14.
I Will Sing of the Lord. Philippians 2:8-9, 11.
I Will Walk in the Presence of God. Psalm 116:1-19.
If God Is for Us. Romans 8:31-39.
If You, O God. Psalm 130:1-4, 6-8.
Keep Me Safe, O God. Psalm 16:1-5, 7-11.
Let All the Earth. Psalm 66:1-7, 16-20.
Let All Who Fear the Lord. Isaiah 41:13.
Look Toward Me. Psalm 25:1-2, 15-16.
The Lord Is Kind and Merciful. Psalm 103:2-4, 6, 8-11, 13, 19-20.
The Lord Is My Light. Psalm 27:1, 4, 7-9, 14.
The Lord Is My Shepherd. Psalm 23:1-6.
Lord It Is Good to Give Thanks to You. Psalm 92:2-5, 13-16.
Magnificat. Luke 1:46-55.
My Soul Is Thirsting for You. Psalm 63:1-9.
Never Shall a Soul. Joel 2:28-32.
One Bread, One Body. I Corinthians 10:16-17.
Only in God. Psalm 62:1-2, 8, 11-12.
Our God Has Done Great Things for Us. Psalm 126:1-6.
Praise the Lord, My Soul. Psalm 103:1-2, 8, 14-15, 21.
Psalm 16. Psalm 16:1-5, 7-11.
Psalm 23. Psalm 23:1-6.
Psalm 27. Psalm 27:7-9, 13-14.
Psalm 33. Psalm 33:1-2, 4-7, 12-13, 18-22.
Psalm 63. Psalm 63:1-9.
Psalm 66. Psalm 66:1-7, 16-20.
Psalm 89. Psalm 89:1-6, 16-19, 21-22, 25, 27.
Psalm 92. Psalm 92:2-5, 13-16.
Psalm 96. Psalm 96:1-5, 7-13.
Psalm 103. Psalm 103:2-4, 6, 8-11, 13, 19-20.
Psalm 104. Psalm 104:1-3b, 5-6, 10-14, 24, 27-28, 30-31, 33-34.
Psalm 116. Psalm 116:1-19.
Psalm 118. Psalm 118:1-4, 8-9, 13-17, 21-24, 26.
Psalm 126. Psalm 126:1-6.
Psalm 128. Psalm 128:1-6.
Psalm 130. Psalm 130:1-4, 6-8.
Redeemer Lord. Psalm 22:1-2, 6.
Rescue Me From My Enemies. Psalm 129:1-4.
Rise Up, Jerusalem. Isaiah 60:1-4.
Sing to the Lord. Psalm 96:2-5, 7-9.
A Song of Hope. Jeremiah 29:10-14.
The Sparrow Finds a Home. Psalm 84:3-4.
The Steadfast Love. Isaiah 30:15, 18, 27.
This is My Body. I Corinthians 11:24-25.
This is the Day. Psalm 118:1-4, 8-9, 13-17, 21-24, 26.
To His Angels. Psalm 91:2, 5, 10-12, 14-15.
Turn to Me. Isaiah 45:22-23.
Why, O Lord. Exodus 32:11, 13-14.

Foley, John B. and Bob Dufford.
Praise God. Psalm 19:1.
Folk Hymn–Ancient Gaelic.
Ar nathir. Matthew 6:9-13.
The Lord's Prayer. Matthew 6:9-13.
Folkemer, Stephen P.
Psalm 145. Psalm 145:1-3, 8-9, 13b-14, 17-18, 21.
Forsyth, Josephine.
The Lord's Prayer. Matthew 6:9-13.
Foss, Lukas.
Awake, O North Wind. Song of Songs 4:16.
By Night On My Bed. Song of Songs 3:1, 3.
Come My Beloved. Song of Songs 7:11.
Set Me as a Seal. Song of Songs 8:6-7.
Foster, Myles B.
Eye Hath Not Seen, Nor Ear Heard. John 14:15.
If Ye Then Be Risen With Christ. Colossians 3:1-2.
Is it Nothing to You? Lamentations 1:12.
Seek Ye First the Kingdom of God. Matthew 6:31-33.
There Were Shepherds. Luke 2:8-11, 14.
Why Seek Ye the Living Among the Dead? Luke 24:5-6a.
Fragar, Russell.
Show Me Your Ways. Psalm 25:4-5 (based on).
Fraley, Christopher Lee.
Psalm 25. Psalm 25:00.
Franck, César.
Agnus Dei. Psalm 51:1-41, 10-12.
Ave Maria. Luke 1:28, 30-31, 42.
Be Thou Still. Psalm 46:10.
Bless the Lord, O My Soul. Psalm 103:2-4, 19.
Hear My Cry, O God. Psalm 56:4a.
Lord, Have Mercy. Psalm 51:1-4, 10-12.
Franck, Melchior.
Mache dich auf, werde Licht. Isaiah 60:1.
Siehe, eine Jungfrau ist schwanger. Matthew 1:23.
Franco, Johan.
The Lord's Prayer. Matthew 6:9-13.
Franz, Robert.
Let Not Your Heart Be Troubled. John 14:12.
The Lord of Love (ed. and arr. K. K. Davis and N. Loring). Psalm 23:00.
Fredrickson, Carl.
Bless the Lord. Psalm 103:1-5, 13, 17a, 20-22.
Garment of Praise. Isaiah 61:1-3.
Freed, Isadore.
O Lord, How Excellent is Thy Name. Psalm 8:00.
Psalm 8. Psalm 8:00.
Freedman, Harry.
Psalm 137. Psalm 137:00.
Freud, Joyce.
Peter Was a Fisherman (arr. Lyndell Leatherman). Matthew 4:18.
Freudenthal, Josef.
The Earth Is Lord's. Psalm 24:1-6.
A Lamp unto My Feet. Psalm 119:50.
Last Words of David. II Samuel 23:1-5.
Let Us Sing Unto the Lord. Psalm 95:00.
The Lord Is My Shepherd. Psalm 23:00.
The Lord's Blessing. Psalm 67:00.
The Precepts of Micah. Micah 6:6-8.
Frey, Richard E.
Bow Down Thine Ear, O Lord. Psalm 86:1-3, 5.
In Thee O Lord Do I Put My Trust. Psalm 18:2.
Incline Your Ear. Isaiah 55:1-3.

Freylinghausen, J. A. and Theodore Beck.
Lift Up Your Heads, You Mighty Gates. Psalm 24:1a.
Fromm, Herbert.
Lamentation of David. II Samuel 19:27.
Praise Ye the Lord. Psalm 92:00.
Psalm 1. Psalm 1:00.
Psalm 42. Psalm 42:1-4a.
Psalm 121. Psalm 121:00.
Psalm 149. Psalm 149:1-4.
Unto the Hills. Psalm 121:00.
Frost, Richard.
The Wonder of His Care. Psalm 8:00.
Fryxell, Regina H.
Psalm 67. Psalm 67:00.
Fyock, Joan A.
Look to the Mountains. Psalm 121:00.
Trust in God. Psalm 37:00.

Gabriel, Charles H.
His Eye Is on the Sparrow. Matthew 10:29-31.
Galbraith, J. Lamont.
How Beautiful upon the Mountains, op. 41, no. 3. Psalm 104:33.
I Sought the Lord. Psalm 34:4.
Galbraith, Robert.
I Wait upon Thee. I Peter 3:18, 19.
Gardner, Aldelaide.
The Lord Is My Shepherd (arr. Bob Mitchell). Psalm 23:00.
Gardner, Daniel.
Exalt the Lord Our God. Psalm 99:9.
Gardner, Irene Justine.
Bow Down Thine Ear. Psalm 86:1-3, 5-6, 11.
Garlick, Anthony.
Psalm 4. Psalm 4:00.
Psalm 17. Psalm 17:00.
Psalm 23. Psalm 23:00.
Psalm 28. Psalm 28:00.
Garrett, Les.
This Is the Day. Psalm 118:24.
Gaskill, Clarence.
Our Father. Matthew 6:9-13.
Gaslini, Giorgio.
Magnificat (1963). Luke 1:46-47.
Gast, Lothar.
Wir rühmen uns allein des Kreuzes. Psalm 111:2, 4, 5-9.
Gates, B. Cecil.
The Lord's Prayer. Matthew 6:9-13.
Gates, Crawford.
For I Am Called By Thy Name. Jeremiah 15:16.
A New Commandment I Give Unto You. John 13:34-35.
To Obey Is Better than Sacrifice. I Samuel 15:22.
Gaul, Alfred Robert.
Ascribe Unto the Lord Worship and Power. Psalm 96:7-8.
Come Ye Blessed. Matthew 25:34.
Eye Hath Not Seen. Isaiah 64:4.
My Soul Is Athirst for God. Psalm 42:2-3.
Now Go Your Ways. Ruth 1:8.
O Gracious Lord. Ruth 1:8.
These Are They Which Came Out of Great Tribulation. Revelation 7:14-15.
Thou Art the Guide of Our Youth. Psalm 23:6.
To the Lord Our God Belong Mercies. Daniel 9:9.
Gay, Roert.
No Other Name. Psalm 96:8.
Geisler, Johann Christian.
Bless the Lord, O My Soul. Psalm 103:00.
Gellman, Steven.
Psalm 121. Psalm 121:00.
Gersmehl, Mark and Scott Douglas.
We Will See Him As He Is. I John 3:2.
Gideon, Miriam.
The Labor of Thy Hands, no. 1. Psalm 127:00.
The Labor of Thy Hands, no. 3. Psalm 128:00.
Woman of Valor, no. 2. Proverbs 31:10, 25, 28, 31.
Gieseke, Richard W.
God's Own Time. Acts 17:28.
Rejoice in the Lord Always. Philippians 4:4-7.
Wedding Song. Ruth 1:16-17.
Gilbert, Harry M.
God of Righteousness. Psalm 4:1.
Gilbert, N.
The Lord Is My Shepherd. Psalm 23:00.
Giovanni, Bassani.
Ascribe to the Lord. Psalm 96:8, 10.
Glick, Srul Irving.
Seven Tableaux from the Song of Songs. Song of Songs 1:00 - 8:14.
Gluck, Christoph von.
As Pants the Hart. Psalm 42:1-4.
Thanks Be to God. I Corinthians 15:57.
Gober, Belle Biard.
I Will Lift Up Mine Eyes. Psalm 121:00.
Godard, Benjamin.
Be Merciful, O Lord. Psalm 67:00.
Goemanne, Noel.
A Time for Everything. Ecclesiastes 3:1-8.
Golde, W.
I Will Lift Up Mine Eyes. Psalm 121:1-2.
Goldman, Edward M.
By the Rivers of Babylon. Psalm 137:00.
Psalm 23. Psalm 23:00.
Psalm 97. Psalm 98:00.
Psalm 150. Psalm 150:00.
O Sing unto the Lord a New Song. Psalm 98:00.
Goldman, Maurice.
Entreat Me Not to Leave Thee. Ruth 1:16-17.
I Am My Beloved's. Song of Songs 2:10-13.
Song of Ruth. Ruth 1:16-17.
Gollner, Ronald E.
Great is the Lord. Psalm 145:3a.
Goode, Jack.
Psalm 23. Psalm 23:00.
Psalm 147. Psalm 147:00.
Thou Art My God. Psalm 63:00.
Gordigiani, L.
O Come Hither, and Hearken. Psalm 66:14-15.
Entreat Me Not to Leave Thee. Ruth 1:16-17.
O Sing unto the Lord a New Song. Psalm 98:00.
Goss, Lari.
Cornerstone. Isaiah 9:6c.
Gottlieb, Jack.
And You Shall Love. Deuteronomy 6:5-9.
Come, My Beloved. Song of Songs 7:10-14.
How Lovely Are Your Tents. Numbers 24:5.
Ma Tovu. Numbers 24:5.
Veahavta. Deuteronomy 6:5-9.

Gounod, Charles.
Ave Maria. Luke 1:28, 30-31, 42.
Cross of Calvary (sacred text). Luke 1:28, 30-31, 42.
Entreat Me Not to Leave Thee. Ruth 1:16-17.
God is Spirit. Psalm 51:16-17.
The King of Love My Shepherd Is. Psalm 23:00.
O Come to Me. Matthew 5:3-4, 6, 8.
The Peace of God. John 14:27.
The Vision of St. John. Revelation 21:1, 2.
Graafsma, Debbye.
To Him Who Sits on the Throne. Revelation 5:13.
Graff, Leta Bishop.
The Inhabitants Shall Not Say I Am Sick. Isaiah 33:24.
Graham, Robert.
My Shepherd. Psalm 23:00.
Grant, Amy and Wes King.
Seek First. Matthew 6:33.
Grantham, Donald.
How Lovely Is Thy Dwelling Place. Psalm 84:00.
Green, Keith.
Create in Me a Clean Heart. Psalm 51:10-12 (adapted).
Create in Me a Clean Heart (arr. Bill Syarda). Psalm 51:10-13.
Green, Steve and Jon Mohr.
Other Side of the Grave. Romans 6:00.
Greenbaum, Matthew.
Psalm 84. Psalm 84:00.
Greene, Maurice.
Blessed Are They That Dwell in Thy House. Psalm 84:4-5.
Blessed Is the Man. Psalm 1:1, 4.
I Will Lay Me Down in Peace. Psalm 4:8.
I Will Sing Unto the Lord. Psalm 146:2.
The Lord's Name Is Praised. Psalm 113:3-4.
O Praise the Lord. Psalm 103:20.
O That My Ways. Psalm 119:4-5, 18.
Praise the Lord, O My Soul. Psalm 103:1,2-4.
Praised Be the Lord. Psalm 68:19.
Salvation Belongeth Unto the Lord. Psalm 3:8.
Show Me Thy Ways, O Lord. Psalm 25:4.
The Sun Shall Be No More Thy Light. Isaiah 60:19.
Thou Hast Charged. Psalm 119:4-5, 18.
Greenfield, Alfred M.
Blessed Be Thou Lord God of Israel. I Chronicles 29:10-11, 13-14.
Greif, Jean Anthony.
We Are the Light of the World (arr. Randall DeBruyn). Matthew 5:3-10, 16.
Grier, Gene and Lowell Everson.
The Lord Is My Shepherd. Psalm 23:00.
Griffin, Charles B.
Soggetto Cavato. I Corinthians 13:1-11, 13.
Grimm, Heinrich.
Hosianna, dem Sohne David. Matthew 21:9.
Groton, Frederic.
Entreat Me Not. Ruth 1:16-17.
Groves, Kandela.
He Is Our Peace. Ephesians 2:14.
Gulliksen, Kenn.
Charity. I Corinthians 13:1-7, 11-13.

Haan, Raymond H.
The Shepherd Song. Psalm 23:1-2.
Haas, David.
Blest Are They. Matthew 5:3-12.
Christ Will Be Your Light. Ephesians 5:8-15.
Deep Within. Jeremiah 31:33.
Go Out to All the World. Psalm 117:00.
God Is My Light. Psalm 27:4, 13-14.
God's Command. Psalm 112:1-4, 6-7, 9.
The Goodness of God. Psalm 34:1-6, 8.
Happy Are They Who Believe. John 20:29.
Happy Are They Who Honor the Lord. Psalm 128:00.
Hear, O Israel. Deuteronomy 6:4-5.
I Am the Resurrection. John 11:25-26.
I Was Glad. Psalm 122:00.
I Will Praise You, Lord. Psalm 30:1-3, 10-12.
I Will Sing. Psalm 71:1, 5, 8, 15.
If Today You Hear His Voice. Psalm 95:1-2, 6-9.
In the Shadow of Your Wings. Psalm 63:1-8.
Initiation Acclamation. Ephesians 4:5-6.
Like a Little Child. Psalm 42:2-3, 12.
The Lord Upholds My Life. Psalm 54:1-4.
Lord, Send Out Your Spirit. Psalm 104:1, 24, 30-31, 34.
Lord, You Have the Words. Psalm 19:7-10.
The Lord's Prayer I. Matthew 6:9-13.
The Love of the Lord. Romans 8:35, 38-39.
Magnificat. Luke 1:46-55.
The Mountain I See. Psalm 121:00.
My Soul Is Still. Psalm 131:00.
The Name of God. Psalm 116:00.
Nations and Heavens. Psalm 113:00.
Now, the Acceptable Time. Joel 2:12.
Psalm 113. Psalm 113:00.
Psalm 121. Psalm 121:00.
Seek First the Kingdom. Matthew 6:28-32.
Song of the Risen One. Matthew 11:4-5.
The Stars Declare His Glory. Psalm 19:00.
Tell Out, My Soul. Luke 1:46-55.
There Is One Lord. Ephesians 4:5-6.
The Water I Give. John 4:14-15.
We Are Called. Micah 6:8.
We Will Rise Again. Isaiah 40:11, 26, 29-30.
Where There Is Love. I Corinthians 13:4-7, 10, 13.
Whereever You Go. Ruth 1:16-17.
Who Can This Be? Mark 5:39-41.
You Alone Are the Word. John 6:68.
You Are God's Work of Art. Ephesians 2:10.
You Are My Rock. Psalm 18:2-3, 6, 35.
You've Searched Me. Psalm 139:1-2, 7-10.
Haas, David and Marty Haugen.
All the Ends of the Earth. Psalm 98:1-6.
His Love Is Everlasting. Psalm 136:1-9, 24-26.
Proclaim to All the Nations. Psalm 96:1-4, 9-10.
Haeussler, Paul.
Let Not Your Heart Be Troubled. John 14:1-2, 27.
Halberstam, Rabbi E.
He Guideth Me in the Path of Righteousness (arr. Velvel Pasternak). Psalm 23:3.
Yanchéni (arr. Velvel Pasternak). Psalm 23:3.
Halberstam, Rabbi S.
Sah'énu (arr. Velvel Pasternak). Psalm 90:14.
Satisfy Us in the Morning (arr. Velvel Pasternak). Psalm 90:14.
Hall, Pam Mark.
The Now and the Not Yet. I John 3:2a.
Hallquist, Gary.
Song of Ruth (arr. Paul Johnson). Ruth 1:16-17.
Hamblen, Bernard.
Ave Maria. Luke 1:28, 30-31, 42.
Beside Still Waters. Psalm 23:00.
Hear Thou My Prayer. Psalm 86:1a, 4a, 6-7, 13.

The Lord's Prayer. Matthew 6:9-13.
On Eagle's Wings. Isaiah 40:28-31.
Teach Me, O Lord. Psalm 119:00.
This Is My Commandment. John 15:00.
I Know That My Redeemer Liveth. Job 19:25-26.
Hammerschmidt, Andreas.
Eile mich, Gott, zu erretten. Psalm 70:2-6.
Es danken dir, Gott, die Voelker. Psalm 67:3-7.
Fürchte euch nicht. Luke 2:10-11.
Herzlich lieb Hab' ich dich. Psalm 18:2-6.
I Am the Resurrection. John 11:25-26.
Ich bin die Auferstehung. John 11:25-26.
Let the People Praise Thee, O God. Psalm 67:3-7.
Lobe den Herren, meine Seele. Psalm 103:2-4.
Hancock, Vicki.
Unto Thee, O Lord, Do We Give Thanks. Psalm 75:1.
Handel, G. F.
All They That See Him, Laugh Him to Scorn. Psalm 22:7.
All We Like Sheep Have Gone Astray. Isaiah 53:6.
And Lo! The Angel of the Lord. Luke 2:9.
And the Angel Said Unto Them. Luke 2:10-11.
And the Glory of the Lord. Isaiah 40:5.
Arm, Arm, Ye Brave! I Macabees 3:58.
Awake Thou That Sleepest (arr. Carl Fredrickson). I Corinthians 15:20, 23.
Be Ye Sure (ed. Stan Pethel). Psalm 100:3.
Behold and See. Lamentations 1:12.
Behold the Lamb of God. John 1:29.
Behold, a Virgin Shall Conceive. Isaiah 7:14.
Behold, I Tell You a Mystery. I Corinthians 15:51-52a.
Blessed Are They That Consider the Poor. Psalm 41:1-4.
Blessed Are They That Fear the Lord. Psalm 128:1-2.
But Thou Didst Not Leave. Psalm 16:10.
But Who May Abide. Malachi 3:2.
Come to the Waters (arr. Carl Fredrickson). Isaiah 55:1, 3.
Come Unto Him. Matthew 11:28-29.
Come, Let Us Make a Joyful Noise (arr. Carl Fredrickson). Psalm 95:00.
Comfort Ye. Isaiah 40:1-3.
The Enemy Said. Exodus 15:9.
Er weidet seine Herde. Isaiah 40:11.
Every Day Will I Give Thanks. Psalm 145:2, 9.
Every Valley. Isaiah 40:4.
For Behold, Darkness Shall Cover the Earth. Isaiah 60:2-3.
For Look as High as Heaven Is. Psalm 97:10.
For Look as High as the Heaven. Psalm 95:00.
For This Our Truest Interest. Psalm 95:1-2.
For unto Us a Child is Born. Isaiah 9:6.
Gleich wie der Rauch schnell verweht. Psalm 68:00.
Gloria. Luke 2:14.
God Is a Constant Sure Defense. Psalm 9:9-10.
God Sent His Son Into the World. John 3:16-17.
God So Loved the World. John 3:16-17.
God's Tender Mercy Know No Bounds. Psalm 57:10.
He Shall Feed His Flock. Isaiah 40:11.
He That Dwelleth in Heaven. Psalm 2:4.
He Was Cut Off. Isaiah 53:8.
He Was Despised. Isaiah 53:3.
How Beautiful Are the Feet. Romans 10:15.
I Know That My Redeemer Liveth. Job 19:25-26.
I Will at All Times Praise the Lord. Psalm 34:1, 4, 8.
Ich weiss, dass mein Erlöser lebet. Job 19:25-26.
If God Be for Us. Romans 8:31, 33-34.
Kommt her zu ihm. Matthew 11:28-29.
Lead Me, Lord (arr. Carl Fredrickson). Psalm 5:8.
Like as the Smoke Vanisheth. Psalm 68:00.
The Lord Is My Strength. Exodus 15:2.
The Lord Preserveth Souls. Psalm 97:10.
Make Me a Clean Heart, O God. Psalm 51:10-12.
My Father, My Father, Look upon My Anguish. Matthew 26:42.
My Shepherd. Psalm 23:00.
O Come, Let Us Sing. Psalm 99:9.
O Come Let Us Worship. Psalm 95:6-8.
O Death, Where Is Thy Sting? I Corinthians 15:55-56.
O Magnify the Lord. Psalm 99:9.
O Praise the Lord. Psalm 103:21.
O Sing unto God. Psalm 68:4.
O Sing unto the Lord (Psalm 96). Psalm 93:4.
O singt unserm Gott. Psalm 68:00.
O Thou That Tellest Good Tidings to Zion. Isaiah 40:9.
O Worship the Lord. I Chronicles 16:29.
The People That Walked in Darkness. Isaiah 9:2-3.
Powerful Guardian (arr. Carl Fredrickson). Psalm 84:12.
Praise Him, All Ye That in His House Attend. Psalm 135:1-2.
Rejoice Greatly, O Daughter of Zion. Zechariah 9:9-10.
Righteous and Equity. Psalm 89:15.
Sing Out Your Joy to God (ed. Hal H. Hopson). Psalm 81:1-3.
Sing unto the Lord (duet). Psalm 96:1-4 (based on).
Sing with Songs of Joy. Psalm 42:4b.
And Suddenly There Was with the Angel. Luke 2:13.
Supplication (arr. Keith W. Bissell). Psalm 64:1.
That God Is Great. Psalm 135:5.
Their Sound Is Gone Out. Romans 10:18.
Then Shall Be Brought to Pass. I Corinthians 15:54.
Then Shall the Eyes of the Blind. Isaiah 35:5-6.
There Upon a Manger Bed (arr. Carl Fredrickson). Matthew 2:1-2, 11.
There Were Shepherds. Luke 2:8.
Thou Art Gone Up On High. Psalm 68:18.
Thou Didst Blow. Exodus 15:4.
Thou Shalt Break Them. Psalm 2:9.
Thou Shalt Bring Them In. Exodus 15:17.
Thus Saith the Lord. Haggai 2:6, 7.
Thy Mercy, Lord. Psalm 135:00.
Thy Rebuke Hath Broken His Heart. Psalm 69:20.
The Trumpet Shall Sound. I Corinthians 15:52b-53.
Unto Which of the Angels Said He at Any Time. Hebrews 1:5.
Walk Humbly With Thy God (arr. Carl Fredrickson). Ephesians 5:2.
Was betrübst du dich. Psalm 42:6.
Wash Me Throughly from My Wickedness. Psalm 51:2.
Waves of the Sea. Psalm 93:4.
Why Do the Nations. Psalm 2:1-2.
Worthy Is the Lamb That Was Slain. Revelation 5:12-13.
Handy, William Christopher.
They That Sow in Tears. Psalm 126:1-2, 5-6.
Hanks, Billie, Jr.
The Heavens Declare His Glory. Psalm 19:00.
Hanson, Howard.
God Is Our Refuge and Strength. Psalm 46:00.
O Clap Your Hands, All Ye People. Psalm 47:00.
O Lord, Our Lord, How Excellent Is Thy Name. Psalm 8:00.
O Lord, Rebuke Me Not in Thine Anger. Psalm 6:00.
Hanson, Jens.
Psalm 3. Psalm 3:00.

Harker, F. Flaxington.
Arise, Shine, for Thy Light Is Come. Isaiah 60:1-3, 13, 21.
As it Began to Dawn. Matthew 28:1-7.
Blest Are the Pure in Heart. Matthew 5:8.
Consider, and Hear Me. Psalm 13:00.
Glory to God in the Highest. Luke 2:10-14.
God Shall Wipe Away All Tears. Revelation 21:00.
He Shall Feed His Flock. Isaiah 40:11.
How Beautiful Upon the Mountains. Isaiah 52:7.
I Will Lift Up Mine Eyes to the Hills. Ephesians 4:7..
Like as the Hart Desireth the Water-Brooks. Psalm 42:1-4.
They That Sow in Tears Shall Reap in Joy. Psalm 126:5-6.
Turn Ye Even to Me with All Your Heart. Joel 2:12.
Harlan, Benjamin.
With Wings as Eagles (arr. Tom Fettke). Isaiah 40:28-31.
Worthy is the Lamb. Revelation 5:12-13.
Harrah, Walt.
No More Night. Hebrews 11:13-16.
Harris, Cuthbert.
Save Me, O God. Psalm 69:1, 3, 29.
Harris, Don and Martin J. Nystrom.
Don't Grow Weary (arr. Carl Seal). Galations 6:9a.
Harris, Ed.
Shepherd Alluluia. Psalm 23:1-2.
Hart, Don.
Go to All the World. Matthew 28:18-20.
Hart, Theron Wolcott.
The Healing of Blind Bartimaeus. Mark 10:46-52.
The Healing of the Woman. Mark 5:24-29, 34.
Raising the Son of the Widow. Luke 7:11-16.
Hartley, Evaline.
Charity. I Corinthians 13:1-6, 8, 13.
Hartley, John and Gary Sadler.
This Is My Prayer. I Chronicles 4:10.
Hartley, Walter S.
Adagio ma non troppo. Psalm 43:1-3.
Allegro. Psalm 12:1-4, 9.
Allegro con brio. Psalm 145:1-3, 8-10, 21.
Andante con moto. Psalm 40:1-4.
Andante molto. Psalm 63:1-5.
Haskins, V.
Love Never Faileth (arr. Carl Fredrickson). I Corinthians 13:00.
Hassler, Hans Leo.
Cantate Domino (arr. Kenny Williams). Psalm 96:00.
Hatch, Verna.
My Soul Doth Magnify the Lord! Luke 1:46-55.
Hatch, Wilbur.
Behold! What Manner of Love. I John 3:1-3.
Hatton, Ray D.
Love the Lord. Deuteronomy 6:5.
Haugen, Marty.
Canticle of the Sun. Psalm 19:1a.
Come Unto Me. Matthew 6:28-32.
Come, O Come, Let Us Sing. Psalm 95:1-2, 6-9.
Create in Me. Psalm 51:1, 10-12, 15.
Creation. Genesis 1:00.
God Mounts His Throne. Psalm 47:1-2, 5-8.
In the Morning I Will Sing. Psalm 63:1b-9.
The Love of the Lord. Romans 8:35, 38-39.
My Soul Is Thirsting. Psalm 63:1b-9.
Shepherd Me, O God. Psalm 23:00.
Speak, O Lord. John 6:68.
You Will Show Me the Path of Life. Psalm 16:1-2, 6-7, 9-11.
Your Love is Never Ending. Psalm 136:00.
Hausman, Ruth L.
Suffer the Little Children. Mark 10:13-16.
Hawkins, Floyd.
Let Thy Mantle Fall On Me. II Kings 2:9-13.
Haydn, F. Joseph.
And God Created Man. Genesis 1:27.
And God said, Let the Earth Bring Forth Grass. Genesis 1:11.
And God said, Let the Earth Bring Forth Living Creatures. Genesis 1:24.
And God said, Let the Waters Bring Forth Abundantly. Genesis 1:20.
And God said, Let the Waters Under the Heavens. Genesis 1:9.
Benedictus. Matthew 21:9.
The Heavens Are Telling (arr. Douglas E. Wagner). Psalm 19:1.
How Lovely Is Thy Dwelling Place (arr. Carl Fredrickson). Psalm 84:1-2, 4.
In the Beginning. Genesis 1:1-3.
Trust in the Lord (arr. Carl Fredrickson). Proverbs 3:1, 5-6.
Hayford, Jack.
Tell Ye This Story (arr. Paul Johnson). Exodus 13:14.
Until He Comes Again. I Corinthians 11:23-26.
Head, Michael.
Acquaint Now Thyself With Him. Job 22:21.
Ave Maria. Luke 1:28, 30-31, 42.
Be Merciful unto Me. Psalm 57:00.
Behold, I Send an Angel. Exodus 23:20, 22, 25.
Beloved, Let Us Love One Another. I John 4:7.
I Will Lift Up Mine Eyes. Psalm 121:00.
The Lord's Prayer. Matthew 6:9-13.
Make a Joyful Noise. Psalm 100:00.
Thus Spake Jesus. John 17:1, 5, 11, 21, 23.
Heiller, Anton.
Pater Noster. Matthew 6:9-13.
Held, Wilbur.
The King of Love. Psalm 23:00.
Helder, Bartholomaeus.
The Lord Is My Shepherd (arr. Paul Bunjes). Psalm 23:00.
Helfman, Max.
Set Me as a Seal Upon Thy Heart. Song of Songs 8:6-7.
The Voice of My Beloved. Song of Songs 2:10-18.
Helvering, Sandi Patti, Phil McHugh, and Gloria Gaither.
In the Name of the Lord. Matthew 21:9.
Who Will Call Him Kings of Kings. Matthew 28:1-10.
Henschel, George.
The Lord's Prayer. Matthew 6:9-13.
Herbert, Muriel.
Sing unto the Lord All the Earth. Psalm 96:00.
Herbst, Johannes.
Abide in Me. John 15:4.
Bleibet in mir. John 15:4.
Du solst erfahren. Isaiah 60:16.
I Will Go in the Strength of the Lord (ed. Donald M. McCorkle). Psalm 71:16a.
See Him, He is the Lamb of God. John 1:29.
Siehe das ist Gottes Lamm. John 1:29.
And Thou Shalt Know It. Isaiah 60:16.
Hildach, Eugen.
Where'er Thou Goest. Ruth 1:16-17.
Hillert, Richard.
He Shall Give His Angels Charge Over You. Psalm 91:9-12, 15-16.

Himmel, F. H.
Incline Thine Ear to Me. Psalm 70:1-5.
Hines, Jerome.
The Lord's Prayer. Matthew 6:9-13.
Hobby, Robert A.
I Will Bless the Lord at All Times. Psalm 34:1-11.
Psalm 34. Psalm 34:1-11.
Hoffmeister, Leon Abbott.
Arise, O Lord. Psalm 9:10, 19-20.
Behold the Tabernacle of God. Revelation 21:3-4.
The Birth of Christ. Luke 1:30-32.
How Long Wilt Thou Forget Me, O Lord? Psalm 13:1-5.
I Will Lift Up Mine Eyes. Psalm 121:00.
The Lord's Prayer. Matthew 6:9-13.
Holler, John.
The King of Love My Shepherd Is. Psalm 23:00.
Honegger, Arthur.
Benedica Dominum in Omni. Psalm 34:00.
Confitebor tibi, Domine. Psalm 138:00.
Eripe Me Domine, ab homine malo. Psalm 140:0.
Hope, Lawrence.
When I Survey the Wondrous Cross. Galatians 6:14.
Hopekirk, Helen.
God Is a Spirit. John 4:23-24.
Hopson, Hal H.
Gentle Shepherd, Kind and True. Luke 15:3-10.
The Gift of Love. I Corinthians 13:1, 3.
Give Thanks to the Lord. Psalm 106:1, 2.
I Lift Up My Eyes to the Hills. Psalm 121:00.
Jesus Fed the Hungry Thousands. Matthew 14:13-21.
Lord, From the Depths I Call to You. Psalm 130:1-4.
Neath Vine and Fig Tree. Isaiah 2:1-4.
Psalm 84. Psalm 84:00.
The Treasure and Pearl. Matthew 13:44-45.
Horman, John D.
Tell All the World. Psalm 9:1-2.
Horowitz, Rabbi M.
Eso énai, no. 1 (arr. Velvel Pasternak). Psalm 121:1-2.
For the Lord Has Comforted Zion (arr. Velvel Pasternak). Isaiah 51:3.
I Will Lift Up Mine Eyes (arr. Velvel Pasternak). Psalm 121:1-2.
The Jews Had Lightness (arr. Velvel Pasternak). Esther 8:16.
Joyfully Shall You Draw (arr. Velvel Pasternak). Isaiah 12:3.
Ki Nicham, no. 2 (arr. Velvel Pasternak). Isaiah 51:3.
The Law of the Lord is Perfect. Psalm 19:8.
La-y'hudim, no. 2 (arr. Velvel Pasternak). Esther 8:16.
Tõras Hasem t'mimo, no. 3 (arr. Velvel Pasternak). Psalm 19:8.
Ushavtem Mayim (arr. Velvel Pasternak). Isaiah 12:3.
Horvit, Michael.
The Prophecy of Amos. Amos 9:7-15.
Sing to God. Psalm 68:4.
Horwood, Michael S.
Psalm 121. Psalm 121:00.
Hovhaness, Alan.
Out of the Depths, op. 142, no. 3. Psalm 130:1-6.
Hovland, Egil.
Magnificat. Luke 1:46-55.
Howard, Tom.
How Lovely Is Your Dwelling Place. Psalm 84:00.
Psalm 13. Psalm 13:1-2.
Psalm 84. Psalm 84:00.
When Heaven's Locked in Silence. Psalm 13:1-2.
Howell, Charles T.
By the Waters of Babylon. Psalm 137:1-5.
Hoy, Dawn Riske.
Psalm 148. Psalm 148:00.
Hudson, Bob.
Humble Thyself in the Sight of the Lord. I Peter 5:6.
Huhn, Bruno S.
Be Glad, O Ye Righteous. Psalm 32:11.
Be Thou Exalted. Psalm 21:13.
Great Is the Lord. Psalm 47:1-2, 6-7.
Hear Me When I Call. Psalm 4:1.
The Lord Is My Strength. Psalm 118:14, 24, 26, 28-29.
Huijbers, Bernard.
As a Deer. Psalm 42:1-5, 8.
Song of All Seed. Mark 4:1-34.
Hummel, Ferdinand.
Alleluia! (arr. Carl Fredrickson). Psalm 23:1-2.
Humphreys, Don.
Arise, Shine for Thy Light Is Come. Isaiah 60:1.
The Beatitudes. Matthew 5:1-10.
Behold What Manner of Love. I John 3:1-3.
God Is Love. I John 4:16.
Great and Marvelous. Revelation 15:3-4.
He Sent His Word and Healed Them. Psalm 107:20.
He That Dwelleth in the Secret Place. Psalm 91:1-2, 4-5, 11.
The House of God. Psalm 127:1.
How Excellent Is Thy Loving Kindness. Psalm 36:7-10.
I Sought the Lord. Psalm 34:1-4, 8.
I Will Lift Up Mine Eyes Unto the Hills. Psalm 121:00.
Let This Mind Be in You. Philippians 2:1-2, 5.
Light of the World. Ephesians 5:14.
The Lord Is My Light. Psalm 27:1, 4-6.
The Lord Is My Shepherd. Psalm 23:00.
Lord, Thou Hast Been Our Dwelling Place. Psalm 90:00.
Man. Genesis 1:27.
My Prayer. Psalm 19:14.
Praise Ye the Lord. Psalm 106:1-4.
Put on the Whole Armour of God. Ephesians 6:10-13.
The Ransomed of the Lord. Isaiah 35:00.
Rejoice in the Lord. Philippians 4:4-5, 7-8.
Rest in the Lord. Psalm 37:4-7a.
Seek Ye the Lord. Isaiah 55:6.
Truth. Psalm 100:5.
Hurd, Bob.
All the Ends of the Earth. Psalm 98:1,3-6.
Arise, O Jerusalem (arr. Barbara Bridge and Dominic MacAller). Isaiah 65:13, 25.
As the Deer Longs. Psalm 42:1-4.
Be it Done unto Me. Luke 1:26-28.
Be With Me. Psalm 91:1-2, 10-12, 14-15.
Be With Me, O God. Psalm 16:10.
Come unto Me. Isaiah 62:3.
Create in Me. Psalm 51:3-4, 9, 12, 14.
Each Time I Think of You. Isaiah 46:3-5.
Envía Tu Espíritu. Psalm 104:30.
Everlasting Your Love. Psalm 136:1, 4-6, 8-9.
Flow River Flow. Isaiah 35:1-6.
Fracción Del Pan. Psalm 34:9.
From My Mother's Womb. Psalm 22:2-3, 10-11, 17.
Gather Your People. Isaiah 2:3-4.
God's Eye Is on the Sparrow. Job 11:16.
I Want to Praise Your Name. Psalm 148:00.
If Today (arr. Bellamy). Psalm 95:1-2, 6-9.
If You Belong to Me. Luke 18:22.

Let All the Earth Cry Out. Psalm 66:1-3, 5-6, 9, 19-20.
Let Us Share This Bread of Life. I Corinthians 12:13, 27.
Like a Weaned Child. Psalm 62:6.
Mi Dios, Mi Dios. Psalm 22:2, 8-11, 17-20, 23, 25.
My Soul Is Thirsting. Psalm 63:1-8.
Our Blessing Cup. Psalm 116:1, 3, 5, 12-13, 15-18.
Psalm 25. Psalm 25:1, 4-5, 8-10, 14.
Psalm 51. Psalm 51:3-4, 12, 14, 17, 19.
Psalm 85. Psalm 85:8-9, 11-14.
Psalm 91. Psalm 91:1-2, 10-12, 14-15.
Psalm 95. Psalm 95:1-2, 6-9.
Pueblo De Dios. Psalm 122:1.
Ready the Way. Isaiah 35:1-6.
Return to Me. Hosea 11:00.
Roll Down the Ages. Isaiah 42:1-17.
Shelter Me, O God. Psalm 61:3.
Show Us Your Kindness. Psalm 85:8-9, 11-14.
Taste and See. Psalm 34:2-4, 9.
They Who Do Justice. Psalm 15:1.
This Is the Day. Psalm 118:1-2, 16-17, 22-23.
To You, O God, I Lift Up My Soul. Psalm 25:1, 4-5, 8-10, 14.
Unless a Grain of Wheat. John 12:24.
We Are All Parts of One Body. I Corinthians 12:5, 12, 26.
Where There Is Love. I John 4:16, 20, 21.
Where You Go. Ruth 1:16-17.
The Word is in Your Heart. Matthew 4:4.

Hurd, Bob and Paul Ford.
Our Father. Matthew 6:9-13.

Hurd, Bob and Dominic MacAller.
I Have Seen the Lord. Job 19:25-27.
No Longer I. Galatians 2:19-20.
O, How I Long to See. Psalm 17:15.

Hurd, David.
How Dear to Me Is Your Dwelling. Psalm 84:1-7, 9.
Psalm 84. Psalm 84:1-7, 9.

Hustad, Donald.
Spirit of God. Galatians 5:25.
This Is My Commandment. John 15:12.

Ingles, David.
Garment of Praise. Isaiah 61:3b.

Inwood, Paul.
Center of My Life. Psalm 16:1-2, 7-11.
Evening Psalm. Psalm 141:1-5, 8-9.
Holy Is God. Psalm 117:00.
I Will Praise You, O Lord. Psalm 30:1, 3, 4-5, 8-12.
Let My Prayer Rise Before You. Psalm 141:1-5, 8-9.
O Blessed Are Those. Psalm 128:1-5.
Remember Your Mercy, Lord. Psalm 25:4-9.
Ring Out Your Joy. Psalm 95:1-8.
You, Lord, Have the Message. Psalm 19:7-10.

Ippolitof-Ivanof, Mikhail.
Bless the Lord, O My Soul (arr. William Stickles). Psalm 103:1-4.

Irvine, Jessie S.
Crimond. Psalm 23:00.
The Lord's My Shepherd, I'll Not Want. Psalm 23:00.

Isaacson, Michael.
B'Ni. Proverbs 3:1-6.
My Son. Proverbs 3:1-6.
Psalm 23. Psalm 23:00.

Isensee, Paul R.
The Lord's Prayer. Matthew 6:9-13.

Isham, Royce.
I Am the True Vine. John 15:1, 2, 4-6 (based on).

Jackson, Stanley.
Teach Me, O Lord. Psalm 119:00.

Jadassohn, Solomon.
Arioso from 100th Psalm. Psalm 100:3.
Erkennet, erkennt, dass der Herr ist Gott. Psalm 100:3.
God Hath Made Us All. Psalm 100:3.

Jefferies, George.
Praise the Lord, O My Soul. Psalm 104:1, 2, 33-34.

Jeffreys, George.
O quam suave (ed. Peter Aston). Philippians 2:9-10.
Speciosus forma (ed. Peter Aston). Psalm 45:2.

Jennings, Kenneth.
I Lift Up My Eyes to the Hills. Psalm 121:00.

Jensen, Adolf.
Lift Up Thine Eyes (arr. Carl Fredrickson). Psalm 121:00.

Jernigan, Dennis L.
At the Name of Jesus. Philippians 2:10-11.

Jewell, Lucina.
In My Father's House Are Many Mansions. John 14:1-3, 6a.

Johnson, David N.
The Lord's Prayer. Matthew 6:9-13.
Souls of the Righteous. Wisdom of Solomon 3:1-3.

Johnson, Gary.
Does Anybody Love the Children? Mark 10:13-16.
In Remembrance of Me. I Corinthians 11:23-26.

Johnson, Paul.
Love Theme. I Corinthians 13:1-7, 13.

Joncas, Michael.
All the Ends of the Earth. Psalm 98:1-6.
Be Merciful, O Lord. Psalm 51:1-4, 10-12.
Come to Me. Matthew 11:28-30.
Eternal Is His Mercy. Psalm 136:00.
Every Nation On Earth. Psalm 72:1-2, 7-8, 10-11, 12-13.
Go Out to the World. Matthew 28:19-20.
Guiding Me. Psalm 121:00.
How Lovely Is Your Dwelling Place. Psalm 84:1-8, 10-11.
I Have Loved You. Psalm 24:3.
I Will Praise the Lord. Psalm 146:2-10.
Let the King of Glory Come. Psalm 24:7-8.
Let Us Go Rejoicing. Psalm 122:00.
The Lord Is Near. Psalm 27:1, 4-5.
Lord, to Whom Shall We Go? John 6:68.
May the Angels. Psalm 27:1, 4-5.
On Eagle's Wings. Psalm 91:1-7, 11-12.
Our Blessing Cup. Psalm 34:9a.
Psalm 23. Psalm 23:00.
Send Forth Your Spirit. Psalm 104:1, 24, 29-33.
Take and Eat. Psalm 118:22.
You Have Searched Me. Psalm 139:1-18, 23.

Jones, Hilton Kean.
Happy Are the Lowly Poor. Matthew 5:1-16.

Jones, Kelsey.
Psalm Forty-Nine. Psalm 49:00.

Jongen, Joseph.
Deux Abraham. Psalm 128:00.

Jordan, Alice.
Bless the Lord, O My Soul. Psalm 103:00.

Jorgensen, Philip.
The Lord's Prayer. Matthew 6:9-13.

Joy, Jeanne Alden.
The River of Water of Life. Revelation 22:1, 14, 17.
Thanks Be to God (arr. Carl Fredrickson). Romans 8:2, 6.
Ye Shall Not Sorrow Any More. Revelations 21:4.

Kahn, Erich I.
Psalm 13. Psalm 13:00.
Psalm 126. Psalm 126:00.
Kalmanoff, Martin.
The Lion and Lamb. Isaiah 11:7.
The Lord Is My Shepherd. Psalm 23:00.
Kantor, Daniel.
Ave Maria (arr. Rob Glover). Luke 1:28.
Karg-Elert, Sigfrid.
Der erste Psalm. Psalm 1:00.
Katz, I.
Vaanachnu lõ néda (arr. Velvel Pasternak). Psalm 25:6.
We Know Not What to Do (arr. Velvel Pasternak). Psalm 25:6.
Kaufmann, Julius.
I Will Magnify Thee (arr. Carl Fredrickson). Psalm 145:1, 15-18.
Kavanaugh, John.
All Things Have Their Time. Ecclesiastes 3:1-8.
A Banquet Is Prepared. Psalm 23:00.
God Is Love. I John 4:16.
To You I Lift Up My Soul. Psalm 25:1-2a.
Kavanaugh, Patrick.
The Beatitudes. Matthew 5:1-12.
Kayden, Mildred.
Psalm 121. Psalm 121:00.
Keaggy, Phil.
The Survivor. Psalm 31:13-15.
Kehati, Pinchas.
From Whence Shall Come My Help? (arr. Velvel Pasternak). Psalm 121:1-2.
Mé-aylin yovõ ezri (arr. Velvel Pasternak). Psalm 121:1-2.
My Soul Thirsteth for God (arr. Velvel Pasternak). Psalm 42:3.
Tsomo Nafshi (arr. Velvel Pasternak) Psalm 42:3.
Keil, Kevin.
Psalm 128. Psalm 128:00.
We Long to See Your Face. Psalm 24:1-6.
Kellermeyer, David M.
A Prayer of Moses. Psalm 90:1-2, 4, 10, 12, 14, 17.
Kendrick, Graham.
For This Purpose. I John 3:8b.
Kendrick, Virginia.
I Will Lift Up Mine Eyes. Psalm 121:00.
Look Unto Me, Saith Our God. Isaiah 45:4-6, 11-13.
Kent, James.
It Is a Good Thing to Give Thanks to the Lord. Psalm 92:1-3.
Kiel, Friedrich.
For My Soul Is Athirst. Psalm 42:2.
He Was Oppress'd. Isaiah 53:7.
Turn Again to Thy Rest. Psalm 116:7-8.
Kieserling, Richard.
I Am the Bread of Life. John 6:51.
Kingsley, Gershon.
I Will Give Thanks unto the Lord. Psalm 9:2-3.
The Lord is My Shepherd. Psalm 23:00.
Prepare to Meet Thy God. Amos 5:24.
Rise Up My Love. Song of Songs 2:10-12.
Teach Me, O Lord. Psalm 86:11-13.
Kinscella, Hazel Gertrude.
Yea, Though I Walk through the Valley. Psalm 23:4.
Kirk, Theron.
The Eyes of All Wait upon Thee. Psalm 145:15-16, 18.
Kirkland, Terry.
God's Good Time. Ecclesiastes 3:1-9.
Jesus and the Children. Matthew 19:13-14.
The Lord's Prayer. Matthew 6:9-13.
Klang, E.
Rochõk Mishuosi (arr. Velvel Pasternak). Psalm 22:2.
Thou Art Far From My Help (arr. Velvel Pasternak). Psalm 22:2.
Klass, Leon V.
The People Who Walked in Darkness. Isaiah 9:1.
Klein, Manuel.
Ho! Everyone That Thirsteth. Isaiah 55:1.
Knapp, Phoebe C.
Open the Gates of the Temple. Job 19:25a.
Koch, Frederick.
Arise, Shine. Isaiah 60:1-3.
Be Not Afraid. II Chronicles 20:15b, 17.
The Bread of Life. John 6:00.
Feed My Lambs. John 21:00.
For Everything Its Season. Ecclesiastes 3:1-8.
The Lord Is My Light. Psalm 27:1, 3, 5.
Koch, John.
God Be Merciful unto Us. Psalm 67:00.
I Will Lift Up Mine Eyes. Psalm 121:00.
The Lord Is My Shepherd. Psalm 23:00.
Make a Joyful Noise unto the Lord. Psalm 100:00.
Praise the Lord . Psalm 150:00.
Koprowski, Peter Paul.
Psalm 42. Psalm 42:00.
Koschat, Thomas.
The Lord is My Shepherd (arr. Donald H. Ripplinger). Psalm 23:00.
Kosche, Kenneth T.
Come, Let Us Fix Our Eyes on Jesus. Hebrews 12:2.
Comfort, My People. Isaiah 40:00.
God's Angels. Psalm 91:11-12.
How Good and Pleasant It Is. Psalm 133:1.
Rejoice in the Lord Always. Philippians 4:4-5.
Kranzler, E.
L'Cho Ezbach, no. 2 (arr. Velvel Pasternak). Psalm 116:17.
To Thee I Offer Thanksgiving (arr. Velvel Pasternak). Psalm 116:17.
Krapf, Gerhard.
At the Time of the Banquet. Luke 14:16-24.
Be Merciful, Even as Your Father Is Merciful. Luke 6:36-42.
Confitebor Tibi. Isaiah 12:00.
Father Abraham, Have Mercy On Me. Luke 16:19-31.
Jesus Said to the Widow, "Do Not Weep." Luke 7:11-17.
Master, We Toiled All Night. Luke 5:1-11.
O Lord, I Will Praise Thee. Isaiah 12:00.
Krebs, Karl August.
The Lord's Prayer. Matthew 6:9-13.
Vater unser. Matthew 6:9-13.
Kretz, Vivian A.
Thou Wilt Keep Him in Perfect Peace. Isaiah 26:3-4.
Krieg, Melita.
Behold the Upright. Psalm 37:22a, 23, 31, 33-37.
The Way of Righteousness. Psalm 25:4, 7.
The World of Our God Shall Stand. Matthew 6:19-21, 24, 33.
Krismann, Bob.
His Mercy Endures (arr. Craig S. Kingsbury). Psalm 130:1-3.
Krugman, E. M.
Hasom nafshénu (arr. Velvel Pasternak). Psalm 66:9.
He Kept Us Alive (arr. Velvel Pasternak). Psalm 66:9.

Kufferschmid, Steve.
Come to the Table. Luke 22:14-30.
Kulla, Hans.
Ave Maria (ed. Paul R. Ladd, Jr.). Luke 1:28, 31, 34-35, 38.
Kuntz, Michael.
Der 62 Psalm. Psalm 62.00.

Laderman, Ezra.
Behold the Wicked Man. Psalm 7:14-15.
From the End of the Earth. Psalm 61:1.
Look Away from Me. Psalm 39:12b-13a.
Thou Didst Set the Earth. Psalm 104:5.
What I Did Not Steal. Psalm 69:4b.
Lafferty, Karen.
Seek Ye First. Matthew 6:33.
LaForge, Frank.
And There Were Shepherds Abiding in the Fields. Luke 2:8-14.
Bless the Lord. Psalm 103:00.
But the Hour Cometh. John 4:23-24, 35-36.
Come Near Ye Nations. Isaiah 34:1.
Come unto Me. Matthew 11:28.
Hast Thou Not Known. Isaiah 40:28-31.
He Shall Judge Thy People. Psalm 72:2-3, 6-11.
Hymn of Thanks and Praise. Psalm 118:1, 10, 14-17, 19, 21.
I Will Extol Thee. Psalm 145:00.
If Ye Abide in Me. John 15:7, 9-10, 12.
Let the Heavens Rejoice. Psalm 96:1-2, 6, 9, 13.
Make a Joyful Noise. Psalm 100:00.
Suffer the Little Children. Matthew 19:1-2, 13-15.
Teach Me, O Lord. Psalm 119:33-34, 37.
Thy Mercy, O Lord, Is in the Heavens. Psalm 36:5-7, 11.
What Shall I Render unto the Lord. Psalm 116:12-14, 17-19.
Ye Are the Light of the World. Matthew 5:14-16, 43-45, 48.
Lagourgue, Charles.
Psalm 92. Psalm 92:00.
Lake, Ruth.
Therefore the Redeemed. Isaiah 51:11.
LaMontaine, John.
Behold, a Virgin Shall Be With Child. Matthew 1:23.
His Left Hand Is under My Head, and His Right Hand Doth Embrace Me. Song of Songs 2:6.
I Am the Rose of Sharon and the Lily of the Valley. Song of Songs 2:1-3a.
I Sat Down under the Shadow. Song of Songs 2:3b-5.
The Lord is My Shepherd, op. 36, no. 2. Psalm 23:00.
My Beloved Is Mine and I am His. Song of Songs 2:16-17.
O My Dove, That Art in the Clefts of the Rock. Song of Songs 2:14.
Rise Up, My Love, My Fair One, and Come Away. Song of Songs 2:10b-13.
The Voice of My Beloved! Behold, He Cometh. Song of Songs 2:8-10a.
Landry, Rev. Carey.
Like a Seal on Your Heart (arr. Margaret Pizzuti). Song of Songs 8:6-7.
Lane, Richard.
Rejoice in the Lord. Philippians 4:4, 8.
Lansing, A. W.
As Pants the Hart. Psalm 42:00.
Seek Ye the Lord. Isaiah 55:6-7.
Larson, Lloyd.
Death, Where Is Your Sting? I Corinthians 15:51-52, 55, 57.
O Come, Let Us Sing to the Lord. Psalm 95:1-6.
O Praise the Lord! Psalm 117:1.
Larson, Sonia.
Psalm 103. Psalm 103:1-4.
Sing Allelu, Alleluia! Matthew 28:1-10.
Lawson, Gordon.
Psalm 23. Psalm 23:00.
Leavitt, John.
Jesus My Shepherd. Psalm 23:00.
The Lord Is My Light. Psalm 27:00.
Lederer, Charles.
Psalm 104. Psalm 104:00.
Ledner, Michael.
You Are My Hiding Place. Psalm 32:7.
Lee, John.
Thine Be the Glory. Matthew 6:9-13.
Leech, Bryan Jeffrey.
The Greatest of These Is Love (arr. Ruth Morris Bray). I Corinthians 13:1.
Leichtling, Alan.
The Fear of the Lord. Proverbs 1:7-9.
The Lord By Wisdom Founded Earth. Proverbs 2:19-22.
Lekberg, Sven.
And a Very Great Multitude. Matthew 21:8, 9.
How Long Wilt Thou Forget Me, O Lord? Psalm 13:00.
I Will Lift Up Mine Eyes. Psalm 121:00.
O Come, Let Us Sing unto the Lord. Psalm 95:1-7.
O Lord, Thou Hast Searched Me. Psalm 139:1, 4, 8.
Lepke, Charma Davies.
Great and Marvelous Are Thy Works. Revelation 15:1.
Leslie, Henry.
Come unto Him. Matthew 11:28-30.
Lewis Jr., Ross.
In My Father's House (arr. Bo Williams). John 14:2-3.
Liddle, Samuel.
How Lovely Are Thy Dwellings. Psalm 84:1-3, 8, 10.
Like as the Hart. Psalm 42:00.
The Lord Is My Shepherd (arr. Niel Jenkins). Psalm 23:00.
Liebergen, Patrick M.
Psalm 95. Psalm 95:1-3.
Liljestrand, Paul.
Whither Thou Goest. Ruth 1:16-17.
Lindh, Jody W.
Behold, God Is My Salvation. Isaiah 12:2, 4b-5.
Lift Up Your Heads. Psalm 24:7-10.
Lister, Mosie.
The Lord Is in this Place. Genesis 28:16-17.
Liszt, Franz.
God Shall Wipe Away All Tears (arr. Carl Fredrickson). Isaiah 25:8-9.
Ninety-First Psalm (arr. Carl Fredrickson). Psalm 91:1-4, 11.
Lorenz, Ellen Jane.
When I Survey the Wondrous Cross. Galatians 6:14.
Lovelace, Austin C.
The Beauty of the Lord. Psalm 90:17.
Faith Is. Hebrews 11:1-2, 13, 16b.
The Great White Host. Revelation 7:9-10, 13-16.
Have You Not Known? Isaiah 40:28-31.
How Beautiful upon the Mountains. Isaiah 52:7-9.
I Lift Mine Eyes Unto the Hills. Psalm 121:1-4.
The Love of God. Psalm 23:4.
My Shepherd Will Supply My Need. Psalm 23:1-2.
My Soul Is Filled with Joy. I Samuel 2:1-10.
O God, in All Thy Might. I Corinthians 13:9, 12.
O Love That Casts Out Fear. John 4:14.
Seek Ye the Lord. Isaiah 55:6-7.

Sing a New Song! Psalm 98:1-3.
Song of Hannah. I Samuel 2:1-10.
Than Eye Hath Seen. I Corinthians 2:9-10.
Wedding Song. Matthew 19:6.
You Crown the Year with Goodness. Psalm 65:00.

Lowe, Augustus F.
Be Still. Psalm 46:10.
O Lord How Lovely. Psalm 8:1.
Psalm 8. Psalm 8:1.
Psalm 23. Psalm 23:00.
Sanctuary. Psalm 91:1-2, 4, 9, 11.

Lowenbraun, S.
If I say, "My foot slippeth" (arr. Velvel Pasternak). Psalm 94:18.
Im omarti, no. 1 (arr. Velvel Pasternak). Psalm 94:18.

Lucke, Katharine E.
Blessed Is the Man. Psalm 1:00.

Lully, Jean Baptiste.
Great Peace Have They. Psalm 119:135, 165.
Our God Has Borne Our Troubles. Isaiah 53:4-5.

Lund, Lynn S.
The Lord Is My Shepherd. Psalm 23:1-6 (based on).

Lundy, Damian.
Song for a Young Prophet (arr. Malcolm Archer). Jeremiah 1:00.

Luther, Martin.
God Is Our Refuge and Our Strength (arr. Thomas J. Fleming). Psalm 46:1-7.

Lutkin, Peter C.
The Lord Bless You and Keep You. Numbers 6:24.
The Lord Bless You and Keep You (arr. William Stickles). Numbers 6:24.

Luzzi, Luigi.
Ave Maria. Luke 1:28, 30-31, 42.
Sing Hallelujah with Glad Rejoicing. Luke 1:28, 30-31, 42.

Lyles, Dwight and Niles Borop.
Proclaim the Glory of the Lord. Psalm 145:1-13.

Lynch, Mike.
Forever I Will Sing, Psalm 89:1-2, 15-16.
I Believe That I Shall See. Psalm 25:1.
I Lift Up My Eyes (arr. Dennis Richardson). Psalm 121:00.
In the Land There Is a Hunger. Psalm 62:2.
Let My Tongue Be Silenced. Psalm 137:1-4, 6.
Sing to the Lord. Psalm 27:1.
We Are Called. Jeremiah 1:5.

Lynes, Frank.
The Earth Is the Lord's. Psalm 24:1-5, 7-9.
Seek Ye the Lord. Isaiah 55:6.
Send Out Thy Light. Psalm 43:1-4.

Lynn, Lorna.
The Greatest of These is Love. I Corinthians 13:4-7, 13.

Lyon, A. Laurence.
Behold the Lamb of God. Matthew 11:28.

Lyon, James.
Oh, Lord, Our Heavenly King. Psalm 8:00.

MacDermid, James G.
Acquaint Now Thyself With Him. Job 22:21.
Arise, Shine for Thy Light Is Come. Revelation 3:20.
As the Rain Cometh Down. Isaiah 55:1, 3, 10-11.
Behold What Manner of Love. Genesis 1:26, 27.
Bring Ye All the Tithes Into the Storehouse. Psalm 127:1.
Cans't Thou By Searching Find Our God? Job 11:7, 13-15, 17.
Doth Not Wisdom Cry? Proverbs 8:00.
For the Mountains Shall Depart. Isaiah 55:6.
God Is Our Refuge. Psalm 46:1-3, 6-7, 9-10.
God So Loved the World. John 3:5-7, 16.
God That Made the World. Acts 27:22, 24, 28.
He Sent His Word. John 1:1.
He That Dwelleth in the Secret Place of the Most High. Psalm 91:1, 5-6, 9, 10-12.
I Am the True Vine. John 15:1-3, 5-7.
I Will Lift Up Mine Eyes. Psalm 121:00.
In My Father's House Are Many Mansions. John 14:2-4, 27.
Is Not This the Fast. Isaiah 58:1, 3-6, 8-9.
Let Not the Wise Man Glory in His Wisdom. Jeremiah 31:31, 33-34.
Lift Up Your Eyes to the Heavens. Isaiah 51:6.
Love. Genesis 1:3.
Make a Joyful Noise. Psalm 100:00.
My New Name. Revelation 3:10-12.
My Speech Shall Distill as the Dew. Deuteronomy 32:1-3.
The Ninety-First Psalm. Psalm 91:1, 5-6, 9, 10-12.
The Ransomed of the Lord. Isaiah 35:00.
The Shadow of Thy Wings. Psalm 36:5-9.
Sing, O Daughters of Zion. Zephaniah 3:00.
Sing unto the Lord a New Song. Psalm 148:1-6, 9, 11.
The Spirit of the Lord God Is upon Me. Isaiah 61:1, 2.
They Shall Run and Not Be Weary. Isaiah 40:6, 8, 28-31.
Thine, O Lord is the Greatness. I Chronicles 29:11-13.
Thou Wilt Keep Him in Perfect Peace. Isaiah 26:3-4, 13-14.
Thy Word Is a Lamp. Psalm 119:105.
Trust in the Lord With All Thine Heart. Proverbs 3:5-6, 19-20, 25-26.
Whither Shall I Go from Thy Spirit. Psalm 139:7-12.

MacFadyen, Alexander.
Bow Down Thine Ear, O Lord. Psalm 86:1-4, 6-7, 11-12.

MacGimsey, Robert.
Our Father. Matthew 6:9-13.
Shadrach. Daniel 3:00 (based on).
Think On These Things. Philippians 4:8-9.

Mader, Clarence.
Happy Is the Man. Proverbs 3:13-23.
I Waited Patiently for the Lord. Psalm 40:1-4, 8, 9b, 10b, 11-12, 16.
The Lord Is My Shepherd. Psalm 23:00.

Mahnke, Allan.
Fling Wide the Gates. Psalm 24:7-10.
Psalm 16. Psalm 16:5-11.
Psalm 24. Psalm 24:7-10.
Psalm 25. Psalm 25:1.
Psalm 27. Psalm 27:1-3.
Psalm 32. Psalm 32:5-8.
Psalm 47. Psalm 47:1-2, 5-7.
Psalm 61. Psalm 61:1.
Psalm 67. Psalm 67:00.
Psalm 85. Psalm 85:8-13.
Psalm 86. Psalm 86:10-12, 15.
Psalm 89. Psalm 89:1-4, 15-18.
Psalm 99. Psalm 99:1-5.
Psalm 116. Psalm 116:5-9.
Psalm 116:10-17. Psalm 116:10-17.
Psalm 126. Psalm 126:1-6.
Psalm 131. Psalm 131:00.
Psalm 139. Psalm 139:7-10.
Psalm 149. Psalm 149:1-4.

Malotte, Albert Hay.
The Beatitudes. Matthew 5:3-6.
Hast Thou Not Known? Isaiah 40:28-31.
The Lord's Prayer. Matthew 6:9-13.
The Lord's Prayer (arr. David Hamilton). Matthew 6:9-13.
Only Thee, O Lord. Psalm 25:1, 4-5.
Padre Nuestro (arr. Steve Green). Matthew 6:9-13.
Unto Thee, O Lord. Psalm 25:1, 4-5.
Manion, Tim.
Blessings on the King. Isaiah 52:7-8.
I Lift Up My Soul. Psalm 25:1, 4-6, 8-9.
Lord of Glory. Song of Songs 2:8.
This Alone. Psalm 27:1, 4, 6, 14.
The Twenty-Third Psalm. Psalm 23:00.
Manney, Charles F.
Teach Me, O Lord. Psalm 119:33-34, 37.
Manookin, Robert P.
Prayer of Dedication. Matthew 23:37 (based on).
Who Are These Arrayed in White Robes? Revelation 7:13-17.
Manuel, Ralph.
Hark, the Voice of Jesus Calling. Isaiah 6:8.
Manzo, Laura.
They Shall Soar Like Eagles. Isaiah 40:29-31.
Marcello, Benedetto.
As Pants the Wearied Hart. Psalm 42:00.
The Heavens Declare God's Glory. Psalm 19:00.
I Will Lift Up My Soul (arr. Barbara Owen). Psalm 25:1-2a, 4-5.
O Sing unto the Lord. Psalm 95:1.
Marks, J. Christopher.
Out of the Deep. Psalm 130:00.
Marot, Clement.
Il faut que de tour mes espirits. Psalm 138:00.
Marsh, Donald.
Beloved. Matthew 24:42.
Martin, Gilbert M.
My Shepherd Is Jehovah. Psalm 23:00.
Martin, Joseph M.
Come, Sing unto the Lord. Psalm 96:1-3, 11-12.
Martinson, Joel.
God So Loved the World. John 3:16-17.
The Lord Is My Shepherd. Psalm 23:00.
Psalm 85. Psalm 85:9-14.
Taste and See the Goodness of the Lord. Psalm 34:1-8.
Marzo, Eduardo.
Unto Thee O Lord. Psalm 25:00.
Mascagni, Pietro.
Ave Maria (arr. Eduardo Marzo). Luke 1:28, 30-31.
Ave Maria (arr. Steven Mercurio). Luke 1:28, 30-31.
Mason, Babbie.
Bless the Lord. Psalm 103:1.
Jesus the One and Only. Philippians 2:6-11.
Mason, Lowell.
A Charge to Keep Have I (arr. Rhonda Sandberg). Leviticus 8:35.
Matesky, Thelma.
Behold, How Good and How Pleasant. Psalm 133:00.
I Will Praise Thee With My Whole Heart. Psalm 138:00.
Matthews, H. Alexander.
Lord, I Have Loved the Habitation of Thy House. Psalm 26:8.
The Lord Is My Light. Psalm 27:00.
The Lord Is My Shepherd. Psalm 23:00.
Matthews, Thomas.
The Lord Is My Shepherd. Psalm 23:00.
Mayfield, Larry.
O Father in Heaven. Matthew 6:9-13.
McAfee, Don.
The Earth Is Lord's. Psalm 24:1-5.
How Excellent Is Thy Name. Psalm 8:1, 3-8.
If I Am Without Love. I Corinthians 13:1-7.
A Living Sacrifice. Romans 12:1-2.
O Clap Your Hands. Psalm 47:1, 5-8.
Psalm 139. Psalm 139:00.
The Two Commandments. Matthew 22:37-39.
When All Things Began. John 1:5.
McArthur, Edwin.
Bless the Lord, O My Soul. Psalm 103:1-3.
God Is a Spirit. John 4:23-24.
McConnell, Doug.
Set Me as a Seal. Song of Songs 8:6, 8.
McCray, James.
Love Is. . . Psalm 128:00.
Set Me as a Seal. Song of Songs 2:16.
McDonald, Boyd.
Psalm 47. Psalm 47:00.
McFeeters, Raymond.
A Psalm of Praise. Psalm 100:00.
McGuire, Bobby.
Communion Song. Luke 22:17-20.
McGuire, Dony.
Upon This Rock. Matthew 16:13-18, 25.
McNeil, Edith.
The Steadfast Love of the Lord. Lamentations 3:22-23.
Mead, Sr. Janet.
The Lord's Prayer. Matthew 6:9-13.
Medema, Ken.
O Rest in the Lord (arr. Mark Hayes). Psalm 37:1.
Sing to the Lord. Psalm 34:3.
Meek, Kenneth.
The Lord Is My Shepherd. Psalm 23:00.
Meininger, F. C.
Ave Maria. Luke 1:28, 30-31, 42.
Mendelowitz, F.
The Law of the Lord is Perfect (arr. Velvel Pasternak). Psalm 19:8.
Tōras Hasem t'mimo, no. 1 (arr. Velvel Pasternak). Psalm 19:8.
Mendelssohn, Felix.
Be Thou Faithful unto Death. Revelation 2:10.
Bread of Life. John 6:35.
But the Lord Is Mindful of His Own. Acts 9:2.
Cast Thy Burden on the Lord (arr. Lynn Hodges). Psalm 55:21.
Consume Them All, Lord Sabaoth. Exodus 32:10.
Dann werden die Gerechten leuchten. Matthew 13:43.
Doch der Herr, er leitet die Irrenden recht. Psalm 25:8-9, 12-13.
Draw Near, All Ye People (arr. Lynn Hodges). I Kings 18:36-37.
Es ist genug! I Kings 19:4, 10.
For I Had Gone Forth. Psalm 42:3-4.
For Know Ye Not That Ye Are His Temple. I Corinthians 3:16-17.
For My Soul Thirsteth for God. Psalm 42:2.
For the Lord Is a Mighty God (arr. Hal H. Hopson). Psalm 95:3-6.
For the Lord Is a Mighty God (arr. James McKelvy). Psalm 95:3-6.

For the Lord Will Lead. Psalm 25:8-9, 12-13.
For the Mountains Shall Depart. Isaiah 54:10.
Go Up, Child (arr. Lynn Hodges). I Kings 18:43-44.
God Hath Led His People On. Deuteronomy 32:11.
Gott sei mir gnädig. Psalm 51:1, 10-11, 13, 15, 17.
He Counteth All Your Sorrows. Psalm 107:2, 14-15, 19.
He, Watching Over Israel (arr. Lynn Hodges). Psalm 121:3.
Hear My Prayer. Psalm 55:1-5.
Hear Ye, Israel. Isaiah 49:7.
Herr Gott Abrahams. I Kings 18:36-37.
Höre, Israel. Isaiah 49:7.
How Beautiful on the Mountains (arr. Carl Fredrickson). Isaiah 52:7.
I Praise Thee, O Lord, My God. Psalm 86:12-13.
I to the Hills Will Lift My Eye (ed. Hal H. Hopson). Psalm 121:00.
I Waited for the Lord. Isaiah 40:1.
I Waited for the Lord (arr. William Stickles). Isaiah 40:1.
I Will Sing of Thy Great Mercies. Psalm 89:1.
I Will Sing of Thy Mercies (ed. Gordon Young). Psalm 89:1.
Ich harrete des Herrn. Isaiah 40:1.
If with All Your Hearts. Deuteronomy 4:29.
If Your Heart and Soul Both Truly Seek Me (arr. Leonard Van Camp). Deuteronomy 4:29.
If Your Heart and Soul Both Truly Seek Me. Job 23:3.
In His Hands Are All the Corners of the Earth. Psalm 95:4.
Is Not His Word Like a Fire? Jeremiah 23:29.
Ist nicht des Herrn Wort wie ein Feuer? Jeremiah 23:29.
It Is Enough. I Kings 19:4, 10.
It Is Enough (arr. Lynn Hodges). I Kings 19:4, 10.
Ja, es sollen wohl Berge weichen. Isaiah 54:10.
Jerusalem (ed. Lloyd Pfautsch). Matthew 23:37.
Jerusalem! Jerusalem! Thou That Killest the Prophets. Matthew 23:37.
The King of Love My Shepherd Is (arr. Carl Fredrickson). Psalm 23:00.
Lift Thine Eyes (arr. Carl Fredrickson). Psalm 121:1-4.
Lift Thine Eyes to the Mountains (adapted Carl Deis). Psalm 121:1-4.
Lord God of Abraham. I Kings 18:36-37.
Lord God of Abraham (arr. Lynn Hodges). I Kings 18:36-37.
Lord, Our Creator (arr. Lynn Hodges). Psalm 8:9.
The Lord Shall Bless Thee With Abundance. Psalm 115:14-15.
The Lord's Prayer (arr. Michael Johnson). Matthew 6:9-13.
My Tears Have Been My Meat. Psalm 42:3-4.
Now Trust in the Lord (arr. Leonard Van Camp). Psalm 37:1, 4-5, 7.
O Christ the Way. John 8:32.
O Come, Let Us Worship. Psalm 95:00.
O for the Wings of a Dove. Psalm 55:6-7.
O God, Have Mercy. Psalm 51:1, 10-11, 13, 15, 17.
O Lord They Prophesy Against Thee. Exodus 32:10.
O Rest in the Lord. Psalm 37:1, 4-5, 7.
O Rest in the Lord (arr. Lynn Hodges). Psalm 37:1, 4-5, 7.
O Rest in the Lord (arr. Hal H. Hopson). Psalm 37:1, 4-5, 7.
O Wherefore Do Ye These Things? I Corinthians 3:16-17.
Praise Thou the Lord, O My Spirit. Psalm 103:1-2.
Saget es, die ihr erlöst seid. Psalm 107:2, 14-15, 19.
Sing Ye Praise. Psalm 107:2, 14-15, 19.
Then Shall the Righteous Shine. Matthew 13:43.
So ihr mich von ganzem Herzen suchet (arr. Leonard Van Camp). Deuteronomy 4:29.
The Sorrows of Death. Psalm 116:3.
Strikke des Todes. Psalm 116:3.
There Is Nothing (arr. Lynn Hodges). I Kings 18:43-44.
They Have Taken Away My Lord. John 20:13-15.
Thy Secret Place (arr. Carl Fredrickson). Psalm 91:00.
Tulerunt Dominum meum. John 20:13-15.
Why Art Thou Cast Down, O My Soul? Psalm 43:3-5.
Woe unto Them Who Forsake Him! Hosea 7:13.
Woe. Woe unto Them Who Forsake Him! Hosea 7:13.
Ye Have Taken Away My Lord. John 20:13.
Ye People Rend Your Hearts. Jeremiah 29:13.
Zerreisset eure Herzen. Jeremiah 29:13.

Merbecke, John.
The Lord's Prayer (arr. Everett Jay Hilty). Matthew 6:9-13.

Mercadante, S.
Blessed is He That Cometh. Mark 11:9-10.
Salve Maria. Mark 11:9-10.

Meyers, Don.
Trust in the Lord. Proverbs 3:5-6.

Michaels, John.
O Bless the Lord (arr. Craig S. Kingsbury). Psalm 148:1-3, 7, 9-10, 12-13.

Milhaud, Darius.
Cantate de Psaume. Psalm 129:00.

Millard, H.
Ave Maria. Luke 1:28, 30-31, 42.
Ave Maria (arr. Gottlieb Harms). Luke 1:28, 30-31, 42.
Hear Us, O Father. Luke 1:28, 30-31, 42.

Miller, Merle.
Create in Me a Clean Heart. Psalm 51:10-12.
Seek the Lord. Psalm 34:12-14, 19.
Solomon's Prayer. I Kings 3:5, 7, 9, 10-14.
Think on These Things. Philippians 4:4.

Mills, Pauline Michael.
Thou Art Worthy. Revelation 4:10-11.
Thou Art Worthy (arr. Fred Bock). Revelation 4:10-11.

Misetich, Marianne.
As the Deer Longs. Psalm 42:1-4.
Comfort My People. Isaiah 40:4.
Here Is Your God. Isaiah 35:6-7.
Holy One of Israel. Isaiah 41:18-19.
I Have Waited for the Lord. Psalm 40:1.
A Joyful Sound. Psalm 150:1-5.
Let Not Your Hearts. John 14:1-3, 6, 14.
Like a Shepherd. Isaiah 40:11.
This Is the Day. Psalm 118:24.

Mitchell, Hugh.
Thy Loving Kindness. Psalm 63:3-4.

Mitchell, Raymond Earle.
The Tabernacle of God Is With Men. Revelation 21:1, 4, 5, 6.

Moe, Daniel.
The Greatest of These Is Love. I Corinthians 13:1-7.

Moen, Don.
All We Like Sheep. Isaiah 53:6.
Worthy the Lamb That Was Slain. Revelation 5:12-13.

Mohr, Jon.
He Who Began a Good Work in You. Philippians 1:6.
He Who Began a Good Work in You (arr. Steven V. Taylor). Philippians 1:6.

Molique, Wilhelm Bernhard.
I Will Extol Thee, My God. Psalm 145:1, 3, 16, 18-20.
It Is of the Lord's Great Mercies. Psalm 9:13.
Lead Me, Lord. Psalm 5:8.
Lead Me, O Lord. Psalm 5:8.

Monroe, Charles F.
Unto Thee, O Lord. Psalm 25:1-4.
Montemayor, Judy Horner.
God Is My Refuge. Psalm 46:1-2.
Montgomery, James and Thomas Koshat.
The Lord Is My Shepherd. Psalm 23:00.
Moore, Bob.
In the Shadow of Your Wings. Psalm 63:2-6.
We Are a Chosen People. Colossians 3:12-15.
Moore, Gary and Michael W. Smith.
The Throne. Revelation 5:13.
Moore, Harlan.
Restore the Joy. Psalm 51:23.
Morawetz, Oskar.
My God Why Have You Forsaken Me? Psalm 22:00.
Psalm 22. Psalm 22:00.
Morris, David.
Now unto Him. Jude 1:24-25.
Mosenthal, Joseph.
I Will Magnify Thee, O God. Psalm 30:2.
Mourant, Walter.
The Hour Cometh. John 4:23-24.
Mozart, W. A.
Agnus Dei. John 1:29.
Behold the Son of God. John 3:13-15, 17-18.
Come, Be Joyful (arr. Hal H. Hopson). Psalm 100:12.
Laudamus te. Psalm 145:1-2.
Laudate Dominum. Psalm 117:00.
Laudate Dominum (arr. Doreen Rao). Psalm 117:00.
Mighty Are Your Works, O God (arr. Hal H. Hopson). Psalm 8:1.
Wait on the Lord. Psalm 37:7.
Mueller, Carl F.
Create in Me a Clean Heart. Psalm 51:10-13.
The Lord Is My Shepherd. Psalm 23:00.
The One Hundredth Psalm. Psalm 100:00.
Whither Shall I Go from Thy Spirit. Psalm 139:00.
Mulligan, Harold Vincent.
Hear My Cry. Psalm 61:00.
Mullins, Rich.
Awesome God. Genesis 1:1-3.
The Just Shall Live (arr. Robert Sterling). Psalm 16:10.
That Where I Am, There You. . . John 14:1-6.
Murray, Jim and Daniel L. Schutte.
All My Days. Psalm 8:2-7.
Murray, Lyn.
When I Survey the Wondrous Cross. Galatians 6:14.
Myers, Gordon.
Beloved, Let Us Love One Another. I John 4:7-8.
Except the Lord Build the House. Psalm 127:1.
The Lord's Prayer. Matthew 6:9-13.
Thanksgiving. Revelation 5:13b.

Nagy, Russell.
And the Angel Said. Luke 1:27-31.
The Lord's Prayer. Matthew 6:9-13.
Naplan, Allan E.
Hine Ma Tov. Psalm 133:1.
Nazareth, Aniceto.
Without Seeing You. John 6:68.
Neidlinger, W. H.
He That Dwelleth in the Secret Place. Psalm 91:1, 9-11, 14, 16.
Nelhybel, Vaclav.
Be Not Far from Me. Psalm 22:11.
Blessed Is the Man. Psalm 1:00.
Hear Me When I Call. Psalm 25:4-5.
Hear My Voice. Psalm 61:1-2.
The Lord Is My Rock. Psalm 18:2.
Nelson, Greg and Bob Farrell (Sandi Patti Helvering).
Who Will Call Him Kings of Kings. Matthew 28:1-10.
Nelson, Greg and Phil McHugh.
Power in Jesus Name. Isaiah 45:23b.
Nelson, Jeff.
The Lord Is My Light. Psalm 27:1.
Nelson, Rachelle.
Ana Dodi. Song of Songs 2:10-11.
Nelson, Ronald A.
Angels. Psalm 91:11-12.
Hosanna! Matthew 21:9.
I Will Not Leave You Comfortless. John 14:18.
Let Thy Work Appear. Psalm 90:16-17a.
Not Two, But One. Matthew 19:6.
To You, O Lord, I Lift Up My Soul. Psalm 25:1a, 3-5, 19.
Nevin, George.
I Am the Good Shepherd. John 10:11-16.
Nibley, Reid.
Jesus, the Very Thought of Thee. Psalm 103:34 (based on).
Norbet, Gregory.
Mountains of My Soul. Psalm 121:1-2.
Shepherd Song. Psalm 23:00.
Those Who Hear My Words. John 12:24, 32, 35.
Norbet, Gregory and Mary David Callahan.
Wherever You Go. Ruth 1:16-17.
Nystedt, Knut.
Teach Me, O Lord. Psalm 119:33-35, 44-45, 171-172.
Tenebrae factae sunt. Matthew 27:45-46.
Nystrom, Martin.
As the Deer. Psalm 42:1-7.

O'Carroll, Fintan and Christopher Walker.
Celtic Alleluia. I John 4:8, 11-12, 16.
O'Connor, Roc.
Guide Me, O God (arr. Jeanne Cotter). Psalm 23:4.
In Praise of His Name. Psalm 100:4.
In the Shadow of Your Wings. Psalm 27:1, 4, 7-9, 13.
Jesus the Lord. Acts 17:28.
Lift Up Your Hearts. Psalm 66:1-6.
A Prayer for Mercy. Psalm 51:2-3, 10-12, 15.
Psalm Fifty-One. Psalm 51:2-3, 10-12, 15.
Trust in the Lord. Isaiah 40:28-31.
O'Connor-Morris, Geoffrey.
Psalm 91. Psalm 91:00.
Thanksgiving. Psalm 103:1-5, 19.
Olds, W. B.
The Bread of Life. John 6:00.
He Sent His Word and Healed Them. Psalm 107:20.
Ore, Charles W.
Answer Me When I Call. Psalm 4:00.
Blessed is the Man. Psalm 1:00.
The Lord is My Shepherd. Psalm 23:00.
Turn Thee Unto Me. Psalm 25:00.
Orland, Henry.
From Psalm 49. Psalm 49:00.
O'Shields, Michael.
I Will Call Upon the Lord. II Samuel 22:4.
The Lord Liveth. II Samuel 22:4.

Otte, Paul R.
Your Decrees Are My Song. Psalm 119:49-50, 54-56.
Overby, Rolf Peter.
Come, My Beloved. Song of Songs 7:11-13.
Overholt, Ray.
Ten Thousand Angels (arr. Tom Fettke). Matthew 26:47 through 27:1, 50.
Owens, Carol.
Freely, Freely. Matthew 10:8.
Owens, Jimmy.
Behold the Man. Isaiah 53:3.
Behold the Man (arr. Tom Fettke). Isaiah 53:3.
Clap Your Hands. Psalm 47:1.
If My People Will Pray. II Chronicles 7:14.
Owens, Jimmy and Jamie Collins.
The Battle Belongs to the Lord. I Samuel 17:47.
Owens, Sam Batt.
Dominus regit me. Psalm 23:00.
Psalm 23. Psalm 23:00.
Oxley, Harrison.
Lord, How Gracious. Psalm 85:1-2, 10-13.

Pachelbel, Johann.
Deposuit potentes (arr. Jerald B. Stone). Luke 1:52.
Esurientes (arr. Jerald B. Stone). Luke 1:53.
Et misericordia (ed. Jerald B. Stone). Luke 1:53.
Sing to the Lord New Song. Psalm 98:1-3, 9.
Paer, Ferdinando.
Beatus vir. Psalm 111:00.
Page, Anna Laura.
Creation Will Be at Peace. Isaiah 11:6-9.
Hallelujah! Praise Ye the Lord. Psalm 150:2-6.
Paris, Harry Allen.
Behold, What Manner of Love. I John 3:1-3.
Paris, Twila.
Come Worship the Lord. Psalm 106:1.
Exalt the Name (with *He is Exalted*). Psalm 99:2-3.
He is Exalted. Psalm 99:2-3.
Holy is the Lord. Psalm 99:3.
How Beautiful. Isaiah 52:7-9.
You Have Been Good. Psalm 89:1.
Parker, Clifton.
Blessed is the People. Psalm 89:1, 15-16.
I Will Lift Up Mine Eyes Unto the Hills. Psalm 121:00.
If Thou Prepare Thine Heart. Job 11:13-19.
Parker, Harold.
Thou Visitest the Earth. Psalm 65:9.
Parker, Horatio W.
Glorious Jerusalem. Isaiah 40:1.
Parks, Marty.
The Love of Christ. Ephesians 3:18 (other).
Parry, C. H. H.
The Lord is Long-suffering. Psalm 103:8.
Pasternak, Velvel.
Above the Voices of Many Waters. Psalm 93:4.
And He Hath Put a New Song in My Mouth. Psalm 40:4.
And Thou Shalt Rejoice in Thy Feast. Deuteronomy 16:14.
Dignity and Honor Are Her Garb. Proverbs 31:25-28.
El n'komõs. Psalm 94:1-2.
Eshes Chayil. Proverbs 31:10-17.
God of Vengeance. Psalm 94:1-2.
How Goodly Are Your Tents. Numbers 24:5.
It Was Turned to the Contrary. Esther 9:1.
Kén bakõdesh. Psalm 63:2-3.
The Law of the Lord Is Perfect. Psalm 19:8-9.
L'Cho Ezbach, no. 1. Psalm 116:17.
Lift Up Your Heads. Psalm 24:7.
Ma Tõvu. Numbers 24:5.
Men of Blood and Deceit. Psalm 55:24.
Mikõlõs mayim. Psalm 93:4.
Offer the Sacrifices of Righteousness. Psalm 4:6-7.
The Offering of Judah and Jerusalem. Malachi 3:4.
Oz V'Hodor. Proverbs 31:25-28.
Revere the Lord, You, His Holy Ones. Psalm 29:11.
Sheb'shiflénu. Psalm 136:23.
Shiru Lonu. Psalm 137:3.
Sing Praise to God. Psalm 47:7.
Sing Us One of the Songs of Zion. Psalm 137:3.
So I Have Looked for Thee. Psalm 63:2-3.
S'u sh'orim. Psalm 24:7.
Tõras Hasem t'mimo, no. 2. Psalm 19:8-9.
Tõras Hasem t'mimo, no. 4. Psalm 19:8-9.
Vaani evtach boch. Psalm 55:24.
Vayitén b'fi shir chodosh. Psalm 40:4.
V'nahafõch, no. 1. Esther 9:1.
V'or'vo lashem. Malachi 3:4.
V'Somachto B;Chagecho, no. 1. Deuteronomy 16:14.
V'Somachto B;Chagecho, no. 2. Deuteronomy 16:14.
Who Remembered Us When We Were Downcast. Psalm 136:23.
A Woman of Worth. Proverbs 31:10-17.
Yiru Es Adõnoy. Psalm 29:11.
Zamru elõkim. Psalm 47:7.
Zivchu Zivché Tsedek. Psalm 4:6-7.
Patillo, Leon.
Cornerstone. Isaiah 9:6c.
Cornerstone (arr. Steven V. Taylor). Isaiah 9:6c.
Sing Unto the Lord (arr. Tom Fettke). Psalm 96:1-4.
Pearce, Almeda J.
When He Shall Come (arr. Paul Mickelson). Revelation 7:9-15.
Peery, Rob Roy.
God Shall Wipe Away All Tears. Revelation 21:3-4.
Psalm 23. Psalm 23:00.
Where Pastures Green Invite. Psalm 23:00.
Peeters, Flor.
Ave Maria. Luke 1:28, 30-31, 42.
Hail Mary. Luke 1:28, 30-31, 42.
The Lord's Prayer. Matthew 6:9-13.
Pater Noster. Matthew 6:9-13.
Wedding Song. Ruth 1:16-17.
Peloquin, C. Alexander.
I Believe That My Redeemer Lives. Job 19:25-26.
Pelz, Walter L.
Happy Are They Who Dwell in Your House. Psalm 84:3-4, 10-12.
Our Soul Waits for the Lord. Psalm 33:20-22.
Pendleton, Emmet.
Christ Is Lord. Isaiah 9:6.
The Kingdom of God. Matthew 6:33.
Sing unto the Lord. Psalm 50:14.
Song of Ruth. Ruth 1:16-17.
Penhorwood, Edwin.
The Greatest of These Is Love. I Corinthians 13:00.
Penn, Marilyn.
Psalm 93. Psalm 93:00.
Thy Will Be Done. Matthew 6:9-13.
Pergolesi, Giovanni B.
Agnus Dei (ed. and arr. Michael Burkhardt). John 1:29.
Benedictus qui vent (ed. Francesco Cafarelli). Matthew 21:9.

Glory to God (ed. and arr. Michael Burkhardt. Luke 2:14.
Inflammatus et accensus (ed. and arr. Michael Burkahrdt). Luke 2:14.
O Lord, Have Mercy Upon Me. Psalm 10:00.
Sing to the Lord God (ed. and arr. Michael Burkhardt). Psalm 96:1-4.
Perry, Dave and Jean Perry.
Psalm 150. Psalm 150:1-3, 5-6.
Perry, Julian.
How Beautiful Are the Feet. Isaiah 52:7.
Peter, Johann Friedrich.
The Days of All Thy Sorrow (ed. and arr. Thor Johnson and Donald M. McCorkle). Isaiah 60:20.
Der Herr ist in seinem heiligen Temple. Habakkuk 2:20.
I Will Always Trust the Lord (ed. and arr. Karl Kroeger). Psalm 71:14.
I Will Make an Everlasting Covenant (ed. and arr. Thor Johnson and Donald M. McCorkle). Isaiah 55:3.
Ich will immer Harren (ed. and arr. Karl Kroeger). Psalm 71:14.
Ich will mit euch einen ewigen Bund machen (ed. and arr. Thor Johnson and Donald M. McCorkle). Isaiah 55:3.
Lead Me in the Truth. Psalm 25:5.
Leite mich in Deiner Wahrheit. Psalm 25:5.
The Lord is in His Holy Temple. Habakkuk 2:20.
Die Tage Deines Leides (ed. and arr. Thor Johnson and Donald M. McCorkle). Isaiah 60:20.
Peterson, John W.
Come, Holy Spirit (arr. Tom Fettke). Acts 1:8.
Peterson, John W. and Alfred B. Smith.
Surely Goodness and Mercy. Psalm 23:6.
Pethel, Stan.
Sing a New Song. Psalm 149:3.
We Have Seen the Risen Lord. John 20:25.
Petree, Larry and Arlie Petree.
Lazarus, Come Forth. John 11:43.
Pfleuger, Carl.
How Long Wilt Thou Forget Me? Psalm 13:1, 3, 5.
O Salutaris. Psalm 13:1, 3, 5.
Phillips, Leslie.
By My Spirit. Zechariah 4:6.
Phillips, Louis Baker.
Lord, Thou Hast Been Our Dwelling Place. Psalm 90:00.
Phillips, Madalyn.
He is Risen, as He Said. Matthew 28:5-7.
Picket, Frederick.
All Flesh is Grass. Isaiah 40:6-8.
Pinkham, Daniel.
Ave Maria. Luke 1:28, 31.
But of the Times and the Seasons. I Thessalonians 5:1-6.
Go Thy Way, Eat Thy Bread With Joy. Ecclesiastes 9:7-9.
I Will Not Leave You Comfortless. John 14:18, 28.
Let the Word of Christ Dwell in You. Colossians 3:16.
Magnificat. Luke 1:46-55.
Man That is Born of a Woman. Job 14:1-2.
Now it is High Time to Awake. Romans 13:11-12.
Nunc Dimittis. Luke 2:29-32.
Psalm 79. Psalm 80:00.
Rejoice in the Lord Alway. Philippians 4:4-7.
To Everything There Is a Season. Ecclesiastes 3:1-8.
Vanity of Vanities. Ecclesiastes 1:2.
Wedding Song. Song of Songs 8:6-7.
Wherefore Seeing. Hebrews 12:1-2.
Who Shall Separate Us from the Love of Christ. Romans 8:35, 37-39.
Pisk, Paul A.
Lamentation. Jeremiah 5:15-22.
Solomon's Prayer. II Chronicles 6:14, 19-21.
The Spirit of God. II Corinthians 3:9-12.
Plantavsky, Peter.
Hannu und Eli. I Samuel 1:00.
Pohle, David.
Wie der Hirsch schreyet (ed. Helmet Winter). Psalm 42:1-2, 12.
Pooler, Marie.
The Lord's My Shepherd. Psalm 23:00.
My Shepherd Will Supply My Need. Psalm 23:00.
Portugal, Rabbi E.
All Those Who Take Refuge in Thee (arr. Velvel Pasternak). Psalm 5:12.
And the Lord Alone (arr. Velvel Pasternak). Isaiah 2:11.
Ho-ōse g'dōlōs (arr. Velvel Pasternak). Job 9:10.
The Jews Had Lightness (arr. Velvel Pasternak). Esther 8:16.
La-y'hudim, no. 1 (arr. Velvel Pasternak). Esther 8:16.
Nafshénu chik'so (arr. Velvel Pasternak). Psalm 33:20-21.
Our Soul Hath Waited for the Lord (arr. Velvel Pasternak). Psalm 33:20-21.
This is the Day Which the Lord Has Made (arr. Velvel Pasternak). Psalm 118:24.
V'nisgov (arr. Velvel Pasternak). Isaiah 2:11.
V'yism'chu chol chōsé voch (arr. Velvel Pasternak). Psalm 5:12.
Who Does Great Things (arr. Velvel Pasternak). Job 9:10.
Ze Hayōm (arr. Velvel Pasternak). Psalm 118:24.
Posch, Isaac.
Confitebor tibi Domine. Psalm 111:00.
Domine ne in furore tuo. Psalm 6:00.
Ecco Dominus veniet. Zechariah 9:9.
Exsultate justi in Domino. Psalm 33:00.
Magnificat. Luke 1:46-55.
Quemamodum desiderat. Psalm 42:00.
Pote, Allen.
I Am the Vine (arr. Dale Wood). John 15:5-6, 12.
Praise the Lord, O My Soul for Guidance. Psalm 25:4-7.
Poterack, Kurt.
Magnificat. Luke 1:46-55.
Poulsen, James.
Entreat Me Not to Leave You. Ruth 1:16-17.
Powell, Robert J.
Blessed Are Those Who Fear the Lord. Psalm 128:1.
How Long Wilt Thou Forget Me? Psalm 13:1-6.
I Will Sing of the Mercies of the Lord. Psalm 89:1, 5, 8-9, 11, 14-15.
O Give Thanks. Psalm 107:1-2, 43.
Our Heart Shall Rejoice in the Lord. Psalm 33:21.
Praise the Lord, All Ye Nations. Psalm 117:00.
Sing Praises to Our God. Psalm 147:1, 5a, 7a, 12a.
Surely the Lord Is in This Place. Genesis 28:16-17.
Walk in Love. Ephesians 5:2, 8, 11, 15, 19.
The Wisdom, Riches and Knowledge of God. Romans 11:33-36.
Powers, George.
Create in Me. Psalm 51:10-12, 15.
Powers, Margaret Westlake.
Be Still, and Know. Psalm 46:1-6, 10.
Prince, Nolene.
Holy, Holy, Holy Is the Lord of Hosts. Isaiah 6:3.

Protheroe, Daniel.
A Song of Redemption. Isaiah 1:18.
Proulx, Richard.
Ar nathir. Matthew 6:9-13.
Beloved, Let Us Love. I John 4:7-8.
From Whence Shall Come My Help? Psalm 121:00.
I Rejoiced. Psalm 122:00.
The Lord's Prayer. Matthew 6:9-13.
Psalm 121. Psalm 121:00.
Psalm 122. Psalm 122:00.
Wedding Song from Colossians. Colossians 3:15-17.
Purcell, Henry.
The Blessed Virgin's Expostulation. Luke 2:42.
Blow Ye the Trumpet. Joel 2:15.
Lord, What Is Man. Hebrews 2:6.
Loving Kindness. Psalm 36:7-10.
O Lord, Rebuke Me Not. Psalm 6:1-4.
Unto Thee Will I Cry. Psalm 28:1.

Raff, Joseph J.
Behold, the House of God Is with Men. Revelation 21:3-4.
God, Hear My Voice. Psalm 27:7, 9.
Great and Wonderful Are All Thy Works. Revelation 15:3-4.
Thrust in Thy Sickle and Reap. Revelation 14:15-18.
Raigorodsky, Natalie.
I Will Lift Up Mine Eyes. Psalm 121:00.
Raksim, David.
Psalm on the Eve of Battle. Psalm 3:1-4.
Rambo, Dottie.
Behold the Lamb. John 1:29.
I Will Glory in the Cross (arr. Linn and Lyndell Leatherman). Galatians 6:14.
We Shall Behold Him. I Corinthians 15:52.
Rameau, J. P.
Ave Maria. Luke 1:28, 30-31, 42.
Hear Us, O Savior. Luke 1:28, 30-31, 42.
Randegger, Alberto.
Save Me, O God! Psalm 69:1, 3.
Ranzzini.
Lord, How Long Wilt Thou Forget Me? (ed. Gertrude Tingley). Psalm 13:00.
Read, Gardner.
Epistle to the Corinthians. I Corinthians 13:00.
Rebbi of Chernowitzer.
Eso énai, no. 2 (arr. Velvel Pasternak). Psalm 121:1-4.
I Will Lift Up Mine Eyes (arr. Velvel Pasternak). Psalm 121:1-4.
Rebbi of Kaley.
It is Good to Give Thanks (arr. Velvel Pasternak). Psalm 92:2-16.
Tō l'hōdōs (arr. Velvel Pasternak). Psalm 92:2-16.
Redman, Matt.
Better Is One Day. Psalm 84:10.
Reese, Dorothy Dasch.
Let Not Your Heart Be Troubled. John 14:1-2, 27.
Reeves, Jeff.
Sing unto the Lord. Psalm 96:1-4, 7-9.
Reger, Max.
Wohl denen, die Ohne Tadel leben. Psalm 119:1-5, 8.
Reiff, Stanley T.
Let Not Your Heart Be Troubled. John 14:1-3.
Reinthaler, C.
The Lord Will Not Be Ever Wroth. Deuteronomy 4:29.
Why Art Thou Cast Down, O My Soul? Psalm 42:5.
Repp, Ray.
I Lift Up My Eyes. Psalm 121:00.
Revicki, Robert.
Dominus Illuminatis Mea. Psalm 27:1.
The Lord Is My Light and Salvation. Psalm 27:1.
Reznick, Hyman.
A Seal upon Thy Heart. Song of Songs 8:6-7.
Rheinberger, Josef.
Ave Maria. Luke 1:28, 30-31, 42.
Richards, Stephen.
By the Waters of Babylon. Psalm 137:00.
A Lily Among Thorns. Song of Songs 2:2-3.
Psalm 137. Psalm 137:00.
Richner, Thomas.
Rise Up and Walk. Acts 3:1-3.
Riddle, Peter.
Psalm XXIII. Psalm 23:00.
Rider, Dale G.
Every Good and Perfect Gift. James 1:17-22.
Rider, Lucy.
Come, Every One Who is Thirsty. Isaiah 55:1.
Ridge, M. D.
The Greatest of These Is Love. I Corinthians 13:1-8.
Parable. Ecclesiastes 3:1-9.
Praise the Lord. Psalm 113:1-5, 7-9.
Psalm 113. Psalm 113:1-5, 7-9.
Rieth, Mildred F.
Bless Yahweh, O My Soul. Psalm 104:1, 3a, 19, 29.
God, Make a Heart in Me. Psalm 51:10-12, 15.
I Will Bless Yahweh. Psalm 34:1.
Mary's Song. Luke 1:46-55.
O God, You Are My God. Psalm 63:1-5.
O Lord, I Have Waited. Psalm 40:1-10.
Praise the Lord. Psalm 146:1-6.
Yahweh Is My Shepherd. Psalm 23:00.
Riker, Franklin.
Create in Me a Clean Heart, O Lord. Psalm 51:10-15.
Hear, O Heavens, and Give Ear O Earth. Isaiah 1:2, 4, 18-19.
Roberts, J. E.
God Is a Spirit. John 4:23-24.
If With All Your Hearts. Deuteronomy 4:29.
Roberts, John Varley.
Brood O'er Us. Genesis 1:3.
Love. Genesis 1:3.
Peace I Leave with You. John 14:27.
Seek Ye the Lord. Isaiah 55:6-7.
Robinson, McNeil.
In the Beginning Was the Word. John 1:1-14.
Robison, P.
Make a Joyful Noise. Psalm 100:00.
Robyn, Alfred G.
I Sought the Lord. Psalm 34:4.
Let the Words of My Mouth. Psalm 19:15.
Wilt Thou Not Receive Us Again. Psalm 85:6-11.
Rochberg, George.
Behold! Thou Art Fair. Song of Songs 4:1.
Come, My Beloved. Song of Songs 7:11.
Rise Up My Love. Song of Songs 2:10-13b.
Set Me as a Seal. Song of Songs 8:6-7.
Rodríguez, Bernardo.
Ave Maria (arr. Rick Modlin). Luke 1:28, 30-31, 42.
Roff, Joseph.
Entreat Me Not to Leave You. Ruth 1:16.
He Is Like a Tree. Psalm 1:1.

Make a Joyful Noise to the Lord. Psalm 98:4-6.
My Heart Is Steadfast. Psalm 108:1-4.
A Psalm of David. Psalm 108:1-4.
Sing Praise to the Lord. Psalm 149:1-3.
Wait for the Lord. Psalm 27:13-14.
Rogers, Bernard.
Psalm 68. Psalm 68:00.
Rogers, Dawn and Tricia Walker.
Baruch Hashem Adonai. Job 1:21a.
Rogers, Faith Helen.
Whoso Dwelleth in the Secret Place. Psalm 91:1, 5-7, 11-12.
Rogers, James H.
Great Peace Have They Which Love Thy Law. Psalm 119:165, 174-176.
How Long, O Lord, Wilt Thou Forget Me? Psalm 13:1.
Out of the Depths. Psalm 130:00.
They That Sow in Tears. Psalm 126:5-6.
Today If Ye Will Hear His Voice. Isaiah 63:5.
Rogers, Sharon Elery.
Song of Hosanna. Matthew 21:9.
Song of the Redeemed. Revelation 5:8-10.
A Song of Victory. Revelation 14:3.
Rohlig, Harald.
Teach Me Your Ways, Lord. Psalm 25:4-5.
Roma, Caro.
God Shall Wipe Away All Tears. Revelation 7:16.
The Lord's Prayer. Matthew 6:9-13.
Oh! For the Wings of a Dove. Psalm 55:6-7.
The Silent Voice. Psalm 46:10a.
Romer, Charles B.
New Heaven–New Earth (arr. Lyndell Leatherman). Revelation 21:1-7.
Prayer. Matthew 6:9-13.
Root, Frederic.
Love. Genesis 1:3.
Love Never Faileth. I Corinthians 13:00.
Rorem, Ned.
An Angel Speaks to the Shepherd. Luke 2:9-15.
Behold, Bless Ye the Lord. Psalm 134:00.
Gloria. Luke 2:14.
I Cried to the Lord. Psalm 142:00.
The Lord's Prayer. Matthew 6:9-13.
Mourning Scene. II Samuel 1:19-27.
Praise Ye the Lord. Psalm 148:00.
Praise Ye the Lord. Psalm 150:00.
Psalm 120. Psalm 120:00.
A Psalm of Praise. Psalm 100:00.
Resurrection. Matthew 27:28, 62-66.
A Song of David. Psalm 120:00.
Rosenblatt, Yossele.
Shir hamaalõs (arr. Velvel Pasternak). Psalm 126:1-3.
When the Lord Turned Again the Captivity of Zion (arr. Velvel Pasternak). Psalm 126:1-3.
Rosenmüller, Johann.
Der 134th Psalm. Psalm 134:1-4.
Lamentationes Jeremiae Prophetae. Jeremiah 1:1-5.
Ross, Barbara.
You Who Are Thirsty. Isaiah 55:1.
Rotermund, Melvin.
I Am the Resurrection and the Life. John 11:25-26.
Roth, John.
David's Song. Psalm 23:00.
God of Love Beyond All Wonder. Matthew 6:9-13.
Magnificat. Luke 1:46-55.
Roth, Robert N.
Jubilate Deo. Psalm 100:00.
Psalm 100. Psalm 100:00.
Row, Richard D.
I Will Not Leave You Comfortless. John 14:18-21.
Thy Right Hand Shall Hold Me. Psalm 138:00.
Rowan, William.
Prepare the Way of the Lord. Isaiah 40:4-5.
Rowberry, Robert Lee.
How Beautiful Thy Temples, Lord. Psalm 24:3-5 (based on).
I Stand All Amazed. Isaiah 53:4, 5 (based on).
O Galilee. Mark 4:30 (based on).
Rowley, Alec.
O That I Knew Where I Might Find Him. Job 23:3.
Rubbra, Edmund.
The Lord Is My Shepherd. Psalm 23:00.
O Lord, Rebuke Me Not. Psalm 6:00.
Praise Ye the Lord. Psalm 150:00.
Psalm 6. Psalm 6:00.
Psalm XXIII. Psalm 23:00.
Psalm 150. Psalm 150:00.
Rubenstein, Anton.
Comfort Ye My People (arr. Carl Fredrickson). Isaiah 40:1-3.
Give Me an Understanding Heart (arr. Carl Fredrickson). I Kings 3:9.
Rubin, Steffi.
A New Heaven and a New Earth. Revelation 21:1-7.
Rusk, Harriet.
The Lord Is My Shepherd. Psalm 23:00.
Psalm 23. Psalm 23:00.
Ruston, Kevin and Vince Nichols.
I Am the Keeper (arr. Malcom Archer). Isaiah 27:1-5.
Rutenber, C. B.
Come unto Me. Matthew 11:28-30.
I Will Lift Up Mine Eyes. Psalm 121:00.
Let Not Your Heart Be Troubled. John 14:1-3, 19, 20.
Ryder, Dennis.
First John 4:7 and 8. I John 4:7-8.

Sacco, John.
God's Time. Psalm 27:13-14.
Sacco, Peter.
Blessed Are the Peacemakers. Matthew 5:9-10.
Keep Not Thou Silence, O God. Psalm 83:00.
O Lord, How Long Wilt Thou Forget Me. Psalm 13:00.
The Sorrows of Death Compassed Me. Psalm 18:00.
Saint-Saëns, Camille.
Ave Maria. Luke 1:28, 30-31, 42.
Come Blessed Savior. Luke 1:28, 30-31, 42.
Domine, Domine, Adjutor meus. Psalm 19:14b.
Expectans Expectavi Dominum. Psalm 40:1.
I Waited for the Lord (arr. K. Lee Scott). Psalm 40:1.
Patiently Have I Waited for the Lord (arr. K. Lee Scott). Psalm 40:1.
Patiently I Awaited Christ the Lord. Psalm 40:1.
Thou, O Lord, Art My Protector. Psalm 19:14b.
Saltzman, Peter.
Bind Me as a Seal Upon Your Heart. Song of Songs 8:6.
I Am in the Fever of Love. Song of Songs 2:4.
I Am the Rose of Sharon. Song of Songs 2:1.
I Longed for My Love. Song of Songs 3:1-2.
Kiss Me, Make Me Drunk With Your Kisses. Song of Songs 1:2.

Samama, Leo.
My Beloved Spake. Song of Songs 2:10-13.
Thou Hast Ravished My Heart. Song of Songs 3:9-11.
Wedding Cantata. Song of Songs 4:9-11.
Whither Thou Goest. Ruth 1:16-17.
Sandresky, Margaret.
My Soul Doth Magnify. Luke 1:46-47.
Sands, Ernest.
Song of Farewell. Psalm 27:1, 4, 7, 9, 13.
Sankey, Ira D.
The Ninety and Nine (arr. O. D. Hall, Jr.). Luke 15:4-7.
Savioni, Mario.
Magnificat. Luke 1:46-47.
Scarlatti, Alessandro.
Come unto Me. Matthew 7:7-8.
Schack, David.
The Lord Is My Shepherd. Psalm 23:00.
Schalit, Heinrich.
Eili, Eili! Invocation (adapted Kurt Schindler). Psalm 22:2.
O Lord, Return. Psalm 6:00.
Schalk, Carl.
Be Joyful in the Lord, All You Lands. Psalm 100:1.
Go Therefore and Make Disciples of All Nations. Matthew 28:19-20.
Schein, Johann Hermann.
An wasserflüsswen Babylon. Psalm 137:00.
Magnificat anima mea Dominum (ed. Paul Horn). Luke 1:46-47.
Magnificat anima mea Dominum. Luke 1:46-55.
Schiavone, John.
Happy Are You Who Fear the Lord. Psalm 128:00.
Schiller, Benjie Ellen.
Zeh Dodi. Song of Songs 5:16.
Schilling, Hans Ludwig.
Psalm 150 in the form of a Ciacona. Psalm 150:00.
Schinhan, Jan Philip.
Whither Shall I Go from Thy Spirit. Psalm 139:00.
Schlösser, Adolphe.
He That Keepeth Israel. Psalm 91:11.
Schmutz, Albert D.
Arise, Shine, for Thy Light Is Come. Isaiah 60:1-3, 18-19.
Hast Thou Not Known. Isaiah 40:28-31.
I Will Extol Thee. Psalm 145:00.
And in That day Thou Shalt Say. Isaiah 12:00.
Schnecker, P. A.
In His Hands Are All the Corners of the Earth. Psalm 95:4, 6.
Rejoice in the Lord. Psalm 33:1-2, 4-5.
Schockman, Gregg.
Psalm 103. Psalm 103:00.
Schoenbachler, Tim.
Babylon. Psalm 137:00.
Forever I Will Sing. Psalm 89:00.
Glory to God (arr. Sheryl Soderberg). Luke 2:14.
Happy Are They. Psalm 1:00.
Here I Am, Send Me. Psalm 3:00.
I Will Bless the Lord. Psalm 34:1-5, 8.
Send Out Your Spirit (arr. Sheryl Soderberg). Psalm 104:00.
Taste and See. Psalm 34:1-5, 8.
This Is the Day. Psalm 118:24.
Scholtes, Peter.
Holy, Holy, Holy. Isaiah 6:3.
Scholz, Robert.
Set Me as a Seal. Song of Songs 8:6-7.
Schram, Ruth Elaine.
Vanished Like a Vapor. James 4:14.
Schubert, Franz.
Ave Maria. Luke 1:28, 30-31, 42.
The Good Shepherd (arr. Carl Fredrickson). Psalm 23:00.
The Grand Alleluia. I Chronicles 16:29.
The Grand Alleluia (arr. Carl Fredrickson). I Chronicles 16:29.
The Lord Is My Shepherd (arr. K. K. Davis). Psalm 23:00.
Peace Be unto You. Isaiah 26:3.
Schultz, A. L.
Suffer the Little Children. Matthew 19:14.
Schutte, Daniel L.
Before the Sun Burned Bright. Jeremiah 1:4-10.
Behold the Wood. John 12:24, 32.
Blessed Are You. Genesis 48:16.
Blest Be the Lord. Psalm 91:2-7, 10.
City of God. Isaiah 9:6.
Come to Me All Who Are Weary. Matthew 9:11-13.
Come with Me into the Fields. Matthew 9:39.
Ever On My Lips (arr. Bob Harrold). Psalm 34:1.
Give Thanks to the Lord (arr. Randall DeBruyn). Psalm 136:1-4.
Glory and Praise to Our God. Psalm 65:00.
Happy Are the Ones. Psalm 89:15, 18.
Here I Am, Lord. Isaiah 6:8.
How Long, O Lord (arr. Randall DeBruyn). Psalm 13:1.
I Found the Treasure. Matthew 13:44-45.
If the Lord Does Not Build. Psalm 27:00.
Like Cedars They Shall Stand (arr. Randall deBruyn). Psalm 92:1-7, 10, 12-13.
Like the Deer. Psalm 42:1-3.
Lover of Us All. Ephesians 2:7-18.
May the Angels. Luke 24:5.
Meadows and Mountains. Daniel 3:51-90.
My Soul Thirsts. Psalm 63:1-7.
Only This I Want (arr. John B. Foley). Philippians 2:15, 18.
Psalm 150. Psalm 150:00.
Servant Song. Isaiah 49:1-7.
Sing a New Song. Psalm 98:1a, 6.
Though the Mountains May Fall. Isaiah 40:31-32.
Valleys of Green. Psalm 23:00.
What You Hear in the Dark. Matthew 5:13-14.
With Merry Dancing. Psalm 150:1-5.
Yahweh, the Faithful One. Genesis 12:1-2.
You Are Near. Psalm 139:2-8, 13-15, 17-18.
Schutte, Daniel L. and Jim Murray.
All My Days. Psalm 8:2-7.
Schütz, Heinrich.
Angel's Message to the Shepherds. Luke 2:8-13.
Attendite, popule meus, legem meam. Psalm 78:1-3.
Be Not Afraid. Luke 2:10-12.
Blessed Are They. Psalm 1:1-3.
Bring to Jehovah. Psalm 29:1-2.
Bringt her dem Herren. Psalm 29:1-2.
Bringt her dem Herren (arr. Robert Ross). Psalm 29:1-2.
Cantabo Domino in vita mea. Psalm 104:103.
Daily Will I Love Thee. Psalm 18:2-7.
Der Herr ist gross. Psalm 145:3-4.
Eile, mich Gott, zu erretten. Psalm 40:14-18.
Einbitte ich vom Herren. Psalm 27:4.
Erhöre mich, Wenn ich rufe. Psalm 4:2.
Exultavit cor meum. I Samuel 2:1-2.
Feurchte dich nicht. Isaiah 41:10.

Fili mi, Absalom. II Samuel 18:33.
Frohlocket mit Händen. Psalm 47:1-6.
Give God, the Father, Praise. Psalm 29:1-2.
Great Is the Lord (arr. Don McAfee). Psalm 145:3-4.
Habe deine Lust an dem Herren. Psalm 37:1-5.
Haste Thee, Lord God, Haste to Save Me. Psalm 40:14-18.
Hear Me, O Lord. Psalm 4:1.
Der Herr ist mein Licht und mein Heil. Psalm 27:1.
Herr, ich hoffe darauf. Psalm 13:5-6.
Der Herr ist gross (arr. Don McAfee). Psalm 145:3-4.
Der Herr ist gross und sehr löblich. Psalm 145:3, 4.
Herr, nun lassert du deinen, Diener im Friede fahren. Luke 2:29-30.
Der Herr schauet vom Himmel auf der Menschen Kinder. Psalm 14:2, 3.
Herzlich Lieb hab ich dich. Psalm 18:2-7.
Heutet euch. Luke 21:34-36.
Hodie Chistus natus est. Luke 2:11.
I Bow and Bend the Knee. Ephesians 3:14-15.
I Have Been a Young Man and Now Am Aged. Psalm 37:25.
I Will Bless the Lord at All Times. Psalm 34:2-7.
Ich beuge meine Knie. Ephesians 3:14-15.
Ich bin jung gewesen. Psalm 37:25.
Ich danke dem Herren. Psalm 111:00.
Ich danke dem Herren loben allezeit. Psalm 34:1-7.
Ich, Liege und Schlafe. Psalm 3:6-9.
Ich will den Herren loben allezeit. Psalm 34:2-7.
Ihr Heiligen, lobsinget dem Herren. Psalm 30:5-6.
In Te, Domine, Speravi. Psalm 31:2-3.
Jubilate deo omnis terra. Psalm 100:00.
Kleines Geistliches Concert. Psalm 4:1.
Lobet den Herren, der zu Zion wohnet. Psalm 9:11-12.
Lord, Create in Me a Clean Heart. Psalm 51:10-12.
Lord, My Trust Is in Thee. Psalm 13:5-6.
Master, Though Laboring All the Night and Toiling Here. Luke 5:5.
Mein Herz ist bereit. Psalm 57:00.
Meine Seele erhebt den Herren. Luke 1:46-47.
Meine Seele, Warum Hast du uns das getan? Luke 2:48-49.
Meister, wir habe die ganze Nacht gearbeitet. Luke 5:5.
My Son, Wherefore Hast Thou Done This to Us? Luke 2:48-49.
Now Will I Praise the Lord with All My Heart. Psalm 34:1-7.
O God, I Will Praise Thee. Psalm 111:00.
O Holy Ones, Sing Praise. Psalm 30:5-6.
One Thing I Ask of the Lord. Psalm 27:4.
Paratum cor meum. Psalm 107:2-4.
Praise to the Lord God. Psalm 9:11-12.
Praise Ye Jehovah. Psalm 9:11-12.
Praise Ye the Lord. Psalm 30:5-6.
A Psalm of David. Psalm 70:00.
Recitative and Angel's Message to the Shepherds. Luke 2:8-14.
Sacred Concert. Psalm 4:1.
Schaffe in mir, Gott, ein reines Herz. Psalm 51:10-12.
Singet dem Herrn ein neues Leid. Psalm 96:1-4.
To God the Father (arr. Robert Ross). Psalm 29:1-2.
Venite ad Me. Matthew 11:28-30.
Wedding Song. Ruth 1:16.
Wedding Song. Ruth 1:16-17.
Wohl dem der nicht wandelt. Psalm 1:1-3.
Zur Trauung. Ruth 1:16-17.

Schwarz, May.
Magnificat. Luke 1:46-55.
Schweizer, Rolf.
How Good to Offer Thanks. Psalm 92:1-5.
Scott, Charles P.
God Is a Spirit. John 4:23-24.
Suffer the Little Children. Luke 18:15-16.
The Voice of Joy. Psalm 118:14-15.
When I Remember Thee. Psalm 63:5-6.
Scott, John Prindle.
Angels Roll the Rock Away. Matthew 28:5-6.
Arise, Shine. Isaiah 60:00.
Christ is Risen. I Corinthians 5:7-8.
Come Ye Blessed. Matthew 25:34-36.
Consider the Lilies. Matthew 6:28-34.
Depart From Me. Matthew 25:41-45.
The First Easter Morn. Luke 24:00.
God Is a Spirit. John 4:23-24.
He Maketh Wars to Cease. Isaiah 2:4.
He Shall Give His Angel Charge. Psalm 91:1-2, 5-7, 11-12.
I Know in Whom I Have Believed. II Timothy 1:12.
Like as a Father. Psalm 103:13-17.
The Lord Is My Shepherd. Psalm 23:00.
The Messenger of Peace. Isaiah 52:00.
Out of the Depths. Psalm 130:00.
Remember Now Thy Creator. Ecclesiastes 12:1-7.
Repent Ye. Matthew 3:1-2, 7-8, 11-12.
There Were Shepherds. Luke 2:8-15.
Trust Ye in the Lord. Isaiah 26:3-4, 11-12.
The Voice in Wilderness. Isaiah 40:3, 6, 7, 8.
When I Consider the Heavens. Psalm 8:00.
Scott, K. Lee.
Set Me as a Seal. Song of Songs 8:6-7.
Scrivener, Joseph.
Psalm 139. Psalm 139:00.
Scruggs, Randy.
Tell the World That Jesus Loves You. John 3:16.
Searcy, George.
Making War in the Heavenlies. II Corinthians 10:5.
Seaton, Annette.
Those Who Wait on the Lord. Psalm 62:1, 5-7.
Secchi, Antonio.
Bow Down Your Ear. Isaiah 55:00.
Lift Up Your Heads, O Ye Gates! Psalm 24:7-8, 10.
Sedio, Mark.
Teach Me Your Way, O Lord. Psalm 86:11.
Seeger, Charles.
Psalm 137. Psalm 137:00.
Selby, Peter H.
Give Ear Oh Ye Heaven. Deuteronomy 32:1-4, 9-12.
Selby, William.
The Heavens Declare Thy Glory (arr. Barbara Owen). Psalm 19:1.
Selle, Thomas.
Aus der Tiefe. Psalm 130:00.
Herr, wo soll ich hingehen. Psalm 139:7-12.
Ich taufe mit Wasser. John 1:26-27.
Sessions, Roger.
Psalm 140. Psalm 140:00.
Shafferman, Jean Anne and George C. Strattner.
A Lenten Lesson. Matthew 26:36-39, 42.
Shapiro, Rabbi N.
If I say, "My foot slippeth" (arr. Velvel Pasternak). Psalm 94:18.
Im omarti, no. 2 (arr. Velvel Pasternak). Psalm 94:18.

Shapiro, Rabbi Y.
Asé imonu ōs (arr. Velvel Pasternak). Psalm 86:17.
Rejoice Ye With Jerusalem (arr. Velvel Pasternak). Isaiah 66:10.
Simchu es y'rusholayim (arr. Velvel Pasternak). Isaiah 66:10.
Work in Our Behalf a Sign for Good (arr. Velvel Pasternak). Psalm 86:17.
Sharlin, William.
Shir Hashirim. Song of Songs 1:1-2.
Song of Songs. Song of Songs 1:1-2.
Shaw, Martin.
With a Voice of Singing. Isaiah 48:20.
With a Voice of Singing (arr. Jacobson, Maurice). Isaiah 48:20.
Shawn, Allen.
Thou Wilt Keep Him in Perfect Peace. Isaiah 26:3-4.
Sheatz, Elizabeth Q.
The Lord's Prayer. Matthew 6:9-13.
Shelley, Harry Rowe.
And I, John, Saw the Holy City. Revelation 21:1-3.
He That Dwelleth in the Secret Place. Psalm 91:1-2.
I Am Alpha and Omega. Revelation 1:8.
I Jesus, Have Sent Mine Angel. Revelation 22:14, 16.
The King of Love My Shepherd Is. Psalm 23:00.
Shenk, Louis.
The Lord's Prayer. Matthew 6:9-13.
Sheppard, Tim.
Me and My House. Joshua 24:15.
Sherman, Arnold B.
Let Us Love One Another (arr. Dale Wood). I John 4:7-11.
Sibelius, Jean.
The Lord's Prayer (arr. Richard D. Row). Matthew 6:9-13.
Siegel, Arsene.
Keep Thou Not Silence, O God. Psalm 83:1-5, 13-15, 18.
Sifler, Paul.
De Profundis. Psalm 130:00.
Silvia, Giulio.
Benedictus. Matthew 21:9.
Singer, Guy.
Whither Thou Goest. Ruth 1:16-17.
Sinzheimer, Max.
Blessed Are Those Who Fear the Lord. Psalm 128:00.
Sisler, Hampson, A.
Every Good and Perfect Gift. James 1:16-17, 19-20, 22, 25, 27.
Skillings, Otis.
Canticle of the Virgin. Luke 1:46-55.
Mary's Magnificat. Luke 1:46-55.
Whatever Is True. Philippians 4:8-9.
Slater, Jean.
From All That Dwell Below the Skies. Psalm 117:00.
Sleeth, Natalie.
Consider the Lilies. Matthew 6:25-32.
Psalm. Psalm 121:1-2.
Sing a New Song to the Lord. Psalm 98:1a, 4-6.
Smart, Henry.
As Pants the Hart (arr. L. Kessler). Psalm 42:1-2.
The Lord Is My Shepherd. Psalm 23:00.
Smiley, Billy and Bill George.
Worship the King. Psalm 145:1-13.
Smith, G. Alan.
Because You Are God's Chosen Ones. Colossians 3:12-17.
The Lord Comes. Matthew 21:9.
Smith, Gregg.
The Lord Bless Thee and Keep Thee. Numbers 6:24.
The Lord Is My Shepherd. Psalm 23:00.
Smith, Jeffrey.
Psalm 103. Psalm 103:1-5, 11, 17a.
Smith, L.
Psalm 42. Psalm 42:00.
Smith, Leonard E. Jr.
Our God Reigns. Isaiah 52:7.
Smith, Marcus.
Evening Song. Matthew 16:25 (based on).
Home, Dost Thou Beckon? II Corinthians 5:1 (based on).
Softly Beams the Sacred Dawning. Matthew 24:27 (based on).
Smith, Michael W.
Agnus Dei. Revelation 5:12-13.
As It Is in Heaven (The Lord's Prayer). Matthew 6:9-13.
How Majestic Is Your Name. Psalm 8:9.
How Majestic Is Your Name (arr. Tom Fettke). Psalm 8:9.
How Majestic Is Your Name (with *Holy, Holy*) (arr. Steven V. Taylor). Psalm 8:9.
I Am. John 11:25.
Jude Doxology. Jude 1:24-25.
Magnify the Lord. Psalm 34:00.
Sing unto Him. Psalm 105:1-3.
Thy Word (arr. Steven V. Taylor). Psalm 119:105.
Smith, Michael W. and Amy Grant.
Thy Word. Psalm 119:105.
Smith, Michael W. and Gary Moore.
The Throne. Revelation 5:13.
Smith, Michael W. and Deborah D. Smith.
Could He Be the Messiah. Matthew 14:17-21.
Great Is the Lord (arr. Steven V. Taylor). Psalm 145:3a.
Hosanna (arr. Steven V. Taylor). Matthew 21:9.
Smith, Michael W. and Deborah D. Smith, Debbie and Brown Bannister.
Holy, Holy. Isaiah 6:3.
Smith, Timothy Whitworth.
The Twenty-Third Psalm. Psalm 23:00.
Snyder, Virginia.
Let Not Your Heart Be Troubled. John 14:1-3.
Soler, Hanns.
Ave Maria. Luke 1:28, 30-31.
Soler, Joseph.
An ignoratis quia quicumque. Romans 6:3-4.
Fraters: Si Consurrexistis cum Christo. Colossians 3:1-4.
Sonnenberg, Lorraine.
Now Unto the King Eternal. I Timothy 1:17.
Soper, Scott.
I Know That My Redeemer Lives. Job 19:25a.
I Will Always Thank the Lord. Psalm 34:1.
Sowerby, Leo.
Hear My Cry, O God. Psalm 61:1-5, 8.
How Long Wilt Thou Forget Me? Psalm 13:1-6.
I Will Lift Up Mine Eyes. Psalm 121:00.
I Will Lift Up Mine Eyes (arr. John Delorey and Ronald Stalford). Psalm 121:00.
The Lord Is My Shepherd. Psalm 23:00.
O Be Joyful in the Lord. Psalm 100:00.
Psalm 91. Psalm 91:00.
Psalm 100. Psalm 100:00.

Psalm 121. Psalm 121:00.
Psalm 142. Psalm 142:00.
Whoso Dwelleth. Psalm 91:00.
Speaks, Oley.
By Waters of Babylon. Psalm 137:1-5.
Easter Song. Matthew 28:1-6.
How Long Wilt Thou Forget Me? Psalm 13:1, 3, 5.
In the End of the Sabbath. Matthew 28:1-6.
Let Not Your Heart Be Troubled. John 14:1, 27.
The Lord Is My Light. Psalm 27:00.
Thou Wilt Keep Him in Perfect Peace. Isaiah 26:3.
Speir, Randy.
In Him We Live. Psalm 66:1-2.
Spence, William.
The King of Love My Shepherd Is. Psalm 23:00.
Spicker, Max.
In Thee, O God, Do I Put My Trust. Psalm 71:1, 9, 12, 18.
Why Art Thou Cast Down, O My Soul? Psalm 42:5.
Spies, Claudio.
Blessed is the Man. Psalm 1:1-3.
I Will Lift Up Mine Eyes Unto the Hills. Psalm 121:1-8.
I Will Praise Thee, O Lord. Psalm 9:1-2.
O Sing Unto the Lord. Psalm 96:1-3.
Praise the Lord, O My Soul. Psalm 146:1-2.
Spiritual.
Balm in Gilead (arr. Harry T. Burleigh). Jeremiah 8:22 (based on).
Balm in Gilead (arr. William Dawson). Jeremiah 8:22 (based on).
Balm in Gilead (arr. Mark Hayes). Jeremiah 8:22 (based on).
Balm in Gilead (arr. Hall Johnson). Jeremiah 8:22 (based on).
Chariot's Comin' (arr. Jean Anne Shafferman). II Kings 2:11 (based on).
De Blin' Man Stood On De Road An' Cried (arr. Harry T. Burleigh). Mark 10:46, 52 (based on).
Didn't My Lord Deliver Daniel? (arr. Edward Boatner). Daniel 6:22 (based on).
Didn't My Lord Deliver Daniel? (arr. Harry T. Burleigh. Daniel 6:22 (based on).
Don't You Weep When I'm Gone (arr. Harry T. Burleigh). Jeremiah 22:10 (based on).
Ezek'el Saw the Wheel (arr. Margaret Bonds). Ezekiel 1:15 (based on).
Go Down, Moses (arr. Edward Boatner). Exodus 8:1 (based on).
Go Down, Moses (arr. Harry T. Burleigh). Exodus 8:1 (based on).
Go Down, Moses (arr. Michael Johnson). Exodus 8:1 (based on).
Hard Trials (arr. Harry T. Burleigh). Matthew 8:20 (based on).
He's Jus' De Same Today (arr. Harry T. Burleigh). Exodus 14:22 (based on).
I Don't Feel No-Ways Tired (arr. Harry T. Burleigh). Hebrews 11:14 (based on).
I Know De Lord's Laid His Hands On Me (arr. Harry T. Burleigh). Matthew 19:15 (based on).
I Know the Lord Laid His Hands On Me (arr. Edward Boatner). Luke 4:40 (based on).
I Want to Be Ready (arr. Harry T. Burleigh). Acts 2:00 (based on).
John's Gone Down On De Island (arr. Harry T. Burleigh). Revelation 1:00 (based on).
Joshua Fit Da Battle of Jericho (arr. Bond). Joshua 6:00 (based on).
Joshua Fit Da Battle of Jericho (arr. Harry T. Burleigh). Joshua 6:00 (based on).
Joshua Fit Da Battle of Jericho (arr. Mark Hayes). Joshua 6:00 (based on).
Little David, Play On Your Harp (arr. Harry T. Burleigh). Exodus 8:1 (based on).
Lost Sheep (arr. Edward Boatner). Matthew 18:13 (based on).
My Lord, What a Morning (arr. Harry T. Burleigh). Revelation 8:10 (based on).
My Lord, What a Morning (arr. William Dawson). Revelation 8:10 (based on).
My Lord, What a Morning (arr. Mark Hayes). Revelation 8:10 (based on).
My Lord, What a Morning (arr. Hall Johnson). Revelation 8:10 (based on).
Oh, Didn't it Rain (arr. Harry T. Burleigh). Genesis 7:4 (based on).
Ride On, King Jesus (arr. Harry T. Burleigh). Revelation 6:2 (based on).
Ride On, King Jesus (arr. Hall Johnson). Revelation 6:2 (based on).
Swing Low, Sweet Chariot (arr. Edward Boatner). II Kings 2:11 (based on).
Swing Low, Sweet Chariot (arr. Harry T. Burleigh). II Kings 2:11 (based on).
Swing Low, Sweet Chariot (arr. Hall Johnson). II Kings 2:11 (based on).
Take My Mother Home (arr. Hall Johnson). John 19:26-27 (based on).
There Is a Balm in Gilead (arr. William Dawson). Jeremiah 8:22 (based on).
There Is a Balm in Gilead (arr. Mark Hayes). Jeremiah 8:22 (based on).
There Is a Balm in Gilead (arr. Hall Johnson. Jeremiah 8:22 (based on).
They Led My Lord Away (arr. Edward Boatner). Luke 22:54 (based on).
Twelve Gates into the City. Revelation 21:12-13, 22 (based on).
Weepin' Mary (arr. Harry T. Burleigh). John 20:11 (based on).
You Hear the Lambs A-Crying (arr. Edward Boatner). John 21:17 (based on).
You May Bury Me in De Eas' (arr. Harry T. Burleigh). I Corinthians 15:52 (based on).
Sprouse, Bill Jr.
Psalm 5. Psalm 5:1-3.
St. James, Rebecca.
Psalm 139 (arr. Dennis Allen). Psalm 139:1.
St. James, Rebecca and Matt Bronleewe.
For the Love of God. I Corinthians 13:1-3.
Stainer, John.
God So Loved the World. John 3:16-17.
God So Loved the World (arr. Carl Fredrickson). John 3:16-17.
God So Loved the World (arr. Carol McClure). John 3:16-17.
Stanford, Charles Villiers.
O Come Hither. Psalm 46:8-10.
A Song of Battle. Psalm 124:00.
A Song of Hope. Psalm 130:00.
A Song of Trust. Psalm 121:00.
A Song of Wisdom. Ecclesiasticus 24:3-7, 12-14.

Starer, Robert.
Give Thanks unto the Lord. Psalm 136:1-9.
Have Mercy upon Me, O Lord. Psalm 51:1.
Stearns, Peter Pindar.
Beloved, Now Are We the Sons of God. I John 3:2.
Bless the Lord, O My Soul. Psalm 104:1, 24.
Eye Hath Not Seen. I Corinthians 2:9.
I Will Lift Up Mine Eyes. Psalm 121:00.
The Lord Is My Shepherd. Psalm 23:00.
Stearns, Theodore.
I Lift Up Mine Eyes. Psalm 121:1-4.
Stebbins, G. Waring.
Come Now and Let Us Reason Together. Isaiah 1:18, 20, 28.
Steele, David.
I Love You, Lord (arr. Tom Fettke). Psalm 18:1-3, 6.
Steinberg, Ben.
And David Said to Abigail. I Samuel 25:32.
Behold, the Days Come. Amos 9:13, 15.
Esa Einai. Psalm 121:00.
Hinei Yamin Ba-Im. Amos 9:13, 15.
How Goodly Are Thy Tents. Numbers 24:5.
I Will Lift Up Mine Eyes. Psalm 121:00.
Lakol Z'Man. Ecclesiastes 3:1-3.
Lo Yareiu. Isaiah 2:4.
Mah Tovu. Numbers 24:5.
They Shall Not Hurt Nor Destroy. Isaiah 2:4.
To Everything There Is a Season. Ecclesiastes 3:1-3.
Vayomer David L'Avigayil. I Samuel 25:32.
Stephenson, Richard T.
Psalm 103. Psalm 103:1-5, 8, 13.
Stern, Robert.
Al Tifg'i Vi. Ruth 1:16-17.
Stevenson, Frederick.
Hear, O My People. Psalm 81:9-11.
I Sought the Lord. Psalm 34:4.
Light. Wisdom of Solomon 18:14-15.
Stewart, Roy James.
Fill Us with Your Love, O Lord. Psalm 90:12-17.
Happy Are Those Who Fear the Lord. Psalm 128:00.
I Will Walk in the Presence of the Lord. Psalm 116:00.
Let My Tongue Be Silenced. Psalm 137:1-6.
Psalm 33. Psalm 33:00.
Stockhommer, A.
Hal'lu nafshi (arr. Velvel Pasternak). Psalm 146:1.
Praise the Lord, O My Soul (arr. Velvel Pasternak). Psalm 146:1.
Strals, Arnold.
The Lord's Prayer (arr. Les Sands). Matthew 6:9-13.
Strandberg, Newton.
De David. Psalm 100:00.
Strickland, Lily.
As Pants the Hart. Psalm 42:00.
Incline Your Ear. Isaiah 55:1, 3, 12.
Strommen, Carl.
The Lord's Prayer. Psalm 23:00.
Suben, Joel.
Make a Joyful Noise. Psalm 100:00.
Sullivan, Sir Arthur.
And God Shall Wipe Away All Tears. Revelation 21:4-5a.
Come Ye Children. Hebrews 12:6, 11.
Daughters of Jerusalem. Luke 23:28-29a.
How Many Hired Servants. Luke 15:17-19.
The Lord Is Risen. Revelation 21:3-5.
Love Not the World. John 14:6a.
The Spirit of the Lord Is upon Me. Luke 4:18, 21.
Trust in the Lord. Proverbs 3:5-6.
Sutermeisster, Heinrich.
Der 70 und 86 Psalm. Psalm 70:00.
Sweney, J.
The Lord Is My Light. Psalm 27:1.
Swift, Robert F.
Hast Thou Not Known? Isaiah 40:28-31.

Talbot, John Michael.
1 Corinthians 13. I Corinthians 13:1-7.
Father, I Put My Life in Your Hands. Psalm 31:00.
Forever Will I Sing. Psalm 89:00.
Give Thanks to the Lord. Psalm 107:1.
Happy Are Those Who Fear the Lord. Psalm 128:00.
I Am the Bread of Life. John 6:35.
I Am the Good Shepherd. Psalm 23:00.
I Am the Resurrection. John 11:25-26.
I Am the Vine. John 15:1-8.
I Rejoiced When I Heard Them Say. Psalm 122:00.
Let Us Sing to the Lord. Exodus 15:1.
The Lilies of the Field. Matthew 6:28, 31.
Lord, Every Nation On Earth Shall Adore You. Psalm 72:00.
The Lord Is My Shepherd. Psalm 23:00.
Lord, It Is Good. Psalm 92:00.
The Lord Will Bless His People. Psalm 29:00.
The Lord's Prayer. Luke 6:13.
May God Bless Us. Psalm 67:00.
My God, My God. Psalm 22:00.
My Heart is Ready. Psalm 108:00.
My Yoke Is Easy. Matthew 11:28-30.
Only in God. Psalm 62:00.
Our Blessing Cup. Psalm 116:12-14.
Send Us Out. Matthew 28:18-20.
The Spirit of the Lord. Isaiah 61:1.
Take Up Your Cross. Luke 9:23-27.
Taste and See. Psalm 34:1-8.
Today Is Born Our Savior. Psalm 96:1-3.
With the Lord There Is Mercy. Psalm 130:00.
Word of God Became Man. Psalm 148:00.
Talma, Louise.
Cantata: All the Days of My Life. Psalm 27:4.
Talmud, Rabbi Y.
Be Not Ashamed (arr. Velvel Pasternak). Psalm 42:11a.
Behold How Good and How Pleasant it is (arr. Velvel Pasternak). Psalm 133:1.
Hiné ma tõv, no. 1 (arr. Velvel Pasternak). Psalm 133:1.
Lõ Sevõshi (arr. Velvel Pasternak). Psalm 42:11a.
Tamblyn, William.
King of Glory. Psalm 24:00.
Tapp, Freda.
Thou Art a Shield for Me. Psalm 3:1-3.
Tappe, Stephen.
Psalm 100. Psalm 100:00.
Tarsi, Boaz.
Ashrei Ha'Ish. Psalm 1:1-3.
Happy Is the Man. Psalm 1:1-3.
Taub, Rabbi S. E.
And Thou Shalt Rejoice in Thy Feast (arr. Velvel Pasternak). Deuteronomy 16:14.
The Lord Bless You From Zion (arr. Velvel Pasternak). Psalm 128:5.

V'Somachto B;Chagecho, no. 3 (arr. Velvel Pasternak). Deuteronomy 16:14.
Y'vorech'cho Hasem (arr. Velvel Pasternak). Psalm 128:5.
Taylor, Raynor.
The Lord Is My Shepherd. Psalm 23:00.
Tecson, Andrew.
Sing unto the Lord. Psalm 98:1-2, 4, 7, 9.
Telemann, Georg Philipp.
Ein jeder Lauft, der in den Schranken kauft. I Corinthians 6:11.
Ew'ge Qwelle, milder Strom. James 1:17-22.
Hemmet den Eifer, verbannet die Rache. Romans 13:8-10.
Ich habe meine Augen auf zu den Bergen. Psalm 121:00.
Ich will den Herren loben allezeit. Psalm 34:2-5, 7.
Ihr Volkers, Hört. Isaiah 60:1-6.
Jauchzet dem Herrn, alle Welt. Psalm 100:00.
Jauchzt, ihr Christen, seid vergnügt. I Corinthians 15:50-58.
Kleines Magnificat. Luke 1:46-47.
Laudate pueri Dominum. Psalm 113:1-4.
The Lord Will I Bless for All My Days. Psalm 34:2-5, 7.
O Blest Is He Who Reveres the Lord. Psalm 112:1b-3.
Sing Now to God. Psalm 98:00.
Sing to the Lord, Rejoice! (arr. Hal H. Hopson). Psalm 147:1, 15.
Singet dem Herrn. Psalm 98:00.
Wohl dem, der den Herrn fürchtet. Psalm 112:1b-3.
Terndrup, Craig.
Blow the Trumpet in Zion. Joel 2:1.
Thiman, Eric H.
The God of Love My Shepherd Is. Psalm 23:00.
Happy Is the Man (Proverbs). Proverbs 3:13, 15-18.
Happy Is the Man (Psalms). Psalm 1:00.
How Lovely Are Thy Dwellings Fair. Psalm 134:00.
Thou Wilt Keep Him in Perfect Peace. Isaiah 26:3-4.
The Wilderness. Isaiah 35:1-2, 6-8, 10.
Thomas, Donn and Charles Williams.
A Shield About Me. Psalm 3:3.
Thompson, Randall.
My Soul Doth Magnify the Lord! Luke 1:46-47.
Thompson, William H.
Peace I Leave With You. John 14:1, 27.
Thomson, Sydney.
When I Survey the Wondrous Cross. Galatians 6:14.
Thomson, Virgil.
By Night. Song of Songs 3:1-2.
I Am My Beloved's. Song of Songs 6:3.
My Shepherd Will Supply My Need. Psalm 23:00.
O My Dove. Song of Songs 2:14.
Return, O Shulamite! Song of Songs 6:13.
Thou That Dwellest in the Garden. Song of Songs 8:13.
Thorne, Francis.
Magnificat. Luke 1:46-47.
Nunc Dimittis. Luke 2:29-32.
Prepare Ye the Way of the Lord. Isaiah 40:3-5.
Thornton, William.
As the Apple Tree. Song of Songs 2:3-6.
Happy Are They. Psalm 1:00.
I Sought Him. Song of Songs 3:1-3.
Psalm 1. Psalm 1:00.
Rise Up, My Love. Song of Songs 2:10-13.
Wear Me as a Seal. Song of Songs 8:6-7a, 10.
Thurman, Geoffrey P.
Jehovah. Matthew 6:28-34.
Jehovah (arr. Steven V. Taylor). Matthew 6:28-34.
Timmings, William.
Turn Thy Face From My Sins. Psalm 51:9-11.
Tindall, Adrienne M.
Aleph. Psalm 119:1-7.
Beth. Psalm 119:10-13, 15.
Blessed Are the Undefiled in the Way. Psalm 119:1-7.
Fear Not! Isaiah 41:10.
He. Psalm 119:33-36, 38, 40.
Hear, O Israel. Deuteronomy 6:4-5.
How Good and How Pleasant It Is. Psalm 133:1.
I Am Persuaded. John 3:16-17.
And I Saw a New Heaven. Revelation 21:1-5.
Jod. Psalm 119:73-74, 76-77, 80.
The Lord is My Light. Psalm 27:1, 2b, 3, 4a, 5.
Lord, Make Me an Instrument. Psalm 85:8.
The Lord's My Shepherd, I'll Not Want. Psalm 23:1-6.
Love Never Fails. I Corinthians 13:4-8, 13.
Mem. Psalm 119:97, 99, 101-103.
The Mists of Adam Dreaming. I Corinthians 15:45, 53, 49.
Nun. Psalm 119:105-106, 108, 110-112.
Psalm 23. Psalm 23:1-6.
Psalm 133. Psalm 133:1.
Remember the Word unto Thy Servant. Psalm 119:49-52, 54-55.
Teach Me, O Lord, the Way of Thy Statutes. Psalm 119:33-36, 38, 40.
Thy Hands Have Made Me and Fashioned Me. Psalm 119:73-74, 76-77, 80.
Trust in the Lord. Proverbs 2:1-5.
Unto Thee O Lord. Psalm 24:3-5.
With My Whole Heart Have I Sought Thee. Psalm 119:10-13, 15.
Zain. Psalm 119:49-52, 54-55.
Toch, Ernst.
There Is a Season to Everything. Ecclesiastes 3:1-8.
Toolan, Sr. Suzanne.
Great Is the Lord (arr. Randall deBruyn). Isaiah 52:7.
I Am the Bread of Life. John 6:35, 51, 53.
Topliff, Robert.
Consider the Lilies. Matthew 6:25-26, 28-29.
Tornioli, Marcantonio.
Salvum me fac deus (ed. Karl Gustav Fellerer). Psalm 69:00.
Traditional Folk Song–Hasidic.
Enter in the Wilderness. Isaiah 40:3-5.
Praise the Lord (arr. Samuel Adler). Psalm 113:1-5.
Traditional English Thanksgiving Canon (arr. Anna Laura Page). Psalm 117:00.
Trapp, Lynn.
Nunc Dimittis. Luke 2:29-32.
Psalm 19. Psalm 19:8-10.
Psalm 86. Psalm 86:5-6, 9-10, 15-16.
Psalm 89. Psalm 89:2-3, 16-19.
Psalm 141. Psalm 141:1-5, 8-9.
Psalm 145. Psalm 145:1-2, 8-11, 13-14.
Travers, John.
Ascribe unto the Lord (arr. Harrison Oxley). Psalm 96:7-9.
O Worship the Lord (arr. Harrison Oxley). Psalm 96:7-9.
Triplett, Robert F.
I Will Sing of Thy Steadfast Love. Psalm 89:1-5, 15-18, 52.
The Lord is My Shepherd. Psalm 23:00.
Trowbridge, J. Eliot.
I Am Alpha and Omega. Revelation 1:8.

Tschaikovsky, Peter I.
Lift Up Your Eyes (arr. Carl Fredrickson). Isaiah 51:7-8.
Lord Is My Shepherd (arr. Richard Maxwell and Fred Feibel). Psalm 23:00.
Tucker, Margaret R.
Psalm 48. Psalm 48:1, 4, 9, 11-13.
Upon Mount Zion Sits Our God. Psalm 48:1, 4, 9, 11-13.
Tunney, Dick.
How Excellent Is Thy Name (arr. Steven V. Taylor). Psalm 8:1.
Tunney, Dick and Melodie Tunney.
Come Before Him. I Chronicles 16:29.
For unto Us. Isaiah 9:6.
In Majesty He Will Come with Majesty. I Corinthians 15:52.
Majesty. I Corinthians 15:52.
O Magnify the Lord. Psalm 34:3.
Tunney, Dick, Melodie Tunney, and Paul C. Smith.
How Excellent Is Thy Name. Psalm 8:1.
Tunney, Melodie.
Sound His Praise (arr. Jospeh Linn). Psalm 150:6.
Twinn, Sydney.
I Will Lift Up Mine Eyes. Psalm 121:00.

Ultan, Lloyd.
I Will Give You Shepherds. Joshua 1:8-9.
Wedding Song. Song of Songs 2:10-13.
Underhill, Charles D.
Suffer the Little Children. Mark 10:13-14.
Unknown.
Bless the Lord, O My Soul (arr. Tom Fettke). Psalm 103:1.
Sing unto the Lord (arr. Tom Fettke). Psalm 96:1, 4.
Urspringer, Steven and Jay Robinson.
Arise Shine. Isaiah 60:1.
Uszler, Marienne.
Speak Lord (arr. Tim Schoenbachler). Psalm 119:00.

Vale, Alliene G.
The Joy of the Lord. Nehemiah 8:10.
Valentini, Giovanni.
Hodie Christus natus est. Luke 2:11.
Vance, Margaret.
God Bless the King. Luke 19:28-39.
VanDewater, Beardsley.
The Good Shepherd. Psalm 23:00.
The Penitent. Luke 15:11-25.
Praise the Lord, O My Soul. Luke 18:10-14.
VanDyke, May.
As a Shepherd. Isaiah 40:11.
God Is a Spirit. Psalm 104:00.
In the Beauty of Holiness. Psalm 113:3.
Love. Matthew 22:37-39.
Seek Ye the Lord. Isaiah 55:6-7.
VanNuys, Rena.
Whither Shall I Go. Psalm 139:7-10, 12, 14, 23-24.
Vantine, Patricia.
Behold What Manner of Love. I John 3:1.
VanVollenhoven, Hanna.
Hear Me Speedily, O Lord! Psalm 27:1.
VanWoert, Rutger.
Be Not Far From Me, Oh God. Isaiah 45:1-2, 22.

Vaughan Williams, Ralph.
And It Came to Pass in Those Days, ño. 4. Luke 2:1,4-7.
The Bird's Song. Psalm 23:00.
Let Us Now Praise Famous Men. Sirach 44:00.
The Pilgrim's Psalm. Psalm 18:32, 37.
The Song of Leaves of Life and Water of Life. Revelation 2:7.
Watchful's Song. Psalm 121:00.
Vejvanovsky, Pavel Josef.
Haec dies quam fecit Dominus. Psalm 118:24.
Vessels, Dennis.
My Refuge (arr. Sheryl Soderberg). Psalm 31:1-5.
Viadana, Ludovico.
Cantemus Domino. Exodus 15:1-2.
Vieker, Jon D.
Come, Holy Spirit. Psalm 104:24, 28a, 30.
Vierdanck, Johann.
Gloria (ed. and arr. Michael Burkhardt). Luke 2:14.
Vivaldi, Antonio.
And to All Goodwill (arr. Vernon M. Whaley). Luke 2:14b.
Behold, the Hungry He Fills. Luke 1:53.
Esurientes. Luke 1:53.
Esurientes implevit (arr. Richard Walters). Luke 1:53.
Et in Terra Pax Hominibus (arr. Vernon M. Whaley). Luke 2:14b.
Gloria (arr. Vernon M. Whaley). Luke 2:14a.
Glory to God (arr. W. Daniel Landes). Luke 2:14.
Laudamus Te (arr. Vernon M. Whaley). Psalm 145:1-2.
Lord, to Thee Do I Lift My Soul. Psalm 86:4-6, 12.
Peccator videbit (ed. Richard Walters). Psalm 112:10.
We Praise You God (arr. Vernon M. Whaley). Psalm 145:1-2.
Vogel, Howard.
Behold, How Fair and Pleasant. Song of Songs 7:6.
Vree, Marion.
Psalm 23. Psalm 23:00.

Wagner, Douglas E.
Blessed Is the Man. Psalm 1:1-3.
Clap Hands, Be Glad! Psalm 47:1.
The Earth Is the Lord's. Psalm 24:1-8.
For the Mountains Shall Depart. Isaiah 54:13.
Walfish, H.
He Will Bless the House of Israel (arr. Velvel Pasternak). Psalm 115:12.
Y'Voréch (arr. Velvel Pasternak). Psalm 115:12.
Walker, Christopher.
Because the Lord Is My Shepherd. Psalm 23:00.
Bless the Lord, O My Soul. Psalm 104:1, 5-6, 10-12, 24, 29-31, 34.
Faith, Hope and Love. John 13:5-7.
Give Me a New Heart, O God. Psalm 51:00.
I Rejoiced. Psalm 122:00.
Like a Child Rests. Psalm 131:00.
Lord, Be with Us. Psalm 33:4-22.
May God Bless and Keep You. Numbers 6:22-27.
My God, My God. Psalm 22:8-9, 17-20, 23-24.
Nunc Dimittis. Luke 2:29-32.
O Lord, I Will Sing. Psalm 63:1-8.
O My Soul, Bless the Lord. Psalm 103:1-4.
Send Forth Your Spirit, O Lord. Psalm 104:1, 5-6, 10-12, 24, 29-31, 34.
Taste and See. Psalm 34:1-6, 8.
This Day Was Made By the Lord. Psalm 118:14, 19-24.

Walker, Tricia.
The Heavens Are Telling. Psalm 19:1a.
Sing the Glory of His Name. Psalm 66:1-8.
Walker, W.
Farewell, Dear Companion (arr. Max V. Exner). Luke 2:29-35.
Song of Simeon (arr. Max V. Exner). Luke 2:29-35.
Wallach, Joelle.
Set Me as a Seal upon Your Heart. Song of Songs 8:6-7.
Simëni kachotam al libbecha. Song of Songs 8:6-7.
V'erastich li l'olam. Hosea 2:16-22.
Wallbridge, Richard L. A.
Glory of the Lord. Isaiah 60:1-4.
Walton, William.
Babylon Was a Great City. Revelation 18:10-13.
Ward-Stephens.
Awake Thou That Sleepest. Ephesians 5:14.
Blessed Are the Meek. Matthew 5:5.
Blessed Are the Merciful. Matthew 5:7.
Blessed Are the Peacemakers. Matthew 5:9.
Blessed Are the Poor in Spirit. Matthew 5:3.
Blessed Are the Pure in Heart. Matthew 5:8.
Blessed Are They That Mourn. Matthew 5:4.
Blessed Are They Which Are Persecuted. Matthew 5:10.
Blessed Are They Which Do Hunger. Matthew 5:6.
The Earth is the Lord's. Psalm 24:00.
God is Our Refuge. Psalm 46:00.
He That Dwelleth in the Secret Place. Psalm 91:1-12.
I Will Lift Up Mine Eyes. Psalm 121:00.
In My Father's House Are Many Mansions. John 14:2-4, 27.
The Lord Is My Shepherd. Psalm 23:00.
Love Never Faileth. I Corinthians 13:00.
Love Not the World. I John 2:15a, 17.
Search Me, O God, and Know My Heart. Psalm 139:00.
Ware, Harriet.
The Greatest of These. I Corinthians 13:00.
Warren, Clara.
Hast Thou Not Known Me? John 14:6, 8-9.
Let Us Keep the Feast. Psalm 118:24.
Rise and Walk. Acts 3:1-8.
Warren, Raymond.
Drop, Drop Slow Tears. Luke 7:36-40, 47-48.
Watkins, Margery.
I Will Lift Up Mine Eyes (ed. Wilmans, Wilman). Psalm 121:00.
Watson, Michael.
Babylon. Psalm 137:1.
Watts, Wintter.
Intreat Me Not to Leave Thee. Ruth 1:16-17.
Way, Arthur.
Acquaint Now Thyself With Him. Job 22:21.
Weaver, Powell.
Alleluia. Psalm 150:00.
Joy to the World. Psalm 98:00.
Praise the Lord His Glories Show. Psalm 150:00.
Webb, Charles.
Psalm 23. Psalm 23:00.
Weber, Carl M. von.
Praise the Lord, Ye Heavens (ed. Doroth Allan Park). Psalm 148:00.
Weber, Jim and Niles Borop.
It Is Good. Psalm 92:1-2.
Weinberger, Jaromir.
Psalm 150. Psalm 150:00.
The Way to Emmaus. Luke 24:13-31.
Weiner, Lazar.
Adoration. Deuteronomy 4:39.
Etz Chayim. Proverbs 3:17-18.
L'Cho Adonoy. I Chronicles 29:11.
Mah Tovu. Numbers 24:5.
May the Words. Psalm 19:15.
Mimaamakim. Psalm 130:00.
Out of the Depths. Psalm 130:00.
Ruth. Ruth 1:16-17.
Tov L'Hodos. Psalm 92:2-16.
Weldon, John.
He Will Not Suffer Thy Foot to Be Moved. Psalm 121:3.
The Lord Shall Preserve Thee From All Evil. Psalm 121:8.
Wells, Oliver and Eddie Carswell.
Come Let's Worship Him. I Chronicles 16:8-9.
Wenzel, Eberhard.
Psalm 90. Psalm 90:00.
Wernick, Richard F.
A Prayer for Jerusalem. Psalm 122:2-3, 6-8.
Wesley, Samuel Sebastian.
Lead Me, Lord. Psalm 5:8.
Lead Me, Lord (arr. Fred Bock). Psalm 5:8.
Lead Me, Lord (arr. Mary Hamlin). Psalm 5:8.
Praise the Lord, O My Soul. Psalm 103:1.
Say to Them of a Fearful Heart (arr. Harrison Oxley). Isaiah 35:4.
West, John E.
Like as the Hart. Psalm 42:00.
Wetzler, Robert.
Good Tidings. Isaiah 61:1-3.
The Greatest of These Is Love. I Corinthians 13:00.
How Excellent Is Your Name. Psalm 8:1, 3-5, 9.
The Lord Is My Light. Psalm 27:1-3a.
Psalm 128. Psalm 128:00.
A Wedding Song. Psalm 128:00.
Wexelberg, Shannon.
You Are My Refuge. Psalm 91:1-2.
Whikehart, Lewis E.
O Sing unto the Lord. Psalm 96:00.
Whitaker, James.
Ave Maria. Luke 1:28, 30-31, 42.
White, Louie.
Entreat Me Not to Leave Thee. Ruth 1:16-17.
Whitehouse, Jan.
He Makes All Things New. Revelation 21:5.
Peace I Leave You. John 14:27.
Whitsett, Eleanor.
Jesus Christ, the Same (arr. Gene Thomas). Hebrews 13:8.
Whittemore, Dan.
My Lord Is Leading Me On (arr. Joseph Linn). Psalm 25:4-5.
Wiant, Bliss.
The Great Commission. Isaiah 61:1-3.
Wiemer, Wolfgang.
Der Herr ist Meine Hirt. Psalm 23:00.
Eile, Gott, mich zu erretten. Psalm 70:2-6
Lobe den Herrn, meine Seele. Psalm 103:00.
Wienhorst, Richard.
I Will Sing the Story of Thy Love. Psalm 89:1.
The King of Love My Shepherd Is. Psalm 23:00.
The Lord Is Faithful. Psalm 145:13b-16.
Thou Wilt Keep Him in Perfect Peace. Isaiah 26:3-4.
Wilder, Alec.
By the Rivers of Babylon. Psalm 137:00.

Willan, Healey.
Come Unto Me, All Ye That Labor. Matthew 11:28-30.
Create in Me a Clean Heart, O God. Psalm 51:10-12.
The Lord's Prayer. Matthew 6:9-13.
Rejoice Greatly, O Daughter of Zion. Zechariah 9:9-10.
Willard, Kelly.
Cares Chorus. I Peter 5:7.
I Cast All My Cares upon You. I Peter 5:7.
Williamson, Inez McC.
The Lord's Prayer. Matthew 6:9-13.
Williamson, Malcolm.
King of Love, no. 5. Psalm 23:00.
Psalm 23. Psalm 23:00.
Psalm 24. Psalm 24:7-10.
Who is the King of Glory, no. 4. Psalm 24:7-10.
Willis, Michelle.
Set Me as a Seal. Song of Songs 8:6-7.
Wilson, John Floyd.
Hosanna! Blessed Is He. Mark 11:9-10.
A New Creature. II Corinthians 5:17.
A Worthy Woman. Proverbs 31:25-31.
Wilson, Mark.
Lift Every Voice. Psalm 47:1, 6-7.
Winton, Mary.
Psalm 23. Psalm 23:00.
Whither Shall I Go From Thy Spirit. Psalm 139:7-10.
Wise, Joe.
And the Light Shines. Joel 2:28.
The Lord Is My Shepherd. Psalm 23:00.
Wolaver, Bill.
Rejoice With Exceeding Great Joy. Matthew 2:1-12 (based on).
Wolaver, Bill and Robin.
Make His Praise Glorious. Psalm 66:2.
Wold, Wayne L.
Agnus Dei, Lamb of God. John 1:29.
Gloria in Excelsis Deo. Luke 2:14.
Sanctus and Benedictus. Isaiah 6:3b.
Wolf, Hugo.
Man the Child of God. I Corinthians 2:9-12.
Revelation (arr. K. K. Davis). Revelation 21:9-10.
With an Everlasting Love. Proverbs 3:24.
Wolfe, Jacques.
The Blessed. Matthew 5:3-11.
Bone Come A-knittin'. Ezekiel 37:00.
Joy for All the Ages. Psalm 67:00.
Psalm LXVII. Psalm 67:00.
Wolford, Darwin.
The King of Love My Shepherd Is. I Corinthians 13:3.
Wolford, Julie Lofgren.
The Shepherd. Psalm 23:00.
Wolpe, Stefan.
Isaiah. Isaiah 65:17-22a, 25.
Wood, Dale.
The Beatitudes. Matthew 5:1-10, 12.
In This Moment of Remembrance. Luke 22:19.
Wooler, Alfred.
Behold, God is Mighty. Job 36:5, 6, 7.
Consider and Hear Me. Psalm 13:00.
God Be Merciful to Me. Psalm 51:00.
Hear My Cry, O Lord! Psalm 61:1.
How Beautiful on the Mountains. Romans 10:15.
Let God Arise. Psalm 68:1-3.
The Lord is My Light. Psalm 27:1-3, 5.
O Lord, Rebuke Me Not. Psalm 6:33-37.
Out of the Depths. Psalm 130:00.
Save Me, O God. Psalm 54:00.
Send Out Thy Light. Psalm 43:1-4.
Wright, Norman S.
The Eighth Psalm. Psalm 8:00.
Wyner, Yehudi.
Halleluya. Psalm 66:00.
Lord, Let Me Know My End. Psalm 39:4-5.
Psalm 66. Psalm 66:1-4.
Psalm 119. Psalm 119:25-32.
Wyrtzen, Don.
Worthy is the Lamb. Revelation 5:12.
Worthy is the Lamb. Revelation 5:12-13.

Yardumian, Richard.
Symphony, no. 2. Psalm 130:00.
Young, Carlton.
The Lord's Prayer. Matthew 6:9-13.
Nunc Dimittis. Luke 2:29-32.
O Taste and See. Psalm 34:8.
Processional. Psalm 24:7.
We Have Seen Your Salvation. Luke 2:29-32.
Young, Gordon.
Entreat Me Not to Leave Thee. Ruth 1:16-17.
Young, Ovid.
As a Deer Longs So for Water (arr. Lyndell Leatherman). Psalm 42:1-4.
Young, Philip M.
I Will Greatly Rejoice in the Lord. Isaiah 61:1-3, 10.
Who Shall Come Before the Lord? Psalm 24:1, 3-4, 7.
Young, Walter E.
The Wilderness. Isaiah 1:6, 10.

Zaabriskie, David A.
Pioneer Lullaby. Hosea 13:14 (based on).
Zaimont, Judith Lang.
Psalm 24 (23). Psalm 23:00.
A Woman of Valor. Proverbs 31:10-11, 17, 20, 26, 28, 30.
Zelenka, Jan Dismas.
Laudate pueri. Psalm 113:00.
Zentner, Johannes.
Gloria. Luke 2:14.
Lobgesang der Maria. Luke 1:46-55.
Ziegenhals, Harriet.
You Shall Have a Song. Psalm 100:00.
Zimmermann, Heinz Werner.
Christmas Carol. Psalm 95:1.
Come, Let Us Praise. Psalm 95:1.

Title Index

I Corinthians 13.
Archer, Violet. I Corinthians 13:1-8.
Behrens, Jack. I Corinthians 13:00.
Talbot, John Michael. I Corinthians 13:1-7 (adapted).
Der 62 Psalm. Kuntz, Michael. Psalm. 62:00.
Der 70 und 86 Psalm. Sutermeisster, Heinrich. Psalm 70:00.
Der 134th Psalm. Rosenmüller, Johann. Psalm 134:1-4.

Abide in Christ. Atkins, Jean. John 15:00.
Abide in Me. Herbst, Johannes (arr. Karl Kroeger). John 15:4.
Abide with Me. Bennett, Sir William Sterndale. Luke 24:13.
Abide with Me; 'tis Eventide. Bradshaw, Daniel. Psalm 143:6, 7.
Above the Voices of Many Waters. Pasternak, Velvel. Psalm 93:4.
Abraham and Issac. Britten, Benjamin. Genesis 22:2-19 (based on).
Absalom. DeLong, Richard. II Samuel 18:33.
Acclaim Adonai, All People on Earth. Cohen, Gerald. Psalm 100:00.
Ach, Herr, strafe mich nicht in deinen Zorn. Bernhard, Christoph. Psalm 6:00.
Acquaint Now Thyself With Him.
Head, Michael. Job 22:21.
MacDermid, James G. Job 22:21.
Way, Arthur. Job 22:21.
Acquaint Thyself With Him. Buck, Dudley. Job 22:00.
Ad Matai. Cohen, Gerald. Psalm 82:1-5, 8.
Ad te levavi occulos meus. Couperin, François. Psalm 122:00.
Adagio ma non troppo. Hartley, Walter S. Psalm 43:1-4.
Adoration. Weiner, Lazar. Deuteronomy 4:39.
Agnus Dei.
Bach, J. S. John 1:29.
Bizet, Georges. John 1:29.
Franck, César (arr. Hal H. Hopson). Psalm 51:1.
Mozart, W. A. John 1:29.
Pergolesi, Giovanni B. (ed. and arr. Michael Burkhardt). John 1:29.
Smith, Michael W. Revelation 5:12.
Agnus Dei, Lamb of God. Wold, Wayne L. John 1:29.
Air for Brother James.
Bain, James Leith Macbeth (arr. Walter Rodby). Psalm 23:00.
Bain, James Leith Macbeth (arr. Phyllis Tate). Psalm 23:00.
Bain, James Leith Macbeth (arr. Arthur Trew). Psalm 23:00.
Al Tifg'i Vi. Stern, Robert. Ruth 1:16-17.
Al Tifigi vi Le-Ozveich. Avery, Lawrence. Ruth 1:16-17.
Aleph. Tindall, Adrienne M. Psalm 119:1-17.
All Flesh is Grass. Picket, Frederick. Isaiah 40:6-8.
All Hearts Now Be Joyful. Bach, J. S. Psalm 35:9.
All My Days. Schutte, Daniel L. and Jim Murray. Psalm 8:2-7.
All the Ends of the Earth.
Dufford, Bob. Psalm 98:00 (based on).
Haas, David and Marty Haugen. Psalm 98:1-6.
Hurd, Bob (arr. Craig S. Kingsbury). Psalm 98:1, 3-6.
Joncas, Michael. Psalm 98:1-6.
All They That See Him, Laugh Him to Scorn. Handel, G. F. Psalm 22:7.
All Things Have Their Time. Kavanaugh, John. Ecclesiastes 3:1-8 (based on).
All Things Work Together for Good. Carter, John. Romans 8:28.
All Those Who Take Refuge in Thee. Portugal, Rabbi E. (arr. Velvel Pasternak). Psalm 5:12.
All Thy Works Shall Praise Thee. Benati. Psalm 145:10-12, 17-18.
All We Like Sheep. Moen, Don. Isaiah 53:6 (based on).
All We Like Sheep Have Gone Astray. Handel, G. F. (arr. James Michael Stevens). Isaiah 53:6.
All You Who Pass This Way. Berthier, Jacques (ed. Brother Robert). Lamentations 1:1.
Allegro. Hartley, Walter S. Psalm 12:1-4, 9.
Allegro con brio. Hartley, Walter S. Psalm 145:1-3, 8-10, 21.
Alleluia.
Hummel, Ferdinand (arr. Carl Fredrickson). Psalm 23:1-2.
Weaver, Powell. Psalm 150:00.
Alleluia. Ascendit Deus (Alleluia. God Has Come Up) (ed. James H. Laster). Bencini, Pietro Paolo. Psalm 47:5.
Als wir dort an den Wassern der Stadt Baylon sassen. Dvorák, Antonín. Psalm 137:1-5.
Also hat Gott die Welt geliebt. Buxtehude, Dietrich. John 3:16.
Am I My Brother's Keeper? Barrett-Ayres, Reginald. Genesis 4:9.
Amen, amen dico vobis. Aichinger, Gregor. John 6:54.
Amplius lava me ab inquitate mea. Bach, J. C. F. Psalm 51:2-3.
An ignoratis quia quicumque. Soler, Joseph. Romans 6:3-4.
An wasserflüsswen Babylon. Schein, Johann Hermann (ed. Paul Horn). Psalm 137:00.
Ana Dodi. Nelson, Rachelle. Song of Songs 2:10-11.
And a Very Great Multitude. Lekberg, Sven. Matthew 21:8, 9.
And David Said to Abigail. Steinberg, Ben. I Samuel 25:32.
And God Created Man. Haydn, F. Joseph. Genesis 1:27.
And God Said, Let the Earth Bring Forth Grass. Haydn, F. Joseph. Genesis 1:11.
And God Said, Let the Earth Bring Forth Living Creatures. Haydn, F. Joseph. Genesis 1:24.
And God Said, Let the Waters Bring Forth Abundantly. Haydn, F. Joseph. Genesis 1:20.
And God Said, Let the Waters Under the Heavens. Haydn, F. Joseph. Genesis 1:9.
And God Shall Wipe Away All Tears. Sullivan, Sir Arthur. Revelations 21:4-5a.
And He Hath Put a New Song in My Mouth. Pasternak, Velvel. Psalm 40:4.
And in That Day Thou Shalt Say. Schmutz, Albert D. Isaiah 12:00.
And It Came to Pass in Those Days. Vaughan Williams, Ralph. Luke 2:1, 4-7.
And Jesus Said: It Is Finished. Antes, John. John 19:30.
And Lo! The Angel of the Lord. Handel, G. F. Luke 2:9.
And Lo! The Angel of the Lord Came Upon Them. Handel, G. F. Luke 2:9.
And the Angel Said. Nagy, Russell. Luke 1:27-31.
And the Angel Said unto Them. Handel, G. F. Luke 2:10-11.
And the Glory of the Lord. Handel, G. F. (arr. W. Daniel Landes). Isaiah 40:5.

And the Light Shines. Wise, Joe. Joel 2:28.
And the Lord Alone. Portugal, Rabbi E. (arr. Velvel Pasternak). Isaiah 2:11.
And There Were Shepherds. Boex, Andrew J. Luke 2:8-15.
And There Were Shepherds Abiding in the Fields. LaForge, Frank. Luke 2:8-14.
And There Will Be Signs. Bender, Jan. Luke 21:25-26, 33.
And Thou Shalt Rejoice in Thy Feast.
  Pasternak, Velvel. Deuteronomy 16:14.
  Taub, Rabbi S. E. (arr. Velvel Pasternak). Deuteronomy 16:14.
And to All Goodwill. Vivaldi, Antonio (arr. Vernon M. Whaley). Luke 2:14b.
And You Shall Love. Gottlieb, Jack. Deuteronomy 6:5-9.
Andante con moto. Hartley, Walter S. Psalm 40:1-4.
Andante molto. Hartley, Walter S. Psalm 63:1-5.
An Angel Speaks to the Shepherd. Rorem, Ned. Luke 2:9-15.
Angels. Nelson, Ronald A. Psalm 91:11-12.
Angel's Message to the Shepherds. Schütz, Heinrich. Luke 2:8-13.
Angels Roll the Rock Away. Scott, John Prindle. Matthew 28:5-6.
Angelus Domini.
  Aichinger, Gregor. John 1:14.
  Ferguson, Michael. Matthew 28:2, 5-6.
Ani Chavatselet Hasharon. Bugatch, Samuel. Song of Songs 2:1-5.
Answer Me When I Call. Ore, Charles W. Psalm 4:00.
Answer When I Call. Foley, John B. Psalm 102:1-2, 6-7, 11 (based on).
Ar nathir. Proulx, Richard. Matthew 6:9-13.
Arioso from 100th Psalm. Jadassohn, Solomon. Psalm 100:3.
Arise, My Love. Card, Michael and Scott Brasher. Song of Songs 2:10.
Arise, O Jerusalem. Hurd, Bob (arr. Barbara Bridge and Dominic MacAller). Isaiah 65:13, 25.
Arise, O Lord. Hoffmeister, Leon Abbott. Psalm 9:10, 19-20.
Arise, Shine.
  Burton, Wendell and Marty Goetz. Isaiah 9:2a.
  Humphreys, Don. Isaiah 60:1.
  Koch, Frederick. Isaiah 60:1-3.
  Scott, John Prindle. Isaiah 60:00.
  Urspringer, Steven and Jay Robinson. Isaiah 60:1.
Arise, Shine, for Thy Light Is Come.
  Harker, F. Flaxington. Isaiah 60:1-3,13, 21.
  MacDermid, James G. Revelation 3:20.
  Schmutz, Albert D. Isaiah 60:1-3, 18-19.
Arm, Arm, Ye Brave! Handel, G. F. (arr. Richard Walters). I Macabees 3:58.
As a Deer.
  Derfler, Carl. Psalm 42:1-4.
  Huijbers, Bernard. Psalm 42:1-5, 8.
As a Deer Longs So for Water. Young, Ovid (arr. Lyndell Leatherman). Psalm 42:1-4.
As a Shepherd. VanDyke, May. Isaiah 40:11.
As it Began to Dawn.
  Coombs, Charles Whitney. Matthew 28:1-6.
  Harker, F. Flaxington. Matthew 28:1-7.
As it is in Heaven. Smith, Michael W. Matthew 6:9-13.
As Pants the Hart.
  Gluck, Christoph von. Psalm 42:1-4.
  Lansing, A. W. Psalm 42:00.
  Smart, Henry (arr. L. Kessler). Psalm 42:1.
  Strickland, Lily. Psalm 42:00.
As Pants the Wearied Hart. Marcello, Benedetto. Psalm 42:00.
As the Apple Tree. Thornton, William. Song of Songs 2:3-6.
As the Deer. Nystrom, Martin. Psalm 42:1-7.
As the Deer Longs.
  Hurd, Bob (arr. MacAller and Kingsbury). Psalm 42:1-4.
  Misetich, Marianne. Psalm 42:1-4.
As the Hart Panteth. Blair, Kathleen. Psalm 42:00.
As the Rain Cometh Down. MacDermid, James G. Isaiah 55:1, 3, 10-11.
As the Thirsty Deer at Morning. Burton, Daniel. Psalm 42:1, 8, 11 (based on).
Ascribe to the Lord. Giovanni, Bassani (ed. Gertrude Tingley). Psalm 96:8, 10.
Ascribe unto the Lord. Travers, John. Psalm 96:7-9.
Ascribe unto the Lord Worship and Power. Gaul, Alfred Robert. Psalm 96:7-8.
Asé imonu õs. Shapiro, Rabbi Y. (arr. Velvel Pasternak). Psalm 86:17.
Ashrei Ha'Ish. Tarsi, Boaz. Psalm 1:1-3.
At the Name of Jesus.
  Berry, Cindy (arr. Richard Huggins). Philippians 2:6-11 (adapted).
  Jernigan, Dennis L. Philippians 2:10-11 (based on).
At the Time of the Banquet. Krapf, Gerhard. Luke 14:16-24.
Attendite, popule meus, legem meam. Schütz, Heinrich. Psalm 78:1-3.
Aus der Tiefe. Selle, Thomas (ed. Klaus Vetter). Psalm 130:00.
Aus der Tiefen. Bernhard, Christoph. Psalm 130:00.
Ave Maria.
  Abt, Franz. Luke 1:28, 30-31, 42.
  Amedeo, Leone. Luke 1:28, 30-31, 42.
  Arcadelt, Jacob. Luke 1:28, 32.
  Atkinson, René. Luke 1:28, 42.
  Bizet, Georges. Luke 1:28, 30-31, 42.
  Caccini, Giulio (arr. Steven Mercurio). Luke 1:28, 30-31, 42.
  Cherubini, Luigi. Luke 1:28, 30-31, 42.
  Dorff, Daniel. Luke 1:28, 30-31.
  Dupré, Marcel. Luke 1:28, 30-31, 42 (based on).
  Franck, César. Luke 1:28, 30-31. 42.
  Gounod, Charles. Luke 1:28, 30-31, 42 (based on).
  Hamblen, Bernard. Luke 1:28, 30-31, 42.
  Head, Michael. Luke 1:28, 30-31, 42.
  Kantor, Daniel (arr. Rob Glover). Luke 1:28.
  Kulla, Hans. Luke 1:28, 31, 34-35, 38.
  Luzzi, Luigi. Luke 1:28, 30-31, 42.
  Mascagni, Pietro (arr. Eduardo Marzo). Luke 1:28, 30-31.
  Mascagni, Pietro (arr. Steven Mercurio). Luke 1:28, 30-31.
  Meininger, F. C. Luke 1:28, 30-31, 42.
  Millard, H. Luke 1:28, 30-31, 42.
  Millard, H. (arr. Gottlieb Harms). Luke 1:28, 30-31, 42.
  Peeters, Flor. Luke 1:28, 30-31, 42.
  Pinkham, Daniel. Luke 1:28, 30-31, 42.
  Rameau, J. P. Luke 1:28, 30-31, 42.
  Rheinberger, Josef. Luke 1:28, 30-31, 42.
  Rodríguez, Bernardo (arr. Rick Modlin). Luke 1:28, 30-31, 42.
  Saint-Saëns, Camille. Luke 1:28, 30-31, 42.
  Schubert, Franz. Luke 1:28, 30-31, 42.
  Soler, Hanns. Luke 28, 30-31.
  Whitaker, James. Luke 1:28, 30-31, 42.

Awake, All Ye People. Bach, J. S. I Corinthians 15:20, 26-28.
Awake, Arise. Foley, John B. Isaiah 60:1-4.
Awake, O North Wind. Foss, Lukas. Song of Songs 4:16.
Awake Thou That Sleepest.
Handel, G. F. I Corinthians 15:20, 23.
Ward-Stephens. Ephesians 5:14.
Awesome God. Mullins, Rich. Genesis 1:1-3.

Babylon.
Schoenbachler, Tim. Psalm 137:00.
Watson, Michael. Psalm 137:1.
Babylon Was a Great City. Walton, William. Revelation 18:10-13.
Balm in Gilead.
Spiritual (arr. Harry T. Burleigh). Jeremiah 8:22.
Spiritual (arr. William Dawson). Jeremiah 8:22.
Spiritual (arr. Mark Hayes). Jeremiah 8:22.
Spiritual (arr. Hall Johnson). Jeremiah 8:22.
A Banquet Is Prepared. Kavanaugh, John. Psalm 23:00 (based on).
Barocha. Card, Michael. Numbers 6:24.
Baruch Hashem Adonai. Rogers, Dawn and Tricia Walker. Job 1:21a.
The Battle Belongs to the Lord. Owens, Jimmy and Jamie Collins. I Samuel 17:47.
Be Bold, Be Strong. Chapman, Morris. Joshua 1:9 (based on).
Be Exalted, O God.
Chambers, Brent. Psalm 57:9-11.
Chambers, Brent (arr. Yankitis, Jane). Psalm 57:9-11.
Be Glad, O Ye Righteous. Huhn, Bruno S. Psalm 32:11.
Be it Done unto Me. Hurd, Bob (arr. Craig S. Kingsbury). Luke 1:26-28.
Be Joyful in the Lord, All You Lands. Schalk, Carl. Psalm 100:1.
Be Merciful, Even As Your Father Is Merciful. Krapf, Gerhard. Luke 6:36-42.
Be Merciful, O Lord.
Godard, Benjamin. Psalm 67:00.
Joncas, Michael. Psalm 51:1-4, 10-12.
Be Merciful unto Me. Head, Michael. Psalm 57:00.
Be Not Afraid.
Bertrand, Lucy and Brown Bertrand. Mark 6:50.
Courtney, Craig. Isaiah 43:1-4.
Dufford, Bob. Isaiah 43:2-3.
Dufford, Bob (arr. Theophane Hytreak). Isaiah 43:2-3.
Dufford, Bob (arr. Jack Schrader). Isaiah 43:2-3.
Koch, Frederick. II Chronicles 20:15b-17.
Schütz, Heinrich. Luke 2:10-12.
Be Not Ashamed. Talmud, Rabbi Y. (arr. Velvel Pasternak). Psalm 42:11a.
Be Not Far from Me. Nelhybel, Vaclav. Psalm 22:11.
Be Not Far from Me, Oh God. VanWoert, Rutger. Isaiah 45:1-2, 22.
Be of Good Courage. Beaumont, Vivian. Psalm 31:19, 24.
Be Still. Lowe, Augustus F. Psalm 46:10.
Be Still and Know.
Chapman, Steve Curtis (arr. Bryce Inman). Exodus 15:26b.
Chapman, Steve Curtis and Tom Fettke. Exodus 15:26b.
Chapman, Steve Curtis and Tom Fettke (arr. Lee Herrington). Exodus 15:26b.
Be Still and Know That I Am God.
Bitgood, Roberta. Psalm 46:10a.
Dungan, Olive. Psalm 46:00.
Be Still, and Know. Powers, Margaret Westlake. Psalm 46:1-6, 10.
Be Strong and Take Courage. Chiasson, Basil (arr. Carl Seal). Joshua 1:9.
Be Strong in the Lord. Bach, J. S. Ephesians 6:16-17.
Be Thou Exalted. Huhn, Bruno S. Psalm 21:13.
Be Thou Faithful unto Death. Mendelssohn, Felix. Revelation 2:10.
Be Thou Still. Franck, César. Psalm 46:10.
Be with Me. Hurd, Bob (arr. Craig S. Kingsbury). Psalm 91:1-2, 10-12, 14-15 (based on).
Be with Me, O God. Hurd, Bob (arr. Craig S. Kingsbury). Psalm 16:10.
Be Ye Kind, One to Another. Davis, Katherine K. Ephesians 4:31-32.
Be Ye Sure. Handel, G. F. (ed. Stan Pethel). Psalm 100:3.
The Beatitudes.
Browning, Mortimer. Matthew 5:1-12.
Foley, John B. Matthew 5:3-10.
Humphreys, Don. Matthew 5:1-10.
Kavanaugh, Patrick. Matthew 5:1-12.
Malotte, Albert Hay. Matthew 5:3-6.
Wood, Don. Matthew 5:1-10, 12.
Beatus vir. Paer, Ferdinando. Psalm 111:00.
The Beauty of the Lord. Lovelace, Austin C. Psalm 90:17.
Because the Lord Is My Shepherd. Walker, Christopher. Psalm 23:00.
Because You Are God's Chosen Ones. Smith, G. Alan. Colossians 3:12-17.
Before the Sun Burned Bright. Schutte, Daniel L. Jeremiah 1:4-10.
Begone Satan. Bender, Jan. Matthew 4:10.
Behold, a Virgin Shall Be with Child. LaMontaine, John. Matthew 1:23.
Behold, a Virgin Shall Conceive. Handel, G. F. Isaiah 7:14.
Behold and See. Handel, G. F. Lamentations 1:12.
Behold, Bless Ye the Lord. Rorem, Ned. Psalm 134:00.
Behold, God Is Mighty. Wooler, Alfred. Job 36:5, 6, 7.
Behold, God Is My Salvation. Lindh, Jody W. Isaiah 12:2, 4b-5.
Behold, How Fair and Pleasant. Vogel, Howard. Song of Songs 7:6.
Behold, How Good. Edmunds, John. Psalm 133:00.
Behold, How Good and How Pleasant. Matesky, Thelma. Psalm 133:00.
Behold How Good and How Pleasant It Is. Talmud, Rabbi Y. (arr. Velvel Pasternak). Psalm 133:1.
Behold, I Send an Angel. Head, Michael. Exodus 23:20, 22, 25.
Behold, I Stand at the Door. Bryant, Verna Mae. Revelation 3:20.
Behold, I Tell You a Mystery. Handel, G. F. I Corinthians 15:51-52a.
Behold, the Days Come. Steinberg, Ben. Amos 9:13, 15.
Behold! the Former Things Are Come to Pass. Brown, Allanson G. Y. Isaiah 42:6-7.
Behold, The House of God Is With Men. Raff, Joseph J. Revelation 21:3-4.
Behold, the Hungry He Fills. Vivaldi, Antonio. Luke 1:53.
Behold the Lamb. Rambo, Dottie. John 1:29.
Behold the Lamb of God.
Barker, Clement W. Matthew 3:16.
Dufford, Bob (arr. John B. Foley). Isaiah 53:4.

Handel, G. F. John 1:29.
Lyon, A. Laurence. Matthew 11:28.
Behold the Man.
Baroni, David and Niles Borop. Isaiah 53:3-7.
Owens, Jimmy. Isaiah 53:3.
Owens, Jimmy (arr. Tom Fettke). Isaiah 53:3.
Behold the Son of God. Mozart, W. A. John 3:13-15, 17-18.
Behold the Tabernacle of God. Hoffmeister, Leon Abbott. Revelation 21:3-4.
Behold the Upright. Krieg, Melita. Psalm 37:22a, 31, 33-37.
Behold the Wicked Man. Laderman, Ezra. Psalm 7:14-15.
Behold the Wood. Schutte, Daniel L. John 12:24, 32.
Behold! Thou Art Fair. Rochberg, George. Song of Songs 4:1.
Behold, Thus Is the Man Blessed. Ferris, William. Psalm 128:4-6.
Behold! What Manner of Love.
Hatch, Wilbur. I John 3:1-3.
MacDermid, James G. Genesis 1:26, 27.
Paris, Harry Allen. I John 3:1-3.
Behold What Names of Love.
Baumgartner, H. Leroy. I John 1:1, 5-7, 9.
Cruikshank, Helen M. I John 2:25.
Dubois, Theodore. I John 3:1-2.
Fichthoin, Claude. Matthew 4:4.
Humphreys, Don. I John 3:1-3.
Vantine, Patricia. I John 3:1.
Beloved. Marsh, Donald. Matthew 24:42.
Beloved, Let Us Love.
Busarow, Donald. I John 4:7-8.
Proulx, Richard. I John 4:7-8 (based on).
Beloved, Let Us Love One Another.
Head, Michael. I John 4:7.
Myers, Gordon. I John 4:7-8.
Beloved, Now Are We the Sons of God. Stearns, Peter Pindar. I John 3:2.
Benedica Dominum in Omni. Honegger, Arthur. Psalm 34:00.
Benedicto Nuptialis. Felciano, Richard. Psalm 92:12.
Benedictus.
Bach, J. S. Matthew 21:9.
Haydn, F. Joseph. Matthew 21:9.
Silvia, Giulio. Matthew 21:9.
Benedictus qui vent. Pergolesi, Giovanni B. (ed. Francesco Cafarelli). Matthew 21:9.
Beside Still Waters.
Deacon, Mary. Psalm 23:00.
Hamblen, Bernard. Psalm 23:00.
Beth. Tindall, Adrienne M. Psalm 119:10-13, 15.
Bethlehem Morning. Chapman, Morris. Isaiah 9:6.
Better Is One Day. Redman, Matt. Psalm 84:10.
Beyond the Borders. Cooper, Jim and Regie Hamm. I Chronicles 4:10.
Bind Me as a Seal Upon Your Heart. Saltzman, Peter. Song of Songs 8:6.
The Bird's Song. Vaughan Williams, Ralph. Psalm 23:00.
The Birth of Christ. Hoffmeister, Leon Abbott. Luke 1:30-32.
Bleibet in mir. Herbst, Johannes (ed. Karl Kroeger). John 15:4.
Bless His Holy Name. Crouch, Andraé. Psalm 103:01.
Bless Our God. Foley, John B. Ephesians 1:3-6, 11-13, 17-18.
Bless the Lord.
Barrett, Joanne and Ron E. Long. Psalm 103:1-4.
Christensen, Chris. Psalm 103-1-4.
Fredrickson, Carl. Psalm 103:1-5, 13, 17a, 20-22.
LaForge, Frank. Psalm 103:00.
Mason, Babbie. Psalm 103:1.
Bless the Lord, All Nations. Caldara, Antonio (ed. and arr. Michael Burkhardt). Psalm 100:2.
Bless the Lord, O My Soul.
Barker, Clement W. Psalm 67:00.
Davis, Katherine K. Psalm 103:1-4, 11, 13.
Fauré, Gabriel. Psalm 103:1-4, 19.
Franck, César. Psalm 103:2-4, 19.
Geisler, Johann Christian. Psalm 103.00.
Ippolitof-Ivanof, Mikhail (arr. William Stickles). Psalm 103:1-4.
Jordan, Alice. Psalm 103:00.
McArthur, Edwin. Psalm 103:1-3.
Stearns, Peter Pindar. Psalm 104:1, 24.
Unknown (arr. Tom Fettke). Psalm 103:1.
Walker, Christopher. Psalm 104:1-4 (based on).
Bless Thou the Lord. Benati (ed. Gertrude Tingley). Psalm 103:00.
Bless Yahweh, O My Soul. Rieth, Mildred F. Psalm 104:1, 3a, 19, 29 (based on).
The Blessed. Wolfe, Jacques. Matthew 5:3-11.
Blessed Are the Meek. Ward-Stephens. Matthew 5:5.
Blessed Are the Merciful. Ward-Stephens. Matthew 5:7.
Blessed Are the Peacemakers.
Sacco, Peter. Matthew 5:9-10.
Ward-Stephens. Matthew 5:9.
Blessed Are the Poor in Spirit. Ward-Stephens. Matthew 5:3.
Blessed Are the Pure in Heart. Ward-Stephens. Matthew 5:8.
Blessed Are the Undefiled in the Way. Tindall, Adrienne M. Psalm 119:1-7.
Blessed Are They. Schütz, Heinrich. Psalm 1:1-3.
Blessed Are They That Consider the Poor. Handel, G. F. Psalm 41:1-4.
Blessed Are They That Dwell in Thy House. Greene, Maurice. Psalm 84:4-5.
Blessed Are They That Fear the Lord. Handel, G. F. Psalm 128:1-2.
Blessed Are They That Mourn. Ward-Stephens. Matthew 5:4, 5.
Blessed Are They Which Are Persecuted. Ward-Stephens. Matthew 5:10.
Blessed Are They Which Do Hunger. Ward-Stephens. Matthew 5:6.
Blessed Are Those Who Fear the Lord.
Sinzheimer, Max. Psalm 128:00.
Powell, Robert J. Psalm 128:1.
Blessed Are You. Schutte, Daniel L. Genesis 48:16.
Blessed Are You, O God of Our Fathers. DeLong, Richard. Tobit 8:5-7.
Blessed Be the Lord. Foley, John B. Luke 1:68-79.
Blessed Be Thou Lord God of Israel. Greenfield, Alfred M. I Chronicles 29:10-11, 13-14.
Blessed Is He That Cometh. Mercadante, S. Mark 11:9-10.
Blessed Is the Man.
Clements, John. Psalm 1:1-3.
Greene, Maurice. Psalm 1:1, 4.
Lucke, Katharine E. Psalm 1:00.
Nelhybel, Vaclav. Psalm 1:00.
Ore, Charles W. Psalm 1:00.
Spies, Claudio. Psalm 1:1-3.
Wagner, Douglas E. Psalm 1:1-3.
Blessed Is the People. Parker, Clifton. Psalm 89:1, 15-16.
Blessed to Be a Blessing. Cox, Joe. Mark 10:15-16.
The Blessed Virgin's Expostulation. Purcell, Henry. Luke 2:42.
Blessings on the King. Manion, Tim. Isaiah 52:7-8.
Blest Are the Pure in Heart. Harker, F. Flaxington. Matthew 5:8.
Blest Are They. Haas, David. Matthew 5:3-12.

Blest Be the Lord. Schutte, Daniel L. Psalm 91:2-7, 10 (based on).
Blikke mich an und erbarme Dich meiner, Herr. Dvorák, Antonín. Psalm 25:16-18, 20.
Blow the Trumpet in Zion. Terndrup, Craig. Joel 2:1.
Blow Ye the Trumpet.
Andrews, Mark. Joel 2:12-13, 15-17.
Purcell, Henry. Joel 2:15.
B'Ni. Isaacson, Michael. Proverbs 3:1-6.
Bone Come A-knittin'. Wolfe, Jacques. Ezekiel 37:00 (based on).
Bonum Est Confidere. Berthier, Jacques (ed. Brother Robert). Psalm 92:1-2, 5, 12-13.
Bow Down Thine Ear.
Adler, Samuel. Psalm 86:1-5.
Gardner, Irene Justine. Psalm 86:1-3, 5-6, 11.
Bow Down Thine Ear, O Lord.
Frey, Richard E. Psalm 86:1-3, 5.
MacFadyen, Alexander. Psalm 86:1-4, 6-7, 11-12.
Bow Down Your Ear. Secchi, Antonio. Isaiah 55:00.
Bože! Bože! Písen novou. Dvorák, Antonín. Psalm 144:9.
Bread of Life. Mendelssohn, Felix. John 6:35.
The Bread of Life.
Koch, Frederick. John 6:00.
Olds, W. B. John 6:00.
The Bread That We Break. Dean, Stephen. I Corinthians 10:16-17.
Bring to Jehovah. Schütz, Heinrich (ed. Richard T. Gore). Psalm 29:1-2.
Bring Ye All the Tithes into the Storehouse. MacDermid, James G. Psalm 127:1.
Bringt her dem Herren.
Schütz, Heinrich. Psalm 29:1-2.
Schütz, Heinrich (arr. Ross Robert). Psalm 29:1-2.
Brood O'er Us. Roberts, John Varley. Genesis 1:3.
Brother James's Air.
Bain, James Leith Macbeth. Psalm 23:00.
Bain, James Leith Macbeth (arr. Malcolm Archer). Psalm 23:00.
But of the Times and the Seasons. Pinkham, Daniel. I Thessalonians 5:1-6.
But the Hour Cometh. LaForge, Frank. John 4:23-24, 35-36.
But the Lord Is Mindful of His Own.
DeLong, Richard. II Timothy 2:19.
Mendelssohn, Felix. Acts 9:2.
But Thou Didst Not Leave. Handel, G. F. Psalm 16:10.
But Who May Abide. Handel, G. F. Malachi 3:2.
By My Spirit. Phillips, Leslie. Zechariah 4:6 (and other).
By Night. Thomson, Virgil. Song of Songs 3:1-2.
By Night on My Bed. Foss, Lukas. Song of Songs 3:1, 3.
By the Rivers of Babylon.
Chajes, Julius. Psalm 137:00
Goldman, Edward M. Psalm 137:00.
Wilder, Alec. Psalm 137:00.
By the Shore of the River Babylon, Dvorák, Antonín. Psalm 137:1-5.
By the Still Waters of Babylon. Dvorák, Antonín. Psalm 137:1-5.
By the Waters of Babylon.
Bloch, Ernst. Psalm 137:00.
Dvorák, Antonín. Psalm 137:1-5.
Eville, Vernon. Psalm 137:00.
Howell, Charles T. Psalm 137:1-5.
Richards, Stephen. Psalm 137:00.
By Waters of Babylon.
Bach, J. S. Psalm 137:00.
Speaks, Oley. Psalm 137:1-5.

Cans't Thou By Searching Fine Our God? MacDermid, James G. Job 11:7, 13-15, 17.
Cantabo Domino in vita mea. Schütz, Heinrich. Psalm 104:1-3.
Cantata: All the Days of My Life. Talma, Louise. Psalm 27:4.
Cantate de Psaume. Milhaud, Darius. Psalm 129:00.
Cantate Domino. Hassler, Hans Leo (arr. Kenny Williams). Psalm 96:00.
Cantemus Domino. Viadana, Ludovico. Exodus 15:1-2.
Canticle I–My Beloved Is Mine and I Am His, op. 40. Britten, Benjamin. Song of Songs 2:16 (based on).
Canticle II–Abraham and Isaac, op. 51. Britten, Benjamin. Genesis 22:2-19 (based on).
Canticle of the Sun. Haugen, Marty. Psalm 19:1a.
Canticle of the Virgin. Skillings, Otis. Luke 1:46-55.
Cares Chorus. Willard, Kelly. I Peter 5:7 (based on).
Cast Thy Burden on the Lord. Mendelssohn, Felix (arr. Lynn Hodges). Psalm 55:21.
Celtic Alleluia. O'Carroll, Fintan and Christopher Walker. I John 4:8, 11-12, 16.
Center of My Life. Inwood, Paul. Psalm 16:1-2, 7-11 (based on).
Changed. Fettke, Tom. I Corinthians 15:51-55.
Chant Mode II. Daigle, Gary. Matthew 6:9-13.
A Charge to Keep Have I. Mason, Lowell (arr. Rhonda Sandberg). Leviticus 8:35.
Chariot's Comin'. Spiritual (arr. Jean Anne Shafferman). II Kings 2:11.
Charity.
Gulliksen, Kenn. I Corinthians 13:1-7, 11-13.
Hartley, Evaline. I Corinthians 13:1-6, 8, 13.
A Child's 23rd Psalm. Clatterbuck, Robert C. Psalm 23:00.
Chosen Generation. Clattenburg, Jeannie and Rick Powell. I Peter 2:9.
Christ Is Lord. Pendleton, Emmet. Isaiah 9:6.
Christ Is Risen. Scott, John Prindle. I Corinthians 5:7-8.
Christ Is With Me. Coleman. John 15:4.
The Christ of God. Foley, John B. Luke 9:20-24.
Christ Whose Glory. Butt, James. Malachi 4:2.
Christ Will Be Your Light. Haas, David. Ephesians 5:8-15.
Christmas Carol. Zimmermann, Heinz Werner. Psalm 95:1.
Christmas Prophecy. Burroughs, Bob. Matthew 1:21.
City of God. Schutte, Daniel L. Isaiah 9:6.
Clap Hands, Be Glad! Wagner, Douglas E. Psalm 47:1.
Clap Your Hands. Owens, Jimmy. Psalm 47:1.
Clap Your Hands, All You People. Burton, Daniel. Psalm 47:1.
Clouds and Darkness. Dvorák, Antonín. Psalm 97:2-6.
Come and Sing Praises. Chapman, Morris and Greg Massanart. Psalm 29:1-2 (based on).
Come, Be Joyful. Mozart, W. A. (arr. Hal H. Hopson). Psalm 100:12.
Come Before Him. Tunney, Dick and Melodie Tunney. I Chronicles 16:29.
Come Blessed Savior. Saint-Saëns, Camille. Luke 1:28, 30-31, 42.
Come, Every One Who Is Thirsty. Isaiah 55:1. Rider, Lucy.
Come, Holy Spirit.
Peterson, John W. (arr. Tom Fettke). Acts 1:8.
Vieker, Jon D. Psalm 104:24, 28a, 30.
Come into His Presence. Baird, Lynn. Psalm 95:2.

Come, Let Us Fix Our Eyes on Jesus. Kosche, Kenneth T. Hebrews 12:2.
Come, Let Us Make a Joyful Noise. Handel, G. F. Psalm 95:00.
Come, Let Us Praise. Zimmermann, Heinz Werner. Psalm 95:1.
Come, Let Us Worship and Bow Down. Doherty, Dave. Psalm 95:6-7 (based on).
Come Let's Worship Him. Carswell, Eddie and Oliver Wells. I Chronicles 16:8-9.
Come, My Beloved.
Foss, Lukas. Song of Songs 7:11.
Gottlieb, Jack. Song of Songs 7:10-14.
Overby, Rolf Peter. Song of Songs 7:11-13.
Rochberg, George. Song of Songs 7:11.
Come Near Ye Nations. LaForge, Frank. Isaiah 34:1.
Come Now and Let Us Reason Together. Stebbins, G. Waring. Isaiah 1:18, 20, 28.
Come, O Come, Let Us Sing. Haugen, Marty. Psalm 95:1-2, 6-9.
Come, Sing to the Lord. Cooper, Lowell. Psalm 95:1-7.
Come, Sing unto the Lord. Martin, Joseph M. Psalm 96:1-3, 11-12 (based on).
Come, Take the Water of Life. Fischer, Irwin. Revelations 22:1, 14, 17.
Come to Me.
Beethoven, Ludwig van (adapted). Matthew 11:28-30.
Joncas, Michael. Matthew 11:28-30.
Come to Me All Who Are Weary. Schutte, Daniel L. Matthew 9:11-13.
Come to the Table. Kufferschmid, Steve. Luke 22:14-30.
Come to the Waters.
Cherubini, Luigi (ed. and arr. K. K. Davis and N. Loring). Isaiah 55:1, 3.
Handel, G. F. Isaiah 55:1, 3.
Come unto Him.
Bach, J. S. Matthew 11:28-30.
Handel, G. F. Matthew 11:28-29.
Leslie, Henry. Matthew 11:28-30.
Cady, Gertrude. Matthew 11:28-29.
Chadwick, George Whitefield. Matthew 11:28-30.
Coenen, William. Matthew 11:28-30.
Dvorák, Antonín. Matthew 11:28-30.
Haugen, Marty. Matthew 6:28-32.
Hurd, Bob. Isaiah 62:3.
LaForge, Frank. Matthew 11:28.
Rutenber, C. B. Matthew 11:28-30.
Scarlatti, Alessandro. Matthew 7:7-8.
Come unto Me, All Ye That Labor. Willan, Healey. Matthew 11:28-30.
Come with Me into the Fields. Schutte, Daniel L. Matthew 9:39.
Come Worship the Lord. Paris, Twila. Psalm 106:1.
Come Ye Blessed.
Gaul, Alfred Robert. Matthew 25:34.
Scott, John Prindle. Matthew 25:34-36.
Come Ye Children. Sullivan, Sir Arthur. Hebrews 12:6,11.
Comfort My People.
Kosche, Kenneth T. Isaiah 40:00.
Misetich, Marianne. Isaiah 40:4.
Comfort Ye. Handel, G. F. Isaiah 40:1-3.
Comfort Ye My People.
Dvorák, Antonín. Isaiah 40:1.
Rubenstein, Anton (arr. Carl Fredrickson). Isaiah 40:1-3.
The Commission. Burroughs, Bob. Matthew 9:36b-37.
Communion Song. McGuire, Bobby. Luke 22:17-20.
Confitebor Tibi. Krapf, Gerhard. Isaiah 12:00.
Confitebor tibi Domine.
Honegger, Arthur. Psalm 138:00.
Posch, Isaac (ed. Karl Geiringer). Psalm 111:00.
Consider and Hear Me.
Harker, F. Flaxington. Psalm 13:00.
Wooler, Alfred. Psalm 13:00.
Consider the Lilies.
Bischoff, John W. (ed. Carl Fredrickson). Matthew 6:25c-26, 28b-30.
Scott, John Prindle. Matthew 6:28-34.
Sleeth, Natalie. Matthew 6:25-33.
Topliff, Robert. Matthew 6:25-26, 28-29.
Consume Them All, Lord Sabaoth. Mendelssohn, Felix. Exodus 32:10.
A Contrite Heart. Beethoven, Ludwig van (arr. K. Lee Scott). Psalm 51:00.
Cornerstone.
Goss, Lari. Isaiah 9:6c.
Patillo, Leon. Isaiah 9:6c.
Patillo, Leon (arr. Steven V. Taylor). Isaiah 9:6c.
Could He Be the Messiah? Smith, Michael W. and Deborah D. Smith. Matthew 14:17-21 (based on).
Courage. Butt, James. Joshua 1:5-7.
Covenant Hymn. Daigle, Gary. Ruth 1:16.
Create in Me.
Haugen, Marty. Psalm 51:1, 10-12, 15.
Hurd, Bob. Psalm 51:3-4, 9, 12, 14 (based on).
Powers, George. Psalm 51:10-12, 15.
Create in Me a Clean Heart.
Bannister, Brown. Psalm 51:10-12 (based on).
Bernhard, Christoph. Psalm 51:10-11.
Buxtehude, Dietrich (ed. James Boeringer). Psalm 51:10-12.
Evans, Vincent. Psalm 51:00.
Greeen, Keith. Psalm 51:10-12.
Green, Keith (arr. Bill Svarda). Psalm 51:10-13.
Miller, Merle. Psalm 51:1012.
Mueller, Carl F. Psalm 51:10-13.
Create in Me a Clean Heart, O God.
Barnes, Frederick M. Psalm 51:10-13.
Riker, Franklin. Psalm 51:10-15.
Willan, Healey. Psalm 51:10-12.
Create Me Again. Cooney, Rory. Psalm 51:00 (based on).
Creation. Haugen, Marty. Genesis 1:00.
Creation Hymn. Beethoven, Ludwig van (arr. Harrell). Psalm 8:3-4.
Creation Will Be at Peace. Page, Anna Laura. Isaiah 11:6-9.
Crimond. Irvine, Jessie S. (descant by W. Baird Ross). Psalm 23:00.
Cross of Calvary. Gounod, Charles. Luke 1:28, 30-31, 42.
Cry of the Prophet. Applebaum, Louis. Jeremiah 2:2.

Daily Will I Love Thee. Schütz, Heinrich. Psalm 18:2-7.
Dann werden die Gerechten leuchten. Mendelssohn, Felix. Matthew 13:43.
Darkness and Thunderclouds Are Round About Him. Dvorák, Antonín. Psalm 97:2-6.
Das ist ein köstlich ding, dem Herren danden. Bernhard, Christoph. Psalm 92:2-5.
Daughters of Jerusalem. Sullivan, Sir Arthur. Luke 23:28-29a.
David Mourns for Absalom. Diamond, David. II Samuel 18:33.

David's Psalm. Broones, Martin. Psalm 23:00.
David's Song. Roth, John. Psalm 23:00.
The Days of All Thy Sorrow. Peter, Johann Frederich (ed. and arr. Thor Johnson and Donald M. McCorkle). Isaiah 60:20.
De Blin' Man Stood on De Road An' Cried. Spiritual (arr. Harry T. Burleigh). Mark 10:46, 52 (based on).
De David. Strandberg, Newton. Psalm 100:00.
De Profundis. Sifler, Paul. Psalm 130:00.
Death of a Son. Card, Michael. Psalm 22:00.
Death, Where is Your Sting? Larson, Lloyd. I Corinthians 15:51-52, 55, 57 (based on).
Deep Within. Haas, David. Jeremiah 31:33.
Delight Thyself in the Lord. Fischer, Irwin. Psalm 145:00.
Deliver Us, O God of Israel. Foley, John B. Psalm 25:1-6, 9, 22.
Denn es gehet dem Menschen. Brahms, Johannes. Ecclesiastes 3:19-22.
Depart From Me. Scott, John Prindle. Matthew 25:41-45.
Deposuit potentes.
Bach, J. S. Luke 1:52.
Pachelbel, Johann (arr. Jerald B. Stone). Luke 1:52.
Despite Locked Doors. Balchmetev, Nikolai. John 20:26-29.
Deux Abraham. Jongen, Joseph. Psalm 128:00.
Dialogus auf Ostern: Sie Haben meinen Herrn hinweggenommen. Bernhard, Christoph. John 20:13-17.
Didn't My Lord Deliver Daniel?
Spiritual (arr. Edward Boatner). Daniel 6:22 (based on).
Spiritual (arr. Harry T. Burleigh). Daniel 6:22 (based on).
Dignity and Honor Are Her Garb. Pasternak, Velvel. Proberbs 31:25-28.
Discubuit Jesus. Aichinger, Gregor. Luke 22:14-15.
Divine Calling. Bock, Fred. Romans 10:13-15.
Doch der Herr, er leitet die Irrenden recht. Mendelssohn, Felix. Psalm 25:8-9, 12-13.
Does Anybody Love the Children? Johnson, Gary. Mark 10:13-16.
Domine, Domine, Adjutor meus. Saint-Saëns, Camille. Psalm 19:14b.
Domine ne in furore tuo. Posch, Isaac (ed. Karl Geringer). Psalm 6:00.
Domine, non sum dignus. Aichinger, Gregor. Matthew 8:8.
Domine Salvum fac regem. Couperin, François. Psalm 19:10.
Dominus Illuminatis Mea. Revicki, Robert. Psalm 27:1.
Dominus regit me. Owens, Sam Batt. Psalm 23:00.
Don't Be Afraid. Mark 4:37-39. Bennett, Roger (arr. Russell Maudlin).
Don't Grow Weary (arr. Carl Seal). Harris, Don and Martin J. Nystrom. Galatians 6:9a.
Don't You Know. Borneman, Bruce and Judi. Psalm 150:1.
Don't You Weep When I'm Gone. Spiritual (arr. Harry T. Burleigh). Jeremiah 22:10 (based on).
Doth Not Wisdom Cry? MacDermid, James G. Proberbs 8:00.
Draw Near, All Ye People. Mendelssohn, Felix (arr. Lynn Hodges). I Kings 18:36-37.
Draw Nigh to God. Barker, Clement W. Romans 14:11.
Drop, Drop Slow Tears. Warren, Raymond. Luke 7:36-40, 47-48.
Du, Du bist mire ein Schirm und Schild. Dvorák, Antonín. Psalm 119:114, 115, 117, 120.
Du solst erfahren. Herbst, Johannes (arr. Karl Kroeger). Isaiah 60:16.
Dwelling Place. Foley, John B. Ephesians 1:2.
Each Time I Think of You. Hurd, Bob (ed. Craig S. Kingsbury). Isaiah 46:3-5.
The Earth Is Lord's.
Freudenthal, Josef. Psalm 24:1-6.
McAfee, Don. Psalm 24:1-5.
The Earth is the Lord's.
Lynes, Frank. Psalm 24:1-5, 7-9.
Wagner, Douglas E. Psalm 24:1-8.
Ward-Stephens. Psalm 24:00.
The Earth with All That Dwell Therein. Adler, Samuel. Psalm 24:1-4, 7-10.
Earthen Vessels. Foley, John B. I Corinthians 1:27-29.
Easter Song. Speaks, Oley. Matthew 28:1-6.
Ecco Dominus veniet. Posch, Isaac. Zechariah 9:9.
The Eighth Psalm. Wright, Norman S. Psalm 8:00.
Eili, Eili! Invocation. Schalitt (adapted Kurt Schindler). Psalm 22:2.
Eile mich, Gott, zu erretten.
Hammerschmidt, Andreas. Psalm 70:2-6.
Schütz, Heinrich. Psalm 40:14-18.
Wiemer, Wolfgang. Psalm 70:2-6.
Ein jeder Lauft, der in den Schranken kauft. Telemann, Georg Philipp. I Corinthians 6:11.
Einbitte ich vom Herren. Schütz, Heinrich. Psalm 27:4.
El n'komōs. Pasternak, Velvel. Psalm 94:1-2.
Elohim! Why Hast Thou Forsaken Me? Bloch, Ernst. Psalm 22:00.
The Enemy Said. Handel, G. F. Exodus 15:9 (based on).
Enter in the Wilderness. Traditional Folk Song–Hasidic. Isaiah 40:3-5.
Entreat Me Not. Groton, Frederic. Ruth 1:16-17.
Entreat Me Not to Leave Thee.
Avery, Lawrence. Ruth 1:16-17.
Birch, Robert Fairfax. Ruth 1:16-17.
Damrosch, Leopold. Ruth 1:16-17.
Goldman, Maurice. Ruth 1:16-17.
Gore, Richard T. Ruth 1:16-17.
Gounod, Charles. Ruth 1:16-17.
Roff, Joseph. Ruth 1:16.
White, Louie. Ruth 1:16-17.
Young, Gordon. Ruth 1:16-17.
Entreat Me Not to Leave You. Poulsen, James. Ruth 1:16-17.
Envía Tu Espíritu. Hurd, Bob. Psalm 104:30.
Epistle to the Corinthians. Read, Gardner. I Corinthians 13:00.
Er weidet seine Herde. Handel, G. F. Isaiah 40:11.
Erbarme dich. Bach, J. S. Psalm 139:7-10 (based on).
Erhöre mich, Wenn ich rufe. Schütz, Heinrich. Psalm 4:2.
Eripe Me Domine, ab homine malo. Honegger, Arthur. Psalm 140:00.
Erkennet, erkennt, dass der Herr ist Gott. Jadassohn, Solomon. Psalm 100:3.
Der erste Psalm. Karg-Elert, Sigfrid. Psalm 1:00.
Es danken dir, Gott, die Voelker. Hammerschmidt, Andreas. Psalm 67:3-7.
Es ist genug! Mendelssohn, Felix. I Kings 19:4, 10.
Es wird eine rute aufgehen vom stamm Isai. Bernhard, Christoph. Isaiah 11:1-4.
Esa Einai. Steinberg, Ben. Psalm 121:00.
Eshes Chayil. Pasternak, Velvel. Proberbs 31:10-17.
Eso énai, no. 1. Horowitz, Rabbi M. (arr. Velvel Pasternak). Psalm 121:1-2.
Eso énai, no. 2. Rebbi of Chernowitzer (arr. Velvel Pasternak). Psalm 121:1-4.

Esurientes.
Pachelbel, Johann (arr. Jerald B. Stone). Luke 1:53.
Vivaldi, Antonio (Günter Gralich). Luke 1:53.
Esurientes implevit. Vivaldi, Antonio (arr. Richard Walters). Luke 1:53.
Et exultavit. Bach, J. S. Luke 1:47.
Et exultavit spiritus meus. Bach, J. S. Luke 1:46.
Et in Terra Pax Hominibus. Vivaldi, Antonio (arr. Vernon Whaley). Luke 2:14b.
Et misericordia. Pachelbel, Johann (arr. Jerald B. Stone). Luke 1:53.
Et misericordia ejus. Charpentier, Marc-Antoine (M. Alfred Bichsel). Luke 1:53.
Eternal is His Mercy. Joncas, Michael. Psalm 136:00 (based on).
Eternal Love. Castelnuovo-Tedesco, Maro. Hosea 2:21-22.
Etz Chayim. Weiner, Lazar. Proverbs 3:17-18.
Even Moasu. Chait, B. (arr. Velvel Pasternak). Psalm 118:22.
Evening Psalm. Inwood, Paul. Psalm 141:1-5, 8-9.
Evening Song. Smith, Marcus. Matthew 16:25 (based on).
Ever on My Lips. Schutte, Daniel L. (arr. Bob Harrold). Psalm 34:1 (based on).
Ever Will I Praise. Bach, J. S. II Samuel 22:3.
Everlasting Your Love. Hurd, Bob. Psalm 136:1, 4-6, 8-9.
Every day Will I Give Thanks. Handel, G. F. Psalm 145:2, 9.
Every Good and Perfect Gift.
Rider, Dale G. James 1:17-22.
Sisler, Hampson, A. James 1:16-17, 19-20, 22, 25, 27.
Every Morning in Your Eyes. Cooney, Rory. Psalm 34:1-8 (based on).
Every Nation on Earth. Joncas, Michael. Psalm 72:1-2, 7-8, 10-11, 12-13.
Every Valley.
Beck, John Ness (trans. Craig Courtney). Isaiah 40:4-5.
Dufford, Bob. Isaiah 35:5-6.
Handel, G. F. Isaiah 40:4.
Ew'ge Qwelle, milder Strom. Telemann, Georg Philipp. James 1:17-22.
Exalt the Lord Our God. Gardner, Daniel. Psalm 99:9 (based on).
Exalt the Name (with *He is Exalted*). Paris, Twila. Psalm 99:2-3.
Except the Lord Build the House. Myers, Gordon. Psalm 127:1.
Expectans Expectavi Dominum. Saint-Saëns, Camille. Psalm 40:1.
Exsultate justi in Domino. Posch, Isaac (ed. Karl Geiringer). Psalm 33:00.
Exultavit cor meum. Schütz, Heinrich. I Samuel 2:1-2.
Eye Hath Not Seen.
Faulkner, William M. I Corinthians 2:9.
Gaul, Alfred Robert. Isaiah 64:4.
Stearns, Peter Pindar. I Corinthians 2:9.
Eye Hath Not Seen, Nor Ear Heard. Foster, Myles B. John 14:15.
The Eyes of All Wait upon Thee. Kirk, Theron. Psalm 145:15-16, 18.
The Eyes of All Wait upon Thee, O Lord. Boyce, William. Psalm 145:15-16.
Ezek'el Saw the Wheel. Spiritual (arr. Margaret Bonds). Ezekiel 1:15 (based on).

Faith Is. Lovelace, Austin C. Hebrews 11:1-2, 13, 16b.
Faith, Hope and Love. Walker, Christopher. John 13:5-7.
Far Above Riches. Fettke, Tom. Proverbs 31:10-31.
Farewell, Dear Companion. Walker, W. (arr. Max V. Exner). Luke 2:29-35.
Father Abraham, Have Mercy on Me. Krapf, Gerhard. Luke 16:19-31.
Father, I Put My Life in Your Hands. Talbot, John Michael. Psalm 31:00.
Father, May They All Be One. Foley, John B. John 17:3-4, 21-23.
Father, Mercy. Dufford, Bob. Psalm 51:1-8 (based on).
Fear Not! Tindall, Adrienne M. Isaiah 41:10.
Fear Not, Little Flock. Bach, J. S. Luke 12:24, 27, 29, 32.
Fear Not Ye, O Israel. Buck, Dudley. Jeremiah 31:6, 16.
The Fear of the Lord. Leichtling, Alan. Proberbs 1:7-9.
Fecit potentiam. Bach, C. P. E. Luke 1:51.
Feed My Lambs. Koch, Frederick. John 21:00.
Feed My Sheep. Faulkner, George. John 21:15.
Feurchte dich nicht. Schütz, Heinrich. Isaiah 41:10.
Fili mi, Absalom. Schütz, Heinrich. II Samuel 18:33.
Fill Us With Your Love, O Lord. Stewart, Roy James. Psalm 90:12-17.
The First Commandment. Clifford, Beatrice. Mark 12:28-31.
The First Easter Morn. Scott, John Prindle. Luke 24:00.
First John 4:7 and 8. Ryder, Dennis. I John 4:7-8.
The First Psalm. Bone, Gene / Fenton, Howard. Psalm 1:00.
Fling Wide the Gates. Mahnke, Allan. Psalm 24:7-10.
Flow River Flow. Hurd, Bob. Isaiah 35:1.
For Behold, Darkness Shall Cover the Earth. Handel, G. F. Isaiah 60:2-3.
For Everything Its Season. Koch, Frederick. Ecclesiastes 3:1-8.
For God So Loved. Dauermann, Stuart. John 3:16.
For He Hath Regarded. Bach, J. S. Luke 1:48.
For He That is Mighty. Bach, J. S. Luke 1:49.
For I Am Called By Thy Name. Gates, Crawford. Jeremiah 15:16 (based on).
For I Am Persuaded. Floyd, Carlisle. Romans 8:38, 39.
For I Had Gone Forth. Mendelssohn, Felix. Psalm 42:3-4.
For Know Ye Not That Ye Are His Temple. Mendelssohn, Felix. I Corinthians 3:16-17.
For Look As High As Heaven Is. Handel, G. F. Psalm 97:10.
For Look As High As the Heaven. Handel, G. F. Psalm 95:00.
For Me a Table. Bach, J. S. Psalm 23:5.
For My Soul Is Athirst. Kiel, Friedrich. Psalm 42:2.
For My Soul Thirsteth for God. Mendelssohn, Felix. Psalm 42:2.
For the Lord Has Comforted Zion.
Benet, Ch. (arr. Velvel Pasternak). Isaiah 51:3.
Horowitz, Rabbi M (arr. Velvel Pasternak). Isaiah 51:3.
For the Lord Is a Mighty God.
Mendelssohn, Felix (arr. Hal H. Hopson). Psalm 95:3-6.
Mendelssohn, Felix (arr. James McKelvy). Psalm 95:3-6.
For the Lord Will Lead. Mendelssohn, Felix. Psalm 24:8-9, 12-13.
For the Love of God. St. James, Rebecca and Matt Bronleewe. I Corinthians 13:1-3.
For the Mountains Shall Depart.
Bowling, Blanche. Isaiah 54:10, 13.
MacDermid, James G. Isaiah 55:6.
Mendelssohn, Felix. Isaiah 54:10.
Wagner, Douglas E. Isaiah 54:13.
For This Our Truest Interest. Handel, G. F. Psalm 95:1-2.
For This Purpose. Kendrick, Graham. I John 3:8b.
For unto Us. Tunney, Melodie and Dick Tunney. Isaiah 9:6.

For unto Us a Child Is Born. Handel, G. F. Isaiah 9:6.
For You Are My God. Foley, John B. Psalm 16:2-5, 9, 11 (based on).
Forever I Will Sing.
Foley, John B. Psalm 89:1-6, 16-19, 25, 27.
Lynch, Mike. Psalm 89:1-2, 15-16.
Schoenbachler, Tim. Psalm 89:00.
Talbot, John Michael. Psalm 89:00.
Forgive Our Sins as We Forgive. Fettke, Tom. Matthew 6:12.
Four Phrases From Psalm 91. Bukvich. Psalm 91:1, 4-5, 11.
Fracción Del Pan. Hurd, Bob. Psalm 34:9.
Fraters: Si Consurrexistis cum Christo. Soler, Joseph. Colossians 3:1-4.
Freely, Freely. Owens, Carol. Matthew 10:8 (based on).
Frohlocket mit Händen. Schütz, Heinrich. Psalm 47:1-6.
From All That Dwell Below the Skies. Slater, Jean. Psalm 117:00.
From My Mother's Womb. Hurd, Bob. Psalm 22:2-3, 10-11, 17.
From Psalm 49. Orland, Henry. Psalm 49:00.
From the End of the Earth. Laderman, Ezra. Psalm 61:1.
From the Song of Songs. Blackford, Richard. Song of Songs 2:00.
From Whence Shall Come My Help?
Kehati, Pinchas (arr. Velvel Pasternak). Psalm 121:1-2.
Proulx, Richard. Psalm 121:00.
Fürchte euch nicht. Hammerschmidt, Andreas. Luke 2: 10-11.

Garment of Praise.
Fredrickson, Carl. Isaiah 61:1-3.
Ingles, David. Isaiah 61:3b (based on).
Gather Your People. Hurd, Bob. Isaiah 2:3-4.
Gentle Shepherd. Colgan, Bro. Tobias (arr. Randall DeBruyn). Psalm 23:00.
Gentle Shepherd, Kind and True. Hopson, Hal H. Luke 15:3-10.
The Gift of Love. Hopson, Hal H. I Corinthians 13:1, 3.
Give Ear, O God, Unto My Prayer. Dvorák, Antonín. Psalm 55:1-8.
Give Ear Oh Ye Heaven. Selby, Peter H. Deuteronomy 32:1-4, 9-12.
Give God, the Father, Praise. Schütz, Heinrich. Psalm 29:1-2.
Give Me a New Heart, O God. Walker, Christopher. Psalm 51:00 (based on).
Give Me an Understanding Heart. Rubenstein, Anton (ed. Carl Fredrickson). I Kings 3:9.
Give Thanks to the Lord.
Hopson, Hal H. Psalm 106:1, 2.
Schutte, Daniel L. (arr. Randall DeBruyn). Psalm 136:1-4 (based on).
Talbot, John Michael. Psalm 107:1.
Give Thanks unto God. Boito, A. Psalm 136:1-2 (and other).
Give Thanks unto the Lord. Starer, Robert. Psalm 136:1-9.
Give to God. Foley, John B. Psalm 96:1-5, 7-13.
Gleich wie der Rauch schnell verweht. Handel, G. F. Psalm 68:00.
Gloria.
Handel, G. F. Luke 2:14.
Rorem, Ned. Luke 2:14.
Vierdanck, Johann (ed. and arr. Michael Burkhardt). Luke 2:14.
Vivaldi, Antonio (arr. W. Daniel Landes). Luke 2:14.
Zentner, Johannes. Luke 2:14.
Gloria in Excelsis Deo. Wold, Wayne L. Luke 2:14.
Glorious Jerusalem. Parker, Horatio W. Isaiah 40:1.
Glory and Praise to Our God. Schutte, Daniel L. Psalm 65:00.
Glory of the Lord. Wallbridge, Richard L. A. Isaiah 60:1-4.
Glory to God.
Daigle, Gary. Luke 2:14.
Pergolesi, Giovanni B. (ed. Michael Burkhardt). Luke 2:14.
Schoenbachler, Tim (arr. Sheryl Soderberg). Luke 2:14.
Vivaldi, Antonio (arr. W. Daniel Landes). Luke 2:14.
Glory to God in the Highest. Harker, F. Flaxington. Luke 2:10-14.
Go Down, Moses.
Spiritual (arr. Edward Boatner). Exodus 8:1.
Spiritual (arr. Harry T. Burleigh). Exodus 8:1.
Spiritual (arr. Michael Johnson). Exodus 8:1.
Spiritual (arr. Florence Price). Exodus 8:1.
Go Out to all the World. Haas, David. Psalm 117:00.
Go Out to the World. Joncas, Michael. Matthew 28:19-20.
Go Therefore and Make Disciples of All Nations. Schalk, Carl. Matthew 28:19-20.
Go Thy Way, Eat Thy Bread With Joy. Pinkham, Daniel. Ecclesiastes 9:7-9.
Go to All the World. Hart, Don. Matthew 28:18-20.
Go Up, Child. Mendelssohn, Felix. I Kings 18:43-44.
Go Ye Forth in His Name. Dencke, Jeremiah. Matthew 25:1-6.
God and Man. Bach, J. S. John 17:1, 11.
God Be Merciful to Me. Wooler, Alfred. Psalm 51:00.
God Be Merciful unto Us.
Edwards, Leo. Psalm 67:00.
Koch, John. Psalm 67:00.
God Bless the King. Vance, Margaret. Luke 19:28-39.
God Does All Things Well. Bach, J. S. (arr. David Stocker). Mark 7:37.
God Exalted Him. Fettke, Tom. Philippians 2:5-11.
God Hath Led His People On. Mendelssohn, Felix. Deuteronomy 32:11.
God Hath Made Us All. Jadassohn, Solomon. Psalm 100:3.
God, Hear My Voice. Raff, Joseph J. Psalm 27:7, 9.
God Is a Constant Sure Defense. Handel, G. F. Psalm 9:9-10.
God Is a Spirit.
Hopekirk, Helen. John 4:23-24.
McArthur, Edwin. John 4:23-24.
Roberts, J. E. John 4:23-24.
Scott, Charles P. (ed. Wilman Wilmans). John 4:23-24.
Scott, John Prindle. John 4:23-24.
VanDyke, May. Psalm 104:00.
God Is Love.
Humphreys, Don. I John 4:16.
Kavanaugh, John. I John 4:16.
God Is My Light. Haas, David. Psalm 27:4, 13-14.
God Is My Refuge. Montemayor, Judy Horner. Psalm 46:1-2.
God Is My Salvation. Calder, Lee. Isaiah 12:3-4.
God Is My Shepherd. Dvorák, Antonín. Psalm 23:1-4.
God Is Our Refuge.
MacDermid, James G. Psalm 46:1-3, 6-7, 9-10.
Ward-Stephens. Psalm 46:00.
God Is Our Refuge and Our Strength. Luther, Martin (arr. Thomas J. Fleming). Psalm 46:1-7.
God Is Our Refuge and Strength. Hanson, Howard. Psalm 46:00.
God Is Spirit. Gounod, Charles. Psalm 51:16-17.

God, Let Your Mercy. Foley, John B. Psalm 33:1-2, 4-7, 12-13, 18-22.
God, Make a Heart in Me. Rieth, Mildred F. Psalm 51:10-12, 15 (based on).
God Mounts His Throne. Haugen, Marty. Psalm 47:1, 2, 5-8.
God, My Father. Dubois, Theodore. Matthew 27:46.
God of Abraham. Jongen, Joseph. Psalm 128:00.
God of Love Beyond All Wonder. Roth, John. Matthew 6:9-13.
The God of Love My Shepherd Is. Thiman, Eric H. Psalm 23:00.
God of Righteousness. Gilbert, Harry M. Psalm 4:1.
God of Vengeance. Pasternak, Velvel. Psalm 94:1-2.
God, Send Out Your Spirit. Foley, John B. Psalm 104:1-3b, 5-6, 10-14, 24, 27-28, 30-31, 33-34.
God Sent His Son into the World. Handel, G. F. (ed. Earnest Murphy). John 3:16-17.
God Shall Wipe Away All Tears.
Ambrose, Paul. Isaiah 35:10.
Field, J. T. Revelation 21:4.
Harker, F. Flaxington. Revelation 21:00.
Liszt, Franz (arr. Carl Fredrickson). Isaiah 25:8-9.
Peery, Rob Roy. Revelation 21:3-4.
Roma, Caro. Revelation 7:16.
God Sings in Pleasure. Archer, Violet. Zephaniah 1:00-3:20 (based on).
God So Loved. Eaton, Chris. John 3:16.
God So Loved the World.
Fearis, John S. John 3:16-17.
Fischer, Irwin. John 3:16-17.
Handel, G. F. John 3:16-17 (based on).
MacDermid, James G. John 3:5-17, 16.
Martinson, Joel. John 3:16-17.
Stainer, John. John 3:16.
Stainer, John (arr. Carl Fredrickson). John 3:16-17.
Stainer, John (arr. Carol McClure). John 3:16-17.
God That Made the World. MacDermid, James G. Acts 27:22, 24, 28.
God the Lord My Shepherd Is. Dvorák, Antonín. Psalm 23:1-4.
God's Angels. Kosche, Kenneth T. Psalm 91:11-12 (based on).
God's Command. Haas, David. Psalm 112:1-4, 6-7, 9.
God's Eye Is on the Sparrow. Hurd, Bob. Job 11:16.
God's Good Time. Kirkland, Terry. Ecclesiastes 3:1-9.
God's Love. Burroughs, Bob. John 3:16-17.
God's Own Time. Gieseke, Richard W. Acts 17:28.
God's Poor Ones. Foley, John B. Psalm 34:6, 15, 18.
God's Tender Mercy Know No Bounds. Handel, G. F. Psalm 57:10.
God's Time. Sacco, John. Psalm 27:13-14.
The Good Shepherd.
Schubert, Franz (arr. Carl Fredrickson). Psalm 23:00.
VanDewater, Beardsley. Psalm 23:00.
Good Tidings. Wetzler, Robert. Isaiah 61:1-3.
The Goodness of God. Haas, David. Psalm 34:1-6, 8 (based on).
Gott der Herr ist Hirte mir. Dvorák, Antonín. Psalm 23:1-4.
Gott, der Herr, ist Sonn' und Schild. Bach, J. S. Psalm 84:12.
Gott, erhör' mit Langmust mein Flehn. Dvorák, Antonín. Psalm 61:1, 3-4.
Gott hat Alles. Bach, J. S. Mark 7:37.
Gott ist unser Sonn' und Schild. Bach, J. S. Psalm 84:12.
Gott, o höre, hör' auf mein Gebet. Dvorák, Antonín. Psalm 55:1-8.
Gott sei mir gnädig. Mendelssohn, Felix. Psalm 52:1, 10-11, 13, 15, 17.
The Grand Alleluia. Schubert, Franz (ed. Carl Fredrickson). I Chronicles 16:29.
Great and Marvelous. Humphreys, Don. Revelation 15:3-4.
Great and Marvelous Are Thy Works. Lepke, Charma Davies. Revelation 15:1.
Great and Wonderful Are All Thy Works. Raff, Joseph J. Revelation 15:3-4.
The Great Commission. Wiant, Bliss. Isaiah 61:1-3.
Great Is Our Lord. Cartwright, Marion L. Psalm 147:3-7a, 8-9, 18a.
Great Is the Lord.
Gollner, Ronald E. Psalm 145:3a.
Huhn, Bruno S. Psalm 47:1-2, 6-7.
Schütz, Heinrich. Psalm 145:3, 4.
Smith, Michael W. Psalm 145:3a.
Smith, Michael W. and Deborah D. Smith. Psalm 145:3a.
Toolan, Sr. Suzanne (arr. Randall DeBruyn). Isaiah 52:7.
Great Peace Have They.
Brown, Allanson G. Y. Psalm 119:165-166, 175-176.
Lully, Jean Baptiste. Psalm 119:135, 165.
Great Peace Have They Which Love Thy Law. Rogers, James H. Psalm 119:165, 174-176.
The Great White Host. Lovelace, Austin C. Revelation 7:9-10, 13-16.
The Greatest of These. Ware, Harriet. I Corinthians 13:00.
The Greatest of These Is Love.
Bitgood, Roberta. I Corinthians 13:00.
Clausen, René. I Corinthians 13:1-2, 4-8.
Leech, Bryan Jeffrey (arr. Ruth Morris Bray). I Corinthians 13:1.
Lynn, Lorna. I Corinthians 13:4-7, 13.
Moe, Daniel. I Corinthians 13:1-7.
Penhorwood, Edwin. I Corinthians 13:00.
Ridge, M. D. I Corinthians 13:1-8.
Wetzler, Robert. I Corinthians 13:00.
Greatly Rejoice. Burton, Patti and Wendell Burton. Isaiah 61:10-11.
Guide Me, O God. O'Connor, Roc (arr. Jeanne Cotter). Psalm 23:4.
Guiding Me. Joncas, Michael. Psalm 121:00.

Habe deine Lust an dem Herren. Schütz, Heinrich. Psalm 37:1-5.
Haec Dies quam fecit Dominus. Vejvanovsky, Pavel Josef (ed. Konrad Ruhland). Psalm 118:24.
Hail Holy Mary. Atkinson, René. Luke 1:28, 42.
Hail Mary. Peeters, Flor. Luke 1:28, 30-31, 42.
Hallelujah! Praise Ye the Lord. Page, Anna Laura. Psalm 150:2-6.
Halleluya. Wyner, Yehudi. Psalm 66:00.
Hal'lu. Chait, B. (arr. Velvel Pasternak). Psalm 117:1.
Hal'lu nafshi. Stockhommer, A. (arr. Velvel Pasternak). Psalm 146:1.
Hannu und Eli. Plantavsky, Peter. I Samuel 1:00.
Happy Are the Lowly Poor. Jones, Hilton Kean. Matthew 5:1-16.
Happy Are the Ones. Schutte, Daniel L. Psalm 89:15, 18 (based on).
Happy Are They.
Foley, John B. Psalm 128:1-6.
Schoenbachler, Tim. Psalm 1:00.
Thornton, William. Psalm 1:00.
Happy Are They Who Believe. Haas, David. John 20:29 (based on).

Happy Are They Who Dwell in Your House. Pelz, Walter L. Psalm 84:3-4, 10-12.
Happy Are They Who Honor the Lord. Haas, David. Psalm 128:00.
Happy Are Those Who Fear the Lord.
Stewart, Roy James. Psalm 128:00.
Talbot, John Michael. Psalm 128:00.
Happy Are You Who Fear the Lord. Schiavone, John. Psalm 128:00.
Happy He Who Walketh Ever. Adler, Samuel. Psalm 1:1-3.
Happy Is the Man.
Mader, Clarence. Proberbs 3:13-23.
Tarsi, Boaz. Psalm 1:103.
Thiman, Eric H. Proberbs 3:13, 15-18.
Thiman, Eric H. Psalm 1:00.
Hard Trials. Spiritual (arr. Harry T. Burleigh). Matthew 8:20.
Hariu Ladonai kol haarets. Cohen, Gerald. Psalm 100:00.
Hark, My Beloved. Barkan, Emanuel. Song of Songs 2:8-13.
Hark, the Voice of Jesus Calling. Manuel, Ralph. Isaiah 6:8.
Hasom nafshénu. Krugman, E. M. (arr. Velvel Pasternak). Psalm 66:9.
Hast Thou Not Known (?)
LaForge, Frank. Isaiah 40:28-31.
Malotte, Albert Hay. Isaiah 40:28-31.
Schmutz, Albert D. Isaiah 40:28-31.
Swift, Robert F. Isaiah 40:28-31.
Hast Thou Not Known Me? Warren, Clara. John 14:6, 8-9.
Haste Thee, Lord God, Haste to Save Me. Schütz, Heinrich. Psalm 40:14-18.
Have Mercy Upon Me, O Lord. Starer, Robert. Psalm 51:1.
Have You Not Known? Lovelace, Austin C. Isaiah 40:28-31.
He. Tindall, Adrienne M. Psalm 119:33-36, 38, 40.
He Counteth All Your Sorrows. Mendelssohn, Felix. Psalm 107:2, 14-15, 19.
He Giveth His Beloved Sheep. Benedict, Sir Julius. Psalm 127:2.
He Guideth Me in the Path of Righteousness. Halberstam, Rabbi E. (arr. Velvel Pasternak). Psalm 23:3.
He Has Made Me Glad. Brethorst, Leona Von. Psalm 100:4.
He Hath Shewed Thee O Man. Banks, Harry C. Micah 6:7-8.
He Is Exalted. Paris, Twila. Psalm 99:2-3.
He Is Like a Tree. Roff, Joseph. Psalm 1:1.
He Is Our Peace. Groves, Kandela. Ephesians 2:14.
He Is Risen! Barnes, Frederick M. Matthew 28:1-7.
He Is Risen, As He Said. Phillips, Madalyn. Matthew 28:5-7.
He Is There. Beall, Mary Kay. Psalm 139:7-8.
He Kept Us Alive. Krugman, E. M. (arr. Velvel Pasternak). Psalm 66:9.
He Loved Me. Dolck, Doug and Tom Fettke. Romans 8:35-39.
He Maketh Wars to Cease.
Chadwick, George Whitefield. Psalm 46:9, 10.
Scott, John Prindle. Isaiah 2:4.
He Makes All Things New. Whitehouse, Jan. Revelation 21:5.
He Restoreth My Soul. Blair, Kathleen. Psalm 23:00.
He Sent His Word. MacDermid, James G. John 1:1.
He Sent His Word and Healed Them.
Humphreys, Don. Psalm 107:20.
Olds, W. B. Psalm 107:20.
He Shall Be Like a Tree. Bowling, Blanche. Psalm 1:00.
He Shall Feed His Flock.
Beck, John Ness. Psalm 23:1.
Handel, G. F. Isaiah 40:11.
Harker, F. Flaxington. Isaiah 40:11.
He Shall Give His Angel Charge. Scott, John Prindle. Psalm 91:1-2, 5-7, 11-12.
He Shall Give His Angels Charge Over Thee. Busarow, Donald. Psalm 91:4. 11-12.
He Shall Give His Angels Charge Over You. Hillert, Richard. Psalm 91:9-12, 15-16.
He Shall Judge Thy People. LaForge, Frank. Psalm 72:2-3, 6-11.
He Takes Away the Sins of the World. John 1:29. Fettke, Tom and Phillip P. Bliss.
He That Dwelleth in Heaven. Handel, G. F. Psalm 2:4.
He That Dwelleth in the Secret Place.
Baumgartner, H. Leroy. Psalm 91:1-2, 5-6, 9-10, 14-16.
Davye, John J. Psalm 91:00.
Fisher, William Arms. Psalm 91:1, 4, 7, 10-11.
Humphreys, Don. Psalm 91:1-2, 4-5, 11.
Neidlinger, W. H. Psalm 91:1, 9-11, 14, 16.
Shelley, Harry Rowe. Psalm 91:1-2.
Ward-Stephens. Psalm 91:1-12.
He That Dwelleth in the Secret Place of the Most High. MacDermid, James G. Psalm 91:1, 5-6, 9, 10-12.
He That Keepeth Israel. Schlösser, Adolphe. Psalm 91:11.
He Was Cut Off. Handel, G. F. Isaiah 53:8.
He Was Despised. Handel, G. F. Isaiah 53:3.
He Was Oppress'd. Kiel, Friedrich. Isaiah 53:7.
He Was Wounded. Courtney, Craig. Isaiah 53:3-6.
He, Watching Over Israel. Mendelssohn, Felix (arr. Lynn Hodges). Psalm 121:3.
He Who Began a Good Work in You.
Mohr, Jon. Philippians 1:6.
Mohr, Jon (arr. Steven V. Taylor). Philippians 1:6.
He Will Bless the House of Israel. Walfish, H. (arr. Velvel Pasternak). Psalm 115:12.
He Will Not Suffer Thy Foot to Be Moved. Weldon, John. Psalm 121:3.
Heal Our Land. Brooks, Tom and Robin Brooks. II Chronicles 7:14.
The Healing of Blind Bartimaeus. Hart, Theron Wolcott. Mark 10:46-52.
The Healing of the Woman. Hart, Theron Wolcott. Mark 5:24-29, 34.
Hear Me, O Lord. Schütz, Heinrich. Psalm 4:1.
Hear Me Speedily, O Lord! VanVollenhoven, Hanna. Psalm 27:1.
Hear Me When I Call.
Huhn, Bruno S. Psalm 4:1.
Nelhybel, Vaclav. Psalm 25:4-5.
Hear My Cry. Mulligan, Harold Vincent. Psalm 61:00.
Hear My Cry, O God.
Franck, César. Psalm 56:4a.
Sowerby, Leo. Psalm 61:1-5, 8.
Hear My Cry, O Lord! Wooler, Alfred. Psalm 61:1.
Hear My Crying, O Lord. Dvorák, Antonín. Psalm 61:1, 3-4.
Hear My Prayer.
Dvorák, Antonín. Psalm 55:1-8.
Dvorák, Antonín. Psalm 61:1, 3-4 (duet).
Mendelssohn, Felix. Psalm 55:1-5.
Hear My Voice. Nelhybel, Vaclav. Psalm 61:1-2.
Hear My Words, O Gracious Lord. Adler, Samuel. Psalm 5:1-5, 7.
Hear, O Heavens, and Give Ear O Earth. Riker, Franklin. Isaiah 1:2, 4, 18-19.
Hear, O Israel.
Haas, David. Deuteronomy 6:4-5.
Tindall, Adrienne M. Deuteronomy 6:4-5.

Hear, O Lord, When I Cry With My Voice. Baumgartner, H. Leroy. Psalm 27:7-9, 11, 13-14.
Hear, O My People. Stevenson, Frederick. Psalm 81:9-11.
Hear, Oh Hear My Prayer, Lord. Dvorák, Antonín. Psalm 55:1-8.
Hear, Oh Lord, My Bitter Cry. Dvorák, Antonín. Psalm 61:1, 3-4.
Hear Thou My Prayer. Hamblen, Bernard. Psalm 86:1a, 4a, 6-7, 13.
Hear Us, O Father. Millard, H. Luke 1:28, 30-31, 42.
Hear Us, O Savior. Rameau, J. P. Luke 1:28, 30-31, 42.
Hear Ye, Israel. Mendelssohn, Felix. Isaiah 49:7.
The Heavens Are Telling.
Haydn, F. Joseph. Psalm 19:1.
Walker, Tricia. Psalm 19:1a.
The Heavens Declare God's Glory. Marcello, Benedetto. Psalm 19:00.
The Heavens Declare His Glory. Hanks, Billie, Jr. Psalm 19:00 (based on).
The Heavens Declare Thy Glory. Selby, William (arr. Barbara Owen). Psalm 19:1.
Heed My Call for Help. Foley, John B. Psalm 5:2-3a.
Hemmet den Eifer, verbannet die Rache. Telemann, Georg Philipp. Romans 13:8-10.
Here I Am, Lord. Schutte, Daniel L. Isaiah 6:8 (based on).
Here I Am, Send Me. Schoenbachler, Tim. Psalm 3:00 (based on).
Here Is Your God. Misetich, Marianne. Isaiah 35:6-7.
Herr, auf dich traue ich. Buxtehude, Dietrich. Psalm 31:2-4.
Herr, deine Augen sehen nach dem Glauben. Bach, J. S. Jeremiah 5:3.
Herr Gott Abrahams. Mendelssohn, Felix. I Kings 18:36-17.
Herr, ich hoffe darauf. Schütz, Heinrich. Psalm 13:5-6.
Der Herr ist gross.
Schütz, Heinrich. Psalm 145:3, 4.
Schütz, Heinrich (ed. Bradley L. Almguist). Psalm 145:3.
Der Herr ist gross und sehr löblich. Schütz, Heinrich. Psalm 145:3, 4.
Der Herr ist in seinem heiligen Temple. Peter, Johann Friedrich. Habakkuk 2:20.
Der Herr ist mein Licht und mein Heil. Schütz, Heinrich. Psalm 27:1.
Der Herr ist Meine Hirt. Wiemer, Wolfgang. Psalm 23:00.
Der Herr segne euch. Bach, J. S. Psalm 115:13-15.
Herr, mein Gott, ich sing' en neues Lied. Dvorák, Antonín. Psalm 144:9.
Herr, nun lassert du deinen diener. Buxtehude, Dietrich. Luke 2:29-32.
Herr, nun lassert du deinen, Diener im Friede fahren. Schütz, Heinrich. Luke 2:29-30.
Der Herr schauet vom Himmel auf der Menschen Kinder. Schütz, Heinrich. Psalm 14:2, 3.
Herr, wenn ich nur dich Habe. Buxtehude, Dietrich. Psalm 73:25-26.
Herr, wer wird wohnen in deiner Hütten. Bernhard, Christoph. Psalm 15:00.
Herr, wo soll ich hingehen. Selle, Thomas. Psalm 139:7-12.
Herzlich lieb Hab' ich dich. Hammerschmidt, Andreas. Psalm 18:2-6.
Herzlich Lieb hab ich dich. Schütz, Heinrich. Psalm 18:2-7.
He's Jus' De Same Today. Spiritual (arr. Harry T. Burleigh). Exodus 14:22.
Heutet euch. Schütz, Heinrich. Luke 21:34-36.
Hic est panis. Aichinger, Gregor. John 6:59.
Hine Ma Tov. Naplan, Allan E. Psalm 133:1.
Hiné ma tõv, no. 1. Talmud, Rabbi Y. (arr. Velvel Pasternak). Psalm 133:1.
Hinei Yamin Ba-Im. Steinberg, Ben. Amos 9:13, 15.
His Children. Burns, William K. I John 3:1.
His Eye Is on the Sparrow. Gabriel, Charles H. Matthew 10:29-31.
His Left Hand Is Under My Head, and His Right Hand Doth Embrace Me. LaMontaine, John. Song of Songs 2:6.
His Love Is Everlasting. Haas, David. Psalm 136:1.
His Mercy Endures. Krismann, Bob (arr. Craig S. Kingsbury). Psalm 130:1-3.
His Salvation Is Nigh Them That Fear Him. Bennett, Sir William Sterndale. Psalm 85:9, 12.
His Strength Is Perfect.
Chapman, Steven Curtis and Jerry Salley. Philippians 4:13.
Chapman, Steven Curtis (arr. Steven V. Taylor). Philippians 4:13.
Ho! Everyone That Thirsteth. Klein, Manuel. Isaiah 55:1.
Hodie Christus Natus Est.
Schütz, Heinrich. Luke 2:11.
Valentini, Giovanni. Luke 2:11.
Holy Is God. Inwood, Paul. Psalm 117:00.
Holy Is the Lord. Paris, Twila. Psalm 99:3.
Holy One of Israel. Misetich, Marianne. Isaiah 41:18-19.
Holy, Holy. Smith, Michael W.; Deborah D. Smith; Debbie and Brown Bannister. Isaiah 6:3.
Holy, Holy, Holy.
Dykes, John Bacchus. Psalm 145:10.
Scholtes, Peter. Isaiah 6:3.
Holy, Holy, Holy Is the Lord of Hosts. Prince, Nolene. Isaiah 6:3.
Holy, Holy, Lord God of Hosts. Cherubini, Luigi. Luke 1:28, 30-31, 42.
Home, Dost Thou Beckon? Smith, Marcus. II Corinthians 5:1 (based on).
Ho-õse g'dõlõs. Portugal, Rabbi E. (arr. Velvel Pasternak). Job 9:10.
Höre, Israel. Mendelssohn, Felix. Isaiah 49:7.
Hosanna (!)
Nelson, Ronald A. Matthew 21:9.
Smith, Michael W. Matthew 21:9.
Smith, Michael W. (arr. Steven V. Taylor). Matthew 21:9.
Hosanna! Blessed Is He. Wilson, John Floyd. Mark 11:9-10.
Hosanna! Hosanna! Beall, Mary Kay. Mark 11:9-10.
Hosanna to the Son of David. Carr, Arthur. Matthew 21:9.
Hosianna, dem Sohne David. Grimm, Heinrich. Matthew 21:9.
Hospokin jest muj pastyr. Dvorák, Antonín. Psalm 23:1-4.
The Hour Cometh. Mourant, Walter. John 4:23-24.
The House of God. Humphreys, Don. Psalm 127:1.
How Beautiful. Paris, Twila. Isaiah 52:7-9.
How Beautiful Are the Feet.
Handel, G. F. Romans 10:15.
Handel, G. F. (arr. Harrison Oxley). Romans 10:15.
Handel, G. F. (arr. Richard Peek). Romans 10:15.
Handel, G. F. (arr. Doreen Rao). Romans 10:15.
Handel, G. F. (arr. James Michael Stevens). Romans 10:15.
Perry, Julian. Isaiah 52:7.
How Beautiful Are Thy Dwellings. deLange, S. (ed. Max Spicker). Psalm 84:1.
How Beautiful on the Mountains.
Mendelssohn, Felix (arr. Carl Fredrickson). Isaiah 52:7.
Wooler, Alfred. Romans 10:15.

How Beautiful upon the Mountains.
Fischer, Irwin. Isaiah 52:7, 9.
Harker, F. Flaxington. Isaiah 52:7.
Lovelace, Austin C. Isaiah 52:7-9.
How Beautiful Thy Temples, Lord. Rowberry, Robert Lee. Psalm 24:3-5 (based on).
How Can I Repay the Lord. Dean, Stephen. Psalm 116:1-8, 12-16, 17.
How Dear to Me is Your Dwelling. Hurd, David. Psalm 84:1-7, 9.
How Excellent Is Thy Loving Kindness.
Cowen, Frederic Hymen. Psalm 65:9, 11, 13.
Humphreys, Don. Psalm 36:7-10.
How Excellent Is Thy Name.
McAfee, Don. Psalm 8:1, 3-8.
Tunney, Dick (arr. Steven V. Taylor). Psalm 8:1.
Tunney, Dick and Melodie; Paul C. Smith. Psalm 8:1.
How Excellent Is Your Name. Wetzler, Robert. Psalm 8:1, 3-5, 9.
How Firm a Foundation. Boren, Murry. Isaiah 41:10 (based on).
How Good and How Pleasant It Is. Tindall, Adrienne M. Psalm 133:1.
How Good and Pleasant It Is. Kosche, Kenneth T. Psalm 133:1.
How Good It Is to Give Thanks to God. Foley, John B. Psalm 92:1-6.
How Good to Offer Thanks. Schweizer, Rolf. Psalm 92:1-5.
How Goodly Are Thy Tents. Steinberg, Ben. Numbers 24:5.
How Goodly Are Your Tents. Pasternak, Velvel. Numbers 24:5.
How Great, O Lord, Is Thy Goodness. Benedict, Sir Julius. Psalm 16:11a.
How Long (?)
Card, Michael. Psalm 13:00.
Cohen, Gerald. Psalm 82:1-5, 8.
How Long, O Lord. Schutte, Daniel L. Psalm 13:1.
How Long, O Lord, Wilt Thou Forget Me?
Buck, Dudley. Psalm 13:1-5.
Rogers, James H. Psalm 13:1.
How Long Wilt Thou Forget Me?
Brown, Russell J. Psalm 13:1-5.
Pfleuger, Carl. Psalm 13:1, 3, 5.
Powell, Robert J. Psalm 13:1-6.
Sowerby, Leo. Psalm 13:1-6.
Speaks, Oley. Psalm 13:1, 3, 5.
How Long Wilt Thou Forget Me, O Lord?
Beech, Robert L. Psalm 13:00.
Hoffmeister, Leon Abbott. Psalm 13:1-5.
Lekberg, Sven. Psalm 13:00.
Sacco, Peter. Psalm 13:00.
How Lovely Are Thy Dwellings.
Davis, Katherine K. Psalm 84:1-3.
Liddle, Samuel. Psalm 84:1-3, 8, 10.
How Lovely Are Thy Dwellings Fair. Thiman, Eric H. Psalm 134:00.
How Lovely Are Your Tents. Gottlieb, Jack. Numbers 24:5.
How Lovely Is Thy Dwelling Place.
Carter, John. Psalm 84:1-4.
Grantham, Donald. Psalm 84:00.
Haydn, F. Joseph (ed. Carl Fredrickson). Psalm 84:1-2, 4.
How Lovely Is Your Dwelling Place.
Alstott, Owen. Psalm 84:1-4, 8, 11.
Howard, Tom. Psalm 84:00.
Joncas, Michael. Psalm 84:1-8, 10-11.
How Majestic Is Your Name. Smith, Michael W. Psalm 8:9.
How Majestic Is Your Name. Smith, Michael W. (arr. Tom Fettke). Psalm 8:9.
How Majestic Is Your Name (with Holy, Holy). Smith, Michael W. (arr. Steven V. Taylor). Psalm 8:9.
How Many Hired Servants. Sullivan, Sir Arthur. Luke 15:17-19.
Humble Thyself in the Sight of the Lord. Hudson, Bob. I Peter 5:6 (based on).
Hymn of Thanks and Praise. LaForge, Frank. Psalm 118:1, 10, 14-17, 19, 21.
Hymn of the Last Supper. Demarest, Victoria. Mark 14:24.

I Am. Smith, Michael W. John 11:25.
I Am Alpha and Omega.
Shelley, Harry Rowe. Revelation 1:8.
Trowbridge, J. Eliot. Revelation 1:8.
I Am Crucified with Christ. Elliott, John G. Galatians 3:20.
I Am in the Fever of Love. Saltzman, Peter. Song of Songs 2:4.
I Am My Beloved's.
Goldman, Maurice. Song of Songs 2:10-13.
Thomson, Virgil. Song of Songs 6:3.
I Am Persuaded. Tindall, Adrienne M. John 3:16.
I Am the Bread of Life.
Kieserling, Richard. John 6:51.
Talbot, John Michael. John 6:35.
Toolan, Sr. Suzanne. John 6:35, 51, 53
I Am the Good Shepherd.
Burroughs, Bob. John 10:14, 16a
Elgar, Edward. John 10:10, 14.
Nevin, George. John 10:11-16.
Talbot, John Michael. Psalm 23:00.
I Am the Keeper. Ruston, Kevin and Vince Nichols (arr. Malcolm Archer). Isaiah 27:1-5.
I Am the Resurrection.
Anderson, Jim. John 11:25.
Buxtehude, Dietrich. John 11:25-26.
Haas, David. John 11:25-26.
Hammerschmidt, Andreas. John 11:25-26.
Talbot, John Michael. John 11:25-26.
I Am the Resurrection and the Life. Rotermund, Melvin. John 11:25-26.
I Am the Rose of Sharon. Saltzman, Peter. Song of Songs 2:1.
I Am the Rose of Sharon and the Lily of the Valley.
LaMontaine, John. Song of Songs 2:1-3a.
I Am the True Vine.
Isham, Royce. John 15:1, 2, 4-6.
MacDermid, James G. John 15:1-3, 5-7.
I Am the Vine.
Doig, Don. John 15:1-6.
Pote, Allen (arr. Dale Wood). John 15:5-6, 12.
Talbot, John Michael. John 15:1-8.
I Believe I Will See. Foley, John B. Psalm 27:7-9, 13-14.
I Believe That I Shall See. Lynch, Mike (arr. John Strege). Psalm 25:1.
I Believe That My Redeemer Lives. Peloquin, C. Alexander. Job 19:25-26.
I Bow and Bend the Knee. Schütz, Heinrich. Ephesians 3:14-15.
I Cast All My Cares upon You. Willard, Kelly. I Peter 5:7.
I Cried to the Lord. Rorem, Ned. Psalm 142:00.
I Cried Unto the Lord. Dengler, Lee. Psalm 142:1, 6.
I Don't Feel No-Ways Tired. Spiritual (arr. Harry T. Burleigh). Hebrews 11:14 (based on).

I Found the Treasure. Schutte, Daniel L. Matthew 13:44-45.
I Have Been a Young Man and Now Am Aged. Schütz, Heinrich. Psalm 37:25.
I Have Chosen the Way of Truth. Courtney, Craig. Psalm 119:30-37.
I Have Loved You. Joncas, Michael. Psalm 24:3.
I Have Prayed to Thee. Elgar, Edward. Acts 2:14b, 16-17, 21-23, 32-33, 36.
I Have Seen the Lord. Hurd, Bob and Dominic MacAller. Job 19:25-27.
I Have Seen Water. Ferris, William. Ecclesiasticus 47:2.
I Have Waited for the Lord. Misetich, Marianne. Psalm 40:1.
I Jesus, Have Sent Mine Angel. Shelley, Harry Rowe. Revelation 22:14, 16.
I Journeyed on My Way. Brahms, Johannes. Ecclesiastes 4:1-3.
I Know De Lord's Laid His Hands on Me. Spiritual (arr. Harry T. Burleigh). Matthew 19:15.
I Know in Whom I Have Believed. Scott, John Prindle. II Timothy 1:12.
I Know That My Redeemer Lives. Soper, Scott. Job 19:25a.
I Know That My Redeemer Liveth. Handel, G. F. Job 19:25-26.
I Know the Lord Laid His Hands on Me. Spiritual (arr. Edward Boatner). Luke 4:40.
I Lift Mine Eyes. Adler, Samuel. Psalm 121:00.
I Lift Mine Eyes unto the Hills. Lovelace, Austin C. Psalm 121:1-4.
I Lift Up Mine Eyes. Stearns, Theodore. Psalm 121:1-4.
I Lift Up My Eyes.
Derfler, Carl. Psalm 121:00.
Lynch, Mike (arr. Dennis Richardson). Psalm 121:00.
Repp, Ray. Psalm 121:00.
I Lift Up My Eyes to the Hills.
Hopson, Hal H. Psalm 121:00.
Jennings, Kenneth. Psalm 121:00.
I Lift Up My Soul. Manion, Tim. Psalm 25:1, 4-6, 8-9.
I Longed for My Love. Saltzman, Peter. Song of Songs 3:1-2.
I Love the Lord. Duke, John. Psalm 116:1-5, 7-8.
I Love Thee, Lord, My Strength, op. 2, no. 2. Cornelius, Peter. Psalm 18:00.
I Love You, Lord. Steele, David (arr. Tom Fettke). Psalm 18:1-3, 6.
I Praise Thee, O Lord, My God. Mendelssohn, Felix. Psalm 86:12-13.
I Rejoiced.
Proulx, Richard. Psalm 122:00.
Walker, Christopher. Psalm 122:00.
I Rejoiced When I Heard Them Say. Talbot, John Michael. Psalm 122:00.
I Sat Down Under the Shadow. LaMontaine, John. Song of Songs 2:3b-5.
And I Saw a New Heaven. Tindall, Adrienne M. Revelation 21:1-5.
I See the Lord. Fettke, John. Isaiah 6:1-4.
I Shall Not Want. Ellis, James G. Psalm 23:00.
I Sought Him. Thornton, William. Song of Songs 3:1-3.
I Sought the Lord.
Galbraith. J. Lamont. Psalm 34:4.
Humphreys, Don. Psalm 34:1-4, 8.
Robyn, Alfred G. Psalm 34:4.
Stevenson, Frederick. Psalm 34:4.
I Speak of the Things. Dencke, Jeremiah. Psalm 45:1-2.
I Stand All Amazed. Rowberry, Robert Lee. Isaiah 53:4, 5 (based on).
I to the Hills Will Lift My Eyes. Mendelssohn, Felix (ed. Hal H. Hopson). Psalm 121:00.
I Wait upon Thee. Galbraith, Robert. I Peter 3:18, 19 (based on).
I Waited for the Lord.
Mendelssohn, Felix. Isaiah 40:1.
Mendelssohn, Felix (arr. William Stickles). Isaiah 40:1.
Saint-Saëns, Camille. Psalm 40:1.
Saint-Saëns, Camille (arr. K. Lee Scott). Psalm 40:1.
I Waited for the Lord My God. Burnett, John Y. Psalm 40:1-4.
I Waited Patiently for the Lord. Mader, Clarence. Psalm 40:1-4, 8-9b, 10b, 11-12, 16.
I Want to Be Ready.
Spiritual (arr. Harry T. Burleigh). Acts 2:00.
Spiritual (arr. Phillip McIntyre). Acts 2:00.
I Want to Praise Your Name. Hurd, Bob. Psalm 148:00.
I Was Glad. Haas, David. Psalm 122:00.
I Will Always Thank the Lord. Soper, Scott. Psalm 34:1.
I Will Always Trust the Lord. Peter, Johann Friedrich. Psalm 71:14.
I Will at All Times Praise the Lord. Handel, G. F. (arr. Hal H. Hopson). Psalm 34:1, 4, 8.
I Will Betroth Her Unto Me. Adler, Samuel. Hosea 2:21, 22.
I Will Bless the Lord. Schoenbachler, Tim. Psalm 34:1-5, 8.
I Will Bless the Lord at All Times.
Hobby, Robert A. Psalm 34:1-11.
Schütz, Heinrich. Psalm 34:2-7.
I Will Bless Yahweh. Rieth, Mildred F. Psalm 34:1.
I Will Call Upon the Lord.
O'Shields, Michael. II Samuel 22:4.
O'Shields, Michael (arr. Gary Rhodes). II Samuel 22:4.
I Will Dwell in the House of the Lord. Ewille, Vernon. Psalm 23:00.
I Will Enter His Gates. Brethorst, Leona Von. Psalm 100:4.
I Will Espouse You to Me Forever. DeLong, Richard. Hosea 2:21-23.
I Will Extol Thee.
LaForge, Frank. Psalm 145:00.
Schmutz, Albert D. Psalm 145:00.
I Will Extol Thee, My God. Molique, Wilhelm Bernhard. Psalm 145:1, 3, 16, 18-20.
I Will Extol Thee, O Lord! Costa, Michael. Psalm 30:1-2, 11.
I Will Follow. Avery, Richard and Donald Marsh. Ruth 1:16, 17.
I Will Give Thanks unto the Lord.
Campbell-Tipton, Louis. Psalm 9:1-2, 10.
Kingsley, Gershon. Psalm 9:2-3.
I Will Give You Shepherds. Ultan, Lloyd. Joshua 1:8-9.
I Will Glory in the Cross. Rambo, Dottie (arr. Linn and Lyndell Leatherman). Galatians 6:14.
I Will Go in the Strength of the Lord. Herbst, Johannes (arr. Donald M. McCorkle. Psalm 71:16a.
I Will Greatly Rejoice in the Lord. Young, Philip M. Isaiah 61:1-3, 10.
I Will Lay Me Down in Peace.
Buck, Dudley. Psalm 4:8.
Greene, Maurice. Psalm 4:8.
I Will Lift Mine Eyes. Cornelius, Peter. Psalm 121:00.
I Will Lift Up Mine Eyes.
Barnes, Frederick M. Psalm 121:00.
Dvorák, Antonín. Psalm 121:1-4
Eville, Vernon. Psalm 121:00.
Gober, Belle Biard. Psalm 121:00.
Golde, W. Psalm 121:1-2.

Head, Michael. Psalm 121:00.
Hoffmeister, Leon Abbott. Psalm 121:00.
Horowitz, Rabbi M. Psalm 121:1-2.
Kendrick, Virginia. Psalm 121:00.
Koch, John. Psalm 121:00.
Lekberg, Sven. Psalm 121:00.
MacDermid, James G. Psalm 121:00.
Raigorodsky, Natalie. Psalm 121:00.
Rebbi of Chernowitzer. Psalm 121:1-4.
Rutenber, C. B. Psalm 121:00.
Sowerby, Leo. Psalm 121:00.
Sowerby, Leo (arr. John Delorey and Ronald Stalford). Psalm 121:00.
Stearns, Peter Pindar. Psalm 121:00.
Steinberg, Ben. Psalm 121:00.
Twinn, Sydney. Psalm 121:00.
Ward-Stephens. Psalm 121:00.
Watkins, Margery. Psalm 121:00.

I Will Lift Up Mine Eyes to the Hills. Harker, F. Flaxington. Ephesians 4:7.

I Will Lift Up Mine Eyes unto the Hills.
Burnam, Edna Mae. Psalm 121:1-2.
Humphreys, Don. Psalm 121:00.
Parker, Clifton. Psalm 121:00.
Spies, Claudio. Psalm 121:1-8.

I Will Lift Up My Eyes.
Bartlett, Floy Little. Psalm 121:00.
Conry, Tom. Psalm 63:1-4.
Dengler, Lee. Psalm 121:1-3, 7-8.

I Will Lift Up My Soul. Marcello, Benedetto (arr. Barbara Owen). Psalm 25:1-2a, 4-5.

I Will Magnify Thee. Kaufmann, Julius (arr. Carl Fredrickson). Psalm 145:1, 15-18.

I Will Magnify Thee, O God. Mosenthal, Joseph. Psalm 30:2.

I Will Make an Everlasting Covenant. Peter, Johann Friedrich. Isaiah 55:3.

I Will Not Leave You Comfortless.
Nelson, Ronald A. John 14:18.
Pinkham, Daniel. John 14:18, 28.
Row, Richard D. John 14:18-21.

I Will Praise the Lord. Joncas, Michael. Psalm 146:2-10.

I Will Praise Thee, O Lord. Spies, Claudio. Psalm 9:1-2.

I Will Praise Thee With My Whole Heart. Matesky, Thelma. Psalm 138:00.

I Will Praise You, Lord. Haas, David. Psalm 30:1-3, 10-12.

I Will Praise You, O Lord. Inwood, Paul. Psalm 30:1, 3, 4-5, 8-12.

I Will Sing. Haas, David. Psalm 71:1, 5, 8, 15.

I Will Sing New Songs of Gladness. Dvorák, Antonín. Psalm 144:9.

I Will Sing of the Lord. Foley, John B. Philippians 2:8-9, 11.

I Will Sing of the Mercies. Fillmore, James H. and Tom Fettke (arr. Lee Herrington). Psalm 89:1.

I Will Sing of the Mercies of the Lord. Powell, Robert J. Psalm 89:1, 5, 8-9, 11, 14-15.

I Will Sing of Thy Great Mercies. Mendelssohn, Felix. Psalm 89:1.

I Will Sing of Thy Mercies. Mendelssohn, Felix (ed. Gordon Young). Psalm 89:1.

I Will Sing of Thy Steadfast Love. Triplett, Robert F. Psalm 89:1-5, 15-18, 52.

I Will Sing of Your Steadfast Love. Diemer, Emma Lou. Psalm 89:1-5, 6, 9, 14.

I Will Sing the Story of Thy Love. Wienhorst, Richard. Psalm 89:1.

I Will Sing Unto the Lord. Greene, Maurice. Psalm 146:2.

I Will Walk in the Presence of God. Foley, John B. Psalm 116:1-19.

I Will Walk in the Presence of the Lord. Stewart, Roy James. Psalm 116:00.

I Will Worship the Lord. Birch, Robert Fairfax. Psalm 18:1-6, 49.

And I, John, Saw the Holy City. Shelley, Harry Rowe. Revelation 21:1-3.

Ich armer Mensch. Bach, J. S. Psalm 139:7-10.

Ich beuge meine Knie. Schütz, Heinrich. Ephesians 3:14-15.

Ich bin die Auferstehung. Hammerschmidt, Andreas. John 11:25-26.

Ich bin ein guter Hirt. Bach, J. S. John 10:12.

Ich bin jung gewesen. Schütz, Heinrich. Psalm 37:25.

Ich danke dem Herren. Schütz, Heinrich. Psalm 111:00.

Ich danke dem Herren loben allezeit. Schütz, Heinrich. Psalm 34:1-7.

Ich habe meine Augen auf zu den Bergen. Telemann, Georg Philipp. Psalm 121:00.

Ich harrete des Herrn. Mendelssohn, Felix. Isaiah 40:1.

Ich hebe den Blick zum Berg empor. Dvorák, Antonín. Psalm 121:1-4.

Ich, Liege und Schlafe. Schütz, Heinrich. Psalm 3:6-9.

Ich taufe mit Wasser. Selle, Thomas. John 1:26-27.

Ich wandte mich und sahe an. Brahms, Johannes. Ecclesiastes 4:1-3.

Ich weiss, dass mein Erlöser lebet. Handel, G. F. Job 19:25-26.

Ich will den Herren loben allezeit.
Schütz, Heinrich. Psalm 34:2-7.
Telemann, Georg Philipp. Psalm 34:2-5, 7.

Ich will immer Harren. Peter, Johann Friedrich. Psalm 71:14.

Ich will mit euch einen ewigen Bund machen. Peter, Johann Friedrich. Isaiah 55:3.

Ich will singen von einem Könige. Dencke, Jeremiah. Psalm 45:1-2.

If a Man Die, Shall He Live Again? Cundick, Robert. Job 14:14.

If a Man Loves Me. Bender, Jan. John 14:23.

If God Be for Us.
Burns, William K. Romans 8:31, 35, 37-39.
Handel, G. F. Romans 8:31, 33-34.

If God Is for Us. Foley, John B. Romans 8:31-39.

If God So Clothe the Grass. Bischoff, John W. Matthew 6:25-29.

If I Am Without Love. McAfee, Don. I Corinthians 13:1-7.

If I Forget You, Jerusalem. Cooney, Rory. Psalm 137:1-6.

If I say, "My foot slippeth."
Lowenbraun, S. (arr. Velvel Pasternak). Psalm 94:18.
Shapiro, Rabbi N. (arr. Velvel Pasternak). Psalm 94:18.

If I Take the Wings of the Morning. Fischer, Irwin. Psalm 139:9-11, 14, 17.

If My People Will Pray. Owens, Jimmy. II Chronicles 7:14.

If the Lord Does Not Build. Schutte, Daniel L. Psalm 27:00.

If Thou Prepare Thine Heart. Parker, Clifton. Job 11:13-19.

If Today. Hurd, Bob (arr. Bellamy). Psalm 95:1-2, 6-9.

If Today You Hear His Voice. Haas, David. Psalm 95:1-2, 6-9.

If We Live in the Spirit. Barker, Clement W. Galatians 5:1, 25.

If With All Your Hearts.
Mendelssohn, Felix. Deuteronomy 4:29.
Mendelssohn, Felix (arr. Lynn Hodges). Deuteronomy 4:29.
Roberts, J. E. Deuteronomy 4:29.

If Ye Abide in Me. LaForge, Frank. John 15:7, 9-10, 12.
If Ye Love Me, Keep My Commandments. Fischer, Irwin. John 14:16.
If Ye Then Be Risen With Christ. Foster, Myles B. Colossians 3:1-2.
If You Belong to Me. Hurd, Bob. Luke 18:22.
If You Search With All Your Heart. Courtney, Craig. Jeremiah 29:11-14.
If You, O God. Foley, John B. Psalm 130:1.
If Your Heart and Soul Both Truly Seek Me. Mendelssohn, Felix (arr. Leonard Van Camp). Deuteronomy 4:29.
Ihr Alle. Dvorák, Antonín. Matthew 11:28-30.
Ihr Heiligen, lobsinget dem Herren. Schütz, Heinrich. Psalm 30:5-6.
Ihr Volkers, Hört. Telemann, Georg Philipp. Isaiah 60:1-6.
Il faut que de tour mes espirits. Marot, Clement. Psalm 138:00.
Im omarti, no. 1. Lowenbraun, S. (arr. Velvel Pasternak). Psalm 94:18.
Im omarti, no. 2. Shapiro, Rabbi N. (arr. Velvel Pasternak). Psalm 94:18.
Immanuel. Card, Michael (arr. Marty Parks). Romans 9:2.
In Him We Live. Speir, Randy. Psalm 66:1-2.
In His Hands Are All the Corners of the Earth.
Mendelssohn, Felix. Psalm 95:4.
Schnecker, P. A. Psalm 95:4, 6.
In Love We Choose to Live. Cotter, Jeanne. I Corinthians 13:4.
In Majesty He Will Come with Majesty. Tunney, Dick & Melodie. I Corinthians 15:52.
In My Father's House. Lewis Jr., Ross (arr. Bo Williams). John 14:2-3.
In My Father's House Are Many Mansions.
Jewell, Lucina. John 14:1-3, 6a.
MacDermid, James G. John 14:2-4, 27.
Ward-Stephens. John 14:2-4, 27.
In Praise of His Name. O'Connor, Roc. Psalm 100:4.
In Remembrance of Me.
Johnson, Gary (arr. Cheri Keaggy). I Corinthians 11:23-26.
Linn, Joseph. I Corinthians 11:23-26.
In Te, Domine, Speravi. Schütz, Heinrich. Psalm 31:2-3.
In the Beauty of Holiness. VanDyke, May. Psalm 113:3.
In the Beginning. Haydn, F. Joseph. Genesis 1:1-3.
In the Beginning Was the Word. Robinson, McNeil. John 1:1-14.
In the End of the Sabbath. Speaks, Oley. Matthew 28:1-6.
In the Land There is a Hunger. Lynch, Mike. Psalm 62:2.
In the Morning I Will Sing. Haugen, Marty. Psalm 63:1b-9.
In the Name of the Lord. Helvering, Sandi Patti, Phil McHugh and Gloria Gaither. Matthew 21:9.
In the Shadow of Your Wings.
Haas, David. Psalm 63:1-8.
Moore, Bob. Psalm 63:2-6.
O'Connor, Roc. Psalm 27:1, 4, 7-9, 13.
In Thee, O God, Do I Put My Trust. Spicker, Max. Psalm 71:1, 9, 12, 18.
In Thee O Lord Do I Put My Trust. Frey, Richard E. Psalm 18:2.
In This Moment of Remembrance. Wood, Dale. Luke 22:19.
Incline Thine Ear. Charles, Ernest. Isaiah 55:1, 3.
Incline Thine Ear to Me. Himmel, F. H. Psalm 70:1-5.
Incline Your Ear.
Frey, Richard. Isaiah 55:1-3.
Strickland, Lily. Isaiah 55:1, 3, 12.
Inflammatus et accensus. Pergolesi, Giovanni B. (arr. Michael Burkhardt). Luke 2:14.
The Inhabitants Shall Not Say I am Sick. Graff, Leta Bishop. Isaiah 33:24 (based on).
Initiation Acclamation. Haas, David. Ephesians 4:5-6.
Into Thy Hands. Bach, J. S. Psalm 31:5.
Intreat Me Not to Leave Thee. Watts, Wintter. Ruth 1:16-17.
Is It Nothing to You? Foster, Myles B. Lamentations 1:12.
Is Not His Word Like a Fire? Mendelssohn, Felix. Jeremiah 23:29.
Is Not This the Fast. MacDermid, James G. Isaiah 58:1, 3-6, 8-9.
Isaiah. Wolpe, Stefan. Isaiah 65:17-22a, 25.
Ist nicht des Herrn Wort wie ein Feuer? Mendelssohn, Felix. Jeremiah 23:29.
It Is a Good Thing to Give Thanks to the Lord. Kent, James. Psalm 92:1-3.
It Is a Good Thing to Give Thanks Unto the Lord. Costa, Michael. Psalm 92:1.
It Is a Precious Thing to Thank Our God. Distler, Hugo. Psalm 92:1-3.
It Is Enough. Mendelssohn, Felix. I Kings 19:4, 10.
It Is Good. Weber, Jim and Niles Borop. Psalm 92:1-2.
It Is Good to Give Thanks. Rebbi of Kalev (arr. Velvel Pasternak). Psalm 92:2-16.
It Is Good to Sing Thy Praises. Adler, Samuel. Psalm 92:1-5, 9, 12-15.
It Is Good to Trust and Hope in the Lord. Berthier, Jacques. Psalm 92:1-2, 5, 12-13.
It Is of the Lord's Great Mercies. Molique, Wilhelm Bernhard. Psalm 9:13.
It Was Turned to the Contrary.
Benet, Ch. Esther 9:1.
Pasternak, Velvel. Esther 9:1.
It's Time to Praise the Lord. Borneman, Bruce and Judi. Psalm 150:1.

Ja, es sollen wohl Berge weichen. Mendelssohn, Felix. Isaiah 54:10.
Jane's Song. Burgess, Dan and Harold Decou (arr. Bob Krogstad). Psalm 139:00.
Jauchzet dem Herrn, alle Welt.
Bernhard, Christoph. Psalm 100:00.
Telemann, Georg Philipp. Psalm 100:00.
Jauchzt, ihr Christen, seid vergnügt. Telemann, Georg Philipp. I Corinthians 15:50-58.
Jehovah.
Thurman, Geoffrey P. Matthew 6:28-29.
Thurman, Geoffrey P. (arr. Steven V. Taylor). Matthew 6:28-29.
Jerusalem. Mendelssohn, Felix (ed. Lloyd Pfautsch). Matthew 23:37.
Jerusalem! Jerusalem! Thou That Killest the Prophets. Mendelssohn, Felix. Matthew 23:37.
Jesus and the Children. Kirkland, Terry. Matthew 19:13-14.
Jesus Christ, the Same. Whitsett, Eleanor (arr. Gene Thomas). Hebrews 13:8.
Jesus Fed the Hungry Thousands. Hopson, Hal H. Matthew 14:13-21.
Jesus Has Time. Fettke, Tom. Matthew 18:2-5.
Jesus ist ein guter Hirt. Bach, J. S. John 10:12.
Jesus My Shepherd. Leavitt, John. Psalm 23:00.
Jesus Said to the Widow, 'Do Not Weep.' Krapf, Gerhard. Luke 7:11-17.
Jesus the Lord. O'Connor, Roc. Acts 17:28 (based on).

Jesus the One and Only. Mason, Babbie. Philippians 2:6-11.
Jesus, the Very Thought of Thee. Nibley, Reid. Psalm 104:34 (based on).
Jesus, Lord. DeBruyn, Randall. John 3:16-21.
Jesús, pastor tan dulce. Colgan, Bro. Tobias. Psalm 23:00.
Jesus—He Shall Be Great. Fettke, Tom. Isaiah 7:14.
The Jews Had Lightness.
Horowitz, Rabbi M. (arr. Velvel Pasternak). Esther 8:16.
Portugal, Rabbi E. (arr. Velvel Pasternak). Esther 8:16.
Jod. Tindall, Adrienne M. Psalm 119:73-74, 76-77, 80.
John's Gone Down on de Island. Spiritual (arr. Harry T. Burleigh) Revelation 1:1.
Joshua Fit da Battle of Jericho.
Spiritual (arr. Harry T. Burleigh). Joshua 6:00.
Spiritulal (arr. Bond). Joshua 6:00.
Spiritual (arr. Mark Hayes). Joshua 6:00.
Joy for All the Ages. Wolfe, Jacques. Psalm 67:00.
The Joy of the Lord. Vale, Alliene G. Nehemiah 8:10 (based on).
Joy to the World. Weaver, Powell. Psalm 98:00.
A Joyful Sound. Misetich, Marianne. Psalm 150:1.
Joyfully Shall You Draw. Horowitz, Rabbi M. (arr. Velvel Pasternak). Isaiah 12:3.
Jubilate Deo.
Campra, André. Psalm 100:00.
Roth, Robert N. Psalm 100:00.
Jubilate deo omnis terra. Schütz, Heinrich. Psalm 100:00.
Jubilate Domino. Buxtehude, Dietrich. Psalm 98:4-6.
Jude Doxology. Smith, Michael W. Jude 1:24-25.
The Just Shall Live. Mullins, Rich (arr. Robert Sterling). Psalm 16:10.

Keep Me Safe, O God. Foley, John B. Psalm 16:1-5, 7-11.
Keep Not Thou Silence, O God. Sacco, Peter. Psalm 83:00.
Keep Thou Not Silence, O God. Siegel, Arsene. Psalm 83:1-5, 13-15, 18.
Kén bakõdesh. Pasternak, Velvel. Psalm 63:2-3.
Ki Nicham, no. 1. Benet, Ch. (arr. Velvel Pasternak). Isaiah 51:3.
Ki Nicham, no. 2. Horowitz, Rabbi M. (arr. Velvel Pasternak). Isaiah 51:3.
King of Glory. Tamblyn, William. Psalm 24:00.
King of Love. Williamson, Malcolm. Psalm 23:00.
The King of Love.
Butt, James. Psalm 23:00.
Crawford, John. Psalm 23:00.
Held, Wilbur. Psalm 23:00.
The King of Love My Shepherd Is.
Allen, David Len. Psalm 23:00.
Beck, John Ness. Psalm 23:00.
Gounod, Charles. Psalm 23:00.
Holler, John. Psalm 23:00.
Mendelssohn, Felix. Psalm 23:00.
Shelley, Harry Rowe. Psalm 23:00.
Spence, William. Psalm 23:00.
Wienhorst, Richard. Psalm 23:00.
The Kingdom of God. Pendleton, Emmet. Matthew 6:33.
The Kings. Cornelius, Peter. Matthew 2:10-11.
Kings Shall Bow. Driskell, Gary / Hennis, Marty. Isaiah 45:23.
Kiss Me, Make Me Drunk with Your Kisses. Saltzman, Peter. Song of Songs 1:2.
Kleines Magnificat. Telemann, Georg Philipp. Luke 1:46-47.
Know Ye That the Lord He Is God. Britton, D. Guyver. Psalm 100:00.
Komm, mein Herze steht dir offen. Bach, J. S. John 15:9-10.
Kommt her zu ihm. Handel, G. F. Matthew 11:28-29.

The Labor of Thy Hands, no. 1. Gideon, Miriam. Psalm 127:00.
The Labor of Thy Hands, no. 3. Gideon, Miriam. Psalm 128:00.
Lakol Z'Man. Steinberg, Ben. Ecclesiastes 3:1-3.
Lamb of God. Bizet, Georges. John 1:29.
Lamentation. Pisk, Paul A. Jeremiah 5:15-22.
Lamentation of David. Fromm, Herbert. II Samuel 19:27.
Lamentationes Jeremiae Prophetae. Rosenmüller, Johann. Jeremiah 1:1-5.
Laments. Adler, Samuel. II Samuel 1:19-27.
A Lamp unto My Feet. Freudenthal, Josef. Psalm 119:50.
Last Words of David. Freudenthal, Josef. II Samuel 23:1-5.
Lauda, anima mea. Dobry, Wallace. Psalm 146:00.
Laudamus te.
Bach, J. S. Psalm 145:1-2.
Brixi, Franz Xaver. Psalm 145:1-2.
Mozart, W. A. Psalm 145:1-2.
Vivaldi, Antonio. Psalm 145:1-2.
Laudate Dominum.
Buxtehude, D. Psalm 117:00.
Mozart, W. A. Psalm 117:00.
Mozart, W. A. (arr. Doreen Rao). Psalm 117:00.
Mozart, W. A. (arr. Richard Walters). Psalm 117:00.
Laudate nomen. Cassler, G. Winston. Psalm 135:00.
Laudate, Pueri.
Buxtehude, Dietrich. Psalm 113:1-2, 4-8.
Zelenka, Jan Dismas. Psalm 113:00.
Laudate pueri Dominum.
Telemann, Georg Philipp. Psalm 113:1-4.
The Law of the Lord Is Perfect.
Horowitz, Rabbi M (arr. Velvel Pasternak). Psalm 19:8.
Mendelowitz, F. (arr. Velvel Pasternak). Psalm 19:8.
La-y'hudim, no. 1. Portugal, Rabbi E. (arr. Velvel Pasternak). Esther 8:16.
La-y'hudim, no. 2. Horowitz, Rabbi M. (arr. Velvel Pasternak). Esther 8:16.
Lazarus, Come Forth. Petree, Larry and Arlie Petree. John 11:43.
L'Cho Adonoy. Weiner, Lazar. I Chronicles 29:11.
L'Cho Ezbach, no. 1. Pasternak, Velvel. Psalm 116:17.
L'Cho Ezbach, no. 2. Kranzler, E. (arr. Velvel Pasternak). Psalm 116:17.
Lead Me in the Truth. Peter, Johann Friedrich. Psalm 25:5.
Lead Me, Lord.
Handel, G. F. Psalm 5:8.
Handel, G. F. (arr. Fred Bock). Psalm 5:8.
Handel, G. F. (arr. Carl Fredrickson). Psalm 5:8.
Handel, G. F. (arr. Mary Hamlin). Psalm 5:8.
Molique, Wilhelm Bernhard. Psalm 5:8.
Wesley, Samuel Sebastian. Psalm 5:8.
Wesley, Samuel Sebastian (arr. Fred Bock). Psalm 5:8.
Wesley, Samuel Sebastian (arr. Mary Hamlin). Psalm 5:8.
Lead Me, O Lord. Molique, Wilhelm Bernhard. Psalm 5:8.
Leite mich in Deiner Wahrheit. Peter, Johann Friedrich. Psalm 25:5.
A Lenten Lesson. Shafferman, Jean Anne and George C. Strattner. Matthew 26:36-39, 42.
Let All Praise the Name of the Lord. Cotter, Jeanne. Psalm 148:1-4, 12-13.
Let All the Earth. Foley, John B. Psalm 66:1-7, 16-20.

Let All the Earth Cry Out.
Cooney, Rory. Psalm 66:1-7, 16-20.
Hurd, Bob. Psalm 66:13, 5-6, 9, 19-20.
Let All Who Fear the Lord. Foley, John B. Isaiah 41:13.
Let God Arise. Wooler, Alfred. Psalm 68:1-3.
Let My Prayer Be unto Thee. Davidowitz, M. (arr. Velvel Pasternak). Psalm 69:14.
Let My Prayer Rise Before You. Inwood, Paul. Psalm 141:1-5, 8-9.
Let My Tongue Be Silenced.
Lynch, Mike (arr. Patrick Loomis). Psalm 137:1-4, 6.
Stewart, Roy James. Psalm 137:1-6.
Let Not the Wise Man Glory in His Wisdom. MacDermid, James G. Jeremiah 31:31, 33-34.
Let Not Your Hearts. Misetich, Marianne. John 14:1-3, 6, 14.
Let Not Your Heart Be Troubled.
Chadwick, George Whitefield. John 14:1-2.
Franz, Robert. John 14:1-2.
Haeussler, Paul. John 14:1-2, 27.
Reese, Dorothy Dasch. John 14:1-2, 37.
Reiff, Stanley T. John 14:1-3.
Rutenber, C. B. John 14:1-3, 19, 20.
Snyder, Virginia. John 14:1-3.
Speaks, Oley. John 14:1, 27.
Let Our Praise to You. Archer, Malcolm. Psalm 141:2.
Let the Beauty of the Lord. Fischer, Irwin. Psalm 90:1, 16-17.
Let the Children Come unto Me. Bender, Jan. Mark 10:14.
Let the Heavens Rejoice. LaForge, Frank. Psalm 96:1-2, 6, 8, 13.
Let the King of Glory Come. Joncas, Michael. Psalm 24:7-8.
Let the Peace of Christ Rule in Your Heart. Cagle, Denny (arr. Ken Barker). Colossians 3:15.
Let the People Praise Thee, O God. Hammerschmidt, Andreas. Psalm 67:3-7.
Let the Redeemed. Ellis, Ward L. Psalm 107:2a.
Let the Word of Christ Dwell in You. Pinkham, Daniel. Colossians 3:16.
Let the Words of My Mouth. Robyn, Alfred G. Psalm 19:15.
Let This Mind Be in You. Humphreys, Don. Philippians 2: 1-2, 5.
Let Thy Mantle Fall on Me. Hawkins, Floyd. II Kings 2:9-13.
Let Thy Work Appear. Nelson, Ronald A. Psalm 90:16-17a.
Let Us Go Rejoicing. Joncas, Michael. Psalm 122:00.
Let Us Keep the Feast. Warren, Clara. Psalm 118:24.
Let Us Love One Another. Sherman, Arnold B. (arr. Dale Wood). I John 4:7.
Let Us Now Praise Famous Men. Vaughan Williams, Ralph. Ecclesiasticus 44:00.
Let Us Share This Bread of Life. Hurd, Bob. I Corinthians 12:13, 27.
Let Us Sing to the Lord. Talbot, John Michael. Exodus 15:1.
Let Us Sing Unto the Lord. Freudenthal, Josef. Psalm 95:00.
Libavtini achoti chala. Cohen, Gerald. Song of Songs 4:9-10, 16.
Lied der Ruth. Eben, Petr. Ruth 1:16-17.
Lift Every Voice. Wilson, Mark. Psalm 47:1, 6-7.
Lift Thine Eyes. Mendelssohn, Felix. Psalm 121:1-4.
Lift Thine Eyes to the Mountains. Mendelssohn, Felix (adapted Carl Deis). Psalm 121:1-4.
Lift Up Thine Eyes. Jensen, Adolf (arr. Carl Fredrickson). Psalm 121:00.
Lift Up Your Eyes. Tchaikovsky, Peter I. (arr. Carl Fredrickson). Isaiah 51:7-8.
Lift Up Your Eyes to the Heavens. MacDermid, James G. Isaiah 51:6.
Lift Up Your Heads.
Lindh, Jody W. Psalm 24:7-19.
Pasternak, Velvel. Psalm 24:7.
Lift Up Your Heads, O Ye Gates! Secchi, Antonio. Psalm 24:7-8.
Lift Up Your Heads, You Mighty Gates. Freylinghausen, J. A. and Theodore Beck. Psalm 24:1a.
Lift Up Your Hearts. O'Connor, Roc. Psalm 66:1-6 (based on).
Light. Stevenson, Frederick. Wisdom of Solomon 18:14-15.
Light of the World. Humphreys, Don. Ephesians 5:14.
Like a Child Rests. Walker, Christopher. Psalm 131:00.
Like a Little Child. Haas, David. Psalm 42:2-3, 12
Like a Seal on Your Heart. Landry, Rev. Carey (arr. Margaret Pizzuti). Song of Songs 8:6-7.
Like a Shepherd.
Dufford, Bob. Isaiah 40:9.
Misetich, Marianne. Isaiah 40:11.
Like a Weaned Child. Hurd, Bob. Psalm 62:6.
Like as a Father.
Cowen, Frederic Hymen. Psalm 103:13-14.
Scott, John Prindle. Psalm 103:13-17.
Like as the Hart.
Liddle, Samuel. Psalm 42:00.
West, John E. Psalm 42:00.
Like as the Hart Desireth. Allitsen, M. Frances. Psalm 42:1-3, 5.
Like as the Hart Desireth the Water-Brooks. Harker, F. Flaxington. Psalm 42:1-4.
Like as the Smoke Vanisheth. Handel, G. F. Psalm 68:00.
Like Cedars. Schutte, Daniel L. Psalm 92:1.
Like Cedars They Shall Stand. Schutte, Daniel L. Psalm 92:1-7, 10, 12-13.
Like the Deer. Schutte, Daniel L. Psalm 42:1-3.
The Lilies of the Field. Talbot, John Michael. Matthew 6:28, 31.
A Lily Among Thorns. Richards, Stephen. Song of Songs 2:2-3.
The Lion and Lamb. Kalmanoff, Martin. Isaiah 11:7 (based on).
Little David, Play on Your Harp.
Spiritual (ed. Jay Althouse). Exodus 8:1 (based on).
Spiritual (arr. Harry T. Burleigh). Exodus 8:1 (based on).
Living By Dying. Anthony, Dick. John 12:24-25.
A Living Sacrifice. McAfee, Don. Romans 12:1-2.
Lõ Sevõshi. Talmud, Rabbi Y. (arr. Velvel Pasternak). Psalm 42:11a.
Lo Yareiu. Steinberg, Ben. Isaiah 2:4.
Lo, He Regarded. Bach, C. P. E. Luke 1:48.
Lo, I Unfold unto You a Mystery. Brahms, Johannes. I Corinthians 15:51-52, 54b-55.
Lobe den Herren, meine Seele. Hammerschmidt, Andreas. Psalm 103:2-4.
Lobe den Herrn, meine Seele.
Geisler, Johann Christian. Psalm 103:00.
Wiemer, Wolfgang. Psalm 103:00.
Lobet den Herren, der zu Zion wohnet. Schütz, Heinrich. Psalm 9:11-12.
Lobgesang der maria. Zentner, Johannes. Luke 1:46-55.
Look Away From Me. Laderman, Ezra. Psalm 39:12b-13a.
Look to the Mountains. Fyock, Joan A. Psalm 121:00.
Look Toward Me. Foley, John B. Psalm 25:1-2, 15-16.
Look unto Jesus. Allen, Dennis and Nan Davis. Hebrews 12:1-2.
Look unto Me, Saith Our God. Kendrick, Virginia. Isaiah 45:4-6, 11-13.
Lord, a New Song I Would Fashion. Dvorák, Antonín. Psalm 144:9.

Lord and Savior. Bizet, Georges. John 1:29.
The Lord Be Magnified. Ayala, Bob. Psalm 40:16 (based on).
Lord, Be With Us. Walker, Christopher. Psalm 33:4-22 (based on).
The Lord Bless Thee and Keep Thee. Smith, Gregg. Numbers 6:24.
The Lord Bless You. Bach, J. S. Psalm 115:13-15.
The Lord Bless You and Keep You.
Lutkin, Peter C. Numbers 6:24.
Lutkin, Peter C. (arr. William Stickles). Numbers 6:24.
The Lord Bless You From Zion. Taub, Rabbi S. E. (arr. Velvel Pasternak). Psalm 128:5.
The Lord By Wisdom Founded Earth. Leichtling, Alan. Proverbs 2:19-22.
The Lord By Wisdom Hath Founded Earth. Fischer, Irwin. Proverbs 3:13, 16, 17, 19, 21.
The Lord Comes. Smith, G. Alan. Matthew 21:9.
Lord, Create in Me a Clean Heart. Schütz, Heinrich. Psalm 51:10-12.
Lord, Every Nation on Earth Shall Adore You. Talbot, John Michael. Psalm 72:00.
Lord, From the Depths I Call to You. Hopson, Hal H. Psalm 130:1-4.
Lord, From Your Hand (arr. Bruce Greer). Luke 22:19. English Folk Melody.
Lord God of Abraham. Mendelssohn, Felix. I Kings 18:36-37.
The Lord Has Done Great Things for Them. Bobb, Barry L. Psalm 126:00.
Lord, Have Mercy. Franck, César (arr. Hal H. Hopson). Psalm 51:1-4, 10-12.
Lord, How Gracious. Oxley, Harrison. Psalm 85:1-2, 10-13.
Lord, How Long Wilt Thou Forget Me? Ranzzini. Psalm 13:00.
Lord, I Have Loved the Habitation of Thy House.
Baumgartner, H. Leroy. Psalm 26:8.
Matthews, H. Alexander. Psalm 26:8.
Lord, in Thee Do I Trust. Buxtehude, Dietrich (arr. Clarence Dickinson). Psalm 31:2-4.
The Lord Is Long-suffering. Parry, C. H. H. Psalm 103:8.
Lord, It Is Good. Talbot, John Michael. Psalm 92:00.
The Lord Is a Mighty Warrior. Anonymous (ed. Marilyn Gombosi). Exodus 15:3.
The Lord Is Faithful. Wienhorst, Richard. Psalm 145:13b-16.
The Lord Is in His Holy Temple. Peter, Johann Friedrich. Habakkuk 2:20.
The Lord Is in This Place. Lister, Mosie. Genesis 28:16-17.
The Lord Is Kind and Merciful. Foley, John B. Psalm 103:2-4, 6, 8, 11-13, 19-20.
The Lord Is My Light.
Allitsen, M. Frances. Psalm 27:1, 3, 5.
Allitsen, M. Frances (arr. William David Young and Tom Fettke). Psalm 27:1, 3, 5.
Berthier, Jacques. Psalm 27:1, 3, 5-6.
Buck, Dudley. Psalm 27:1, 3, 5-6.
Courtney, Craig. Psalm 27:1-6.
Edwards, Clara. Psalm 27:00.
Foley, John B. Psalm 27:1, 4, 7-9, 14.
Humphreys, Don. Psalm 27:1-4, 8.
Koch, Frederick. Psalm 27:1, 3, 5.
Leavitt, John. Psalm 27:00.
Matthews, H. Alexander. Psalm 27:00.
Nelson, Jeff. Psalm 27:1a, 3-5, 19.
Speaks, Oley. Psalm 27:00.
Sweney, J. Psalm 27:1.
Tindall, Adrienne M. Psalm 27:1, 2b, 3, 4a, 5.
Wetzler, Robert. Psalm 27:1-3a.
Wooler, Alfred. Psalm 27:1-3, 5.
The Lord Is My Light and Salvation. Revicki, Robert. Psalm 27:1.
The Lord Is My Rock. Nelhybel, Vaclav. Psalm 18:2.
The Lord Is My Shepherd.
Adams, Joseph H. Psalm 23:00.
Arcadelt, Jacob. Psalm 23:00.
Binder, Abraham Wolf. Psalm 23:00.
Bohn, Carl. Psalm 23:00.
Brown, Keith Crosby. Psalm 23:00.
Burton, Daniel. Psalm 23:00.
Childs, Edwin T. Psalm 23:00.
Clarke, Henry Leland. Psalm 23:00.
Courtney, Craig. Psalm 23:00.
Curran, Pearl G. Psalm 23:00.
Davidson, Charles. Psalm 23:00.
Davye, John J. Psalm 23:00.
Dvorák, Antonín. Psalm 23:00.
Edmunds, John. Psalm 23:00.
Foley, John B. Psalm 23:1-6.
Freudenthal, Josef. Psalm 23:00.
Gardner, Aldelaide (arr. Bob Mitchell). Psalm 23:00.
Gilbert, N. Psalm 23:00.
Grier, Gene and Lowell Everson. Psalm 23:00.
Helder, Bartholomaeus (arr. Paul Bunjes). Psalm 23:00.
Humphreys, Don. Psalm 23:00.
Kalmanoff, Martin. Psalm 23:00.
Kingsley, Gershon. Psalm 23:00.
Koch, John. Psalm 23:00.
Koschat, Thomas (arr. Donald H. Ripplinger). Psalm 23:00.
LaMontaine, John. Psalm 23:00.
Liddle, Samuel. Psalm 23:00.
Liddle, Samuel (arr. Neil Jenkins). Psalm 23:00.
Lund, Lynn S. Psalm 23:1-6 (based on).
Mader, Clarence. Psalm 23:00.
Martinson, Joel. Psalm 23:00.
Matthews, H. Alexander. Psalm 23:00.
Matthews, Thomas. Psalm 23:00.
Meek, Kenneth. Psalm 23:00.
Montgomery, James and Thomas Koshat. Psalm 23:00.
Mueller, Carl F. Psalm 23:00.
Ore, Charles W. Psalm 23:00.
Rubbra, Edmund. Psalm 23:00.
Rusk, Harriet. Matthew 6:9-13.
Schack, David. Psalm 23:00.
Schubert, Franz (arr. K. K. Davis). Psalm 23:00.
Scott, John Prindle. Psalm 23:00.
Smart, Henry. Psalm 23:00.
Smith, Gregg. Psalm 23:00.
Sowerby, Leo. Psalm 23:00.
Stearns, Peter Pindar. Psalm 23:00.
Talbot, John Michael. Psalm 23:00.
Taylor, Raynor. Psalm 23:00.
Tchaikovsky, Peter I. (arr. Richard Maxwell and Fred Feibel). Psalm 23:00.
Triplett, Robert F. Psalm 23:00.
Ward-Stephens. Psalm 23:00.
Wise, Joe. Psalm 23:00.
The Lord Is My Strength.
Handel, G. F. Exodus 15:2.
Huhn, Bruno S. Psalm 118:14, 24, 26, 28-29.

The Lord Is Near. Joncas, Michael. Psalm 27:1, 4-5.
The Lord Is Nigh unto Them. Demarest, C. Agnew. Psalm 34:18-19, 21-22.
The Lord Is Risen. Sullivan, Sir Arthur. Revelation 21:3-5.
Lord It Is Good to Give Thanks to You. Foley, John B. Psalm 92:2-5, 13-16.
Lord, Let Me Know My End. Wyner, Yehudi. Psalm 39:4-5.
The Lord Liveth. O'Shields, Michael. II Samuel 22:4.
Lord, Lord Open to Us. Bender, Jan. Matthew 25:1-13.
Lord, Make Me an Instrument. Tindall, Adrienne M. Psalm 85:8.
Lord, Make Me to Know. Brahms, Johannes. Psalm 39:4-7.
Lord My Shield, My Refuge. Dvorák, Antonín. Psalm 119:114-115, 117, 120.
Lord, My Trust Is in Thee. Schütz, Heinrich. Psalm 13:5-6.
Lord, O Harken Unto My Crying. Dvorák, Antonín. Psalm 61:1, 3-5.
Lord of Glory. Manion, Tim. Song of Songs 2:8.
The Lord of Love. Franz, Robert (ed. and arr. K. K. Davis and N. Loring). Psalm 23:00.
Lord, Our Creator. Mendelssohn, Felix. Psalm 8:9.
The Lord Preserveth Souls. Handel, G. F. Psalm 97:10.
The Lord Reigns. Butler, Eugene. Psalm 97:1.
Lord Send Out Your Spirit.
Connolly, Michael. Psalm 104:1.
Haas, David. Psalm 104:1, 24, 30-31, 34.
The Lord Shall Bless Thee With Abundance. Mendelssohn, Felix. Psalm 115:14.
The Lord Shall Preserve Thee From All Evil. Weldon, John. Psalm 121:8.
Lord, Teach Me Thy Statues. Fischer, Irwin. Psalm 119:12, 18, 28, 35, 59, 69.
Lord, Thou Art My Refuge. Dvorák, Antonín. Psalm 119:114-115, 117, 120.
Lord, Thou Hast Been Our Dwelling Place.
Humphreys, Don. Psalm 90:00.
Phillips, Louis Baker. Psalm 90:00.
Lord, to Thee Do I Lift My Soul. Vivaldi, Antonio. Psalm 86:4-6, 12.
Lord, to Whom Shall We Go? Joncas, Michael. John 6:68.
The Lord Upholds My Life. Haas, David. Psalm 54:1.
Lord, What Is Man. Purcell, Henry. Hebrews 2:6.
Lord Who at Cana's Wedding. Buxtehude, Dietrich. John 2:1-10.
The Lord Will Bless His People. Talbot, John Michael. Psalm 29:00.
The Lord Will I Bless for All My Days. Telemann, Georg Philipp. Psalm 34:2-5, 7.
The Lord Will Not Be Ever Wroth. Reinthaler, C. Deuteronomy 4:29.
Lord, You Have the Words. Haas, David. Psalm 19:7-10.
The Lord Your God Is with You. Butler-Moore, Nylea L. Zephaniah 3:17.
Lord, Your Love Has Drawn Us Near. Dean, Stephen. Psalm 116:12.
The Lord's Blessing. Freudenthal, Josef. Psalm 67:00.
The Lord's My Shepherd.
Flowers, Geoffrey E. Psalm 23:00.
Pooler, Marie. Psalm 23:00.
The Lord's My Shepherd, I'll Not Want.
Irvine, Jessie S. Psalm 23:00.
Tindall, Adrienne M. Psalm 23:1-6
The Lord's Name Is Praised. Greene, Maurice. Psalm 113:3-4.
The Lord's Prayer.
Aäddissen, Erol. Matthew 6:9-13.
Albrecht, M. Matthew 6:9-13.
Anderson, Leroy and Alfred Heller. Matthew 6:9-13.
Bach, J. S. Matthew 6:9-13.
Bantock, Granville. Matthew 6:9-13.
Barnes, Milton. Matthew 6:9-13.
Cadzow, Dorothy. Matthew 6:9-13.
Cory, George. Matthew 6:9-13.
Daigle, Gary. Matthew 6:9-13.
Earls, Paul. Matthew 6:9-13.
Flowers, Geoffrey E. Matthew 6:9.
Forsyth, Josephine. Matthew 6:9-13.
Franco, Johan. Matthew 6:9-13.
Gates, B. Cecil. Matthew 6:9-13.
Hamblen, Bernard. Matthew 6:9-13.
Head, Michael. Matthew 6:9-13.
Henschel, George. Matthew 6:9-13.
Hines, Jerome. Matthew 6:9-13.
Hoffmeister, Leon Abbott. Matthew 6:9-13.
Isensee, Paul R. Matthew 6:9-13.
Johnson, David N. Matthew 6:9-13.
Jorgensen, Philip. Matthew 6:9-13.
Kirkland, Terry. Matthew 6:9-13.
Krebs, Karl August. Matthew 6:9-13.
Malotte, Albert Hay. Matthew 6:9-13.
Malotte, Albert Hay (ed. David Hamilton). Matthew 6:9-13.
Mead, Sr. Janet. Matthew 6:9-13.
Mendelssohn, Felix. Matthew 6:9-13.
Mendelssohn, Felix (arr. Michael Johnson). Matthew 6:9-13.
Merbecke, John (arr. Everett Jay Hilty). Matthew 6:9-13.
Myers, Gordon. Matthew 6:9-13.
Nagy, Russell. Matthew 6:9.
Peeters, Flor. Matthew 6:9-13.
Proulx, Richard. Matthew 6:9-13.
Roma, Caro. Matthew 6:9-13.
Rorem, Ned. Matthew 6:9-13.
Sheatz, Elizabeth Q. Matthew 6:9-13.
Shenk, Louis. Matthew 6:9-13.
Sibelius, Jean (arr. Richard D. Row). Matthew 6:9-13.
Strals, Arnold (arr. Les Sands). Matthew 6:9-13.
Strommen, Carl. Psalm 23:00.
Talbot, John Michael. Luke 11:2.
Willan, Healey. Matthew 6:9-13.
Williamson, Inez McC. Matthew 6:9-13.
Young, Carlton. Matthew 6:9-13.
The Lord's Prayer I. Haas, David. Matthew 6:9.
Lost Sheep. Spiritual (arr. Edward Boatner). Matthew 18:13 (based on).
Love.
Birch, Robert Fairfax. Song of Songs 8:6-7.
MacDermid, James G. Genesis 1:3.
Roberts, John Varley. Genesis 1:3.
Root, Frederic W. Genesis 1:3.
VanDyke, May. Matthew 22:37-39.
Love is of God. Baumgartner, H. Leroy. I John 4:7-12, 18-19, 21.
Love Is . . . McCray, James. Psalm 128:00.
Love Never Faileth.
Fauré, Gabriel. I Corinthians 13:1-8.
Haskins, V. I Corinthians 13:00.
Root, Frederic. I Corinthians 13:00.
Ward-Stephens. I Corinthians 13:00.

Love Never Fails. Tindall, Adrienne M. I Corinthians 13:4-8, 13.
Love Not the World.
Sullivan, Sir Arthur. John 14:6a.
Ward-Stephens. I John 2:15a, 17.
The Love of Christ. Parks, Marty. Ephesians 3:18 (other).
The Love of God. Lovelace, Austin C. Psalm 23:4.
The Love of the Lord. Haas, David. Romans 8:35, 38-39.
Love One Another. Fischer, Irwin. I John 4:7.
Love the Lord. Hatton, Ray D. Deuteronomy 6:5.
Love Theme. Johnson, Paul. I Corinthians 13:1-7, 13 (based on).
Lover of Us All. Schutte, Daniel L. Ephesians 2:7-18.
Loving Kindness. Purcell, Henry. Psalm 36:7-10.

Ma Tovu.
Gottlieb, Jack. Numbers 24:5.
Pasternak, Velvel. Numbers 24:5.
Mache dich auf, werde Licht. Franck, Melchior. Isaiah 60:1.
Magnificat.
Bernardi, Steffano. Luke 1:46-47.
Burkhard, Willy. Luke 1:46-47.
Couperin, François. Luke 1:45-55.
Duke, John. Luke 1:46-55.
Foley, John B. Luke 1:46-55.
Gaslini, Giorgio. Luke 1:46-57.
Haas, David. Luke 1:46-55.
Hovland, Egil. Luke 1:46-55.
Pinkham, Daniel. Luke 1:46-55.
Posch, Isaac. Luke 1:46-55.
Poterack, Kurt. Luke 1:46-55.
Roth, John. Luke 1:46-55.
Savioni, Mario. Luke 1:46-57.
Schwarz, May. Luke 1:46-55.
Thorne, Francis. Luke 1:46-47.
Magnificat anima mea Dominum.
Schein, Johann Hermann. Luke 1:46-55.
Schein, Johann Hermann (ed. Paul Horn). Luke 1:46-47.
Magnify the Lord. Smith, Michael W. (arr. Tom Fettke). Psalm 34:00.
Mah Tovu.
Steinberg, Ben. Numbers 24:5.
Weiner, Lazar. Numbers 24:5.
Majesty. Tunney, Dick and Melodie. I Corinthians 15:52.
The Majesty and Glory of Your Name. Fettke, Tom. Psalm 8:1, 3-9.
Make a Joyful Noise.
Head, Michael. Psalm 100:00.
LaForge, Frank. Psalm 100:00.
MacDermid, James G. Psalm 100:00.
Robison, P. Psalm 100:00.
Suben, Joel. Psalm 100:00.
Make a Joyful Noise to the Lord. Roff, Joseph. Psalm 98:4-6.
Make a Joyful Noise unto the Lord. Koch, John. Psalm 100:00.
Make His Praise Glorious. Wolaver, Bill and Robin. Psalm 66:2.
Make Me a Clean Heart, O God. Handel, G. F. Psalm 51:10-12.
Making War in the Heavenlies. Searcy, George. II Corinthians 10:5 (based on).
Man. Humphreys, Don. Genesis 1:27.
Man That is Born of a Woman.
Floyd, Carlisle. Job 14:1, 2, 7-12.
Pinkham, Daniel. Job 14:1-2.
Man the Child of God. Wolf, Hugo. I Corinthians 2:9-12.
Mark the Perfect Man. Barker, Clement W. Isaiah 2:22.
Mary's Magnificat. Skillings, Otis. Luke 1:46-55.
Mary's Song. Rieth, Mildred F. Luke 1:46-55 (based on).
Master, Though Laboring All the Night and Toiling Here. Schütz, Heinrich. Luke 5:5.
Master, We Toiled All Night. Krapf, Gerhard. Luke 5:1-11.
May Adonai Bless You. Cohen, Gerald. Numbers 6:24-26.
May Choirs of Angels Welcome You. Dean, Stephen. Psalm 116:1-8, 15, 18.
May God Bless and Keep You. Walker, Christopher. Numbers 6:22-27.
May God Bless Us. Talbot, John Michael. Psalm 67:00.
May the Angels.
Joncas, Michael. Psalm 27:1, 4-5.
Schutte, Daniel L. Luke 24:5.
May the Words. Weiner, Lazar. Psalm 19:15.
Me and My House. Sheppard, Tim. Joshua 24:15.
Meadows and Mountains. Schutte, Daniel L. Daniel 3:51-90.
Mé-aylin yovõ ezri. Kehati, Pinchas (arr. Velvel Pasternak). Psalm 121:1-2.
Mein Aug' erheb' ich. David, Ferdinand. Psalm 121:00.
Mein Herz ist bereit.
Buxtehude, Dietrich. Psalm 57:00.
Schütz, Heinrich. Psalm 57:00.
Meine Seele erhebet den Herrn. Dencke, Jeremiah. Luke 1:46-50.
Meine Seele erhebt den Herren. Schütz, Heinrich. Luke 1:46-47.
Meine Seele wartet auf den Herrn. Bach, J. S. Psalm 130:6.
Meine Seele, Warum Hast du uns das getan? Schütz, Heinrich. Luke 2:48-49.
Meister, wir habe die ganze Nacht gearbeitet. Schütz, Heinrich. Luke 5:5.
Mem. Tindall, Adrienne M. Psalm 119:97, 99, 101-103.
Men of Blood and Deceit. Pasternak, Velvel. Psalm 55:24.
The Messenger of Peace. Scott, John Prindle. Isaiah 52:00.
Mi Dios, Mi Dios. Hurd, Bob (arr. Dominic MacAller). Psalm 22:2, 8-11, 17-20, 23, 25 (based on).
Mighty Are Your Works, O God. Mozart, W. A. (arr. Hal H. Hopson). Psalm 8:1.
The Mighty God Hath Spoken.
Case, Henry Lincoln. Psalm 50:1-3, 5-6.
Croft, William (arr. Katherine K. Davis). Psalm 150:1,4, 7, 14-15.
Mikõlõs mayim. Pasternak, Velvel. Psalm 93:4.
Mimaamakim. Weiner, Lazar. Psalm 130:00.
Miserere et Jubilate. Archer, Violet. Psalm 13:1-3.
The Mists of Adam Dreaming. Tindall, Adrienne M. I Corinthians 15:45, 53, 49.
Mizmor le David. Neumann, Richard, Arr. Psalm 29:00.
The Mountain I See. Haas, David. Psalm 121:00.
Mountains of My Soul. Norbet, Gregory. Psalm 121:1-2.
Mourning Scene. Rorem, Ned. II Samuel 1:19-27.
My Beloved Is Mine and I Am His.
Britten, Benjamin. Song of Songs 2:16 (based on).
LaMontaine, John. Song of Songs 2:16-17.
My Beloved Spake. Samama, Leo. Song of Songs 2:10-13.
My Dear Brethren, Meet the Demands of This Time. Distler, Hugo. Romans 12:11-12, 18.
My Eyes Have Seen Your Salvation. Berkig, Laurey and Jon Lugo. Luke 2:25-30.
My Eyes Will I to the Hills Lift Up. Dvorák, Antonín. Psalm 121:1-4.

My Father, My Father, Look upon My Anguish. Handel, G. F. Matthew 26:42.
My God, My God.
Talbot, John Michael. Psalm 22:00.
Walker, Christopher. Psalm 22:8-9, 17-20, 23-24.
My God Why Have You Forsaken Me? Morawetz, Oskar. Psalm 22:00.
My Heart Is Breaking With Grief. Berthier, Jacques. Matthew 26:38-39a, 45.
My Heart Is Ready. Talbot, John Michael. Psalm 108:00.
My Heart Is Ready, O God. Ferris, William. Psalm 108:00.
My Heart Is Steadfast. Roff, Joseph. Psalm 108:1-4.
My Lord Is Leading Me On. Whittemore, Dan (arr. Joseph Linn). Psalm 25:4-5
My Lord, What a Morning.
Spiritual (arr. Jay Althouse). Revelation 8:10.
Spiritual (arr. Harry T. Burleigh). Revelation 8:10.
Spiritual (arr. William Dawson). Revelation 8:10.
Spiritual (arr. Mark Hayes). Revelation 8:10.
Spiritual (arr. Hall Johnson). Revelation 8:10.
My New Name. MacDermid, James G. Revelation 3:10-12.
My Prayer. Humphreys, Don. Psalm 19:14.
My Refuge. Vessels, Dennis (arr. Sheryl Soderberg). Psalm 31:1-5.
My Shepherd.
Card, Michael. Psalm 23:00.
Graham, Robert. Psalm 23:00.
Handel, G. F. Psalm 23:00.
My Shepherd is Jehovah. Martin, Gilbert M. Psalm 23:00.
My Shepherd Will Supply My Need.
Lovelace, Austin C. Psalm 23:1-2.
Pooler, Marie. Psalm 23:00.
Thomson, Virgil. Psalm 23:00.
My Son. Isaacson, Michael. Proverbs 3:1-6.
My Son Has Gone Away. Dufford, Bob. Luke 15:11-32.
My Son, Wherefore Hast Thou Done This to Us? Schütz, Heinrich. Luke 2:48-49.
My Soul Doth Magnify. Sandresky, Margaret. Luke 1:46-47.
My Soul Doth Magnify the Lord.
Burns, William K. Luke 1:46-49.
Dencke, Jeremiah. Luke 1:46-50.
Hatch, Verna. Luke 1:46-55.
Thompson, Randall. Luke 1:46-47.
My Soul Is Athirst for God.
Gaul, Alfred Robert. Psalm 42:2-3.
Stickles, William. Psalm 42:2.
My Soul Is Filled with Joy. Lovelace, Austin C. I Samuel 2:1-10.
My Soul Is Longing. Cooney, Rory. Psalm 63:1-5, 7-8.
My Soul Is Still. Haas, David. Psalm 131:00.
My Soul Is Thirsting.
Haugen, Marty. Psalm 63:1b-9.
Hurd, Bob (arr. Dominic MacAller). Psalm 63:1-8.
My Soul Is Thirsting for You. Foley, John B. Psalm 63:1-9.
My Soul Magnifies the Lord. Bambino, Annemarie. Luke 1:46-47.
My Soul Rejoices. Bach, J. S. Luke 1:47.
My Soul Thirsteth for God. Kehati, Pinchas (arr. Velvel Pasternak). Psalm 42:3.
My Soul Thirsts. Schutte, Daniel L. (acc. Thomas Kendzia). Psalm 63:1-7.
My Speech Shall Distill As the Dew. MacDermid, James G. Deuteronomy 32:1-3.
My Spirit Rejoice. Bach, J. S. (arr. Dolores Hruby). Psalm 104:30.
My Spirit Takes Joy. Dufford, Bob (arr. John B. Foley). Luke 1:46.
My Tears Have Been My Meat. Mendelssohn, Felix. Psalm 42:3-4.
My Voice Shalt Thou Hear. Corfe, Joseph. Psalm 5:3.
My Yoke is Easy. Talbot, John Michael. Matthew 11:28-30.

Nafshénu chik'so. Portugal, Rabbi E. (arr. Velvel Pasternak). Psalm 33:20.
The Name of God. Haas, David. Psalm 116:00.
Nations and Heavens. Haas, David. Psalm 113:00.
Neath Vine and Fig Tree. Hopson, Hal H. Isaiah 2:1-4.
Neither Hath This Man Sinned. Elgar, Edward. John 9:3-5.
Never Shall a Soul. Foley, John B. Joel 2:28-32.
The New 23rd Psalm. Carmichael, Ralph. Psalm 23:00.
A New Commandment I Give unto You. Gates, Crawford. John 13:34-35.
A New Creature. Wilson, John Floyd. II Corinthians 5:17.
A New Heaven and a New Earth. Revelation 21:1-7. Rubin, Steffi.
New Heaven-New Earth. Romer, Charles B. (arr. Lyndell Leatherman). Revelation 21:1-7.
The New Jerusalem. Card, Michael and Scott Brasher. Revelation 21:1-4 (based on).
The Ninety and Nine.
Campion, Edward. Luke 15:4-7.
Sankey, Ira D. (arr. O. D. Hall, Jr.). Luke 15:4-7.
The Ninety First Psalm.
Davis, M. Psalm 91:1-5, 9-12.
Liszt, Franz. Psalm 91:1-4, 11.
MacDermid, James G. Psalm 91:1, 5-6, 9, 10-12.
Nisi Dominus aedificaverit domum. Biber, Heinrich Ignaz Franz (ed. Wolfram Stude). Psalm 127:00.
No Longer I. Hurd, Bob and Dominic MacAller. Galatians 2:19-20.
No More Night. Harrah, Walt. Hebrews 11:13-16 (based on).
No Other Name. Gay, Roert (arr. Mosie Lister). Psalm 96:8.
Not a Sparrow Falleth. Abt, Franz. Matthew 10:29-31.
Not Two, But One. Nelson, Ronald A. Matthew 19:6.
The Now and the Not Yet. Hall, Pam Mark. I John 3:2a.
Now Christ Is Risen. Bach, J. S. I Corinthians 15:20, 22.
Now Comes the Day. Conry, Tom (arr. Dominic MacAller). Psalm 118:1, 16-17, 19.
Now Go Your Ways. Gaul, Alfred Robert. Ruth 1:8.
Now It Is High Time to Awake. Pinkham, Daniel. Romans 13:11-12.
Now Let All Christian Men Rejoice. Boex, Andrew J. Luke 2:13-14.
Now That I've Held Him in My Arms. Card, Michael. Luke 2:22-35.
Now, the Acceptable Time. Haas, David. Joel 2:12.
Now Trust in the Lord. Mendelssohn, Felix. Psalm 37:1, 4-5, 7.
Now unto Him. Morris, David. Jude 1:24-25 (based on).
Now unto the King Eternal. Sonnenberg, Lorraine. I Timothy 1:17.
Now Will I Praise the Lord. Dietterich, Philip. Psalm 34:1-6.
Now Will I Praise the Lord With All My Heart. Schütz, Heinrich. Psalm 34:1-7.
Nun. Tindall, Adrienne M. Psalm 119:105-106, 108, 110-112.
Nunc Dimittis.
Burgon, Geoffrey. Luke 2:29-32.
Pinkham, Daniel. Luke 2:29-32.

Thorne, Francis. Luke 2:29-32.
Trapp, Lynn. Luke 2:29-32.
Walker, Christopher. Luke 2:29-32.
Young, Carlton. Luke 2:29-32.

O All Ye Who Travel. Dubois, Theodore. Lamentations 1:12.
O Be Joyful in the Lord. Sowerby, Leo. Psalm 100:00.
O Bless the Lord. Michaels, John (arr. Craig S. Kingsbury). Psalm 148:1-3, 7, 9-10, 12-13.
O Blessed Are Those. Inwood, Paul. Psalm 128:1-5.
O Blest Is He Who Reveres the Lord. Telemann, Georg Philipp. Psalm 112:1b-3.
O Christ the Way. Mendelssohn, Felix. John 8:32.
O Clap Your Hands.
Dengler, Lee. Psalm 47:1-2, 5-7.
McAfee, Don. Psalm 47:1, 5-8.
O Clap Your Hands, All Ye People. Hanson, Howard. Psalm 47:00.
O Come Hither. Stanford, Charles Villiers. Psalm 46:8-10.
O Come Hither, and Hearken. Gordigiani, L. Psalm 66:14-15.
O Come, Let Us Sing. Handel, G. F. Psalm 99:9.
O Come, Let Us Sing to the Lord. Larson, Lloyd. Psalm 95:1-6.
O Come, Let Us Sing unto the Lord. Lekberg, Sven. Psalm 95:1-7.
O Come Let Us Worship.
Handel, G. F. Psalm 95:6-8.
Mendelssohn, Felix. Psalm 95:00.
O Come to Me. Gounod, Charles. Matthew 5:3-4, 6, 8.
O Death How Bitter. Brahms, Johannes. Ecclesiasticus 41:1.
O Death, Where is Thy Sting? Handel, G. F. I Corinthians 15:55-56.
O Dieu donne moi deliverance. DeBese, Theodore. Psalm 140:00.
O Father in Heaven. Mayfield, Larry. Matthew 6:9-13.
O for the Wings of a Dove. Mendelssohn, Felix. Psalm 55:6-7.
O Galilee. Rowberry, Robert Lee. Mark 4:30 (based on).
O Give Thanks. Powell, Robert J. Psalm 107:1-2, 43.
O God, for You I Long. Farrell, Bernadette. Psalm 42:1-6, 8.
O God, Have Mercy. Mendelssohn, Felix. Psalm 51:1, 10-11, 13, 15, 17.
O God, I Will Praise Thee. Schütz, Heinrich. Psalm 111:00.
O God, in All Thy Might. Lovelace, Austin C. I Corinthians 13:9, 12.
O God, Our Help in Ages Past.
Croft, William (arr. Jery Ray). Psalm 90:1-2, 4.
Davies, Henry Walford (arr. Harrison Oxley). Psalm 90:1-2, 4.
O God, You Are My God. Rieth, Mildred F. Psalm 63:1-5.
O Gracious Lord. Gaul, Alfred Robert. Ruth 1:8.
O Holy Ones, Sing Praise. Schütz, Heinrich. Psalm 30:5-6.
O How Amiable Are Thy Dwellings. Coombs, Charles Whitney. Psalm 84:00.
O, How I Long to See. Hurd, Bob (arr. Dominic MacAller). Psalm 17:15.
O Lord, Have Mercy Upon Me. Pergolesi, Giovanni B. Psalm 10:00.
O Lord, How Excellent Is Thy Name. Freed, Isadore. Psalm 8:00.
O Lord, How Long Wilt Thou Forget Me. Sacco, Peter. Psalm 13:00.
O Lord How Lovely. Lowe, Augustus F. Psalm 8:1.
O Lord, How Manifold Are Thy Works. Fischer, Irwin. Psalm 104:1, 2, 4, 24, 30.
O Lord, I Have Waited. Rieth, Mildred F. Psalm 40:1-10.
O Lord, I Love the Habitation of Your House. Bender, Mark. Psalm 26:8.
O Lord, I Will Praise Thee. Krapf, Gerhard. Isaiah 12:00.
O Lord, I Will Sing. Walker, Christopher. Psalm 63:1-8.
O Lord, Most Holy. Abt, Franz. Luke 1:28, 30-31, 42.
O Lord, My God, Thou Art Very Great. Baumgartner, H. Leroy. Psalm 104:1-3, 24.
O Lord, My Heart Is Fixed. Edmunds, John. Psalm 108:1-5.
O Lord, Our Lord, How Excellent Is Thy Name. Hanson, Howard. Psalm 8:00.
O Lord, Rebuke Me Not.
Purcell, Henry. Psalm 6:1-4.
Rubbra, Edmund. Psalm 6:00.
Wooler, Alfred. Psalm 6:33-37.
O Lord, Rebuke Me Not in Thine Anger. Hanson, Howard. Psalm 6:00.
O Lord, Return. Schalit, Heinrich. Psalm 6:00.
O Lord They Prophesy Against Thee. Mendelssohn, Felix. Exodus 32:10.
O Lord, Thou Hast Searched Me. Lekberg, Sven. Psalm 139:1.
O Lord, Thou Hast Searched Me and Known Me. Floyd, Carlisle. Psalm 139:1, 4, 8.
O Lord, Thou Hast Searched Me Out. Bennett, Sir William Sterndale. Psalm 139:1-4.
O Love That Casts Out Fear. Lovelace, Austin C. John 4:14.
O Magnify the Lord.
Handel, G. F. Psalm 99:9.
Tunney, Melodie and Dick. Psalm 34:3.
O My Dove. Thomson, Virgil. Song of Songs 2:14.
O My Dove, That Art in the Clefts of the Rock. LaMontaine, John. Song of Songs 2:14.
O My Father. Dubois, Theodore. Matthew 27:46.
O My Soul, Bless the Lord. Walker, Christopher. Psalm 103:1-4.
O Praise the Lord.
Greene, Maurice. Psalm 103:20.
Handel, G. F. Psalm 103:21.
Larson, Lloyd. Psalm 117:1 (based on).
O Praise the Lord, All Ye Nations. Chait, B. (arr. Velvel Pasternak). Psalm 117:1.
O quam suave. Jeffreys, George (ed. Peter Aston). Philippians 2:9-10.
O Rejoice in the Lord at All Times. Distler, Hugo. Philippians 4:4.
O Rest in the Lord.
Medema, Ken (arr. Mark Hayes). Psalm 37:1.
Mendelssohn, Felix. Psalm 37:1, 4-5, 7.
Mendelssohn, Felix (arr. Lynn Hodges). Psalm 37:1, 4-5, 7.
Mendelssohn, Felix (arr. Hal H. Hopson). Psalm 37:1, 4-5, 7.
O Salutaris. Pfleuger, Carl. Psalm 13:1, 3, 5.
O Savior, Lord of Heaven. Arcadelt, Jacob. Luke 1:28, 32.
O Sing unto God. Handel, G. F. Psalm 68:4.
O Sing unto the Lord.
Dvorák, Antonín. Psalm 98:1, 7-8.
Handel, G. F. Psalm 93:4.
Marcello, Benedetto. Psalm 95:1.
Spies, Claudio. Psalm 96:1-3.
Whikehart, Lewis E. Psalm 96:00.
O Sing Unto the Lord a New Song.
Goldman, Edward M. Psalm 98:00.
Gore, Richard T. Psalm 98:00.
O singt unserm Gott. Handel, G. F. Psalm 68:00.

O Taste and See.
Bach, J. S. Psalm 34:8.
Young, Carlton. Psalm 34:8.
O That I Knew Where I Might Find Him. Rowley, Alec. Job 23:3.
O That My Ways. Greene, Maurice. Psalm 119:4-5, 18.
O Thou Afflicted, and Tossed With Tempest. Benedict, Sir Julius. Isaiah 54:11, 14.
O Thou That Tellest Good Tidings to Zion.
Handel, G. F. Isaiah 40:9.
Handel, G. F. (arr. W. Daniel Landes). Isaiah 40:9.
O Tod, wie bitter bist du. Brahms, Johannes. Ecclesiasticus 41:1-2.
O vos omnes. Dubois, Theodore. Lamentations 1:12.
O Wherefore Do Ye These Things? Mendelssohn, Felix. I Corinthians 3:16-17.
O Worship the Lord.
Handel, G. F. I Chronicles 16:29.
Travers, John. Psalm 96:7-9.
O Ye, that Love the Lord. Barnby, J. Amos 5:15.
Oblak a mrokotá jest vukol Neho. Dvorák, Antonín. Psalm 97:2-6.
Offer the Sacrifices of Righteousness. Pasternak, Velvel. Psalm 4:6-7.
The Offering of Judah and Jerusalem. Pasternak, Velvel. Malachi 3:4.
Oh, Didn't it Rain. Spiritual (arr. Harry T. Burleigh). Genesis 7:4 (based on).
Oh! For the Wings of a Dove. Roma, Caro. Psalm 55:6-7.
Oh, Lord, Have Mercy and Turn Thou Thy Face to Me. Dvorák, Antonín. Psalm 25:16-18, 20.
Oh, Lord, Our Heavenly King. Lyon, James. Psalm 8:00.
Oh, My Shepherd Is the Lord. Dvorák, Antonín. Psalm 23:1-4.
Oh Praise the Lord. Cassler, G. Winston. Psalm 135:00.
Oh, Sing unto the Lord a Joyful Song. Dvorák, Antonín. Psalm 98:1, 7-8.
Oh, That I Had Wings. Barnes, A. M. Psalm 55:6-7.
Old Jerusalem. Chajes, Julius. Psalm 134:00.
The Old Rugged Cross. Bennard, George. I Corinthians 1:22-25 (based on).
Omnes gentes, plaudite. Dobry, Wallace. Psalm 47:00.
On Eagle's Wings.
Hamblen, Bernard. Isaiah 40:28-31.
Joncas, Michael. Psalm 91:1-7, 11-12.
Joncas, Michael (arr. Mark Hayes). Psalm 91:1-7, 11-12.
Joncas, Michael (arr. Lloyd Larson). Psalm 91:1-7, 11-12.
On Laziness. Beale, James. Proberbs 24:30-31, 33-34.
On Slander. Beale, James. Proberbs 26:21-23.
On Truth. Beale, James. Proberbs 12:19.
On Wisdom. Beale, James. Proberbs 22:17-18.
One Bread, One Body. Foley, John B. I Corinthians 10:16-17.
One Hundred Twenty-First Psalm. Crowe, B. Psalm 121:00.
The One Hundredth Psalm. Mueller, Carl F. Psalm 100:00.
One Thing Befalleth the Beasts. Brahms, Johannes. Ecclesiastes 3:19-22.
One Thing I Ask. Dean, Stephen. Psalm 27:1, 3, 5, 7-9, 13-14 (based on).
One Thing I Ask of the Lord. Schütz, Heinrich. Psalm 27:4.
Only in God.
Foley, John B. Psalm 62:1-2, 8, 1-12.
Talbot, John Michael. Psalm 62:00.
Only This I Want. Schutte, Daniel L. (arr. John B. Foley). Philippians 2:15, 18.
Only With Thine Eye. Malotte, Albert Hay. Psalm 91:8-12.
Open the Gates of the Temple. Knapp, Phoebe C. Job 19:25a.
Open to Me the Gates. Bischoff, John W. (ed. Richard D. Row). Isaiah 26:2-3.
Other Side of the Grave. Green, Steve and Jon Mohr. Romans 6:00.
Our Blessing Cup.
Hurd, Bob. Psalm 116:1, 3, 5, 12-13, 15-18.
Joncas, Michael (arr. Craig S. Kingsbury). Psalm 34:9a.
Talbot, John Michael. Psalm 116:12-14.
Our Father.
Dame, William. Matthew 6:9-13.
Dennis, Randall. Matthew 6:9-13.
Gaskill, Clarence. Matthew 6:9-13.
Hurd, Bob and Paul Ford (arr. Craig S. Kingsbury). Matthew 6:9-13.
MacGimsey, Robert. Matthew 6:9-13.
Our Father Who Art in Heaven. Bottenberg, Henry. Matthew 6:9-13.
Our Fathers Hoped in Thee. Boyce, William. Psalm 22:4.-5.
Our God Has Borne Our Troubles. Lully, Jean Baptiste. Isaiah 53:4-5.
Our God Has Done Great Things for Us. Foley, John B. Psalm 126:1-6.
Our God Is Compassion. Cotter, Jeanne. Psalm 145:8-10, 17-18.
Our God Reigns. Smith, Leonard E. Jr. Isaiah 52:7.
Our Heart Shall Rejoice in the Lord. Powell, Robert J. Psalm 33:21.
Our Loving Father. Cornelius, Peter. Luke 15:11-24.
Our Soul Hath Waited for the Lord. Portugal, Rabbi E. (arr. Velvel Pasternak). Psalm 33:20-21.
Our Soul Waits for the Lord. Pelz, Walter L. Psalm 33:20-22.
Out of My Soul's Depth. Campion, Thomas. Psalm 130:00.
Out of the Deep. Marks, J. Christopher. Psalm 130:00.
Out of the Deep Have I Called unto Thee. Bedell, Robert L. Psalm 130:00.
Out of the Depths.
Bantock, Granville. Psalm 130:00.
Burns, William K. Psalm 130:00.
Butler, Eugene. Psalm 130:1-3, 5-6.
Hovhaness, Alan. Psalm 130:1-6.
Rogers, James H. Psalm 130:00.
Scott, John Prindle. Psalm 130:00.
Weiner, Lazar. Psalm 130:00.
Wooler, Alfred. Psalm 130:00.
Out of the Depths I Cry to Thee. English Tune, 17th c. (ed. K. Lee Scott). Psalm 130:00.
Oz V'Hodor. Pasternak, Velvel. Proberbs 31:25-28.

Padre Nuestro. Malotte, Albert Hay (arr. Steve Green). Matthew 6:9-13.
Parable. Ridge, M. D. (arr. Patrick Loomis). Ecclesiastes 3:1-9.
Paratum cor meum. Schütz, Heinrich. Psalm 107:2-4.
Pater Noster.
Chausson, Ernest. Matthew 6:9-13.
Heiller, Anton. Matthew 6:9-13.
Peeters, Flor. Matthew 6:9-13.
The Path of the Just. Barker, Clement W. Isaiah 1:18.
Patiently Have I Waited for the Lord.
Saint-Saëns, Camille. Psalm 40:1.
Saint-Saëns, Camille (arr. Scott, K. Lee). Psalm 40:1.

Patiently I Awaited Christ the Lord. Saint-Saëns, C. Psalm 40:1.
Peace Be unto You.
Elgar, Edward. Luke 24:36c, 49.
Schubert, Franz. Isaiah 26:3.
Peace I Leave With You.
Dichmont, William. John 14:27.
Roberts, John Varley. John 14:27.
Thompson, William H. John 14:1, 27.
Peace I Leave You. Whitehouse, Jan. John 14:27.
The Peace of God. Gounod, Charles. John 14:27.
Peccator videbit. Vivaldi, Antonio (arr. Richard Walters). Psalm 112:10.
The Penitent. VanDewater, Beardsley. Luke 15:11-25.
The People That Walked in Darkness.
Handel, G. F. Isaiah 9:2-3.
Klass, Leon V. Isaiah 9:1.
Peter Was a Fisherman. Freud, Joyce (arr. Lyndell Leatherman). Matthew 4:18.
The Pilgrim's Psalm. Vaughan Williams, Ralph. Psalm 18:32, 37.
Pioneer Lullaby. Zaabriskie, David A. Hosea 13:14 (based on).
The Pledge. Black, Jennie Prince. Ruth 1:16-17.
Popatriz na mne a smilujh se nade mnou. Dvorák, Antonín. Psalm 25:16-18, 20.
Power in Jesus Name. Nelson, Greg and Phil McHugh. Isaiah 45:23b.
Powerful Guardian. Handel, G. F. Psalm 84:12.
Pozdvihuji ocí svych k horám. Dvorák, Antonín. Psalm 121:1-4.
Praise. Barrus, Lemar. Psalm 106:1, 47-48.
Praise and Give Thanks. Adair, Hazel Ferrell. Psalm 107:6, 9.
Praise God. Dufford, Bob and John B. Foley. Psalm 19:1.
Praise God, From Whom All Blessings Flow. Traditional English (arr. Anna Laura Page). Psalm 117:00.
Praise God, Ye Servants of the Lord. Adler, Samuel. Psalm 113:00.
Praise Him! Courtney, Craig. Psalm 145:1-3, 8-9.
Praise Him, All Ye That in His House Attend. Handel, G. F. Psalm 135:1-2.
Praise, My Soul, the King of Heaven. Cassler, G. Winston. Psalm 103:00.
Praise the Lord.
Adler, Samuel. Psalm 150:00.
Koch, John. Psalm 150:00.
Ridge, M. D. Psalm 113:1-5, 7-9.
Rieth, Mildred F. Psalm 146:1-6.
Praise the Lord All ye Nations. Powell, Robert J. Psalm 117:00.
Praise the Lord His Glories Show. Weaver, Powell. Psalm 150:00.
Praise the Lord, My Soul. Foley, John B. Psalm 103:1-2, 8, 14-15, 21.
Praise the Lord, O My Soul.
Floyd, Carlisle. Psalm 146:1-2.
Greene, Maurice. Psalm 103:1, 2-4.
Jefferies, George. Psalm 104:1, 2, 33-34.
Romer, Charles B. Matthew 6:9-13.
Spies, Claudio. Psalm 146:1-2.
Stockhommer, A. (arr. Velvel Pasternak). Psalm 146:1.
VanDeWater, Beardsley. Luke 18:10.
Wesley, Samuel Sebastian. Psalm 103:1.
Praise the Lord, O My Soul for Guidance. Pote, Allen. Psalm 25:4-7.
Praise the Lord Ye Heavens.
Stainer, John (arr. Austin C. Lovelace). Psalm 148:00.
Weber, Carl M. von. Psalm 148:00.
Praise Thou the Lord, O My Spirit. Mendelssohn, Felix. Psalm 103:1-2.
Praise to the Lord God. Schütz, Heinrich. Psalm 9:11-12.
Praise We the Lord. Edmunds, John. Psalm 113:1-5.
Praise Ye Jehovah. Schütz, Heinrich. Psalm 9:11-12.
Praise Ye the Lord.
Bantock, Granville. Psalm 150:00.
Fischer, Irwin. Psalm 148:1, 3, 7, 9, 11-13.
Fromm, Herbert. Psalm 92:00.
Humphreys, Don. Psalm 106:1-4.
Rorem, Ned. Psalm 148:00.
Rorem, Ned. Psalm 150:00.
Rubbra, Edmund. Psalm 150:00.
Schütz, Heinrich. Psalm 30:5-6.
Praised Be the Lord. Greene, Maurice. Psalm 68:19.
Prayer. Curran, Pearl G. James 5:16.
A Prayer for Jerusalem. Wernick, Richard F. Psalm 122: 2-3, 6-8.
A Prayer for Mercy. O'Connor, Roc. Psalm 51:2-3, 10-12, 15 (based on).
Prayer of Dedication. Manookin, Robert P. Matthew 23:37.
Prayer of Jabez. Beck, Joe and Tom Lane. I Chronicles 4:10.
A Prayer of Moses. Kellermeyer, David M. Psalm 90:1-2, 4, 10, 12, 14, 17.
The Precepts of Micah. Freudenthal, Josef. Micah 6:6-8.
Prepare the Royal Highway. Ferguson, John. Isaiah 40:4.
Prepare the Way of the Lord. Rowan, William. Isaiah 40:4-5.
Prepare to Meet Thy God. Kingsley, Gershon. Amos 5:24.
Prepare Ye the Way of the Lord. Thorne, Francis. Isaiah 40:3-5.
Pri rekách babylonskych. Dvorák, Antonín. Psalm 137:1-5.
Processional. Young, Carlton. Psalm 24:7.
Proclaim the Glory of the Lord. Lyles, Dwight and Niles Borop. Psalm 145:1-13.
Proclaim to All the Nations. Haas, David and Marty Haugen. Psalm 96:1-4, 9-10.
The Prophecy of Amos. Horvit, Michael. Amos 9:7-15.
Psalm. Sleeth, Natalie. Psalm 121:1-2.
Psalm 1.
Butt, James. Psalm 1:00.
Cooney, Rory. Psalm 1:1-3.
Fromm, Herbert. Psalm 1:00.
Thornton, William. Psalm 1:00.
Psalm 3. Hanson, Jens. Psalm 3:00.
Psalm 4. Garlick, Anthony. Psalm 4:00.
Psalm 5. Sprouse, Bill Jr. Psalm 5:1-3.
Psalm 6. Rubbra, Edmund. Psalm 6:00.
Psalm 8.
Barnes, Milton. Psalm 8:00.
Cortese, Luigi. Psalm 8:00.
Courtney, Craig. Psalm 8:00.
Freed, Isadore. Psalm 8:00.
Lowe, Augustus F. Psalm 8:1.
Psalm VIII. Courtney, Craig. Psalm 8:00.
Psalm 13.
Barnes, Milton. Psalm 13:00.
Card, Michael. Psalm 13:00.
Howard, Tom. Psalm 13:1-1.
Kahn, Erich I. Psalm 13:00.
Psalm 16.
Foley, John B. Psalm 16:1-5, 7-11.
Mahnke, Allan. Psalm 16:5-11.

Psalm 17. Garlick, Anthony. Psalm 17:00.
Psalm 19. Trapp, Lynn. Psalm 19:8-10.
Psalm 22.
Bloch, Ernst. Psalm 22:00.
Cherwin, David. Psalm 22:00.
Morawetz, Oskar. Psalm 22:00.
Psalm 23.
Adler, Samuel. Psalm 23:00.
Barnes, Frederick M. Psalm 23:00.
Barnes, Milton. Psalm 23:00.
Ben-Haim, Paul. Psalm 23:00.
Berlinski, Hermann (Hernam). Psalm 23:00.
Betts, Lorne. Psalm 23:00.
Binder, Abraham Wolf. Psalm 23:00.
Buss, Duane. Psalm 23:00.
Card, Michael. Psalm 23:00.
Davidson, Charles. Psalm 23:00.
Deutschmann, Gerhard. Psalm 23:00.
Foley, John B. Psalm 23:1-6.
Garlick, Anthony. Psalm 23:00.
Goetz, Marty. Psalm 23:00.
Goldman, Edward M. Psalm 23:00.
Goode, Jack. Psalm 23:00.
Isaacson, Michael. Psalm 23:00.
Joncas, Michael. Psalm 23:00.
Lawson, Gordon. Psalm 23:00.
Lowe, Augustus F. Psalm 23:00.
Owens, Sam Batt. Psalm 23:00.
Peery, Rob Roy. Psalm 23:00.
Riddle, Peter. Psalm 23:00.
Rusk, Harriet. Psalm 23:00.
Tindall, Adrienne M. Psalm 23:1-6.
Vree, Marion. Psalm 23:00.
Webb, Charles. Psalm 23:00.
Williamson, Malcolm. Psalm 23:00.
Winton, Mary. Psalm 23:00.
Psalm XXIII.
Creston, Paul. Psalm 23:00.
Riddle, Peter. Psalm 23:00.
Rubbra, Edmund. Psalm 23:00.
Psalm 24 (23). Zaimont, Judith Lang. Psalm 23:00.
Psalm 24.
Mahnke, Allan. Psalm 24:7-10.
Williamson, Malcolm. Psalm 24:7-10.
Psalm 25.
Hurd, Bob (arr. Dominic MacAller). Psalm 25:1, 4-5, 8-10, 14.
Fraley, Christopher Lee. Psalm 25:00.
Mahnke, Allan. Psalm 25:1.
Psalm 27.
Foley, John B. Psalm 27:7-9, 13-14.
Mahnke, Allan. Psalm 27:1-3.
Psalm 28. Garlick, Anthony. Psalm 28:00.
Psalm 29.
Barnes, Milton. Psalm 29:00.
Neumann, Richard, arr. Psalm 29:00.
Psalm 32. Mahnke, Allan. Psalm 32:5-8.
Psalm 33.
Foley, John B. Psalm 33:1-2, 4-7, 12-13, 18-22.
Stewart, Roy James. Psalm 33:00.
Psalm 34.
Barnard, Mark. Psalm 34:00.
Hobby, Robert A. Psalm 34:1-11.
Psalm 42.
Fromm, Herbert. Psalm 42:1-4a.
Koprowski, Peter Paul. Psalm 42:00.
Smith, L. Psalm 42:00.
Psalm 47.
Mahnke, Allan. Psalm 47:1-2, 5-7.
McDonald, Boyd. Psalm 47:00.
Psalm 47: Clap Your Hands, All You Peoples. Dobry, Wallace. Psalm 47:00.
Psalm 48. Tucker, Margaret R. Psalm 48:1, 4, 9, 11-13.
Psalm 49. Jones, Kelsey. Psalm 49:00.
Psalm 51.
Cooney, Rory. Psalm 51:00.
Hurd, Bob (arr. Domini MacAller). Psalm 51:3-4, 12, 14, 17, 19.
Psalm 61. Mahnke, Allan. Psalm 61:1.
Psalm 63.
Cooney, Rory. Psalm 63:1-5, 7-8.
Foley, John B. Psalm 63:1-9.
Psalm 66.
Cooney, Rory. Psalm 66:1-7, 16-20.
Foley, John B. Psalm 66:1-7, 16-20.
Wyner, Yehudi. Psalm 66:1-4
Psalm 67.
Edwards, Leo. Psalm 67:00.
Fryxell, Regina H. Psalm 67:00.
Mahnke, Allan. Psalm 67:00.
Wolfe, Jacques. Psalm 67:00.
Psalm LXVII. Wolfe, Jacques. Psalm 67:00.
Psalm 68. Rogers, Bernard. Psalm 68:00.
Psalm 79. Pinkham, Daniel. Psalm 80:00.
Psalm 81. Childs, David. Psalm 81:1-4.
Psalm 83. Childs, David. Psalm 83:1-4, 13, 18.
Psalm 84.
Greenbaum, Matthew. Psalm 84:00.
Hopson, Hal H. Psalm 84:00.
Howard, Tom. Psalm 84:00.
Hurd, David. Psalm 84:1-7, 9.
Psalm 85.
Hurd, Bob (arr. Dominic MacAller). Psalm 85:8-9, 11-14.
Mahnke, Allan. Psalm 85:8-13.
Martinson, Joel. Psalm 85:9-14.
Psalm 86.
Mahnke, Allan. Psalm 86:10-12, 15.
Trapp, Lynn. Psalm 86:5-6, 9-10, 15-16.
Psalm 89.
Foley, John B. Psalm 89:1-6, 1-19, 21-22, 25, 27.
Mahnke, Allan. Psalm 89:1-4, 15-18.
Trapp, Lynn. Psalm 89:2-3, 16-19.
Psalm 90.
Barnes, Milton. Psalm 90:00.
Butt, James. Psalm 90:1-2, 4, 16-17.
Wenzel, Eberhard. Psalm 90:00.
Psalm 91.
Childs, David. Psalm 91:1-4.
Courtney, Craig. Psalm 91:1-7, 9-12.
Hurd, Bob (arr. Craig S. Kingsbury). Psalm 91:1-2, 10-12, 14-15.
O'Connor-Morris, Geoffrey. Psalm 91:00.
Sowerby, Leo. Psalm 91:00.
Psalm 92.
Adler, Samuel. Psalm 92:00.
Childs, David. Psalm 92:1-5.

Foley, John B. Psalm 92:2-5, 13-16.
Lagourgue, Charles. Psalm 92:00.
Psalm 93. Penn, Marilyn. Psalm 93:00.
Psalm 95.
Hurd, Bob (arr. Dominic MacAller). Psalm 95:1-2, 6-9.
Liebergen, Patrick M. Psalm 95:1-3.
Psalm 95: Come, Let Us Sing to the Lord. Dobry, Wallace. Psalm 95:1-7.
Psalm 96.
Adler, Samuel. Psalm 96:1-6, 9-13.
Foley, John B. Psalm 96:1-5, 7-13.
Psalm 97. Goldman, Edward M. Psalm 98:00.
Psalm 99. Mahnke, Allan. Psalm 99:1-5.
Psalm 100.
Bernhard, Christoph. Psalm 100:00.
Roth, Robert N. Psalm 100:00.
Sowerby, Leo. Psalm 100:00.
Tappe, Stephen. Psalm 100:00.
Psalm 103.
Foley, John B. Psalm 103:2-4, 6, 8-11, 13, 19-20.
Larson, Sonia. Psalm 103:1-4.
Schockman, Gregg. Psalm 103:00.
Smith, Jeffrey. Psalm 103:1-5, 11, 17A.
Stephenson, Richard T. Psalm 103:1-5, 8, 13.
Psalm 104.
Foley, John B. Psalm 104:1-3b, 5-6, 10-14, 27-28, 30-31, 33-34.
Lederer, Charles. Psalm 104:00.
Psalm 112. Englert, Eugene. Psalm 112:00.
Psalm 113.
Haas, David. Psalm 113:00.
Ridge, M. D. Psalm 113:1-5, 7-9.
Psalm 114. Bloch, Ernest. Psalm 114:00.
Psalm 116.
Foley, John B. Psalm 116:1-19.
Mahnke, Allan. Psalm 116:5-9.
Psalm 116:10-17. Mahnke, Allan. Psalm 116:10-17.
Psalm 118. Foley, John B. Psalm 118:1-4, 8-9, 13-17, 21-24, 26.
Psalm 119. Wyner, Yehudi. Psalm 119:25-32.
Psalm 120. Rorem, Ned. Psalm 120:00.
Psalm 121.
Barnes, Milton. Psalm 121:00.
Barta, Daniel. Psalm 121:00.
Burns, William K. Psalm 121:00.
Childs, David. Psalm 121:00.
Eaton, Chris. Psalm 121:00.
Fromm, Herbert. Psalm 121:00.
Gellman, Steven. Psalm 121:00.
Haas, David. Psalm 121:00.
Horwood, Michael S. Psalm 121:00.
Kayden, Mildred. Psalm 121:00.
Proulx, Richard. Psalm 121:00.
Sowerby, Leo. Psalm 121:00.
Psalm 122. Proulx, Richard. Psalm 122:00.
Psalm 123. Childs, David. Psalm 123:1-5.
Psalm 126.
Brod, Max. Psalm 126:00.
Foley, John B. Psalm 126:1-6.
Kahn, Erich I. Psalm 126:00.
Mahnke, Allan. Psalm 126:1-6.
Psalm CXXVI. Brod, Max. Psalm 126:00.
Psalm 127. Dinn, Freda. Psalm 127:00.
Psalm 128.
Barnes, Milton. Psalm 128:00.
Dailey, William. Psalm 128:00.
Foley, John B. Psalm 128:1-6.
Keil, Kevin. Psalm 128:00.
Wetzler, Robert. Psalm 128:00.
Psalm 130. Foley, John B. Psalm 130:1-4, 6-8.
Psalm 131. Mahnke, Allan. Psalm 131:00.
Psalm 133. Tindall, Adrienne M. Psalm 133:1.
Psalm 137.
Bloch, Ernst. Psalm 137:00.
Freedman, Harry. Psalm 137:00.
Richards, Stephen. Psalm 137:00.
Seeger, Charles. Psalm 137:00.
Psalm 139.
Card, Michael. Psalm 139:00.
Cooney, Rory. Psalm 139:1.
Mahnke, Allan. Psalm 139:7.
McAfee, Don. Psalm 139:00.
St. James, Rebecca (arr. Dennis Allen). Psalm 139:1.
Scrivener, Joseph. Psalm 139:00.
Psalm 140. Sessions, Roger. Psalm 140:00.
Psalm 141. Trapp, Lynn. Psalm 141:1-5, 8-9.
Psalm 142. Sowerby, Leo. Psalm 142:00.
Psalm 145.
Canedo, Ken. Psalm 145:00.
Folkemer, Stephen P. Psalm 145:1-3, 8-9, 13b-14, 17-18, 21.
Trapp, Lynn. Psalm 145:1-2, 8-11, 13-14.
Psalm 146: Praise the Lord, O My Soul. Dobry, Wallace. Psalm 146:00.
Psalm 147. Goode, Jack. Psalm 147:00.
Psalm 148.
Childs, David. Psalm 148:1-6.
Delaney, Maureen. Psalm 148:00.
Hoy, Dawn Riske. Psalm 148:00.
Psalm 149.
Fromm, Herbert. Psalm 149:1-4.
Mahnke, Allan. Psalm 149:1-4.
Psalm 150.
Butt, James. Psalm 150:00.
Goldman, Edward M. Psalm 150:00.
Perry, Dave and Jean Perry. Psalm 150:1-3, 5-6.
Rubbra, Edmund. Psalm 150:00.
Schilling, Hans Ludwig. Psalm 150:00.
Schutte, Daniel L. Psalm 150:00.
Weinberger, Jaromir. Psalm 150:00.
Psalm Fifty-One. O'Connor, Roc. Psalm 51:2-3, 10-12, 14.
Psalm Forty-Nine. Jones, Kelsey. Psalm 49:00.
A Psalm of David.
Roff, Joseph. Psalm 108:1-4.
Schütz, Heinrich. Psalm 70:00.
Psalm of Exaltation. Charles, Ernest. Psalm 27:1, 4, 6.
Psalm of Joy. Anderson, Ronald. Psalm 150:00.
Psalm of Praise. Fischer, Irwin. Isaiah 63:7.
A Psalm of Praise.
McFeeters, Raymond. Psalm 100:00.
Rorem, Ned. Psalm 100:00.
Psalm on the Eve of Battle. Raksim, David. Psalm 3:1-4.
Psalms 22 and 69. Card, Michael. Psalm 22:00.
Pueblo De Dios. Hurd, Bob. Psalm 122:1.
Put on the Whole Armour of God. Humphreys, Don. Ephesians 6:10-13.
Put Thou Thy Trust in the Lord. Camidge, John. Psalm 37:1, 4-5, 7.

Quemamodum desiderat. Posch, Isaac. Psalm 42:00.
Quia fecit mihi magna.
Bach, C. P. E. Luke 1:49.
Bach, J. S. Luke 1:49.
Quia respexit.
Bach, C. P. E. Luke 1:48.
Bach, J. S. Luke 1:48.
Quia respexit humilitatem. Bach, J. S. Luke 1:48.

The Raising of Lazarus.
Barker, Clement W. John 11:1-44.
Davis, Katherine K. John 11:1, 3-4, 15, 17, 41-44.
Raising the Son of the Widow. Hart, Theron Wolcott. Luke 7:11-16.
The Ransomed of the Lord.
Humphreys, Don. Isaiah 35:00.
MacDermid, James G. Isaiah 35:00.
Ready the Way. Hurd, Bob (arr. Craig S. Kingsbury). Isaiah 35:1-6.
Recitative and Angel's Message to the Shepherds. Schütz, Heinrich. Luke 2:8-14.
Redeemer Lord. Foley, John B. Psalm 22:1-2, 6.
Rejoice Greatly, O Daughter of Zion.
Handel, G. F. Zechariah 9:9-10.
Willan, Healey. Zechariah 9:9-10.
Rejoice in the Lord.
Humphreys, Don. Philippians 4:4-5, 7-8.
Lane, Richard. Philippians 4:4, 8.
Schnecker, P. A. Psalm 33:1-2, 4-5.
Rejoice in the Lord Alway,. Pinkham, Daniel. Philippians 4:4-7.
Rejoice in the Lord Always.
Gieseke, Richard W. Philippians 4:4-7.
Kosche, Kenneth T. Philippians 4:4-5.
Rejoice With Exceeding Great Joy. Wolaver, Bill. Matthew 2:1-12 (based on).
Rejoice Ye With Jerusalem. Shapiro, Rabbi Y. (arr. Velvel Pasternak). Isaiah 66:10.
Remember Me. Dolck, Doug. I Corinthians 11:23-26.
Remember Now Thy Creator.
Eggert, Fred E. Ecclesiastes 12:1-8.
Scott, John Prindle. Ecclesiastes 12:1-7.
Remember the Word unto Thy Servant. Tindall, Adrienne M. Psalm 119:49-52, 54-55.
Remember Your Mercy, Lord. Inwood, Paul. Psalm 25:4-9.
Repent Ye. Scott, John Prindle. Matthew 3:1-2, 7, 8, 11, 12.
Requiem. Archer, Violet. Song of Songs 3:1-3.
Rescue Me From My Enemies. Foley, John B. Psalm 129:1-4.
Rest in the Lord. Humphreys, Don. Psalm 37:4-7a.
Restore the Joy. Moore, Harlan. Psalm 51:23.
The Resurrection. Curran, Pearl G. John 20:1, 11, 14-15, 17-20, 26, 30-31.
Resurrection. Rorem, Ned. Matthew 27:28, 62-66.
Return to Me. Hurd, Bob (arr. Craig S. Kingsbury). Hosea 11:00.
Return to Your People, O Lord. Dufford, Bob. Isaiah 64:1, 8-11.
Return, O Shulamite! Thomson, Virgil. Song of Songs 6:13.
Revelation. Wolf, Hugo (arr. K. K. Davis). Revelation 21: 9-10.
Revere the Lord, You, His Holy Ones. Pasternak, Velvel. Psalm 29:11.
Ride On, King Jesus.
Spiritual (arr. Harry T. Burleigh). Revelation 6:2 (based on).
Spiritual (arr. Hall Johnson). Revelation 6:2 (based on).
Righteous and Equity. Handel, G. F. Psalm 89:15.
Ring Out Your Joy. Inwood, Paul. Psalm 95:1-8.
Rise and Walk. Warren, Clara. Acts 3:1-8.
Rise Up and Praise Him. Baloche, Paul and Gary Sadler. Psalm 96:11.
Rise Up and Walk. Richner, Thomas. Acts 3:1-3.
Rise Up, Jerusalem. Foley, John B. Isaiah 60:1-4 (based on).
Rise Up My Love.
Kingsley, Gershon. Song of Songs 2:10-12.
Rochberg, George. Song of Songs 2:10-13b.
Thornton, William. Song of Songs 2:10-13.
Rise Up, My Love, My Fair One, and Come Away.
LaMontaine, John. Song of Songs 2:10b-13.
Rite of Blessing and Sprinkling of Water. Daigle, Gary. Luke 2:14.
River of Life. Butt, James. Revelation 22:1-4.
The River of Water of Life. Joy, Jeanne Alden. Revelation 22:1, 14, 17.
The Robe of Righteousness. Coryell, Marion. Isaiah 61:10.
Rochōk Mishuosi. Klang, E. (arr. Velvel Pasternak). Psalm 22:2.
Roll Down the Ages. Hurd, Bob (arr. Craig S. Kingsbury). Isaiah 42:1-17.
Romans Doxology. Elliott, John G. Romans 11:33, 36.
Roots in the Earth. Cooney, Rory. Psalm 1:1-3.
Ruth. Weiner, Lazar. Ruth 1:16-17.
Ruth (to Naomi). Cook, Gerald. Ruth 1:16-17.

Sacrament. Bach, J. S. Matthew 26:26-29.
Saget es, die ihr erlöst seid. Mendelssohn, Felix (ed. Robert Shaw). Psalm 107:2, 14-15, 19.
Sah'énu. Halberstam, Rabbi S. (arr. Velvel Pasternak). Psalm 90:14.
Salmo VIII. Cortese, Luigi. Psalm 8:00.
Salvation Belongeth unto the Lord. Greene, Maurice. Psalm 3:8.
Salve Maria. Mercadante, S. Mark 11:9-10.
Salvum me fac Deus.
Couperin, François. Psalm 68:1-6, 17-18.
Tornioli, Marcantonio (ed. Karl Gustav Fellerer). Psalm 69:00.
Sanctuary. Lowe, Augustus F. Psalm 91:1-2, 4, 9, 11.
Sanctus and Benedictus. Wold, Wayne L. Isaiah 6:3b.
Satisfy Us in the Morning. Halberstam, Rabbi S. (arr. Velvel Pasternak). Psalm 90:14.
Save Me, O God.
Butler, Eugene. Psalm 69:1-3, 5, 16-17, 29-30.
Charles, Ernest. Psalm 69:00.
Harris, Cuthbert. Psalm 69:1, 3, 29.
Randegger, Alberto. Psalm 69:1, 3.
Wooler, Alfred. Psalm 54:00.
Save Me, O God, By Your Name. Bouman, Paul. Psalm 54:00.
Save Me, O God, for the Waters Are Come in unto My Soul.
Floyd, Carlisle. Psalm 69:1-3, 14-17, 20.
Save Me, O Lord. Clerbois, Roger. Psalm 54:00.
Save Us, O Lord. Dufford, Bob. Psalm 80:1-3, 7, 15-16.
Say to Them of a Fearful Heart. Wesley, Samuel Sebastian. Isaiah 35:4.
Schaffe in mir, Gott, ein rein Herz. Buxtehude, Dietrich. Psalm 51:12-13.

Schaffe in mir, Gott, ein reines Herz.
Bernhard, Christoph. Psalm 51:10-11.
Schütz, Heinrich. Psalm 51:10-12.
Seal My Heart. Castelnuovo-Tedesco, Maro. Song of Songs 8:6-7.
A Seal upon Thy Heart. Reznick, Hyman. Song of Songs 8:6-7.
Search Me and Know Me. Card, Michael. Psalm 139:00.
Search Me, O God. Dvorák, Antonín. Psalm 139:4, 23-24.
Search Me, O God, and Know My Heart. Ward-Stephens. Psalm 139:00.
See Him, He Is the Lamb of God. Herbst, Johannes (arr. Karl Kroeger). John 1:29.
Seek First. Grant, Amy and Wes King. Matthew 6:33.
Seek First the Kingdom. Haas, David (arr. Jeanne Cotter). Matthew 6:28-32.
Seek the Lord.
Campion, Thomas. Isaiah 55:6-7.
Carter, John. Isaiah 55:6-7
Miller, Merle. Psalm 34:12-14, 19.
Seek Ye First. Lafferty, Karen. Matthew 6:33.
Seek Ye First the Kingdom of God.
Fisher, William Arms. Matthew 6:25-33.
Foster, Myles B. Matthew 6:31-33.
Seek Ye the Lord.
DeLong, Richard. Isaiah 55:6-9.
Humphreys, Don. Isaiah 55:6.
Lansing, A. W. Isaiah 55:6-7.
Lovelace, Austin C. Isaiah 55:6-7.
Lynes, Frank. Isaiah 55:6.
Roberts, John Varley. Isaiah 55:6-7.
VanDyke, May. Isaiah 55:6-7.
Sehet, welch eine Liebe. Bach, J. S. I John 3:1-3.
Send Forth Your Spirit. Joncas, Michael. Psalm 104:1, 24, 29-33.
Send Forth Your Spirit, O Lord. Walker, Christopher. Psalm 104:1, 5-6, 10-12, 24, 29-31, 34.
Send Out Thy Light.
Lynes, Frank. Psalm 43:1-4.
Wooler, Alfred. Psalm 43:1-4.
Send Out Your Spirit. Schoenbachler, Tim (arr. Sheryl Soderberg). Psalm 104:00.
Send Us Out. Talbot, John Michael. Matthew 28:18-20.
Servant Song. Schutte, Daniel L. Isaiah 49:1-7.
Set Me as a Seal.
Berman, Judith M. Song of Songs 8:6-7.
Betts, Lorne. Song of Songs 8:6-7.
Clokey, Joseph Waddel. Song of Songs 8:6-7.
DeLong, Richard. Song of Songs 8:6-7.
Foss, Lukas. Song of Songs 8:6-7.
McConnell, Doug. Song of Songs 8:6, 8.
McCray, James. Song of Songs 2:16.
Rochberg, George. Song of Songs 8:6-7.
Scholz, Robert. Song of Songs 8:6-7.
Scott, K. Lee. Song of Songs 8:6-7.
Willis, Michelle. Song of Songs 8:6-7.
Set Me as a Seal upon Thy Heart.
Helfman, Max. Song of Songs 8:6-7.
Wallach, Joelle. Song of Songs 8:6-7.
Seven Tableaux from the Song of Songs. Glick, Srul Irving. Song of Songs 1:00-8:14.
The Shadow of Thy Wings. MacDermid, James G. Psalm 36:5-9.
Shadrach. MacGimsey, Robert. Daniel 3:00 (based on).
Sharon. Bugatch, Samuel. Song of Songs 2:1-5.
Sheb'shiflénu. Pasternak, Velvel. Psalm 136:23.
Shelter Me, O God. Hurd, Bob (arr. Craig S. Kingsbury). Psalm 61:3.
The Shepherd.
Caldwell, Mary E. Isaiah 40:11.
Wolford, Julie Lofgren. Psalm 23:00.
Shepherd Alluluia. Harris, Ed. Psalm 23:1-2.
Shepherd Me, O God. Haugen, Marty. Psalm 23:00.
The Shepherd Psalm. Carter, John. Psalm 23:00.
The Shepherd Song.
Haan, Raymond H. Psalm 23:1-2.
Norbet, Gregory. Psalm 23:00.
The Shepherds. Cornelius, Peter. Luke 2:8-13.
Shepherd's Psalm. Espina, Noni. Psalm 23:00.
Shew Us Thy Mercy, O Lord. Boyce, William. Psalm 85:7.
A Shield About Me. Thomas, Donn and Charles Williams. Psalm 3:3.
Shir hamaalõs. Rosenblatt, Yossele (arr. Velvel Pasternak). Psalm 126:1-3.
Shir Hashirim. Sharlin, William. Song of Songs 1:1-2.
Shiru Lonu. Pasternak, Velvel. Psalm 137:3.
Show Me Thy Ways, O Lord. Greene, Maurice (arr. Laurence H. Davies). Psalm 25:4.
Show Us Your Kindness. Hurd, Bob (arr. Dominic MacAller). Psalm 85:8-9, 11-14.
Show Me Your Ways. Fragar, Russell. Psalm 25:4-5 (based on).
Sicut locutus est ad patres. Charpentier, Marc-Antoine. Luke 1:50.
Sicut Moses. Buxtehude, Dietrich. John 3:14-15.
Siehe das ist Gottes Lamm. Herbst, Johannes (arr. Karl Kroeger). John 1:29.
Siehe, eine Jungfrau ist schwanger. Franck, Melchior. Matthew 1:23.
The Silent Voice. Roma, Caro. Psalm 46:10a.
Simchu es y'rusholayim. Shapiro, Rabbi Y. (arr. Velvel Pasternak). Isaiah 66:10.
Simëni kachotam al libbecha. Wallach, Joelle. Song of Songs 8:6-7.
Simeon. Cornelius, Peter. Luke 2:21-22, 29-33.
Simeon's Song. Card, Michael. Luke 2:22-35.
Sing a Joyful Song. Farrell, Jim (arr. Craig S. Kingsbury). Psalm 145:00.
Sing a New Song.
Dvorák, Antonín. Psalm 98:1, 7-8.
Lovelace, Austin C. Psalm 98:1-3.
Pethel, Stan. Psalm 149:3.
Schutte, Daniel L. Psalm 98:1a, 6.
Sing a New Song to the Lord. Sleeth, Natalie. Psalm 98:1a, 4-6.
Sing Allelu, Alleluia! Larson, Sonia. Matthew 28:1-10.
Sing Hallelujah with Glad Rejoicing. Luzzi, Luigi. Luke 1:28, 30-31, 42.
Sing Now to God. Telemann, Georg Philipp. Psalm 98:00.
Sing, O Daughters of Zion. MacDermid, James G. Zephaniah 3:00.
Sing Out Your Joy to God. Handel, G. F. (ed. Hal H. Hopson). Psalm 81:1-3.
Sing Praise to God. Pasternak, Velvel. Psalm 47:7.
Sing Praise to the Lord. Roff, Joseph. Psalm 149:1-3.
Sing Praises to Our God. Powell, Robert J. Psalm 147:1, 5a, 7a, 12a.

Sing the Glory of His Name. Walker, Tricia. Psalm 66:1-8.
Sing to God. Horvit, Michael. Psalm 68:4.
Sing to the Lord.
Foley, John B. Psalm 96:2-5, 7-9.
Lynch, Mike. Psalm 27:1.
Medema, Ken. Psalm 34:3.
Sing to the Lord a New Song.
Buxtehude, Dietrich. Psalm 96:00.
Courtney, Craig. Psalm 96:1.
Pachelbel, Johann. Psalm 98:1-3, 9.
Sing to the Lord God. Pergolesi, Giovanni B. (arr. Burkhardt, Michael). Psalm 96:1-4.
Sing to the Lord, Rejoice! Telemann, Georg Philipp (arr. Hal H. Hopson). Psalm 147:1, 5.
Sing to the Mountains. Dufford, Bob. Psalm 118:4, 14, 18, 21, 24.
Sing unto Him. Smith, Michael W. Psalm 105:1-3.
Sing unto the Lord.
Cornelius, Peter. Psalm 30:00.
Dengler, Lee. I Chronicles 16:23-25, 27, 31.
Handel, G. F. Psalm 96:1-4 (based on).
Patillo, Leon (arr. Tom Fettke). Psalm 96:1-4.
Pendleton, Emmet. Psalm 50:14.
Reeves, Jeff. Psalm 96:1-4, 6-9.
Tecson, Andrew. Psalm 98:1-2, 4, 7, 9.
Unknown (arr. Tom Fettke). Psalm 96:1, 4.
Sing unto the Lord a New Song. MacDermid, James G. Psalm 148:1-7, 9, 11.
Sing unto the Lord All the Earth. Herbert, Muriel. Psalm 96:00.
Sing Us One of the Songs of Zion. Pasternak, Velvel. Psalm 137:3.
Sing With Songs of Joy. Handel, G. F. (arr. Hal H. Hopson). Psalm 42:4b.
Sing Ye a Joyful Song! Dvorák, Antonín. Psalm 139:4, 23-24.
Sing Ye Praise. Mendelssohn, Felix. Psalm 107:2, 14-15, 19.
Singet dem Herrn.
Buxtehude, Dietrich. Psalm 98:1-4.
Telemann, Georg Philipp. Psalm 98:00.
Singet dem Herren ein neues Leid. Schütz, Heinrich. Psalm 96:1-4.
Singt, singet Gott, dem Herren, neue Lieder. Dvorák, Antonín. Psalm 98:1, 7-8.
Skryse ma a paveza má Ty jsi. Dvorák, Antonín. Psalm 119:114-115, 117, 120.
Slyš, ó Bože! Slyš modlitbu mou. Dvorák, Antonín. Psalm 55:1-8.
Slyš, ó bože, volání me. Dvorák, Antonín. Psalm 61:1, 3-4.
Snatched Away by Jehovah. Bloch, Ernst. Psalm 114:00.
So du willst, so du willst. Bach, J. S. Psalm 130:3-4.
So Great Is His Mercy. Doig, Don. Psalm 103:11-17.
So I Have Looked for Thee. Pasternak, Velvel. Psalm 63:2-3.
So ihr mich von ganzem Herzen suchet. Mendelssohn, Felix. Deuteronomy 4:29.
Softly Beams the Sacred Dawning. Smith, Marcus. Matthew 24:27 (based on).
Soggetto Cavato. Griffin, Charles B. I Corinthians 13:1-11, 13.
Solomon's Prayer.
Miller, Merle. I Kings 3:5, 7, 9, 10-14.
Pisk, Paul A. II Chronicles 6:14, 19-21.
Song for a Young Prophet. Lundy, Damian (arr. Malcolm Archer). Jeremiah 1:00.
Song of All Seed. Huijbers, Bernard. Mark 4:1-34
A Song of Battle. Stanford, Charles Villiers. Psalm 124:00.
A Song of David. Rorem, Ned. Psalm 120:00.
Song of Devotion. Beck, John Ness. Philippians 1:3-11.
Song of Farewell. Sands, Ernest. Psalm 27:1, 4, 6, 14.
Song of Gladness Will I Sing Thee. Dvorák, Antonín. Psalm 144:9.
Song of Hannah. Lovelace, Austin C. I Samuel 2:1-10.
A Song of Hope.
Foley, John B. Jeremiah 29:10-14.
Stanford, Charles Villiers. Psalm 130:00.
Song of Hosanna. Rogers, Sharon Elery. Matthew 21:9.
Song of Joy. Beck, John Ness. Psalm 40:00.
The Song of Leaves of Life and Water of Life. Vaughan Williams, Ralph. Revelation 2:7.
The Song of Moses. Cumming, Richard. Exodus 15:00.
A Song of Redemption. Protheroe, Daniel. Isaiah 1:18.
Song of Ruth.
Eben, Petr. Ruth 1:16-17.
Goldman, Maurice. Ruth 1:16-17.
Hallquist, Gary (arr. Paul Johnson). Ruth 1:16.
Pendleton, Emmet. Ruth 1:16-17.
Song of Simeon. Walker, W. Luke 2:29-32.
The Song of Songs.
Bilchick, Ruth Coleman. Song of Songs 2:11-13.
Sharlin, William. Song of Songs 1:1-2.
Song of the Redeemed. Rogers, Sharon Elery. Revelation 5:8-10.
Song of the Risen One. Haas, David. Matthew 11:4-5.
A Song of Trust. Stanford, Charles Villiers. Psalm 121:00.
A Song of Victory. Rogers, Sharon Elery. Revelation 14:3.
A Song of Wisdom. Stanford, Charles Villiers. Ecclesiasticus 24:3-7, 12-14.
Songs of the Angels. Dufford, Bob. Job 19:25.
The Sorrows of Death. Mendelssohn, Felix (arr. Richard Walters). Psalm 116:3.
The Sorrows of Death Compassed Me. Sacco, Peter. Psalm 18:00.
Souls of the Righteous. Johnson, David N. Wisdom of Solomon 3:1-3.
Sound His Praise. Tunney, Melodie (arr. Joseph Linn). Psalm 150:6.
The Spacious Firmament. Addison, Joseph. Psalm 19:1-6.
The Sparrow Finds a Home. Foley, John B. Psalm 84:3.
Speak Lord. Uszler, Marienne (arr. Tim Schoenbachler). Psalm 119:00.
Speak, O Lord. Haugen, Marty. John 6:68.
Speciosus forma. Jeffreys, George (ed. Peter Aston). Psalm 45:2.
The Spirit Is Willing. Berthier, Jacques. Matthew 26:30.
Spirit of God. Hustad, Donald. Galatians 5:25 (based on).
The Spirit of God. Pisk, Paul A. II Corinthians 3:9-12.
The Spirit of the Lord. Talbot, John Michael. Isaiah 61:1.
The Spirit of the Lord God is upon Me. MacDermid, James G. Isaiah 61:1-2.
The Spirit of the Lord is upon Me. Sullivan, Sir Arthur. Luke 4:18, 21.
The Stars Declare His Glory. Haas, David. Psalm 19:00.
The Steadfast Love. Foley, John B. Isaiah 30:15, 18, 27.
The Steadfast Love of the Lord. McNeil, Edith. Lamentations 3:22-23.
The Stone Which the Builders Rejected.
Chait, B. (arr. Velvel Pasternak). Psalm 118:22.
Farrell, Bernadette. Psalm 118:1-7, 9-22.
Strikke des Todes. Mendelssohn, Felix (arr. Richard Walters).

Psalm 116:3.
S'u sh'orim. Pasternak, Velvel. Psalm 24:7.
And Suddenly There Was With the Angel. Handel, G. F. Luke 2:13.
Suffer the Children to Come unto Me. Fischer, Irwin. Matthew 19:14.
Suffer the Little Children.
Day, Stanley A. Matthew 18:1-4.
Hausman, Ruth L. Mark 10:13-16.
LaForge, Frank. Matthew 19:1-2, 13-15.
Schultz, A. L. Matthew 19:14.
Scott, Charles P. Luke 18:15.
Underhill, Charles D. Mark 10:13-14.
The Sun Goeth Down. Elgar, Edward. Psalm 63:6.
The Sun Shall Be No More Thy Light. Greene, Maurice. Isaiah 60:19.
Supplication. Handel, G. F. (arr. Keith W. Bissell). Psalm 64:1.
Surely Goodness and Mercy. Peterson, John W. and Alfred B. Smith. Psalm 23:6.
Surely He Bore Our Griefs. DeVidal, David. Isaiah 53:4-6.
Surely He Will Care for Me. Carter, John. Matthew 6:28-34.
Surely the Lord Is in This Place.
Colvin, Herbert (arr. Richard Huggins). Genesis 28:16-17.
Powell, Robert J. Genesis 28:16-17.
The Survivor. Keaggy, Phil. Psalm 31:13-15.
Suscepit Israel. Charpentier, Marc-Antoine. Luke 1:54.
Swing Low, Sweet Chariot.
Spiritual (arr. Edward Boatner). II Kings 2:11.
Spiritual (arr. Harry T. Burleigh). II Kings 2:11.
Spiritual (arr. Hall Johnson). II Kings 2:11.
Symphony, no. 2. Yardumian, Richard. Psalm 130:00.

The Tabernacle of God Is With Men. Mitchell, Raymond Earle. Revelation 21:1, 4, 5, 6.
Die Tage Deines Leides. Peter, Johann Frederich. Isaiah 60:20.
Take and Eat. Joncas, Michael. Psalm 118:22.
Take, Eat (Communion Meditation). Bock, Fred. Matthew 26:26-28.
Take My Mother Home. Spiritual (arr. Hall Johnson). John 19:26-27.
Take Up Your Cross. Talbot, John Michael. Luke 9:23-27.
Taste and See.
Hurd, Bob (arr. Kingsbury and MacAller). Psalm 34:2.
Hurd, Bob (arr. Craig S. Kingsbury). Psalm 34:2-4, 9.
Schoenbachler, Tim. Psalm 34:1-5, 8.
Talbot, John Michael. Psalm 34:1-8.
Walker, Christopher. Psalm 34:1-6, 8.
Taste and See That the Lord Is Good. Fischer, Irwin. Psalm 34:8.
Taste and See the Goodness of the Lord. Martinson, Joel. Psalm 34:1-8.
Te Deum. Archer, Violet. Psalm 104:31-34.
Teach Me, O Lord.
Hamblen, Bernard. Psalm 119:00.
Jackson, Stanley. Psalm 119:00.
Kingsley, Gershon. Psalm 86:11-13.
LaForge, Frank. Psalm 119:33-34, 37.
Manney, Charles F. Psalm 119:33-34, 37.
Nystedt, Knut. Psalm 119:33-35, 44-45, 171-172.
Teach Me, O Lord, the Way of Thy Statutes. Tindall, Adrienne M. Psalm 119:33-36, 38, 40.
Teach Me Your Way, O Lord. Sedio, Mark. Psalm 86:11.
Teach Me Your Ways, Lord. Rohlig, Harald. Psalm 25:4-5.
Tecum principium. Bellini, Vincenzo. Psalm 110:00.
Tell All the World. Horman, John D. Psalm 9:1-12.
Tell Out, My Soul. Haas, David. Luke 1:46-55.
Tell the World that Jesus Loves You. Scruggs, Randy. John 3:16.
Tell Ye This Story. Hayford, Jack (arr. Paul Johnson). Exodus 13:14.
Temple of Glory. Barker, Clement W. II Corinthians 6:16.
Ten Thousand Angels. Overholt, Ray (arr. Tom Fettke). Matthew 26:47 through Matthew 27:1, 50.
Tenebrae factae sunt. Nystedt, Knut. Matthew 27:45-46.
Than Eye Hath Seen. Lovelace, Austin C. I Corinthians 2:9-10.
Thanks Be to God.
Gluck, Christoph von. I Corinthians 15:57.
Joy, Jeanne Alden. Romans 8:2, 6.
Thanksgiving.
Myers, Gordon. Revelation 5:13b.
O'Connor-Morris, Geoffrey. Psalm 103:1-5, 19.
Thanksgiving Canon. Traditional English (arr. Anna Laura Page). Psalm 117:00.
That God Is Great. Handel, G. F. Psalm 135:5.
That Where I Am, There You . . . Mullins, Rich. John 14:1-6.
Their Sound Is Gone Out. Handel, G. F. Romans 10:18.
Thema. Bryant, Larry and Lesa Bryant (arr. Robbie Buchanan). Isaiah 9:2-7.
Then Shall Be Brought to Pass. Handel, G. F. I Corinthians 15:54.
Then Shall the Eyes of the Blind. Handel, G. F. Isaiah 35:5-6.
Then Shall the Righteous Shine. Mendelssohn, Felix. Matthew 13:43.
There Is a Balm in Gilead.
Spiritual (arr. William Dawson). Jeremiah 8:22 (based on).
Spiritual (arr. Bruce Greer). Jeremiah 8:22 (based on).
Spiritual (arr. Mark Hayes). Jeremiah 8:22 (based on).
Spiritual (arr. Hall Johnson). Jeremiah 8:22 (based on).
There is a Season to Everything. Toch, Ernst. Ecclesiastes 3:1-8.
There Is a Spirit in Man. Cornelius, Peter. Job 14:1, 32-33.
There Is a Time. Courtney, Craig. Ecclesiastes 3:1-8.
There Is Nothing. Mendelssohn, Felix (arr. Lynn Hodges). I Kings 18:43-44.
There Is One Body. Cotter, Jeanne. Ephesians 4:6-10 (based on).
There Is One Lord. Haas, David. Ephesians 4:5-6.
There upon a Manger Bed. Handel, G. F. Matthew 2:1-2, 11.
There Were Shepherds.
Belcher, Supply (ed. Gordon Myers). Luke 2:8-15.
Foster, Myles B. Luke 2:8-11, 14.
Handel, G. F. Luke 2:8.
Handel, G. F. (arr. W. Daniel Landes). Luke 2:8.
Scott, John Prindle. Luke 2:8-15.
Therefore the Redeemed. Lake, Ruth. Isaiah 51:11.
These Are They Which Came Out of Great Tribulation. Gaul, Alfred Robert. Revelation 7:14-15.
They Have Taken Away My Lord. Mendelssohn, Felix. John 20:13-15.
They Led My Lord Away. Spiritual (arr. Edward Boatner). Luke 22:54 (based on).
They Shall Not Hurt Nor Destroy. Steinberg, Ben. Isaiah 2:4.
They Shall Run and Not Be Weary. MacDermid, James G. Isaiah 40:6, 8, 28-31.
They Shall Soar Like Eagles. Manzo, Laura (arr. Mac Lynch).

Isaiah 40:29-31.
They That Sow in Tears.
Handy, William Christopher. Psalm 126:1-2, 5-6.
Rogers, James H. Psalm 126:5-6.
They That Sow in Tears Shall Reap in Joy. Harker, F. Flaxington. Psalm 126:5-6.
They Who Do Justice. Hurd, Bob (arr. Craig S. Kingsbury). Psalm 15:1.
Thine Be the Glory. Lee, John. Matthew 6:9-13.
Thine, O Lord Is the Greatness. MacDermid, James G. I Chronicles 29:11-13.
Think on These Things.
MacGimsey, Robert. Philippians 4:8-9.
Miller, Merle. Philippians 4:4.
This Alone. Manion, Tim. Psalm 27:1, 4, 6, 14 (based on).
This Day Was Made By the Lord. Walker, Christopher. Psalm 118:14, 19-24.
This Is My Body. Foley, John B. I Corinthians 11:24-25.
This Is My Commandment.
Clark, Palmer John. John 5:5-7, 9.
Hamblen, Bernard. John 15:00.
Hustad, Donald. John 15:12.
This Is My Prayer. Hartley, John and Gary Sadler. I Chronicles 4:10.
This Is the Day.
Brown, Scott Wesley. Psalm 118:24a.
Foley, John B. Psalm 118:1-4, 8-9, 13-17, 21-24, 26.
Garrett, Les. Psalm 118:24.
Hurd, Bob (arr. Dominic MacAller). Psalm 118:1-2, 16-17, 22-23 (based on).
Misetich, Marianne. Psalm 118:24.
Schoenbachler, Tim. Psalm 118:24.
This Is the Day Which the Lord Has Made. Portugal, Rabbi E. (arr. Velvel Pasternak). Psalm 118:24.
This Is the Victory, Even Our Faith. Baumgartner, H. Leroy. I John 5:4-5, 7, 11, 14, 15.
This Must Be the Lamb. Card, Michael. Matthew 27:30.
This Night I Lift My Heart to Thee. Costa, Michael. Psalm 84:4, 10.
This We Declare unto You. Baumgartner, H. Leroy. I John 1:1, 5-7, 9.
Those Who Hear My Words. Norbet, Gregory. John 12:24, 32, 35.
Those Who Wait on the Lord. Seaton, Annette. Psalm 62:1, 5-7.
Thou Art a Shield for Me. Tapp, Freda. Psalm 3:1-3.
Thou Art Clothed With Honor. Bavicchi, John Alexander. Psalm 104:1a-4.
Thou Art Far From My Help. Klang, E. (arr. Velvel Pasternak). Psalm 22:2.
Thou Art Gone Up on High. Handel, G. F. Psalm 68:18.
Thou Art My God. Goode, Jack. Psalm 63:00.
Thou Art the Guide of Our Youth. Gaul, Alfred Robert. Psalm 23:6.
Thou Art Worthy. Mills, Pauline Michael (arr. Fred Bock). Revelation 4:10-11.
Thou Didst Blow. Handel, G. F. Exodus 15:4 (based on).
Thou Didst Set the Earth. Laderman, Ezra. Psalm 104:5.
Thou Hast Charged. Greene, Maurice. Psalm 119:4.
Thou Hast Made the Moon. Bavicchi, John Alexander. Psalm 104:19-23.
Thou Hast Ravished My Heart. Samama, Leo. Song of Songs 3:9-11.
Thou Makest the Spring Gush Forth. Bavicchi, John Alexander. Psalm 104:10-16.
Thou, O Lord, Art My Protector. Saint-Saëns, Camille. Psalm 19:14b.
Thou Shalt Break Them. Handel, G. F. Psalm 2:9.
Thou Shalt Bring Them In. Handel, G. F. Exodus 15:17.
And Thou Shalt Know It. Herbst, Johannes (arr. Karl Kroeger). Isaiah 60:16.
Thou That Dwellest in the Garden. Thomson, Virgil. Song of Songs 8:13.
Thou Visitest the Earth. Parker, Harold. Psalm 65:9.
Thou Wilt Keep Him in Perfect Peace.
Beck, Theodore. Isaiah 26:3-4.
Kretz, Vivian A. Isaiah 26:33-4.
MacDermid, James G. Isaiah 26:3-4, 11-12.
Shawn, Allen. Isaiah 26:3-4.
Speaks, Oley. Isaiah 26:3.
Thiman, Eric H. Isaiah 26:3-4.
Wienhorst, Richard. Isaiah 26:3-4.
Though I Speak With the Tongues of Men. Brahms, Johannes. I Corinthians 13:1-3, 12,-12.
And Though I Wander. Bach, J. S. Psalm 23:00.
Though the Mountains May Fall. Schutte, Daniel L. Isaiah 40:31-32.
Three Times I Asked Him. Fettke, Tom (arr. Dick Bolks). II Corinthians 12:7-10 (based on).
The Throne. Smith, Michael W. and Gary Moore. Revelation 5:13.
Thrust in Thy Sickle and Reap. Raff, Joseph J. Revelation 14:15-18.
Thus Saith the Lord. Handel, G. F. Haggai 2:6, 7.
Thus Spake Jesus. Head, Michael. John 17:1, 5, 11, 21, 23.
Thy Hands Have Made Me and Fashioned Me. Tindall, Adrienne M. Psalm 119:73-74, 76-77, 80.
Thy Loving Kindness. Mitchell, Hugh. Psalm 63:3-4 (based on).
Thy Mercy, Lord. Handel, G. F. Psalm 135:00.
Thy Mercy, O Lord, Is in the Heavens. LaForge, Frank. Psalm 36:5-7, 11.
Thy Rebuke Hath Broken His Heart. Handel, G. F. Psalm 69:20.
Thy Right Hand Shall Hold Me. Row, Richard D. Psalm 138:00.
Thy Secret Place. Mendelssohn, Felix (arr. Carl Fredrickson). Psalm 91:00.
Thy Will Be Done.
Eilers, Joyce. Matthew 6:9-13.
Penn, Marilyn. Matthew 6:9-13.
Thy Word.
Smith, Michael W. and Amy Grant. Psalm 119:105.
Smith, Michael W. and Amy Grant (arr. Steven V. Taylor). Psalm 119:105.
Thy Word Is a Lamp.
Bone, Gene. Psalm 119:54, 55, 97, 103, 105, 125.
Englert, Andrew Lloyd. Psalm 119:105.
MacDermid, James G. Psalm 119:105.
A Time for Everything. Goemanne, Noel. Ecclesiastes 3:1-8 (based on).
To Everything There Is a Season.
Pinkham, Daniel. Ecclesiastes 3:1-8.
Steinberg, Ben. Ecclesiastes 3:1-3.
To God the Father. Schütz, Heinrich (arr. Robert Ross). Psalm 29:1-2.
To Him Who Sits on the Throne. Graafsma, Debbye. Revelation 5:13.
To His Angels. Foley, John B. Psalm 91:2, 5, 10-12, 14-15.
Tō l'hōdōs. Rebbi of Kalev (arr. Velvel Pasternak). Psalm

92:2-16.
To Living Waters, Bright and Clear. Bach, J. S. Psalm 23:2b.
To Obey is Better Than Sacrifice. Gates, Crawford. I Samuel 15:22.
To the Lord Our God Belong Mercies. Gaul, Alfred Robert. Daniel 9:9.
To Thee I Offer Thanksgiving. Kranzler, E. (arr. Velvel Pasternak). Psalm 116:17.
To You I Lift Up My Soul. Kavanaugh, John. Psalm 25:1.
To You, O God, I Lift Up My Soul. Hurd, Bob (arr. Dominic MacAller). Psalm 25:1, 4-5, 8-10, 14.
To You, O Lord. Alstott, Owen. Psalm 25:1, 4-5, 7, 17, 20.
To You, O Lord, I Lift Up My Soul. Nelson, Ronald A. Psalm 25:1a, 3-5, 19.
Today If Ye Will Hear His Voice. Rogers, James H. Isaiah 63:5.
Today Is Born Our Savior. Talbot, John Michael. Psalm 96:1-3.
Tõras Hasem t'mimo, no. 1. Mendelowitz, F. (arr. Velvel Pasternak. Psalm 19:8.
Tõras Hasem t'mimo, no. 2. Pasternak, Velvel. Psalm 19:8-9.
Tõras Hasem t'mimo, no. 3. Horowitz, Rabbi M. (arr. Velvel Pasternak). Psalm 19:8.
Tõras Hasem t'mimo, no. 4. Pasternak, Velvel. Psalm 19:8-9.
Tov L'Hodos. Weiner, Lazar. Psalm 92:2-16.
Transfiguration. Ellis, James G. Luke 9:28-29, 35.
The Treasure and Pearl. Hopson, Hal H. Matthew 13:44-45.
Treasure in Heaven.
Barnes, Edward Shippen. Luke 12:15-20.
Davis, Katherine K. Mark 10:17-24.
The Trees of the Field. Dauermann, Stuart. Isaiah 55:12.
The Trumpet Shall Sound.
Handel, G. F. I Corinthians 15:52b-53.
Handel, G. F. (arr. James Michael Stevens). I Corinthians 15:52b-53.
Trust in God. Fyock, Joan A. Psalm 37:00.
Trust in the Lord.
Davis, Katherine K. Proverbs 3:5-6.
Haydn, F. Joseph. Proverbs 3:1, 5-6.
Meyers, Don. Proverbs 3:5-6.
O'Connor, Roc. Isaiah 40:28-31.
Sullivan, Sir Arthur. Proverbs 3:5-6.
Tindall, Adrienne M. Proverbs 2:1-5.
Trust in the Lord With All Thine Heart. MacDermid, James G. Proverbs 3:5-6, 19-20, 25-26.
Trust Ye in the Lord. Scott, John Prindle. Isaiah 26:3-4, 11-12.
Truth. Humphreys, Don. Psalm 100:5.
Tsomo Nafshi. Kehati, Pinchas (arr. Velvel Pasternak). Psalm 42:3.
Tulerunt Dominum meum. Mendelssohn, Felix. John 20:13-15.
Turn Again to Thy Rest. Kiel, Friedrich. Psalm 116:7-8.
Turn Thee to Me and Have Mercy. Dvorák, Antonín. Psalm 25:16-18, 20.
Turn Thee unto Me. Ore, Charles W. Psalm 25:00.
Turn Thy Face From My Sins. Timmings, William. Psalm 51:9-11.
Turn to Me. Foley, John B. Isaiah 45:22-23.
Turn Ye Even to Me With All Your Heart. Harker, F. Flaxington. Joel 2:12.
Twelve Gates Into the City. Spiritual (arr. Hal H. Hopson). Revelation 21:12-13, 22.
The Twenty-Third Psalm.
Andrews, Mark. Psalm 23:00.
Archer, Violet. Psalm 23:00.
Bedell, Robert L. Psalm 23:00.
Brown, Russell J. Psalm 23:00.
Collister, Robert. Psalm 23:00.
Malotte, Albert Hay. Psalm 23:00.
Smith, Timothy Whitworth. Psalm 23:00.
The Two Commandments. McAfee, Don. Matthew 22:37-39.

Unless a Grain of Wheat.
Farrell, Bernadette. John 12:23-24, 26.
Hurd, Bob (arr. Craig S. Kingsbury). John 12:24.
Until He Comes Again. Hayford, Jack (arr. Lyndell Leatherman). I Corinthians 11:23-26.
Unto the Hills.
David, Ferdinand. Psalm 121:00.
Fromm, Herbert. Psalm 121:00.
Unto Thee I Lift Up My Soul. Cornelius, Peter. Psalm 25:1-2,5, 7.
Unto Thee O Lord.
Malotte, Albert Hay. Psalm 25:1, 4-5.
Marzo, Eduardo. Psalm 25:00.
Monroe, Charles F. Psalm 25:1-4.
Tindall, Adrienne M. Psalm 24:3-5.
Unto Thee, O Lord, Do We Give Thanks. Hancock, Vicki. Psalm 75:1.
Unto Thee Will I Cry. Purcell, Henry. Psalm 28:1.
Unto Us (Isaiah 9) with "Thema". Bryant, Larry (arr. Robbie Buchanan). Isaiah 9:2-7.
Unto Which of the Angels Said He at Any Time. Handel, G. F. Hebrews 1:5.
Upon Mount Zion Sits Our God. Tucker, Margaret R. Psalm 48:1, 4, 9, 11-13.
Upon This Rock. McGuire, Dony. Matthew 16:13-19, 25.
Ushavtem Mayim. Horowitz, Rabbi M. (arr. Velvel Pasternak). Isaiah 12:3.
Usquequo Domine. Couperin, Francois. Psalm 12:00.

Vaanachnu lõ néda. Katz, I. (arr. Velvel Pasternak). Psalm 25:6.
Vaani evtach boch. Pasternak, Velvel. Psalm 55:24.
Vaani s'filosi. Davidowitz, M. (arr. Velvel Pasternak). Psalm 69:14.
Valleys of Green. Schutte, Daniel L. Psalm 23:00.
Vanished Like a Vapor. Schram, Ruth Elaine. James 4:14.
Vanity of Vanities. Pinkham, Daniel. Ecclesiastes 1:2.
Vater unser. Krebs, Karl August. Matthew 6:9-13.
Vayitén b'fi shir chodosh. Pasternak, Velvel. Psalm 40:4.
Vayomer David L'Avigayil. Steinberg, Ben. I Samuel 25:32.
Veahavta. Gottlieb, Jack. Deuteronomy 6:5-9.
Venite ad Me. Schütz, Heinrich. Matthew 11:28-30.
Venite, exultemus. Dobry, Wallace. Psalm 95:1-7.
The Vision of St. John. Gounod, Charles. Revelation 21:1, 2.
V'erastich li l'olam. Wallach, Joelle. Hosea 2:16-22.
V'Erstich. Castelnuovo-Tedesco, Maro. Hosea 2:21-22.
V'nahafõch, no. 1. Pasternak, Velvel. Esther 9:1.
V'nahafõch, no. 2. Benet, Ch. (arr. Velvel Pasternak). Esther 9:1.
V'nisgov. Portugal, Rabbi E. (arr. Velvel Pasternak). Isaiah 2:11.
The Voice in Wilderness. Scott, John Prindle. Isaiah 40:3, 6, 7, 8.
The Voice of Joy. Scott, Charles P. Psalm 118:14-15.
The Voice of My Beloved. Helfman, Max. Song of Songs 2:10-18.
The Voice of My Beloved! Behold, He Cometh. LaMontaine, John. Song of Songs 2:8-10a.
The Voice of Thy Watchman. Elgar, Edward. Isaiah 52:8-9.

Von der Welt verlang' ich nichts. Bach, J. S. I John 3:1-3.
V'or'vo lashem. Pasternak, Velvel. Malachi 3:4.
V'Somachto B;Chagecho, no. 1. Pasternak, Velvel. Deuteronomy 16:14.
V'Somachto B;Chagecho, no. 2. Pasternak, Velvel. Deuteronomy 16:14.
V'Somachto B;Chagecho, no. 3. Taub, Rabbi S. E. (arr. Velvel Pasternak). Deuteronomy 16:14.
V'yism'chu chol chõsé voch. Portugal, Rabbi E. (arr. Velvel Pasternak). Psalm 5:12.

Wait for the Lord. Roff, Joseph. Psalm 27:13-14.
Wait on the Lord. Mozart, W. A. Psalm 37:7.
Walk Humbly With Thy God. Handel, G. F. Ephesians 5:2.
Walk in Love. Powell, Robert J. Ephesians 5:2, 8, 11, 15, 19.
Walk in the Way of the Lord. Butler, Eugene. Isaiah 2:5.
Was betrübst du dich. Handel, G. F. Psalm 42:6.
Was it a Morning Like This? Croegaret, Jim. Matthew 28:1-8.
Wash Me Throughly From My Wickedness. Handel, G. F. Psalm 51:2.
Watchful's Song. Vaughan Williams, Ralph. Psalm 31:5.
The Water I Give. Haas, David. John 4:14-15.
Water of Life. Dean, Stephen. Isaiah 55:1-3.
Waves of the Sea. Handel, G. F. Psalm 93:4.
The Way of Righteousness. Krieg, Melita. Psalm 25:4, 7.
The Way to Emmaus. Weinberger, Jaromir. Luke 24:13-31.
We Are a Chosen People. Moore, Bob. Colossians 3:12-25.
We Are All Parts of One Body. Hurd, Bob (arr. Dominic MacAller). I Corinthians 12:5, 12, 16.
We Are Called.
Haas, David (arr. Patrick Loomis). Micah 6:8.
Lynch, Mike. Jeremiah 1:5.
We Are Glad. Courtney, Craig. Psalm 126:00.
We Are the Earth. Dick, Colleen R. (arr. Craig S. Kingsbury). Psalm 90:2-6.
We Are the Light of the World. Greif, Jean Anthony (arr. Randall DeBruyn). Matthew 5:3-10, 16.
We Bring the Sacrifice of Praise. Dearman, Kirk. Psalm 50:14.
We Have Seen the Risen Lord. Pethel, Stan. John 20:25.
We Have Seen Your Salvation. Young, Carlton. Luke 2:29-32.
We Know Not What to Do. Katz, I. (arr. Velvel Pasternak). Psalm 25:6.
We Long to See Your Face. Keil, Kevin. Psalm 24:1-6.
We Praise You God. Vivaldi, Antonio (arr. Vernon M. Whaley). Psalm 145:1-2.
We Shall All Be Changed. Fettke, Tom and Bob Ashton. I Corinthians 15:51-52.
We Shall Be Like Him. Cross, Phil and Carolyn Cross. I John 3:2.
We Shall Behold Him. Rambo, Dottie. I Corinthians 15:52.
We Will Rise Again. Haas, David. Isaiah 40:11, 26, 29-30.
We Will See Him as He Is. Gersmehl, Mark and Scott Douglas. I John 3:2.
Wear Me As a Seal. Thornton, William. Song of Songs 8:6-7a, 10.
Wedding Cantata. Samama, Leo. Song of Songs 4:9-11.
Wedding Song.
Bender, Jan. Psalm 128:1-4.
Gieseke, Richard W. Ruth 1:16-17.
Lovelace, Austin C. Matthew 19:6.
Peeters, Flor. Ruth 1:16-17.
Pinkham, Daniel. Song of Songs 8:6-7.
Schütz, Heinrich. Ruth 1:16.
Schütz, Heinrich. Ruth 1:16-17.
Ultan, Lloyd. Song of Songs 2:10-13.
A Wedding Song. Wetzler, Robert. Psalm 128:00.
Wedding Song From Colossians. Proulx, Richard. Colossians 3:15-17.
Weepin' Mary. Spiritual (arr. Harry T. Burleigh). John 20:11.
Weh der Seele. Bach, J. S. Jeremiah 5:3.
Wenn ich mit Menschen und mit Engelszungen. Brahms, Johannes. I Corinthians 13:1-3, 12-13.
Wer mich liebet, der wird mein Wort halten. Bach, J. S. John 15:9-10.
Were Not Our Hearts Burning Within Us. Conry, Tom. Luke 24:32.
What I Did Not Steal. Laderman, Ezra. Psalm 69:4b.
What Shall I Render to the Lord? Courtney, Craig. Psalm 116:7-8, 12-14, 18-19.
What Shall I Render Unto the Lord. LaForge, Frank. Psalm 116:12-14, 17-19.
What You Hear in the Dark. Schutte, Daniel L. Matthew 5:13-14.
Whatever is True. Skillings, Otis. Philippians 4:8-9.
When All Things Began. McAfee, Don. John 1:5.
When From the Lips of Truth. Brown, Keith Crosby. I John 1:1-3.
When He Shall Come. Pearce, Almeda J. (arr. Paul Mickelson). Revelation 7:9-15.
When Heaven's Locked in Silence. Howard, Tom. Psalm 13:1-2.
When I Consider the Heavens. Scott, John Prindle. Psalm 8:00.
When I Remember Thee. Scott, Charles P. Psalm 63:5-6.
When I Survey the Wondrous Cross.
Hope, Lawrence. Galatians 6:14 (based on).
Lorenz, Ellen Jane. Galatians 6:14 (based on).
Murray, Lyn. Galatians 6:14 (based on).
Thomson, Sydney. Galatians 6:14 (based on).
When Israel Went Out of Egypt. Edmunds, John. Psalm 114:1.
When the Lord Turned Again the Captivity of Zion.
Rosenblatt, Yossele (arr. Velvel Pasternak). Psalm 126:1-3.
Where is the Profit? Anthony, Dick. Matthew 16:26.
Where Pastures Green Invite. Peery, Rob Roy. Psalm 23:00.
Where There is Love.
Haas, David (arr. Craig S. Kingsbury). I Corinthians 13:4-7, 10, 13.
Hurd, Bob (arr. Dominic MacAller). I John 4:16, 20, 21.
Where You Go. Hurd, Bob (arr. Craig S. Kingsbury). Ruth 1:16-17.
Where'er Thou Goest. Hildach, Eugen. Ruth 1:16-17.
Whereever You Go. Haas, David. Ruth 1:16-17.
Wherefore Seeing. Pinkham, Daniel. Hebrews 12:1-2.
Wherever You Go. Norbet, Gregory and Mary David Callahan. Ruth 1:16-17.
Whither Shall I Go. VanNuys, Rena. Psalm 139:7-10, 12, 14, 23-24.
Whither Shall I Go From Thy Spirit.
Demarest, Alison. Psalm 139:00.
MacDermid, James G. Psalm 139:7-12.
Mueller, Carl F. Psalm 139:00.
Schinhan, Jan Philip. Psalm 139:00.
Winton, Mary. Psalm 139:7-10.
Whither Thou Goest.
Cassler, G. Winston. Ruth 1:16-17.
Dewey, Richard A. Ruth 1:16.
Engel, James. Ruth 1:16-17.
Liljestrand, Paul. Ruth 1:16.
Samama, Leo. Ruth 1:16-17.

Singer, Guy. Ruth 1:16-17.
Who Are These Arrayed in White Robes? Manookin, Robert P. Revelation 7:13-17.
Who Can This Be? Haas, David. Mark 5:39-41.
Who Does Great Things. Portugal, Rabbi E. (arr. Velvel Pasternak). Job 9:10.
Who Hath Believed Our Report? Dauermann, Stuart. Isaiah 53:1-11.
Who Is the King of Glory. Williamson, Malcolm. Psalm 24:7-10.
Who Remembered Us When We Were Downcast. Pasternak, Velvel. Psalm 136:23.
Who Shall Come Before the Lord? Young, Philip M. Psalm 24:1, 3-4, 7.
Who Shall Separate Us? Doig, Don. Romans 8:35, 38-39.
Who Shall Separate Us from the Love of Christ. Pinkham, Daniel. Romans 8:35, 37-39.
Who Will Call Him Kings of Kings. Nelson, Greg and Bob Farrell. Matthew 28:1-10.
Whoso Dwelleth. Sowerby, Leo. Psalm 91:00.
Whoso Dwelleth in the Secret Place. Rogers, Faith Helen. Psalm 91:1, 5-7, 11-12.
Whosoever Does Not Receive the Kingdom. Bender, Jan. Mark 10:14-15.
Why Art Thou Cast Down, O My Soul?
  Mendelssohn, Felix. Psalm 43:3-5.
  Reinthaler, C. Psalm 42:5.
  Spicker, Max. Psalm 42:5.
Why Do the Nations. Handel, G. F. Psalm 2:1-2.
Why, O Lord. Foley, John B. Exodus 32:11, 13-14.
Why Seek Ye the Living Among the Dead? Foster, Myles B. Luke 24:5-6a.
Wie der Hirsch schreyet. Pohle, David (ed. Helmet Winter). Psalm 42:1-2, 12.
The Wilderness.
  Thiman, Eric H. Isaiah 35:1-2, 6-8, 10.
  Young, Walter E. Isaiah 1:6, 10.
Wilt Thou Not Receive Us Again. Robyn, Alfred G. Psalm 85:6-11.
Wings of Dawn. Cooney, Rory. Psalm 139:1-2, 5, 7-9, 11-18, 23-24.
Wir müssen durch viel Trusal. Bach, J. S. (trans. Hal H. Hopson). Psalm 35:9.
Wir rühmen uns allein des Kreuzes. Gast, Lothar. Psalm 111:2, 4, 5-9.
The Wisdom, Riches and Knowledge of God. Powell, Robert J. Romans 11:33-36.
With a Voice of Singing.
  Shaw, Martin. Isaiah 48:20.
  Shaw, Martin (arr. Maurice Jacobson). Isaiah 48:20.
With an Everlasting Love. Wolf, Hugo. Proverbs 3:24.
With Merry Dancing. Schutte, Daniel L. Psalm 150:1-5.
With My Whole Heart Have I Sought Thee. Tindall, Adrienne M. Psalm 119:10-13, 15.
With the Lord There Is Mercy. Talbot, John Michael. Psalm 130:00.
With Thee There Is Forgiveness. Cowen, Frederic Hymen. Psalm 130:4-6.
With Wings as Eagles. Harlan, Benjamin (arr. Tom Fettke). Isaiah 40:28-31.
Without Seeing You. Nazareth, Aniceto. John 6:68.
Woe Unto the Foolish Prophets. Barker, Clement W. Ezekiel 13:3.
Woe unto Them Who Forsake Him! Mendelssohn, Felix (arr. Richard Walters). Hosea 7:13.
Woe, Woe unto Them Who Forsake Him! Mendelssohn, Felix. Hosea 7:13.
Wohl dem, der den Herrn fürchtet. Telemann, Georg Philipp. Psalm 112:1b, 3.
Wohl dem der nicht wandelt. Schütz, Heinrich. Psalm 1:1-3.
Wohl denen, die Ohne Tadel leben. Reger, Max. Psalm 119:1-5, 8.
Wolken und Finsternis hullen Sein Antlitz. Dvorák, Antonín. Psalm 97:2-6.
A Woman of Valor.
  Adler, Samuel. Proverbs 31:20, 28-30.
  Gideon, Miriam. Proverbs 31:10, 25, 28, 31.
  Zaimont, Judith Lang. Proverbs 31:10-11, 17, 20, 26, 28, 30.
A Woman of Worth. Pasternak, Velvel. Proverbs 31:10-17.
The Wonder of His Care. Frost, Richard. Psalm 8:00.
The Wonders of Universe. Cesti, Marcantonio. Psalm 8:00.
The Word Is in Your Heart. Hurd, Bob (arr. Craig S. Kingsbury). Matthew 4:4.
Word of God Became Man. Talbot, John Michael. Psalm 148:00.
Words of Love. Fettke, Tom. John 1:1, 3, 7-8, 14.
Work in Our Behalf a Sign for Good. Shapiro, Rabbi Y. (arr. Velvel Pasternak). Psalm 86:17.
The World of Our God Shall Stand. Krieg, Melita. Matthew 6:19-21, 24, 33.
Worship the King. Smiley, Billy and Bill George. Psalm 145:1-13.
Worthy is the Lamb.
  Chapman, Morris. Revelation 5:12-13.
  Dufford, Bob. Revelations 5:2-5, 9, 12-13.
  Harlan, Benjamin. Revelation 5:12-13.
  Wyrtzen, Don. Revelation 5:12.
  Wyrtzen, Don. Revelations 5:12-13.
Worthy Is the Lamb That Was Slain. Handel, G. F. (arr. James Michael Stevens). Revelation 5:12-13.
Worthy the Lamb That Was Slain. Moen, Don. Revelation 5:12-13.
A Worthy Woman. Wilson, John Floyd. Proberbs 31:25-31.

Yahweh Is My Shepherd. Rieth, Mildred F. Psalm 23:00.
Yahweh, the Faithful One. Schutte, Daniel L. Genesis 12:1-2.
Yanchéni. Halberstam, Rabbi E. (arr. Velvel Pasternak). Psalm 23:3.
Ye Are the Light of the World. LaForge, Frank. Matthew 5:14-16, 43-45, 48.
Ye Have Taken Away My Lord. Mendelssohn, Felix. John 20:13.
Ye Now Are Sorrowful. Brahms, Johannes. Wisdom of Solomon 51:35.
Ye People Rend Your Hearts.
  Mendelssohn, Felix. Jeremiah 29:13.
  Mendelssohn, Felix (arr. Lynn Hodges). Jeremiah 29:13.
Ye Shall Know the Truth. Fischer, Irwin. John 8:2, 12, 31-32, 36.
Ye Shall Not Sorrow Any More. Joy, Jeanne Alden. Revelation 21:4.
Yea, Like as a Father Pitieth His Own Children, no. 4. Boyce, William. Psalm 103:13.
Yea, Though I Walk Through the Valley. Kinscella, Hazel Gertrude. Psalm 23:4.
Yes, I Shall Arise. Alstott, Owen. Psalm 27:4, 8.
Yihyu L'Ratzon. Davidson, Charles. Psalm 19:15.
Yiru Es Adõnoy. Pasternak, Velvel. Psalm 29:11.

You Alone Are the Word. Haas, David. John 6:68.
You Are God's Work of Art. Haas, David. Ephesians 2:10.
You Are My Hiding Place. Ledner, Michael. Psalm 32:7.
You Are My Refuge. Wexelberg, Shannon. Psalm 91:1-2.
You Are My Rock. Haas, David (arr. J. Hylton). Psalm 18:2-3, 6, 35.
You Are Near. Schutte, Daniel L. Psalm 139:2-8, 13-15, 7-18.
You Are the Chosen of the Lord. Fedak, Alfred V. Colossians 3:12-17.
You Are the People of God. Becker, Gerhardt C. Colossians 3:12-14, 17.
You Are the Salt of the Earth. Avery, Richard. Matthew 5:13-16 (based on).
You Crown the Year with Goodness. Lovelace, Austin C. Psalm 65:00.
You Have Been Good. Paris, Twila. Psalm 89:1.
You Have Captured My Heart, My Own, My Bride. Cohen, Gerald. Song of Songs 4:9-10, 16.
You Have Searched Me. Joncas, Michael. Psalm 139:1-18, 23.
You Hear the Lambs A-Crying. Spiritual (arr. Edward Boatner). John 21:17.
You Know My Folly. Dengler, Lee. Psalm 69:5-6.
You, Lord, Have the Message. Inwood, Paul. Psalm 19:7-10.
You May Bury Me in De Eas'. Spiritual (arr. Harry T. Burleigh). I Corinthians 15:52 (based on).
You Shall Have a Song. Ziegenhals, Harriet. Psalm 100:00.
You Who Are Thirsty. Ross, Barbara. Isaiah 55:1 (based on).
You Will Show Me the Path of Life. Haugen, Marty. Psalm 16:1-2, 6-7, 9-11.
Your Decrees Are My Song. Otte, Paul R. Psalm 119:49-50, 54-56.
Your Love Is Never Ending. Haugen, Marty. Psalm 136:00.
You've Searched Me. Haas, David. Psalm 139:1-2, 7-10.
Y'Voréch. Walfish, H. (arr. Velvel Pasternak). Psalm 115:12.
Y'varech'cha. Cohen, Gerald. Numbers 6:24-26.
Y'vorech'cho Hasem. Taub, Rabbi S. E. (arr. Velvel Pasternak). Psalm 128:5.

Zain. Tindall, Adrienne M. Psalm 119:49-52, 54-55.
Zamru elõkim. Pasternak, Velvel. Psalm 47:7.
Ze Hayõm. Portugal, Rabbi E. (arr. Velvel Pasternak). Psalm 118:24.
Zeh Dodi. Schiller, Benjie Ellen. Song of Songs 5:16.
Zerreisset eure Herzen. Mendelssohn, Felix. Jeremiah 29:13.
Zion Hears Her Watchman Crying. Bach, J. S. Isaiah 52:8.
Zion hört die Wächter singen. Bach, J. S. Isaiah 52:8.
Zivchu Zivché Tsedek. Pasternak, Velvel. Psalm 4:6-7.
Zpívetje Hospodinu píen novou. Dvorák, Antonín. Psalm 98:1, 7-8.
Zur Trauung. Schütz, Heinrich. Ruth 1:16-17.

Collections

10 Hymns and Gospel Songs for Solo Voice: For Concerts, Contests, Recitals and Worship (arr. Mark Hayes). Alfred (2000) MH: AL019086; ML: AL019191

10 Wedding Solos: Popular & Contemporary Christian. Hal Leonard (1995) HL00740004

12 Sacred Songs. G. Schirmer (1993) HL 50482062

22 Sacred Gems for Piano, Voice & Guitar. Santorella Publications (1998) T559

24 Songs for Solo Ministry (arr. Tom Fettke). Lillenas (2000) MB-809

25 Contemporary Solos (arr. Dennis Allen). Lillenas (1999) MB-830, 083-419-9904

25 Inspirational Easter Favorites (ed. Byrce Inman). Word (2001) 080 689 395284

25 More Contemporary Favorites for Duet (arr. Bryce Inman). Word (1991) 301 0207 492

25 Songs for Two-Part Choir (arr. Steven V. Taylor). Word (1988) 301 0145 012

25 Songs for Two-Part Choir, vol. II (arr. Steven V. Taylor). Word (1990) 301 0197 012

32 Wedding Songs (arr. Leslie D. Cradlaugh). Remich Music (1960) 27

40 Contemporary Hits. Word (1989) 3010167490

42 Songs for All Occasions (ed. Bryce Inman). Word (1993) 301 0249 497

50 Contemporary Favorites for Low Voice (ed. Bryce Inman). Word (1991) 301 0208 499

50 EZ Inspirational Favorites. Word (2002) HL00209882

50 Great Christian Duets (arr. Bryce Inman). Word (1995) 301 0293 496

50 Great Low Voice Solos (ed. Bryce Inman). Word (1995) 301 0282 494

50 Great Low Voice Solos (ed. Bryce Inman). Word (1997) 301 0356 498

50 Great Songs of Commitment (ed. Bryce Inman). Word (1997) 301 0356 498

50 Great Wedding Favorites (comp. and ed. Bryce Inman). Word (1997) 302 0334 494

52 Sacred Songs You Like to Sing. G. Schirmer (1939) 1642

56 Songs You Like to Sing. G. Schirmer (1937) 1596

60 Great Solos for Low Voice (arr. Tom Fettke). Lillenas (1999) 083-419-9750

Album of 12 Sacred Solos. G. Schirmer (1907)

Album of Negro Spirituals: Arranged for Solo Voice By H. T. Burleigh. Franco Colombo (Belwin Mills) (1969), H-32-1432-703, L-32-1433-703

Album of Sacred Songs. G. Schirmer (1918) H-1384; L-1385

Album of Sixteen Sacred Duets. G. Schirmer (1917, 1939)

All-American Gospel (arr. Michael Johnson). Creative Concepts Publishing (1996) 07-1105

All the Best Songs of Praise & Worship (comp. Ken Bible, Marty Parks, John Mathias, and George Baldwin). Lillenas (2001) MB-856

Alto Arias from Oratorios, vol. 1 (comp. Irving Brown). G. Schirmer (1977) 3108

America Worships: Songs from the Heart of the Church. Maranatha! (1993) 38597-9004-7

American Art Songs. Associated (1946)

And the Light Shines: Joe Wise. GIA (1982) G-2590

Andrea Bocelli-Arie Sacre. Nuova Carisch (1999) 1855

Anthology of Sacred Song, vol. 1, Soprano (ed. Max Spicker). G. Schirmer (1929) 15794

Anthology of Sacred Song, vol. 2, Alto (ed. Max Spicker). G. Schirmer (1929) 15891

Anthology of Sacred Song, vol. 3, Tenor (ed. Max Spicker). G. Schirmer (1929) 15830

Anthology of Sacred Song, vol. 4, Bass (ed. Max Spicker). G. Schirmer (1929) 15941

Anthology (Sandi Patti). Hal Leonard (1991) HL00490473

The Art Song (ed. Alice Howland and Poldi Zeitlin). Consolidated Music (1960) 040025

Art Songs for School and Studio, Second year (ed. M. Glenn and A. Spouse). Oliver Ditson (1934)

Art Songs of the Hymnal, vol. 1-3 (arr. Harris). Woodland Music Press (1990)

As Sung By. Laurel Press (Lorenz) (1985) PP 114

Baritone Arias from Oratorios, vol. 1 (comp. Irving Brown). G. Schirmer (1977) 3112

The Baroque Songbook (ed. Earnest Murphy). McAfee Music (1973) DM00099

Bass Arias from Oratorios, vol. 2 (comp. Irving Brown). G. Schirmer (1977) 3115

The Best Contemporary Christian Songs Ever. Hal Leonard (1999) HL00310558

The Best Gospel Songs Ever. Hal Leonard (1999) HL00310558

The Best of Popular Wedding Music. Warner Bros. (1998) F3007SMC

The Best of Times (arr. Richard Huggins). Word (1995) 301 0291 019

Bible Songs. Hal Leonard (2001) HL00310739

The Big Book of Contemporary Christian Favorites. Hal Leonard (1995) HL00310021

The Big Book of Hymns: 125 Favorite Hymns. Hal Leonard (1999) HL00310510

The Big Book of Love and Wedding Songs. Hal Leonard (1992) HL00311567

Bond of Love: Contemporary Songs for Christian Weddings. Lillenas (1979) MB-464

The Bride's Guide to Wedding Music. Hal Leonard (1992) HL00310615

Bring Us Back (arr. Mosie Lister). Integrity (1988) 083-417-2615

Canticles of Christmas (arr. T. W. Dean and R. Dean). Gamut (1961) SC353

Carols for Two (comp. Jean Anne Shafferman). Alfred (1997) 11536 book; 16021 book/CD

A Celebration of Melody (comp. Mary E. Caldwell). Triune (Lorenz) (1982) TUO140

Choice Sacred Duets for All Voices, vol. I, II. Oliver Ditson (1936) 431-40070

Choice Sacred Songs for Home or Church Services. Willis (1952)

Choice Sacred Songs (ed. Wilmans). Oliver Ditson (1936), H:431-40098, L:431-40099

A Choir Book for Advent (ed. Paul R. Ladd). GIA (1990) G-3365

The Choirbook for Saints and Singers (ed. Carlton R. Young). Agape (Hope) (1980) 939

Christian Wedding Duets. Hal Leonard (2001) HL00740110

Christian Wedding Songbook. Hal Leonard (1996) HL00310681

Christian Wedding Songs. Hal Leonard (2001) HL00310680

Christmas for Solo Singers (comp. and ed. Jay Althouse). Alfred (1997)

Christmas Song Album, vol. 1. Boosey & Hawkes (1982) VAB202

Christmas Song Album, vol. 2. Boosey & Hawkes (1984) VAB218

The Church Soloist–A Collection. Hope (1995) 806

The Church Soloist (ed. Eric H. Thiman). Novello (1981) 170305

Church Soloists Favorites, bk 1 (arr. Carl Fredrickson). R. D. Row (1963) H-RB 65; L-RB 66

The Church Year in Song (comp. & ed. Ruth Michaelis). G. Schirmer (1978) 3104

Classical Carols (arr. Richard Walters). Hal Leonard (1992) HL00747024

Classical Contest Solos: Baritone/Bass. Hal Leonard (1997) HL00740076

Classical Contest Solos: Mezzo-Soprano. Hal Leonard (1997) HL00740074

Classical Contest Solos: Soprano. Hal Leonard (1997) HL00740073

The Classical Singer's Christmas Album. Hal Leonard (1992) H: HL00747022; L: HL00747021

Classics (Twila Paris). Star Song (1990) SS 8945

The Collection (Amy Grant). Word (1986) 301-0119496

Come and Journey. GIA (1985) G-2886

Come to Me. GIA (1990) G-3373

Come to Set Us Free. OCP (1987) 8702

Come With a Singing Heart: Sacred Solos for Medium Voice (ed. John Carter and Mary Kay Beall). Hope (1992) 1053

The Communion Soloist. Fred Bock (1989) BG0867

The Complete Ave Maria. Hal Leonard (1992) 00747023

The Complete Lord's Prayer for Every Busy Accompanist. Hal Leonard (1990) HL00481088

The Complete Wedding Music Collection. Warner Bros. (2000) F3222SME

Complete Wedding Songbook for Organ. Hal Leonard (1987) HL00212194

Contemporary American Sacred Songs. G. Schirmer (1985) 3537

Contemporary Chart Toppers: Featuring 35 Contemporary Christian Hits. Word (1998) 00309580

Contemporary Christian Classics, vol 1. Lorenz (1982) MTB 101

Contemporary Christian Classics, vol 2. Lorenz (1982) PP 113

Contemporary Christian Hits. Warner Bros. (2001) MFM0136

Contemporary Christian Today (ed. Milton Okun). Cherry Lane Music (1993) 02502109

Contemporary Christmas Collection (comp. and ed. Bryce Inman). Word (1991) 301 0209 495

Contemporary Low Voice: Solo arr. of current favorites and new songs (Ken Bible). Lillenas (1990) MB

Ditson Treasury of Sacred Songs (comp. J. C. Randolph). Ditson (1934)

A Dozen Duets (ed. Leonard Van Camp). Laudamus (Intrada) (1997) LA-128

Duet Album (ed. V. Morris and V. Anderson). Boosey & Hawkes (1944) VAB-7

Duetbook: Twelve Duets for two equal voices and piano. (arr. Donald Ripplinger). Presser (1985) 491-00199

Duets For All Seasons (arr. Tom Fetke). Lellenas (1998) MB-800

A Dwelling Place: Basic Music Book. North American Liturgy Resources (1976) SJ-76M

Earthen Vessels. North American Liturgy Resources (1975)

Easy Songs For The Beginning Baritone/Bass. Hal Leonard (2000) HL50483759

Eleven Scriptural Songs from the 20th Century. Coburn Press (Presser) (1975) 4911

The Essential Wedding Book (arr. Jerry Ray). Alfred Publishing (1990) 0-6002

Everlasting Your Love: Liturgical Music for Worship. OCP (1988) 8897

Everybody's Favorite Sacred Songs (ed. Michael Whitehall). Amsco (1940) AM 40189

Everything for the Church Soloist (ed. Jack Schrader). Hope (1981) 804

Everything for the Wedding Soloist (ed. Jack Schrader). Hope (1981) 911

Exodus Songbook (comp. Carlton Young). Agape (Hope) (1976) 19

Exodus (ed. Bryce Inman). Word (1998) 080689 319280

Face to Face: Worship for Men. Maranatha! (1993) 38597-1006-7

Famous Sacred Songs. Allens (Presser) (1944) 1189

Favorite Hymns. Hal Leonard (1991) HL00490436

Favorite Sacred Classics for Solo Singers (comp. and ed. Patrick M. Liebergen). Alfred (1995) ML-11481, MH-11482

Favorite Wedding Classics for Solo Singers (ed. and arr. Patrick M. Liebergen). Alfred (2001), MH-19898; ML-19901

Favorites of Mahalia Jackson. Hal Leonard (1955) HL00307150

Festive Arias for soprano, mezzo-soprano and trumpet (comp Scott Foss). Roger Dean (2001) 30/1676R

Fifty Contemporary Favorites for Low Voice (ed. Bryce Inman). Word (1991) 301 0208 499

The Finest Moments. Word (1989) 3010178492

The First Book of Baritone/Bass Solos (comp. Joan Frey Boytim). G. Schirmer (1991) 50481176

The First Book of Baritone/Bass Solos, vol. II (comp. Joan Frey Boytim). G. Schirmer (1993) 50482067

The First Book of Mezzo-Soprano/Alto Solos (comp. Joan Frey Boytim). G. Schirmer (1991) 50481174

The First Book of Mezzo-Soprano/Alto Solos, vol. II (comp. Joan Frey Boytim). G. Schirmer (1993) 50482065.

The First Book of Soprano Solos (comp. Joan Frey Boytim). G. Schirmer (1991) 50481173

The First Book of Soprano Solos, vol. II (comp. Joan Frey Boytim). G. Schirmer (1993) 50482064

The First Book of Tenor Solos, vol. II (comp. Joan Frey Boytim). G. Schirmer. (1993) 50482066

Five Vocal Gems for Bass, vol. 1. HLH Music (1992) ANT103

Five Vocal Gems for Mezzo-Soprano and Alto, vol. 1. HLH Music (1992) ANT101

Five Vocal Gems for Soprano, vol. 1. HLH Music (1992) ANT100

Five Vocal Gems for Tenor, vol. 1. HLH Music (1992) ANT102

For All the Saints: Songs for the Christian Funeral (comp. and ed. Jack Schrader) Hope (1984) 44

Forty Eight Duets of the 17th-19th Century Arranged for Medium Voice (ed. Victor Prahl). E. C. Schirmer (1970) 156

From This Day Forward (comp. Fred Bock). Fred Bock Music (1983) B-G0589

Glorious Praise: Great Songwriters and Songs (comp. Cox). Hal Leonard (1988) HL00359895

Gospel & Inspirational Showstoppers. Warner Bros. (1992, 1997) F3283SMB

Great Hymns Treasury. Hal Leonard (1997) HL00310167

Great is Your Name. Mayhew (1992) 1425342

Greatest Hits (comp. Randy Cox). Hal Leonard (1988) HL003581865

Greatest Songs of Sandi Patty (comp. and ed. Bryce Inman). Word (2000) HL00309755

High Voice Treasury: Contemporary and Traditional Favorites (arr. Lloyd Larson). Lillenas (1996) MB 733

Holy is God. OCP (1988) 8758

Homeland Harmony. Homeland (1988) HB8802

Homeland Harmony, vol. 2. Homeland (1991) HB9104

How Can I Keep from Singing (ed. John Leavitt). Concordia (2001) 97-6921U2; 97-6958U2 w/CD

How Majestic is Your Name (ed. Fred Bock). Carl Fischer (1983) SGB501

Hymn Classics (arr. Richard Walters). Hal Leonard (1993) HL00747048

Hymns & Voices. Sparrow (1995) 70090

Hymns From the Crossroads. Carl Fischer (1965) 04516

Hymns: A Portrait of Christ (ed. Bill Wolaver). Sparrow (1992) 70069

I Can Only Imagine (ed. Bryce Inman). Word (2002) 00309894

I Will Sing of My Redeemer: Medium Voice Solos for All Occasions (arr. Marty Parks). Lillenas (1998) MB-801

I'll Lead You Home (trans. Bryce Inman). Word (1995) 701 0106

Inspirational Chart Toppers (comp. & ed. Bryce Inman). Word (1999) 00309712

Inspirational Selections. Hal Leonard (1987) HL00199098

The Jaci Velasquez Songbook (trans. and ed. Bryce Inman). Word (1998) 00309679

Jesus, Lord: Liturgical Music for Worship. OCP (1985) 8503GC

Joy, Joy, Joy: Famous Hymns & Sacred Songs. Creative Concepts Publishing (1997) 07-1107

The Joy of Wedding Music (comp. Denes Agary). Yorktown Music Press (1990) YK21533

A Joyous Wedding Celebration (arr. Bryan Jeffrey Leech). Fred Bock Music (1992) BG0855

Kirchen-Arien und Lieder. C. F. Peters (n.d.) H-7230

Library of Vocal Classics for Medium Voice (comp. Appleby & Pickow). Amsco (1994) AM91735

Lift Up Your Voice (ed. Stearns). Coburn Press (Presser) (1971) 32-2-716

The Lord Is My Light (comp. Ken Bible). Lillenas (1985) BCMB-530

Lord of Light. North American Liturgy Resources (1981)

The Low Voice Book: 24 Contemporary and Gospel Favorites (arr. Peter Moss). Lillenas (1995) MB-702

Low Voice Classics: 101 Solos (collected Tom Fettke). Lillenas (1985) MB-545

Low Voice Treasury: 101 Contemporary & Time-honored Favorites (comp. Tom Fettke). Lillenas (1982)

Marian Anderson Album of Songs and Spirituals (ed. Franz Rupp). G. Schirmer (1948) 1917

Mark Hayes Vocal Solo Collection: 10 Spirituals for Solo Voice, vol. 1. Alfred (1998), MH-17958; ML-17963

Michael Crawford–On Eagle's Wings. Warner Bros. (1998) PF9812

More Than Wonderful. Hal Leonard (1984) HL00240556

Morning Like This. Word (1986) 3010110499

Music for Solemn Moments (arr. Jerry Ray). Alfred (1994) 11726

Music for the Master (ed. Craig Courtney). Beckenhorst Press (1988) VC1

My God and King. Mayhew (1991) 1405529

My Utmost for His Highest – Quiet Prayers. Word (1996) 301 0327 498

The New Complete Wedding Songbook. Hal Leonard (1987)

The New Love & Wedding Songbook (The Ultimate Series). Hal Leonard (1986) HL00361445

New Testament Songs. Hope (1970) 501

O Sing to the Lord! Vocal Solos for the Christian Year. Abingdon Press (1996) ISBN 0-687-05573-3

The Oratorio Anthology: Alto/Mezzo-Soprano (comp. and ed. Richard Walters). Hal Leonard (1994) HL00747059

The Oratorio Anthology: Baritone/Bass (comp. and ed. Richard Walters). Hal Leonard (1994) HL00747061

The Oratorio Anthology: Soprano (comp. and ed. Richard Walters). Hal Leonard (1994) HL00747058

Oratorio Anthology: Tenor (comp. and ed. Richard Walters). Hal Leonard (1994) HL00747060

Oratorio Repertoire (ed. Nicholas Douty), vol. 1, soprano. Theodore Presser (1923)

Oratorio Repertoire (ed. Nicholas Douty), vol. 2, alto. Theodore Presser (1923)

Oratorio Repertoire (ed. Nicholas Douty), vol. 3, tenor. Theodore Presser (1923)

Oratorio Repertoire (ed. Nicholas Douty), vol. 4, bass. Theodore Presser (1923)

Our God Reigns: The Praise and Worship Collection. Hal Leonard (1984) HL00360740

Our Praise to You. Mayhew (1991) 1405521

People Need the Lord. Hal Leonard (1994) HL00306138

The Perfect Wedding Songbook (comp. Len Handler). Cherry Lane Music (1991) CL7950

Praise Classics: Lord of Hosts. Maranatha! (1993) 38597-1001-7

The Praise Collection (ed. Bryce Inman). Word (1999) 00309718

Praise: A Collection of Worship and Praise. Hal Leonard (n.d.) HL00240775

The Prayer of Jabez. Hal Leonard (2001) HL00306458

Psalms for Bass and O Perfect Love. The Leo Sowerby Foundation (Presser) (n.d.) (n.#.)

Ray Boltz: The Classics. Word Music (2000) HL08739064

Reflections and Meditations (comp. Mark Barnard). Unity (1995) 30/1104U

Rejoice Now My Spirit (comp. and ed. K. Lee Scott). Augsburg Fortress (1992) MH: 11-10228, ML: 11-10229

Return to Me: Music for Funerals and Healing, vol. 1. OCP (1992) 9303

Romantic American Art Songs. G. Schirmer (1990) HL50481219

Sabbath Song (comp. Clayne W. Robison). Sonos (Jackman Music) (1997) 00434

Sacred Classics. Hal Leonard (1992) H: HL00740051; L: HL00740052

The Sacred Collection (ed. Richard Walters). Hal Leonard (2001). H: 00740155, L: 00740156

Sacred Duet Masterpieces, vol. 1 (ed. Carl Fredrickson). R. D. Row (1955) 58

Sacred Duet Masterpieces, vol. 2 (ed. Carl Fredrickson). R.D. Row, (1955) 59

Sacred Duet Masterpieces, vol. 3 (ed. Carl Fredrickson). R.D. Row (1955) 60

Sacred Duets, vol. 1 (ed. Shakespeare). John Church (Presser) (1907) 32-40000

Sacred Duets, vol. 2 (ed. Shakespeare). John Church (Presser) (1907) 400001

The Sacred Hour of Song (arr. Mark Harrell). Carl Fischer (1939) H-02933, M-02983

Sacred Song Masterpieces, bk 1 (ed. Carl Fredrickson). R. D. Row (1959) H-RB49, L-RB50

Sacred Song Masterpieces, bk 2 (ed. Carl Fredrickson). R. D. Row (1964) H-RB75, L-RB76

Sacred Songs Especially Suitable for Christian Science Services. Huntzinger (1952) 1133

Sacred Songs for All Occasions (ed. Carl Fredrickson). R. D. Row, H: RB61, L: RB62

Sacred Songs for Easter (arr. William Stickes). Ethel Smith Music (1952) ES 1016

Sacred Songs for General Use. Huntzinger (1930)

Sacred Songs for the Soloist: 20 Songs on Religious Texts for Medium High Voice (comp. and ed. David Patrick). Boosey & Hawks (1996) 10320

Sacred Songs for the Soloist: 20 Songs on Religious Texts for Medium Low Voice (comp. and ed. David Patrick). Boosey & Hawks (1996) 10321

Sacred Songs, Nine Solos for Medium Voice (comp. and ed. Dale Wood). Sacred Music Press (1988) PP196

Sacred Songs. Abingdon (1963) APM-633

Sacred Songs: A Standard Collection of Sacred Solos by the Best Composers (ed. W. J. Henderson). John Church (Presser) (1903) vol. 1-4

Sacred Vocal Duets for High and Low Voice (ed. Lloyd Larson). Hope (2000) 8065

The Sanctuary Soloist, vol. 1 (ed. Fred Bock). Fred Bock Music (1964) H-574; L-575

The Sanctuary Soloist, vol. 2 (ed. Fred Bock). Fred Bock Music (1980) H-767, L-768

The Sanctuary Soloist, vol. 3 (ed. Fred Bock). Fred Bock Music (2001) H: BG0972; L: BG0973

Sandi Patti Medium Voice Collection. Word (1988) 3010140495

Schirmer's Singer's Library: Alto Arias from Oratorios (comp. Brown), vol. 1. Hal Leonard (1977) 3108

Schirmer's Singer's Library: Alto Arias from Oratorios (comp. Brown), vol. 2. Hal Leonard (1977) 3109

Schirmer's Singer's Library: Baritone Arias from Oratorios (comp. Brown), vol. 1. Hal Leonard (1977) 3112

Schirmer's Singer's Library: Baritone Arias from Oratorios (comp. Brown), vol. 2. Hal Leonard (1977) 3113

Schirmer's Singer's Library: Bass Arias from Oratorios (comp. Brown), vol. 1. Hal Leonard (1977) 3114

Schirmer's Singer's Library: Bass Arias from Oratorios (comp. Brown), vol. 2. Hal Leonard (1977) 3115

Schirmer's Singer's Library: Soprano Arias from Oratorios (comp. Brown), vol. 1. Hal Leonard (1977) 3106

Schirmer's Singer's Library: Soprano Arias from Oratorios (comp. Brown), vol. 2. Hal Leonard (1977) 3107

Schirmer's Singer's Library: Tenor Arias from Oratorios (comp. Brown), vol. 1. Hal Leonard (1977) 3110

Schirmer's Singer's Library: Tenor Arias from Oratorios (comp. Brown), vol. 2. Hal Leonard (1977) 3111

Schirmer's Favorite Sacred Duets. G. Schirmer (1955) HL50328980

Scriptural Solos for All Seasons (comp. Ken Bible). Lillenas (1980) BCMB-491

The Second Book of Baritone/Bass Solos (comp. Joan Frey Boytim). G. Schirmer (1994) HL50482071

The Second Book of Mezzo-Soprano/Alto Solos (comp. Joan Frey Boytim). G. Schirmer (1994) HL50482069

The Second Book of Soprano Solos (comp. Joan Frey Boytim). G. Schirmer (1994) HL50482068

The Second Book of Tenor Solos (comp. Joan Frey Boytim). G. Schirmer (1994) HL50482070

Select Vocal Solos for the Church Musician. Abingdon (1964) 308

Selected Duets for Contest, set 1, (ed. Gene and Audrey Grier). Heritage (Lorenz) (1991) PP327

Selected Sacred Songs for General Use. Willis/Huntzinger (1930), H-1013, L-1012

Seven Wedding Songs. Concordia (1980) H-97-5576-19, L-97-5577

Seventeen Sacred Songs for Church and General Use (ed. Walter Kirby). G. Schirmer (1938) H-1935; L-1934

Seventeen Sacred Songs Suitable for Christian Science Services. G. Schirmer (1938) H-1935; L-1934

Simple Songs for Young Singers (comp. Aaron Adams). Triune (Lorenz) (2001) 45/1101K

Sing a Song of Joy (ed. K. Lee Scott). Augsburg (1989). MH:11-8194; ML: 11-8195

Sing and Worship: 20 Distinctive Sacred Solos (arr. William Stickles). Boston (1961) 12590

Sing of the Lord's Goodness. OCP (1986) 8627

Sing Solo Christmas (ed. John Carol Case). Oxford (1987) H-ISBN 0 19 345783 0

Sing Solo Sacred (arr. and ed. Neil Jenkins). Oxford (1997) ISBN 0-19-345785-7

Sing Solo Tenor (ed. Robert Tear). Oxford (1986) ISBN 0 19 345778 4

Sing Unto the Lord, vol. I. (ed. K. K. Davis and N. Loring). Carl Fischer (1948) O3534

Sing Unto the Lord, vol. II. (ed. K. K. Davis and N. Loring). Carl Fischer (1948) O3535

Singer's Christian Wedding Collection. Hal Leonard (1996). H:HL 00740109; L:HL00740108

Singer's Repertoire: Songs of Faith. G. Schirmer (1985) 3536

Singer's Wedding Anthology. Hal Leonard (1995) HL00740008

Singer's Wedding Anthology-Duets. Hal Leonard (1995) HL00740005

Smokey Mountain Gospel Favorites. Hal Leonard Corporation (1996) HL00310161

The Solo Book: A Treasury of Inspirational Classics (arr. Tom Fettke). Lillenas (1996) MB-732

The Solo Psalmist. Sacred Music Press (1969) PP 98

Solo Singer (comp. Peter D. Tkach). Kjos (1958)

Soloist's Practical Library of Sacred Songs (ed. Row), bk 1. R. D. Row (1959) H: RB47, L: RB48

Soloist's Practical Library of Sacred Songs (ed. Row), bk 2. R. D. Row (1959) H: RB73, L: RB74

Solos for Christian Science Services (comp. Hunt). Ditson (1913)

Solos for the Church Soloist (ed. Lloyd Pfautsch). Lawson Gould (1961) LG000877

Solos for the Church Year: A Collection of Sacred Songs (ed. Lloyd Pfautsch). Lawson Gould (1957)

Solos from the Great Oratorios for Soprano (comp. and ed. Bernard Taylor). G. Schirmer (1968) 46149

Solos from the Word (comp. Ken Bible). Lillenas (1999) MB-825

The Song Book, vol. III (ed. Comp. Cason and Greer). Word (1985) 1009549X

Song of the Year: A Collection of Dove Award-Winning Songs 1969-1999, 3rd ed. Hal Leonard (2000) HL00490326

Songs For A Christian Wedding. Hal Leoanrd (2001) HL00310682

Songs for Bass in a Comfortable Range (ed. Leonard Van Camp). Carl Fischer (1990) O5201

Songs for Christian Science Services (ed. Don Humphrey). R. D. Row (1960) H-8006, L-8006A.

Songs for Low Voice in a Comfortable Range (ed. Leonard Van Camp). Carl Fischer (1990) O5183

Songs for Praise and Worship. Word (1992) 301 0203 497

Songs for Youthful Tenors of All Ages (ed. Leonard Van Camp). Laudamus Press (1993) LA-129

Songs from the Loft. Word Music (1993) 301 0256 493

Songs of Praise by Contemporary Composers (ed. and comp. Darwin Wolford). Harold Flammer (Shawnee) (1975) IA 5052

Songs of the Chassidim II (ed. & arr. Velvel Pasternak) Bloch (1971)

Spirituals For Church and Concert (arr. Phillip McIntyre). FitzSimons (1990) F0144

Spirituals for Solo Singers (ed. Jay Althouse). Alfred (1997) MH: 16915; ML: 16916

Spirituals for Two (comp. Jean Anne Shafferman). Alfred (1997) 16189; 16; 16191 book/CD

Steve Green: People Need the Lord. Sparrow (1994) HL00306138

The Sunday Solo (comp. Gertrude Tingley). G. Schirmer (1965) 2596

Sunday Soloist, vol. 3, (ed. Bryce Inman). Word (1994) M: 301 0265 492; L: 301 0268 491

The Sunday Worship Duet Book (arr. Tom Fettke). Lillenas (1993) MB-656

Take the Nations: Produced and Arranged for Solo Voice (arr. Ronald E. Gollner and Bob Book). Lorenz (2000) 30/1531RA

Ten Sacred Songs (ed. Hans T. David). C. F. Peters (1954) P6084

Thirty Spirituals (arr. Hall Johnson). G. Schirmer (1949) HL50328310

Three Swedish Folk Hymns for Medium Voice (arr. Ferguson). Augsburg (1990) 11-5360

Time for Joy: Contemporary Songs for Weddings. Word (1980) 3010025491

To Be Your Bread. David Haas. GIA (1985) G-2887

Together (comp. Strader and DeCou). Belwin (1983) L04017

Top 25 Heart Seekers – Praise Songs (ed. Phil Kristianson and George Pavlov). Maranatha! (2001) 00309874

Traditional & Popular Wedding Music. Warner Bros. (1997) MF9720

True Believer. Sparrow (1995) 70089

Twelve Sacred Songs. Hal Leonard (1993) H: HL5042062, L: HL5042063

Twenty Favorites of Steven Curtis Chapman. Sparrow (1992) 70065

The Two Part Collection (adapted Keith Christopher). Word (1994) 301 0277 016

The Ultimate Series: New Love & Wedding Songbook. Hal Leonard (1986) HL00361445.

United As One, vol. 1. OCP (1990) 9297

United As One, vol. 2. OCP (1990) 9749

The Very Best of Michael W. Smith. Word (1992) 30102340494

The Very Best of Sandi Patti. Word (1992) 3010232497

Very Special Sacred Songs (arr. John L. Haag). Creative Concepts (1993) 07-1039

Vocal Solos for Funerals and Memorial Services (ed. Wilbur Held). Augsburg (1992) 11-10226

The Way of Wisdom (trans. Phil Perkins). Sparrow (1990) 70048

We Will Serve the Lord (ed. Beth Lynch). Kavelin Music (1954) MB 112

The Wedding and Love. Hal Leonard (1990) HL00490377

Wedding Blessings (ed. Paul Bunjes). Concordia (1952) H: 97-9238, L: 97-9240

Wedding Bouquet (ed. Bernard Taylor). G. Schirmer (1958) H: 2311; L: 2312

Wedding Classics. Hal Leonard (1992). H: HL00740053; L: HL00740054

Wedding Collection (ed. Cuellar and DeLisa). Warner Bros. (1993) F3279P2X

Wedding Collection: 52 Solos arranged for Low Voice (ed. Bryce Inman). Word (1992) L-301 0225 490

Wedding Collection: 52 Solos arranged for Medium Voice (ed. Bryce Inman). Word (1992), M-301 0199 49X

Wedding Duets: 22 Arrangements for Medium Voice (ed. Bryce Inman). Word (1995) 301 0283 490

A Wedding Garland (arr. Barry O'Neal). G. Schirmer (1977) HL50333800.

Wedding Music, vol. 2. Benson (1987) B00754

Wedding Music: 49 Solos and Duets arranged for Low Voice (comp. & ed. Bryce Inman and Ken Barker). Word (1999) L-080689 33286

Wedding Music: 49 Solos and Duets Arranged for Medium/ High Voice (comp. and ed. Bryce Inman and Ken Barker). Word (1999) HL-080689 334283

Wedding Songs of Love and Friendship. Hal Leonard (1983) HL00361489

When Love is Found (ed. Jeanne Cutter & David Haas). GIA (1993) G-3745

When the Lord in Glory Comes. GIA (1993) G-4005

Who Calls You By Name: Music for Christian Initiation, vol. 1. GIA (1988) G-3193

Who Calls You By Name: Music for Christian Initiation, vol. 2. GIA (1991) G-3622

Whom God Hath Joined Together. Fred Bock (1972) B-G0670

Wings of Faith. Kevin Mayhew (Brodt) (1992) 1425341

With a Voice of Singing. Kevin Mayhew (Brodt) (1990) 1425245

With All My Heart. Word (1990) L: HL301 0186 495

The World's Greatest Hymns for Piano & Voice. Alfred (1993) 6662

World's Favorite Sacred Songs for Church and Home (comp. Albert Gamse). Ashley Publications (1961) 11

WOW The 90's Songbook. Word (2000) 00309791

WOW Worship Songbook, (blue). Integrity (1999) 15836

WOW Worship Songbook, (orange). Integrity (2000) 17236

WOW Worship Green Songbook. Integrity (2001) 19556

About the Compilers

James H. Laster is Professor Emeritus at Shenandoah Conservatory of Shenandoah University, Winchester, Virginia, where he has taught since 1973. Previous teaching positions were at Grove City College in Pennsylvania; the Community School of Tehran, Iran; and the Beirut College for Women, Beirut, Lebanon. At Shenandoah, he taught courses in choral literature, choral conducting, music theory, and was a choral conductor. Prior to retirement, he also worked as a reference librarian in Shenandoah's Alson Smith, Jr. Library. In addition to his academic career, he has been an organist/choirmaster in various churches, most recently at Trinity Episcopal Church, Upperville, Virginia, where he served for 25 years.

Laster holds a B.A. with majors in music history and biology from Maryville College, Maryville, Tennessee; an M.A. in musicology and a Ph.D. in church music from George Peabody College, Nashville, Tennessee; a certificate in organ from the Mozarteum Summer-Academy, Salzburg, Austria, and an M.S. in library science (music emphasis) from Catholic University, Washington, D.C.

His publications include choral works published by Concordia, Augsburg, Boosey & Hawkes, and Treble Clef Press. Other publications include: *A Catalogue of Choral Music Arranged in Biblical Order; A Catalogue of Choral Music Arranged in Biblical Order – Supplement; A Catalogue of Vocal Solos and Duets Arranged in Biblical Order; A Discography of Treble Voice Recordings* and most recently, *So You're the New Musical Director: An Introduction to Conducting a Broadway Musical,* all published by Scarecrow Press. An annotated bibliography of materials dealing with the women's chorus, co-authored with Dr. Nancy Menk, is published as #149 (Part I), #150 (Part II), #166 (Part III), and #175 (Part IV) of *The Research Memorandum Series.* He is currently compiling an annotated bibliography of music for organ and instruments, which is under contract to Scarecrow Press. A history of the women's chorus at the collegiate level in the United States since 1880 is an on-going research project.

Laster is a member of ACDA, AGO and ASCAP, and is a member of Actors' Equity Association and Screen Actors Guild. Acting credits include numerous stage roles, film and TV, as well as commercials and voice-over work.

Diana Reed Strommen, B.A., B.M., M.Mus.Ed., is a graduate of the University of Wisconsin-Stevens Point (*Phi Kappa Phi, Pi Kappa Lambda, Outstanding Graduate Assistant*), Indiana University, and St. Olaf College. Prior to her recent relocation to Georgia, she held positions as General Manager for the Central Wisconsin Symphony Orchestra, and Director of Youth Choirs, serving as the Coordinator of Worship Music for Trinity Lutheran Church for more than a decade.

An artist/teacher of voice, clinician, and adjudicator, Strommen is a full member of NATS, and ACDA with more than 20 years served in the teaching of private voice. As former adjunct faculty for the UWSP Conservatory for Creative Expression and faculty of the Wausau Conservatory of Music, Strommen was known in the mid-west for her work with changing voices and as a specialist in sacred vocal music. She is a member of the Atlanta Symphony Orchestra Chorus and Chamber Chorus.

Strommen resides in Marietta, Georgia with her husband and two teenage children. Her current position is as Youth Ministry Administrator for First Presbyterian Church, Marietta, Georgia.